JERUSALEM
BESIEGED

JERUSALEM
BESIEGED

From
ANCIENT CANAAN
to
MODERN ISRAEL

ERIC H. CLINE

THE UNIVERSITY OF MICHIGAN PRESS   ANN ARBOR

Copyright © by the University of Michigan 2004
All rights reserved
Published in the United States of America by
The University of Michigan Press
Manufactured in Singapore
⊗ Printed on acid-free paper

2007   2006   2005   2004   4   3   2   1

A CIP catalog record for this book is available from the British Library.

Library of Congress Cataloging-in-Publication Data

Cline, Eric H.
    Jerusalem besieged : from ancient Canaan to modern Israel /
Eric H. Cline.
        p.   cm.
    Includes bibliographical references and index.
    ISBN 0-472-11313-5 (cloth : alk. paper)
      1. Jerusalem—History, Military.   I. Title.
DS109.9.C63   2004
956.94'42—dc22   2004007661

Text design by Jillian Downey

Dedicated to my family

Pray for the peace of Jerusalem:

"May they prosper who love you.
Peace be within your walls,
and security within your towers."
For the sake of my relatives and friends
I will say, "Peace be within you."

(Psalm 122:6–8, New Oxford Annotated Bible)

ACKNOWLEDGMENTS

I WOULD LIKE to gratefully acknowledge the following individuals who all assisted in the preparation of this book in one way or another: Elizabeth Fisher, John Ziolkowski, Marc Saperstein, Dina Rizk Khoury, Max Ticktin, Samia Montasser, and Nancy Kocher of George Washington University; Shmuel Ben-Gad and the staff of the Gelman Library at George Washington University, as well as the staff members of the various libraries within the Washington Research Library Consortium; Israel Finkelstein, David Ussishkin, and Oded Lipschits of Tel Aviv University; Baruch Halpern and Ann Killebrew of Pennsylvania State University; Jodi Magness of the University of North Carolina at Chapel Hill; Rose Mary Sheldon of the Virginia Military Institute; Uzi Baram of the New College of Florida; P. Kyle McCarter of Johns Hopkins University; Peter Warnock of the University of Missouri; Holt Parker and Barbara Burrell of the University of Cincinnati; James Russell of the University of British Columbia; Louis Feldman of Yeshiva University; Morris Silver of the City College of New York; Oded Borowski of Emory University; Victor Matthews of Southwest Missouri State University; Rhoads Murphey of the University of Birmingham, England; Ezra Marcus of the University of Haifa; Michael Oren of the Shalem Center in Jerusalem; Paul Scham of the Truman Institute for Peace in Jerusalem; Allen Packwood and Rachel Lloyd of the

Churchill Archives Centre; Jack Meinhardt and Molly Dewsnap Meinhardt of the Biblical Archaeology Society; Yigal Carmon and Angi Jacobs of the Middle East Media Research Institute; Gregory Nagy and the staff of the Center for Hellenic Studies and Alice-Mary Talbot and Deborah Brown of Dumbarton Oaks, both in Washington, DC; and Simone Bercu, Solomon Borodkin, Jane Cahill, Douglas Feith, Jake Fratkin, Michael Klitsch, Lewis Lipkin, Alan Mairson, John and Carol Merrill, Sandra Scham, and Colin Winston.

I owe much to the many scholars, authors, and historians of Jerusalem who have gone before me, and I hope that I have properly and adequately documented all of the many primary and secondary sources used in the writing of this book; apologies are offered in advance if any grievous errors or omissions of attribution remain. I have also tried to take into account all of the feedback received from colleagues, friends, family, and audience members on various earlier drafts and public presentations of sections from this manuscript; in particular I would like to thank Uzi Baram, Oded Lipschits, Jodi Magness, John Merrill, Paul Scham, and Rose Mary Sheldon, who each read and commented on rough drafts of various chapters.

Without a doubt, this book would not be in its present form without the guiding hands of Geoff Skinner and Martin J. Cline, editors extraordinaire, to whom I owe a debt beyond words. I would also like to thank my agent, Nina Graybill, and the people at the University of Michigan Press, especially Chris Collins, Sarah Mann, Collin Ganio, Erin Snoddy, Jessica Sysak, Peter Sickman-Garner, and Michael Kehoe. Last but certainly not least, I am indebted to my immediate family—Diane, Hannah, and Joshua—who have had to live with me and all the besiegers of Jerusalem for the past few years.

Visits to Jerusalem itself were made during even-numbered summers from 1994 to 2000, before and after the excavation seasons at Megiddo. Financial support for research and writing was provided by a grant from the Center for Hellenic Studies in Washington, DC, for the summer of 2001; by a Junior Scholar Incentive Award from George Washington University for the summer of 2002; and by both another Junior Scholar Incentive Award and a University Facilitating Fund grant from George Washington University for the summer of 2003. All of this financial assistance is very gratefully acknowledged.

All of the maps used in this book were produced by Mark Stein of Mark Stein Studios; although some are new, most were first published in Professor Karen Armstrong's book *Jerusalem: One City, Three Faiths* (New York: Alfred A. Knopf, 1996) and are reproduced here with her permission. David Roberts's Jerusalem lithographs were photographed by Aaron Levin and are reproduced here by kind permission of George Lintzeris and his Petra Fine Art gallery in Baltimore, Maryland (http://www.petrafineart.net), who carefully and lovingly saw to the restoration of the original prints. The upper portion of the cover illustration is from a photograph by Ammar Awad, *Tear Gas at the Dome of the Rock*, April 2, 2004, used here by permission from Reuters; the lower portion of the cover art is from a lithograph by Louis Haghe (ca. 1850 CE), based in turn upon the original oil painting *The Siege and Destruction of Jerusalem by the Romans under the Command of Titus*, A.D. 70, by David Roberts (ca. 1847–49 CE); the lithograph was restored and digitally enhanced by Robert E. Browning and is reproduced here courtesy of Mr. Browning and American Vision (http://www.americanvision.org).

CONTENTS

xv *Abbreviations*

xvii *List of Maps*

xix *List of Illustrations*

xxi *List of Tables*

1 Introduction: A Lonely Ship on a Hostile Sea
JERUSALEM UNDER SIEGE

CHAPTER 1
11 A Rock and a High Place
DAVID AND THE JEBUSITES, 1000 BCE

CHAPTER 2
36 The End of the Beginning
NEBUCHADNEZZAR AND THE NEO-BABYLONIANS, 586 BCE

CHAPTER 3
68 Oil upon Troubled Waters
THE MACCABEAN REBELLION, 165 BCE

CHAPTER 4
96 In Blood and Fire
THE FIRST AND SECOND JEWISH REVOLTS, 70 AND 135 CE

CHAPTER 5

136 The "Holy House"
THE ARRIVAL OF ISLAM, 638 CE

CHAPTER 6

164 For God, Gold, and Glory
THE CRUSADERS AND SALADIN, 1099 AND 1187 CE

CHAPTER 7

201 The Sultan and the City
SELIM I AND THE OTTOMANS, 1516 CE

CHAPTER 8

235 Peace to Their Ashes, Honor to Their Memory
ALLENBY AND THE ALLIED FORCES, 1917 CE

CHAPTER 9

267 Jerusalem of Gold
THE ARAB-ISRAELI WARS, 1948 AND 1967 CE

CHAPTER 10

299 Speak Tenderly to Jerusalem
THE INTIFADAS AND BEYOND

311 *Notes*
361 *Bibliography*
397 *Index*

ABBREVIATIONS

AE	*American Ethnologist*
AHR	*American Historical Review*
AJHG	*American Journal of Human Genetics*
AO	*Archaeology Odyssey*
ASQ	*Arab Studies Quarterly*
AUSS	*Andrews University Seminary Studies*
BA	*Biblical Archaeologist*
BAR	*Biblical Archaeology Review*
BASOR	*Bulletin of the American Schools of Oriental Research*
BeO	*Bibbia e Oriente*
BN	*Biblische Notizen*
BR	*Bible Review*
CBQ	*Catholic Biblical Quarterly*
EHR	*English Historical Review*
GRBS	*Greek, Roman, and Byzantine Studies*
HTR	*Harvard Theological Review*
IEJ	*Israel Exploration Journal*
IOS	*Israel Oriental Studies*
JAOS	*Journal of the American Oriental Society*
JAS	*Journal of Archaeological Science*
JBL	*Journal of Biblical Literature*

JHS	*Journal of Hebrew Scriptures*
JJS	*Journal of Jewish Studies*
JNES	*Journal of Near Eastern Studies*
JPS	*Journal of Palestine Studies*
JQR	*Jewish Quarterly Review*
JRAS	*Journal of the Royal Asiatic Society of Great Britain and Ireland*
JRS	*Journal of Roman Studies*
JSAI	*Jerusalem Studies in Arabic and Islam*
JSOT	*Journal for the Study of the Old Testament*
JSQ	*Jewish Studies Quarterly*
JSS	*Journal of Strategic Studies*
LDA	*Les Dossiers d'Archeologie*
NT	*Novum Testamentum*
PEQ	*Palestine Exploration Quarterly*
PNAS	*Proceedings of the National Academy of Sciences of the United States of America*
QDAP	*Quarterly of the Department of Antiquities in Palestine*
RB	*Revue Biblique*
SCI	*Scripta Classica Israelica*
ST	*Studia Theologica*
TA	*Tel Aviv*
UF	*Ugarit-Forschungen*
VT	*Vetus Testamentum*
WI	*Die Welt des Islams*
ZAW	*Zeitschrift für die Alttestamentliche Wissenschaft*
ZDPV	*Zeitschrift des Deutschen Palästina-Vereins*
ZPE	*Zeitschrift für Papyrologie und Epigraphik*

MAPS

1. The ancient Near East   4
2. Ancient Canaan   14
3. Ancient Jerusalem   23
4. Jerusalem under David and Solomon   31
5. The kingdoms of Israel and Judah   40
6. Jerusalem during the First Temple period, 1000–586 BCE   43
7. Jerusalem and Judah, after 722 BCE   47
8. Jerusalem and the province of Yehud during the Persian period   71
9. Jerusalem at the time of Nehemiah   72
10. The Hasmonean kingdom   83
11. Jerusalem in the Hasmonean period   84
12. Herodian Jerusalem, 4 BCE–70 CE   103
13. Roman Palestine   107
14. Aelia Capitolina, 135–326 CE   133
15. Byzantine Jerusalem, 326–638 CE   140
16. Moslem Jerusalem, 638–1099 CE   152
17. Crusader Jerusalem, 1099–1187 CE   169
18. The Islamization of Jerusalem under the Ayyubids, 1187–1250 CE   209
19. Development in Mamluke Jerusalem, 1250–1517 CE   217

20. Suleiman's Jerusalem, 1540 CE   222
21. Allenby's Jerusalem, 1917 CE   244
22. The city boundary of Jerusalem, 1948–67 CE   271
23. The frontiers of the state of Israel, 1949–67 CE   283
24. Divided Jerusalem, 1948–67 CE   287

ILLUSTRATIONS

1. Jerusalem from the south   24
2. Jerusalem from the north   24
3. The "Tower of David" (perhaps the Tower of Hippicus)   104
4. The "Pool of Bethesda" (perhaps part of the Antonia)   104
5. The "Church of the Purification" (perhaps on
   the site of Justinian's "Nea" church)   141
6. The "Mosque of Omar" (the Dome of the Rock)   153
7. Jerusalem from the Mount of Olives   170
8. The Damascus Gate   170
9. The entrance to the citadel   210
10. Jerusalem, from the road leading to Bethany   245

TABLES

Table 1. Jerusalem Conflicts from 2000 BCE to 2000 CE   8
Table 2. Chronology from 1000 BCE to 582 BCE   67
Table 3. Chronology from 586 BCE to 63 BCE   94
Table 4. Chronology from 1077 CE to 1840 CE   234

INTRODUCTION

A Lonely Ship on a Hostile Sea

TODAY THE STRUGGLE for Jerusalem and for all of Israel continues without respite, perpetuating four thousand years of confrontation in the heart of the land once called Canaan. Where once the ancient weapons were bronze swords, lances, and battle-axes, they are now stun grenades, helicopter gunships, remotely detonated car bombs, and suicidal young men and women armed with explosives. Although the individuals and their weapons may have changed, the underlying tensions and desires have not. And the end is not yet in sight. Meron Benvenisti, the former deputy mayor of Jerusalem, has described the rival Jewish and Moslem claims to the Temple Mount as "a time bomb . . . of apocalyptic dimensions."[1]

Jerusalem Besieged is the story of four thousand years of struggles for control of Jerusalem, a city central to three major religions and held sacred by hundreds of millions of people throughout the world. No other city in the world has been more bitterly fought over throughout its history. Although frequently called the "city of peace," this is likely a mistranslation and certainly a misnomer, for the city's existence has been anything but peaceful. As Norman Corwin has written:

Yerushalayim
The sound mellifluous, but the city behind the syllables never
  for long serene
The austere, the beautiful, the vexed city . . .[2]

There have been at least 118 separate conflicts in and for Jerusalem during the past four millennia—conflicts that ranged from local religious struggles to strategic military campaigns and that embraced everything in between. Jerusalem has been destroyed completely at least twice, besieged twenty-three times, attacked an additional fifty-two times, and captured and recaptured forty-four times. It has been the scene of twenty revolts and innumerable riots, has had at least five separate periods of violent terrorist attacks during the past century, and has only changed hands completely peacefully twice in the past four thousand years.[3]

Jerusalem stands on the eastern edge of the Judaean hills that protrude like a spine down the middle of modern Israel and the West Bank, separating the western coastal region from the Great Rift Valley and the desert to the east. Although in ancient times there were probably good agricultural and pastoral lands near the site, the bleak Judaean wilderness lay not too far to the east. Indeed, even today the view to the east from any high point in the modern city of Jerusalem is of the barren Judaean desert, with rocks shimmering in the heat. The remains of flora and fauna embedded in the ancient strata of the city testify that the environment was not much different in 1000 BCE.[4]

At the site where the city was built, two ridges run side by side from north to south. The original city was small, covering only about twelve acres at the southern end of the eastern ridge. This area of Jerusalem is known in modern Hebrew as ʿir David (the "City of David"). Immediately to the east of the first city was the Kidron Valley, in which lay the Gihon Spring that provided water all year round. To the west, the Central Valley separated the city from the second (western) ridge, and to the south lay the Hinnom Valley.[5] Thus deep valleys—really ravines—surrounded the city on all sides but the north.

The existence of the Gihon Spring and the protection afforded by the deep valleys were probably the principal reasons why the Canaanites originally settled in this relatively forsaken spot sometime in the third millennium BCE. At first glimpse, there is little else to commend the site. It was well off the main trade routes that stretched between Egypt to the south and the regions of Anatolia and Mesopotamia to the north and east. It was in a region bereft of most natural resources and was distant from the seaports that lined the Mediterranean.

When the city expanded later, in the first millennium BCE, centuries after the time of David and Solomon, it incorporated the western ridge within the city limits, together with the Central Valley (between the two ridges), which then ran right through the center of the expanded city. Over time the valley filled with debris, and today it is barely noticeable. The city of this early period was still protected on three sides by steep ravines, but the northern aspect—without such natural defenses—had to be defended by a series of man-made walls.[6]

Strabo, the famous geographer writing in the first century CE, described Jerusalem as being in a spot that "was not such as to excite jealousy, nor for which there could be any fierce contention" (Strabo 16.2.36).[7] How wrong he was! Battles for control of the city began as early as the second millennium BCE, but their relevance to the modern world begins in earnest when the Israelites, led by the young warrior king David, engaged in an epic battle with the Jebusites for control of Jerusalem sometime around 1000 BCE. In the three millennia that have passed since David captured the city and made it his capital, Jerusalem has been fought over again and again.

Why is this? Why have dozens of armies—from minor tribes as well as great civilizations—fought to conquer and rule Jerusalem? It lay far from major ports and did not dominate any historically important trade routes. It sat on the edge of a barren and forbidding desert poorly suited for the building of an important commercial center or strategic military base. The answer may lie on a hill called the Temple Mount—known in Arabic as the Haram al-Sherif (the "Noble Sanctuary")—that looks down upon the surrounding city; Gershom Gorenberg has called it "the most contested piece of real estate on earth."[8]

On this mount stands a great rock that is central to the story of the struggles for Jerusalem. It has seen kingdoms rise and fall, great empires come and go. It once lay within the Temple of King Solomon and later inside Herod's Temple. Today, this great stone still has a commanding presence on the Temple Mount. It now lies beneath the golden-roofed

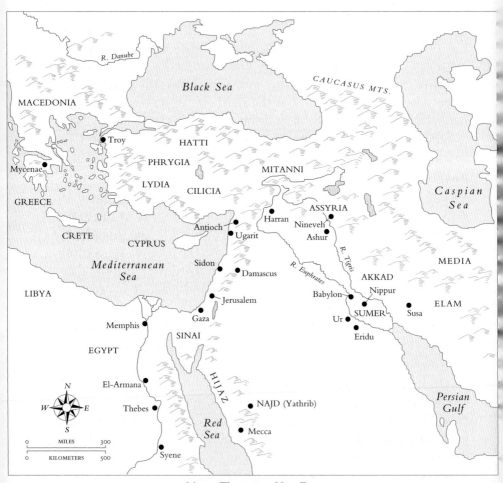

Map 1. The ancient Near East

Dome of the Rock and is a vital part of the third most sacred site of the Islamic world. According to Moslem tradition, the Prophet Mohammed ascended to the furthest reaches of heaven from this rock. According to Jewish tradition, this is the rock upon which Abraham offered his son Isaac as a sacrifice to God. It was here that David brought the sacred ark of the covenant of his people.

Legend has it that the Israelites toiled by the rock to build the great temple for Solomon, that it was bathed with the tears of Judaeans bound for exile in the fields of Babylon, and that it was stained with the blood of Crusaders and Saracens engaged in holy warfare. This is the rock that has outlasted all those who came to besiege Jerusalem—David and Shishak, Sennacherib and Nebuchadnezzar, Vespasian and Titus, Crusaders and Saracens, Moslems and Mamlukes, Ottomans and British.

If the story of the rock is the story of the Temple Mount, it is also the story of the city of Jerusalem. The major thesis of *Jerusalem Besieged* is that most of the battles that have raged over Jerusalem during the past four millennia were inspired by the desire of one or another group to establish cultural and religious hegemony over the region, whose focal point has always been the Temple Mount and the rock that stands upon it. Thus the battles for control of Jerusalem were usually fought because the city was an important political and religious center rather than because of any inherent military or commercial value it had.

Many of these conflicts have reverberated down through the pages of history to the present time. Again, Norman Corwin writes:

Utter the word Jerusalem
And voltages thrill in the cell banks of history
And stored occasions leap to life like the dry bones
　　of Ezekiel . . .[9]

In this ancient city, the battles of yesterday have frequently become part of the propaganda of today, and so events that took place eight hundred or even three thousand years ago still exert a dramatic and significant influence. Israeli officials celebrate David's conquest of Jerusalem from the Jebusites about 1000 BCE as marking the city's beginnings under Jewish rule. But such prominent Palestinians as

Yasser Arafat, describing themselves as descendants of the original Jebusites who fought against the Israelites, see the conquest of the city by David as the first skirmish in a three-thousand-year-long battle between the Palestinians and the Israelis.

Similarly, Saddam Hussein hailed the destruction of Jerusalem by Nebuchadnezzar in 586 BCE and its recapture from the Crusaders by Saladin in 1187 CE as precedents for his own actions and intentions. In Iraq, laser shows, billboards, and statuary depicted Hussein as the modern successor to these ancient warriors. Theodor Herzl, Max Nordau, Vladimir Jabotinsky, and other Zionists intent on founding the modern state of Israel invoked stirring images of heroic Maccabean warriors from 167 BCE and of Bar Kokhba facing the legions of the Roman Empire in 135 CE. Osama bin Laden styled himself on grainy videotapes as a latter-day Saladin, battling Western Crusaders in the Middle East a thousand years after the fact and proclaiming his determination to bring Jerusalem under Moslem sovereignty once again.

And so military occupations and religious conflicts continue in Jerusalem, as they have done unrelentingly for four thousand years, with no end in sight. It seems that not much has changed in the nearly 3,400 years since Abdi-Heba, the beleaguered Canaanite ruler of Urusalim, exclaimed to the Egyptian pharaoh, "I am situated like a ship in the midst of the sea!" The modern state of Israel, which only recently celebrated its fiftieth anniversary, has been described as a besieged island surrounded by a sea of hostile Arab forces.[10] Will it last even as long as did the Crusader kingdom of Jerusalem? The future of the new state of Palestine, whose birthing pangs are still being felt, is even less certain; its twin outposts in the Gaza Strip and the West Bank can similarly be depicted as islands surrounded by a sea of increasingly hostile Israeli forces.

Jerusalem Besieged presents a perspective that sweeps across the centuries yet focuses on a single location. Its aim is to put these four millennia of conflicts into context in order to begin to understand how past events may have contributed to the current political and religious strife in the region. The book's particular emphasis upon those conflicts that have been used (and, more frequently, misused) as propaganda by modern military and political leaders demonstrates how some are still reflected in the social and political environment of the Middle East today.

Although this is a work targeted for the general reader interested in the troubled history of Jerusalem, it may nevertheless be of interest and use to others who are more engaged and involved in the current conflicts roiling the Middle East. A more discerning view of the past might enable a clearer examination of the problems of the present and might perhaps help in the evaluation and determination of directions for the future. It may be that the fires that burned in this bitterly contested city can serve to illuminate the way ahead.

TABLE 1. Jerusalem Conflicts from 2000 BCE to 2000 CE

Date	Opponents	Action/Result
About 1350 BCE	Abdi-Heba vs. Canaanites/Habiru	Possibly attacked
About 1120 BCE	Joshua and the Israelites vs. the Jebusites	Possibly attacked
About 1100 BCE	Tribe of Judah vs. the Jebusites	Possibly attacked and captured
About 1100 BCE	Tribe of Benjamin vs. the Jebusites	Possibly attacked and captured
About 1000 BCE	**King David and the Israelites** vs. the Jebusites	Besieged; captured
925 BCE	**Egyptian pharaoh Shishak/Shoshenq** vs. Rehoboam of Judah	Probably besieged; ransom or tribute paid
875 BCE	Baasha of Israel against Asa of Judah	Threatened; possibly attacked
800 BCE	**Hazael of Aram** vs. Jehoash (Joash) of Judah	Attacked
785 BCE	**Jehoash (Joash) of Israel** vs. Amaziah of Judah	Attacked
734 BCE	Rezin of Syria and Pekah of Israel vs. Ahaz (Jehoahaz) of Judah	Threatened; possibly attacked and besieged
701 BCE	**Sennacherib and the Neo-Assyrians** vs. Hezekiah of Judah	Besieged; ransom or tribute paid
598 BCE	**Nebuchadnezzar and the Neo-Babylonians** vs. Judaeans	Attacked; deportation
597 BCE	**Nebuchadnezzar and the Neo-Babylonians** vs Judaeans	Besieged; captured; deportation
586 BCE	**Nebuchadnezzar and the Neo-Babylonians** vs. Judaeans	Besieged; destroyed; deportation
582 BCE	**Nebuchadnezzar and the Neo-Babylonians** vs. Judaeans	Possibly attacked; deportation
312 BCE	**Ptolemy I** vs. Jerusalem inhabitants	Attacked; captured
201 BCE	**Antiochus III** vs. Ptolemy IV	Attacked; captured
200 BCE	**Ptolemy IV** vs. Antiochus III	Attacked; captured
200 BCE	**Antiochus III** vs. Ptolemy IV	Besieged; captured
180 BCE	Seleucus IV/Heliodorus vs. **Judaeans**	Possibly apocryphal revolt
172 BCE	Judaean uprising vs. Menelaus and Lysimachus	Revolt
169 BCE	**Jason** vs. Menelaus	Attacked
169 BCE	**Antiochus IV Epiphanes** vs. Judaeans	Attacked; captured
167 BCE	**Antiochus IV Epiphanes** vs. Judaeans	Attacked; captured
164 BCE	**Judah Maccabee** vs. Antiochus IV	Attacked; Temple Mount captured
162 BCE	Judah Maccabee vs. Antiochus V	Akra attacked
162 BCE	Judah Maccabee vs. **Antiochus V**	Temple attacked
145 BCE	Jonathan vs. Demetrius I	Akra attacked
142–41 BCE	**Simon** vs. Tryphon	Akra attacked and destroyed
135 BCE	**Antiochus VII** vs. John Hyrcanus	Besieged; ransom or tribute paid
94–88 BCE	**Alexander Jannaeus** vs. Jerusalem inhabitants	Revolt (and civil war)
67 BCE	**Aristobulus II** vs. Hyrcanus II	Attacked, captured
65 BCE	**Hyrcanus II, Antipater, and Aretas III** vs. Aristobulus II	Besieged
63 BCE	**Pompey and Hyrcanus II** vs. Aristobulus II	Besieged; captured
57, 56, and 55 BCE	**Gabinius** vs. Hasmoneans	Revolt

TABLE 1—*Continued*

Date	Opponents	Action/Result
54 BCE	**Crassus** vs. Judaeans	Revolt
40 BCE	**Parthians and Antigonus** vs. Phasael and Herod	Besieged; captured
37 BCE	**Herod the Great** vs. Antigonus	Besieged; captured
4 BCE	Judaeans vs. **Herod**	Revolt
4 BCE	Judaeans vs. **Archelaus**	Revolt
4 BCE	Judaeans vs. **Varus**	Revolt
4 BCE	Judaeans vs. **Sabinus and Varus**	Revolt
26 CE	Judaeans vs. **Pontius Pilate**	Riot/protests
27 CE	Judaeans vs. **Pontius Pilate**	Riot/protests
41 CE	Judaeans vs. Caligula	Protests
48 CE	Judaeans vs. **Cumanus**	Riot
58 CE	Judaeans and Paul vs. Romans	Riot
66 CE	Judaeans vs. **Florus and Gallus**	Revolt
66 CE	Idumeans and Zealots vs. **moderate Judaeans**	Civil war; Roman garrison besieged
68–70 CE	Simon bar Giora vs. John of Gischala vs. Eleazar bar Simon	Civil war
70 CE	**Titus and the Romans** vs. Judaeans	Besieged; destroyed
132–35 CE	Judaeans vs. **Hadrian**	Revolt; city renamed
614 CE	**Shahr-Baraz and the Persians** vs. Byzantines	Besieged; captured
629 CE	**Heraclius and Byzantines** vs. Persians	Attacked; captured
638 CE	**Caliph Umar and the Umayyads** vs. Byzantines	Besieged; captured
745 CE	**Abbasids** vs. Umayyads	Attacked
807–15 CE	Desert tribes vs. Abbasids	Revolts
841–42 CE	**Abu Harb Tamim** vs. Abbasids	Revolt
938 CE	Moslems vs. Christians	Riot
966 CE	Anti-Christian riots (**Ikhshidids vs. Christians)**	Riots
About 973 CE	**Fatimids** vs. Abbasids	Presumed attacked; captured
975 CE	**Alptakin and alliance** vs. Fatimids	Reportedly attacked; possibly captured
1009 CE	Anti-Christian persecutions	Riots
1024 CE	**Arab rebels** vs. Fatimids	Attacked
1025 CE	**Fatimids** vs. Arab rebels	Recaptured
1073 CE	**Seljuks (Turcomans)** vs. Fatimids	Besieged; captured
1076 CE	**Fatimids** vs. Seljuks (Turcomans)	Revolt
1077 CE	**Seljuks (Turcomans)** vs. Fatimids	Attacked; recaptured
1098 CE	**Fatimids** vs. Seljuks (Turcomans)	Besieged; captured
1099 CE	**First Crusade** vs. Fatimids	Besieged; captured
1187 CE	**Saladin** vs. Crusaders	Besieged; captured
1191–92 CE	Saladin vs. Crusaders (Richard the Lion Heart)	Peace treaty signed
1229 CE (February)	**Frederick II and Sixth Crusade** vs. Moslems	Bloodless conquest; peace treaty
1229 CE (February to March)	Moslems vs. **Crusaders**	Attacked

(continued)

TABLE 1—*Continued*

Date	Opponents	Action/Result
1239 or 1240 CE	**Moslems** vs. Crusaders	Besieged; captured
1241 or 1243 CE	**Crusaders** vs. Moslems	Attacked; captured
1244 CE	**Khwarizmian Turks** vs. Crusaders	Besieged; captured
1246–47 CE	**Khwarizmians** vs. Egyptians	Attacked; captured
1246–47 CE	**Egyptians** vs. Khwarizmians	Attacked; captured
1246–47 CE	**Kerakians** vs. Egyptians	Attacked; captured
1247–48 CE	**Egyptians** vs. Kerakians	Attacked; captured
About 1248–50 CE	**Aleppoans/Damascenes** vs. Egyptians	Attacked; captured
1253–54 CE	**Egyptians** vs. Damascenes/Aleppoans	Returned peacefully
1254 CE	**Damascenes/Aleppoans** vs. Egyptians	Attacked; captured
1260 CE	**Mongols** vs. Damascenes/Aleppoans	Attacked; captured
1260 CE	**Mamlukes** vs. Mongols	Attacked; recaptured
1300 CE	**Mongols** vs. Mamlukes	Attacked
1348 CE	**Bedouin** vs. Mamlukes	Attacked
1480 CE	**Bedouin** vs. Mamlukes	Attacked
1516 CE	**Selim I and the Ottomans** vs. Mamlukes	Captured
About 1590 CE	**Bedouins** vs. governor of Jerusalem	Attacked
1625 CE	**Mohammed ibn Faroukh** vs. Ottomans	Attacked; captured
1627–28 CE	**Ottomans** vs. Mohammed ibn Faroukh	Attacked; recaptured
1703 CE	*Naqib al-ashraf* **revolt** vs. pasha of Jerusalem	Revolt
1705 CE	*Naqib al-ashraf* revolt suppressed	Attacked; recaptured
1757 CE	**Greek Orthodox Jerusalemites** vs. Catholic Jerusalemites	Riot
1798 CE	**Moslem Jerusalemites** vs. Catholic Jerusalemites	Riot
1806–7 CE	**Governor of Sidon** vs. Jerusalem rebels	Revolt
1819 CE	Moslem Jerusalemites vs. Greek Orthodox Jerusalemites	Riot
1821 CE	Moslem Jerusalemites vs. Greek Orthodox Jerusalemites	Riot
1825 CE	**Jerusalem inhabitants** vs. Ottomans	Revolt
1826 CE	Jerusalem inhabitants vs. **Ottomans**	Attacked; recaptured
1831 CE	**Mohammed Ali and the Egyptians** vs. Ottomans	Attacked; captured
1834 CE	Jerusalem inhabitants vs. **Egyptians**	Revolt
1840 CE	**Ottomans** vs. Egyptians	Attacked; captured
1917 CE	**Allenby and the Allies** vs. Ottomans and Germans	Attacked; captured
1920 CE	Arabs vs. Jews	Riot
1921 CE	Arabs vs. Jews	Riot
1929 CE	Arabs vs. Jews	Riot
1936–39 CE	Arabs vs. Jews and British (Arab Revolt)	Revolt; terrorist attacks
1942–6 CE	Jews (Irgun) vs. British and Arabs	Terrorist attacks
1947–48 CE	**Israelis** vs. Arabs	Attacked; besieged; captured
1949–66 CE	**Israelis** vs. Arabs	Terrorist attacks
1967 CE	**Israelis** vs. Arabs	Attacked; captured
1987–93 CE	First Intifada: Palestinians vs. Israelis	Revolt; terrorist attacks
2000 CE–present	Second Intifada: Palestinians vs. Israelis	Revolt; terrorist attacks

Note: Winners, if any, are marked in bold. "Besieged" = surrounded and with supplies cut off for more than a few days.

I

A ROCK AND A HIGH PLACE

The taut rope stretched upward into the darkness, twisting and creaking softly, as Joab began the long climb to the opening at the top of the narrow water shaft. The climb was difficult and dangerous, but if Joab succeeded, the way into the heart of Jerusalem would be open before him. But that would be only half the journey. He would still have to evade the guards lining the high walls and open the gates to the army waiting silently outside—an army ready to strike and take the citadel for David, their King. If Joab succeeded, the army of the Hebrews would surprise the Jebusite garrison and conquer Jerusalem. Joab would become the General of David's armies.

IS THIS ACTUALLY what took place when David launched his attack against Jerusalem and the Jebusites one dark night about the year 1000 BCE? The tale of Joab's upward climb into the heart of Jerusalem, as described in the Bible,[1] is the subject of scholarly debate, but it is clear that one day or night some three thousand years ago, one of the pivotal battles of history began. The biblical account of David's battle against the Jebusites and his capture of their city is a dramatic tale of skill and courage. The victory described set the stage for the predominance of the Israelites in the region for the next four hundred years, until they in turn were conquered by the Neo-Babylonians. It is a tale that still reverberates today in the conflict between Israelis and Palestinians.

POLITICS AND PROPAGANDA

"Our forefathers, the Canaanites and Jebusites," declared Yasser Arafat, chairman of the Palestine Liberation Organization and president of the Palestinian Authority, "built the cities and planted the land; they built the monumental city of Bir Salim [Jerusalem] . . ." His trusted confidant and advisor, Faisal Husseini, agreed. "First of all," he said, "I am a Palestinian. I am a descendant of the Jebusites, the ones who came before King David. This [Jerusalem] was one of the most important Jebusite cities in the area. . . . Yes, it's true. We are the descendants of the Jebusites." Husseini, well-known in the Arab world as the son of a war hero, a member of a respected Jerusalem family, and a distant cousin of Yasser Arafat, was the Palestinian Authority minister for Jerusalem affairs before he suffered a fatal heart attack while visiting Kuwait in May 2001. He was especially fond of referring to himself as a descendant of the ancient Jebusites, the "original landlords of Jerusalem."[2]

Arafat and Husseini were using a new tactic in the attempt, begun by the Palestinian Authority a decade or more earlier, to gain control of modern Jerusalem. Their initial targets were the notepads and tape recorders of news reporters. Their ultimate targets were especially Americans and also the peoples of Europe and the Middle East. By claiming descent from the ancient Jebusites, they were effectively avowing that the Palestinian people can trace their lineage to a people that held an already ancient Jerusalem when the Israelites conquered the city and made it the capital of their fledgling kingdom. They were implying that King David's capture of the city from the Jebusites about 1000 BCE was simply the first time that the Jews took Jerusalem from its rightful Palestinian owners.[3]

Not to be outdone in the propaganda campaign, Israeli politicians opened fire with a media onslaught of their own. They gave top billing to King David in the "Jerusalem 3000" advertising campaign for celebrations that began in 1995, and they identified David's conquest of the city in about 1000 BCE as marking the foundation of Jerusalem. To their Palestinian opponents, this was political propaganda that conveniently ignored the earlier Canaanite and Jebusite occupations of Jerusalem that extend the history of the city back an additional two thousand years.[4]

David's capture of Jerusalem three thousand years ago is thus relevant—or claimed to be relevant—to the conflict between Jews and Arabs in Israel today. The modern contestants are stretching and embroidering the faded cloth of history. The ancient conflict between the Israelites and Jebusites is being recast as the original battle between Israelis and Palestinians for control of Jerusalem. Just what was this battle? Who were the Jebusites? And why were King David and the Israelites so determined to capture the city? Let us begin with a description of the land of Canaan three thousand years ago.

A LAND OF MILK AND HONEY

During the transition between the Late Bronze and Early Iron Ages, Canaanites, Jebusites, Israelites, and other Semitic and non-Semitic groups inhabited the ancient Levant, in the region that encompasses modern Israel, Syria, Lebanon, and Jordan. This was the land of Canaan (*Ka-na-na, Ki-na-a*), according to ancient documents found in Egypt, Syria, and Mesopotamia (located in what is now modern Iraq and northern Syria). *Canaan* is also the name used in the Hebrew Bible.[5]

Among the peoples living in the land of Canaan at this time were the Philistines. They were descendants of the Peleset—members of an elusive group of marauding brigands known to archaeologists as the Sea Peoples. It is from the Peleset and the Philistines that our word *Palestine* comes—*Philistia* became Neo-Assyrian *Palashtu*, Roman *Syria Palastina*, Arabic/Moslem *Filastin*, and, eventually, British *Palestine*.

Little is known about the origins of the Sea Peoples, but Egyptian inscriptions record that they ravaged the lands bordering the eastern Mediterranean and Aegean seas, laying waste to cities great and small. Many archaeologists believe that the Sea Peoples were instrumental in bringing to an end the Late Bronze Age and civilized life in the Aegean and eastern Mediterranean in about 1200 BCE. By their looting and

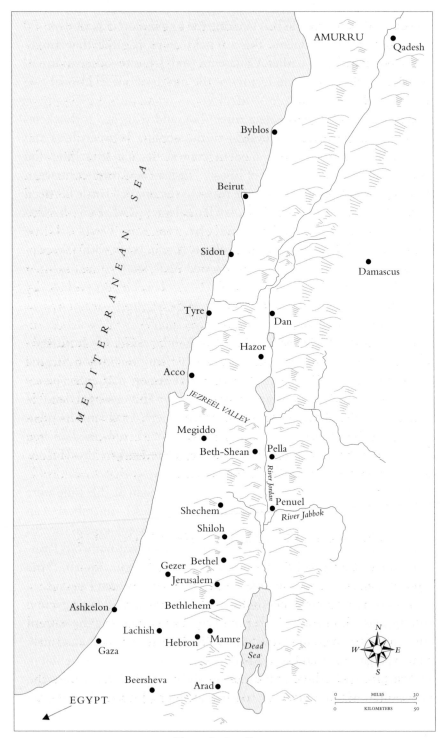

Map 2. Ancient Canaan

pillaging, they ushered in the so-called Dark Ages in the Aegean world and parts of the Near East. Gone forever from those lands were the great powers of the second millennium BCE—the Mycenaeans and Minoans of the Aegean, the Hittites of Anatolia (modern Turkey), the original Babylonians and Assyrians of Mesopotamia, and the Egyptians of the Eighteenth Dynasty.[6]

Mighty Egypt had been brought to its knees in trying to repel successive waves of Sea Peoples attacking by both land and sea. With the collapse of their civilization, the Egyptian overlords of Canaan fled, leaving behind smoking ruins of once-beautiful palaces and fortified cities. The Hittites of central Anatolia, whose sway had once extended as far south as Qadesh in Syria, had been defeated at home, and their capital city of Hattusas, near modern Ankara, lay in ruins. The once-proud Assyrians and Babylonians of Mesopotamia remained in their cities by the banks of the Tigris and Euphrates Rivers and were beset by nomadic tribes that earlier would not have dared attack them. Pleas for help drafted by the king of Ugarit, the largest and most prosperous seaport in northern Syria, went unheard, as his clay tablet lay in the baking kiln, unfired and unsent, when Ugarit was violently destroyed about the year 1186 BCE. "My father, the enemy ships are already here," he had written to the king of Cyprus on the unsent tablet. He continued: "they have set fire to my towns and have done very great damage in the country. . . . Consider this, my father, there are seven enemy ships that have come and done very great damage. Now if there are more enemy ships let me know about them so that I can decide what to do."[7]

CANAANITES, JEBUSITES, AND ISRAELITES

After the withdrawal of the Egyptians and the other great empires, the land of Canaan—now inhabited only by small city-states and petty kingdoms busy fighting among themselves—was a plum ripe for the picking. The Sea Peoples had created a power vacuum in which small tribes and ethnic groups were free to flourish without fear of suppression by larger states and kingdoms.

The principal ethnic groups left in the land of Canaan were the Canaanites and their assorted cousins, including Jebusites and Amorites, together with the unrelated Philistines. The Canaanites may have been one of the "indigenous" peoples of this land. It is not known when exactly they arrived, although they may have already been in place five thousand years ago, by about 3000 BCE. Like the later Phoenicians, the Canaanites were known for the purple dye they manufactured from murex shells, particularly in the coastal regions around the area that is now Sidon and Tyre in modern Lebanon. Indeed, the very name *Canaanite*, like the name *Phoenician*, may have meant "purple" in the original languages of the area.[8]

The origins of the Jebusite peoples are rather more obscure than those of their Canaanite cousins and are even more hotly debated by scholars. So far, only one intriguing suggestion has merited more than a brief discussion. That is the possibility that the Jebusites were distantly related to the Hittites, who ruled ancient Anatolia (modern Turkey) from 1700 BCE to 1200 BCE and whom the Bible surprisingly—and erroneously—places in the land of Canaan itself. The evidence for this relationship is largely circumstantial but is appealing.[9]

An appointment calendar distributed by Faisal Husseini's Palestine Association for Studies of International Affairs in Jerusalem declares, "About the year 4000 BC, the Jebusites, a Canaanite subgroup, founded Jebus—Jerusalem—in the place where it is located today."[10] However, archaeological evidence suggests that Jerusalem was not founded until about 3000 BCE, thus contradicting Husseini's calendar. Moreover, most scholars agree that Jerusalem was under Canaanite—perhaps specifically Amorite—control at the time of the so-called Egyptian Execration Texts from the nineteenth and eighteenth centuries BCE. That conclusion is drawn from the names for the rulers of Jerusalem in the lists of those cursed.

The two sets of so-called Execration Texts list the Syria-Palestinian towns, regions, and rulers that the Egyptians regarded as enemies and upon which they hoped to cast ritual spells and curses. The first, earlier, set of names was written on terra-cotta bowls, while the second set of names was inscribed on terra-cotta figurines in the shape of prisoners. In both instances, the objects were ritually smashed and buried. Only when archeologists reassembled those ceramic jigsaw puzzles could they read the hieroglyphic texts painted or inscribed on the original objects.

Within the earlier set of Execration Texts—those on the bowls—

was written, ". . . the Ruler of Jerusalem, Yaqir-Ammu, and all the retainers who are with him; the Ruler of Jerusalem, Saz-Anu [Sas-Anu or Shaz-Anu], and all the retainers who are with him." The second set of texts—those on the figurines—also include the city of Jerusalem, but in this case only the first syllable of the ruler's name, "Ba . . . ," is still preserved. In both sets, the city's name is given in Egyptian hiero-glyphs as *rwsh3mm*, which has been transliterated by various scholars as *Rushalimum, Urushamem,* or *Urusalim.* Virtually all scholars accept that this is to be translated into English as "Jerusalem." From these texts, moreover, the names of the early rulers of Jerusalem have been interpreted as being of West Semitic—even specifically Amorite—origin.[11]

Although it is impossible to say exactly when the Jebusites took over Jerusalem from their Canaanite or Amorite cousins, scholarly sugges-tions have usually ranged from 2000 BCE to 1200 BCE. At the very least, if the biblical text is to be believed, they were in control of Jerusalem by the time of David, in the late eleventh century BCE.[12]

The date of the first appearance of the Israelites in the land of Canaan is perhaps the most complex and controversial issue. Numer-ous scholars have weighed in on this particular topic, suggesting hypotheses that include an exodus and military conquest as described in the Hebrew Bible, a peaceful infiltration by seminomads, a peasant's revolt by villagers in the highlands against Canaanite overlords, a grad-ual development into "Israelites" from within the local Canaanite pop-ulation, and so on. All we know for certain is that an inscription on a victory monument of Pharaoh Merneptah claims that the Egyptians defeated a people called "Israel" who were living in the land of Canaan by about the year 1207 BCE.[13]

Regardless of the antecedent events and the means by which they entered the picture, by the twelfth and eleventh centuries BCE the Israelites were poised to take advantage of the political and military vacuum created by the marauding Sea Peoples.

THE FIRST BATTLES FOR JERUSALEM

Textual records show that battles for Jerusalem had already occurred hundreds of years before David captured the city. For example, among the (so-called) Amarna Letters sent to the Egyptian pharaoh by Abdi-Heba, the Canaanite ruler of Jerusalem about 1350 BCE, is one in which he writes "the war against me is severe and so I am not able to go in to the king, my lord" (Amarna Letter EA 286).[14]

The Amarna Letters date to the reigns of the Egyptian pharaohs Amenhotep III and his son Akhenaten. They were found in Egypt in 1887 by a peasant woman digging in the fields at modern Tell el-Amarna (ancient Akhetaten) in Egypt, located halfway between the cities of Cairo and Luxor. Most of these ancient letters are copies of correspondence between the Egyptian pharaohs and the rulers of other kingdoms and empires—Babylonia, Assyria, the Hittites, and so on. Within the Amarna archive, there are also letters sent to the Egyptian pharaohs by petty rulers in Canaan who owed them allegiance. Among these was Abdi-Heba of Jerusalem, who was a "mayor" (hazannu) on paper but a minor king in actuality. From his extensive correspondence—he sent at least six letters to the Egyptian pharaoh and was mentioned in two others—it is clear that the name of his city was Urushalim (Jerusalem) and that he was its ruler at this time, ca. 1350 BCE.[15]

Abdi-Heba, who says that he came to power by courtesy of "the strong arm" of the pharaoh (Amarna Letters EA 286, 288), was frequently at odds with his neighbors, and the conflicts he wrote of almost certainly would have involved attacks on Jerusalem itself. In another letter to the Egyptian pharaoh, he sent a similar message.

> . . . message of Abdi-Heba, your servant . . . May the king give thought to his land; the land of the king is lost. All of it has attacked me. . . . I am situated like a ship in the midst of the sea. (Amarna Letter EA 288)

We know that Abdi-Heba's cry for help was not in vain. He received assistance from the pharaoh in the form of a company of fifty archers who were apparently stationed in Jerusalem for some time. The Amarna letters are thus the earliest written records that we possess of conflicts for Jerusalem.

Details of other conflicts that involved Jerusalem before the time of David may be gleaned from the biblical accounts, if they can be trusted.

For instance, the Book of Joshua says that Joshua defeated the king of Jerusalem, a man named Adonizedek, at a battle fought at Gibeon, a site located some distance north of Jerusalem. This was the famous twelfth-century BCE battle in which Joshua commanded the sun to stand still, in order to allow the Israelites more time to kill the enemy soldiers and the five Amorite kings who led them. We are told that Adonizedek was the head of this coalition and that he and the other kings were executed after the battle.[16]

Although the Bible says that Joshua killed the king of Jerusalem, the text is silent on the question of whether or not Joshua captured the city. Modern authorities are divided on this issue, particularly since many of the events portrayed in the Books of Joshua and Judges are problematic in terms of historical accuracy. Many scholars suggest that while Joshua may have captured the surrounding area, Jerusalem itself successfully resisted and Joshua did not take the city. This would mirror situations found elsewhere in Canaan at this time—for instance, Joshua is said to have killed the kings of Megiddo, Taanach, Shimron, Yoqneam, and other cities in the Jezreel Valley without being able to drive out the Canaanites.[17]

DAVID: MAN AND KING

After Joshua's success, the stage was set for David's entrance into both the city and the history of Jerusalem: "And David and all Israel went to Jerusalem, that is Jebus, where the Jebusites were the inhabitants of the land" (1 Chronicles 11:4).[18]

The visual image of David for much of the Western world has been formed by Michelangelo's statue of a beautiful, lean and muscular youth, although that was sculpted some 2,500 years after the man himself lived. Much has been written about King David and the Israelites. David especially has been both adored and reviled in the writings of the last three thousand years. In the past decade alone, he has been called a mythological phantom, a savior, and even a serial killer. The historian Baruch Halpern says bluntly that David "was not someone whom it would be wise to invite to dinner!"[19] And yet, for many, David remains one of the most popular and romantic figures in the Bible, celebrated by the stories of his deeds and adventures. The litany of his achievements is extraordinary: his famous slaying of the mighty Philistine warrior Goliath, when David was but a young boy armed with only a slingshot; his heady ascent from lowly musician to high-ranking advisor within the royal court, eventually to become husband to the king's daughter; his years as an outlaw and mercenary in the wilderness, fleeing the wrath of King Saul; and finally his becoming king.

Those are the stories of myth and legend, recorded in a wonderful biblical biography. However, until recently there has been no archaeological evidence to confirm that a man called David was ever king of the Hebrews or even that David ever existed. Then, in 1993 and 1994, archaeologists excavating at Tel Dan in northern Israel discovered an inscription that commemorates a military campaign in Israel by Hazael of Aram about the year 841 BCE and that mentions the "House of David." This is important supporting evidence from a nonbiblical source that David and the royal lineage that followed him did exist.[20]

The biblical biography presents the following account of how David ascended to the throne of Judah. Saul, the beloved former king, had been killed in battle with the Philistines high on the slopes of Mount Gilboa in the Jezreel Valley. Saul's son Jonathan and three other sons had died in the battle as well. Saul's remaining son, Ishbaal (also called Ishbosheth), assumed command of the northern part of the kingdom, which was called Israel, while David took control of the southern region, called Judah. In time, David gained control of both north and south and established what is often called the United Monarchy.

At first, David situated the capital of his kingdom at Hebron, site of the tomb of the patriarchs, deep in the heart of Judah, in the southern reaches of his lands. David ruled from there for nearly seven years, until the northward growth of his kingdom persuaded him to move to a more central and politically neutral location. The city of Jerusalem was admirably suited for his purposes. It lay in a no-man's-land on the borders of territory governed by the tribes of Judah and Benjamin. It had not yet played a significant role in the history of the Jews and was thus an acceptable seat of government from which to rule both Israel in the north and Judah in the south. It had water and natural defenses. There was only one problem: it was not yet his. But that was a situation soon to be remedied.

DAVID'S BATTLE FOR JERUSALEM: THE BIBLE AND JOSEPHUS

The story of David's battle for Jerusalem, known primarily from the biblical sources, is quickly told.[21] The account in 2 Samuel is usually translated as follows:

> And the king and his men went to Jerusalem against the Jebusites, the inhabitants of the land, who said to David, "You will not come in here, but the blind and the lame will ward you off"—thinking, "David cannot come in here." Nevertheless David took the stronghold of Zion, that is, the city of David. And David said on that day, "Whoever would smite the Jebusites, let him get up the water shaft to attack the lame and the blind, who are hated by David's soul." Therefore it is said, "The blind and the lame shall not come into the house." And David dwelt in the stronghold, and called it the city of David. And David built the city round about from the Millo inward. (2 Samuel 5:6–9)

The account in 1 Chronicles retells this story and adds a few additional details, primarily those concerning the exploits of Joab.

> And David and all Israel went to Jerusalem, that is Jebus, where the Jebusites were the inhabitants of the land. The inhabitants of Jebus said to David, "You will not come in here." Nevertheless David took the stronghold of Zion, that is, the city of David. David said, "Whoever shall smite the Jebusites first shall be chief and commander." And Joab the son of Zeruiah went up first, so he became chief. And David dwelt in the stronghold; therefore it was called the city of David. And he built the city round about from the Millo in complete circuit; and Joab repaired the rest of the city. (1 Chronicles 11:4–8)

If accounts found elsewhere in the Bible are to be believed, Joab may already have been David's trusted lieutenant at the time of his entry into the city.[22]

A traditional interpretation of the biblical text is that David believed he would only be able to capture the Jebusite citadel—the "stronghold of Zion"—by means of a deception. Thus he sent a few chosen men led by Joab to climb up the forty-foot vertical conduit of the water shaft (now known as "Warren's Shaft") and through the underground tunnel system leading from the Gihon Spring in the Kidron Valley to the Jebusite settlement high up on the ridge. After entering the citadel in this manner (perhaps just before dawn, when the senses of the guards were dulled), Joab and his men would have quickly dispatched the sentries and thrown open the gates to David's waiting army.

There is not yet any unequivocal archaeological evidence to corroborate the Bible's story of David's attack on Jerusalem.[23] Furthermore, interpretations of the biblical account are largely dependent upon how the Hebrew word *tsinnor* is translated. This word has been variously interpreted as meaning "water shaft," "ditches," "gutter," "trident," "grappling hook," and so on.[24] Professor P. Kyle McCarter of Johns Hopkins University interprets the word quite differently—as "windpipe"—and has suggested a completely different translation for 2 Samuel 5:6–10, a translation based upon variants found in the Dead Sea Scrolls.

> Then the king and his men went to Jerusalem, to the Jebusites, the inhabitants of the region; but they told David, "You shall not come in here!" (For the blind and the lame had incited them, saying, "David shall not come in here!") So David seized the stronghold of Zion, which is now the City of David, and [he] said at that time, "Whoever smites a Jebusite, let him strike at the windpipe, for David hates the lame and the blind!" (This is the reason it is said, "No one who is blind or lame shall come into the temple.") David occupied the stronghold and called it the City of David. He built a city around it from the Millo inward. David continued to grow greater and greater, because Yahweh Sabaoth was with him. (2 Samuel 5:6–10; translation following McCarter 1984, 135)

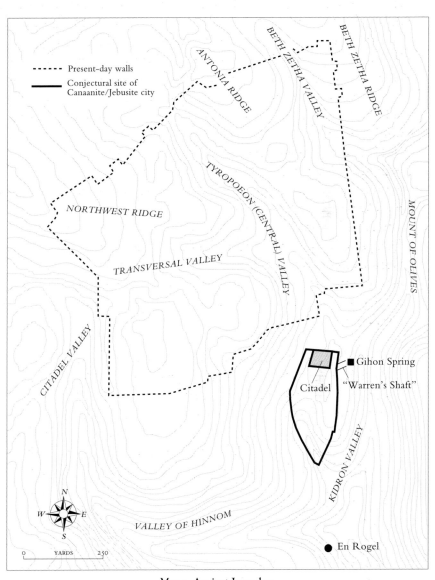

- - - - Present-day walls

━━━━ Conjectural site of
Canaanite/Jebusite city

BETH ZETHA VALLEY

BETH ZETHA RIDGE

ANTONIA RIDGE

TYROPOEON (CENTRAL) VALLEY

MOUNT OF OLIVES

NORTHWEST RIDGE

TRANSVERSAL VALLEY

CITADEL VALLEY

Gihon Spring

Citadel   "Warren's Shaft"

KIDRON VALLEY

N
W   E
S

0   YARDS   250

VALLEY OF HINNOM

En Rogel

Map 3. Ancient Jerusalem

Fig. 1. Jerusalem from the south. (Painting by David Roberts, Esq., R.A.)

Fig. 2. Jerusalem from the north. (Painting by David Roberts, Esq., R.A.)

This is an interesting interpretation of the biblical text, but some recent archaeological evidence now once again favors the interpretation of *tsinnor* as meaning "water shaft," with Joab infiltrating through a system of underground water-carrying tunnels. Israeli archaeologists Roni Reich and Eli Shukron have published evidence showing that the original underground tunnel system connecting Jerusalem with its water source at the Gihon Spring predates the time of David by a good eight centuries. Not only was this water system originally a Canaanite construct, but its origins date to the eighteenth century BCE—approximately the same time that Egypt was cursing the name of Jerusalem in the Execration Texts. In addition, Reich and Shukron identified the remains of massive fortified towers that surrounded and protected the Gihon Spring, also dating from the eighteenth century BCE onward. However, they have shown that "Warren's Shaft"—the vertical water shaft that can still be seen today—was probably not incorporated into the water system until at least two hundred years after the time of King David.[25]

Few additional archaeological remains have survived in the area where the Jebusite fortress and city once stood. As well as the removal (for reuse) of construction materials from earlier buildings, massive erosion and later rebuilding have largely destroyed the ancient site. However, stretches of the Middle Bronze Age city wall were discovered by both an Israeli archaeologist, Yigal Shiloh, and a British archaeologist, Kathleen Kenyon. Kenyon also uncovered a massive stone structure, nicknamed the "Stepped-Stone Structure." Although this was probably built sometime during the fourteenth and thirteenth centuries BCE, it was sufficiently massive to perhaps have been incorporated into the fortifications of the Jebusites—Kenyon has suggested that it may even have been part of the foundations for the stronghold of Zion itself. It is clear that formidable fortifications protecting both the settlement and the water supply, perhaps stout enough to require a stratagem to broach the citadel, were present in Bronze Age Jerusalem. They were probably still present in some form at the time of David's attack in the eleventh century BCE.[26]

With these new archaeological discoveries, it is tempting to reexamine and perhaps once again embrace the traditional biblical account of David's capture of Jerusalem. Joab did not climb up "Warren's Shaft" in order to infiltrate the stronghold of Zion, since the shaft was not in use until well after the time of David. However, Joab could have entered the underground tunnel system down by the Gihon Spring in the Kidron Valley or at any point where access to the system could be gained. He could then have made his way through the centuries-old Canaanite tunnels into the heart of the citadel and then—as Odysseus did for the Greek army at Troy—opened the fortress gates from within to admit David's army. So, for the moment, unless new evidence is unearthed, it is reasonable to accept the translation "Whoever would smite the Jebusites, let him get up the water shaft to attack the lame and the blind, who are hated by David's soul" (2 Samuel 5:8).

There are other uncertainties in the interpretation of the biblical account of David, Joab, and the battle for Jerusalem. One is the meaning of the word *Millo*, which appears at least six times in the Hebrew Bible—for example, at 2 Samuel 5:9: "And David dwelt in the stronghold, and called it the city of David. And David built the city round about from the Millo inward."[27] The best guess is that the word is derived from the Hebrew word meaning "fill" and that it refers to earth that David and Solomon heaped up as a foundation for the structures and fortifications that they built.[28] But that is just a guess. Another unanswered question is how to interpret the reference to "the blind and the lame" among the Jebusites (2 Samuel 5:6–8). Given the uncertainties in the biblical account, it is important to know whether there are other historical documents that can shed light on these questions. There is such a document, but it has to be read with caution and even a degree of skepticism.

Josephus, the Jewish general turned Roman historian and apologist, wrote the only other ancient account of the Israelites' conquest of Jerusalem. He did so during the reigns of the Flavian emperors Vespasian and Titus—the same emperors who built the Colosseum in Rome, probably in part with money from the sacking of Jerusalem and the Second Temple in 70 CE.[29] Thus his account dates from the latter half of the first century CE, nearly 1,100 years after the Israelites wrested control of Jerusalem from the Jebusites.

Now the Jebusites, who were the inhabitants of Jerusalem, and were by extraction Canaanites, shut their gates, and placed the blind, and the lame, and all their maimed persons, upon the wall, in way of derision of the king, and said that the very lame themselves would hinder his entrance into it. This they did out of contempt of his power, and as depending on the strength of their walls. David was hereby enraged, and began the siege of Jerusalem, and employed his utmost diligence and alacrity therein, as intending by the taking of this place to demonstrate his power, and to intimidate all others that might be of the like [evil] disposition toward him. So he took the lower city by force, but the citadel held out still; whence it was that the king, knowing that the proposal of dignities and rewards would encourage the soldiers to greater actions, promised that he who should first go over the ditches that were beneath the citadel, and should ascend to the citadel itself and take it, should have the command of the entire people conferred upon him. So they all were ambitious to ascend, and thought no pains too great in order to ascend thither, out of their desire of the chief command. However, Joab, the son of Zeruiah, prevented the rest; and as soon as he was got up to the citadel, cried out to the king, and claimed the chief command. (Josephus *Antiquities of the Jews* 7.3.61–64)[30]

There are some interesting differences in interpretation and nuance between the biblical account of the battle and the general's story. Josephus interprets the Hebrew word *tsinnor* as meaning "ditches" rather than "water shaft." He states flatly that David captured the lower city before successfully taking the citadel that stood on the northern aspect of the city—an embellishment that does not appear in the biblical texts. Furthermore, Josephus presents a cogent interpretation of the presence of "the blind and the lame" among the Jebusite defenders of the city. The blind and the lame were placed on the battlements as a deliberate act of defiant contempt toward the arrogant Israelites massed outside the walls of the city. The clear message would have been, "We can ward off your puny army with just our blind and lame."

However, many other interpretations of the reference to "the blind and the lame" exist. One is that these "walking wounded" were the only Jebusite soldiers left to defend the citadel. Another, suggested by the famous Israeli warrior and archaeologist Yigael Yadin, is that the

Jebusites were threatening that the Israelites would be struck blind and lame if they dared to attack.[31]

How much credence can be put on Josephus's interpretation of events that occurred more than a millennium before he put pen to papyrus? Hebrew was probably Josephus's native language, and he might well have read or heard accounts of the battle that have long since disappeared. He knew the topography of the city, although it was a city that had changed dramatically in a thousand years. And he knew military strategy. Josephus had been a highly regarded general in the Jewish army before he surrendered ignominiously to the Romans in about 67 CE. Was he an accurate historian, or did he simply write down a version of familiar biblical accounts that were somewhat different from current translations of the Bible?

These questions are unanswered still, and in the end, no one can say with authority which account—the Bible's or Josephus's—is the more reliable. In part this is because there is also currently considerable controversy as to when exactly the biblical stories, including those of 2 Samuel and 1 Chronicles, were written. The short answer is that they were probably written after 1000 BCE and perhaps as late as the seventh century BCE, at the time of Josiah's reign over Judah—that is, at some considerable time after the events they describe.[32] But nobody knows for certain.

Moreover, because there are only the two ancient documentary sources describing David's capture of Jerusalem, some scholars have questioned whether either of these stories can be trusted.[33] However, the Aramaic stele discovered at Tel Dan that mentions the "House of David" has now provided important supporting evidence that David and the royal lineage that followed him did in fact exist. Professor Nadav Naʾaman, the eminent Tel Aviv University ancient historian, has stated that, in his opinion, the facts "strongly support the biblical claims (a) that David conquered Jerusalem and made it his capital; [and] (b) that he founded the royal dynasty of Jerusalem."[34]

ATTACK FROM THE NORTH

We do not know for certain the plan of David's attack on Jerusalem. However, the location of the city among its surrounding hills and valleys places certain constraints on the movements of military forces. As already noted, the ancient city was located on the southern spur of the easternmost of two ridges running side by side from north to south. Steep ravines flanked the eastern ridge on three sides. The only approach to the city of Jerusalem in 1000 BCE was from the north— the only side not defended by a natural barrier. This northern aspect had to be defended by man-made walls and other constructs.[35] To thwart aggressors, the Jebusite citadel called the "stronghold of Zion," mentioned by both Josephus and the biblical accounts, was probably located near the northern edge of the city. We are told that about three thousand years ago, David and his men took the citadel and conquered the city.

Since the basic topography did not change much over the years, an attack primarily from the north was the tactic employed by many conquerors of Jerusalem long after David—conquerors who included Nebuchadnezzar, Antiochus VII, Pompey, Herod, Cestius Gallus, Titus, the Crusaders, Saladin, the Ottomans, the British, the Arab Legion, and the Israelis. However, the visitor to modern Jerusalem will be disappointed in any search for the features of the landscape that almost certainly determined David's final point of attack, because of the expansion of the city over the centuries and the filling in of the Central Valley, which originally separated the two ridges. Nevertheless, even now, thousands of years after the battle, the eastern, western, and southern aspects of the city are still surrounded by valleys or ravines, while the north has no natural defenses.

THE AFTERMATH OF THE BATTLE

With David's victory, Judaism officially came to Jerusalem. However, the biblical account suggests that Jebusites continued to live in Jerusalem even after David's conquest. Neither Josephus nor the Bible mentions a massacre of the city's inhabitants. Presumably they were left alive, since Josephus would almost certainly have remarked upon their slaughter, as he does in connection with sieges elsewhere—most famously that of Masada in 74 CE, where the Jews reportedly took their own lives rather than surrender to the Roman armies.[36] The Jebusites are mentioned only a few more times in the biblical accounts[37] and disappear from them completely by the time of the Babylonian Exile (586 BCE). They have, however, experienced an extraordinary historical rebirth 2,600 years later, in the Palestinian propaganda campaigns of the late twentieth and early twenty-first centuries CE.

According to the biblical account, after David captured the stronghold of Zion, he purchased an adjoining piece of land on the summit of the eastern ridge—an area known as Mount Moriah, just to the north of the city—from Araunah (or Ornan) the Jebusite.[38] The land included a threshing floor, and upon it stood the rock where Abraham, following his God's commandments, had been prepared to sacrifice his son Isaac. David built an altar on the mount, to which he moved the sacred ark of the covenant of the Hebrews. The ark was made of acacia wood, covered with gold, and adorned with cherubim. Within it, the Bible says, was a copy of the Ten Commandments given to Moses on Mount Sinai.

When it was first brought to Jerusalem, the ark was housed in the Tabernacle—an elaborately decorated, multicolored tent that functioned as a movable home and shrine for the god of the Hebrews. David had it set up on the former threshing floor.[39] Decades later, David's son Solomon built the First Temple in this same place, over Abraham's rock,[40] and he installed the ark within the holy of holies—the innermost part of the Temple. More than 1,600 years later—and long after the destruction of Solomon's Temple—Moslems identified this same rock as the one from which Mohammed ascended to heaven while on his famous Night Journey, and they built over it a great edifice now called in English the "Dome of the Rock." Araunah's threshing floor thus eventually became known as the "Temple Mount" and later, in Arabic, as the "Haram al-Sherif"—a holy place for both Judaism and Islam. The area is sacred to Christians as well—in part because of its relationship to Abraham, David, and Solomon, but more particularly because of the later stories of Jesus' involvement with the Second Temple during the time of Herod in the first century CE.

The land on Mount Moriah may already have been a Jebusite holy place at the time that David acquired it from Araunah and converted it into an Israelite "high place" with Abraham's rock as its central feature.[41] Such adoption of sites holy to one religion by another has certainly not been unusual in the history of humankind. Examples are

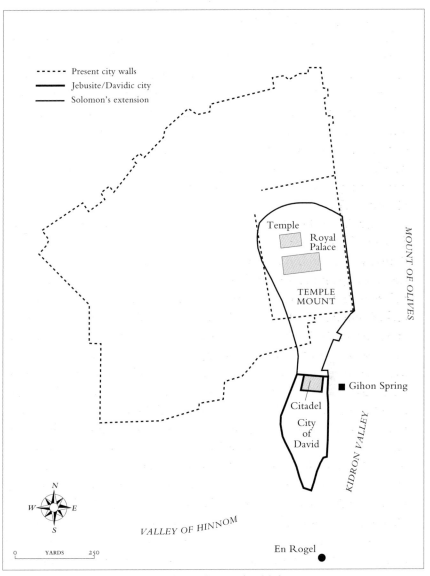

Map 4. Jerusalem under David and Solomon

legion: the construction of Roman temples at Greek shrines, the replacement of Roman temples by Christian churches, and the conversion of Christian churches to Islamic mosques in various parts of the Middle East, the Mediterranean area, and even Europe. Even so, the Temple Mount in Jerusalem may be unique.[42] It has seen the worship of the Canaanite and Jebusite gods, the God of the Hebrews, and now Allah—all over a continuous span of perhaps five thousand years. Jerusalem may first have been sited to take advantage of a year-round water supply and natural defenses. David may have made it his capital because it was centrally located between the two halves of his kingdom and was politically neutral. But today, the city is remarkable for almost certainly holding the world's record for the longest unbroken history of worship at a single site. And probably no other place has commanded the religious allegiance of so many different beliefs.

A MOMENT IN THE SUN

With the capture of Jerusalem, David finally had a capital city from which he could govern his entire territory. Although there is currently an ongoing controversy within archaeological circles as to the size of the city and the extent of the actual territory controlled by David during his reign,[43] it is clear that by moving the ark of the covenant to Jerusalem, David made the city both a religious and a political focal point for his people.

The physical union of Israel and Judah (the joining of north and south known as the United Monarchy), with Jerusalem as its political and religious capital, lasted only through the reigns of David and Solomon—less than a century. However, the importance of this union has endured far longer than the alliance itself. Its reverberations are still being felt today. "Next year in Jerusalem!" has been the cry of Jews for the two thousand years of the Diaspora that followed the Roman destruction of the Second Temple in 70 CE. Jews, longing for their ancestral home, took Jerusalem as a symbol of ambition and hope during the long years of an exile that lasted until the modern state of Israel was founded in 1948. By that time, the Canaanites, Jebusites, and Amorites were long gone. The "stiff-necked" Hebrews, as the Bible calls them (Exodus 33:3–5; 34:9), had outlasted them all.[44]

PALESTINIANS AND ISRAELIS:
WHO ARE THESE PEOPLE?

Few would seriously challenge the belief that most modern Jews are descended from the ancient Hebrews.[45] However, even this simple and ostensibly indisputable claim requires a caveat, because of the often repeated notion that Ashkenazi Jews might be descended from the royal Khazars of southern Russia, who converted to Judaism in the eighth century CE. Even though some scientific doubt—in the form of modern DNA studies—has been cast on the supposed Khazar-Ashkenazi link, the issue continues to be researched and debated.[46]

The origin of the Arab peoples living in the region of modern Israel is even less certain. The calendar distributed by Faisal Husseini, the former minister for Jerusalem affairs of the Palestinian Authority, said, "The Jebusites, who were among the Semitic peoples of Canaan, are the people from whom the Palestinians of today [are] descended." In 1994, the Palestinian scholar Kamil Asali wrote: "The Arabs of Jerusalem, as of those of all of Palestine, are in their majority the descendants of those who lived in the country since time immemorial."[47] But—as mentioned earlier—these claims that modern Palestinians are descended from the ancient Jebusites are made without any supporting evidence. Although some would disagree,[48] historians and archaeologists have generally concluded that most, if not all, modern Palestinians are probably more closely related to the Arabs of Saudi Arabia, Yemen, Jordan, and other countries than they are to the ancient Jebusites, Canaanites, or Philistines. The major movements of those Arabs into the region occurred after 600 CE, more than 1,600 years after David and the Israelites had vanquished the original inhabitants of the land.

In 1997, Rashid Khalidi, then professor of Middle East history and director of the Center for International Studies at the University of Chicago, who has also served as an adviser to various Palestinian delegations, put it bluntly:

There is . . . a relatively recent tradition which argues that Palestinian nationalism has deep historical roots. As with other national movements, extreme advocates of this view . . . anachronistically read back into the history of Palestine over the past few centuries, and even millennia, a nationalist consciousness and identity that are in fact relatively modern. . . . Among the manifestations of this outlook are a . . . predilection for seeing in peoples such as the Canaanites, Jebusites, Amorites, and Philistines the lineal ancestors of the modern Palestinians.[49]

WHAT'S IN A NAME?

The confusion about toponyms and identities (some might call it a deliberate political ambiguity) comes from the fact that the same words—*Palestine* and *Palestinians, Israel* and *Israelis/Israelites*—are now used to designate both the ancient and the modern places and peoples. But the small state of modern Palestine, geographically speaking, is not the same as ancient Palestine, just as modern Israel and ancient Israel are different entities. Ancient Israel was only the northern portion of what is today modern Israel; the southern half of the ancient kingdom in which Jerusalem was sited was known as Judah. Ancient Philistia, home to the Iron Age Philistines, lay primarily along the southern coast of modern Israel, in the approximate area of the Gaza Strip today, as did the Neo-Assyrian province of Palashtu in the early first millennium BCE. In contrast, the Roman province of Syria Palastina was the entire region that lay between Syria and Egypt, an area far larger than the Gaza Strip and West Bank, which currently make up modern Palestine.

As Philip Davies, professor in the Department of Biblical Studies at the University of Sheffield, has noted:

> . . . names and historical identities do not belong together in the simple way that such arguments suppose. For instance, Scotland takes its name from a people (the ancient Scots), who crossed the Irish Sea and settled in Ireland; to the extent that the Scots are descended from any ancient people, these are the Picts, while the Irish are the descendants of the ancient Scots. . . . Modern Palestinians share a label with ancient Philistines, and modern Israelis with Israelites, but in neither case is there really a very strong connection. . . . populations change a lot in the ancient Near East and labels need to be used with due caution . . .[50]

When discussing the ancestry of both modern Palestinians and Israelis, it is important to keep in mind both the tumultuous history of this region over time and the massive waves of migration that have taken place during the past four thousand years. It is necessary to remember the turbulence and movement of peoples during the Neo-Assyrian, Neo-Babylonian, and early Roman periods of the first millennium BCE; the coming of Islam in the first millennium CE; the Moslem, Crusader, Mongol, Mamluke, and Ottoman invasions from the ninth to the sixteenth centuries CE; and, most recently, the movements of both Jews and Arabs in and out of the area in just the past century. As a result of assimilation, annihilation, and acculturation, it is highly unlikely that anyone living in the area today, whether Palestinian or Israeli, can provide a legitimate pedigree definitively extending back to any of the original inhabitants of the "land flowing with milk and honey" (Exodus 3:8, 17; 13:5)—whether Canaanites, Jebusites, Philistines, or Israelites.[51]

2

THE END OF THE BEGINNING

IN FEBRUARY 2001 Ariel Sharon was elected prime minister of Israel. The next day, Saddam Hussein announced the formation of a "Jerusalem Army," to be made up of seven million Iraqis who had volunteered "to liberate Palestine" from Israeli rule. At first many analysts dismissed this as propaganda "in the fantasy drama staged by Saddam." However, in August 2001 the Associated Press reported that thousands of Iraqis had taken to the streets, waving guns and calling for the "liberation of Palestine" under the leadership of Hussein. The banners of the demonstrators read "Here we come Saddam. . . . here we come Jerusalem." By February 2003, as members of the "Jerusalem Army" marched again in Mosul, official Iraqi sources claimed that two and a half million recruits had completed their training in the previous two years.[1]

This was not a new theme for the president of Iraq. In 1979 Saddam Hussein was quoted (in an interview with Fuad Matar, his semiofficial biographer) as saying:

Nebuchadnezzar stirs in me everything relating to pre-Islamic ancient history. And what is most important to me about Nebuchadnezzar is the link between the Arabs' abilities and the liberation of Palestine. Nebuchadnezzar was, after all, an Arab from Iraq, albeit ancient Iraq. Nebuchadnezzar was the one who brought the bound Jewish slaves from Palestine. That is why whenever I remember Nebuchadnezzar I like to remind the Arabs, Iraqis in particular, of their historical responsibilities. It is a burden that should not stop them from action, but rather spur them into action because of their history. So many have liberated Palestine throughout history, before and after the advent of Islam.[2]

Although Nebuchadnezzar was neither Arab nor Moslem, Saddam Hussein's "Nebuchadnezzar Imperial Complex," as psychologist Erwin R. Parson called it, was remarkably consistent. In the late 1980s he promoted the Iraqi arts festival called "From Nebuchadnezzar to Saddam Hussein." He also had a replica of Nebuchadnezzar's war chariot built and had himself photographed standing in it. He ordered images of himself and Nebuchadnezzar beamed, side by side, into the night sky over Baghdad as part of a laser light show. He spent millions rebuilding the ancient site of Babylon, Nebuchadnezzar's capital city, provoking excited anticipation among Christian fundamentalists who saw this as one of the signs of the End Times and the imminent approach of Armageddon.[3]

Who was Nebuchadnezzar and why was he an enduring role model for the president of Iraq? The brief answer is that Nebuchadnezzar—more precisely Nebuchadnezzar II—was a Neo-Babylonian ruler during the late seventh and early sixth centuries BCE. His historical importance derives, at least in part, from the fact that his army destroyed Jerusalem in 586 BCE, after which he expelled the Jews from their ancestral lands. He was responsible for the five-decade-long Babylonian Exile of the Jews—an exile that had a lasting effect on their subsequent history and on the history of the region. The story is an interesting one. But to appreciate it properly, an understanding is first needed of some things about the world of the Near East at the beginning of the sixth century BCE and about some of the events of the preceding four hundred years—the centuries following David's conquest of Jerusalem from the Jebusites.

THE FIRST MILLENNIUM BCE—
FROM 1000 TO 586 BCE

According to the biblical account, David ruled as king over the combined kingdoms of Judah in the south and Israel in the north for about thirty years after his conquest of Jerusalem in about 1000 BCE. His son Solomon succeeded to the throne about 970 BCE and ruled for about forty years. During Solomon's reign—so tradition says—the United Monarchy grew increasingly powerful, as he undertook an ambitious building program throughout the lands of Judah and Israel. He is said to have built large regional centers at Megiddo, Hazor, and Gezer and to have constructed the First Temple of the Jews on the sacred mount in Jerusalem. Not everyone still agrees with this traditional story, however. Archaeologists are now calling much of this scenario into question, and some wonder whether Solomon even existed.[4]

According to the Bible, however, the monarchies of David and Solomon marked a golden age in the history of Judah and Israel. It was a time of unprecedented growth and prosperity. The twelve tribes of Israel—ten in the north and two in the south, composed of the descendants of the twelve sons of Jacob—were now a powerful force in the region, and Jerusalem, their capital, soon became an important administrative center. But power and prosperity were to be short-lived. After King Solomon's death, a succession of kings—some from the lineage of David—ruled over the lands of Judah and Israel for the next four hundred years. As the Books of Kings record, those years were filled with internecine conflicts between the two kingdoms and with a series of catastrophes as internal combatants and outside forces sought to control the lands (see table 2).

After King Solomon's death, his son Rehoboam succeeded to the throne of the United Monarchy of the Jews. But a peaceful reign was not in the cards for the newly crowned king. He had to reckon with Egypt—the great empire to the south. And soon the first of a series of catastrophes overwhelmed the United Monarchy.

> In the fifth year of Rehoboam, Shishak king of Egypt came up
> against Jerusalem; he took away the treasures of the house of the
> LORD, and the treasures of the king's house; he took away every-

thing. He also took away all the shields of gold which Solomon had made . . . (1 Kings 14:25–26)

The Bible's "Shishak" is most likely Pharaoh Shoshenq, a Libyan mercenary who founded the Twenty-second Dynasty of Egypt.[5] In addition to the biblical reference, Shoshenq's campaign is recorded in an inscription found in the great Temple of Karnak in Egypt, which claims that he attacked Canaanite cities in the south, in the north, and along the coastal plains late in the tenth century BCE—around 925 BCE.

SHISHAK/SHOSHENQ AND JERUSALEM

According to the inscription carved on the wall of the Temple of Amon at Karnak in Egypt, Pharaoh Shoshenq campaigned in Syria-Palestine against as many as 150 villages and towns. However, most were located either in the northern kingdom of Israel or in the southern area of the Negev. Few, if any, were located in Judah, and the question of his conquest of Jerusalem itself is still debated.[6] The account in 2 Kings is brief, but the more elaborate tale told by "the Chronicler" (the writer of the biblical Books of Chronicles) states:

> In the fifth year of King Rehoboam, because they had been unfaithful to the LORD, Shishak king of Egypt came up against Jerusalem with twelve hundred chariots and sixty thousand horsemen. And the people were without number who came with him from Egypt—Libyans, Sukkiim, and Ethiopians. And he took the fortified cities of Judah and came as far as Jerusalem. . . . So Shishak king of Egypt came up against Jerusalem; he took away the treasures of the house of the LORD and the treasures of the king's house; he took away everything. He also took away the shields of gold which Solomon had made . . . (2 Chronicles 12:2–9)

This account told by the Chronicler records an elaborate invasion by a huge Egyptian army—comprising some twelve hundred chariots, sixty thousand cavalry, and untold numbers of infantry.[7] However, the

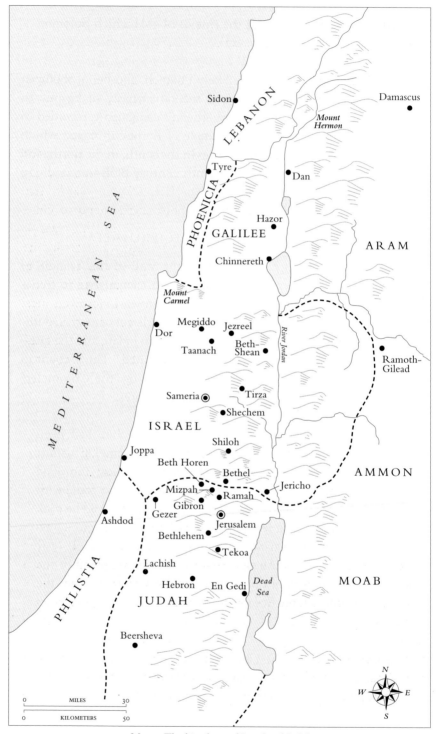

Map 5. The kingdoms of Israel and Judah

detailed inscription of the campaign seems not to mention the city of Jerusalem, and the Chronicler's tale is unsubstantiated by any other contemporary accounts. Thus, while many biblical scholars accept the account of Shishak's attack on Jerusalem and the looting of the treasures of the Temple and palace, others have suggested that only a part of this tale can be believed.

Nadav Naᵓaman and Donald Redford—one a prominent ancient historian and the other a respected Egyptologist—have suggested that a fragmentary inscription discovered at Karnak may indicate that there was a rebellion in Syria-Palestine at approximately this time. They speculate, first, that Rehoboam invited Shishak/Shoshenq to come with an Egyptian army to restore order in the lands, which he did by campaigning primarily in the northern kingdom of Israel and the southern area of the Negev; second, that the treasures from the Temple and the palace in Jerusalem were not taken forcibly but were instead a payment made by Rehoboam to Shishak/Shoshenq for services rendered; and finally, that the author of 2 Chronicles manufactured his story by borrowing details from the 701 BCE campaigns of Sennacherib, the Neo-Assyrian.[8] It remains to be seen if further research will prove any of their interpretations correct.

ACT 1—ENTER ISRAEL

A few years before the invasion by Shishak and the Egyptian army, the tribes of the northern kingdom of Israel (see map 5), angry over taxes instituted by King Rehoboam, broke away to form an independent kingdom. The northerners may already have been unhappy with the central administration in Jerusalem in the time of King Solomon.[9] After the split—and for the next two hundred years—Israel in the north and Judah in the south were separate entities frequently at each other's throats. For most of this period, Israel was the dominant force, with a more numerous population and a comparatively large land area. Blessed with rich arable soil and a more equable climate, the kingdom of Israel was prosperous and powerful, while the kingdom of Judah, bearing the twin burdens of poor soil and a more arid climate with unpredictable rainfall, remained a relatively impoverished backwater.

A new golden age began for the kingdom of Israel some time

between the ninth and eighth centuries BCE. At one point—about 853 BCE—the kingdom was sufficiently powerful to help confront and thwart the forces of the Neo-Assyrian Empire in its attempt to expand westward from Mesopotamia.[10] But the power and prosperity of the northern kingdom did not endure. The Hebrew Bible tells how the people of Israel fell from grace almost immediately. Embracing both their neighbors' women and alien gods, the Israelites took foreign wives and forsook the covenant with their "one true God." They built cult centers to new gods and resurrected idolatry. From the perspective of the biblical writers, that King Ahab took the Phoenician princess Jezebel as his wife showed the marked change for the worse in mores.

The Bible (not surprisingly) reports that the tribes of the north eventually had to pay for their sinful ways (see the Book of Judges and the Books of Kings). Certainly, bloody feuds ensued as successive contenders sought to rule the kingdom. Chaos often ruled in the north and sometimes overran the south as well. Several attacks were made on Jerusalem itself by northern rulers during the ninth and eighth centuries BCE.

AN ATTACK HERE, AN ATTACK THERE . . .

The reported attacks on Jerusalem during the ninth and eighth centuries BCE are known only from the Hebrew Bible and have yet to be corroborated by any other source. The first attack was by Baasha, the king of Israel, who reportedly marched on Judah as far as the northern outskirts of Jerusalem about 875 BCE. To thwart his ambitions, Asa, the king of Judah, formed an alliance with Ben-hadad, king of Syria, bribing him with the treasures of the Temple.[11]

The second attacker—Hazael, king of Aram-Damascus (corresponding to parts of modern Syria)—was seen by the biblical writers as an instrument of divine punishment for the transgressions of the northern kingdom. He conquered some or all of Israel around 841 BCE in a campaign that swept across the Jordan River and over the coastal plains.[12] Some years later, Hazael threatened to besiege Jerusalem. According to the account in 2 Kings, he was bought off by Jehoash (Joash) of Judah, who, like several before him, used the treasures of the Temple. Accord-

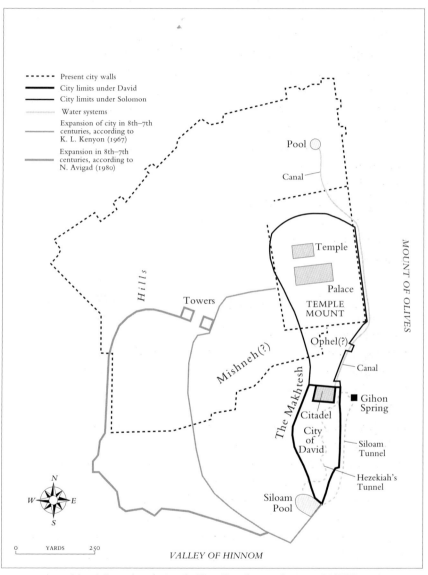

Legend

- Present city walls
- City limits under David
- City limits under Solomon
- Water systems
- Expansion of city in 8th–7th centuries, according to K. L. Kenyon (1967)
- Expansion in 8th–7th centuries, according to N. Avigad (1980)

Pool

Canal

Temple

Palace

TEMPLE MOUNT

Hills

Towers

Ophel(?)

Mishneh(?)

Canal

The Makhtesh

Gihon Spring

Citadel

City of David

Siloam Tunnel

Hezekiah's Tunnel

Siloam Pool

MOUNT OF OLIVES

N
W — E
S

0   YARDS   250

VALLEY OF HINNOM

Map 6. Jerusalem during the First Temple period, 1000–586 BCE

ing to the Chronicler, however, the bribe was of no avail. Jerusalem was attacked, and Jehoash was murdered in a palace coup.[13]

The Hebrew Bible then tells of yet another king named Jehoash (Joash)—a king of Israel, not Judah—who "broke down the wall of Jerusalem." Once again the treasures of the Temple were looted. This was said to have occurred during the reign of the Judaean king Amaziah, around 785 BCE.[14]

Sometime later, the increasing threat from the expanding Neo-Assyrian Empire prompted a Judaean king named Azariah—or Uzziah—to strengthen the fortifications of Jerusalem. He added various towers; put balistae and catapults "on the towers and the corners, to shoot arrows and great stones"; and raised a large army (2 Chronicles 26:9–15). Whether the expected attack ever took place is unknown.

In 734 BCE, during the reign of Ahaz (Jehoahaz) of Judah, a complex political situation arose. Pekah, the king of Israel, and Rezin, the king of Aram-Damascus in Syria, conspired to attack Judah and to lay siege to Jerusalem. Ahaz, apparently in desperation, turned to Tiglath-Pileser III, the Neo-Assyrian king, for assistance, and once again the treasury of the Temple was emptied in order to pay the necessary bribe.[15] The bribe (or perhaps a tribute paid subsequently) is recorded on a building inscription of Tiglath-Pileser III: "In all the countries which . . . [I received] the tribute of . . . Mitinti of Ashkelon, Jehoahaz (Ia-u-ha-zi) of Judah (Ia-u-da-a-a) . . ."[16]

Then a new king ascended to the throne of the Neo-Assyrian Empire, Shalmaneser V (727–722 BCE). He decided to crush these troublesome people in Israel once and for all. Apparently he had some justification. As far as the Neo-Assyrians were concerned, Israel was a minor but annoying vassal state situated in an important buffer zone between Mesopotamia and Egypt.[17] The king of Israel at that time, Hoshea by name, had attempted to play the two great powers in the region, Egypt and Assyria, against each other. Moreover, he had neglected to pay the usual tribute to his Neo-Assyrian overlords.

Shalmaneser's reaction was swift. He laid siege to Samaria, the capital of the northern kingdom, and conquered the city after three years of fighting. To minimize the possibility of future annoyances and to secure the area, Shalmaneser instituted a program of deporting the conquered population of Israel. His successor, Sargon II (722–705

BCE)—who may have marched as far south as Jerusalem[18]—also continued the policy of deportation. The conquerors exiled and dispersed the ten tribes of the northern kingdom and resettled their lands with other peoples: "And the king of Assyria brought people from Babylon, Cuthah, Avva, Hamath, and Sepharvaim, and placed them in the cities of Samaria instead of the people of Israel" (2 Kings 17:24).[19] These ten tribes became the lost tribes of Israel and were never to be heard from again (discounting anecdotal tales to the effect that some of them eventually turned up as Native Americans and Welshmen).

The Hebrew Bible's account of the post-Solomonic period may not always be historically accurate or precise,[20] but there is little question that by 720 BCE the northern kingdom was no longer an independent Israelite domain. However, the southern kingdom of Judah and its capital city of Jerusalem still existed. With the northern kingdom of Israel in ruins and its people dispersed, the next act belonged to the kingdom of Judah.

ACT 2—ENTER JUDAH

In the view of the authors of the Bible, the descendants of Judah, one of the twelve sons of Jacob, were destined to rule over the other tribes.[21] These descendants resided in the southern kingdom. And indeed, with the fall of the northern kingdom of Israel late in the eighth century BCE, the kingdom of Judah awakened from its torpor and entered a period of exceptional growth and prosperity.

Jerusalem became the administrative and religious capital of a powerful kingdom. Its population swelled from the influx of refugees fleeing the devastated northern kingdom of Israel.[22] However, the transformation from the sleepy capital of a quiet backwater to the central city of a regional powerhouse was not to be easy. The vassal states and provinces of the Neo-Assyrian Empire surrounded the land of Judah, and the last decades of the eighth century BCE saw Judah's relationship with that great empire alternating between cooperation and defiance.

A pattern of growth-rebellion-destruction-regrowth characterized Judah during the next century. In 705 BCE, rebellion flared as a chance to break free of the Neo-Assyrian grip presented itself. The powerful Neo-Assyrian king Sargon II died, leaving the throne to his young untested son, Sennacherib, at a moment when the Neo-Assyrian Empire was preoccupied with troubles in its eastern domains. Once again, a king of the Jews, Hezekiah, attempted to play the two great regional powers, Egypt and Assyria, against each other. Apparently, the failure of Hoshea's similar strategy fifteen years earlier did not discourage Hezekiah, who entered into an arrangement with an anti-Assyrian coalition that was backed by Egypt: "[Hezekiah] rebelled against the king of Assyria and would not serve him" (2 Kings 18:7).[23] But his hopes of greatness and independence were soon to be dashed.

"LIKE A BIRD IN A CAGE"

In 701 BCE, four years after Hezekiah came to an agreement with an anti-Assyrian coalition, Sennacherib retaliated and invaded the lands of Judah with massive forces. Records from Assyria tell of widespread destruction throughout the lands of Judah. The Bible tells us that Jerusalem itself did not fall to the conquering armies, and an inscription of Sennacherib's that details the campaign reads:

> In my third campaign, I marched against Hatti [Syria-Palestine]. . . . As for Hezekiah, the Judaean, who had not submitted to my yoke, I besieged forty-six of his fortified walled and surrounding small towns, which were without number. . . . I took out 200,150 people, young and old, male and female, horses, mules, donkeys, camels, cattle and sheep, without number, and counted them as spoil. Himself [Hezekiah], I locked him up within Jerusalem, his royal city, like a bird in a cage.[24]

We know from both the Hebrew Bible and Neo-Assyrian inscriptions that Sennacherib besieged the city at least once (and perhaps twice, some would argue). It seems that the siege(s) did not result in the city being taken. Sennacherib never claimed that he actually captured Jerusalem. If he had, he would probably have depicted its conquest in his lavish palace in Nineveh, where he memorialized the capture of Lachish—the second most important city in Judah—in a huge relief inscribed on stone panels totaling sixty feet long by nine feet high. The panels, now primarily in the British Museum, depict the

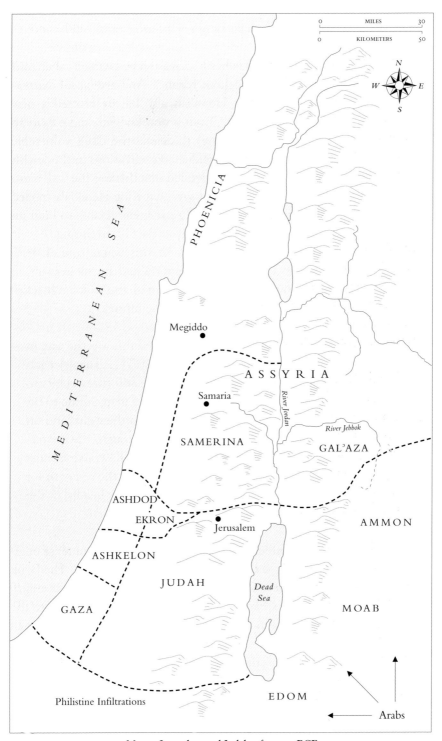

Map 7. Jerusalem and Judah, after 722 BCE

siege in gory detail, with siege ramps, battering rams, and captives being flayed alive.[25]

Hezekiah prepared for Sennacherib's invasion by laying in abundant supplies in Jerusalem and throughout Judah.[26] Archaeological excavations in Jerusalem suggest that Hezekiah also hastily erected a new fortification wall (the "Broad Wall," as it is now known—more than 20 feet thick and at least 130 feet long) to defend the city's vulnerable north side. Nahman Avigad, who conducted excavations in the Jewish Quarter of Jerusalem in the 1970s, suggested that this was the wall mentioned in the Book of Isaiah, where it says that King Hezekiah "pulled houses down to fortify the wall" (Isaiah 22:10). Hezekiah also built an additional access to the city's water supply at the Gihon Spring.[27]

The construction through solid rock of this water tunnel, now known as "Hezekiah's Tunnel," was immortalized in an inscription carved into its roof. Now in a museum in Istanbul, the "Siloam Inscription" tells of the triumphant completion of the tunnel.

> . . . when the tunnel was driven through. And this was the way in which it was cut through: While [. . .] were still [. . .] axe[s], each man toward his fellow, and while there were still three cubits to be cut through, [there was heard] the voice of a man calling to his fellow, for there was an overlap in the rock on the right [and on the left]. And when the tunnel was driven through, the quarrymen hewed [the rock], each man toward his fellow, axe against axe; and the water flowed from the spring toward the reservoir for 1,200 cubits, and the height of the rock above the head[s] of the quarrymen was 100 cubits.[28]

As Finkelstein and Silberman have pointed out, this immense engineering feat did not escape the notice of the biblical writers. The Book of 2 Kings states, "The rest of the deeds of Hezekiah, and all his might, and how he made the pool and the conduit and brought water into the city, are they not written in the Book of the Chronicles of the kings of Judah?" (2 Kings 20:20).[29]

Sennacherib's own inscriptions give no reason why he left Judah before capturing Jerusalem. However, the biblical account in 2 Kings tells us that Hezekiah apparently regretted attempting rebellion and sent a bribe aimed at persuading Sennacherib to spare Jerusalem.

> And Hezekiah king of Judah sent to the king of Assyria at Lachish, saying, "I have done wrong; withdraw from me; whatever you impose on me I will bear." And the king of Assyria required of Hezekiah king of Judah three hundred talents of silver and thirty talents of gold. And Hezekiah gave him all the silver that was found in the house of the LORD, and in the treasuries of the king's house. At that time Hezekiah stripped the gold from the doors of the temple of the LORD, and from the doorposts which Hezekiah king of Judah had overlaid, and gave it to the king of Assyria. (2 Kings 18:14–16)

The amount of the bribe approximately matches the amount of tribute recorded by Sennacherib in his own inscriptions, although he says there that Hezekiah paid him eight hundred talents of silver (rather than only three hundred), in addition to the thirty talents of gold and other items.[30]

The Bible also gives other accounts of the Neo-Assyrian incursion. In one, Sennacherib's army stands outside the walls of Jerusalem, and his representative informs the inhabitants of the city that resistance will be futile.[31] This is in turn followed by a plague that drives off the Assyrians.

> And that night the angel of the LORD went forth, and slew a hundred and eighty-five thousand in the camp of the Assyrians; and when men arose early in the morning, behold, these were all dead bodies. Then Sennacherib king of Assyria departed, and went home, and dwelt at Nineveh. (2 Kings 19:32–36; see also 2 Chronicles 32:20–21)[32]

Sennacherib's invasion profoundly disrupted life in Judah, as did his deportation of as many as 200,150 people (if his inscription can be believed)—surely a considerable proportion of the population. Archaeological surveys indicate that Judah had trouble recovering from Sennacherib's campaign.[33] Perhaps as a result of the thorough disruption, no further rebellions and, thus, no further conflicts involving the city of Jerusalem are recorded until the time of Nebuchadnezzar, a century later. By that time, the Neo-Babylonians had replaced the Neo-Assyrians as the new power in the region, and they soon eclipsed the disruption caused by Sennacherib with their own, more massive series of interventions, through the agency of Nebuchadnezzar II.

In the aftermath of Sennacherib's invasion, some towns and villages were rebuilt, but many were left in ruins for years. Parts of Judah were given to Philistine coastal city-states. Three years after the invasion, King Hezekiah died, and his son Manasseh ascended the throne. Manasseh reinstituted a policy of cooperation with the Neo-Assyrian Empire, and the kingdom of Judah began to thrive once more. The kingdom sat astride important trade routes and soon became an important participant in the commerce between Assyria to the north and Arabia to the south. Olive oil, spices, and luxury goods were brought along caravan routes that ran through Judah, and some of the wealth stayed in the kingdom. The century that followed Manasseh's accession was a period of relative prosperity for Judah. It was also a time of great religious reform, primarily during the reign of Josiah (639–609 BCE): ". . . and all the shrines also of the high places that were in the cities of Samaria, which kings of Israel had made, provoking the LORD to anger, Josiah removed" (2 Kings 23:19–20).[34] Josiah was to be the last independent king of Judah descended from the lineage of David; those who followed him would be puppet kings controlled by foreign masters.

SETTING THE STAGE

For centuries the small kingdoms and city-states of the Levant had been in thrall to either the Neo-Assyrians to the north or the Egyptians to the south. Their fortunes waxed and waned as the relative strengths and ambitions of the two superpowers changed over time. In the last years of the seventh century (700–601 BCE), the Neo-Assyrian Empire was crumbling—a result of challenges from nomadic tribes on its northern border, the growing power of the Neo-Babylonians, and an internal civil war. At the same time, Egypt, which had once been the greatest power in the region but had declined in recent decades, was beginning to awaken from a long sleep.

Around 656 BCE, a pharaoh named Psammetichus I had founded the Twenty-sixth Dynasty of Egypt and thrown off the yoke of the Neo-Assyrian domination of his kingdom. He expanded his domain northward into the areas that had once belonged to Egypt but were now under the Neo-Assyrian thumb. As they drove northward, the Egyptians recaptured their long-lost territory in the area that they once called Canaan. When Psammetichus died in 610 BCE, he was succeeded by his son, Pharaoh Necho II. It was Necho who sent Josiah of Judah to his doom, killing him in a famous encounter at Megiddo in the Jezreel Valley in 609 BCE. As the Hebrew Bible says, "In his days, Pharaoh Necho, king of Egypt, went up to the king of Assyria, to the river Euphrates. King Josiah went to meet him; and Pharaoh Necho slew him at Megiddo, when he saw him" (2 Kings 23:29).[35]

After Josiah's death in 609 BCE, Judah suffered a period of tremendous turbulence. The great powers of the north and the south struggled for control of the Levant. Moreover, as that conflict worked itself out, with the Egyptian Empire expanding and the Neo-Assyrian Empire crumbling, a new power was emerging in Mesopotamia. In 605 BCE Nebuchadnezzar II and the Neo-Babylonians entered the stage (see table 2).

The Neo-Babylonians were making their first appearance in the Near East and would introduce a new twist to the centuries-old plot of the successive advances and retreats of the Neo-Assyrians and the Egyptians. Their civilization—like those of the earlier Babylonians, the Assyrians, and the Neo-Assyrians before them—was born in the lands between the Tigris and Euphrates Rivers in Mesopotamia. As the seventh century ended and the sixth century dawned, their new empire was still young but was growing in strength. It was not long before the Neo-Babylonians cast covetous eyes on the lands to the west and south of their homeland.

Apprehensive about the newcomer, the Neo-Assyrian and Egyptian kingdoms briefly united to engage the common enemy—the Neo-Babylonian army led by Nebuchadnezzar. The ensuing battle of Carchemish took place in 605 BCE in what is now modern Syria. Nebuchadnezzar won the day, and both the Neo-Assyrians and the

Egyptians were forced to flee in disarray. The battle proved to be the deathblow to the tottering Neo-Assyrian Empire. Within a few years, Nebuchadnezzar and the Neo-Babylonians came to control virtually the entire Levant.

Nebuchadnezzar, who had been crown prince at the time of the battle at Carchemish, ascended to the throne in Babylon almost immediately afterward and ruled for the next forty-three years (605–562 BCE). He quickly expanded his empire southward, marching into Judah and destroying the city of Ashkelon in 604 BCE. In 601 BCE he again fought Pharaoh Necho II and the Egyptian forces. As far as can be deduced from the so-called *Babylonian Chronicles*—a contemporary record kept by the Neo-Babylonian priests of the chief events for each year during much of this period—neither side was able to claim a clear-cut victory, and each sustained heavy casualties, afterward withdrawing from the field of battle to recover and regroup.[36]

According to information gleaned from the Book of 2 Kings in the Hebrew Bible and from the *Babylonian Chronicles*, it seems that Jehoiakim, king of Judah, was a faithful vassal of Nebuchadnezzar for the first few years, from about 604 to 601 BCE.[37] However, following the self-destructive pattern of his predecessors, Jehoiakim eventually rebelled. In 601 BCE, following the Babylonian failure to conquer Egypt, Jehoiakim withheld from Nebuchadnezzar the annual tribute due from the kingdom of Judah. His motive for so provoking his overlord, the king of a rich and powerful empire, is uncertain. Jehoiakim may already have been pro-Egyptian in his leanings, since he owed his seat on the Judaean throne to the Egyptians rather than to the newly arrived Neo-Babylonians. Perhaps he thought that the Neo-Babylonians' failure to achieve a clear-cut victory in the battle of 601 BCE indicated weakness; if so, he was mistaken. In any event, it is certain that Nebuchadnezzar did not take kindly to his vassal's insubordination.

According to both biblical and other sources, Nebuchadnezzar retreated to Babylon after his encounter with the Egyptians in 601 BCE. He allowed fully three years to elapse before he set out for the Levant again; this time his purpose was to bring the kingdom of Judah to heel. When he finally acted, he did so with determination; the Neo-Babylonian Empire could not countenance a disaffected independent kingdom situated so close to the border of the Egyptian enemy. The king of Judah had seriously misjudged the prevailing political wind, and Jerusalem was about to pay the price. Judah and Jerusalem became a "contested periphery," caught once again between the grinding stones of great powers to the north and south.[38]

NEBUCHADNEZZAR AND JEHOIAKIM, 598 BCE

The Jewish historian Josephus claimed to know what happened upon Nebuchadnezzar's return from Babylon, although the historian was writing some six centuries after the actual events took place. According to Josephus's account, Nebuchadnezzar attacked Jerusalem in 598 BCE and put Jehoiakim to death for rebelling and failing to pay tribute. He also exiled or put to death many of the leading citizens of the city. Josephus described the events as follows:

> the king of Babylon made an expedition against Jehoiakim. . . . when he [Nebuchadnezzar] was come into the city, he did not observe the covenants he had made, but he killed such as were in the flower of their age, and such as were of the greatest dignity, together with their king Jehoiakim, whom he commanded to be thrown before the walls, without any burial; and made his son Jehoiachin king of the country, and of the city: he also took the principal persons in dignity for captives, three thousand in number, and led them away to Babylon; among which was the prophet Ezekiel, who was then but young. And this was the end of king Jehoiakim, when he had lived thirty-six years, and of them reigned eleven. But Jehoiachin succeeded him in the kingdom, whose mother's name was Nehushta; she was a citizen of Jerusalem. He reigned three months and ten days. (Josephus *Antiquities of the Jews* 10.6.96–98)

The Bible gives us a somewhat more ambiguous account of Jehoiakim's final days, so that the manner and place of his death are matters of debate. We are told variously: "Against him [Jehoiakim] came up Nebuchadnezzar king of Babylon, and bound him in fetters to take him to Babylon" (2 Chronicles 36:6); "In his days, Nebuchadnezzar king of Babylon came up . . . and the LORD sent against him [Jehoiakim] bands of the Chaldeans [Neo-Babylonians] . . . and sent them against Judah to destroy it" (2 Kings 24:1–2); and "So Jehoiakim slept with his fathers, and Jehoiachin his son reigned in his stead" (2 Kings 24:6).[39]

According to Josephus, after Nebuchadnezzar conquered Jerusalem in 598 BCE, he took away to Babylon three thousand "principal persons" as captives, including the prophet Ezekiel.[40] The worst, however, was yet to come, for Nebuchadnezzar laid siege to Jerusalem at least twice more—in 597 and 586 BCE.

NEBUCHADNEZZAR AND JEHOIACHIN, 597 BCE

After the death of Jehoiakim, his son, eight (or possibly eighteen) years old, ascended to the throne of Judah. His reign was short-lived, even by the standards of the Levant in the sixth century BCE. Sometime around the middle of March in 597 BCE, Nebuchadnezzar once again swept into the lands of Judah. Three sources attest to that: the *Babylonian Chronicles*, the Bible, and Josephus. The entry for the seventh year of Nebuchadnezzar's reign in the *Babylonian Chronicles* reads as follows:

> The seventh year: In the month Kislev, the king of Akkad mustered his army and marched to Hattu [Syria-Palestine]. He encamped against the city of Judah and on the second day of the month Adar he captured the city (and) seized (its) king. A king of his own choice he appointed in the city (and) taking vast tribute he brought it into Babylon.[41]

The recording of the exact date for the capture of Jerusalem—the second day of the month Adar (March 16)—is extremely unusual in the Neo-Babylonian records and perhaps reflects the importance of the conquest. From start to finish, Nebuchadnezzar's campaign lasted no more than three months.[42] It has been estimated that it would have taken the Neo-Babylonian army about eight weeks to march from

Babylon to Jerusalem—a distance of about sixteen hundred kilometers (one thousand miles)—if the army were able to march an average of thirty kilometers (about nineteen miles) each winter day. If so, the city capitulated after a siege that lasted no more than a month.[43]

Although no details of the siege are given, the account in the Hebrew Bible agrees with that of the *Babylonian Chronicles*. The biblical history tells us that Nebuchadnezzar himself arrived when the siege was already underway.

> At that time the servants of Nebuchadnezzar king of Babylon came up to Jerusalem, and the city was besieged. And Nebuchadnezzar king of Babylon came to the city, while his servants were besieging it; and Jehoiachin the king of Judah gave himself up to the king of Babylon, himself, and his mother, and his servants, and his princes, and his palace officials. The king of Babylon took him prisoner in the eighth year of his reign, and carried off all the treasures of the house of the LORD, and the treasures of the king's house, and cut in pieces all the vessels of gold in the temple of the LORD, which Solomon king of Israel had made, as the LORD had foretold. (2 Kings 24:10–13)

The biblical account states that, in addition to young king Jehoiachin, Nebuchadnezzar carried away approximately ten thousand captives from the conquered city.

> He [Nebuchadnezzar] carried away all Jerusalem, and all the princes, and all the mighty men of valor, ten thousand captives, and all the craftsmen and the smiths; none remained, except the poorest people of the land. And he carried away Jehoiachin to Babylon; the king's mother, the king's wives, his officials, and the chief men of the land, he took into captivity from Jerusalem to Babylon. And the king of Babylon brought captive to Babylon all the men of valor, seven thousand, and the craftsmen and the smiths, one thousand, all of them strong and fit for war. And the king of Babylon made Mattaniah, Jehoiachin's uncle, king in his stead, and changed his name to Zedekiah. (2 Kings 24:14–17)[44]

Josephus was even more precise in his estimate of the number of Jews carried in exile to Babylon: 10,832. He wrote as follows:

> But a terror seized on the king of Babylon, who had given the kingdom to Jehoiachin, and that immediately; he was afraid that he [Jehoiachin] should bear him [Nebuchadnezzar] a grudge, because of his killing his father, and thereupon should make the country revolt from him; so he [Nebuchadnezzar] sent an army, and besieged Jehoiachin in Jerusalem; but because he [Jehoiachin] was of a gentle and just disposition, he did not desire to see the city endangered on his account, but he took his mother and family, and delivered them to the commanders sent by the king of Babylon, and accepted of their oaths, that neither should they suffer any harm, nor the city; which agreement they did not observe for a single year, for the king of Babylon did not keep it, but gave orders to his generals to take all that were in the city captives, both the youth and the handicraftsmen, and bring them bound to him; their number was ten thousand eight hundred and thirty-two; as also Jehoiachin, and his mother and friends. And when these were brought to him, he kept them in custody, and appointed Jehoiachin's uncle, Zedekiah, to be king . . . (Josephus *Antiquities of the Jews* 10.7.99–102)

After the conquest of Jerusalem, Nebuchadnezzar dedicated the "precious vessels of the house of the LORD" (2 Chronicles 36:10)—taken from the Temple Mount in Jerusalem—in the Temple of Marduk at Babylon. He installed the newly renamed Zedekiah (brother of Jehoiakim and a son of the late King Josiah) on the throne of Judah to rule as a puppet king in Jerusalem. Perhaps Nebuchadnezzar hoped that Zedekiah, recalling his father's death at the hands of the Egyptians at Megiddo two decades earlier, would be inclined to establish a court that was more pro-Babylonian in outlook than those of his predecessors.[45] That is exactly what Zedekiah did, at least for the first years of his reign. But he, like some of his predecessors on the throne of Judah, seems to have had little understanding of realpolitik. He, too, thought that he could successfully challenge the mightiest empire in the Levant. Like Jehoiakim and Jehoiachin before him, Zedekiah misjudged the power and determination of the Neo-Babylonian monarch. And as he and his subjects were soon to learn, the price of rebellion would be high and would have to be paid out over many years in exile.

NEBUCHADNEZZAR AND ZEDEKIAH

The *Babylonian Chronicles* break off after Nebuchadnezzar's eleventh year of rule (594/593 BCE). Consequently, reliance must be put on the biblical account and the later commentary of Josephus for the story of Zedekiah's rebellion against Nebuchadnezzar. However, there is archaeological evidence to support the tales of the destruction of Jerusalem that followed Nebuchadnezzar's ruthless suppression of the rebellion in 586 BCE.

The Bible records that Zedekiah was twenty-one years old when he became king in Jerusalem, that his rule lasted eleven years (597–586 BCE), and that he rebelled against the Neo-Babylonians.[46] There is evidence that Zedekiah began to plot revolution not long after he ascended the throne. Some scholars believe that he may have convened a meeting of potential anti-Babylonian allies as early as 594 BCE, within three years of assuming the mantle of kingship. According to the Bible, he invited to a gathering in Jerusalem delegations from "the king of Edom, the king of Moab, the king of the sons of Ammon, the king of Tyre, and the king of Sidon" (Jeremiah 27:1–3). If successful, this gathering would have created an anti-Babylonian coalition encompassing modern Israel, Jordan, and coastal Lebanon (see maps 1 and 2). However, this early attempt seems to have been aborted before it could come to fruition, and Zedekiah's real rebellion probably did not begin until several years later—in 591 BCE at the earliest and possibly not until 589 BCE.[47]

THE SIEGE OF JERUSALEM, 587–586 BCE

It seems that, at first, Nebuchadnezzar was slow to respond to the insurrection in Judah. His campaign to put it down did not begin until the tenth day of the tenth month (Tebet) in Zedekiah's ninth year of rule—equivalent to January 15, 587 BCE. Three nearly identical biblical accounts tell the story of the campaign. Josephus's history, written several centuries later, also deals with it.[48]

As Nebuchadnezzar's forces swept down from Babylonia, they destroyed the cities of Judah one by one. Archaeological evidence from many sites in modern Israel paints a grim picture of destruction throughout the land. Rubble-strewn houses with fire-blackened toppled walls were all that remained of once prosperous villages. Lachish and Azekah were among the last cities of Judah to face this onslaught.[49] Then it was Jerusalem's turn. Josephus records that Nebuchadnezzar's siege of Jerusalem lasted a total of eighteen months. Both he and the biblical accounts agree that it ended about July 18, 586 BCE—on the ninth day of the fourth month (Tammuz) of Zedekiah's eleventh year of rule.[50]

It is generally thought that Zedekiah broke his allegiance and his word to Nebuchadnezzar at the instigation of the Egyptians and that he expected the Egyptian army to come to his assistance once his revolution began. According to Josephus, Egyptian forces did at first attempt to relieve the siege of Jerusalem but were defeated by Nebuchadnezzar's army. He wrote thus:

> Now when Zedekiah had preserved the league of mutual assistance he had made with the Babylonians for eight years, he broke it, and revolted to the Egyptians, in hopes, by their assistance, of overcoming the Babylonians. When the king of Babylon knew this, he made war against him: he laid his country waste, and took his fortified towns, and came to the city Jerusalem itself to besiege it. But when the king of Egypt heard what circumstances Zedekiah his ally was in, he took a great army with him, and came into Judea, as if he would raise the siege; upon which the king of Babylon departed from Jerusalem, and met the Egyptians, and joined battle with them, and beat them; and when he had put them to flight, he pursued them, and drove them out of all Syria. (Josephus *Antiquities of the Jews* 10.7.108–10)

A brief passage in the Hebrew Bible lends some support to Josephus's account: "The army of Pharaoh had come out of Egypt; and when the Chaldeans [Neo-Babylonians] who were besieging Jerusalem heard news of them, they withdrew from Jerusalem" (Jeremiah 37:5; see also 37:11–15). Some question whether the ill-fated Egyptian intervention ever actually took place.[51] In any event, Nebuchadnezzar's siege of Jerusalem either continued uninterrupted or was resumed shortly after the brief interruption by the Egyptians.

Brief biblical accounts and Josephus give details of the assault on Jerusalem. The siege tactics appear to have been the standard ones used by the Neo-Babylonian armies in their conquest of other Judaean cities and, indeed, to have been much the same as those employed by the Neo-Assyrians in their conquest of the Levant more than a century earlier.[52] Josephus's account is as follows:

> Now the king of Babylon was very intent and earnest upon the siege of Jerusalem; and he erected towers upon great banks of earth, and from them repelled those that stood upon the walls; he also made a great number of such banks around the whole city, whose height was equal to those walls. . . . And this siege they endured for eighteen months, until they were destroyed by the famine, and by the darts which the enemy threw at them from the towers. (Josephus *Antiquities of the Jews* 10.8.131–34)

The biblical accounts agree that siege-works—and perhaps ramps and a dike—were built to surround the city. "Nebuchadnezzar king of Babylon came with all his army against Jerusalem, and laid siege to it; and they built siege-works against it round about," says 2 Kings 25:1 (see also Jeremiah 32:24, 52:4; Ezekiel 4:1–2). Jeremiah records that the Jerusalemites defended their city in part by tearing down some of their houses "to make a defense against the siege mounds and before the sword" (Jeremiah 33:4). Only after a breach had finally been made in the fortification walls surrounding Jerusalem were Nebuchadnezzar's forces able to enter the city. The inhabitants, reduced by famine and disease, offered little resistance: "On the ninth day of the fourth month the famine was so severe in the city that there was no food for the people of the land. Then a breach was made in the city" (2 Kings 25:3–4; see also Jeremiah 32:24, 39:2, 52:6–7).[53]

Some scholars have suggested that the western wall of the city was too formidable to be breached and that it was probably the northern fortifications that ultimately gave way before the onslaught of Nebuchadnezzar's forces. Certainly, it was the northern wall that had proved vulnerable in earlier conquests of the city. Modest support for this thesis also comes from two observations: after the city had been taken, the Neo-Babylonian commanders met at the "Middle Gate," which was apparently situated on the northern wall of the Temple Mount; in addition, during the fighting, Zedekiah had positioned himself at the Gate of Benjamin, which is thought to have been located on the northern side of the city.[54]

The biblical accounts give little reason to believe that Nebuchadnezzar's men showed any sensitivity toward women, the old, or places of worship.

> Therefore he [the LORD] brought up against them the king of the Chaldeans [Nebuchadnezzar], who slew their young men with the sword in the house of their sanctuary, and had no compassion on young man or virgin, old man or aged; he gave them all into his hand. (2 Chronicles 36:17)

The biblical accounts also tell how Zedekiah then fled Jerusalem under cover of darkness but was caught near Jericho and brought before Nebuchadnezzar, in the city of Riblah in Syria. Zedekiah was condemned to be blinded; but first he was forced to witness the execution of his own sons. Their final terrified moments on earth were the last sight he ever saw. He was then bound in chains and taken as a prisoner to Babylon.[55]

FAMINE, DISEASE, AND A REVEALING CESSPOOL

By the end of Nebuchadnezzar's siege of Jerusalem in 586 BCE, the inhabitants were starving and racked by disease. They may have been reduced to cannibalism. The Bible describes the desperate situation: "The hands of compassionate women have boiled their own children; they became their food in the destruction of the daughter of my people" (Lamentations 4:10; see also Ezekiel 5:10–17; Lamentations 2:20, 4:4).

Sometimes archaeological evidence can confirm textual sources such as the Bible. Occasionally, confirmatory evidence comes in unusual forms. Recent excavations in the area of Jerusalem now known as the Jewish Quarter uncovered four ancient latrines. At least one dates to the time of Nebuchadnezzar's destruction of the city in 586 BCE. Made of limestone and set into the floor, the seat had two holes—a small one, perhaps for small children or for male urination, and a larger one directly above a cesspool lined with plaster.[56]

Analysis of the contents of the cesspool has shown that the inhabitants of the city were no longer eating their usual diet of lentils, peas, wheat, and barley. Instead, they were eating "backyard" plants. Pollen samples taken from the cesspool come from the mustard family (cabbage, mustard, radishes, turnips), the carrot family (parsley, caraway, coriander, cumin, dill), the mint family (hyssop thyme, marjoram, sage, mint), and the so-called composite family (lettuce, endive, artichokes, chicory). While many of these plants are domesticated, the archaeologists who have investigated the site suggest that "during the Babylonian siege, supplies of cultivated staples were disrupted and people were forced to consume whatever wild potherbs they could find."[57]

The analysis of the fecal matter in the cesspool below the toilet seat also revealed an unusually large number of eggs from two types of human intestinal parasites: tapeworms and whipworms.[58] Tapeworm infestation comes from eating raw or undercooked meat. Whipworm infections are usually the result either of living in unsanitary conditions or of eating food contaminated with human excrement, such as unwashed vegetables grown utilizing human fecal matter as fertilizer. The existence of both types of parasites in the same cesspool has led the archaeologists to hypothesize that there was only limited water available for washing hands and produce and only limited fuel available for cooking meat. They have also suggested that a lack of water and fuel and a dependence on wild or "backyard" plants rather than cultivated crops suggest that Nebuchadnezzar's siege of Jerusalem was as effective as the biblical account indicates.[59] However, in the fecal matter within this cesspool, there is no evidence of the ingestion of human body parts (i.e., of cannibalism).

THE NINTH OF AB

There was a delay of approximately one month between the fall of Jerusalem on the ninth of Tammuz (July 18), 586 BCE, and the destruction of the city and the Temple. Oded Lipschits, a historian at Tel Aviv University, has suggested that the Neo-Babylonians used the time to loot the city and deport its inhabitants, as recorded in the biblical text.[60]

> In the fifth month, on the seventh day of the month—which was the nineteenth year of King Nebuchadnezzar, king of Babylon— Nebuzaradan, the captain of the bodyguard, a servant of the king of Babylon, came to Jerusalem. And he burned the house of the LORD, and the king's house and all the houses of Jerusalem; every great house he burned down. And all the army of the Chaldeans [Neo-Babylonians], who were with the captain of the guard, broke down the walls around Jerusalem. (2 Kings 25:8–10; see also 2 Chronicles 36:19; Jeremiah 39:8, 52:12–14)

While there are discrepancies in the biblical accounts as to the exact date of these events, the destruction of the Temple itself is traditionally said to have taken place on the ninth of Ab (August 16), 586 BCE.[61]

Archaeological discoveries have confirmed the magnitude of the destruction that followed Nebuchadnezzar's capture of Jerusalem. Huge stones lie scattered on the ground next to the remains of the walls brought down by battering rams. Broken pottery lies on the floors of destroyed homes, covered by a thick layer of ash and burnt debris. Arrowheads are to be found in the houses and by the northern fortifications of the city. The destruction was complete. No mansions or palaces remained.[62] The Temple was destroyed, its treasures looted and carried off to Babylon. Among the several biblical accounts, that in 2 Chronicles is briefest and starkly to the point: "And all the vessels of the house of God, great and small, and the treasures of the house of the LORD, and the treasures of the king and of his princes, all these he brought to Babylon" (2 Chronicles 36:18). The description in 2 Kings is more detailed.

> And the pillars of bronze that were in the house of the LORD, and the stands and the bronze sea that were in the house of the LORD, the Chaldeans [Neo-Babylonians] broke in pieces, and

carried the bronze to Babylon. And they took away the pots, and the shovels, and the snuffers, and the dishes for incense and all the vessels of bronze used in the temple service, the firepans also, and the bowls. What was of gold the captain of the guard took away as gold, and what was of silver, as silver. (2 Kings 25:13–15; see also Jeremiah 52:17–19).

The conflicts over Jerusalem in 598/597 BCE and 587/586 BCE followed the same cycle of events. Each time, the Judaean king (and his kingdom) were successively vassal, rebel, and victim. However, there are clear differences of detail between the Neo-Babylonian siege of 597 and that of 586 BCE. Nebuchadnezzar's campaign of 597 BCE took no more than three months, whereas his campaign of 587/586 BCE lasted at least eighteen months, which perhaps suggests that the fortifications of Jerusalem were strengthened between the two sieges.

Considering that Nebuchadnezzar attacked and laid siege to Jerusalem several times during a sixteen-year period (598–582 BCE), it is not surprising that he finally dealt decisively with the city and its troublesome inhabitants by meting out destruction and exile. One scholar has concluded that Nebuchadnezzar's destruction of Jerusalem in 586 BCE was "no impulsive revenge or punishment for the rebellion." Rather, it was "a calculated act with political goals: to remove the House of David from government after they had proven disloyal, and to destroy Jerusalem which had proven again and again to be the center of resistance to Babylonian rule."[63]

THE EXILE AND BEYOND

And the rest of the people who were left in the city and the deserters who had deserted to the king of Babylon, together with the rest of the multitude, Nebuzaradan the captain of the guard carried into exile. . . . He took into exile in Babylon those who had escaped from the sword, and they became servants to him and to his sons until the establishment of the kingdom of Persia . . . (2 Kings 25:11 and 2 Chronicles 36:20; see also Jeremiah 39:9, 52:15)

And so began the Babylonian Exile. The Book of Ezekiel and part of the Book of Isaiah tell us of the exiles' life in Babylonia. It lasted only about fifty years, but it had an enormous impact, not only on the history of the Jewish people, but also on the evolution of religious thought in the Western world. It was probably during and after this period (586–539 BCE) that the Pentateuch and the Deuteronomistic History of the Hebrew Bible were edited into their final form and that religious practices that became the foundations of Second Temple Judaism— and ultimately of early Christianity—evolved.[64]

The deportation of the leading citizens of Jerusalem and Judah to Babylon was a step-by-step process. The first three phases took place in 598, 587, and 586 BCE. The final phase took place four years later, in 582 BCE, when Nebuchadnezzar once again sent troops to Judah and perhaps Jerusalem: "in the twenty-third year of Nebuchadnezzar, Nebuzaradan the captain of the guard carried away captive of the Jews seven hundred and forty-five persons" (Jeremiah 52:30).[65]

At this time, the lands of Judah might have been annexed into the Neo-Babylonian province of Samaria. However, some of the Judaeans chose instead to escape the Babylonian yoke by fleeing to Egypt. The prophet Jeremiah tells us that "all the people, both small and great, . . . arose, and went to Egypt" (2 Kings 25:26), and we know of a colony of Jews living at this time on the island of Elephantine located at the first cataract of the Nile River.[66]

Jeremiah asserts that, overall, "all the persons [deported] were four thousand and six hundred" (Jeremiah 52:30). However, this number conflicts with the figures given elsewhere in the Hebrew Bible. It also seems low considering that as many as four separate deportations took place between 598 BCE and 582 BCE. In all, rather than 4,600 deportees, the biblical accounts add another 10,000 to the total, claiming that at least 14,600 Judaeans were deported over the course of Nebuchadnezzar's incursions: 3,023 in 598 BCE; 10,000 in 597 BCE; 832 in 586 BCE; and 745 in 582 BCE. It may be that as many as 20,000 were deported.[67] Some scholars have estimated that there were about 75,000 people living in Judah at the time of the Neo-Babylonian incursions, including 15,000 in Jerusalem. If accurate, this would mean that about 70 percent of the population still remained in Judah even after the final set of deportations in 582 BCE.[68] However, regardless of how much of the population remained in Judah as a whole, there is no doubt that the city of Jerusalem and its environs were eviscerated by the Neo-Babylonian deportations. According to Oded Lipschits, "the destruction of Jerusalem and the end of the kingdom of Judah brought about the gravest demographic crisis in the history of the kingdom of Judah."[69]

Those who were left in Judah were not a random sampling of the preconquest population but were from the predominantly rural lower classes. The biblical accounts suggest that the Babylonians were very selective about those they chose for exile and those they left behind.

> Nebuzaradan, the captain of the guard, left in the land of Judah some of the poor people who owned nothing, and gave them vineyards and fields at the same time. (Jeremiah 39:10; see also Jeremiah 40:7–12, 52:16; 2 Kings 25:12, 22)

Consequently, there were now three distinct populations of Judaeans—the elite who had been carried off to Babylon, the lower classes that remained behind in Judah, and those who had fled to Egypt to escape the conquerors.[70] This would lead to problems during the period of restoration that followed the conquest of the Neo-Babylonian Empire in 539 BCE by Cyrus the Great of Persia, as we shall see in the next chapter.

A REPETITION OF HISTORY?

In forming his so-called Jerusalem Army to "liberate Palestine," Saddam Hussein appeared to be positioning himself not only as the successor to Nebuchadnezzar but also as a successor to Cyrus the Great. Just as Cyrus ended the Babylonian Exile of the Jews in 538 BCE, so Saddam boasted that he would end the exile of the Palestinian refugees.

Although, as mentioned earlier, analysts frequently dismissed Saddam Hussein's actions as mere propaganda in a "fantasy drama," some who remember the past recalled that Nebuchadnezzar twice successfully laid waste to Jerusalem twenty-five hundred years ago.[71] Even if Saddam Hussein's "Jerusalem Army" was more wishful thinking than serious threat, his stated intention to "liberate" Jerusalem was hard to ignore. Was he planning to make history repeat itself? To many people around the world, it certainly seemed a distinct possibility, but the capture of Saddam Hussein by U.S. forces in December 2003 ensured that he would not be repeating Nebuchadnezzar's destructions of Jerusalem.

TABLE 2. Chronology from 1000 BCE to 582 BCE

About 1000 BCE	David conquers Jerusalem and reigns as king over the United Monarchy of Israel and Judah.
About 970 BCE	Solomon succeeds to the throne and rules for about forty years.
About 930 BCE	The northern kingdom of Israel breaks away to become independent. Pharaoh Shoshenq, founder of the Twenty-second Dynasty in Egypt, may have threatened or even sacked Jerusalem in 925 BCE.
From about 925 BCE to about 720 BCE	The northern kingdom of Israel is dominant, and the southern kingdom of Judah languishes as a backwater. There are numerous attacks on Israel between the ninth and eighth centuries BCE.
About 850 BCE	Israel is sufficiently powerful to confront the forces of the Neo-Assyrian Empire.
About 841 BCE	Hazael, king of Aram-Damascus, conquers some or all of Israel. But the kingdom of Israel gradually recovers.
About 720 BCE	Shalmaneser V and Sargon II, Neo-Assyrian kings, conquer Israel. They send the ten tribes of Israel into exile and repopulate their lands with foreigners. The ten tribes are lost to history.
After 720 BCE	The southern kingdom of Judah, with Jerusalem as its capital, begins to emerge as a regional power.
701 BCE	Hezekiah, the king of Judah, tries to throw off the yoke of the Neo-Assyrian Empire, but Sennacherib, the Neo-Assyrian king, defeats him and destroys his cities.
698 BCE	Hezekiah's son Manasseh comes to the throne and knuckles under to the Neo-Assyrians. A period of prosperity ensues.
639 BCE	The Neo-Assyrian Empire is in decline. Josiah comes to the throne of Judah and institutes religious reforms but is slain by the Egyptians in 609 BCE as their empire expands northward.
605 BCE	Nebuchadnezzar crushes the Egyptian and Neo-Assyrian forces at the battle of Carchemish, and the Neo-Babylonians emerge as the dominant regional power.
598 BCE	Nebuchadnezzar besieges Jerusalem for the first time, kills King Jehoiakim, and takes Judaean captives into exile.
597 BCE	Nebuchadnezzar besieges Jerusalem for the second time, takes King Jehoiachin and more Judaean captives into exile, and appoints a puppet king.
586 BCE	Nebuchadnezzar besieges Jerusalem for the third time; takes King Zedekiah and still more Judaean captives into exile. The Babylonian Exile of the Jews begins.
582 BCE	Nebuchadnezzar sends troops to Judah yet again; takes still more Judaean captives into exile.

3

OIL UPON TROUBLED WATERS

IN 1896 Theodor Herzl—the father of modern Zionism—published an influential pamphlet entitled *The Jewish State*. In its conclusion, he wrote: "Therefore I believe that a wondrous breed of Jews will spring up from the earth. The Maccabees will rise again." Vladimir Jabotinsky, one of the more controversial figures within the Zionist movement, added an epilogue: "Yes, they have arisen—'the children of those whose ancestor was Judah, lion of the Maccabees.' They have indeed arisen and washed away with their own blood the shame which previously stained and humbled dying Jews."[1]

Although the Maccabean rebellion began in 167 BCE, it is really the story of a three-hundred-year-long conflict between the already ancient religious culture of the Jews and the newer Hellenistic culture introduced by Alexander the Great and his successors. It is also the story of conflicts between the great regional powers to the north and to the south of Judaea for control of that historical crossroads. As would happen frequently over the millennia, the lands and peoples of Judaea were caught between opposing powers. The Maccabean rebellion was in part an effort to free Judaea from those powerful external influences. The revolt resulted in the creation of an independent Jewish kingdom—the largest since the time of David and Solomon, nearly a thousand years earlier. The new kingdom would be the last independent

Jewish political and religious state until the creation of modern Israel more than two thousand years later.

The story of the Maccabees, of their rebellion against their Greek overlords, and of their leader Judah "the Hammer" is celebrated each year during Hanukkah, the Jewish Festival of Lights. During this celebration, religious Jews tell the story of a small flask of oil that miraculously lasted eight days as the Maccabees cleansed and rededicated the Second Temple in Jerusalem after recapturing it from the Seleucid king Antiochus IV in 164 BCE. The eight-branched candelabrum known as a menorah (or, more accurately, as a Hanukkiah) represents the oil lamp that the flask fueled.

The historical significance of the Maccabean rebellion is not as great as either David's conquest of Canaan or the Neo-Babylonian conquest of Judah described in the two previous chapters. However, certain elements of the rebellion reverberated in later history, informing both religious celebrations and parts of the political ideology that underpinned the establishment of the modern state of Israel.[2] In order to understand the significance of this rebellion, it is necessary to review briefly the historical context in which it occurred (see table 3).

FROM CYRUS TO ALEXANDER

The Neo-Babylonian king Nebuchadnezzar conquered the land of Judah and its capital, Jerusalem, several times, the last time in about 586 BCE. He destroyed the Temple that Solomon had built on the sacred mount in Jerusalem, and he took many Jewish captives into exile in Babylonia. Other Jews fled to Egypt. Those who remained behind were forced to share the land with foreign peoples moved in by Babylon. However, within fifty years, Cyrus the Great conquered the faltering Neo-Babylonian Empire, and the Persians became the new rulers of the land of Judah. After its annexation to the Persian Empire, Judah became the Persian province of Yehud—and its people were given the name *Yehudim*, from which ultimately comes the modern term *Jews*.[3]

In 538 BCE, Cyrus allowed the Jews exiled in Babylon to return to their homeland. The returning exiles were influential in determining the future form of religious orthodoxy, but this led to conflicts with their brethren who had remained behind in the Judaean homeland and with those who had fled to Egypt. The groups had developed differently while they were apart. Later, Cyrus issued a royal decree for the restoration of the Temple in Jerusalem that had been destroyed by the Neo-Babylonians, and he returned the gold and silver vessels that Nebuchadnezzar had plundered from the Temple treasury. However, in the process of building the Second Temple—which was completed in 516 BCE under the direction of Zerubbabel and which then served Jerusalem (following a renovation by Herod) until its destruction by the Romans in 70 CE—further conflicts arose between those who had been exiled and those who had remained behind.[4]

The internal conflicts and squabbling went on for decades, until at least 445 BCE, when Nehemiah—a Jew and cupbearer to the Persian king—learned about the sorry state of affairs in Jerusalem from a visiting delegation. He petitioned the king, Artaxerxes I, who had replaced Cyrus on the throne of Persia, for permission to go to the city and supervise the rest of the rebuilding process.[5] Artaxerxes agreed to his request and appointed him governor (*peha*) of the province of Yehud. It is said that the citizens of Jerusalem responded to the newly arrived Nehemiah's exhortations and rebuilt the walls of the City of David in the amazingly brief period of fifty-two days.[6] This apparently miraculous achievement can be interpreted (depending on the standpoint of the commentator) as suggesting either that the magnitude of the task was not very great or that the Jews had some divine help. If the latter, one must assume that they had recovered divine favor after their many earlier falls from grace.[7]

Apart from the internecine squabbling, the period of the Persian rule, beginning in the late sixth century BCE and spanning nearly two hundred years, was a relatively tranquil period for the Jews and for Jerusalem.[8] Inevitably, however, it came to an end when a new leading character appeared on the stage of the Western world. Late in the fourth century BCE, Alexander the Great came of age. Striking out from his birthplace in Macedonia, located to the north of modern Greece, he began a series of conquests that would leave him in command of most of the known Western world and some of the Eastern world as well.

Alexander defeated the Persians in a series of battles between 334

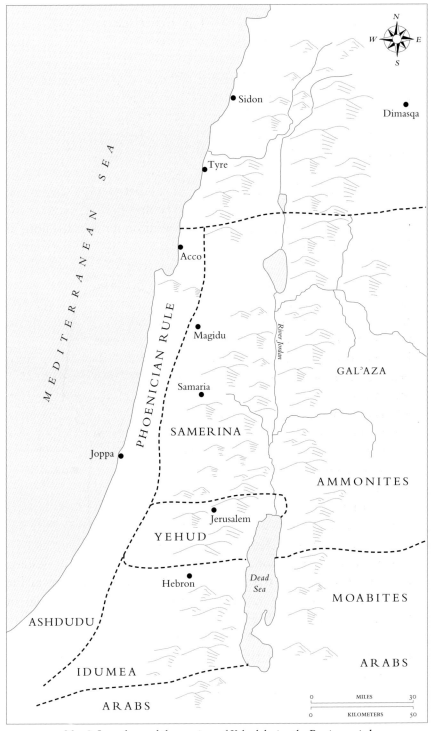

Map 8. Jerusalem and the province of Yehud during the Persian period

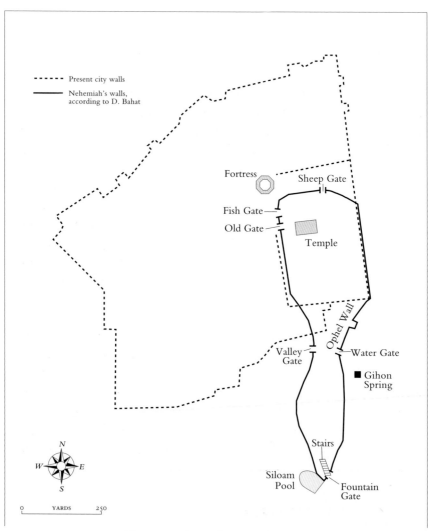

Present city walls
Nehemiah's walls,
according to D. Bahat

Fortress
Sheep Gate
Fish Gate
Old Gate
Temple
Ophel Wall
Valley Gate
Water Gate
Gihon Spring
Stairs
Siloam Pool
Fountain Gate

N
W E
S

0 YARDS 250

Map 9. Jerusalem at the time of Nehemiah

and 323 BCE and took control of the remnants of their empire, including the Persian province of Yehud. There are tales, almost certainly apocryphal, telling of a visit by Alexander to Jerusalem. Josephus says of Alexander: "when he had taken Gaza, [he] hurried to go up to Jerusalem. . . . And when he went up into the temple, he offered sacrifice to God, according to the high priest's direction, and magnificently treated both the high priest and the priests" (Josephus *Antiquities of the Jews* 11.8.325–36). Similar stories are found in the Babylonian Talmud and elsewhere, but most evidence indicates that Alexander proceeded directly to Egypt after taking Gaza and did not dally for a religious exercise in Jerusalem. Certainly, Alexander had a rather hectic schedule between the time that he fought at the Issus River in northern Syria in 333 BCE and at Gaugamela in Mesopotamia in 331 BCE.[9]

Following Alexander's conquest of the Persian Empire, Jerusalem came under Greek rule. The next phase of its history, during the Hellenistic period, is known as the time of the Diodochoi (the "Successors"). It began with Alexander's death in Babylon in 323 BCE and was a period characterized by upheaval, as Alexander's successors fought over his empire. Along with sophisticated Hellenistic civilization came murderous feuds between two of the rival dynasties established by Alexander's generals—the Ptolemies in Egypt and the Seleucids in the Levant and Mesopotamia. Each dynasty regarded Jerusalem and the surrounding territory as its own, and violence reigned intermittently in Judaea for the next three centuries. Once again, Judaea was a "contested periphery," tugged first one way and then another by rival powers to the north and south. Jerusalem would be ground zero for more than twenty conflicts between rivals for rule during the Hellenistic age (323–30 BCE). Some of these conflicts were important prologues to the main drama of the Maccabean rebellion.

THE BATTLES OF THE DIODOCHOI

The action began in 312 BCE, when Ptolemy I—Alexander's general who had inherited control of Egypt—decided to add Judaea to his fiefdom. Josephus records that Ptolemy's success in capturing Jerusalem was at least in part because he attacked on the Sabbath day, when the

Jews were prevented from fighting by their religious beliefs. Apparently, Ptolemy also gained access to the city by claiming that he wished to sacrifice at the Temple, thus compounding his religious affront.[10] It is necessary to recall, however, that Josephus was writing several hundred years after the events he describes.

> Ptolemy . . . seized upon Jerusalem, and for that end made use of deceit and treachery; for as he came into the city on a Sabbath day, as if he would offer sacrifices he, without any trouble, gained the city, while the Jews did not oppose him, for they did not suspect him to be their enemy; and he gained it thus, because they were free from suspicion of him, and because on that day they were at rest and quietness; and when he had gained it, he ruled over it in a cruel manner. (Josephus *Antiquities of the Jews* 12.1.3–4; see also Josephus *Against Apion* 1.209–12)

Ptolemy's Sabbath attack was a stratagem that would be repeated several times by other would-be conquerors of Jerusalem during the following centuries (and which would culminate in the attack on Israel during Yom Kippur in 1973 CE, twenty-three hundred years after Ptolemy). As a result, when the Maccabees and their dynasty came to power in the second century BCE, they decreed that defensive warfare would thenceforth be permitted on the Sabbath.[11]

The Ptolemies incorporated Judaea into their territory after the conquest of Jerusalem and ruled it from Egypt. Their rule was unchallenged for more than a century, until the rise of King Antiochus III in Syria-Mesopotamia. Antiochus the Great, as this young king was known, inherited the throne of the Seleucid dynasty. Antiochus ruled in an area that now comprises modern Syria and its adjacent neighbors. He had an ambition to be a second Alexander and decided to challenge the authority of the Ptolemies in the Levant, a region that bordered the western and southern reaches of his own kingdom. In 201 BCE Antiochus attacked Jerusalem as part of a campaign of annexation of the territories of Ptolemy IV of Egypt. The campaign was only one incident among several that occurred during two decades of warfare between the great powers of Egypt and Syria-Mesopotamia. As usual, Jerusalem was caught in the middle.

Helped by Jewish supporters inside the city, Antiochus briefly captured and held Jerusalem against the Egyptian forces, but he was expelled the following year, in 200 BCE. Undeterred, he besieged the city again and captured it later that same year.[12] Josephus, describing these troubled years, uses the analogy of a "ship in a storm" to describe the predicament of the region's indigenous population.

> Now it happened that in the reign of Antiochus the Great, who ruled over all Asia, that the Jews . . . suffered greatly, and their land was sorely harassed; for while he was at war with Ptolemy Philopater, and with his son, who was called Epiphanes, it fell out that these nations were equally sufferers, both when he was beaten, and when he beat the others: so that they were very like to a ship in a storm, which is tossed by the waves on both sides; and just thus were they in their situation in the middle between Antiochus's prosperity and its change to adversity. (Josephus *Antiquities of the Jews* 12.3.129–30)

After Antiochus's victory over Ptolemy IV, Jerusalem and its surrounding territory came into the hands of the Seleucid kings. They would remain there until the Maccabean rebellion some thirty-five years later. However, before that happened, a rather unusual—and possibly apocryphal—incident is said to have occurred sometime around 180 BCE.[13]

The Apocrypha consists of those books that for some reason were not included in most versions of the Hebrew Bible or the New Testament. The Book of 2 Maccabees in the Apocrypha says that during the reign of King Seleucus IV, the king sent a man named Heliodoros to gather up the treasures contained within the Temple and carry them away. The Temple on the Mount was clearly not a safe place to keep valuable goods, for its treasures are said to have been plundered in earlier times by Shoshenq of Egypt, Sennacherib of Neo-Assyria, and Nebuchadnezzar of Neo-Babylonia, among many others. Indeed, the sacred treasures were looted or used for bribes at least seventeen times during the thousand years that the First and Second Temples existed (from about 960 BCE to 70 CE).[14]

However, on this occasion, the sacrilegious nature of Heliodorus's mission seems to have resulted in a divine intervention, if the account in 2 Maccabees is to be believed.

> For there appeared . . . a magnificently caparisoned horse, with a rider of frightening mien, and it rushed furiously at Heliodorus and struck at him with its front hoofs. Its rider was seen to have armor and weapons of gold. Two young men also appeared to him, remarkably strong, gloriously beautiful and splendidly dressed, who stood on each side of him and scourged him continuously, inflicting many blows on him. When he suddenly fell to the ground and deep darkness came over him, his men took him up and put him on a stretcher and carried him away, this man who had just entered the aforesaid treasury with a great retinue and all his bodyguard but was now unable to help himself; and they recognized clearly the sovereign power of God. While he lay prostrate, speechless because of the divine intervention and deprived of any hope of recovery, they praised the Lord who had acted marvelously for his own place. And the temple, which a little while before was full of fear and disturbance, was filled with joy and gladness, now that the Almighty Lord had appeared. (2 Maccabees 3:25–30)

Apparently, however, divine intervention could not be consistently relied upon to protect the treasures of the Temple, for they were successfully plundered less than eight years later.

ONIAS III, JASON, AND MENELAUS

The story of the Maccabean rebellion itself is an interesting one, whose basic plotline involves the repeated interference by the Seleucid monarchy in the religious practices of the Jews. The Seleucids, the Syrian-Mesopotamian heirs of Alexander the Great's conquest of the Near East, were Hellenistic in their cultural outlook and were thus regarded as pagans by the Jews. Information on the events preceding the rebellion comes from several interrelated sources: 1 and 2 Maccabees in the Apocrypha, books 12–14 of Josephus's *Antiquities of the Jews*, and book 1 of Josephus's *The Jewish War*.[15]

The circumstances that eventually led to the Maccabean revolt involved, once again, the Temple in Jerusalem. This time, a struggle for the position of high priest set events in motion. The tale begins with the ouster of Onias III from his position as high priest in the Temple at Jerusalem. As the story goes, his own brother, Jason, bribed the new Seleucid ruler, Antiochus IV Epiphanes (whose name can be translated as "the God made manifest"), who had come to the throne in Syria in 175 BCE. Jason promised Antiochus a large sum of money in return for appointment as high priest of the Jews. Antiochus duly dismissed Onias and appointed Jason. But Jason was not a typical high priest. He set about the construction of structures in the Hellenistic style, including a gymnasium close to the Temple.[16] Not surprisingly, this offended the generality of Orthodox Jews.

Three years after his appointment, Jason sent the promised money to the Seleucid king, entrusting its delivery to a priest named Menelaus. This was a mistake. Menelaus wanted the position of high priest for himself and offered King Antiochus his own bribe to remove Jason from his position. Money (or rather the promise of it) talked, Jason walked, and Menelaus was installed as the high priest of the Temple. Soon, matters became even more interesting. With the aid of his brother Lysimachus, Menelaus promptly—in 172 BCE—stole and sold gold and silver vessels from the Temple treasures in order to pay the bribe that he had promised to Antiochus. When word of this rascally behavior leaked out, the people of Jerusalem rebelled, seizing an opportunity when Menelaus was away from the city. Lysimachus was forced to send three thousand armed soldiers to put down the uprising. Although the rebellion was eventually suppressed, Lysimachus was killed in the conflict. His brother Menelaus, using methods tried and tested, ultimately bribed his way out of the ensuing scandal and retained his position as high priest.[17]

ANTECEDENTS AND ABOMINATIONS

While the high priest scandals were transpiring, the Seleucids in Syria and the Ptolemies in Egypt were continuing their long struggle for control of the ancient Near East. In November of 170 BCE, Antiochus invaded Egypt, perhaps in response to an initial act of aggression by

Ptolemy VI. Almost immediately, false rumors spread that Antiochus had been killed in battle. Jason, the high priest who had been deposed by Menelaus two years earlier and "driven as a fugitive into the land of Ammon" (2 Maccabees 4:26), seized what he thought was an opportunity to regain his former position. He emerged from hiding and instigated a rebellion. [18]

Attacking Jerusalem, Jason "took no less than a thousand men and suddenly made an assault upon the city." Then, "when the troops upon the wall had been forced back and at last the city was being taken, Menelaus took refuge in the citadel" (2 Maccabees 5:5). Although Jason "kept relentlessly slaughtering his fellow citizens . . . [he] did not gain control of the government . . . and in the end got only disgrace from his conspiracy, and fled again into the country of the Ammonites" (2 Maccabees 5:6–7). Eventually, he died in exile, while reportedly beseeching the Spartans in Greece to come to his aid.[19]

In the meantime, by September of 169 BCE, Antiochus had heard of Jason's rebellion in Jerusalem, and he reacted fiercely.

> When news of what had happened reached the king, he took it to mean that Judaea was in revolt. So, raging inwardly, he left Egypt and took the city by storm. And he commanded his soldiers to cut down relentlessly every one they met and to slay those who went into the houses. Then there was killing of young and old, destruction of boys, women, and children, and slaughter of virgins and infants. Within the total of three days eighty thousand were destroyed, forty thousand in hand-to-hand fighting; and as many were sold into slavery as were slain. Not content with this, Antiochus dared to enter the most holy temple in all the world, guided by Menelaus, who had become a traitor both to the laws and to his country. He took the holy vessels with his polluted hands, and swept away with profane hands the votive offerings which other kings had made to enhance the glory and honor of the place. . . . So Antiochus carried off eighteen hundred talents from the temple . . . (2 Maccabees 5:11–21; see also Josephus *Antiquities of the Jews* 12.5.246–47).

The account in 1 Maccabees adds:

After subduing Egypt, Antiochus . . . went up against Israel and came to Jerusalem with a strong force. He arrogantly entered the sanctuary and took the golden altar, the lamp stand for the light, and all its utensils. He took also the table for the bread of the Presence, the cups for drink offerings, the bowls, the golden censers, the curtain, the crowns, and the gold decoration on the front of the temple; he stripped it all off. He took the silver and the gold, and the costly vessels; he took also the hidden treasures which he found. Taking them all, he departed to his own land. (1 Maccabees 1:20–24)

Thus, Jason's rebellion was suppressed and Menelaus was reinstated as high priest. Antiochus took revenge on the city and slaughtered or sold into slavery tens of thousands of inhabitants. And the Temple treasures were once again plundered of precious vessels, objects, and coins.

Antiochus's forces returned to attack Jerusalem again a few years later, probably in 167 BCE. This second attack was also associated with a Seleucid attempt to invade Egypt. This time, the king sent his military commander Apollonius to Jerusalem, with twenty-two thousand soldiers. Apollonius employed the same stratagem as had Ptolemy I almost 150 years earlier: he attacked on the Sabbath.

When this man arrived in Jerusalem, he pretended to be peaceably disposed and waited until the holy sabbath day; then, finding the Jews not at work, he ordered his men to parade under arms. He put to the sword all those who came out to see them, then rushed into the city with his armed men and killed great numbers of people. (2 Maccabees 5:25–26)[20]

After his second conquest of Jerusalem, Antiochus once again dealt harshly with the city and its inhabitants. He ordered parts of the city wall to be torn down, and he ordered the construction of a new fortress—called the Akra—in which he installed a garrison of soldiers to keep the city and its inhabitants in order. Although the precise location of the fortress is a matter of debate,[21] it is certain that it stood for some two decades as a symbol of Seleucid power over the Jews.

Other measures introduced by Antiochus were no less onerous. In particular, he promulgated a series of restrictions on Jewish religious practices. He forbade ritual circumcision and the observance of the Sabbath and of religious festivals. He ordered the destruction of the books of Jewish law and forced the Jews to eat pork and to worship idols—representations of Greek gods. Those who did not obey were savagely beaten or killed—some strangled, others crucified. Antiochus instructed his emissary to "pollute the temple in Jerusalem and call it the temple of Olympian Zeus" (2 Maccabees 6:2). Josephus tells us that Antiochus placed an altar within the Temple itself and "killed swine upon it" (Josephus *Antiquities of the Jews* 12.5.253; see also 1 Maccabees 1.41–64; 2 Maccabees 6.1–10).[22]

Antiochus's motives may have been not only to punish the Jews but also to Hellenize and "civilize" them. However, the Jews saw matters differently. They saw their conqueror's actions simply as religious persecution and part of a larger attempt to convert them to paganism. The stage was set for rebellion.

The Maccabean rebellion began in 167 BCE and exploded in full force two years later. Mattathias the Hasmonean and his five sons from the village of Modein, some seventeen miles to the northwest of Jerusalem, were the leaders of the revolt against the Seleucid overlords. One of the sons, Judah "the Hammer," would emerge as the leader of the Jews during the most crucial early years of the rebellion, while his brother Simon led the revolution to its successful conclusion twenty years later.

THE MACCABEAN REVOLT

It is reported in 1 Maccabees and by Josephus that in the year 167 BCE, Mattathias killed a Seleucid army commander who had ordered a pagan sacrifice. He also killed a fellow villager who had agreed to take part in the sacrifice. Mattathias and his five sons—known collectively as the Hasmoneans after their family name—were soon joined by other Jews in a struggle for religious freedom. They allied themselves together to fight the forces of the pagan Seleucid Antiochus IV and called themselves Hasidim, or "pious ones."[23]

This brief story is a greatly simplified (and possibly mythologized) version of events that involved complex social, economic, and political factors, as well as purely theological considerations. Furthermore, the conflict did not simply involve religious Jew against pagan Seleucid. It was to a certain extent an internecine war, in which fellow Jews who refused to join the Maccabees' revolt were also targeted.[24]

Mattathias died within the first year of the rebellion, and its leadership passed to Judah, the third of his five sons. Judah remained leader until his death on the battlefield six years later, in 160 BCE.

> Then Judah his son, who was called Maccabeus, took command in his place. All his brothers and all who had joined his father helped him; they gladly fought for Israel. He extended the glory of his people. Like a giant he put on his breastplate; he girded on his armor of war and waged battles, protecting the host by his sword. He was like a lion in his deeds, like a lion's cub roaring for prey. He searched out and pursued the lawless; he burned those who troubled his people. Lawless men shrank back for fear of him; all the evildoers were confounded; and deliverance prospered by his hand. . . . He went through the cities of Judah; he destroyed the ungodly out of the land; thus he turned away wrath from Israel. He was renowned to the ends of the earth; he gathered in those who were perishing. (1 Maccabees 3:1–9)

During the first two years of the revolt, Judah and his followers fought a series of battles against the Seleucid forces, with mixed fortune. None of these early battles involved Jerusalem, and it was not until 164 BCE that Judah Maccabee was finally able to attack and enter the city.[25] The account in 1 Maccabees reports that once there, he found "the sanctuary desolate, the altar profaned, and the gates burned." The account continues: "In the courts they saw bushes sprung up as in a thicket, or as on one of the mountains. They saw also the chambers of the priests in ruins" (1 Maccabees 4:38).

Although the Temple was apparently abandoned, the nearby Akra fortress was still garrisoned by hostile Seleucid soldiers, who harassed Judah and his men as they set about cleansing and rededicating the desecrated Temple.[26] The account in 1 Maccabees reports that then, early in the morning of the twenty-fifth of Chislev (December) in 164

BCE, Judah and his men "rose and offered sacrifice, as the law directs, on the new altar of burnt offering which they had built." The account continues:

> At the very season and on the very day that the Gentiles had pro-
> faned it, [the altar] was dedicated with songs and harps and lutes
> and cymbals. All the people fell on their faces and worshiped and
> blessed Heaven, who had prospered them. So they celebrated the
> dedication of the altar for eight days, and offered burnt offerings
> with gladness; they offered a sacrifice of deliverance and praise.
> (1 Maccabees 4:52–56; see also 2 Maccabees 10:1–8; Josephus
> *Antiquities of the Jews* 12.7.316–23)

The rededication was accomplished exactly three years after Antiochus IV had ordered blasphemous sacrifices within the Temple
precincts.[27] When the Temple was ready, Judah and his brothers
decreed that their eight-day-long dedication of the altar should be celebrated each year in a festival that is now called Hanukkah, or the Festival of Lights. The work of the Maccabees was not finished with the
dedication of the altar. They had to protect their hard-won gains. And
so they "fortified Mount Zion with high walls and strong towers round
about . . . and . . . stationed a garrison there to hold it" (1 Maccabees
4:60–61). Even so, the Maccabees apparently fortified and held only
the area of the Temple Mount itself, leaving the Seleucids in command
of the rest of the city, with their forces in the Akra fortress.

Jerusalem was thus a divided city, and despite minor shifts—back
and forth between the Judaeans and the Seleucids—in the balance of
power, an effective stalemate continued for several years. In 162 BCE
the Maccabees attempted to capture the Akra, using "siege towers and
other engines of war" (1 Maccabees 6:18–21), but they failed. The
same year, the Seleucids were more successful in laying siege to the
Temple with "siege towers, engines of war to throw fire and stones,
machines to shoot arrows, and catapults" (1 Maccabees 6:51–54). At
one point in the prolonged conflict, there was a temporary cease-fire
that the Seleucids immediately violated by tearing down walls that surrounded the Temple and protected the Maccabean garrison.[28]

In 160 BCE, at a small town called Elasa, north of Jerusalem, the

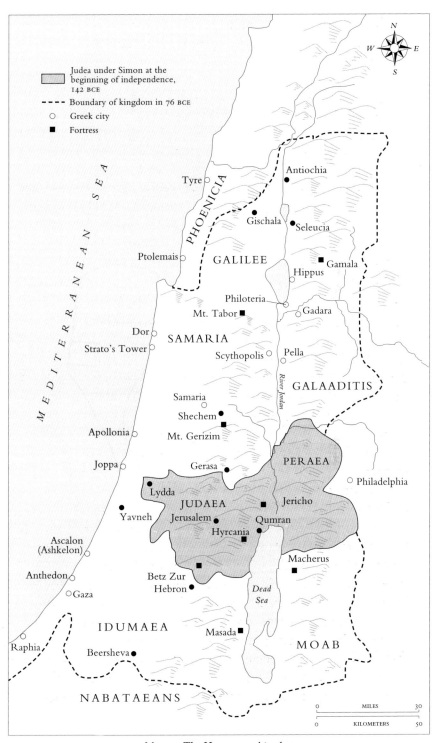

Map 10. The Hasmonean kingdom

Judea under Simon at the beginning of independence, 142 BCE

Boundary of kingdom in 76 BCE

○ Greek city

■ Fortress

N
W *E*
S

MEDITERRANEAN SEA

PHOENICIA

Tyre ○

Antiochia ●

Gischala ●
Seleucia ●

Ptolemais ○

GALILEE

Hippus ○
Gamala ■

Philoteria ○
Mt. Tabor ■
Gadara ○

Dor ○
Strato's Tower ○

SAMARIA

Scythopolis ○
Pella ○

River Jordan

GALAADITIS

Samaria ○
Shechem ●
Mt. Gerizim ■

Apollonia ○

Joppa ○

Gerasa ●

PERAEA

Philadelphia ○

Lydda ●

JUDAEA

Jericho ■

Yavneh ●
Jerusalem ●
Hyrcania ■
Qumran ●

Ascalon
(Ashkelon) ○

Macherus ■

Anthedon ○

Betz Zur ■
Hebron ●

*Dead
Sea*

Gaza ○

IDUMAEA

Masada ■

MOAB

Raphia ○

Beersheva ●

NABATAEANS

MILES 30
KILOMETERS 50

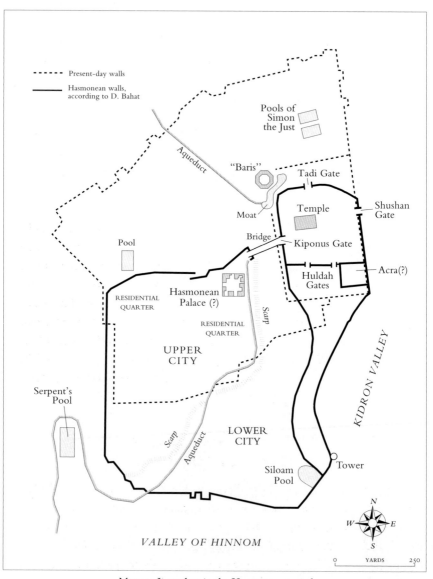

Map 11. Jerusalem in the Hasmonean period

Judaean and Seleucid forces met in battle, and Judah "the Hammer" was killed.

> The battle became desperate, and many on both sides were wounded and fell. Judah also fell, and the rest fled. Then Jonathan and Simon took Judah their brother and buried him in the tomb of their fathers at Modein, and wept for him. And all Israel made great lamentation for him; they mourned many days and said, "How is the mighty fallen, the savior of Israel!" Now the rest of the acts of Judah, and his wars and the brave deeds that he did, and his greatness, have not been recorded, for they were very many. (1 Maccabees 9:17–22; see also Josephus *Antiquities of the Jews* 12.11.426–34)

And so Judah Maccabee was dead before the rebellion was concluded and before an independent Hasmonean kingdom was established.[29] The mantle of leadership passed to Judah's brothers—first to Jonathan and then to Simon Maccabee. Judah is usually given most credit for the success of the rebellion, perhaps because of his part in the rededication of the Temple and the establishment of the Hanukkah celebration, but it was Simon who finally destroyed the Seleucid fortress in Jerusalem. That was a key event in the establishment of an independent Jewish state. It did not happen until 142–41 BCE, twenty-five years after the rebellion first began—and some eighteen years after the death of Judah.[30]

JONATHAN, SIMON, AND THE FALL OF THE AKRA

Between the appearances of the two major Maccabean actors, Judah and Simon, there was a seventeen-year-long interval in which their brother Jonathan occupied the stage. Jonathan became the leader of the Maccabees after Judah's death in 160 BCE and continued in this role until 143 BCE. About midway through his reign, he moved his headquarters to Jerusalem and began to refortify the city.[31]

Then, in 145 BCE, Jonathan laid siege to the Seleucid fortress in Jerusalem. Although he failed to capture it, he succeeded in obtaining concessions from Demetrius, the reigning Seleucid king, by dint of his strength in arms and by showering the king with gifts, including gold, silver, and clothing. The concessions included confirming Jonathan's position as high priest and demanding no more than three hundred talents of tribute from all of Judaea, Samaria, and Galilee.[32] When a new king, Antiochus VI, came to the throne of Syria-Mesopotamia, he continued the laissez-faire policy of his predecessor with regard to Jerusalem. Jonathan used the opportunity to strengthen the defenses of the city, under the eyes of the Seleucid garrison in the Akra fortress.[33]

In 143 BCE Jonathan was treacherously killed by a Seleucid general named Tryphon, who subsequently usurped the Seleucid throne for himself.[34] After the death of Jonathan, Simon, the last of the five sons of Mattathias, became the leader of the Maccabean rebellion. His initial move was to complete Jonathan's refortification of Jerusalem.[35] Then he laid siege to the Akra, as his brother had done. The Book of 1 Maccabees describes Simon's capture of the Akra in late 142 and early 141 BCE.

> The men in the citadel at Jerusalem were prevented from going out to the country and back to buy and sell. So they were very hungry, and many of them perished from famine. Then they cried to Simon to make peace with them, and he did so. But he expelled them from there and cleansed the citadel from its pollutions. On the twenty-third day of the second month, in the one hundred and seventy-first year [141 BCE], the Jews entered it with praise and palm branches, and with harps and cymbals and stringed instruments, and with hymns and songs, because a great enemy had been crushed and removed from Israel. And Simon decreed that every year they should celebrate this day with rejoicing. He strengthened the fortifications of the temple hill alongside the citadel, and he and his men dwelt there. (1 Maccabees 13:49–52)

Josephus's account of these events tells that the Akra was demolished stone by stone and that even the "mountain" upon which it was constructed was leveled. Although Josephus's account is disputed by some modern scholars, the Akra's destruction was certainly so complete that the fortress has never been located by archaeologists. Its precise location remains uncertain.[36]

Simon's accomplishments were many. Within two years of taking command, he had finished the rebuilding of Jerusalem's defenses. His next, perhaps even more daunting task was to oversee the transition from a twenty-year-long insurrection, with all its turbulence, to the establishment of an independent Hasmonean kingdom, with himself as monarch.[37]

But although he had some success, Simon did not reign for long. His own son-in-law, Ptolemy (not to be confused with the various Egyptian rulers of the same name), led a brief rebellion against the newly appointed king, murdering Simon at a banquet in Jericho in 135 BCE. Simon's wife and two of his sons were also either slaughtered or imprisoned. However, a third son, John Hyrcanus, was not present at the banquet. He soon put down the incipient rebellion and was accordingly hailed as his father's successor and as the next Hasmonean ruler. He was to play an important role in the new kingdom. He built upon his father's legacy and expanded the borders of the new Jewish nation. He was so successful that his territory may ultimately have been larger even than that traditionally ascribed to the kingdom of David and Solomon nearly a thousand years earlier.[38]

JOHN HYRCANUS AND ANTIOCHUS VII

Most modern scholars agree that the Maccabean revolt was more than just a struggle for religious freedom. It was also a struggle for national liberation and political independence. Ultimately it became a struggle for the establishment of a free Jewish state. This was to be a state independent of both the Seleucid and the Ptolemaic dynasties to the north and south of the Judaean homeland.[39] However, the Seleucid monarchs were determined to suppress the fledgling Hasmonean kingdom. In 135 BCE, just as John Hyrcanus assumed power, Antiochus VII invaded Judaea and besieged Jerusalem. Once again a would-be conqueror of the city took advantage of its weak defenses on the northern side. Josephus tells the story of the battle.

Antiochus . . . invaded Judea in . . . the first year of the principality of Hyrcanus. . . . And when he had burnt the country, he shut up Hyrcanus in the city, which he surrounded with seven encampments; but did nothing at the first, because of the strength of the walls, and because of the valor of the besieged. . . . However, about the north part of the wall, where it happened the city was upon a level with the outward ground, the king raised a hundred towers of three stories high, and placed bodies of soldiers upon them; and as he made his attacks every day, he cut a double ditch, deep and broad, and confined the inhabitants within it as within a wall . . . (Josephus *Antiquities of the Jews* 13.8.236–39)

Josephus tells how John Hyrcanus eventually saved the day by bribing the Seleucids. In this, he seems to have broken with tradition by using silver taken from the Tomb of David rather than the treasures of the Temple. No doubt, the Temple treasures were depleted as a consequence of looting and earlier misappropriations.[40] In any event, the payment of silver was part of a treaty agreement between Hyrcanus and Antiochus VII—an agreement that also included the giving of hostages and the dismantling of Jerusalem's city walls. In addition, Hyrcanus was forced to join Antiochus in a war against the Parthians, a war that would end in the death of Antiochus and enable Hyrcanus to return to Jerusalem and regain his position as king.[41]

John Hyrcanus ruled from 135 to 104 BCE. The intervention of Antiochus apart, his reign was a period of prosperity and expansion for the kingdom. The Hasmoneans regained and ruled over territories in Samaria to the north, Transjordan to the east, and Edom/Idumea to the south. The inhabitants of Idumea were forcibly converted to Judaism (and from this population would come the future king Herod the Great less than a century later).

It is ironic that the Jews became ever more Hellenized during this period of independence from Seleucid overlords—the acculturation that they had so strongly resisted for the previous three decades. Now they embraced many of the very elements that the Seleucid kings had previously tried to introduce, including public squares, an agora (or marketplace), and perhaps a gymnasium. As the population of Jerusalem grew to as many as thirty-five thousand inhabitants, the city expanded to the west. Fine houses and a palace were built on the western hill of Jerusalem, overlooking the Temple Mount.[42] (Nahman Avigad, an archaeologist at the Hebrew University of Jerusalem, excavated a fortified tower and an attached 160-foot-long stretch of wall on the western hill after the 1967 war. Since the walls built by Jonathan and Simon had been torn down under the terms of the treaty with Antiochus in 135 BCE, this structure is probably part of the fortifications that Hyrcanus or his son Alexander Jannaeus built sometime after the death of Antiochus VII in 129 BCE.)[43]

FROM ALEXANDER JANNAEUS TO POMPEY

Following the death of John Hyrcanus, Alexander Jannaeus ascended to the throne and ruled as both high priest and king from 103 to 76 BCE. His reign was turbulent. It saw the continuing expansion of the Hasmonean kingdom, as well as a vicious civil war between the Sadducees and Pharisees (two rival sects of Judaism), which embroiled the kingdom for half a decade.

The Pharisees rebelled against Jannaeus's rule sometime around the year 94 BCE. The rebellion erupted at the Feast of Tabernacles as Alexander was conducting a sacrifice at the Temple in Jerusalem. Josephus tells the story.

> As to Alexander, his own people were rebellious against him; for at a festival which was then celebrated, when he stood upon the altar, and was going to sacrifice, the nation rose upon him, and pelted him with citrons [which they then had in their hands, because] the law of the Jews required that at the Feast of Tabernacles everyone should have branches of the palm tree and citron tree. . . . They also reviled him, as [being] derived from a captive, and so unworthy of his dignity and of sacrificing. (Josephus *Antiquities of the Jews* 13.13.372)

Enraged, Alexander Jannaeus responded by executing six thousand of the rebels in Jerusalem and erecting a wooden barricade around the Temple precinct, permitting only his own Sadducee priests to enter the area. That sparked a civil war that raged for the next six years.[44] Most of the fighting took place outside Jerusalem. However, in about 88 BCE, the last members of the rebellious Pharisees surrendered. Alexander Jannaeus dealt savagely with them within the city precincts.

> . . . he brought them to Jerusalem, and did one of the most barbarous actions in the world to them; for as he was feasting with his concubines, in the sight of all the city, he ordered about eight hundred of them to be crucified; and while they were living, he ordered the throats of their children and wives to be cut before their eyes. This was indeed by way of revenge for the injuries they had done him; which punishment yet was of an inhuman nature . . . (Josephus *Antiquities of the Jews* 13.14.380–81)

Although the internal revolt was now crushed, the king's problems were not over. The period that followed was no less turbulent. As a series of foreign armies invaded, he either had to fight or negotiate.

When Alexander Jannaeus died in 76 BCE, his widow, Salome Alexandra, ruled briefly in his place. Then, in 67 BCE, their two sons disputed the succession to the throne. Hyrcanus II and Aristobulus II vied for power in what seems to have been a classic case of sibling rivalry and jealousy.[45] Hyrcanus II ruled first but was immediately attacked by his brother. Defeated and taking refuge on the Temple Mount, Hyrcanus II negotiated a deal by which he would be permitted to live—albeit as a private citizen—while Aristobulus II took over as both king and high priest.

While all this was unfolding, a new player, named Antipater, appeared on the stage and introduced a twist into the plot of the ongoing drama. Antipater was an Idumean, whose father had been appointed governor of Idumea by Alexander Jannaeus. (The peoples of Idumea, originally from an area to the south of Judaea, had been conquered and forcibly converted to Judaism by John Hyrcanus nearly half a century earlier, as mentioned above.) Antipater persuaded Hyrcanus II that he had relinquished his throne to his brother too easily. He arranged for a three-way alliance between himself, Hyrcanus II, and King Aretas III, ruler of the Nabateans in Petra. In 65 BCE, the three allies and their armies—which reportedly numbered as many as fifty thousand men—attacked Aristobulus II and laid siege to Jerusalem, trapping the king and his followers on the Temple Mount.[46]

At this point, Pompey, the great Roman general, also made his entrance onto the Judaean stage. Pompey would soon be part of the First Triumvirate, along with Julius Caesar and Crassus. For the moment, however, he had been in the Near East hunting down the pirates of Cilicia (in southeastern Turkey) who had been attacking the grain ships sailing between Rome and Egypt. Having rapidly succeeded in his mission, Pompey tarried in the region, attacking, conquering, and signing treaties with a number of small kingdoms in the area that now comprises Turkey, Armenia, and Syria.

Both Hyrcanus II and Aristobulus II sent delegations, armed with bribes, to Pompey. Aristobulus's emissaries were apparently the more persuasive, and the Romans, led by one of Pompey's lieutenants, Scaurus, forced Hyrcanus II to raise the siege of the Temple Mount, allowing Aristobulus II and his men to escape. But the matter was not yet settled, and the plot took a new twist when Pompey arrived in person some time later.

After a meeting with delegations from both sides, Pompey changed sides and allied himself with Hyrcanus II.[47] The upshot was that Aristobulus II was thrown into prison, and his followers were trapped once again on the Temple Mount—besieged this time by Pompey and his Romans as well as by Hyrcanus II and his followers. This siege lasted for three months in 63 BCE. Like earlier besiegers, the Romans concentrated their attack on the north side of the Temple Mount.

> Pompey pitched his camp within [the wall], on the north part of the temple, where it was most practicable; but even on that side there were great towers, and a ditch had been dug, and a deep valley circled it, for on the parts towards the city were precipices, and the bridge on which Pompey had gotten in was broken down. However, a bank was raised, day by day, with a great deal of labor, while the Romans cut down materials for it from the places around. And when this bank was sufficiently raised, and the ditch filled up, though but poorly, by reason of its immense depth, he brought his mechanical engines and battering rams from Tyre,

and placing them on the bank, he battered the temple with the stones that were thrown against it. (Josephus *Antiquities of the Jews* 14.4.60–62)

The geographer Strabo confirms that the defensive ditch built by the Romans was large—perhaps as much as 60 feet deep and 250 feet wide. The Romans—the world's most skilled and assiduous military engineers—apparently used the Sabbath to do much of the work of filling in the ditch and building the ramp for the siege engines. They correctly believed that the Jews were restricted to defensive fighting on that day and could not engage an enemy that was not directly attacking, even one that was clearly doing work to facilitate a future attack. Josephus says as much.

And had it not been our practice, from the days of our forefathers, to rest on the seventh day, this bank could never have been perfected, by reason of the opposition the Jews would have made; for though our law gives us leave then to defend ourselves against those that begin to fight with us and assault us, yet it does not permit us to meddle with our enemies while they do any thing else. (Josephus *Antiquities of the Jews* 14.4.63)

When a battering ram finally brought down one of the defensive towers protecting the Temple Mount, the Romans poured in through the breech. In the ensuing slaughter, twelve thousand followers of Aristobulus II were killed—some by the Romans and some by Jews loyal to Aristobulus's brother, Hyrcanus II. When the Temple itself was overrun, the Romans "cut the throats of those that were in the temple . . . at their very altars" (Josephus *Antiquities of the Jews* 14.4.66–67).

Pompey then committed a remarkable sacrilege by entering the Temple and the holy of holies deep within, seeing "all that which it was unlawful for any other men to see but only for the high priests. . . . the golden table, the holy candlestick, and the pouring vessels, and a great quantity of spices; and . . . two thousand talents of sacred money . . ." (Josephus *Antiquities of the Jews* 14.4.72). However, on the next day, he ordered that the Temple be cleansed, allowed worship to begin again, and restored the high priesthood to Hyrcanus II. Hyrcanus's brother did not fare so well. Aristobulus II was taken as a prisoner to Rome and forced to march in Pompey's triumphal parade through the city in 61 BCE.[48]

The Romans were in Judaea to stay, and soon the region became Roman territory—eventually it became part of the Roman province of Syria Palastina. However, remnants of resistance continued even after the Roman conquest in 63 BCE. For instance, Aristobulus II and his son managed to escape the Romans and staged brief rebellions in the years from 57 to 55 BCE. These brief flare-ups occasionally involved Jerusalem and required intervention by the successive Roman governors of Syria—including Gabinius and then Crassus. Josephus reports that Crassus took advantage of the situation to loot the Temple in Jerusalem in 54 BCE, taking away "the money that was in the temple, which Pompey had left, being two thousand talents." Josephus continues: "[He] was disposed to spoil it of all the gold belonging to it, which was eight thousand talents. He also took a beam, which was made of solid beaten gold, of the weight of three hundred minae . . ." (Josephus *Antiquities of the Jews* 14.7.105–6).[49] Crassus apparently needed the money to pay his soldiers, for he was on his way to fight the Parthians, a campaign that would turn out to be one of the most disastrous and humiliating in the history of the Roman Republic.

THE AFTERMATH

The Maccabean rebellion and the subsequent brief flowering of an independent Jewish state in the Near East during the first century BCE had two important repercussions—one purely religious and the other a complex mixture of the political and religious. The purely religious consequence is that the story of the Maccabees and their rebellion against the Greek overlords is still celebrated each year during the religious holiday of Hanukkah.

Politically, the Maccabean rebellion against the Seleucid Empire was important to the development of Zionism and to the founders of modern Israel. Zionism is defined by the 1967 *Random House Dictionary of the English Language* as "A world-wide Jewish movement for the establishment in Palestine of a national homeland for the Jews." The

TABLE 3. Chronology from 586 BCE to 63 BCE

586 BCE	Nebuchadnezzar besieges Jerusalem for the third time; takes King Zedekiah and still more Judaean captives into exile. The Babylonian Exile of the Jews begins.
About 539 BCE	Cyrus the Great of Persia conquers the Neo-Babylonian Empire; the Persians take control of Judah and allow Jews to return to Jerusalem.
About 516 BCE	The Second Temple is completed, replacing the First Temple built by Solomon and destroyed by Nebuchadnezzar.
Between 334 and 323 BCE	Alexander the Great conquers the Persian Empire; Jerusalem and Judah come under Greek rule.
Between 323 and 30 BCE	For 300 years there is a series of battles among Alexander's successors for control of the Near East. These are the conflicts of the so-called Diodochoi (the "Successors"). For example, in 312 BCE Ptolemy I, the heir to Egypt, conquers Jerusalem; his successors rule for more than a century until challenged by the Seleucid king Antiochus III in 201 BCE.
About 175 BCE	Antiochus III begins dabbling in the affairs of the Judaean high priest in Jerusalem.
167 BCE	The Maccabean rebellion begins, continuing for about twenty years with victories and defeats.
141 BCE	Simon Maccabee destroys the Seleucid fortress in Jerusalem and establishes an independent Jewish kingdom ruled by the Hasmonean dynasty.
135–104 BCE	John Hyrcanus of the Hasmonean dynasty rules the kingdom and expands its borders. His kingdom becomes more Hellenized.
63 BCE	The Roman general Pompey conquers Jerusalem in the process of resolving a conflict between two brothers for the succession to the Hasmonean throne. The Romans do not leave after the conquest.
63 BCE and after	The independent Hasmonean kingdom disappears, and Judaea eventually becomes the Roman province of Syria Palastina.

modern movement had ancient and medieval roots but began to grow most vigorously late in the nineteenth century. The early Zionist leaders—Herzl, Jabotinsky, and Max Nordau—frequently invoked the Maccabean rebellion against oppressive Hellenistic overlords and the later revolt of Bar Kokhba against the Romans as examples of Jews fighting successfully against oppressive authoritarian regimes to establish their own independent state. Those historical examples struck a responsive chord with the leaders of the Zionist movement. After all, their objective was to establish an independent Jewish nation in the very region where the Maccabees had lived and ruled more than two thousand years earlier.[50]

Scholars have pointed out that with the beginnings of the Zionist movement, the Maccabean rebellion began to be used as a propaganda device in support of the movement's objectives. Those objectives were more political than religious. In this, they may not have differed greatly from those of the Jewish rebellion two thousand years earlier. Although the Maccabean revolt began as a religious struggle, it evolved into a nationalistic struggle for independence. Neither in the modern Zionist movement nor in the Maccabean rebellion did the active participants speak with a single voice. Many in the Jewish population of Judaea two thousand years ago were in favor of independence from oppressive Seleucid overlords, but fewer favored being ruled by the Hasmoneans—as either kings or high priests. The Hasmoneans were neither descendants of the house of David nor members of the traditional priestly family of Zadok. And yet the members of the House of Hasmon successfully (if briefly) ruled as both high priests and kings, in a manner and style not seen since the days of David and Solomon.[51]

The reign of independent Hasmonean monarchs came to an end with Pompey's conquest of Jerusalem in 63 BCE. The independent kingdom had lasted only about eighty years. History might have taken a different path if Aristobulus II and Hyrcanus II had not asked Pompey to intervene in their conflict, instead settling their differences by themselves.[52] Is it possible that this historical anecdote has some relevance for the feuding peoples of the Middle East today?

4

IN BLOOD AND FIRE

IN THE BASEMENT of a house on Tiferet Israel Street in the Jewish Quarter of Jerusalem, Nahman Avigad and his team of archaeologists found the severed arm of a young woman in her twenties who had died nearly two thousand years ago. That was all, just an arm—with the hand and fingers still attached. It lay in a room filled with ash and soot. In a nearby room, a spear was propped up against the wall. Other rooms contained utensils of daily living, all covered by a thick layer of ash and debris from the fire that destroyed the ancient dwelling.

The house had belonged to a well-to-do family, probably by the name of Bar Kathros. Coins were scattered on the floor. Some bore the inscription "Year Four/Of the Redemption of Zion," indicating that they were minted in 69 CE, in the fourth year of the First Jewish Revolt against the Romans. One year later, the rebellion had been crushed and Jerusalem lay in ruins, destroyed by Titus and the Roman legions.

Almost two millennia after the Roman destruction, Avigad wrote:

Beyond the image of the destruction, each of us pictured in his mind the scene so vividly described by Josephus: the Roman soldiers spreading out over the Upper City, looting and setting the houses ablaze as they slaughtered all in their path. The owner of this house, or one of its inhabitants, had managed to prepare his spear; another member of the household did not manage to escape from the house, and died in the flames. The tangible evidence, surprising in its freshness and shocking in its realism, gave us the feeling that it had all happened only yesterday.[1]

Hundreds of years after the Maccabean rebellion against the Greeks in 167 BCE, the Jews rose up in two more attempts to throw off the shackles of a foreign imperial power—this time the Roman Empire. The Maccabean rebellion had been successful, albeit briefly; but these two further rebellions, against Rome, were to end in disaster. The First Jewish Revolt against the Romans was crushed in 70 CE, and the Second Jewish Revolt, known as the Bar Kokhba Rebellion, also ended in defeat for the Jews, in 135 CE. All three uprisings—spanning a period of three hundred years—had as their basis perceived or actual interference with the cultural and religious practices of the Jewish peoples of Judaea.

Much later, the memory of these three rebellions would serve as a rallying cry for the Zionist movement at the end of the nineteenth and beginning of the twentieth centuries. But first, the two Jewish revolts against the Roman Empire would also impact directly upon subsequent world history—in the form of the final Jewish Diaspora. The Romans, increasingly annoyed with their unruly and stiff-necked Jewish subjects, were ultimately to destroy their Temple and principal city and to enslave or exile those they did not put to the sword. The Jews, thus exiled from their homeland, dispersed to many lands over the ensuing centuries, in a Diaspora that still has its repercussions to the present day.[2]

THE JEWISH REBELLIONS AND ZIONISM

The early Zionist movement had as its primary objective the return of Jews to their ancient homeland. The movement was ultimately successful in establishing the modern state of Israel, which has attempted to serve as a haven for many from those Jewish populations first dispersed nearly two millennia ago. At the end of the nineteenth century, a young poet named Yaakov Cahan wrote *Ha-biryonim* (The hooligans), which reads in part:

We arose, returned, we, the biryonim!
We came to redeem our oppressed land
With a strong hand, we demand our right!
In blood and fire did Judaea fall;
In blood and fire shall Judaea rise.[3]

The last two of the preceding lines were adopted as a motto by Bar-Giora and its offshoot HaShomer (whose name means "the guard"), two secret Zionist organizations whose primary purpose was to provide labor and armed guards for the new Jewish settlements being established in Palestine during the early years of the twentieth century.[4] The poet's portrayal of the new Zionist movement as a phoenix rising from the two-thousand-year-old ashes of the Roman destruction of Jerusalem was also a motif at the core of speeches given by leaders of the movement. Theodor Herzl stressed the First Jewish Revolt of 66–70 CE in an address in Vienna in 1896.

You know that our history, the history of the Diaspora, began in the year 70 after the birth of Christ. The military campaign of Titus, . . . which ended with the Jews being carried off as captive slaves, is the actual beginning of that part of Jewish history which concerns us closely, for we are still suffering from the consequences of those events. The enslavement born of that war affected not only those who were living at that time, not only those who shared the actual responsibility for the war: The effects of this captivity have been felt for 60 generations.[5]

Max Nordau emphasized the Second Jewish Revolt of 132–35 CE, saying:

Bar Kokhba was a hero who refused to suffer any defeat. When victory was denied him, he knew how to die. Bar Kokhba was the last embodiment in world history of a battle-hardened and bellicose Jewry.[6]

What was it about these two Jewish revolts for independence that served as a focus for both Zionist ideology and propaganda? To answer this question, it is necessary to go back to 40 BCE and the man who would become known as Herod the Great.

ANTIPATER, HEROD, AND PHASAEL

The Romans first entered the city of Jerusalem in 63 BCE. A conflict for control of the city—between Antipater, whose father had been appointed governor of Idumea by the Hasmonean king Alexander Jannaeus, and Aristobulus II, the king's son—drew Pompey and the Romans to Jerusalem like flies to honey.

The Romans came to Judaea to resolve a power struggle and stayed to govern. But they were not immune to conflicts of their own. In Rome, civil war erupted soon after the First Triumvirate fell apart by 50 BCE. Antipater, who continued to harbor ambitions for high office, backed Julius Caesar in the conflict. When Caesar defeated Pompey in 49 BCE, Antipater was appointed commissioner of Judaea. The Romans also appointed two of Antipater's sons, Herod and Phasael, as tetrarchs (district commissioners). Antipater's old ally Hyrcanus II became high priest of the Temple. Now apparently secure in his position, Antipater undertook the rebuilding of the walls of Jerusalem that were destroyed in the earlier conflicts. However, this was a turbulent period, and five years later, both Caesar and Antipater were murdered—Caesar by fellow members of the Roman Senate and Antipater by Malichus, an old enemy.[7]

While the Second Triumvirate was coming to power in Rome, Herod and Phasael took over their father's position and ruled jointly in Judaea. But feuds between families often die hard, and almost immediately Herod and Phasael faced a rebellion instigated by Antigonus, the younger son of their father's old enemy Aristobulus II. Aristobulus and his family had been imprisoned in Rome after losing the struggle for power with Antipater. Now, with Rome in turmoil, the moment was ripe for Antigonus to escape. Free, he turned to the Parthians in Mesopotamia to seek help in regaining his ancestors' kingdom, promising them a thousand talents in cash and five hundred of the most beautiful women in his future kingdom if they helped him capture Jerusalem.[8] The Parthians, a warlike people who had consistently defeated the Roman legions in battle, were at this time marching on the Roman province of Syria—an area that encompassed modern Syria, Lebanon, Jordan, and Israel. They agreed to the bargain offered, and soon Antigonus, the Parthians, and a number of sympathetic Judaeans began a siege of Jerusalem, in 40 BCE.[9]

At first the defense of the city went well for Herod and Phasael. Their soldiers defeated the invaders in a skirmish fought in the marketplace and then chased Antigonus and his men into the Temple. (Coincidentally, Antigonus's father, Aristobulus II, had suffered the same indignity decades earlier.) Herod's men were also victorious in a number of vicious street battles and in at least one sally outside the city, where they "put many ten thousands to flight, some flying into the city, and some into the temple, and some into the outer fortifications" (Josephus *Antiquities of the Jews* 14.13.339).[10] But then the Parthian reinforcements arrived—five hundred horsemen immediately outside the city walls and a much larger Parthian army camped farther north in Galilee.

Phasael received a delegation from the Parthians and was persuaded to go, along with the high priest Hyrcanus, to Galilee, for a meeting with the Parthian satrap Barzapharnes. Herod, ever suspicious and vigilant, remained behind in Jerusalem, under the watchful eye of Parthian cavalry. His suspicions were justified. Phasael and Hyrcanus were taken prisoner by the Parthians in breach of truce. Herod himself narrowly avoided capture. He and his men escaped from Jerusalem under cover of night and made their way to Masada, where Herod left his immediate family—including his fiancée, Mariamne—with eight hundred troops. Then, accompanied by a strongly armed escort, he set out for Rome, to argue his case before the Senate and to ask for assistance.

During the long journey to Rome, Herod received the news that his brother Phasael had been forced to commit suicide while in Parthian custody and that Antigonus had disfigured Hyrcanus II by biting (or cutting) off his ears. Thus disfigured, Hyrcanus could no longer serve as high priest of the Jews.[11]

HEROD RETURNS

With Herod off in Rome, Phasael dead, and Hyrcanus mutilated, Antigonus occupied Jerusalem and assumed the throne. Once again, a king of the Hasmonean dynasty ruled Judaea, but Antigonus's tenure was to be brief. When Herod appeared before the Senate in Rome, the powerful triumvir Mark Antony and two other patricians spoke eloquently on his behalf. The Senate was impressed and awarded Herod the title "King of the Jews." Herod immediately began the long trip back to Judaea. Arriving late in 40 BCE or early in 39 BCE, he rescued his family from the fortress at Masada and then began a campaign to reclaim his kingdom, city by city.[12] Eventually he was ready to lay siege to Jerusalem, the capital of Judaea. To take the city proved to be no easy task.

Herod's siege of Jerusalem began in 37 BCE, three years after he became "King of the Jews." He set up camp outside the north wall of the city—the most vulnerable spot, as history had repeatedly shown. He had an immense army at his disposal. Mark Antony had ordered Sossius, the Roman governor of Syria, to gather an army to help Herod. Herod himself brought thirty thousand troops, probably consisting of Galilean and Idumean soldiers, Syrian auxiliaries, and assorted mercenaries. Josephus reports, "They all met together at the walls of Jerusalem, and encamped at the north wall of the city, being now an army of eleven legions, armed men on foot, and six thousand horsemen, with other reinforcements out of Syria" (Josephus *Antiquities of the Jews* 14.16.469; see also *Jewish War* 1.17.345–46). However, they were facing fanatical defenders—Jews who were willing to die for Antigonus, the last of the Hasmoneans, and to defend their Temple yet again.[13] It took five months for Herod and Sossius to capture the city. But finally, after building siege towers, digging ditches, and raising up earthworks, Herod's men broke through the walls of Jerusalem, probably on a Sabbath day during the summer of 37 BCE.[14] A massacre ensued; the defenders were slaughtered in the streets, alleyways, and houses of Jerusalem and even on the Temple Mount. Josephus reports that there was "no pity taken of either infants or the aged, nor did they spare so much as the weaker sex," that "nobody restrained their hand from slaughter, but, as if they were a company of madmen, they fell upon persons of all ages, without distinction" (Josephus *Antiquities of the Jews* 14.16.480; see also *Jewish War* 1.18.352). Although many of the houses and shops of the city were looted and set on fire in the aftermath of the battle, Herod managed to save the Temple and its treasures.[15]

Antigonus surrendered to Sossius and then, bound in chains, was brought before Mark Antony in Antioch. Herod argued persuasively that Antigonus must die. Antony agreed, and the last of the Hasmonean rulers of Judaea was tied to a cross, whipped, and beheaded.[16]

Herod was once again in control of Jerusalem and Judaea. This time, he would remain in power for thirty years. He proved to be an ambitious builder. He rebuilt the city walls of Jerusalem so that the area enclosed was at least 190 and perhaps as much as 230 acres.[17] The population at this time has been estimated to be thirty to forty thousand permanent inhabitants, with additional thousands flocking to the city during religious festivals.[18]

Earlier in his reign (about 35 BCE), Herod had a fortress constructed in Jerusalem, just north of the Temple Mount, where the city was most vulnerable. This fortress was called the Antonia after Herod's good friend and patron Mark Antony. It was massive, with a huge tower at each corner, and was manned by Roman infantry able to look down upon the Temple and the Jewish worshipers below. This facility was to prove useful to the Romans a little more than sixty years after Herod's death, when the First Jewish Revolt took place.

About 23 BCE, Herod built a large palace in Jerusalem—defended by three towers, which he named Phasael, Mariamne, and Hippicus after his brother, his wife, and a good friend, respectively. Then, about 19 BCE, Herod undertook his most ambitious building project in the city—renovating the Second Temple up on the Temple Mount. The Second Temple had originally been completed in 516 BCE by Zerubbabel and the Jews who returned from Babylon. It was nearly five hundred years old by the time of Herod and was showing signs of its age. Herod decided not only to restore the structure but also to enlarge it. It was intended to be one of the wonders of the world.

First, the platform upon which the Temple stood was doubled in size, so that the space available for construction covered thirty-five acres—an area the size of fifteen American football fields.[19] This was achieved by filling in the Central—or Tyropoeon—Valley, which had originally run through the center of the city and had been the western border of the Temple Mount (see chapter 1). In addition, underground arches were constructed and paved over, in order to expand and sup-

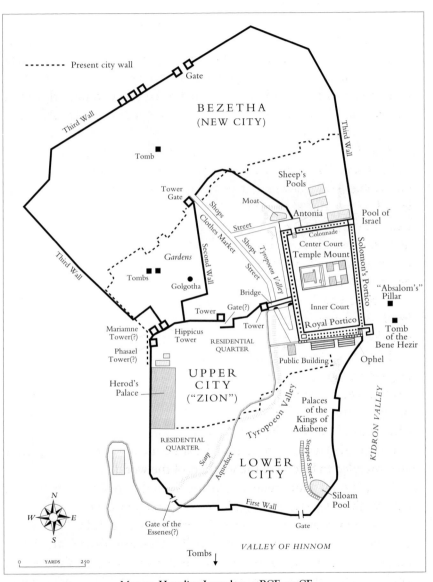

Map 12. Herodian Jerusalem, 4 BCE–70 CE

Fig. 3. The "Tower of David" (perhaps the Tower of Hippicus). (Painting by David Roberts, Esq., R.A.)

Fig. 4. The "Pool of Bethesda" (perhaps part of the Antonia). (Painting by David Roberts, Esq., R.A.)

port the Temple Mount platform to the south. (Today these underground arches are erroneously called "Solomon's Stables": they were not built by Solomon, and they were not used as stables until the Crusader period more than a thousand years later.) New retaining walls were then built further out on the north, south, and west sides, while the original eastern retaining wall was extended to meet the new walls. Evidence of these constructions can still be seen today, two millennia after they were first commissioned. The so-called Kotel, or Western/Wailing Wall, at which modern Jews can be seen praying, is the western retaining wall built by Herod, while the area known to Moslems as the Haram al-Sherif—upon which stand the Dome of the Rock and the al-Aqsa Mosque—is thought faithfully to reflect the platform that Herod built.[20]

In order to permit continuity of religious services within the Temple, Herod had all the building materials prepared beforehand, and to ensure that there was no violation of the sacred areas, he had a thousand priests trained as masons and carpenters to work on the holiest parts of the building. Although work on the entire Temple complex took at least forty-six years—and perhaps as many as eighty years—to complete,[21] the sanctuary within the Temple was completed in only eighteen months, and the Temple itself was finished in eight years.

Sometime around the year 10 BCE, Herod held the dedication ceremony for the reconstructed Temple (which is still called the Second Temple although, in reality, it was the third major Temple to be constructed on the site).[22] According to Josephus, it was a marvel of architectural beauty.

> Now the outward face of the temple in its front wanted nothing that was likely to surprise either men's minds or their eyes; for it was covered all over with plates of gold of great weight, and, at the first rising of the sun, reflected back a very fiery splendor, and made those who forced themselves to look upon it to turn their eyes away, just as they would have done at the sun's own rays. But this temple appeared to strangers, when they were coming to it at a distance, like a mountain covered with snow; for as to those parts of it that were not gilt, they were exceeding white.

Apparently it was also practical in design, for Josephus goes on to say, "On its top it had spikes with sharp points, to prevent any pollution of it by birds sitting upon it" (Josephus *Jewish War* 5.5.222–24).

Today, little remains of Herod's great building projects. They were nearly all destroyed by the Romans in 70 CE when they crushed the First Jewish Revolt and laid waste the city of Jerusalem. Only the massive retaining walls of the Temple Mount, the foundations of the palace, and the base of one of its defensive towers,[23] located just inside the Jaffa Gate in the Old City of Jerusalem, were left by the conquering Romans.[24]

Herod—suffering from constant fever, intestinal ulcers, a pain in his colon, swollen feet, an inflamed abdomen, difficulty breathing, and "a putrefaction of his genitals, that produced worms" (Josephus *Jewish War* 1.33.656; see also *Antiquities of the Jews* 17.6.168–69)—died in the year 4 BCE.[25] Shortly before his death, he faced a minor rebellion. He had ordered a huge golden eagle to be fastened above the entrance to the Temple, as a symbol of Rome and its domination of Judaea. Such a graven image violated the religious laws governing the Temple sanctuary. A group of young men—hearing that Herod was on his deathbed and urged on by two respected rabbis—climbed down from the Temple roof on ropes, swarmed onto the gate, and chopped down the hated eagle. While some of the young men managed to escape, the Temple guards quickly arrested about forty others and the two rabbis. One of Herod's last acts was to sentence to death all those who had been arrested. The two rabbis and those who had been directly involved in chopping down the eagle were burned alive; the rest were executed more humanely—but they were executed nonetheless.[26]

During Passover of the year that Herod died, the Jewish inhabitants of Jerusalem rioted once again, largely as a reaction to the executions of the rabbis and others. Archelaus, one of Herod's three surviving sons, ordered his soldiers to restore order. They did so, killing some three thousand inhabitants and pilgrims in the process.[27]

THE WAR OF VARUS

Archelaus departed for Rome, where the emperor Augustus was to rule on the validity of Herod's will. But five weeks into the journey, he

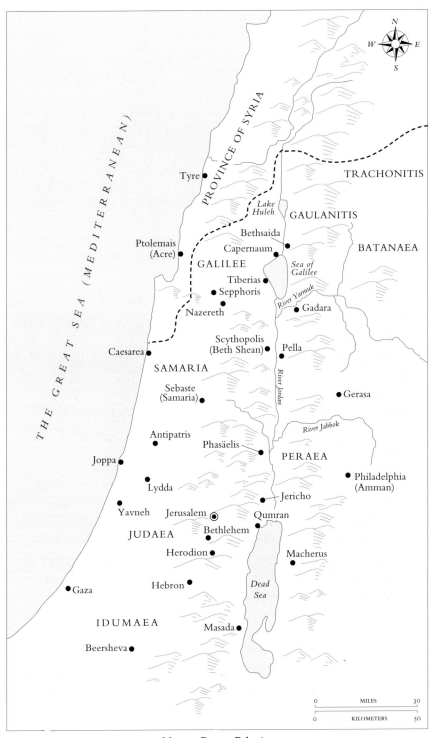

Map 13. Roman Palestine

received word that the inhabitants of Jerusalem were in rebellion yet again. Varus, the Roman governor of Syria, marched to Jerusalem to restore order in Archelaus's absence. The mission accomplished, Varus returned to Syria and left a temporary caretaker named Sabinus in charge of Jerusalem, with a legion of Roman soldiers to enforce his rule.

But Sabinus, whom Josephus described as "Caesar's steward for Syrian affairs," harbored ambitions of his own. He used the legionaries to seize various properties that had belonged to Herod. This had the effect of further enraging the inhabitants of Jerusalem, and open rebellion soon flared again. Retreating to the safety of one of the fortified towers, Sabinus sent a message for help to Varus and ordered the Roman soldiers to crush the rebellion. In the ensuing chaos, the Romans entered the Temple and ransacked its treasures. Josephus says that Sabinus himself took four hundred talents from the Temple treasury.[28]

The looting of the Temple served to further inflame the inhabitants of Jerusalem. When Varus arrived with two additional legions and four troops of horsemen, he found Sabinus barricaded in Herod's palace, besieged by an angry mob. However, with an army of probably more than ten thousand at his disposal, Varus soon crushed the revolt. To emphasize the futility of rebellion to the unruly Jews, he then crucified two thousand of the captured rebels. This so-called "War of Varus" was in reality the speedy putting down of a minor rebellion.[29] In time, Archelaus returned from Rome, having been appointed *ethnarch* ("ruler" or "governor")—rather than king—by Augustus. He was now formally in charge of Judaea, Idumea, and Samaria, where peace reigned once again.

PONTIUS PILATE

All remained reasonably quiet in Jerusalem for the thirty years following the "War of Varus," in part because Augustus, ever watchful for potential rebels, deposed Archelaus in 6 CE and sent him into exile in Gaul. The territory was made into a Roman province and governed by a Roman procurator. The transition to provincial status was a significant event in the history of the region.[30] It was during this period that Jesus—who scholars now think was probably born in either 7 or 4 BCE—grew to adulthood.

Although the emperor Augustus died in the year 14 CE, the Roman Empire continued to expand. His successors, who remained in power until 68 CE, are known formally as the Julio-Claudian dynasty. They were a noteworthy group that included the suspicious and vengeful Tiberius, the insane Caligula, the gullible and easily manipulated Claudius, and—last but certainly not least—the egregious Nero, who sang (rather than "fiddled") while Rome burned in the Great Fire of 64 CE: "Viewing the conflagration from the tower of Maecenas, and exulting, as he said, 'with the beauty of the flames,' he sang the whole time the 'Sack of Ilium,' in his regular stage costume" (Suetonius *Life of Nero* 38).[31]

During the reign of the emperor Tiberius, the situation in Jerusalem deteriorated once again. At that time, Pontius Pilate—the Pontius Pilate of New Testament infamy—was procurator of Judaea, the fifth man to hold the office. Not long after being appointed, probably about 26 CE, he sent five hundred Roman soldiers from Caesarea south to Jerusalem to relieve the regular garrison. This seemingly innocuous movement of troops inflamed the Jewish inhabitants of Jerusalem, perhaps principally because the military standards of this cohort prominently featured a depiction of the emperor Tiberius. Thus the Roman soldiers were, intentionally or not, displaying graven images within the walls of the holy city and dangerously close to the Temple itself. Such a display was seen as a violation of Jewish law.[32] A group of inhabitants of Jerusalem marched to Caesarea and demanded that the offending standards be removed. After several days, Pilate agreed and peace was restored—this time without any bloodshed.[33] But peace was not to last long. The very next year, Pilate confiscated some of the Temple treasures, ostensibly to help pay for repairs to an aqueduct. The Jews, appalled at this new sacrilege, gathered in protest. Pilate—anticipating such a reaction—had instructed his soldiers to fall upon the crowd at once and before they could begin rioting.

> [He] gave the soldiers that signal which had been beforehand agreed on; who laid upon them [the Jews] much greater blows than Pilate had commanded them, and equally punished those that were disorderly, and those that were not; nor did they spare them in the least; and since the people were unarmed, and were

caught by men prepared for what they were about, there were a great number of them killed by this means, and others of them ran away wounded. And thus an end was put to this rebellion. (Josephus *Antiquities of the Jews* 18.3.61–62)[34]

Only a few years after this, the events involving Jesus that are familiar from the accounts in the New Testament took place in Jerusalem. The event that is perhaps best known took place on the grounds of the Temple itself.

And Jesus entered the temple of God and drove out all who sold and bought in the temple, and he overturned the tables of the money-changers and the seats of those who sold pigeons. He said to them, "It is written, 'My house shall be called a house of prayer'; but you make it a den of robbers." And the blind and the lame came to him in the temple, and he healed them. (Matthew 21:12–14; see also Mark 11:15–16; Luke 19:45–46)[35]

The Gospels also say that Jesus accurately predicted the ultimate siege and fall of Jerusalem. Matthew wrote:

Jesus left the temple and was going away, when his disciples came to point out to him the buildings of the temple. But he answered them, "You see all these, do you not? Truly, I say to you, there will not be left here one stone upon another, that will not be thrown down." (Matthew 24:1–3; see also Mark 13:1–2; Luke 21:5–6)

The destruction of the city by the Romans would occur some forty years later; meanwhile, several turbulent decades lay ahead.[36]

PRELUDES TO A REBELLION

In 41 CE, the emperor Caligula, who evidently lacked sensitivity and modesty in about the same degree, ordered that a colossal gilded statue of himself was to be placed within the sanctuary on the Temple Mount. Caligula's motives have long been debated. The most frequent suggestion—first recorded by Josephus—was Caligula's growing resentment at the refusal of the Jews to worship him as a god, as did the rest of the empire. Therefore, it is argued, he decided to force the issue by placing his statue within the Temple. Faced with large demonstrations of protesting Jerusalemites, Caligula deliberated on his order—reportedly changing his mind several times. The issue was only resolved by his sudden death.[37]

With Caligula's death, Judaea once again became a kingdom, and Herod Agrippa—the grandson of Herod the Great—became its king. He, too, is best known for his building activities—in particular, the construction of the so-called Third Wall of Jerusalem. Not completed until long after Agrippa's death and only shortly before the outbreak of the First Jewish Revolt, the wall was apparently intended to defend the northern side of Jerusalem and to bring within the city new suburbs that lay to the north. As such, its construction must have expanded the area covered by Jerusalem to at least 310, and perhaps as much as 450, acres.[38]

When Cumanus, another Roman appointee, began his procuratorship a few years after Agrippa's death, yet another incident occurred that led to bloodshed in Jerusalem—this time during Passover of 48 CE. Josephus records that "on the fourth day of the feast [of Passover], a certain [Roman] soldier let down his breeches, and exposed his privy members to the multitude, which put those that saw him into a furious rage . . ." Events quickly got out of hand, prompting Cumanus to call out the army. The mob turned tail to flee, but the passageways out of the area where they had assembled were narrow, and so, as Josephus says, "a great number [of Jerusalemites] were pressed to death in those narrow passages; nor indeed was the number fewer than twenty thousand that perished in this disturbance" (Josephus *Antiquities of the Jews* 20.5.108–12).[39]

Another riot occurred a few years later when the apostle Paul arrived in Jerusalem in 58 CE. He was arrested by the Romans for "causing a disturbance," prompted by his presence in the Temple. (Might we draw a parallel between Paul's provocative visit to the Temple Mount in 58 CE and that by Ariel Sharon nearly two thousand years later?) Legend says that Paul died in Rome several years later, during Nero's persecution of Christians in 64 CE, when the emperor was searching for scapegoats upon whom to blame the Great Fire.[40]

THE SACRILEGE OF FLORUS
AND THE FIRST REVOLT

It is obvious that, over many decades, conflicts between the Jewish inhabitants of Jerusalem and their Roman overlords occurred at frequent intervals. The spark that usually ignited such conflagrations was the Jews' perception that the Romans were treading heavily upon their sacred grounds or religious practices. The First Jewish Revolt, although of greater magnitude than earlier confrontations, was similar in cause.[41]

The revolt started when Florus, the Roman procurator who was based in Caesarea, took seventeen talents from the sacred treasury of the Temple in the year 66 CE. Josephus speculated that Florus deliberately provoked the Jews into rebelling, in order to cover up his own actions (which may have included embezzlement and extortion, among other activities). It is also possible that Florus was ordered by Nero himself to provoke the Jews into rebellion, so as to justify intervention by the Roman army and the curbing of their growing power.[42] Josephus brings his book *The Antiquities of the Jews* to a close on the following note:

> . . . it was this Florus who necessitated us to take up arms against the Romans, while we thought it better to be destroyed at once, than by little and little. Now this war began in the second year of the government of Florus, and the twelfth year of the reign of Nero. But then what actions we were forced to do, or what miseries we were enabled to suffer, may be accurately known by such as will peruse those books which I have written about the Jewish war. (Josephus *Antiquities of the Jews* 20.11.257–58)

Josephus takes up the story of the confrontation between Jews and Romans in his book *The Jewish War*, which is the main source of information about the First Jewish Revolt.[43] According to Josephus, Florus claimed that he took the money because the Jews were behind in the payment of tribute to Nero. While that may have been true, Florus seems to have been a rapacious individual with quite a talent for extortion.[44] In any event, the inhabitants of Jerusalem rose up again to protest at yet another sacrilegious theft from the Temple's treasury. Florus came to Jerusalem in an attempt to quell the protest, but when moderate measures failed, he unleashed his soldiers, giving them carte blanche to plunder the city market and its surroundings and to kill anyone whom they met while so doing.

> So the soldiers, taking this exhortation of their commander in a sense agreeable to their desire of gain, did not only plunder the place they were sent to, but forcing themselves into every house, they slew its inhabitants; so the citizens fled along the narrow lanes, and the soldiers slew those that they caught, and no method of plunder was omitted; they also caught many of the quiet people, and brought them before Florus, whom he first chastised with stripes [whipping], and then crucified. Accordingly, the whole number of those that were destroyed that day, with their wives and children, (for they did not spare even the infants themselves,) was about three thousand and six hundred. (Josephus *Jewish War* 2.14.305–7)[45]

The next day, Florus sent his men out again, and "the horsemen trampled them [the inhabitants] down, so that a great many fell down dead by the strokes of the Romans, . . . and a terrible destruction there was among those that fell down, for they were suffocated, and broken to pieces by the multitude of those that were uppermost" (Josephus *Jewish War* 2.15.326–27).[46] At this point, the conflict escalated. The Jews, standing on the roofs of their houses, threw darts down upon the Roman soldiers, who were forced to retreat back to Florus's palace. Florus, seeing the need for reinforcements, returned to Caesarea and sent a message to Cestius Gallus, the Roman governor of Syria, asking for assistance in putting down the "rebellion." The inhabitants of Jerusalem also wrote to Cestius Gallus, explaining their side of the story.[47]

In the meantime, a civil war erupted among the Jews of Jerusalem. The high priests, along with the "men of power" and those who desired peace with the Romans, took control of the upper city. Those who were rebellious, as Josephus puts it, were in control of the lower city and the Temple, where they ceased the twice-daily sacrifices made on behalf of the Roman emperor (Josephus *Jewish War* 2.17.422–24).[48] For a week, the two sides threw stones and darts at each other and occasionally engaged in hand-to-hand combat. Then, probably in early August of 66 CE, the rebels "made an assault upon [the fortress of] Antonia, and besieged the [Roman] garrison which was in it [for] two days, and then took the garrison, and slew them, and set the citadel on fire; after which they marched to the palace, whither the king's soldiers were fled, and parted themselves into four bodies, and made an attack upon the walls" (Josephus *Jewish War* 2.17.430–31).[49]

Following the massacre of the Roman garrison, the civil war within the city resumed. Eventually, after much loss of life, those desiring peace with the Romans defeated the rebels.[50] But some of the rebels— known as the Sicarii—ultimately escaped to the fortress at Masada, which they made their base for raiding the surrounding countryside for several more years.[51]

CESTIUS GALLUS AND THE TWELFTH LEGION

At the time of the civil war in Jerusalem, a more serious insurgency began to grow, in Egypt as well as Palestine. In response, the Romans massacred thousands of Jews in cities near Jerusalem—notably Ashkelon, Ptolemais (Akko/Acre), and Caesarea—as well as in distant cities, such as Alexandria.[52] Faced with a growing conflagration within his domain, Cestius Gallus, the Roman governor of Syria, ordered the Twelfth Legion (Legio XII Fulminata, "the Thunderbolt") from its base in Antioch. He added soldiers from other legions as well, and it has been estimated that his total fighting force numbered close to thirty thousand infantry and horsemen. In September of 66 CE, he marched into Galilee.[53]

By mid-October, his army was encamped about six miles from Jerusalem. The inhabitants were busy celebrating the Feast of Tabernacles. Josephus tells what happened next.

> . . . as for the Jews, when they saw the war approaching their metropolis, they left the feast, and betook themselves to their arms; and taking courage greatly from their multitude, went in a

sudden and disorderly manner to the fight, with a great noise, . . . [and] that rage which made them forget the religious observation [of the Sabbath] made them too hard for their enemies in the fight: with such violence therefore did they fall upon the Romans, as to break into their ranks, and to march through the midst of them, making a great slaughter as they went, insomuch that . . . five hundred and fifteen of the Romans were killed, of which number four hundred were footmen, and the rest horsemen, while the Jews lost only twenty-two . . . (Josephus *Jewish War* 2.19. 517–19)[54]

It was a great victory for the Jews, but it was not the end of the conflict. Cestius Gallus moved his forces closer and established a position on Mount Scopus. He then set fire to the northern suburbs and the timber market. Entering the upper city, he pitched his camp near the royal palace.[55] His soldiers spent the next five days attacking the walls surrounding the lower city, but they were unable to breach them. On the sixth day, Cestius Gallus attempted to storm the Temple but failed. However, his force did get close enough to undermine the northern wall surrounding the sanctuary, and his soldiers "got all things ready for setting fire to the gate of the temple" (Josephus *Jewish War* 2.19.537). Then, quite suddenly and inexplicably, Cestius Gallus gave up and withdrew—"he retired from the city, without any reason in the world," as Josephus says (Josephus *Jewish War* 2.19.540).[56]

The Jews followed and attacked the retreating Roman army. Eventually they ambushed the Romans in a narrow pass near Beth Horon. This was the same place where Joshua had pursued the five Amorite kings more than a thousand years earlier and where Judah Maccabee had defeated a Syrian army just over two hundred years earlier.[57] The result was similar this time. The Roman troops were massacred. Josephus reports that the Jerusalemites and their allies "had themselves lost a few only, but had killed of the Romans five thousand and three hundred footmen, and three hundred and eighty horsemen." He added, "This defeat happened . . . in the twelfth year of the reign of Nero" (Josephus *Jewish War* 2.19.555). The Twelfth Legion was nearly wiped out, and Cestius Gallus himself either died or took his own life a few days after the defeat.[58]

Suetonius reports that the Jews captured the Twelfth Legion's eagle standard (*aquila* in Latin): "the people of Judaea took to themselves; accordingly they revolted and after killing their governor, they routed the consular ruler of Syria as well, when he came to the rescue, and took one of his eagles" (Suetonius *Life of Vespasian* 4).[59] The eagle standard was the most important of all those carried by each Roman legion. On the pole of the standard, which bore a golden eagle at its top, was affixed the abbreviation "SPQR," which stood for *senatus populusque romanus*—in English, "the Senate and the people of Rome." The ultimate disgrace for any Roman legion was to have its eagle standard captured in battle. That happened only very rarely, and an eagle's loss usually meant that the legion had been annihilated.[60] Rome did not suffer such humiliation lightly, and the capture of this eagle may have sealed Jerusalem's fate. It is possible that the later campaigns of Vespasian and of Titus—which culminated in the destruction of Jerusalem in 70 CE—were as much attempts to recover the lost eagle or at least to avenge its loss as they were attempts to quell the unruly Judaeans.[61] It is interesting to speculate that if the Jews had not captured the eagle standard of the Twelfth Legion, the Second Temple might still be standing today.

VESPASIAN AND A
CIVIL WAR INTERREGNUM

Nero dispatched Vespasian—one of his most trusted generals—to suppress the Jewish rebellion. Vespasian immediately headed for Antioch in Syria, to take command of the Roman forces. At the same time, he sent his son Titus to Alexandria in Egypt, to fetch the Roman soldiers stationed there. All of these troops—which now included the Roman Fifth, Tenth, and Fifteenth Legions and assorted allied forces—assembled in the city of Ptolemais (modern Acre on the coast of Israel, north of Jerusalem) in the spring of 67 CE. Numbering nearly sixty thousand, the combined force then headed for Judaea.[62]

Vespasian decided to isolate Jerusalem and to leave the attack on it until last. Heading into Galilee, he began the task of conquering one rebel city after another—Gadara, then Jotapata, then Japha. During the difficult siege of Jotapata, Josephus—considered by the Romans to be among the best of the Judaean generals—was captured and brought before Vespasian. Josephus escaped execution and soon become part of Vespasian's entourage. It is said that he accomplished this, at least in part, by predicting that Vespasian would soon succeed Nero as Roman emperor. Later, Josephus shed his Hebrew name and Judaean clothing and adopted the emperor's family name and Roman attire. Thus Joseph ben Mattathias (or Yosef bar Mattathyahu in Aramaic) became Flavius Josephus—and a Jewish general was reborn as a Roman author and apologist.[63]

Vespasian continued his campaign in Judaea. He marched south down the coast to capture Joppa (near modern Tel Aviv); then headed north by way of the Sea of Galilee and took the hilltop city of Gamala (located on what is now the Golan Heights); and then returned to Galilee, where he captured the city of Gischala. Eventually he conquered the entire region of Idumea, including Jericho.[64] By late summer of 68 CE, Vespasian was firmly established in Caesarea on the coast, having subdued most of the country. He was now ready to deal with Jerusalem.[65]

The Jerusalemites had ample warning that Vespasian was on his way, and they could have prepared their defenses accordingly. But while the Roman armies were marching around Judaea, the inhabitants of Jerusalem had once again been engaged in yet another bitter civil war. Josephus devotes much of books 4 and 5 in his *Jewish War* to describing this activity, which he likens to "a wild beast grown mad, which, . . . fell now upon eating its own flesh" (Josephus *Jewish War* 5.1.4). The Jerusalemites split into three factions, led by Simon bar Giora, John of Gischala, and Eleazar bar Simon, respectively. Each faction then began fighting the other two. In doing so, not only did they divide their forces and their leadership, but they also performed foolish actions, including burning their own food supplies.

And now there were three treacherous factions in the city, the one parted from the other. Eleazar and his party, that kept the sacred firstfruits, came against John in their cups. Those that were with John plundered the populace, and went out with zeal against

Simon. This Simon had his supply of provisions from the city, in opposition to the rebellious. When, therefore, John was assaulted on both sides, he made his men turn about, throwing his darts upon those citizens that came up against him, from the passages he had in his possession, while he opposed those that attacked him from the temple by his engines of war. And if at any time he was freed from those that were above him, which happened frequently, from their being drunk and tired, he sallied out with a great number upon Simon and his party; and this he did always in such parts of the city as he could come at, until he set on fire those houses that were full of grain, and of all other provisions. The same thing was done by Simon, when, upon the other's retreat, he attacked the city also; as if they had, on purpose, done it to serve the Romans, by destroying what the city had laid up against the siege, and by thus cutting off the nerves of their own power. Accordingly, it so came to pass, that all the places that were about the temple were burned down, and were become an intermediate desert space, ready for fighting on both sides of it; and that almost all that grain was burned, which would have been sufficient for a siege of many years. So they were taken by the means of the famine, which it was impossible they should have been, unless they had thus prepared the way for it by this procedure. And now, as the city was engaged in a war on all sides, from these treacherous crowds of wicked men, the people of the city, between them, were like a great body torn in pieces. The aged men and the women were in such distress by their internal calamities, that they wished for the Romans, and earnestly hoped for an external war, in order to their delivery from their domestic miseries. (Josephus *Jewish War* 5.1.21–28)[66]

Vespasian was apparently aware of the tensions and the internecine warfare within Jerusalem. It is thought that this was one of the reasons that he left the attack on the city until last.[67] But just before Vespasian finally decided to send his forces against the city, he received word that Emperor Nero was dead. He now had a greater preoccupation than the fate of Jerusalem. He postponed his attack and hurried back to Rome. There, in what is known as the "Year of the Four Emperors" (68–69

CE), first Galba, then Otho, then Vitellius, and finally Vespasian succeeded each other as emperor. When the dust finally settled late in 69 CE, Vespasian was established in Rome as sole emperor. He and then his sons Titus and Domitian would rule as the Flavian dynasty for twenty-seven years, until 96 CE.

Thus, not until 70 CE was Vespasian able to return to the unsettled issue of Jerusalem. Since the business of running the empire required his presence in Rome, he put his son Titus at the head of the army sent to finish off the city and its troublesome inhabitants.

THE SIEGE BEGINS

It has been estimated that the army that Titus led against Jerusalem numbered as many as sixty-five thousand men.

> He found awaiting him in Judaea three legions, Vespasian's old troops, the Fifth, the Tenth, and the Fifteenth. He reinforced these with the Twelfth from Syria and with some soldiers from the Twenty-second and the Third which he brought from Alexandria; these troops were accompanied by twenty cohorts of allied infantry, eight squadrons of cavalry, as well as by the princes Agrippa and Sohaemus, the auxiliaries sent by King Antiochus, and by a strong contingent of Arabs, who hated the Jews with all that hatred that is common among neighbors. . . . With these forces Titus entered the enemy's land: his troops advanced in strict order, he reconnoitered at every step and was always ready for battle; not far from Jerusalem he pitched camp. (Tacitus *Histories* 5.1)[68]

The army included the remnants of the Twelfth Legion, the one that had been all but destroyed and had lost its eagle standard in 66 CE. Josephus notes the presence of "that twelfth legion which had been formerly beaten with Cestius; which legion, as it was otherwise remarkable for its valor, so did it march on now with greater alacrity to avenge themselves . . . remembering what they had formerly endured" (Josephus *Jewish War* 5.1.41).

On the march, Titus's army must have been a fearsome sight.

. . . the reinforcements that were sent by the kings marched first, having all the other reinforcements with them; after whom followed those that were to prepare the roads and measure out the camp; then came the commander's baggage, and after that the other soldiers, who were completely armed to support them; then came Titus himself, having with him another select body; and then came the pikemen; after whom came the horsemen belonging to that legion. All these came before the engines; and after these engines came the tribunes and the leaders of the cohorts, with their select bodies; after these came the ensigns, with the eagle; and before those ensigns came the trumpeters belonging to them; next [there] came the main body of the army in their ranks, every rank being six deep; the servants belonging to every legion came after these; and before these last their baggage; the mercenaries came last, and those that guarded them brought up the rear. (Josephus *Jewish War* 5.2.47–49)

Upon approaching Jerusalem, the Roman army set up camp about four miles from the city. Titus then chose six hundred horsemen to accompany him in scouting out the defenses. He must have been astounded when the inhabitants charged out of the gates and surrounded his force. According to Josephus, it was only through Titus's own bravery that the Romans were able to extricate themselves: "[Titus] turned his horse about, and cried out aloud to those that were about him to follow him, and ran with violence into the midst of his enemies, in order to force his way through them" (Josephus *Jewish War* 5.2.2). Although he wore no armor, Titus managed to escape serious injury and make his way back to the Roman camp. However, the success of the surprise attack gave heart to the inhabitants of Jerusalem.[69]

The northern side of the city now had a wall bristling with ninety defensive towers. Josephus reports:

[Titus] set the strongest part of his army near to that wall which lay on the north quarter of the city, and near to the western part of it, and made his army seven deep, with the footmen placed before them, and the horsemen behind them, each of the last in three ranks, whilst the archers stood in the midst in seven ranks.

. . . However, the tenth legion continued in its own place, upon the Mount of Olives. (Josephus *Jewish War* 5.3.130–35)[70]

Meanwhile, the city's inhabitants waited until the last possible moment to cease fighting each other and face their common enemy.

There were three generals, three armies: the outermost and largest circuit of the walls was held by Simon [bar Giora], the middle of the city by John [of Gischala], and the temple was guarded by Eleazar [bar Simon]. John and Simon were strong in numbers and equipment, Eleazar had the advantage of position: between these three there was constant fighting, treachery, and arson, and a great store of grain was consumed. Then John got possession of the temple by sending a party, under pretence of offering sacrifice, to slay Eleazar and his troops. So the citizens were divided into two factions until, at the approach of the Romans, foreign war produced concord. (Tacitus *Histories* 5.12; see also Josephus *Jewish War* 5.6.248–57)[71]

Josephus lists approximately 23,400 fighting men in all of the various factions within the city, and Tacitus says, "the total number of the besieged of every age and both sexes was six hundred thousand" (Tacitus *Histories* 5.13; see also Josephus *Jewish War* 5.6.248–50). This is a surprisingly (perhaps unbelievably) high number, even if it included pilgrims come to celebrate Passover in 70 CE, since the estimated population of Jerusalem just forty years earlier was about eighty thousand. In any event, these inhabitants soon began to feel the pressures of a besieging army camped immediately outside the walls of the city.[72]

DEEP SILENCE AND A DEADLY NIGHT

As previously noted, in 1970 Nahman Avigad's archaeological team found a woman's arm in the "Burnt House." The rest of her body was never found. Avigad suggests that her other body parts were simply "scattered and swept away by later activities in antiquity." He and other historians have assumed that the house was destroyed and the woman killed by the Romans during the capture of the city.[73]

It was probably in early May of 70 CE that the battle for Jerusalem began in earnest.

> [Titus] gave his soldiers leave to set the suburbs on fire, and ordered that they should bring timber together, and raise banks against the city. . . . when he had parted his army into three parts, in order to set about those works, he placed those that shot darts and the archers in the midst of the banks that were then raising; before whom he placed those engines that threw javelins, and darts, and stones, that he might prevent the enemy from sallying out upon their works, and might hinder those that were upon the wall from being able to obstruct them. So the trees were now cut down immediately, and the suburbs left naked. (Josephus *Jewish War* 5.6.262–64).

The Romans set up three large wooden towers that were fifty cubits (slightly more than seventy feet) in height and covered with plates of iron. In these they placed archers and as some of their smaller "war engines" that threw darts and flung stones.

The Jerusalemites used their own few war engines and conducted sorties to fight in hand-to-hand combat against the Roman soldiers and engineers.[74] But the Romans possessed larger and better "engines" than those of the city's defenders. Those of the Tenth Legion—stationed on the Mount of Olives—were especially impressive.

> . . . those that threw darts and those that threw stones were more forcible and larger than the rest, by which they not only repelled the excursions of the Jews, but drove those away that were upon the walls also. Now the stones that were cast were of the weight of a talent, and were carried two furlongs and further. The blow they gave was no way to be sustained, not only by those that stood first in the way, but by those that were beyond them for a great space . . . (Josephus *Jewish War* 5.6.269–70)

On the fifteenth day of the siege, the Romans broke through the outermost of the three walls protecting Jerusalem. They promptly tore down most of this wall and demolished much of the northern part of the city. Titus then established his camp within the city itself.[75] Five days later, with the help of battering rams, the Romans stormed and then breached the second wall. Titus, with a thousand armed men at his back, "did not permit his soldiers to kill any of those they caught, nor to set fire to their houses" (Josephus *Jewish War* 5.8.334). The inhabitants of Jerusalem took this as a sign of weakness and promptly counterattacked, driving Titus and his men back beyond the second wall. It took the Romans another four days to recapture the second wall, at which point Titus ordered it torn down and turned his attention to breaching the final, innermost wall.[76]

In the meantime, the defenders of the city, now crowded into the portions of the city still remaining to them, were suffering from the longer-term effects of the siege. Josephus tells us that famine became so severe that "children pulled the very morsels that their fathers were eating out of their very mouths, and what was still more to be pitied, so did the mothers . . . to their infants." His account continues:

They also invented terrible methods of torments to discover where any food was, and they were these[:] to stop up the passages of the privy parts of the miserable wretches, and to drive sharp stakes up their fundaments; and a man was forced to bear what it is terrible even to hear, in order to make him confess that he had but one loaf of bread, or that he might discover a handful of barley-meal that was concealed . . . (Josephus *Jewish War* 5.10.430–36)

Some of the inhabitants crept out of the city by night in order to gather wild plants and herbs. Titus set ambushes to capture them, and when they were caught, they "were first whipped, and then tormented with all sorts of tortures, before they died, and were then crucified before the wall of the city" (Josephus *Jewish War* 5.11.449). Josephus says that five hundred or more Jews were caught and executed in this manner each day.[77]

But the Jews were not without their minor victories. They were at least temporarily successful in undermining one of the Roman siege embankments. The Romans had been working for seventeen days to build such embankments to attack the innermost wall. By the twenty-ninth day of the Roman month of Artemisius (probably mid-June of 70

CE), they had built "four great banks"—which brought the Romans' troops and engines up to the height of the defenders'. These banks served as platforms for the attack towers and battering rams. The Fifth Legion built one in the area of the Antonia fortress, and the Twelfth Legion constructed another nearby. The Tenth Legion built a third one some distance away to use in attacking the upper city, and a fourth was constructed by the Fifteenth Legion about fifty feet beyond the third, near "the high priest's monument"—a well-known monument dedicated to John Hyrcanus, the earlier Hasmonean ruler. The Jews managed to undermine the embankment of the Fifth Legion, bringing it crashing down "with a prodigious noise" in a cloud of smoke, dust, and fire.[78]

At this point, Titus ordered a wall built around the entire city in order to tighten the siege. Josephus says that this was done in a matter of days, although it is thought that this wall may have been as much as four and a half miles long.[79]

> So all hope of escaping was now cut off from the Jews, together with their liberty of going out of the city. Then did the famine widen its progress, and devoured the people by whole houses and families; the upper rooms were full of women and children that were dying by famine, and the lanes of the city were full of the dead bodies of the aged; the children also and the young men wandered about the market-places like shadows, all swelled with the famine, and fell down dead, wheresoever their misery seized them. As for burying them, those that were sick themselves were not able to do it; and those that were hearty and well were deterred from doing it by the great multitude of those dead bodies. . . . A deep silence also, and a kind of deadly night, had seized upon the city . . . (Josephus *Jewish War* 5.12.512–15)

Josephus claims that "no fewer than six hundred thousand [dead bodies] were thrown out at the gates" (Josephus *Jewish War* 5.13.569). This seems like an inflated number, but the message is clear—the Roman siege was effective, and at least as many people were dying of starvation as were dying on the points of Roman spears and arrows.

In the meantime, John of Gischala, one of the Jewish leaders, had taken control of the Temple and its immediate area. He sacrilegiously seized and began to melt down many of the sacred utensils—described by Josephus as "many of those vessels which were necessary for such as ministered about holy things, the caldrons, the dishes, and the tables." Josephus postulates, "I suppose, that had the Romans made any longer delay in coming against these villains, that the city would either have been swallowed up by the ground opening upon them, or been overflowed by water, or else been destroyed by such thunder as the country of Sodom perished by" (Josephus *Jewish War* 5.13.566).[80]

The Romans pulled the noose around Jerusalem ever tighter. In late July, Titus launched an assault on the Antonia fortress and captured it, after much fighting over several days. Titus ordered his soldiers to demolish the Antonia, even to its very foundations. They did such a good job that archaeologists today are still not completely certain where the Antonia stood.[81]

The next dish on the Roman menu was the Temple itself. Within a week of capturing the Antonia fortress, the Romans began to build siege embankments abutting the Temple and its precincts. Josephus says that "one bank was near to the north-west corner of the inner temple[;] another was at that northern edifice which was between the two gates; and of the other two, one was at the western passage of the outer court of the temple; the other against its northern passage" (Josephus *Jewish War* 6.2.150–51). The Jewish defenders put up a valiant fight, which Josephus describes in great detail, singling out a few instances of defenders or attackers who acted particularly heroically. (Josephus *Jewish War* 6.2.152–76)

Meanwhile, the famine continued to take its toll of the inhabitants of Jerusalem.[82] By now, "their hunger was so intolerable, that it obliged them to chew everything, while they gathered such things as the most sordid animals would not touch, and endured to eat them; nor did they at length abstain from girdles and shoes; and the very leather which belonged to their shields they pulled off and gnawed" (Josephus *Jewish War* 6.3.197). Josephus recounts with horror the story of a woman named Mary.

> . . . it was now become impossible for her to find any more food anyway, while the famine pierced through her very bowels and marrow, . . . She then attempted a most unnatural thing; and

snatching up her son, who was a child sucking at her breast, she . . . killed her son, and then roasted him, and ate the one half of him, and kept the other half by her concealed. Upon this the rebellious came in presently, and smelling the horrid scent of this food, they threatened her that they would cut her throat immediately if she did not show them what food she had gotten ready. She replied that she had saved a very fine portion of it for them, and nonetheless uncovered what was left of her son. But they were seized with a horror and amazement of mind, and stood astonished at the sight, when she said to them, "This is mine own son, and what has been done was mine own doing! Come, eat of this food; for I have eaten of it myself! Do not you pretend to be either more tender than a woman, or more compassionate than a mother; but if you be so scrupulous, and do abominate this my sacrifice, as I have eaten the one half, let the rest be reserved for me also. (Josephus *Jewish War* 6.3.204–11)[83]

When the siege embankments near the Temple were completed, Titus gave orders for the battering rams to be brought up. When the rams proved ineffective against the massive stonework, he ordered that the gates of the Temple be set on fire. Then, when the timbers of the gates were burning and the metal encasing them was molten from the heat, the Roman soldiers dashed in. A bitter battle left them in control of the outer courts of the Temple, with the defenders driven into the inner temple, wherein lay the inner courts and the sanctuary.[84]

It took only a few more days, in the last week of August 70 CE, for the Roman soldiers to break into the inner temple. Josephus reports that in the ensuing battle, the defenders "were everywhere killed." He describes the gruesome scene: "Around the altar lay dead bodies heaped one upon another; down the steps of the sanctuary flowed a stream of blood, and the bodies of those killed above went sliding to the bottom" (Josephus *Jewish War* 6.4.259).[85] The sanctuary itself was set on fire—reportedly not as an act of high policy but by an ordinary Roman soldier throwing a piece of burning wood into it. Soon the entire Temple was on fire. Titus later claimed that he had never meant to destroy the Temple and that he had ordered his men to try to save it.[86] But it was too late; the Temple was consumed by the flames, and for the second time in their history, the holiest place of the Jews was destroyed by an imperial power. The date was August 28, 70 CE—the ninth of Ab, according to the Hebrew calendar. Tradition holds that the Temple of Solomon was destroyed on the very same date more than six hundred and fifty years earlier.[87] Josephus wrote, "But as for that house [i.e., the Temple], God had, for certain, long ago doomed it to the fire; and now that fatal day was come, according to the revolution of ages" (Josephus *Jewish War* 6.4.250).

With the Temple complex in flames, "the Romans, judging that it was in vain to spare what was round about the holy house, burnt all those places, as also the remains of the cloisters and the gates." They also "burnt down the treasury chambers, in which was an immense quantity of money, and an immense number of garments, and other precious goods there reposited" (Josephus *Jewish War* 6.5.281–82). The fires burned so fiercely that the outline of stone arches were burnt into the southern wall of the Temple Mount, where they can still be seen today.[88] Josephus reports: "While the Temple blazed, the victors plundered everything that fell in their way and slaughtered wholesale all who were caught. No pity was shown for age, no reverence for rank; children and greybeards, laity and priests alike were massacred" (Josephus *Jewish War* 6.5.271).[89] Six thousand people died within the Temple complex that day; some hacked to death, others burned alive. At the end, the Roman soldiers brought their military standards into the smoldering ruins of the Temple, set them up near the remnants of the eastern gate, and made sacrifices to them.[90] Nothing could have spoken more eloquently of the defeat of the Jews.

It took another month for the Romans to subdue the rest of Jerusalem—mostly the upper city. Titus ordered his soldiers to kill the inhabitants, plunder the entire city, and then set it on fire. It was now the end of September in 70 CE. It was perhaps at this time that a young woman, whose arm was to be unearthed nearly two thousand years later, lost her life inside the burnt house of Bar Kathros.[91]

. . . when they went in numbers into the lanes of the city with their swords drawn, they slew those whom they overtook without and set fire to the houses whither the Jews were fled, and burned every soul in them, and laid waste a great many of the rest; and when they were come to the houses to plunder them, they found in them entire families of dead men, and the upper rooms full of dead corpses, that is, of such as died by the famine; they then stood in a horror at this sight, and went out without touching anything. But although they had pity for such as were destroyed in that manner, yet had they not the same for those that were still alive, but they ran everyone through whom they met with, and obstructed the very lanes with their dead bodies, and made the whole city run down with blood, to such a degree indeed that the fire of many of the houses was quenched with these men's blood. (Josephus *Jewish War* 6.8.404–6)[92]

THE LOOT

Upon Titus's return to Rome in 71 CE, a triumphal parade was held in which hundreds of Jewish prisoners were forced to march—including the captured leaders Simon bar Giora and John of Gischala—and during which the booty from the Judaean campaign was carried through the streets of Rome. Among the items in the booty were objects taken from the Temple in Jerusalem.

For there was here to be seen a mighty quantity of silver, and gold, and ivory, . . . running along like a river. . . . those that were taken in the temple of Jerusalem, they made the greatest figure of them all; that is, the golden table, of the weight of many talents; the candlestick also, that was made of gold, . . . and the last of all the spoils, was carried the Law of the Jews [i.e., the Torah]. (Josephus *Jewish War* 7.5.134–50).[93]

To celebrate his victory, Titus built a triumphal arch at the eastern end of the forum in Rome, near where the triumphal procession had marched. Among the objects depicted was the candelabrum taken from the Temple in Jerusalem. The accompanying inscription was not entirely accurate, but it was only a little exaggerated: "The Roman Senate and people [dedicate this] to the Emperor Titus. . . . he subdued the Jewish people and destroyed the city of Jerusalem, which all generals, kings, and peoples before him had either attacked without success or left entirely unassailed."[94]

After the public display of the Temple objects, Vespasian built a temple to Peace, inside which he stored "those golden vessels and instruments that were taken out of the Jewish temple, as ensigns of his glory" (Josephus *Jewish War* 7.5.161). Subsequently, new coins were issued by order of the emperor, including many that depicted a captive Jewish woman under a palm tree and bore the inscription *Judaea Capta*, "Judaea captured," or the inscription *Judaea Devicta*, "Judaea vanquished."[95] According to a recently deciphered inscription, Vespasian and Titus may have also used some of the Judaean loot—perhaps specifically from the Temple treasury—to pay for the construction of the Colosseum in Rome.[96]

The holiest place of the Jews had been looted on at least seventeen separate occasions between the time the First Temple was built by Solomon in the tenth century BCE and the time the Second Temple was destroyed by Titus in the first century CE, but never before had the extent of the depredation been so huge.[97] The exact amount of plunder taken from the Temple in 70 CE is unknown, but it was so vast that thereafter "in Syria a pound weight of gold was sold for half its former value" (Josephus *Jewish War* 6.6.317).[98]

THE IMMEDIATE AFTERMATH OF THE SIEGE

Josephus says that the number of those taken captive during the First Jewish Revolt was ninety-seven thousand and that, in all, the number of those that perished during the siege of Jerusalem was eleven hundred thousand. Of these, he notes:

> the greater part . . . were indeed of the same nation [with the citizens of Jerusalem], but not belonging to the city itself; for they were come up from all the country to the Feast of Unleavened Bread [i.e., Passover], and were on a sudden shut up [in the city] by an army . . . (Josephus *Jewish War* 6.9.420–21)

Almost certainly, the number of casualties given by Josephus—more than a million people—is an exaggeration, for there were still sufficient Judaeans left to defy the Romans over the next thirty years.[99] Nevertheless, it is likely that the Judaeans lost a substantial portion of their population at this time. The majority of those captured were either taken to Rome, sent to the mines in Egypt, sold into slavery, or killed by wild animals or at the hands of gladiators in amphitheaters around the Roman Empire.

> . . . of the young men he [Titus] chose out the tallest and most beautiful, and reserved them for the triumph [the parade in Rome]; and as for the rest of the multitude that were above seventeen years old, he put them into bonds, and sent them to the Egyptian mines. Titus also sent a great number into the provinces, as a present to them, that they might be destroyed upon their theaters, by the sword and by the wild beasts; but those that were under seventeen years of age were sold for slaves. (Josephus *Jewish War* 6.9.417–18)

Meanwhile, Titus ordered the Roman soldiers to demolish most of what remained of Jerusalem, thus fulfilling the prophecy reportedly made by Jesus forty years earlier: "Truly, I say to you, there will not be left here one stone upon another, that will not be thrown down" (Matthew 24:1–3; see also Mark 13:1–2; Luke 21:5–6). Israeli archaeologists excavating just outside the Temple Mount have found thousands of stones—some weighing between three and five tons—that had once been part of the Temple Mount's huge retaining walls but that had been deliberately thrown down and now lay in heaps amid the ruins of the ancient streets. One archaeologist later wrote:

> Standing there on a street from the Second Temple period with the ashlars of Herod's monumental walls at my feet—stones that had been torn out of the wall by rampaging soldiers—I could almost feel the horror and savagery of those days of destruction when Jerusalem and the Temple Mount, the jewel at its center, were laid low.[100]

The Romans left standing only the three towers built by Herod—Phasael, Mariamne, and Hippicus—and what remained of the western wall of the city. The towers were spared so that future generations might see how strongly fortified Jerusalem had been at the time that Titus captured it. The wall was left to serve as protection for the camp of the Tenth Legion (Legio X Fretensis), which Titus left behind to garrison the ruined city.[101]

So Josephus writes: "And thus was Jerusalem taken, in the second year of the reign of Vespasian . . . This was the end which Jerusalem came to . . . ; a city otherwise of great magnificence, and of mighty fame among all mankind" (Josephus *Jewish War* 6.10.435–7.1.4). But it was not really the end of Jerusalem; merely the end of the five-hundred-year-long period when the Second Temple loomed large over the city and over Judaea as a whole. Nor was this the final end of the First Jewish Revolt—Masada and two other fortresses were to hold out against the Romans for several more years after the destruction of Jerusalem.[102] Indeed, the final end of Judaean resistance to Roman rule still lay sixty years in the future, during the reign of the emperor Hadrian, when the Second Jewish Revolt took place.

THE SECOND JEWISH REVOLT

The Second Jewish Revolt—also called the Bar Kokhba Rebellion, after its charismatic leader—lasted from 132 to 135 CE. By this time, Josephus was dead, but archaeology and the pages of other ancient authors—especially the work of the Roman historian Dio Cassius, that of the church historian Father Eusebius, and Hadrian's biography in the *Scriptores Historiae Augustae*—provide much information about the rebellion.[103]

The main events of the Second Jewish Revolt were as follows. When the Roman emperor Hadrian visited Jerusalem during a grand tour of the eastern part of his empire in 129–30 CE, he announced that the city would henceforth be known as Aelia Capitolina—named for the emperor himself, Aelia Hadrianus, and the cult of the Capitoline of Rome. This announcement was met with intense resentment. Rebellion soon broke out in Judaea. There may have been other factors contributing to this revolt, possibly including a ban on circumcision. But Hadrian's announcement that he would "refound" and rename the city was probably the last and most inflammatory of a series of provocative pronouncements.[104]

The uprising lasted three years, from 132 to 135 CE, and was led by Bar Kokhba, whom some—including the famous rabbi Akiba—

regarded as the Messiah. The name *Bar Kokhba* meant "son of the star" and was a nom de guerre for the rebel leader. Letters and scrolls discovered by archaeologists in the past fifty years indicate that his real name was probably Shim'on Bar Kosiba. Whatever he was called, he was an effective leader. It has been estimated that it took as many as eighty thousand Roman soldiers to suppress his revolt. After years of successful guerilla fighting, Bar Kokhba and his followers made a final stand at Bethar, a few miles from Jerusalem. There, they were killed by the Romans.[105]

During the course of the revolt, Bar Kokhba and the Jewish rebels apparently inflicted heavy losses on the Roman troops, for Dio Cassius says: "Many Romans, moreover, perished in this war. Therefore Hadrian in writing to the senate did not employ the opening phrase commonly affected by the emperors, 'If you and your children are in health, it is well; I and the legions are in health'" (Dio Cassius *Historia Romana* 69.14). Much has been made of this statement, for it is most unusual and must reflect an extraordinary number of casualties suffered by the Romans during their campaign against Bar Kokhba. However, the Judaeans fared far worse. Dio Cassius says that fifty important outposts and 985 famous villages were burned to the ground during the Roman suppression of the Second Jewish Revolt. Moreover, "five hundred and eighty thousand [Judaean] men were slain in the various raids and battles, and the number of those that perished by famine, disease and fire was past finding out" (Dio Cassius *Historia Romana* 69.12–14). Dio Cassius also says that the Romans sold so many Judaean prisoners as slaves that the price of slaves in the Mediterranean area dropped drastically in the years following the suppression of the revolt; so many Judaeans were carried off that "almost the whole of Judaea was made desolate."[106]

It is still a matter of debate whether Bar Kokhba and his men ever captured Jerusalem during the course of this rebellion.[107] However, with the revolt suppressed, Hadrian finally made good his earlier pronouncement. A new—and renamed—city was built upon the ruins of Jerusalem left by the siege of 70 CE. It was constructed on the typical Roman colonial plan, with a broad north-south avenue called the Cardo Maximus and an equally broad east-west avenue called the Decumanus. Today, in the Old City of Jerusalem, the plan can still be

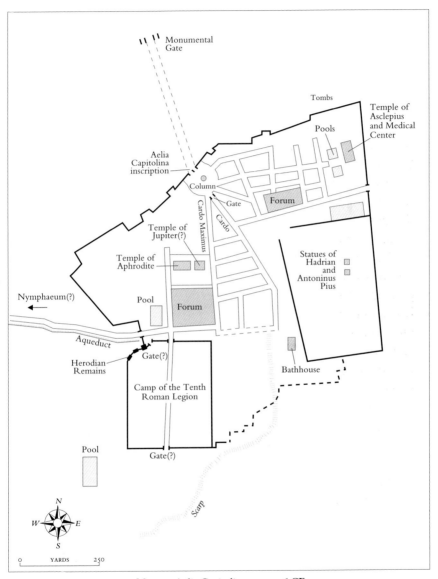

Map 14. Aelia Capitolina, 135–326 CE

traced, and the remains of those avenues can be seen. A statue of Hadrian may have been set up on the Temple Mount, and a Temple to Jupiter was built somewhere in the city. The emperor expelled all remaining Jews from Jerusalem and forbade them to ever live there again. Jerusalem was now renamed Aelia Capitolina, and Judaea was renamed Syria Palastina (or simply Palastina).[108] And so the Diaspora of the Jews began.

SIXTY GENERATIONS

The two Jewish rebellions against the Romans had lasting effects. When Titus suppressed the First Revolt, he destroyed the Second Temple. That single act has had repercussions on Jewish religious life over the centuries. Without a central temple of worship, smaller synagogues were built in the many places in which Jews found themselves. But the Second Revolt has had the more profound effect on world events. When Hadrian expelled the Jews from Jerusalem, he initiated a Diaspora that spread the Jews across the world into countless countries and into contact with scores of different cultures. There was no Jewish homeland for nearly two thousand years—from 135 CE until the establishment of the modern state of Israel in 1948. For many, their sojourn was often painful, and they frequently found themselves as unwanted guests in foreign lands. Many of the exiles longed for a return to the ancient homeland, and a strong movement for a return of the Jews to Palestine—once the lands of Judaea—arose at the end of the nineteenth century. For religiously observant Jews, each year the Passover service still concludes with the words "Next year in Jerusalem."

That there is a link between Bar Kokhba's rebellion and the modern world has not been lost on politicians. Prime Minister David Ben-Gurion declared in 1948, just after the establishment of the state of Israel, "The chain that was broken in the days of Shimon Bar Kokhba and Akiba ben Yosef was reinforced in our days, and the Israeli army is again ready for the battle in its own land, to fight for the freedom of the nation and the homeland."[109] But some scholars and politicians have taken issue with this glorification of Bar Kokhba and the Second Jewish Revolt, arguing that it should be seen for what it truly was—a disastrous undertaking with the foregone conclusion of defeat and exile at the hands of the Romans.

One critic in particular is an Israeli former chief of military intelligence turned university professor named Yehoshafat Harkabi. He sparked a national debate in Israel in 1980 when he published a book entitled in its subsequent English translation *The Bar Kokhba Syndrome: Risk and Realism in International Politics*.[110] Harkabi argued that Bar Kokhba's defeat was one of the three greatest disasters of the Jews in antiquity—the other two being the destructions of the First and Second Temples—and should be identified as such, rather than held up as an event to be revered. He also portrayed Bar Kokhba as an irresponsible zealot, rather than a glorious national defender, and charged him with dragging the Judaeans into "national suicide."[111]

Whatever their wisdom, it is clear that the rebellions of the Jews against the Romans still resonate today, even after two millennia. As the *New York Times* once said, "For Israelis, Bar Kokhba isn't ancient history."[112] The noted author and historian Neil Asher Silberman wrote recently that the First Jewish Revolt in particular is "a searing human nightmare that has—despite time, social transformation, historical distance, and coldly dispassionate scholarship—simply refused to fade away."[113] As for the Second Jewish Revolt, Yehoshafat Harkabi put it bluntly, "The catastrophe of the Bar Kokhba Rebellion is not merely an appendix to the Temple destruction, but a separate calamity in its own right, parallel to, and to my mind, an even greater tragedy than the earlier event."[114]

5

THE "HOLY HOUSE"

THE RECENT TREND toward citing ancient conflicts and ancient history in support of modern propaganda has led to some remarkable, not to say extraordinary, calls upon and distortions of the history of Jerusalem. For instance, at the failed Camp David peace summit in July 2000, Yasser Arafat announced: "The Temple didn't exist in Jerusalem, it existed in Nablus. . . .There is nothing there [i.e., no trace of a temple on the Temple Mount]." Bill Clinton, Ehud Barak, and Dennis Ross—the former president of the United States, prime minister of Israel, and U.S. special envoy to the Middle East, respectively—have all recalled Arafat's statement with varying degrees of astonishment. Arafat repeated his assertion to the French president, Jacques Chirac, on September 20, 2000, saying: "But the ruins of the Temple don't exist! Our studies show that these are actually Greek and Roman ruins."[1]

Similarly, in January 2001, Ekrima Sabri, the Grand Mufti of Jerusalem, who is the chief Moslem cleric at the Haram al-Sherif (Temple Mount) and thus the highest-ranking religious figure within the Palestinian Authority in Jerusalem, was quoted in the *Jerusalem Post* as saying, "There are no historical artifacts that belong to the Jews on the Temple Mount." That same month, he was also quoted in the German periodical *Die Welt* as saying: "There is not [even] the smallest indication of the existence of a Jewish temple on this place [the Temple Mount] in the past. In the whole city, there is not a single stone indicating Jewish history."[2]

A few months later, Adnan Husseini, director of the Islamic Waqf in Jerusalem, said of the Haram al-Sherif: "it is God's will that it is a mosque. It is not for me to go against Him. There is no compromise, from the Islamic side. This place is a mosque. It is a place for Moslems to pray and no one else."[3] The Islamic Waqf in Jerusalem is the trust that has been responsible for overseeing the Haram al-Sherif ever since Moshe Dayan signed an agreement granting them that authority immediately after the capture of the Old City of Jerusalem during the Six-Day War in 1967.[4]

At the heart of these denials lie the rival religious claims to the Temple Mount—or, as Moslems have it, the Haram al-Sherif. It is an intriguing confluence and a definitive example of continuity of religion that the al-Aqsa Mosque and the Dome of the Rock are located—however emphatic the denials of Arafat, Sabri, and Husseini—just where most archaeologists and ancient historians believe that the Temples of Solomon and Herod once stood.[5] Built more than twelve hundred years ago, within a century of the Moslem conquest of the city in 638 CE, these two Islamic houses of worship are physical reminders of the fact that Jerusalem is not only holy to Jews and Christians but also one of the three most sacred places in Islam. How did this come to be? The beginnings of an answer are to be found in Roman and Byzantine Jerusalem, when the city was renamed Aelia Capitolina.

A MOUNT IN RUINS

After the destruction of the Temple of the Jews by Titus in 70 CE, the Romans may have erected a statue of the emperor Hadrian, as well as a temple to Jupiter, as mentioned earlier.[6] Those were gone by the Byzantine period, and except for one abortive attempt to rebuild the Temple during the time of the emperor Julian (the Apostate) around 361 CE (an effort that came to an end with the death of the emperor in a skirmish against the Persians in 363 CE), the mount remained in ruins for the next five centuries.[7]

The ninth-century Christian historian Eutychius believed, as do some modern scholars, that leaving the Temple Mount in ruins was a deliberate policy of the Eastern Roman emperors in Constantinople during the Byzantine period. Eutychius wrote:

> The place of the rock and the area around it were deserted ruins and they [the Romans] poured dirt over the rock so that great was the filth about it. The Byzantines, however, neglected it and did not hold it in veneration, nor did they build a church over it because Christ our Lord said in his Holy Gospel "Not a stone will be left upon a stone which will not be ruined and devastated." And for this reason the Christians left it as a ruin and did not build a church over it.[8]

The ruins would serve as a visual reminder of Jesus' prophecy of the destruction of the Temple (which Eutychius paraphrased): ". . . there will not be left here one stone upon another, that will not be thrown down" (Matthew 24:1–3). This explanation of events seems reasonable, for at that time there was an ongoing struggle between Judaism and Christianity, particularly when it came to Jerusalem. During most of the Byzantine era, Hadrian's edict prohibiting Jews from entering or living in Jerusalem remained in force. Indeed, it was not until two hundred years after Hadrian that the first exception was finally made—on one day of each year. Jews were allowed into the city and onto the Temple Mount to mourn on the anniversary of the destruction of the Temple, the ninth of the month of Ab. Of course, they had to pay for the privilege of ascending the mount.[9]

Meanwhile, except for the Temple Mount, the city of Jerusalem flourished and grew in importance between the second and sixth centuries CE. It was during this period that Jerusalem first became a holy city to Christian believers. Soon after 200 CE, Christian pilgrims began coming to Jerusalem in droves, and so new churches, monasteries, and hospices to house the pilgrims became necessary.[10] The ninth-century Byzantine chronicler Theophanes the Confessor provides some details, reporting that in the fourth century CE, the Roman emperor Constantine "ordered Makarios, bishop of Jerusalem, . . . to search out . . . the site of the holy Resurrection and that of Golgotha of the skull and the life-giving wood." Theodosius says further that Constantine's "god-minded mother," Helena, "had a vision which ordered her to go to Jerusalem and to bring to light the sacred sites which had been buried by the impious." Theodosius reports: "She begged her son Constantine to fulfill these commands sent to her from God. And he acted in obedience to her."[11]

In large part because of Helena's visions, Constantine erected many monumental buildings in Jerusalem during the fourth century CE, including the original Church of the Holy Sepulcher (335 CE) and the Church of St. Sion—referred to as the "mother of all churches." A second royal lady, Eudocia, wife of the Roman emperor Theodosius II, was responsible for another elaborate building program in Jerusalem, during the years that she resided in the city (443–60 CE). She is credited with extending the walls of the city to include the new Christian suburbs, ordering the construction of the first patriarchal palace (where the bishop of Jerusalem was to live), and building both a large hospice, to accommodate the growing numbers of pilgrims, and a great basilica, in which she herself was buried. Finally, the Byzantine emperor Justinian oversaw a third era of monumental construction in Jerusalem, during the sixth century CE (527–65 CE). The part of the western hill known as Mount Zion was rebuilt, and the population of the city grew to about sixty thousand. Jerusalem's population would not be so large again until the twentieth century. Among Justinian's most important additions to the city was the New Church of St. Mary, which became known simply as the Nea (Greek for "new").[12]

Thus Jerusalem once again became a religious center, this time for Christian pilgrims rather than Jews. The Christians, like the Jews before them, believed that they alone possessed knowledge of God's final revelations. Another prophet (Mohammed) and another religion (Islam) would soon challenge them in this belief. But first, as a different empire looked toward the Levant, there was to be yet another battle for the holy city of Jerusalem.

THE PERSIAN CONQUEST OF JERUSALEM

During the centuries when Jerusalem was known as Aelia Capitolina, ruled first from Rome and then from Byzantium (later Constantinople), the city was relatively untroubled and peaceful. That peace came

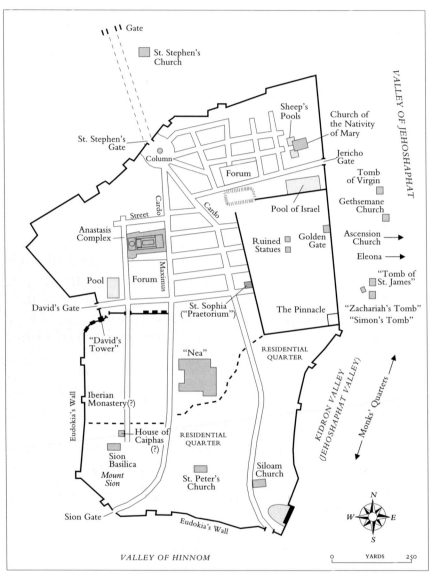

Map 15. Byzantine Jerusalem, 326–638 CE

Fig. 5. The "Church of the Purification" (perhaps on the site of Justinian's "Nea" church). (Painting by David Roberts, Esq., R.A.)

to an abrupt end in the seventh century CE, during the reign of the emperor Heraclius, when the Persians overran the city in a bloody conflict known as the Sasanian conquest.

The Sasanids of Persia (modern Iran) had been fighting on and off against the Roman and Byzantine Empires for nearly the entire four centuries of their existence (224–642 CE). This state of almost perpetual warfare ended early in the seventh century CE, when Islam arose as a new—and soon to be dominant—power in the Middle East. But before the Persian armies were crushed by the forces of Islam, they took on the despised Byzantines once more. Although most of the fighting took place far to the north, primarily in Mesopotamia (modern Iraq and northern Syria), in 614 CE the Persians—led by their general nicknamed Shahr-baraz (the Wild Boar)—came down in a devastating wave upon Palestine and, eventually, Jerusalem.[13]

When the Christian patriarch Zacharias saw the Persian army camped outside the walls of Jerusalem, he prepared to surrender the city. However, a group of young Christians decided instead to defend the city. The ensuing siege began on April fifteenth and lasted for about three weeks. By early May, the Persians had "shot from their balistas with such violence that . . . they broke down the city wall."[14]

Several eminent scholars have suggested that the breach in the wall was made not by ballistas or even battering rams but, rather, via a tunnel that was dug to undermine the wall. Within the tunnel were wooden posts to support the roof. Upon completion of the tunnel, the posts were set on fire. Eventually the roof collapsed, bringing down that portion of the city wall immediately above it, thus creating the crucial breach. The breach was apparently made in the northeast wall, possibly near the present-day Damascus Gate. Here, in excavations conducted next to the city wall, modern archaeologists have found thick layers of destruction debris. A "patch" can also be seen in the wall itself—in one section, the masonry is markedly different and is an obvious attempt to repair a hole.[15] This was the same general area that was later breached by the Crusaders in 1099 CE and then again by Saladin in 1187 CE, although these later breaches may have been made a little further east, adjacent to Herod's Gate.

The monk Antiochus Strategius, a contemporary witness whose

detailed narrative is preserved in both Georgian and Arabic versions, reports what happened next.

> Thereupon the evil foemen [the Persians] entered the city in great fury, like infuriated wild beasts and irritated serpents. The men however who defended the city wall fled and hid themselves in caverns, fosses, and cisterns in order to save themselves; and the people in crowds fled into churches and altars; and there they destroyed them. For the enemy entered in mighty wrath, gnashing their teeth in violent fury; like evil beasts they roared, bellowed like lions, hissed like ferocious serpents, and slew all whom they found. Like mad dogs they tore with their teeth the flesh of the faithful, and respected none at all, neither male nor female, neither young nor old, neither child nor baby, neither priest nor monk, neither virgin nor widow . . .[16]

It is said that the Byzantines made their final—and ultimately futile—stand against the Persians on the Temple Mount itself. The Persian soldiers then went on a rampage that lasted for three full days. According to Strategius,

> . . . the evil Persians . . . slaughtered tender infants on the ground, and then with loud yelps called their parents. Their parents bewailed the children with vociferations and sobbings, but were promptly despatched along with them. Any that were caught armed were massacred with their own weapons. Those who ran swiftly were pierced with arrows, the unresisting and quiet they slew without mercy. They listened not to appeals of supplicants, nor pitied youthful beauty, nor had compassion on old men's age, nor blushed before the humility of the clergy. On the contrary they destroyed persons of every age, massacred them like animals, cut them in pieces, mowed sundry of them down like cabbages, so that all alike had severally to drain the cup full of bitterness. Lamentation and terror might be seen in Jerusalem. Holy churches were burned with fire, others were demolished, majestic altars fell prone, sacred crosses were trampled underfoot, life-giv-

ing icons were spat upon by the unclean. Then their wrath fell upon priests and deacons: they slew them in their churches like dumb animals . . .[17]

Strategius first says that "many tens of thousands" died during the siege and during the following three days in which the city was destroyed by the Persians. He then gives a detailed and formal accounting of just how many died in each part of the city, concluding that the final total killed by the Persians in Jerusalem was 66,509 people. Other accounts say that approximately 57,000 died.[18]

Included in Strategius's account is a detailed inventory that lists the Christian victims buried in each of thirty-five separate locations by a pious man named Thomas "the Undertaker" and his wife and followers. One of these sites is the Pool of Mamilla, where Strategius says at least 4,500 (and perhaps as many as 24,500) bodies were buried. In recent excavations conducted outside the Jaffa Gate, in the vicinity of the Pool of Mamilla, Jerusalem archaeologist Roni Reich discovered a small chapel built in front of a cave. Inside the chapel, opposite the opening to the cave, was a fragmentary inscription in Greek reading, "For the redemption and salvation of those, God knows their names." The cave turned out to be a burial crypt, for Reich found it two-thirds full of human bones "heaped in complete disarray." The skeletons were all of young men, apparently Christians if the cross-shaped pendants found with the bones and the chapel itself are any indication. The mass burial took place sometime after 610 CE, as indicated by a gold coin minted in Constantinople during the reign of the Byzantine emperor Phocas (602–10 CE) which was found among the bones. It seems most likely that the skeletons found by Reich are the remains of Christian inhabitants of Jerusalem who lost their lives during the Persian invasion and sack of the city in 614 CE and who were buried by Thomas and his followers near the Pool of Mamilla, as recorded by the monk Strategius.[19]

Although the Persians were Zoroastrians and the inhabitants of Jerusalem were at the time mainly Christians, this was one of the relatively few instances in the history of the city when its conquest was not sparked by religious differences between attackers and defenders. Although the Persian emperor seemed to have harbored anti-Christian sentiment, which he had expressed when he sacked Antioch earlier, his conquest of Jerusalem was primarily an episode in the prolonged struggle for domination between the Roman/Byzantine and Persian/Sasanian Empires.[20]

However, neither the extent of Jewish involvement nor the motivation of Jewish participants in the Persian capture and destruction of Jerusalem in 614 CE have yet been satisfactorily resolved. It seems clear that there were Jewish soldiers in the Persian army, and there are indications that at least some of these took part in the Persian invasion of Palestine. Some scholars have suggested that the Jews actively participated in this war on the side of the Persians, not as mercenaries, but "as a nation with its own stake in the victory, since they regarded the war as a struggle for national liberation." It has been further suggested that "Khosrau II was perceived as a latter-day Cyrus." Thus, just as the Persians under their king Cyrus the Great had liberated the Jews from their Babylonian oppressors in the sixth century BCE, so it may have been hoped that the Persians under King Khosrau II would liberate the Jews from their Byzantine oppressors a thousand years later, in the seventh century CE. Indeed, Khosrau II did act as had his illustrious predecessor and allowed the Jews to return to the city of Jerusalem, a city from which they had been banished virtually since the time of Hadrian five centuries earlier.[21]

With the Persian capture of Jerusalem, the Christian population that survived—including the patriarch Zacharias—was sent into exile, just as the Jews had been exiled centuries before by the Romans. Reports speak of as many as thirty-five thousand captives being taken away to Persia. Many churches and other religious structures were heavily damaged and even torn down—including the "Nea," Justinian's New Church of St. Mary, which reportedly had been built using materials taken from the Temple Mount and which had long been resented by the Jews of Palestine.[22] However, the Persians were not to control Jerusalem for long, and Jewish reoccupation of the city was short-lived. Indeed, there are some reports that, as a result of Christian influence at the Persian court, the Persians themselves had a change of heart and banished the Jews from the city as early as 617 CE.[23]

The Byzantine emperor Heraclius mounted a counterattack against the Persian Empire by 622 CE. Eventually he won a great victory near the ruins of ancient Nineveh in what is now modern Iraq and advanced into Persia proper. The Persian king Khosrau II was quickly dethroned and then assassinated, leaving Heraclius free to march on Syria and Palestine. In 629 CE, he recaptured Jerusalem. There are no details extant of the actual fighting, apart from a reported massacre of those Jews who had managed to remain in the city. Indeed, there may not have been much other fighting, for some accounts say that the new Persian king, Kawad Sheroe, entered into a pact with Heraclius, giving Jerusalem and other captured territories back to him.[24]

Heraclius himself is said to have led the triumphant Byzantine army into Jerusalem on March 21, 629 CE, carrying the relic of the Holy Cross to the ruins of the Church of the Holy Sepulcher. The ninth-century Byzantine chronicler Theophanes the Confessor briefly describes these events.

> In this year . . . the emperor proceeded to Jerusalem, taking with him the venerable and life-giving Cross so as to offer thanks to God. . . . On entering Jerusalem, the emperor reinstated the patriarch Zacharias and restored the venerable and life-giving Cross to its proper place. After giving many thanks to God, he drove the Jews out of the Holy City and ordered that they should not have the right to come within three miles of the Holy City.[25]

Although Jerusalem was now back in Christian hands, the Byzantine reoccupation would, in its turn, be brief, for the armies of Islam appeared on the horizon less than a decade later. The Byzantine hold on the Levant, weakened by decades of struggle with the Persians, loosened, and the Byzantines soon fell prey to the new invaders.

THE COMING OF ISLAM

As with the other great religions, the origins of Islam are known only from its scriptures and historical traditions. There are few, if any, writings of contemporary objective observers to verify its origins. Having said that, the Moslem historical tradition is that the archangel Gabriel came to Mohammed one night during the month of Ramadan and commanded him to recite a text—a text that was subsequently contained within the first four verses of the ninety-sixth chapter of the Koran. The Koran (or Qur'an) is the scripture that, according to Moslem belief, was given to Mohammed by God.[26]

According to this tradition, Mohammed was born about 571 CE in Mecca, a small oasis town in western Arabia, a land then comprised mostly of barren desert relieved only by widely scattered oases and crossed by a few caravan routes. Again according to tradition, Mohammed was nearly forty years of age when the archangel Gabriel first approached him in 610 CE, and it was more than a decade later, in the year 622 CE, when—because of persecution from his own tribesmen—he moved with a small band of his followers to Yathrib, another oasis town, to the north of his birthplace. The move became known as the Hijra (the "migration"). The Moslem calendar begins with this event, so that Year One (AH 1) is approximately equal to the year 622 CE of the Christian calendar.[27]

The town of Yathrib grew to be a center of the Moslem faith and was soon renamed al-Medina ("the City"). In Medina, Mohammed assumed the roles of religious, political, and military ruler of his sect. His power grew, and within eight years he returned to Mecca at the head of a small army. In Mecca he replaced "pagan" idol worship with the new religion. He called this new religion Islam ("surrender" or "submission" to God). Those who followed it were known as Moslems ("those who surrender" or "those who submit" to God). With Mohammed's move back to Mecca, the spread of Islam formally began.[28]

According to the Moslem view, the purposes of Mohammed's apostolate were to reveal God's final revelations to the world, to abolish idolatry, and to restore a true monotheism that had become degraded in other faiths. According to this view, Mohammed was the apostle of God—the last of the Prophets—and the world would receive no more of God's revelations after his death. The adherents of this new religion believed that they alone knew the one true God, and they believed that earlier revelations to both the Christians and the Hebrews were only parts of the whole truth. They specifically rejected the idea that Jesus was the Son of God, since in their view God had no need of offspring.[29]

Mohammed died in 632 CE. His followers chose a successor—Abu

Bakr—who took the title *khalifa*, meaning "successor" or "deputy." This set the stage for the development of the caliphate, which for some time was the supreme office of the Islamic world. According to Moslem historians, at the time of Mohammed's death the religion had spread only to parts of the Arabian Peninsula. But within little more than a century, the followers of Mohammed, enjoined to spread the word of the Prophet, conquered a vast area including all of the lands and cities that had once been Israel and Judah. Islam then laid claim to Jerusalem—to the Temple Mount and its great rock.[30]

SIEGE AND CONQUEST

Abu Bakr's reign as the first caliph was brief, but before his death he declared a "holy war" (*jihad*) and the Moslem period of conquests began in earnest. At this early stage in the history of Islam, the Moslem sages developed a theory concerning jihad in order to justify Islam's rapid and militaristic expansion, which appeared to violate the Koran's basic message of peace and its condemnation of aggressive warfare. As Professor Karen Armstrong has succinctly said, these Moslem jurists "taught that because there was only one God there should be only one state in the world that must submit to the true religion." Armstrong continues:

It was the duty of the Muslim state (the House of Islam) to con-quer the rest of the non-Muslim world (the House of War) so that the world could reflect the divine unity. Every Muslim must par-ticipate in this jihad and the House of Islam must never compro-mise with the House of War. . . . Until the final domination of the world was accomplished, therefore, Muslims were in a perpetual state of war.[31]

Under the aegis of this philosophy, the forces of Islam eventually spread—throughout the seventh and early eighth centuries CE—across the entire Middle East, east to Asia, to North Africa, and into Spain. Syria-Palestine was among the first areas to be invaded, and Moslem armies quickly overran much of it. By December 634 CE, the Greek patriarch Sophronius of Jerusalem complained that he could not safely travel the five miles to Bethlehem to celebrate Christmas, because of the Islamic armies that stood in the way.[32]

Abu Bakr was succeeded that same year (634 CE) by Umar ibn al-Khattab, a man who was to play a decisive role in the evolution and spread of the Moslem faith. Umar initiated an administration that evolved into a functioning imperial government. In addition to the title *khalifa,* he adopted the additional title—or was addressed as—*amir al-mu'minin* (commander of the faithful)—a title frequently used by subsequent caliphs.[33] According to Moslem tradition, Umar reigned for only ten years before he was killed in battle at the relatively young age of fifty-three, but during his brief rule, the Moslem empire began expanding significantly. By August 636 CE, most of Palestine was in Moslem hands.[34] Jerusalem lay directly ahead on the road to further expansion.

Both Moslem and Christian sources describe the Moslem conquest of Jerusalem in 638 CE. Baladhuri, who lived during the ninth century CE, is considered to be among the most distinguished of Arab chroniclers. He wrote that the siege of Jerusalem began late in the summer of 636 CE, with Amr ibn al-As in command of the Moslem army. The city was strongly defended by a Byzantine garrison supplemented by local inhabitants. Even when, a year into the siege, Moslem reinforcements led by Abu Ubaydah ibn Jarrah arrived, the city continued to hold out against the invaders. Finally, in the spring of 638 CE (AH 17), Jerusalem surrendered, but only after the inhabitants insisted that Caliph Umar appear in person to accept the capitulation.[35]

The Byzantine chronicler Theophanes the Confessor also says that the siege lasted for two years: "In this year Umar undertook his expedition into Palestine, where the Holy City having been continuously besieged for two years (by the Arab armies), he at length became possessed of it by capitulation."[36] The ninth-century Iraqi historian Ya'qubi adds:

On his return into Jordan, Abu Ubaydah besieged the people of Aelia, which is the Holy House [Jerusalem]. They prolonged their resistance and Abu Ubaydah wrote to Umar to inform him of the delays and of the patience of the people of Aelia. Some say that the people of Aelia requested of him that it be the caliph himself who concluded peace with them. Abu Ubaydah assured himself of their sincerity by demanding of them promises by a solemn treaty, and then he informed Umar. . . . Umar came to the region of Damascus, then he went to the Holy House [Jerusalem], took it without struggle and sent the inhabitants the following written message. "In the name of God, the Compassionate, the Merciful. This is a writing of Umar ibn al-Khattab to the inhabitants of the Holy House. You are guaranteed your life, your goods, and your churches, which will be neither occupied nor destroyed, as long as you do not initiate anything blameworthy." He had it confirmed by witnesses . . . (Ya'qubi *History II* 161, 167)[37]

Caliph Umar entered Jerusalem to receive the capitulation of the city from the patriarch Sophronius himself. The caliph was reportedly clad in plain garments and either on foot or modestly mounted (riding a camel, horse, donkey, or mule), depending upon the source.[38] A modern version of the Islamic conquest of Jerusalem states: "[U]mar, the second Muslim Caliph, entered Jerusalem at the invitation of its inhabitants. He was one of the very few men in history to capture Jerusalem without shedding a drop of human blood."[39] Older—and probably more trustworthy—versions from Islamic sources hold that Umar did indeed enter Jerusalem peacefully in 638 CE (AH 17), but they make it clear that his entrance was preceded by a two-year-long siege of the city. It is unlikely in the extreme that the siege was without bloodshed. If the history of earlier prolonged sieges of Jerusalem is any guide, it is more likely than not that many of the inhabitants died of starvation or in sorties against the surrounding Moslem armies. Umar's "bloodless capture" of the city was thus probably similar to that of the British general Edmund H. H. Allenby, who deliberately entered Jerusalem humbly and on foot thirteen hundred years later, but only after a bloody six-week-long military offensive had established his authority, secured the city, and assured his personal safety.

With the surrender of Jerusalem to Umar, the city entered its fourth phase of religious occupation. The original Canaanite and Jebusite city had given way to the Jewish city of David and Solomon, which in turn had given way to the Christian city of Constantine and Justinian. Now the Christian city became an Islamic city. For this was by no means merely the conquest of just another metropolis. This was the securing of a place already sacred to Islam. Thus "another religion and another language now joined those which professed the sanctity of Jerusalem."[40] Umar must have hoped that the Islamic rule of Jerusalem would last forever, and—interrupted only by the Crusader occupation of less than a century—it did in fact last for the next thirteen hundred years, until the final collapse of the Ottoman Empire in 1917.[41]

FROM THE FIRST *QIBLA* TO THE "FURTHER MOSQUE"

Jerusalem's place in the sacred theology of Islam was assured well before Caliph Umar entered the city in 638 CE. The first *qibla* (direction of prayer) that Mohammed proposed for Moslems—probably in about 621 CE, while he was still in Mecca—was toward Jerusalem, in part because the Temple of Solomon had been built there.[42]

A variety of ancient sources report that when Umar entered Jerusalem, he asked to be taken to the Temple Mount, wanting to see the site where Solomon's Temple had once stood. Astonished to be shown a mound covered only with rubbish, dung, and the shattered remains of destroyed buildings, Umar knelt down and began to clean the area himself, putting handfuls of refuse into his own cloak and then carrying away the accumulated garbage and debris. His followers followed suit, and soon the ancient Temple Mount was cleansed of the detritus of five centuries. Plainly, the account has something of legend about it, and a more organized and less picturesque clearance must have been entailed, but it seems that Umar's arrival saw a change in the importance and a great improvement in the state of the Temple Mount. Some traditions say that Umar then erected a temporary mosque on the Mount, which is why the present Dome of the Rock—built by the Umayyad caliph Abd al-Malik in 691 CE—is occasionally misidentified as the "Mosque of Omar."[43]

Although the Koran never mentions Jerusalem by name,[44] it does tell of a nocturnal journey taken by Mohammed in which he traveled from the Holy Mosque in Mecca to the "Further Mosque" (*al-masjid al-aqsa*). In time, this "Further Mosque" came to be associated with the al-Aqsa Mosque in Jerusalem—built on the Haram al-Sherif (Temple

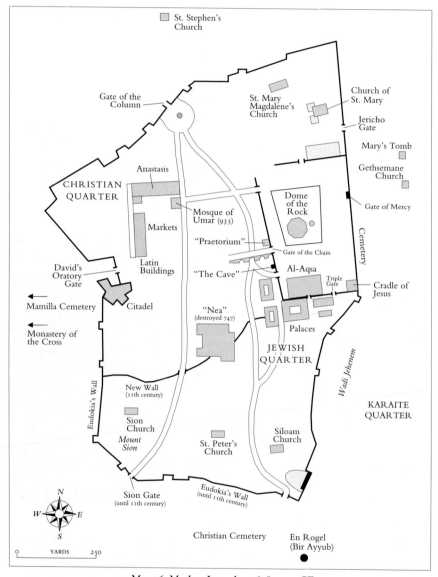

St. Stephen's
Church

Gate of the
Column

St. Mary
Magdalene's
Church

Church of
St. Mary

Jericho
Gate

Mary's Tomb

Anastasis

Gethsemane
Church

CHRISTIAN
QUARTER

Dome
of the
Rock

Gate of Mercy

Mosque of
Umar (935)

Markets

"Praetorium"

Gate of the Chain

Cemetery

Latin
Buildings

"The Cave"

Al-Aqsa

David's
Oratory
Gate

Triple
Gate

Cradle of
Jesus

◄ Mamilla Cemetery

Citadel

"Nea"
(destroyed 747)

◄ Monastery of
the Cross

Palaces

JEWISH
QUARTER

Wadi Jehenem

KARAITE
QUARTER

New Wall
(11th century)

Eudokia's Wall

Sion
Church

Mount
Sion

St. Peter's
Church

Siloam
Church

Sion Gate
(until 11th century)

Eudokia's Wall
(until 11th century)

N
W E
S

Christian Cemetery

En Rogel
(Bir Ayyub)

0   YARDS   250

Map 16. Moslem Jerusalem, 638–1099 CE

Fig. 6. The "Mosque of Omar" (the Dome of the Rock). (Painting by David Roberts, Esq., R.A.)

Mount) by Abd al-Malik's son, the Umayyad caliph al-Walid (705–15 CE). Later Moslem traditions say that Mohammed's steed al-Buraq (Lightning), upon which he rode to the "Further Mosque," was at one point tethered to what is now the Western (or Wailing) Wall while Mohammed stopped to pray at the Temple Mount. Led by the archangel Gabriel, Mohammed then ascended to the heavens from the sacred rock upon the Temple Mount—either by way of a "celestial ladder" or astride al-Buraq. Once in the heavens, Mohammed met various prophets and other eminent figures who had gone before him, including Adam, Abraham, Noah, Elijah, Joseph, Moses, Aaron, John the Baptist, and Jesus. An indentation that can still be seen in the sacred rock today is said to be either al-Buraq's hoofprint or a mark made by the end of the ladder, depending upon which version of the story is being told.[45]

The Dome of the Rock and the al-Aqsa Mosque were constructed on the Haram al-Sherif within a century of Umar's conquest of Jerusalem. Together they formed one of Islam's first great complexes of religious buildings and ensured continuity of religion on what had been the Temple Mount. Arab scholars of the ninth and tenth centuries CE debated the motivations of Abd al-Malik and al-Walid, the father-and-son caliphs who were responsible for this development. It is likely that their motivations were complex. For instance, it seems quite probable that the Dome of the Rock was meant both to compete with such Christian structures as the Church of the Holy Sepulcher and to attract Moslem pilgrims who might otherwise have gone to Mecca or Medina. The buildings were perhaps also meant to make the statement that the religion of Islam represented God's final revelation, superseding his earlier revelations to the Hebrews and Christians and correcting the errors to which the earlier religions had become prey. Thus, within the Dome of the Rock, the inscribed verses of the Koran explicitly deny the Christian concept of the Trinity, reading, "Praise be to God, who begets no son, and has no partner in [his] dominion." There are also specific inscriptions warning the Hebrews of errors in their beliefs. Regardless of the motivations of the builders, Jerusalem's status as the third most holy city in Islam was secure and has lasted from the eighth century CE to the present.[46]

The earliest Moslem rulers of Jerusalem appear to have called the city *Iliya*, a variation on its Roman name, *Aelia*. Over the centuries the name gradually changed to *Madinat Bayt al-Maqdis* (city of the holy house), or simply *Bayt al-Maqdis* (the holy house), similar to the Hebrew designation of the Temple (and sometimes the city) as *Beit ha-Miqdash* (the house of the sanctuary). Eventually the name was further shortened to *al-Maqdis* and then finally became simply *al-Quds* (the holy, probably borrowed from or related to the Hebrew *ha-Qodesh*), by which name the city is still known in the Arabic-speaking world today.[47]

It should be emphasized that Jerusalem's religious importance was not reflected in its political standing. During the Byzantine era, Palestine had been divided into three parts: Palaestina Prima, Palaestina Secunda, and Palaestina Tertia. Palaestina Prima included the coastal area, Judaea, and Samaria. Its capital was not Jerusalem but the city of Caesarea, further north on the coast. The new Moslem conquerors left the Byzantine system of administration in Palestine relatively intact, so that Byzantine Palaestina Prima, in which Jerusalem lay, now simply became Moslem Jund Filastin. However, just as Byzantine Jerusalem had reported to the administrative capital of Caesarea, so now Moslem Jerusalem reported to the new city of Ramla, after the latter was founded in about 715 CE.[48] But that did nothing to lessen the city of Jerusalem's religious importance.

The infancy of Islam, like that of Judaism and Christianity before it, was troubled and turbulent, with quarrelsome rival factions claiming unique knowledge of the true orthodoxy. Shiites, Sunni, Fatimids (named after the Prophet's daughter Fatima), and other factions each believed that they understood the Prophet's true message and were the rightful ones to choose his successors and deputies. Later, converts to Islam from the central steppes of Asia added their own imprint on the religion. Throughout all the turmoil surrounding the evolution of Islam in its first few centuries of existence, Jerusalem, because of its religious significance, was often a much coveted prize. During the many wars fought between rival Islamic factions, dynasties, and kingdoms in Egypt and the Middle East during the eighth through the eleventh centuries CE, as well as during the wars fought against the hated Byzantines, major conflicts and smaller uprisings and rebellions rocked Jerusalem more than ten times before the coming of the Crusaders (see table 1).[49]

The eighth through the eleventh centuries CE were thus turbulent times for Islam: each faction sought to establish its own orthodoxy as primal, and Islam came into conflict with Byzantine Christianity. At first, immediately after the death of Mohammed in 632 CE, the position of caliph was not hereditary. The first four caliphs were chosen by a group of close associates of the Prophet. Sunni Moslems regard this period of Moslem history as a religiously correct "golden age" and consider the first four caliphs to be "the rightly guided ones."[50] But the times were dangerous, and three of the first four caliphs were assassinated. With the founding of the Umayyad dynasty in 661 CE—and for as long as that dynasty endured—the caliphate became de facto an inherited position. But the legitimacy of the Umayyad caliphate was contested. The Shiite Moslems regarded them as usurpers who had taken the caliphate from its rightful possessors—the descendants of Ali ibn Abi Talib, the cousin and son-in-law of the Prophet. Other sects also challenged the legitimacy of the Umayyads, and within five decades of the founding of the dynasty, they were under attack by several other Islamic factions.[51]

In 744 CE, a little more than thirty years after the al-Aqsa Mosque was built by caliph al-Walid, a series of mutinies against the Umayyads swept across Palestine. Jerusalem was not spared in this upheaval. Theophanes the Confessor, the Byzantine chronicler, recounts that in 745 CE, the Umayyad caliph Marwan II destroyed the walls of several rebellious cities, including Jerusalem: "He destroyed the walls of Heliopolis, Damascus, and Jerusalem, killed many important people, and mutilated the people who remained in those cities."[52] But further strife lay ahead, and Marwan II was to be the last of the Umayyad caliphs.

Between 747 and 750 CE, Abu Moslem, a freed Persian slave and the leader of a militant Islamic sect, led a revolt that overthrew the Umayyad forces and established the Abbasid caliphate. This caliphate would soon rule throughout the Moslem world. The religious zeal of the Abbasids was based upon the premise that the descendants of the

Prophet's uncle al-Abbas were the rightful leaders of Islam and that the Umayyads had been degenerate usurpers of the Prophet's succession.[53]

The Abbasids ruled first from Damascus and later from Baghdad. They occasionally visited Jerusalem after the establishment of their dynasty. It is said that around the year 800 CE, the fifth Abbasid caliph, Harun al-Rashid—made famous by the tales of *A Thousand and One Nights*—received gifts brought to the city of Jerusalem by European delegations dispatched by the emperor Charlemagne, although there seems to be no truth to the tradition that Charlemagne himself visited the city.[54] The suzerainty of the Abbasids was fragile, however, and the early years of the ninth century CE saw defections in Spain and North Africa and in the Levant.

Between the years 807 and 815 CE, Palestine was rocked by another series of revolts, this time led by Moslem desert tribesmen opposed to the Abbasid dynasts. Although these revolts were eventually suppressed, various churches in Jerusalem were attacked and looted during the period.[55] Then, during the years 841–42 CE, a new and greater rebellion against the Abbasid rulers embroiled the Palestinian countryside. This time it was a peasant revolt, primarily of Bedouins and farmers. Abu Harb Tamim, nicknamed al-Mubarqa ("the Veiled"), led the revolt and vowed to restore the Umayyads to power. Jerusalem was caught up in the rebellion. At one point the entire population fled the city, as the rebels looted and plundered stores, homes, churches, and mosques. The Church of the Holy Sepulcher was almost set on fire before the rebels were bought off by a large bribe in gold offered by the patriarch of Jerusalem. Eventually Abu Harb was caught and the rebellion was quelled.[56]

By the mid-tenth century CE, Moslem armies were actively engaged in fighting Christian Byzantine armies in various parts of the Middle East. Repercussions from their victories and defeats were frequently felt in Jerusalem. Peace in Jerusalem was thus interrupted in 938 CE, when Christians were attacked during a Palm Sunday procession and churches in the city were set on fire and badly damaged.[57] Similarly, when the Byzantine armies won a series of victories in the field against the forces of Islam toward the end of May 966 CE, the Moslem governor of Jerusalem—who was also annoyed that his demand for larger bribes had not been met by the patriarch of the city—initiated a series of anti-Christian riots in the city. Once again churches were attacked and burned in Jerusalem. The Church of the Holy Sepulcher was looted and was so damaged that its dome collapsed. Rioters even killed the patriarch, John VII, who was discovered hiding inside an oil vat within the Church of the Resurrection.[58]

Nine years later, in 975 CE, a Byzantine army led by Emperor John Tzimisces came within a whisker of attacking Jerusalem, but the campaign came to an abrupt end when John suddenly returned home, only to die in early January of 976 CE—perhaps poisoned by his wife. By this time the Fatimids were the dominant Islamic faction in the Middle East. This caliphate had its roots in Yemen. The Fatimid name derives from the belief held by its adherents that the rightful caliph should be directly descended from the Prophet through his daughter Fatima. The first Fatimid caliph had been enthroned already by 908 CE. The rule of his first two successors was limited to North Africa, but by 969 CE, the fourth caliph had extended his dominion to Egypt and had established the newly built city of Cairo as his capital.[59]

By the time the Byzantine emperor John Tzimisces was threatening to march on Jerusalem in 975 CE, the Fatimids controlled most of Palestine, although their rule was hotly contested by a number of other Islamic factions. While there is little information available for a presumed Fatimid capture of Jerusalem, it probably took place by 973 CE, at about the same time that Ramla and the rest of Palestine fell. The Fatimids, realizing that Jerusalem's defenses needed to be improved, strengthened the city walls, but apparently to no avail. While the threat posed by John's army never materialized, there are indications that the city was captured that same year by Alptakin, a Turkish commander based in Damascus who was loosely allied with John and the Byzantines. According to Moslem sources, Alptakin led an alliance of Turkish regiments, Qarmatians, and Bedouin tribes, and he reportedly captured all of Palestine, including Jerusalem, in 975 CE. It is unclear how long, if at all, Alptakin held Jerusalem, but it was apparently back in Fatimid hands by the early 980s CE, if not earlier.[60]

A few decades later, anti-Christian persecution in Jerusalem reached a peak when the Egyptian Fatimid caliph al-Hakim—whose later worship would give rise to the Druze religion—ordered that all

Christian and Jewish religious buildings in the city be destroyed. The Church of the Holy Sepulcher was attacked once again and was finally burned to the ground on the twenty-eighth of September in 1009 CE.[61]

The repercussions of this savage act of repression were felt a full quarter-century later, when the Christian population of Jerusalem and Palestine supported a Bedouin uprising against the Fatimid rulers. In 1024 CE a rebel leader named Hassan ibn Mufarrij attacked Ramla and probably Jerusalem as well. The Fatimids recaptured the area in 1025 CE, however, and finally suppressed the rebellion by 1029 CE.[62] Peace then reigned in Jerusalem for a time. However, by the middle of the eleventh century CE, a new Islamic power was on the rise—the Turks.

Perhaps the most prominent of the Turkish (or Turcoman) tribes was the Seljuk tribe, named for its leading family. Sometime around the end of the tenth century CE, the Seljuks settled around Bukhara in central Asia (the region of modern Uzbekistan) and adopted Islam as their religion. At first they served as warriors for various Moslem dynasties, but they eventually struck out on their own and swiftly rose to positions of power within the Islamic world. Seljuk warriors defeated Byzantine armies at the Battle of Manzikert in eastern Asia Minor (modern Turkey) in 1071 CE and soon challenged other Islamic factions for dominance.[63]

In 1070 CE, a Turcoman army led by Atsiz ibn Uwaq invaded Palestine, which was still under the control of the Egyptian Fatimid dynasty. Ibn al-Athir, the thirteenth-century Moslem chronicler of the Crusades and author of the enormous *Kamil at-Tawarihh* (The collection of histories),[64] gives the following brief account.

> During this year Atsiz ibn Uwaq al-Khwarizmi . . . invaded Syria. He gathered the Turks and went to Palestine. He conquered the city of Ramla and from there proceeded to Jerusalem, which he besieged. It was garrisoned by Egyptian troops. He conquered it and took the neighboring lands . . . (Ibn al-Athir *Kamil* 68)[65]

Most scholars now believe that it took Atsiz several years of besieging Jerusalem before the city finally fell in the summer of 1073 CE. It seems that the city ultimately surrendered without there being any decisive battle, perhaps in part because the Fatimid governor of the city at the time was himself a Turk and perhaps in part because the inhabitants were too exhausted to hold out any longer.[66]

Reportedly, Atsiz and the Turcomans at first were restrained in dealing with the city's inhabitants, but once they were in firm control, massacres, looting, and wanton destruction became commonplace happenings for some years. Desperate, the inhabitants of Jerusalem rebelled in 1076 CE, with the help of the Fatimids, and took hostage the Turcoman wives and children left behind in the city while their soldier-husbands were off fighting elsewhere. When Atsiz returned and regained control of the city in 1077 CE (by means of a promise to the inhabitants, which he promptly broke), a bloodbath ensued. By the time the killing was over, three thousand of the rebellious inhabitants of Jerusalem had been slaughtered.[67] Again, Ibn al-Athir gives a brief account.

> He [Atsiz] went to Jerusalem and learnt that the people there had ill-treated his men and those he had left in charge. They had blockaded them in the Sanctuary of David (on him be peace). At his approach, the populace fortified the city to resist him and insulted him. He attacked and broke into the city by force and sacked it. Large numbers were killed, even those who had taken refuge in the Aqsa Mosque and the Haram. He spared only those who were in the Dome of the Rock." (Ibn al-Athir *Kamil* 103)[68]

Tales of these and other atrocities committed in Jerusalem—including the news that the Turcomans had established their military headquarters on the Temple Mount itself—eventually reached Europe and spurred first Pope Gregory VII and then Pope Urban II (in 1095 CE) to call for a Crusade to retake Jerusalem from the Moslem "infidels."[69] However, it took the Crusaders three long years to reach the Holy Land. By this time the Turcomans were no longer in control of Jerusalem. The Fatimids had recaptured the city on the twenty-sixth of August in 1098 CE, after a siege that lasted at least forty days. The Fatimid forces from Egypt were led by the vizier al-Afdal himself. They used forty siege engines—described as "war machines"—to destroy one or more sections of the city wall, whereupon the Turcomans sued for peace and then reportedly abandoned the city. Ibn al-Athir records the conflict as follows:

> Taj ad-Daula Tutush was the Lord of Jerusalem but had given it . . . to the amir Suqman ibn Artuq the Turcoman. When the Franks defeated the Turks at Antioch the massacre demoralized them, and the Egyptians, who saw that the Turkish armies were being weakened by desertion, besieged Jerusalem under the command of al-Afdal ibn Badr al-Jamali. Inside the city were Artuq's sons, Suqman and Ilghazi, their cousin Sunij and their nephew Yaquti. The Egyptians brought more than forty siege engines to attack Jerusalem and broke down the walls at several points. The inhabitants put up a defence, and the siege and fighting went on for more than six weeks. In the end the Egyptians forced the city to capitulate. . . . Suqman, Ilghazi, and their friends were well treated by al-Afdal, who gave them large gifts of money and let them go free.[70]

Most modern scholars are of the opinion that the Fatimid vizier al-Afdal had originally favored the Crusaders and had hoped that they would form a buffer state between himself and the Seljuk Turks. When he realized that this would not happen and that the Crusaders were intent on capturing Jerusalem, he decided to beat them to it.[71]

Only one year later, after al-Afdal had installed Iftikhar ad-Daula as the Egyptian governor in charge of defending Jerusalem, the Crusaders laid siege to the city. By the time the Crusaders arrived in 1099 CE, "the inhabitants of Jerusalem had been through so many violent reversals during the previous two hundred years that they had acquired a lordly indifference to such relatively minor vicissitudes."[72]

REVISIONISM AND JERUSALEM'S MOSLEM HISTORY

Not surprisingly, the centuries-long Moslem inhabitation of Jerusalem has had repercussions that are being felt to the present day, when the city is once again in contention between Moslems and non-Moslems. This time, of course, Moslems and Jews are both laying claim to the city's holiest place—known as the Haram al-Sherif to the Moslems and as the Temple Mount to the Jews. This contest has led to some interesting revisions of the history of Jerusalem, such as Yasser Arafat's contention "The Temple didn't exist in Jerusalem, it existed in Nablus."[73]

When Ekrima Sabri, the Grand Mufti of Jerusalem, echoed Yasser Arafat's assertion that the Temple had never existed in Jerusalem—he was quoted in the *Jerusalem Post* as saying, "There are no historical artifacts that belong to the Jews on the Temple Mount"—it was quickly pointed out to him that a booklet published in 1930 in Jerusalem by the Supreme Moslem Council had declared that a link between the Haram al-Sherif and Solomon's Temple was beyond dispute. The booklet states: "The site is one of the oldest in the world. Its sanctity dates from the earliest times. Its identity with the site of Solomon's Temple is beyond dispute."[74] When this wording from the 1930 booklet was republished in the *Jerusalem Post* and shown to the mufti, he denied that the booklet had meant to imply any such link between the Haram al-Sherif and Solomon's Temple.[75] Two months later, the mufti reiterated his original statement, telling the *Boston Globe* in March 2001: "The Temple Mount was never there. . . . There is not one bit of proof to establish that. We do not recognize that the Jews have any right to the wall or to one inch of the sanctuary. . . . Jews are greedy to control our mosque . . . If they ever try to, it will be the end of Israel."[76]

However, these recent disingenuous statements denying that Solomon's Temple was located in Jerusalem or on the Temple Mount are directly contradicted by Islam's own early names for Jerusalem, especially *Madinat Bayt al-Maqdis* (city of the holy house) and *Bayt al-Maqdis* (the holy house). As Professor Moshe Gil has pointed out, the Arabic name *Bayt al-Maqdis* "was applied to the Temple Mount, to the city [of Jerusalem] as a whole, and—frequently—to all of Palestine."[77]

The stakes are large, and the import of the revisionist statements issued by Yasser Arafat and Ekrima Sabri should not be underestimated. Benny Morris, of Ben Gurion University, puts it bluntly: "Arafat denies that any Jewish temple has ever stood there [on the Temple Mount]—and this is a microcosm of his denial of the Jews' historical connection and claim to the Land of Israel/Palestine."[78] Needless to say, however, the situation is far more complex than any of these modern leaders care to acknowledge, for the histories of Jews, Christians, and Moslems in Jerusalem are inextricably intertwined, and no one of them can be denied without doing violence to the whole nexus. One scholar summed up the complex and convoluted situation by using the following archaeological example:

> The vicissitudes of history are truly a matter to ponder: a Byzantine emperor [Justinian] used the remains of the Temple Mount to build an enormous church [the Nea] and did his best to cover the fact; the Jews of the country destroyed the church at the first opportunity [after the Persian conquest in 614 CE]; the Moslems built in the area of the Temple Mount using the remains of that same destroyed church; and after hundreds of years of silence, Israeli scholars redeemed this intricate tale from the depths of oblivion. That is the way of archaeology in Jerusalem.[79]

6

FOR GOD, GOLD, AND GLORY

IN THE CONTINUING struggle for power in the Moslem world of the eleventh century CE, the Turcomans had wrested control of Jerusalem from the Fatimid caliphs in 1077 CE. They killed some three thousand of the city's inhabitants, including many Christians. The slaughter caused Pope Gregory VII and his successor Pope Urban II to call for Christians to retake Jerusalem from the Moslem "infidels." Those who flocked to the papal banner—motivated by religious fervor and perhaps also by a sense of adventure or by the desire for booty—were called Crusaders, for they had "taken up the cross" (Latin *crux*) in preparation for a holy war.

THE CALL TO ARMS

In 1095 CE Pope Urban II called the faithful to what he saw as a pious work. He issued a call to arms to the Christians of Europe. He first spoke at Clermont in France and then sent emissaries throughout Europe to repeat his message. The pope graphically—and with many inaccuracies and exaggerations—described an alarming situation in Jerusalem.

From the confines of Jerusalem and the city of Constantinople a horrible tale has gone forth and very frequently has been brought to our ears, namely, that a race from the kingdom of the Persians, an accursed race, a race utterly alienated from God, a generation forsooth which has not directed its heart and has not entrusted its spirit to God, has invaded the lands of those Christians and has depopulated them by the sword, pillage and fire; it has led away a part of the captives into its own country, and a part it has destroyed by cruel tortures; it has either entirely destroyed the churches of God or appropriated them for the rites of its own religion. They destroy the altars, after having defiled them with their uncleanness. They circumcise the Christians, and the blood of the circumcision they either spread upon the altars or pour into the vases of the baptismal font. When they wish to torture people by a base death, they perforate their navels, and dragging forth the extremity of the intestines, bind it to a stake; then with flogging they lead the victim around until the viscera having gushed forth the victim falls prostrate upon the ground. Others they bind to a post and pierce with arrows. Others they compel to extend their necks and then, attacking them with naked swords attempt to cut through the neck with a single blow. What shall I say of the abominable rape of the women? To speak of it is worse than to be silent. The kingdom of the Greeks is now dismembered by them and deprived of territory so vast in extent that it cannot be traversed in a march of two months. On whom therefore is the labor of avenging these wrongs and of recovering this territory incumbent, if not upon you? You, upon whom above other nations God has conferred remarkable glory in arms, great courage, bodily activity, and strength to humble the hairy scalp of those who resist you. . . . This royal city, therefore, situated at the centre of the world, is now held captive by His enemies, and is in subjection to those who do not know God, to the worship of the heathens. She seeks therefore and desires to be liberated, and does not cease to implore you to come to her aid. From you especially she asks succor, because, as we have already said, God has conferred upon you above all nations great glory in arms. Accordingly undertake this journey for the remission of your sins, with the assurance of the imperishable glory of the kingdom of heaven.[1]

The response to Pope Urban II's call for a Crusade to rescue the Holy Land probably exceeded his expectations. By 1096 CE nobles and commoners had left their castles and their hovels to join in the sacred mission to liberate the holy city from the infidel conquerors.[2] As it happened, when the first Crusaders reached Jerusalem three years later, the Turcomans, who had been responsible for the much-publicized slaughter of Christians and the desecration of their shrines, were no longer in command of Jerusalem. An army of the Fatimid caliphate of Egypt had defeated them and expelled them from the city a year earlier, as described above. To the Crusaders, however, one Moslem was much like another, and the term *Saracen* could conveniently embrace them all.

MODERN CONTINUATIONS

Politicians, scholars, and journalists from both the Middle Eastern and the Western worlds have sometimes compared modern Israelis to these earlier Christian Crusaders, stating that "Israel is the new Crusader state of the Middle East." In virtually every instance, the comparison is intended to be pejorative.[3] President Anwar al-Sadat of Egypt, in particular, drew frequent parallels between the "Zionists/Israelis" and the Crusaders, in a number of speeches that he gave between 1971 and 1975. In an address to the Egyptian Parliament given on June 3, 1971, Sadat said: "The Zionist occupation that we are undergoing will not come to its end once our territories are retrieved. This is a new Crusade that will last in our generation and the coming generations . . ." Two months later, in a radio broadcast on August 30, 1971, Sadat drew an even bleaker picture: "Today, we are facing a Zionist invasion, which is fiercer than the Crusades, because it is backed by world Zionism . . . [and] also by the U.S." And on May 1, 1972, at a celebratory rally in Alexandria broadcast on the radio, he made the link explicit, avowing that the Federation of Arab Republics had concocted a strategy "to counter . . . this Zionist-Crusader invasion."[4] Although it is not quite the parallel that Sadat sought to invoke, it is perhaps justifiable to view both the modern Jewish state and the ancient Crusader kingdom of Jerusalem as besieged lands surrounded by hostile Arab forces. The Latin kingdom of Jerusalem, like modern Israel, was undeniably "an island in the sea of Islam."[5]

The self-styled Moslem religious leader Osama bin Laden has taken to extremes the theme of ancient and modern infidel interlopers in lands that rightfully belong to Islam. He sees himself—as do many others in the Arab world of the twenty-first century—as a second Saladin, the legendary Moslem warrior who recaptured Jerusalem from the Crusaders in 1187 CE.

In August 1996, bin Laden issued his first religious ruling (*fatwa*), entitled "Declaration of War against the Americans Occupying the Land of the Two Holy Places." In it he said:

> Today we work . . . to lift the iniquity that had been imposed . . . by the Zionist-Crusader alliance, particularly after they have occupied the blessed land around Jerusalem, route of the journey of the Prophet . . . and the land of the two Holy Places [Saudi Arabia]. We ask Allah to bestow us with victory, He is our Patron and He is the Most Capable. . . . Our Lord, the people of the cross [Crusaders] had come with their horses and occupied the land of the two Holy places. And the Zionist Jews fiddling as they wish with the Al Aqsa Mosque, the route of the ascendance of the messenger of Allah. . . . Our Lord, shatter their gathering, divide them among themselves, shake the earth under their feet and give us control over them . . .[6]

Osama bin Laden is not the only modern leader to recently invoke the Crusades. In declaring a war on terrorism in the days immediately following bin Laden's September 2001 attacks on the World Trade Center and the Pentagon, President George W. Bush stated with considerable emotion: "This crusade, this war on terrorism, is going to take a while. . . . we will rid the world of the evil-doers." The president later said that he regretted using the word *crusade* —because of its negative connotations, particularly in the Arab world, and because it implied that the West was engaging in a holy war of its own in countering bin Laden's call for a jihad.[7]

Osama bin Laden may have been hoping that the history of the region will repeat itself. For the early Christian Crusaders, the capture of Jerusalem marked the beginning of a turbulent and generally unsatisfactory period. Regarded as unwanted interlopers and surrounded by hostile Arab forces, the Crusaders eked out a meager existence in the Holy Land for less than two hundred years, from 1099 to 1291 CE. The forces of Saladin vanquished their army and recaptured the city of Jerusalem in 1187. The Crusaders had ruled in the holy city for only eighty-eight years. Modern Israelis have now ruled the same city for little more than fifty years.

THE CAPTURE OF JERUSALEM

Fulcher of Chartres, a Crusader/priest/historian, is one of several primary sources for descriptions of the First Crusade. Other European accounts of the capture of Jerusalem include those of Archbishop William of Tyre, Peter Tudebode (a French priest), and Raymond of Aguilers (a chaplain). There is also an interesting account called the Gesta, written by an anonymous Crusader. Its complete title is Gesta francorum et aliorum Hierosolymytanorum, meaning "The Deeds of the Franks and the Other Pilgrims to Jerusalem." The Gesta, written sometime between 1100 and 1103 CE, is one of the earliest and most important accounts and is used by many later writers, including Peter Tudebode and probably Fulcher of Chartres and William of Tyre.[8] There are also descriptions of the First Crusade by contemporary and later Moslem observers and writers, including Ibn al-Athir, Ibn al-Qalanisi, Ibn al-Jawzi, and Ibn Muyassar.[9] From these sources, we can piece together a picture of events that took place some nine hundred years ago.

The First Crusade, under the leadership of Godfrey of Bouillon, was mostly made up of French noblemen, with a scattering of other European nobility and Norman English. This army of "Franks," as they are referred to in Islamic sources, made their way from Europe, across the breadth of Asia Minor (Turkey), and down the coast of what is now Syria and Lebanon and was once the territory that comprised Roman Palestine. After three years of arduous travel and nearly constant fighting, on June 7, 1099 CE, they saw before them the walls of Jerusalem, bristling with heavily armed Fatimid defenders imported from Egypt and under the command of the governor of the city, Iftikhar ad-Daula.[10] One participant described the events thus:

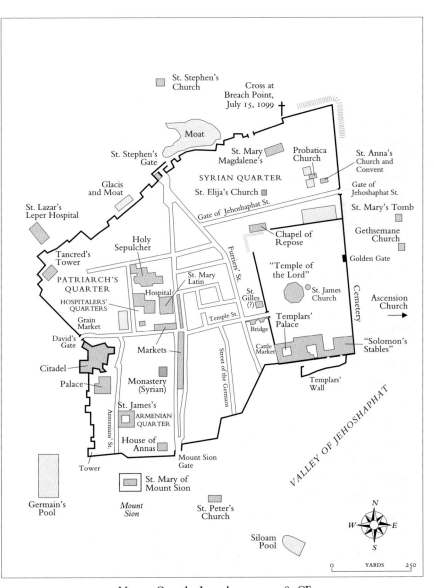

St. Stephen's
Church

Cross at
Breach Point,
July 15, 1099

Moat

St. Stephen's
Gate

St. Mary
Magdalene's

Probatica
Church

St. Anna's
Church and
Convent

SYRIAN QUARTER

Glacis
and Moat

St. Elija's Church

Gate of
Jehoshaphat St.

St. Lazar's
Leper Hospital

Gate of Jehoshaphat St.

St. Mary's Tomb

Holy
Sepulcher

Chapel of
Repose

Gethsemane
Church

Tancred's
Tower

Furriers' St.

"Temple of
the Lord"

Golden Gate

PATRIARCH'S
QUARTER

St. Mary
Latin

St.
Gilles
(?)

St. James
Church

Cemetery

Ascension
Church

HOSPITALERS'
QUARTERS

Hospital

Temple St.

Templars'
Palace

Grain
Market

Bridge

David's
Gate

Markets

Cattle
Market

"Solomon's
Stables"

Citadel

Palace

Monastery
(Syrian)

Templars'
Wall

St. James's

Street of the Germans

VALLEY OF JEHOSHAPHAT

Armenians' St.

ARMENIAN
QUARTER

House of
Annas

Mount Sion
Gate

Tower

St. Mary of
Mount Sion

Germain's
Pool

Mount
Sion

St. Peter's
Church

N
W   E
S

Siloam
Pool

0   YARDS   250

Map 17. Crusader Jerusalem, 1099–1187 CE

Fig. 7. Jerusalem from the Mount of Olives. (Painting by David Roberts, Esq., R.A.)

Fig. 8. The Damascus Gate. (Painting by David Roberts, Esq., R.A.)

Rejoicing and exulting, we reached the city of Jerusalem on Tuesday, on the third day of the week, the eighth day before the Ides of June, and began to besiege the city in a marvelous manner. Robert the Norman besieged it from the north side, near the church of St. Stephen, which was built on the very spot where that first martyr won eternal happiness by being stoned in Christ's name. Next to the Norman Count was Robert, Count of Flanders, while Duke Godfrey and Tancred besieged the city from the west. The Count of St. Gilles located himself on the south, on Mount Zion, near the church of St. Mary, the mother of the Lord, where Christ once supped with His disciples.[11]

Thus the siege of the city began with the Crusaders attacking simultaneously from the northern and western sides and with additional troops located on Mount Zion. The attack from the north—historically the most vulnerable side of the city—first succeeded in gaining access to the city.

On June 10, the third day of the siege, a foraging party of Crusaders unexpectedly met a group of about two hundred enemy soldiers. Says the anonymous author of the *Gesta:* "the soldiers of Christ fought these unbelievers. With the Lord's help, they fought so valiantly that they killed many of the enemy and captured thirty horses."[12]

The Crusaders were then told by a hermit on the Mount of Olives that they would achieve victory if they attacked the city immediately, even before they had siege engines and other machines of war, since they would be protected and strengthened by their faith.[13] Apparently his vision was inaccurate—or their faith alone was not enough—as the Crusaders found out to their dismay when they attacked on June 13.

On the second day of the following week, we made an attack on the city, and so bravely did we fight that, if scaling ladders had been ready for our use, the city most certainly would have fallen into our hands. As it was, we pulled down the outer wall and placed one ladder against the main wall, upon which some of our men ascended and fought hand to hand with swords and lances against the Saracen defenders of the city. Many of our men were killed in this attack, but more of the enemy.[14]

The Moslem defenders had deliberately poisoned or blocked all of the wells around the city, and the Crusaders, short of supplies, were tortured by both hunger and thirst as they suffered in front of the walls of Jerusalem for ten more days. Finally, relief seemed at hand when ships from Genoa anchored at Joppa (modern Jaffa) with fresh supplies of food and water. But to fetch the supplies, the Crusaders had to fight their way to the coast and back—sometimes against vastly superior numbers of the enemy. Eventually they succeeded, and together with reinforcements and fortified with victuals, drink, and wood taken from one of the ships (which was deliberately dismantled), the Crusaders concentrated once more on the siege of Jerusalem.

The Crusaders resumed the building of "machines" and "siege engines,"[15] which William of Tyre says had been under construction since the first week of the siege.

> Thus, with great enthusiasm and diligence, they constructed, from the material at hand, towers and hurling machines called mangons or petraries and also battering rams and scrophae for the purpose of overthrowing the walls. . . . other nobles and distinguished men, with banners unfurled, led the people to places where low bushes and shrubs indigenous to the country were to be found. From these, pliant twigs and withes were cut and carried back to the camp on the backs of horses, asses, and all kinds of pack animals, there to be made into wickerwork coverings to supplement the more important work of the builders. There was great activity everywhere. All labored with untiring zeal; nor was there in that great company a single idle man or one who indulged in leisure, but everyone without distinction did the work best suited to his condition.[16]

In the meantime, the Moslem defenders of the city were also constructing machines of war. William of Tyre reports:

> The besieged, likewise, were ever on the alert to meet wile with wile and made good use of every device for resistance. There was in the city an adequate supply of beams cut from tall trees, which, before the Christians arrived, had been brought in with wise fore-

thought for the defense of Jerusalem. In emulation of our example, they built from these, inside the walls, machines equal to ours in height, but of better material. This they did with the greatest enthusiasm, that their engines might not be inferior to ours either in construction or in material. Guards were maintained constantly on the walls and towers, who watched intently all that was done in our army, especially in regard to devices which pertained to engines of war. Every detail observed was at once reported to the chief men of Jerusalem, who strove with emulous skill to imitate the work of the Christians, that they might meet all our efforts with equal ingenuity. This was comparatively easy, for the people of Jerusalem had at their command many more skilled workmen and building tools, as well as larger supplies of iron, copper, ropes, and everything else necessary, than had our people. All citizens were compelled by a general edict to assist in the work.[17]

According to Peter Tudebode, the Crusaders had an opportunity to test the limits of one of their war machines when they captured a Moslem spy.

On a certain day the enemy sent a Saracen for the purpose of spying on the building of war machines of the Christians. But Syrians and Greeks, seeing the Saracen, pointed him out to the Crusaders. . . . After grabbing him, the Christians interrogated the Saracen through an interpreter, asking him why he had come. In reply the captive said: "The Saracens sent me here to discover what were your inventions." In response the Christians pronounced judgment. They took the spy with bound hands and feet and placed him on the bottom of a machine called a petrary. They thought that with all of their might they could propel him within Jerusalem. They found it impossible, for he was ejected with such force that his bonds broke before he came to the walls and he was dismembered.[18]

Finally, after nearly four weeks, the Crusaders were ready for a decisive assault on the city. Although there may have been as many as forty to sixty thousand Crusaders present at the beginning of the siege of Jerusalem, Raymond of Aguilers—who wrote his account sometime before 1105 CE—contends that by the time of the final assault, "at the most we did not have more than twelve thousand able to bear arms, for there were many poor people and many sick." He reports, "There were twelve or thirteen hundred knights in our army, as I reckon it, not more." He also claims that they were vastly outnumbered by the Moslem defenders in Jerusalem: "according to our estimate and that of many others, there were sixty thousand fighting men within the city, not counting the women and those unable to bear arms, and there were not many of these."[19] William of Tyre provides a similar estimate.

> The number of pilgrims of both sexes and of every age and condition is said to have been about forty thousand, but in this great throng there could not have been more than twenty thousand foot soldiers and fifteen hundred knights. The rest of the multitude consisted of a helpless throng, sick and feeble. [Meanwhile,] reports said that within Jerusalem there were forty thousand brave warriors, splendidly equipped.[20]

The Crusaders were now ready, but there remained one last thing to do before the assault could begin. The anonymous Crusader who wrote the *Gesta* reports: "before we made this assault on the city, the bishops and priests persuaded all, by exhorting and preaching, to honor the Lord by marching around Jerusalem in a great procession, and to prepare for battle by prayer, fasting, and almsgiving." This they did on Friday, July 8.[21] The image of the Crusaders marching barefoot in a great procession around the city was powerful and has been depicted in various art forms over the centuries.

Immediately before the final assault, the Crusaders made a crucial decision to concentrate their efforts against the northern side of the city. Raymond of Aguilers explains the Crusader tactics.

> The besieged Saracens observed the completed siege weapons and so bolstered the weak spots that a successful attack seemed hopeless. Godfrey and the counts of Flanders and Normandy now noted the Saracen buildup, and consequently throughout the

night before the set day of attack shifted their siege weapons, both wattles and towers, to a position between the church of the Blessed Stephen and the Valley of Jehoshaphat [Kidron]. Believe me, the disjointing, transporting over a mile, and erecting of these machines was no small job. The Saracens were thunderstruck next morning at the sight of the changed position of our machines and tents, and, I hasten to add, so were we, the faithful, who saw the hand of the Lord in this.[22]

The northern side of the city, as past battles had shown, was the weakest part of Jerusalem's defenses. Raymond clarifies the Crusaders' reasoning.

To brief you on the move to the north, I must say that two factors motivated the change of position. The flat surface offered a better approach to the walls by our instruments of war, and the very remoteness and weakness of this northern place had caused the Saracens to leave it unfortified.[23]

The siege engines were dragged to the new location on Saturday night, July 9, and were then, according to the anonymous Crusader, "equipped and covered" on July 10–12, 1099 CE. He continues:

Both day and night, on the fourth and fifth days of the week [July 13–14], we made a determined attack on the city from all sides. . . . Early on the sixth day of the week [July 15] we again attacked the city on all sides, but as the assault was unsuccessful, we were all astounded and fearful. However, when the hour approached on which our Lord Jesus Christ deigned to suffer on the Cross for us, our knights began to fight bravely in one of the towers— namely, the party with Duke Godfrey and his brother, Count Eustace. One of our knights, named Lethold, clambered up the wall of the city, and no sooner had he ascended than the defenders fled from the walls and through the city. Our men followed, killing and slaying even to the Temple of Solomon, where the slaughter was so great that our men waded in blood up to their ankles . . .[24]

More details are given in the other Crusader accounts. Raymond of Aguilers provides a particularly detailed and graphic description.

Our men began to undermine the towers and walls. From every side stones were hurled from the tormenti and the petrariae, and so many arrows that they fell like hail. The servants of God bore this patiently, sustained by the premises of their faith, whether they should be killed or should presently prevail over their enemies. The battle showed no indication of victory, but when the machines were drawn nearer to the walls, they hurled not only stones and arrows, but also burning wood and straw. The wood was dipped in pitch, wax, and sulphur; then straw and tow were fastened on by an iron band, and, when lighted, these firebrands were shot from the machines. [They were] all bound together by an iron band, I say, so that wherever they fell, the whole mass held together and continued to burn. Such missiles, burning as they shot upward, could not be resisted by swords or by high walls; it was not even possible for the defenders to find safety down behind the walls. Thus the fight continued from the rising to the setting sun in such splendid fashion that it is difficult to believe anything more glorious was ever done. . . . Night brought fear to both sides. The Saracens feared that we would take the city during the night or on the next day, for the outer works were broken through and the ditch was filled, so that it was possible to make an entrance through the wall very quickly. On our part, we feared only that the Saracens would set fire to the machines that were moved close to the walls, and thus improve their situation. So on both sides it was a night of watchfulness, labor, and sleepless caution: on one side, most certain hope, on the other doubtful fear.[25]

The statement that the "outer works were broken through and the ditch was filled" is interesting. There is indeed archaeological evidence that a lower outer wall had been built around much of the city, including the northern side, with a ditch constructed between it and the main defensive wall. This lower outer wall may have been built as early as 1073 CE, immediately after the Seljuk conquest of the city, as attested by later visitors, such as Ekkehard of Aura.[26] Once this wall had been breached and the ditch filled in, it was only a matter of time before the Crusaders took the city. Raymond of Aguilers continues the story of the attack.

When the morning [of the fifteenth] came, our men eagerly rushed to the walls and dragged the machines forward. . . . a knight on the Mount of Olives began to wave his shield to those who were with the Count and others, signaling them to advance. Who this knight was we have been unable to find out. At this signal our men began to take heart, and some began to batter down the wall, while others began to ascend by means of scaling ladders and ropes. Our archers shot burning firebrands, and in this way checked the attack that the Saracens were making upon the wooden towers of the Duke and the two Counts. These firebrands, moreover, were wrapped in cotton. This shower of fire drove the defenders from the walls. Then the Count quickly released the long drawbridge which had protected the side of the wooden tower next to the wall, and it swung down from the top, being fastened to the middle of the tower, making a bridge over which the men began to enter Jerusalem bravely and fearlessly. Among those who entered first were Tancred and the Duke of Lorraine, and the amount of blood that they shed on that day is incredible. All ascended after them, and the Saracens now began to suffer.[27]

Thus, sometime between 9:00 A.M. and noon on the morning of July 15, 1099 CE, the first Crusaders poured into the city of Jerusalem, sensing victory after three long years of travail. Al-Athir—one of our principal Moslem sources for the siege—put it succinctly: "Jerusalem was taken from the north on the morning of Friday 22 Sha'ban 492/July 15, 1099."[28]

Soon the remaining Crusaders broke into the city. The anonymous Crusader reports: "The Emir who commanded the Tower of St. David surrendered . . . and opened that gate at which the pilgrims had always been accustomed to pay tribute. But this time the pilgrims entered the city, pursuing and killing the Saracens up to the Temple of Solomon, where the enemy gathered in force."[29] The "Temple of Solomon" into which the Moslem defenders fled—and to which many documenters of the First Crusade refer—was of course neither Solomon's Temple, which Nebuchadnezzar had destroyed in 586 BCE, nor even Herod's Temple, which the Romans had destroyed in 70 CE. It was, in fact, the al-Aqsa Mosque. But there was no sanctuary to be had there for the Moslem defenders. Several chroniclers described the slaughter that took place on the Temple Mount, apparently just after the midday prayers had come to an end.

> After the other [Crusader] leaders had slain all whom they encountered in the various parts of the city, they learned that many had fled for refuge to the sacred precincts of the Temple. Thereupon as with one accord they hurried thither. A crowd of knights and foot soldiers was introduced, who massacred all those who had taken refuge there. No mercy was shown to anyone, and the whole place was flooded with the blood of the victims. (William of Tyre)[30]

> What happened there? If I tell the truth, it will exceed your powers of belief. So let it suffice to say this much, at least, that in the Temple and porch of Solomon, men rode in blood up to their knees and bridle reins. (Raymond of Aguilers)[31]

> Our men followed, killing and slaying even to the Temple of Solomon, where the slaughter was so great that our men waded in blood up to their ankles. . . . The battle raged throughout the day, so that the Temple was covered with their blood. When the pagans had been overcome, our men seized great numbers, both men and women, either killing them or keeping them captive, as they wished. (Anonymous Crusader)[32]

> Nowhere was there a place where the Saracens could escape the swordsmen. On the top of Solomon's Temple, to which they had climbed in fleeing, many were shot to death with arrows and cast headlong from the roof. Within this Temple about ten thousand were beheaded. If you had been there, your feet would have been stained up to the ankles with the blood of the slain. What more

shall I tell? Not one of them was allowed to live. They did not spare the women and children. (Fulcher of Chartres)[33]

One might speculate that the Crusaders probably viewed this slaughter as a just punishment for those who, according to Urban II, "[spread] the blood of the circumcision . . . upon the altars or . . . pour [it] into the vases of the baptismal font." In any event, after three days of an orgy of bloodlust, the Crusaders had killed virtually every inhabitant of Jerusalem—not only Moslems, but also Jews, who were burned alive in their synagogue.[34]

There were few survivors of the massacre. William of Tyre mentions a group of Moslem defenders led by the Egyptian governor Iftikhar ad-Daula who, together with their wives and children, had taken refuge in the Tower of David by the Jaffa Gate. They surrendered to Raymond of Toulouse days after the Crusaders had taken the city. After paying a large bribe, they were allowed to leave unharmed for the coastal city of Ascalon.[35]

The anonymous Crusader completes his account of the conquest of Jerusalem in an understated manner: "Afterward, the army scattered throughout the city and took possession of the gold and silver, the horses and mules, and the houses filled with goods of all kinds."[36] Fulcher of Chartres and Peter Tudebode agree, reporting, respectively, that the Crusaders "entered the homes of the citizens, seizing whatever they found in them" and that some "ran through all the city taking gold, silver, horses, mules, and houses packed with all kinds of riches."[37] Fulcher of Chartres also says that Tancred, a twenty-one-year-old Norman Crusader who led a band of heavily armed men to the Temple Mount and who was directly responsible for the slaughter within the al-Aqsa Mosque, ransacked the Dome of the Rock (Fulcher's "Temple of the Lord"). Although Fulcher says that Tancred later "returned everything or something of equal value to its holy place," Ibn al-Athir says that Tancred stole "more than forty silver candelabra, each of them weighing 3600 drams, and a great silver lamp weighing forty-four Syrian pounds, as well as a hundred and fifty smaller silver candelabra and more than twenty gold ones, and a great deal more booty."[38]

Both Fulcher of Chartres and William of Tyre relate a gruesome tale of Crusader greed. A rumor apparently swept through the Crusader forces that the Moslems had swallowed their gold coins before the city fell. Fulcher of Chartres reports:

> After they had discovered the cleverness of the Saracens, it was an extraordinary thing to see our squires and poorer people split the bellies of those dead Saracens, so that they might pick out besants [gold coins] from their intestines, which they had swallowed down their horrible gullets while alive. After several days, they made a great heap of their bodies and burned them to ashes, and in these ashes they found the gold more easily.[39]

The aftermath of the battle was a horrible sight. William of Tyre records the gruesome scene.

> It was impossible to look upon the vast numbers of the slain without horror; everywhere lay fragments of human bodies, and the very ground was covered with the blood of the slain. It was not alone the spectacle of headless bodies and mutilated limbs strewn in all directions that roused horror in all who looked upon them. Still more dreadful was it to gaze upon the victors themselves, dripping with blood from head to foot, an ominous sight which brought terror to all who met them. . . . The rest of the soldiers roved through the city in search of wretched survivors who might be hiding in the narrow portals and byways to escape death. These were dragged out into public view and slain like sheep. Some formed into bands and broke into houses where they laid violent hands on the heads of families, on their wives, children, and their entire households. These victims were either put to the sword or dashed headlong to the ground from some elevated place so that they perished miserably.[40]

So many inhabitants of the city were slain in the three-day-long orgy of killing that the streets of Jerusalem were still littered with corpses long afterward. Peter Tudebode reports that the dead were collected, stacked in "mounds like houses" outside the city walls, and then burned. There were too many bodies, however, and Fulcher of Chartres says that the stench from the corpses left rotting in the sun was still overwhelming when he visited the city after celebrating mass in Bethlehem on December 24, 1099 CE, more than five months after the capture of the city.[41]

The number of those killed during the massacre is uncertain. The earliest Islamic sources are not specific, but the figure of seventy thousand appears in writings soon thereafter. By the time later Islamic authors give their accounts, the number has swelled to one hundred thousand, of whom seventy thousand were killed in the al-Aqsa Mosque alone. "The Franks killed more than 70,000 people in the Aqsa mosque, among them a large group of Moslem imams, religious scholars, devout men and ascetics from amongst those who had left their homelands and lived in the vicinity of that Holy Place," says al-Athir.[42] However, according to Professor Adrian Boas, that number far exceeded "even the highest estimate of the entire population of Jerusalem at the time of the siege"—usually given as thirty to forty thousand, including those who had fled into the city for protection. Crusader sources, such as Fulcher of Chartres and William of Tyre, say that only (!) ten thousand were killed in the "Temple of Solomon" and that another ten thousand were killed elsewhere in the city.[43]

Even by the bloody standards of Jerusalem's earlier history, the massacre of the Moslems by the Crusaders during those hot summer days of July 15–18, 1099 CE, was notorious. This event resonates still in the turbulence of the Middle East today, which helps to explain why President George W. Bush's remark about undertaking a "crusade" in the aftermath of the September 2001 attacks on the World Trade Center and the Pentagon elicited such an angry, knee-jerk reaction in both the Islamic and the European worlds.[44]

Urban II—the pope who had unleashed these Crusaders—never learned what had been done in Jerusalem in the name of Christianity, for he died on July 29, before news of the capture of the city and the massacre had reached him.[45] There is little doubt that he would have approved. On the other side, tales of the disastrous loss of Jerusalem and the manner of its fall spread across the Moslem world, gradually gathering a momentum that ninety years later would unleash powerful and vengeful forces under Salah ad-Din—better known to the Western world as Saladin. These forces would retake Jerusalem from the Crusaders. In the meantime, the Crusaders, with only a tenuous hold on conquered Palestine, busied themselves rebuilding the city of Jerusalem in a Christian image.

CRUSADER RENOVATIONS

After the capture of Jerusalem, the Crusaders undertook much building and rebuilding— especially of churches, including the Church of the Holy Sepulcher and St. Anne's Church.[46] The most significant "renovations" of religious buildings were those made to the Dome of the Rock, the al-Aqsa Mosque, and the Temple Mount/Haram al-Sherif as a whole.

Godfrey of Bouillon, who was appointed the first Crusader leader of Jerusalem, used the al-Aqsa Mosque as his residence. Godfrey took the title "advocate of the Holy Sepulcher" rather than calling himself king. Within two decades, in 1119 CE, the mosque became the headquarters for the Knights Templar (or simply Templars). The Templars were so named because of their proximity to the original location of Solomon's Temple, and they promptly renamed the al-Aqsa Mosque as the Templum Salomonis (Temple of Solomon) or the Palatium Salomonis (Palace of Solomon). The Templars, founded by Hugh de Payens in 1118 CE, were an elite group who combined the functions of a religious order and a military unit. The members, with the dual roles of knights and monks, were originally sworn to protect pilgrims journeying to the Holy Land. Similar orders of warrior-monks also founded during this period included the Hospitallers and the Teutonic Knights. The relations between the various groups were not always chivalrous or friendly.[47]

The Crusaders added additional wings to the original building of the al-Aqsa Mosque and also used the underground vaults that Herod the Great had constructed to support his southern expansion of the Temple Mount. The vaults became stables for their horses—a purpose for which they were admirably suited, but not one for which they had originally been intended. Ultimately, more than a thousand horses and their grooms were housed there. As a result of a modern confusion about the origin of the vaults, this area of the Haram al-Sherif is known today as the "Stables of Solomon," although it has nothing to do with Solomon.[48]

Meanwhile, the Dome of the Rock, located just a few meters from the al-Aqsa Mosque, on the Haram al-Sherif, was used as a residence by Daimbert, archbishop of Pisa. He had arrived a few months after the capture of Jerusalem, as the official papal legate. Daimbert immediately assumed the position of patriarch of Jerusalem. Later, beginning in 1115 CE, the Dome of the Rock was converted into a church. Christian paintings, mosaics, and icons were placed inside, and an altar was built on top of the rock. The rock itself was covered in marble, and an iron grille was placed around it to prevent pilgrims from removing chips as souvenirs. The Koranic inscriptions were covered over with Latin texts, and a huge golden cross was positioned on top of the dome, replacing the crescent that had been displayed there previously. The church became known as the Templum Domini (Temple of the Lord) and was finally consecrated in 1142 CE.[49]

THE MOSLEM RECONQUEST

In the aftermath of the Crusaders' capture of Jerusalem, the Moslem world was temporarily at a loss for a response. Efforts to unify against the Crusaders, to expel them from the Holy Land, and to recapture Jerusalem came to fruition only slowly. It took another eighty-eight years and the emergence of a heroic figure in Islamic history for the Moslems to recapture Jerusalem, and it took nearly two hundred years to drive the last of the Crusaders from the Holy Land.

The story of Saladin's recapture of Jerusalem begins a generation or more earlier, with a Turkish Seljuk officer named Zangi. Zangi gradually accumulated territory, eventually ruling over a small empire in northern Syria and Mesopotamia. He seized Mosul (in what is now modern Iraq) in 1127 CE and Baalbek (in Syria) in 1139 CE. Upon his death, his son, Nur al-Din, inherited and quickly enlarged his realm. By 1154 CE Nur al-Din had captured Damascus, and by 1163 CE he had set his sights on controlling a united Egypt and Syria. He dispatched an army to invade Egypt, commanded by a trusted Kurdish officer named Shirkuh. Reluctantly accompanying Shirkuh was his nephew, Yusuf Salah ad-Din bin Ayyub—now better known as Saladin.[50]

Saladin was born in or near the small village of Tikrit (in what is now modern Iraq) in the year 1138 CE. This village and its environs are perhaps better known to modern readers as the birthplace and hometown of Saddam Hussein. Saladin was only twenty-six years old when Nur al-Din first ordered Shirkuh to invade Egypt in 1164 CE. After numerous attempts, Shirkuh and Saladin managed to capture and hold Cairo five years later, allowing the formerly ruling Fatimid caliphs to remain as puppet rulers in nominal control of the city and of Egypt. When Shirkuh died in suspicious circumstances a few months later, Saladin took over his position and served both as "adviser" to the Fatimid caliphs and as the representative of Nur al-Din. He gradually increased his power and eventually became vizier of Egypt as well as commander in chief of the Syrian armies.

In 1172 CE Saladin simply abolished the Fatimid caliphate and took over as the unchallenged master of Egypt. Thereafter, Nur al-Din was never quite sure of the extent of Saladin's loyalty. Nur al-Din died two years later. Saladin then came quickly from Egypt and took Syria for himself, doing away, in the process, with both Nur al-Din's successors and his own rivals.[51]

Almost immediately upon his accession to this powerful position, Saladin began planning a jihad against the Crusaders, with the goal of driving them out of the Holy Land and retaking Jerusalem. In this mission, Saladin was following the exhortations of a legal scholar in Damascus named al-Sulami, who had published a book in 1105 CE, just after the coming of the Crusaders. Al-Sulami's work, titled *The Book of Holy War*, gave an updated definition for *jihad*. He resuscitated the concept of a "holy war"—a concept that had been in abeyance within Islam since the middle of the eighth century CE, when the first concerted drive to extend Islam across the known world had come to an end. Al-Sulami spelled out the new rules for conducting a jihad, which Saladin took to heart and eventually put into practice.[52]

Al-Sulami largely blamed the internecine wars between Moslem factions for the Crusaders' success, and he foresaw that a unified Moslem front would be required if the Crusaders were to be expelled from the Holy Land. He was under no doubt that this could be accomplished. He wrote: "One knows for sure their [the Crusaders'] weakness, the small amount of cavalry and equipment they have at their disposal and the distance from which their reinforcements come. . . . It is an opportunity which must be seized quickly." Several decades before

Zangi, Nur al-Din, and then Saladin came to lead the Moslem forces, al-Sulami foresaw the need for such leaders.

> The sovereign . . . must devote himself to his relations with the sovereigns of other countries, Syria, the Jazira, Egypt and adjacent regions, for terror [of the Crusaders] can reconcile the old hatreds and secret hostilities of the inhabitants of these countries as well as turn them away from their rivalries and mutual jealousies.[53]

Al-Sulami saw the Crusades as a test of the Moslem faithful and of their willingness to undertake jihad. Although he did not live to see his teachings put into action, al-Sulami provided an outline that Saladin was to follow.

> The early jurists emphasized the offensive Jihad, or the Jihad against enemies in countries that are nearby or remote. However, if an enemy attacks the Moslems, as this enemy [the Crusaders] has done, then pursuing him in areas that he has conquered from us is a just war aimed at protecting lives, children, and families and at preserving those parts that are still under our control.[54]

Al-Sulami's definition of *jihad* as a "just war" provided the basis for Moslem attacks against the Crusaders, on the grounds that they were simply trying to recapture lands previously lost and to protect lands, lives, and families not yet lost. Al-Sulami's arguments were similar to those of another twelfth-century CE Moslem theologian, al-Ghazzali, who argued that jihad was a duty to be undertaken by every free and able Moslem, that any attack on the Crusaders was to be construed as defensive rather than aggressive, and that actions should be collective.

> If a Moslem community bordering on or facing the enemy is strong enough to repel the enemy, then jihad is a collective obligation incumbent upon all members of that community . . . However, if that particular community is too weak to repel the evil of the enemy, then it is incumbent upon the neighboring Moslem communities to help the beleaguered one.[55]

Saladin, taking these injunctions to heart, urged that Moslem leaders should put aside their differences and unite against the Crusaders in order to recapture the city of Jerusalem and the lands of Syria and Palestine. In 1175 CE he ordered al-Qadi al-Fadil, his chief administrator (*wazir*), to draft a document whose principal theme was a jihad against the Crusaders. In it, Saladin outlined his strategy for unifying Egypt, Syria, Mesopotamia, Yemen, and North Africa in the name of the Abbasid caliph and with the express aim of recovering the Holy Land and Jerusalem. He added, "And with God's help, we will be able to release, from captivity, the [al-Aqsa] mosque from which God has lifted His Messenger to the Heaven." But it took twelve years for Saladin to subdue his Moslem rivals, create a united Islamic front, and turn his attention to the recapture of Jerusalem.[56]

SALADIN'S RECAPTURE OF JERUSALEM

The story of Saladin's recapture of Jerusalem is told by a number of different twelfth- and thirteenth-century CE Moslem authors, as well as by the contemporary Crusader chronicler Ernoul and the thirteenth-century anonymous Christian author(s) of the *Libellus*. The Moslem authors include Ibn al-Athir (1160–1233 CE), author of the enormous *Kamil at-Tawarihh* (The collection of histories); Imad al-Din al-Isfahani (1125–1201 CE), who served as personal secretary to Nur al-Din and then Saladin; and Ibn Shaddad (1145–1234 CE), who first came to Saladin's attention by writing a treatise in 1188 CE entitled *The Virtues of the Jihad*. Ibn Shaddad was immediately hired upon his presenting that work to Saladin. He spent the rest of his life serving Saladin, becoming his official biographer. Another account of the reconquest was written much later by the fifteenth-century CE Egyptian historian al-Maqrizi (1364–1442 CE).[57]

On July 4, 1187 CE, Saladin's men annihilated Crusader forces gathered on the double hill known as the "Horns of Hattin," near the western shore of the Sea of Galilee. In this battle, the Crusaders suffered their worst defeat ever at the hands of a Moslem army. Virtually their entire fighting force and many of their leaders were killed. Other prominent Crusaders were taken prisoner, including Guy de Lusignan, the reigning king of Jerusalem, and Reynald of Chatillon, the lord of

Kerak (in Syria). Although Guy was later released, Saladin personally executed Reynald for having broken an earlier truce and for attacking Moslem caravans, including one in which Saladin's own sister was traveling. It was, in fact, these earlier actions by Reynald that had given Saladin an immediate cause for launching a jihad against the Crusaders.[58]

After the victory at Hattin, Saladin and his army marched to the coast, capturing cities as they advanced. They reached the southern city of Ascalon by September 5, and the city and surrounding region quickly succumbed to their strength in arms. They next turned their attention to Jerusalem.

Al-Athir tells of a group of Crusaders on sortie from Jerusalem who surprised and then attacked the vanguard of Saladin's army while the Moslem forces were marching from Ascalon to Jerusalem. The Moslems sustained heavy losses, and one of Saladin's favorite commanders was killed.[59] Saladin himself recalled this campaign.

> We moved to the region of Jerusalem and Asqalan; recovered all its fortresses and citadels as well as all its cities. These are: Haifa, Caesarea, Arsuf, Jaffa, al-Ramla, Lydda . . . and al-Khalil (Hebron). We also invested ᶜAsqalan, the city famous for its fortifications, for fourteen days, and recovered it through surrender. The banners of monotheism have been raised on top of its towers and walls. It has been settled with Moslems after being evacuated from the infidels and polytheists. . . . Nothing is left for recovery in the coastal area from Jubayl (Byblos) to the borders of Egypt, except Jerusalem. May God make its recovery easy. If God wills (that we recover Jerusalem), we will turn to Tyre.[60]

Ernoul, the contemporary Crusader chronicler who was in Jerusalem during this crucial period, claims that a delegation seeking a peaceful solution went to Saladin in early September 1187 CE, on the very day that he captured the coastal city of Ascalon. Saladin offered the Jerusalem Crusaders generous terms, including desperately needed supplies from his own stores, and offered to allow them to retain control of the city and surrounding land until Pentecost. He also said that if they could obtain help and reinforcements, he would allow them to retain control of the city indefinitely, but if they were left on their own without external assistance, they would be required to surrender the city to him. According to Ernoul, the delegates rejected Saladin's offer, saying they would never give up Jerusalem.[61]

All accounts agree that by late September 1187 CE, Saladin's forces were in position before the walls of Jerusalem. When they appeared there on September 20, the Crusader defenders of the city were woefully undermanned. The majority of the Crusaders had returned to Europe immediately after the victorious capture of Jerusalem in 1099 CE, leaving at most a skeleton crew of perhaps three hundred knights and three thousand armed men in the city.[62] There were even fewer Crusader knights in the city on the day that they confronted the Moslem forces, since many had been killed at the battle of Hattin a few months earlier.

When Balian of Ibelin—one of the few Crusader leaders to have escaped from the debacle at Hattin—was admitted into Jerusalem through the good graces of Saladin, he found only two other knights who had also survived the slaughter at Hattin. Balian had promised Saladin that he would only enter Jerusalem in order to rescue his wife and children and that he would only stay in the city one night. However, once inside the city, he sent a message to Saladin, saying that he had been pressed into service by the patriarch and was not being allowed to leave. Saladin agreed to release him from the oath. Balian began vigorously organizing the defense of the city. Among his first actions was the quick promotion to knighthood of fifty sons of the nobility—any who were over the age of fifteen—and of perhaps as many as sixty of the town's leading citizens.[63]

Despite the lack of knights, the total number of armed men in the city had been bolstered by additional foot soldiers, survivors from the doomed Crusader force at Hattin. The overall population inside the walls was further augmented by refugees from the surrounding countryside and by displaced inhabitants from other lost cities, such as Ascalon, as well as Darum, Ramla, Gaza and elsewhere. All of these, says al-Athir, sought protection against the oncoming Moslem army. There may have been as many as one hundred thousand people inside the walls of Jerusalem by the time Saladin arrived, but Ibn Shaddad puts the number of able-bodied defenders at only sixty thousand fighting men (cavalry and infantry), while Imad al-Din and al-Athir put the number of defenders at seventy thousand.[64]

Ibn Shaddad, Saladin's official biographer, gives a concise account of the events that next transpired.

> He [Saladin] descended on the city on Sunday 15 Rajab 583 [September 20, 1187]. He took up position on the western side. It was crammed with fighting men, both mounted and foot soldiers. Experienced sources estimated the number of soldiers who were there at more than 60,000, apart from women and children. Then, because of an advantage he saw, he transferred to the north side, which move took place on Friday 20 Rajab [September 25].[65]

Ernoul and Imad al-Din agree that Saladin spent the first five to seven days attacking the western side of the city, before switching to the north side.[66] Imad al-Din graphically describes this first week of engagements on the western side and lauds the courage of the defending Crusaders.

> The hearts of the unbelievers thudded, the faction of polytheists was in a confusion of breathless anguish, destiny performed the miracle. There were in Jerusalem at the time 70,000 Frankish troops, both swordsmen and archers, and champions of error armed with lances, their pliant points quivering, ready to defend the city. They challenged (us) to combat and barred the pass, they came down into the lists like enemies, they slaughtered and drew blood, they blazed with fury and defended the city, they fumed and burned with wrath, they drove us back and defended themselves, they became inflamed and caused us harm, groaned and incited, called for help in foreign tongue, entrenched themselves and acted like men enraged with thirst, whirled about and crossed, advanced and retreated, rolled about and grieved, cried out and yelled in the conflict, immolated themselves in their tragedy and flung themselves on death. They fought grimly and struggled with all their energy, descending to the fray with absolute resolution, they wielded the sockets of their spears to

give their thirsty points the water of the spirit to drink; they dealt with those that had lost their nerve, and passed round the goblets of death; they hurled themselves into battle to cut off limbs, they blazed and set fire to things, they clustered together and obstinately stood their ground, they made themselves a target for arrows, and called on death to stand by them. They said: "Each of us is worth twenty, and every ten is worth a hundred! We shall bring about the end of the world in defence of the Church of the Resurrection, we shall despise our own safety in desire for her survival." So the battle continued and the slaughter with spear and sword went on.[67]

Saladin eventually realized his tactical error in assaulting the western side of Jerusalem: the sun was directly in the eyes of his men during the Crusader morning attacks, and the Moslems themselves could only mount afternoon attacks because of the blinding rays.[68] He ordered his men to move to the northern side of the city, as so many besieging forces had done in earlier battles for Jerusalem. On September 25, the two sides again "began the fiercest struggle imaginable," as "each side looked on the fight as an absolute religious obligation."[69] Each morning, the Crusader cavalry emerged from the city and engaged Saladin's forces; each evening, they retreated inside.

Al-Athir says that the Moslems were eventually enraged by the death of one of their leaders in battle.

[The Moslems] charged like one man, dislodged the Franks [Crusaders] from their positions and drove them back into the city. When the Moslems reached the moat they crossed it, came up under the walls and began to breach them, protected by their archers and by continuous artillery fire which kept the walls clear of Franks and enabled the Moslems to make a breach and fill it with the usual materials. When the Franks saw how violently the Moslems were attacking, how continuous and effective was the fire from the ballistas and how busily the sappers were breaching the walls, meeting no resistance, they grew desperate, and their leaders assembled to take counsel.[70]

Ibn Shaddad tells a similar tale.

> He [Saladin] set up trebuchets and pressed hard on the city with assaults and a hail of missiles. Eventually, he undermined the city wall on the side next to the Valley of Gehenna in the northern angle. The enemy saw the indefensible position they had fallen into and the signs were clear to them that our true religion would overcome the false. Their hearts were downcast on account of the killing and imprisonment that had befallen their knights and men-at-arms and the fall and conquest of their fortresses. They realized that their lot was ineluctable and that they would be killed by the sword that had killed their brethren. Humbled, they inclined towards seeking terms.[71]

The Crusader chronicles written by Ernoul and others give further details of the final days of Crusader Jerusalem. Ernoul says that the decisive battle for control of the northern wall of the city lasted one week. Saladin sent sappers to undermine and breach the northern wall, while ten thousand archers shot volleys of arrows to protect the men manning the siege engines, and ten thousand mounted cavalrymen waited to fend off any charges made by the Crusaders. Desperate, the Crusader defenders tried to drive off the attackers by using stones, molten lead, arrows, and spears, but eventually Saladin's men made a thirty-meter-long breach in the wall—about the length of an American football field. It is interesting to note that Saladin's men, perhaps deliberately, breached the defensive wall at precisely the same spot where the Crusaders had entered the city eighty-eight years earlier—and near to where the forces of the Sasanian Persian king Khosrau II penetrated the wall when they captured the city nearly six centuries earlier, in 614 CE.[72]

One Crusader account said: "There used to be a stone cross which our knights had once erected on the walls in memory of their victorious capture of this city. . . . Those savages destroyed this with a missile from a catapult, and flattened no small part of the wall with it."[73] The famous cross in question had been erected by Godfrey of Bouillon, the first Crusader leader of Jerusalem, to mark the spot through which the

Crusaders broke through the wall of the city in 1099 CE. According to the eminent scholar Joshua Prawer, when the forces of Saladin breached the defensive wall, "the undermined section of wall fell into the moat and with it the famous cross which marked the place at which the Crusaders had entered the city eighty-eight years before."[74]

The Crusaders, realizing that the end was near, held an emergency meeting. In the end, they authorized Balian of Ibelin to meet with Saladin and present their terms of surrender. Ernoul says that Balian met with Saladin twice over the course of two days. During the first meeting, the fighting was still fierce. At one point, Moslem forces overran the main northern wall of the city, raising their flag high above it. Seeing this, Saladin asked Balian why he was negotiating for the surrender of the city when it had already fallen to the Moslems. Immediately thereafter, the Crusaders counterattacked and drove the Moslems back from the wall once again. Enraged at this turn of events, Saladin dismissed Balian from his presence.[75] When Balian returned the following day, he painted a grim picture for Saladin of the Crusaders' decision to fight to the death if they were not allowed to ransom their way to freedom. Al-Athir relates the conversation.

> Balian said: "Know, O Sultan, that there are very many of us in this city, God alone knows how many. . . . if we see that death is inevitable, then by God we shall kill our children and our wives, burn our possessions, so as not to leave you with a dinar or a drachma or a single man or woman to enslave. When this is done, we shall pull down the Sanctuary of the Rock and the Masjid al-Aqsa and the other sacred places, slaughtering the Moslem prisoners we hold—5,000 of them—and killing every horse and animal we possess. Then we shall come out to fight you like men fighting for their lives, when each man, before he falls dead, kills his equals; we shall die with honor, or win a noble victory!"[76]

Saladin recognized the seriousness of the Crusader threats and agreed to accept the surrender of the city. Ibn Shaddad gives a brief account of the rather anticlimactic outcome of the negotiations.

An agreement was reached through an exchange of messages between the two sides. The sultan received the surrender on Friday 27 Rajab [October 2]. The eve had been the [date of the] Prophetic Ascension which is written about in the Noble Koran. Observe this remarkable coincidence, how God facilitated its restoration to Moslem hands on the anniversary of the Prophet's Night-Journey.[77]

Thus, Saladin received the surrender of the Crusaders and retook Jerusalem on October 2, 1187 CE, the precise anniversary of Mohammed's nocturnal journey, when the prophet journeyed to the "Further Mosque" and thence up to the heavens, mounted on his steed al-Buraq.[78]

THE AFTERMATH

Although Saladin had originally sworn to take the city as the Crusaders had, in fire and blood, in the end he allowed himself to be persuaded by Balian to let the surviving Crusaders go in peace, as long as they were able to pay the ransom that he demanded. Those who were not able to pay would be enslaved. Al-Athir records the discussion that took place between Saladin and his council of advisers.

Then Saladin took counsel with his advisers, all of whom were in favor of his granting the assurances requested by the Franks, without forcing them to take extreme measures whose outcome could not be foreseen. "Let us consider them as being already our prisoners," they said, "and allow them to ransom themselves on terms agreed between us." The Sultan agreed to give the Franks assurances of safety on the understanding that each man, rich and poor alike, should pay ten dinar, children of both sexes two dinar and women five dinar. All who paid this sum within forty days should go free, and those who had not paid at the end of the time should be enslaved. Balian ibn Barzan [Balian of Ibelin] offered 30,000 dinar as ransom for the poor, which was accepted, and the city surrendered on Friday 27 rajab/2 October 1187, a memorable day on which the Moslem flags were hoisted over the walls of Jerusalem.[79]

Balian ransomed eighteen thousand people with his thirty thousand dinars. Many others were able to ransom themselves as well, but Imad al-Din reports that there were about one hundred thousand people in the city and that not all were able to pay. The Moslems watched aghast as the Latin patriarch of Jerusalem ransomed only himself by paying the required ten dinars and then left the city with all of his possessions, including, as al-Athir reports, "treasures from the Dome of the Rock, the Masjid al-Aqsa, the Church of the Resurrection and others." Says al-Athir, "God alone knows the amount of the treasure; he also took an equal quantity of money." Al-Athir comments: "Saladin made no difficulties, and when he was advised to sequestrate the whole lot for Islam, replied that he would not go back on his word. He took only the ten dinar from him, and let him go, heavily escorted, to Tyre." Thus the patriarch left without ransoming other townspeople, although his treasures would certainly have given freedom to a great many.[80]

A number of high-ranking Moslems—including Saladin's own brother—asked to be given captives as gifts. They then proceeded to free them, and several thousand captive Crusaders were released in this way. Al-Athir records that those who still could not pay and who were subsequently taken away as prisoners by the Moslems after the forty days of grace expired numbered sixteen thousand men, women, and children. Imad al-Din differs slightly, saying that there were fifteen thousand prisoners—seven thousand men and eight thousand women and children.[81]

The contrast between the bloodbath and looting that took place when the Crusaders captured Jerusalem in 1099 CE and the far more civilized way in which Saladin treated the city and its inhabitants in 1187 CE is striking. Saladin even assigned 150 of his own officers to escort three groups of Crusader refugees who had been ransomed—50 to the group led by the Knights Templar, 50 to the group led by the Hospitallers, and 50 to the group led by Balian and the patriarch. These Moslem officers were ordered to see that the Crusader refugees reached Christian-occupied territory safely.[82]

As the Crusaders left Jerusalem and as the Moslems entered the city on the Friday after their victory (October 9, 1187 CE), some of the more daring Moslems climbed to the top of the Dome of the Rock and took down the great gilded cross that the Crusaders had placed there. The ensuing Moslem shouts of joy from inside the city were matched by the Crusaders' cries of grief from outside the walls. Al-Athir says that the combination of shrieks, groans, and cries was "so loud and piercing . . . that the earth shook."[83]

Initially, Saladin ordered that the Church of the Holy Sepulcher be closed, but he reopened it a few days later. For the next five years (until Richard the Lionheart negotiated a treaty with Saladin in 1192 CE), pilgrims had to pay a fee of ten bezants in order to enter the church and worship.[84]

Immediately after securing the city, Saladin ordered that all of the Moslem shrines in Jerusalem—which had been much abused during the reign of the Crusaders—be restored. The living quarters, storerooms, and latrines that the Knights Templar had built against the al-Aqsa Mosque were torn down. The Dome of the Rock was "cleansed of all pollution," according to al-Athir, and the marble slabs with which the Crusaders had covered the rock were removed (although the iron grille was left in place and can still be seen today). A wooden *minbar* (prayer rostrum or pulpit) that Nur al-Din had ordered built long before, in anticipation of the day that the Moslems would retake Jerusalem, was brought from Aleppo and installed in the al-Aqsa Mosque. The minbar remained in place for eight hundred years, until 1969 CE, when it was destroyed in a fire set in the mosque by a crazed Australian fundamentalist Christian.[85]

CRUSADERS AND SARACENS *RECIDIVUS*

It is probably fair to say that the contrast between the reprehensible actions of the Crusaders during their conquest of Jerusalem in 1099 CE and the comparatively graceful behavior of Saladin during his victorious recapture of the city in 1187 CE is still very much alive in the memories of many Middle Eastern Moslems. Certainly, these events are still invoked today by Moslem fundamentalists such as Osama bin Laden.

With Saladin as a model, Osama bin Laden has, by his lights, been engaged in a jihad, using the same definition of "aggressive defense" first formulated eight hundred years ago by al-Sulami and al-Ghazzali. While *jihad* does have a multitude of definitions, including pacifistic meanings such as "spiritual, inward-looking devotion,"[86] under al-Sulami's definition, a jihad is not merely a defensive action but involves active aggression in combating perceived threats to Islam anywhere in the world. It is a duty to be undertaken by all Moslems.

Indeed, in an interview with CNN in 1997—one of his earliest public statements after issuing his 1996 religious ruling *(fatwa)*—bin Laden said, "In our religion it is our duty to make jihad so that God's word is the one exalted to the heights and so that we drive the Americans away from all Moslem countries."[87] Others have embraced a similar definition, so that as recently as March 2003, the Islamic Research Academy at Cairo's Al-Azhar University, the preeminent seat of Sunni Moslem learning in the Arab world, declared, "According to Islamic law, if the enemy steps on Moslems' land, jihad becomes a duty on every male and female Moslem." Moreover, the academy called upon "Arabs and Moslems throughout the world to be ready to defend themselves and their faith."[88]

It has also become obvious that Osama bin Laden's use of the term *Crusaders* is deliberate in the extreme; he has been calling the Americans "Crusaders" ever since his first fatwa, issued in 1996. By so labeling the Israelis and the American forces in Saudi Arabia and elsewhere in the Middle East, he—like Saladin—could use al-Sulami's twelfth-century CE definition of a jihad as a "just war" to be fought against Western Crusaders. Thus, on February 23, 1998, bin Laden and his World Islamic Front issued a second fatwa. This time it was entitled "Declaration of the World Islamic Front for Jihad against the Jews and the Crusaders." In this fatwa, bin Laden said:

> The ruling to kill the Americans and their allies—civilians and military—is an individual duty for every Moslem who can do it in any country in which it is possible to do it, in order to liberate the al-Aqsa Mosque and the holy mosque [Mecca] from their grip, and in order for their armies to move out of all the lands of Islam, defeated and unable to threaten any Moslem. This is in accordance with the words of Almighty God . . .[89]

Bin Laden's message remained constant in the ensuing years. He continued to use the term *Crusader*, deliberately evoking an image of Crusader brutality and thereby invoking an immediate reaction of fear and hatred in many Moslems. A few weeks after the attacks on the World Trade Center in New York and on the Pentagon on September 11, 2001, bin Laden said: "The new Jewish crusader campaign is led by the biggest Crusader Bush under the banner of the Cross. This battle is considered one of the battles of Islam . . ."[90] On December 27, 2001, he said: "It has become clear that the West in general—led by America—bears an unspeakable crusader grudge against Islam." He continued, "[This is] the most dangerous, fiercest, and most savage Crusade war launched against Islam."[91] Additional statements along the same lines were made in 2002 and in the first months of 2003. Finally, in February 2003, on the eve of the Second Gulf War, bin Laden said:

We are following with utmost concern the Crusaders' preparations to occupy the former capital of Islam [Baghdad], loot the fortunes of the Moslems and install a puppet regime on you that follows its masters in Washington and Tel Aviv like the rest of the treacherous puppet Arab governments as a prelude to the formation of Greater Israel.[92]

However, even taking into account the recent photographs from Abu Ghraib prison in Iraq, bin Laden's comparison of American actions in the Middle East with the historical reality of the Crusaders' behavior in capturing Jerusalem is distorted and an exaggeration.

SALADIN IN THE MODERN WORLD

Osama bin Laden is not the only modern Arab leader to seek to emulate or to compare himself to Saladin. In this category are also Gamal Abdel Nasser of Egypt, Hafez Assad of Syria, Yasser Arafat of Palestine, and, most ironically, Saddam Hussein of Iraq. (The last habitually neglects to mention that Saladin was a Kurd.)[93]

President Nasser of Egypt reportedly compared his 1956 struggle against the combined forces of Britain, France, and Israel to that of Saladin's struggle against the forces of the Third Crusade (which also included English and French soldiers, but no Israelis).[94] In 1993, President Assad of Syria unveiled a bronze equestrian statue of Saladin, surrounded by captured Crusader leaders in chains. The monument is surrounded by pictures of Assad, with writings proclaiming loyalty to the descendant of Saladin.[95] Journalist Amy Dockser Marcus painted the following picture of Assad in an October 1996 article published in the *Wall Street Journal.*

> Take Syria's President Hafez Assad. He likes to seat foreign visitors in front of an ancient mosaic he had restored and installed in a reception room in his palace. The archaeological find portrays the 1187 battle when Salah al Din—who once ruled from his Imperial seat in ancient Syria—defeated the Christian armies of the Crusaders, forcing their retreat from the Holy Land. In speeches, Mr. Assad frequently cites the example of Salah al Din as support for the hard-line approach he has taken in his dealings with the Israelis, who he views as latter-day Crusaders.[96]

As for Yasser Arafat, in November 2000, journalist Yossi Klein Halevi wrote in the *Los Angeles Times,* "In the West Bank city of Nablus, I saw a massive street banner depicting Arafat riding a white steed and clutching a sword, a modern Saladin on his way to Jerusalem."[97] Ehud Barak, the former prime minister of Israel, stated in an interview with revisionist historian Benny Morris in 2002, "Arafat sees himself as a reborn Saladin—the Kurdish Moslem general who defeated the Crusaders in the twelfth century—and Israel as just another, ephemeral Crusader state."[98] Indeed, the very fact that the Crusader kingdoms in the Holy Land were so ephemeral is an important strand in the thinking of those in the Arab world who hope that the state of Israel will be similarly short-lived.

With regard to Saddam Hussein, Dr. Ofra Bengio, a senior research fellow at the Moshe Dayan Center for Middle Eastern and African Studies at Tel Aviv University, has pointed out that a colloquium on Saladin was held at Tikrit in July 1987 with the title "The Battle of Liberation—from Saladin to Saddam Hussein." That same year, Bengio notes, a Baghdad publisher produced a children's book entitled *The Hero Saladin.* The cover showed a picture of Saddam Hussein, with sword-wielding horsemen in the background. After a brief account of Saladin's life, emphasizing his reconquest of Jerusalem, the rest of the booklet focused on Saddam Hussein, whom it called "the noble and heroic Arab fighter Saladin II Saddam Hussein," consistently referring to him thereafter as "Saladin II."[99] In addition, at least one of Saddam Hussein's opulent palaces in the Mansour area of Baghdad still featured massive bronze busts of Saddam and Saladin on opposite corners of the building just before the outbreak of the Second Gulf War in 2003.[100]

Saladin's appeal to modern Moslem leaders is not surprising. He represents one of the few successful attempts by Islamic forces to defeat and expel unwanted Westerners from the Middle East during the past millennium. Along with Neo-Assyrian and Neo-Babylonian leaders whose armies conquered the ancient Near East and Egypt in the first millennium BCE, Saladin represents an additional—and much more recent—model for modern Moslem political and military leaders. "It's not that the Middle East's leaders are suddenly big believers in the Bible or avid readers of history books," says Efraim Karsh, a professor at King's College at the University of London and author of a political biography of Saddam Hussein. "The obsession with the past," he says, "is geared toward reinforcing the modern foundations of power."[101]

Some of the more militant Moslem leaders may also be familiar with Saladin's vision of a united Islamic world stretching from the Indian Ocean to Europe. Ibn Shaddad, Saladin's biographer, reports that Saladin once said to him:

> My desire is that, once I have conquered the rest of the coast [the Frankish-Syrian coast and Tyre], I'll . . . then set sail to the islands of this sea [the Mediterranean], where I will follow the infidels and fight them until I die, or until no infidel is left on the face of this earth.[102]

It is therefore perhaps not surprising that bin Laden's communiqué in February 2003 included the following statement:

> True Moslems should act, incite and mobilize . . . in order to break free from the slavery of these tyrannic and apostate regimes, which is enslaved by America, in order to establish the rule of

Allah on Earth. Among regions ready for liberation are Jordan, Morocco, Nigeria, the country of the two shrines [Saudi Arabia], Yemen and Pakistan.[103]

Clearly, bin Laden continues to embrace the idea of a world-wide jihad, similar to that envisioned by Saladin in the twelfth century CE and, previously, by Abu Bakr in the seventh century CE. The current worldwide agitation by Islamic militants, stretching from the Philippines and Indonesia to Egypt, the Middle East, Chechnya, Kashmir, India, Spain, and beyond, would seem to suggest that the world is now witnessing a third wave of jihad, a would-be successor to the early Islamic conquests and Saladin's reconquests.[104]

7

THE SULTAN AND THE CITY

IN NOVEMBER 1977, for the first time in modern history, the head of an Arab state visited Jerusalem and addressed the Knesset, the parliament of the nation of Israel. In a historic speech, President Anwar el-Sadat of Egypt spoke of the unique role of the holy city: "I have come to Jerusalem, the city of peace, which will always remain as a living embodiment of coexistence among believers of the three religions."[1] It was a tentative first step along what has been a long and difficult road toward peace between Arabs and Jews.

Less than one year later, along with Prime Minister Menachem Begin of Israel and President Jimmy Carter of the United States, Sadat signed the Camp David Peace Accords. In March 1979 Sadat signed the Egyptian-Israeli Peace Treaty. Jerusalem was deliberately mentioned only briefly—and just in passing—within the Camp David accords and not at all in the subsequent peace treaty, yet the Egyptian president may have had reservations about making any perceived concessions with respect to the Holy City, for he reportedly compared himself to an infamous figure in the Arab world, al-Malik al-Kamil, the nephew of Saladin who surrendered Jerusalem without a fight to Frederick II and the Crusaders in 1229 CE, as part of a peace treaty.[2]

Sadat's premonition that he would be vilified for his part in the diplomatic process turned out to be tragically accurate. On October 6,

1981, during a military review celebrating the Suez crossing by Egyptian troops in 1973, Islamic fundamentalists assassinated the Egyptian president. To understand fully the comparison and the degree of hostility in much of the Arab world occasioned by the actions alike of Sadat and al-Kamil, it is necessary to return to Jerusalem just after its recapture by Saladin and his Moslem forces in 1187 CE.

SALADIN AND JERUSALEM DURING THE THIRD CRUSADE

In the thirteen-hundred-year span from 638 CE to 1917 CE, Westerners controlled Jerusalem for less than a century. In 1187 CE, Moslem forces under Saladin had wrested control of the city from the Crusaders. Four years later, in 1191 CE, Saladin began to refortify the city.

The need was clear. The loss of the Holy City had sparked a new wave of Crusader activity. In 1189 CE, Emperor Frederick Barbarossa had set out at the head of a German Crusade. By August 1189 the Franks, led by Guy of Lusignan, the former king of Jerusalem, had the coastal city of Acre (near modern-day Haifa) under siege, and other Crusader contingents had begun to arrive at Tyre, in what is now modern Lebanon. Barbarossa's Crusade collapsed when he fell off his horse and drowned during the march to the Holy Land. But he was not the last Crusader; in 1190 CE Philip Augustus, king of France, and Richard Coeur-de-Lion (Richard the Lionheart), king of England and the most inspirational Frankish war leader, had set off on a Crusade.

Meanwhile, the initially tiny force of Crusaders besieging Acre had been reinforced not only by the rest of the Frankish remnant already in the Holy Land but by soldiers from all over Christendom—including the leading Italian city-states, various Scandinavian countries, France and Germany. When first Phillip and then Richard arrived, the besieging army grew to some one hundred thousand. And they were almost all fighting men; this was a thoroughly military undertaking, determined to secure the Holy Land, to recover the True Cross, and to retake Jerusalem. The charismatic and arrogant Richard appointed himself leader of the Crusade, and after prodigies of valor and a huge loss of life on both sides, he forced the surrender of Acre on July 12, 1191—little more than a month after his arrival. He then, just a few weeks later, added to the evil reputation of the Crusaders among Moslems by slaughtering the surrendered survivors of the Acre garrison on the specious excuse that the large ransom he demanded for them—two hundred thousand dinars and the True Cross—had not been paid. Richard had probably decided it would be better if the prisoners were dead than a burden on his forces and a potential threat after being freed.[3]

Saladin, meanwhile, had not been idle as the new Crusade threat loomed. Correctly anticipating that Richard and the knights of the Third Crusade would be formidable and ruthless foes in their inevitable attempt to retake Jerusalem, he ordered the construction of a new, deeper moat and a new city wall, as well as the restoration of several defensive towers. Imad al-Din, the personal secretary to Nur al-Din and then Saladin, reports that two thousand Crusader captives were brought in specifically to be used in this project.

But, in fact, the Crusaders lost their chance to take Jerusalem. They had successes, taking the coastal area, and, indeed, they secured a notable victory over Saladin's much larger army at Arsuf. They began marching against Jerusalem twice, in December 1191 and June 1192. But their army was much diminished, and their leaders were much preoccupied with the division of the territorial spoils they had secured. And Richard, a consummate soldier, recognized that Saladin's preparations at Jerusalem and a "scorched-earth" policy of well and spring poisoning that had made the surrounding area a desert meant that a successful siege was impossible. Also, he wanted to get home: he was at odds with many of the other leaders, especially the leaders of the Syrian Franks, and he knew that his brother, John, left as regent in England, was rebelling and seeking his throne.[4]

The feared siege and assault by Richard therefore never materialized; he never got closer than the nearby peak of Nebi Samwil, from which he refused to look at Jerusalem, averting his eyes from the city that he could not capture. In September of 1192 CE, Richard and Saladin signed a three-year truce that permitted the Christians to retain control of the coastal region of Palestine and allowed them access to visit Jerusalem. Having in that limited sense successfully "regained" the city for the Crusaders, Richard sailed for England, only to be shipwrecked, imprisoned, and held for ransom by former Crusader leaders whom his arrogance had offended at Acre, before finally arriving home more than a year later.[5] While Richard was suffering the vicissitudes of his homeward journey, Saladin died in the year 1193 CE. Over the next sixty years, many different forces would rule in Jerusalem (see table 4, at the end of this chapter).

THE AYYUBIDS

Saladin's immediate successors were members of his own family, known as the Ayyubids. They soon divided among themselves the territories he had conquered;[6] they continued to contend with those Crusaders still remaining in the Middle East. The Ayyubid rulers of Jerusalem and the surrounding countryside had a brief respite from battles with the Franks when the Fourth Crusade targeted Constantinople rather than Syria-Palestine in 1204 CE.

By 1217 CE, however, the Fifth Crusade was underway, the Holy Land once again in the Crusaders' sights. Two years later, the rulers of Jerusalem, Saladin's brother al-Adil and nephew al-Muʾazzam, ordered the destruction of the defensive walls—even though they had finished rebuilding them just seven years earlier. They apparently believed that despite their defenses, there was a good chance of a Crusader victory, and they did not wish to hand over a fortified city. Other contested sites, including the fortress on Mount Tabor in the Jezreel Valley, near the ancient site of Megiddo (biblical Armageddon), were dismantled by the Ayyubids at the same time and for the same reason. Ironically, the Crusaders had in fact failed in their attempt to capture the Mount Tabor fortress, although it was one of the primary objectives of the Fifth Crusade.[7]

The tale of the deconstruction of the walls of Jerusalem is told by the thirteenth-century writer Ibn Wasil, who wrote: "[al-Muʾazzam] gathered the masons and sappers and undermined the walls and its towers, and destroyed them—except David's Tower, which he left." The historian Abu Shama reports:

> they began on the walls on the first day of Muharram and there occurred in the city an outcry like [that of] Judgment Day. Secluded women and girls, old men and women, and young men

and boys went out to the [Dome of the] Rock and the Aqsa and they cut their hair and ripped their clothing to such an extent that the Rock and the Aqsa mihrab were filled with hair.

The Moslem inhabitants then fled the city, scattering to Egypt, Syria, and elsewhere. Ibn Wasil says, "After these events, al-Malik al-Mu³azzam began to transfer the armories and weapons, and the like, and its (Jerusalem's) destruction was a hard blow to the Moslems and they sorrowed greatly."[8]

A BLOODLESS CONQUEST

Although the Ayyubids had quickly prepared for the loss of their city, the Crusaders did not attempt to capture Jerusalem until nearly a decade—and a new Crusade—later. In 1225 CE, the Holy Roman emperor, Frederick II Hohenstaufen, married Isabel of Brienne—the young queen of Jerusalem (although the city no longer came with the title)—and began preparations to lead the Sixth Crusade. Paradoxically, the pope excommunicated Frederick in 1227 CE, just before the latter departed for the Holy Land, in part because of delays in his departure and in part because of a falling-out over other matters.

Al-Mu³azzam, hearing of the Crusaders' plans to return, ordered the destruction of the few remaining defenses of Jerusalem sometime during 1227 or 1228 CE. It is likely that the demolition only involved the citadel, as the last remaining significant fortified structure in the city. And so Jerusalem was nearly defenseless when Frederick II and the Crusaders arrived in the Holy Land in early 1229 CE.[9]

Frederick soon began negotiating for the surrender of the city. When al-Mu³azzam died suddenly and his brother al-Kamil took his place, the stage was set for a negotiated peace. Ibn Wasil describes a situation in which the issues involved were remarkably similar to those that prevail today in the confrontation between the Israelis and the Palestinian Authority.

Then followed the negotiations between al-Malik al-Kamil and the Emperor of which the object had been fixed earlier when al-Kamil and the Emperor first met, before the death of al-Malik al-

Muʾazzam. The Frankish King refused to return home except on the conditions laid down, which included the surrender of Jerusalem and of part of the area conquered by Saladin, whereas al-Malik al-Kamil was by no means prepared to yield him these territories. It was finally agreed that he should have Jerusalem on condition that he did not attempt to rebuild the walls, that nothing outside it should be held by the Franks, and that all the other villages within its province should be Moslem, with a Moslem governor resident at al-Bira, actually in the province of Jerusalem. The sacred precincts of the city, with the Dome of the Rock and the Masjid al-Aqsa were to remain in Moslem hands, and the Franks were simply to have the right to visit them, while their administration remained in the hands of those already employed in it, and Moslem worship was to continue there.[10]

This was one of the few times in the history of Jerusalem that the city changed hands without bloodshed. Al-Kamil and Frederick II signed the Treaty of Jaffa on February 18, 1229 CE. The treaty created a truce between Christians and Moslems that lasted for more than ten years. Under its terms, Jerusalem was effectively ceded to the Holy Roman emperor, Frederick II. The Crusaders controlled all of Jerusalem, except for the Temple Mount/Haram al-Sherif, which remained in Moslem hands with the proviso that the Crusaders were to be permitted to visit the site.[11]

The Crusaders understandably considered the treaty and the acquisition of Jerusalem as a great victory. For Moslems across the Middle East, however, it was considered a disaster, and Sultan al-Kamil was reviled as a traitor in many parts of the Islamic world.[12] Ibn Wasil wrote:

> After the truce the Sultan sent out a proclamation that the Moslems were to leave Jerusalem and hand it over to the Franks. The Moslems left amid cries and groans and lamentations. The news spread swiftly throughout the Moslem world, which lamented the loss of Jerusalem and disapproved strongly of al-Malik al-Kamil's action as a most dishonourable deed, for the reconquest of that noble city and its recovery from the hand of

the infidel had been one of al-Malik an-Nasir Saladin's most notable achievements—God sanctify his spirit!—But al-Malik al-Kamil of noble memory knew that the Moslems could not defend themselves in an unprotected Jerusalem, and that when he had achieved his aim and had the situation well in hand he could purify Jerusalem of the Franks and chase them out.[13]

The fifteenth-century CE Egyptian historian al-Maqrizi tells a similar story, concluding, "When the rulers had thus agreed, a truce was concluded between them for a period of ten years, five months, and forty days, commencing on the twenty-eighth of Rabi° al-Awwal of this year of 626 [February 24, 1229]."[14]

Because Jerusalem has changed hands without bloodshed so rarely in history, this event has prompted considerable discussion among historians. Some have argued that the truce that al-Kamil engineered was a good tactical decision. He himself explained:

We have only . . . conceded to them [the Crusaders] some churches and some ruined houses. The sacred precincts, the venerated Rock and all the other sanctuaries to which we make our pilgrimages remain ours as they were; Moslem rites continue to flourish as they did before, and the Moslems have their own governor of the rural provinces and districts.[15]

Al-Kamil told his fellow Moslems that the treaty was advantageous since it swapped Jerusalem for assurances that Egypt would not be attacked. Moreover, a city as defenseless as Jerusalem could easily be retaken at any time. As if in fulfillment of his predictions, shortly after the treaty was signed, Moslems from Hebron and Nablus attacked the city, forcing the inhabitants to take refuge in the Tower of David until Crusader forces from Acre came to their aid.[16] Indeed, disunity among Moslem factions may have inhibited al-Kamil's ability to mount a strong defense in the first place, and some scholars have suggested that he simply needed Crusader military support against his Moslem rivals more than he needed to retain control of Jerusalem.[17]

There were those in the Christian world who were not happy with the manner in which the Sixth Crusade had played out. In particular, the pope refused to acknowledge Frederick's treaty with al-Kamil, in part because of distaste for a bloodless victory and suspicions about a negotiated settlement and in part because the excommunicated Frederick could not be considered a true representative of the church. Lack of papal support notwithstanding, Frederick entered Jerusalem on March 17, 1229 CE, and had himself crowned king of Jerusalem. But his glory was short-lived. He left the country less than six weeks later, disgusted by the lack of support from the church and its military orders, including the Templars and the Hospitallers.[18] Perhaps the lesson to be drawn from this episode is that truce negotiators in the context of Jerusalem, then as now, are frequently reviled by the more extreme elements of their respective sides.

AYYUBID CONQUESTS AND QUARRELS

Al-Kamil died in 1238 CE (AH 635). During the ensuing quarrels between rival Ayyubid rulers over territory in Egypt, Palestine, and Syria, the Ayyubid ruler of Kerak in Syria invaded the region of Palestine. His name was al-Nasir Daʾud, and he besieged Jerusalem in 1239 CE, either just before or just after the expiration of the treaty crafted by al-Kamil. He conquered the city relatively easily, since only the Tower of David remained as a defensive fortification. The Crusaders had been trying to repair the city's fortifications, but they had not completed the task when al-Nasir's forces appeared on the horizon. Ibn al-Furat, a famous Moslem chronicler of the times, reports:

> He [al-Nasir Daʾud] collected a huge army and brought it down against Jerusalem on Tuesday, the 17th of Jumada I of that same year (15 December 1239). The Franks had built up and fortified a tower there known as the Tower of David. Daʾud set up mangonels against it and pressed it hard until it was surrendered to him on Monday, the 8th of Jumada II (5 January 1240). So he took Jerusalem and set up in it a governor of his own.[19]

Al-Maqrizi, the fifteenth-century CE Egyptian historian, places the siege a little earlier in time and says that al-Nasir Daʾud took the main part of the city on December 7 and the Tower of David on December

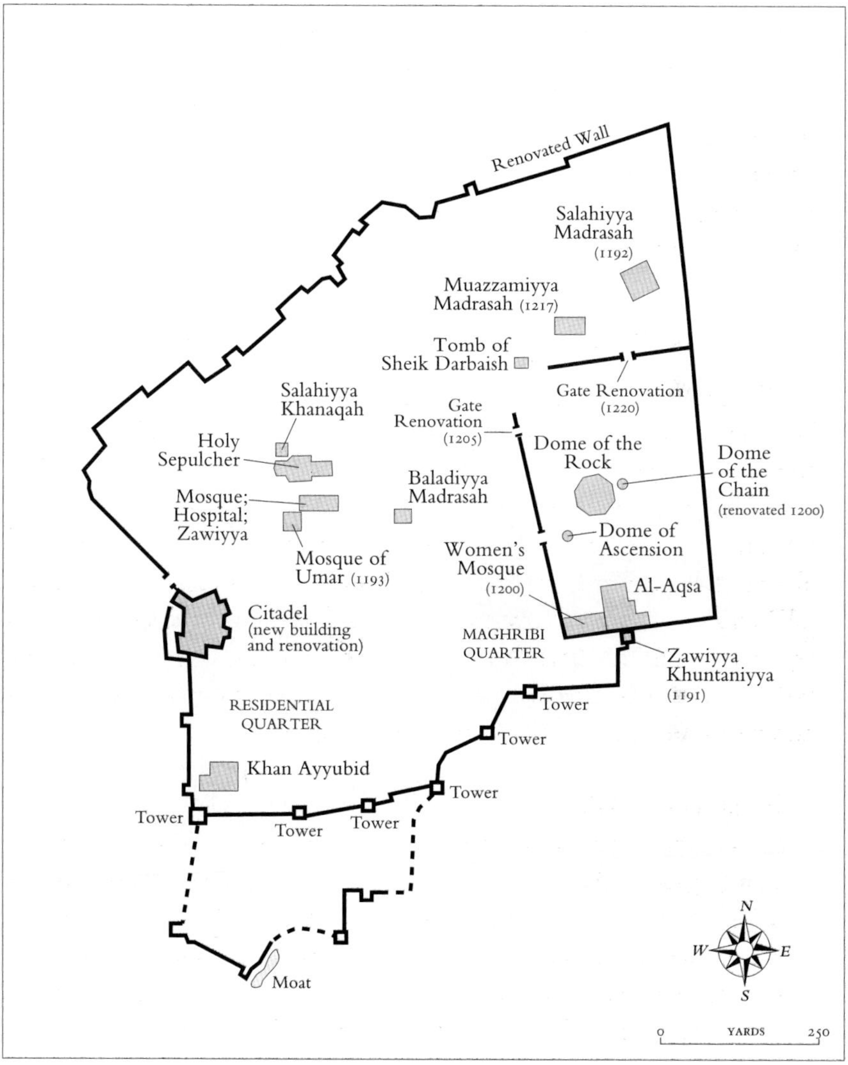
Renovated Wall
Salahiyya Madrasah (1192)
Muazzamiyya Madrasah (1217)
Tomb of Sheik Darbaish
Gate Renovation (1220)
Salahiyya Khanaqah
Gate Renovation (1205)
Holy Sepulcher
Dome of the Rock
Dome of the Chain (renovated 1200)
Baladiyya Madrasah
Mosque; Hospital; Zawiyya
Mosque of Umar (1193)
Dome of Ascension
Women's Mosque (1200)
Al-Aqsa
Citadel (new building and renovation)
MAGHRIBI QUARTER
Zawiyya Khuntaniyya (1191)
RESIDENTIAL QUARTER
Tower
Tower
Tower
Khan Ayyubid
Tower
Tower
Tower
Tower
Moat
N
W
E
S
0
YARDS
250

Map 18. The Islamization of Jerusalem under the Ayyubids, 1187–1250 CE

Fig. 9. The entrance to the citadel. (Painting by David Roberts, Esq., R.A.)

15, 1239 CE. He reports that the siege took twenty-one days in all, and he states: "The Franks were granted their lives, but not their properties. Al-Nasir destroyed David's Tower, took possession of Jerusalem, and drove out the Franks, who returned to their country."[20]

Although the Crusaders were forced to evacuate the city once again, they were almost immediately the beneficiaries of quarrels between rival Ayyubids—the rulers of Kerak, Damascus, Homs, and Egypt.

> Jerusalem remained in his [al-Nasir Daʾud's] possession until he made an arrangement with . . . the ruler of Damascus . . . and . . . the ruler of Homs, to make peace with the Franks in order to persuade them to help them to fight against . . . the ruler of Egypt. These kings gave the Franks Safad (Saphet), al-Shaqif (Beaufort) and Jerusalem, and the Franks entered Jerusalem, raised the Cross on the Rock and drove out the Moslems who lived by the shrine to Hebron.[21]

Thus, as part of an agreement to help al-Nasir Daʾud and his allies from Damascus and Homs in their civil war against al-Malik al-Salih Ayyub of Egypt, the Crusaders, under the leadership of Theobald (or Thibaut) of Navarre and Champagne, returned to rule Jerusalem yet again, perhaps as soon as 1241 CE and certainly by 1243 CE. This time, the Crusaders also regained control of the Temple Mount. Al-Maqrizi, the Egyptian historian, complains that they "set wine bottles on the Rock" and "hung bells in the al-Aqsa mosque."[22]

The new agreement allowing the Crusaders to return to Jerusalem was bitterly denounced in much of the Moslem world. In many respects, the reaction was a replay of that of twelve years earlier, when al-Kamil handed the city to the Crusaders. It was also a dress rehearsal for the response to Anwar Sadat's visit to the Israeli Knesset some 730 years later. In any event, the Crusaders retained control of Jerusalem only briefly, for in 1244 CE a new set of Islamic warriors invaded the Levant.

ENTER THE KHWARIZMIAN WARRIORS

Ibn al-Furat, the chronicler, wrote:

Jerusalem remained in their [Crusader] hands until the Khwarizmians came to Syria in the year 641 [1243–44] after having made an agreement with al-Malik al-Salih, the ruler of Egypt, and they attacked Jerusalem and killed those of the Franks who were in it, cleansing the Rock of their filth. That was in the year 642 [1244–45].[23]

The Khwarizmians are better known to the Western world as the Tatars. Originally from the steppes of central Asia, they had been driven westward into the area of modern-day Turkey by the Mongols under Genghis Khan. They had embraced Islam when they encountered the faith in their journeys westward. They were a warlike people and soon pushed outward from their base in Anatolia.[24]

The Egyptian Ayyubid ruler, al-Malik al-Salih Ayyub, formed an alliance with these Khwarizmian invaders and sent them against his opponents, including the Crusaders in Jerusalem and the Ayyubid rulers in Kerak, Damascus, and Homs in Syria.[25] Ibn al-Furat provides an account of the invasion and destruction.

Al-Malik al-Salih Najm al-Din Ayyub, the ruler of Egypt, sent a message to the Khwarizmians, inviting them to Egypt. They set out from the east with the intention of entering his service and they crossed the Euphrates at the start of this year. Their leaders were the emir Husam al-Din Baraka Khan, Khan Bardi, Sarukhan and Kushlukhan, and their army numbered more than ten thousand riders.[26]

According to this account, the Khwarizmians divided their force of ten thousand men into two parts, both of which headed into Syria— one toward Baalbek and the other toward Damascus. En route, they "sacked and ravaged every place they passed, killing and taking prisoners." The Ayyubid rulers of Damascus, Kerak, and Homs cut short their southern campaigns against the Egyptians and returned to their own cities to confront this new menace. Meanwhile, many of the Crusaders in Jerusalem "took to flight." Those who fled—about three hundred in all—were probably wise, for when the Khwarizmians arrived at Jerusalem on July 11, 1244 CE, most of the unfortified city fell almost immediately. Only the defenders who sought refuge in the Tower of David were able to hold out, until August 23, 1244 CE, when even they were killed or taken captive. Ibn al-Furat reports:

> The Khwarizmians then attacked Jerusalem and put the Christians there to the sword, may God curse them. Not a man was spared and women and children were taken as captives. They entered the chief Christian church known as Qumama (Holy Sepulcher) and destroyed the tomb which the Christians believe to be that of the Messiah, and they ransacked its Christian and Frankish graves, and the royal graves that it contains, burning the bones of the dead. Thus they brought healing relief to the hearts of a believing people, may God Almighty give them the best of rewards on behalf of Islam and, of its people.[27]

The Khwarizmians killed as many as six thousand Crusaders during their conquest of Jerusalem. As Ibn al-Furat notes, they burned the churches, pillaged the houses, and dug up the bones of dead Christians. Afterward they purified the Haram al-Sherif and other Moslem shrines. The Khwarizmians then continued on to Gaza, where they sent word to the Egyptian sultan, asking for Egyptian reinforcements to help them destroy his Ayyubid rivals in Damascus, Homs, and Kerak.

In October 1244 CE, the rival Ayyubid contingents met in a great battle at Gaza, where the Khwarizmian and Egyptian armies defeated the combined Moslem and Crusader forces from Damascus, Homs, and Acre. A few surviving Crusaders fled to Jerusalem after the battle. The Khwarizmians followed and again besieged the Crusaders in the Tower of David, "until they took and killed them." Subsequently, al-Malik al-Salih Ayyub of Egypt appointed a governor in Jerusalem and gave its lands to the Khwarizmians. The Crusaders never returned, and Christians would not again govern in Jerusalem until the arrival of the British during World War I, nearly seven hundred years later.[28]

Ibn al-Furat tells us, however, that the Khwarizmians "continued to follow a course of wanton destruction" until they were finally defeated by the ruler of Aleppo in the territory of Homs in Syria in 1246–47 CE. A small number of Khwarizmian survivors returned to Jerusalem and seized control of it from their former allies, the Egyptians, but immedi-

ately, according to Ibn al-Furat, "an army came out to them from Egypt
... and, after annihilating this remnant, they [the Egyptians] recovered
Jerusalem."[29]

CHAOS REIGNS

The situation in Jerusalem in the mid-thirteenth century CE continued to be unstable. Al-Nasir Daʾud of Kerak took the city from the
Egyptians in the year AH 644 (1246–47 CE), but Egyptian forces
recaptured the city one year later. However, the Egyptian sultan died
soon thereafter, and his son, Turanshah, was murdered in 1250 CE by
his own rebellious Mamlukes—the slave-soldiers so favored by the
Egyptian sultans of the thirteenth century. The Mamlukes were almost
all of Turkish origin, having been bought and brought to Egypt as children. They were greatly feared as formidable and usually fiercely loyal
warriors, who frequently served as the sultan's bodyguard. Once they
had overthrown their Egyptian masters, the Mamlukes took over Egypt
and ruled much of the Middle East for the next 250 years, though they
did not always control Jerusalem (see table 4).[30]

Meanwhile, the Ayyubid ruler of Aleppo and Damascus, al-Malik
al-Nasir Yusuf, captured Jerusalem sometime between 1248 CE and
1250 CE. He offered the city once again to the Crusaders—now led by
Louis IX, king of France—in exchange for an alliance against the
Mamlukes, but his offer was rejected. Two years later, in 1253 CE, al-
Nasir Yusuf returned Jerusalem and all of Palestine west of the Jordan
River to the Mamluke sultan of Egypt, only to take it back again by
force in the following year, 1254 CE.[31] Ibn al-Furat gives a condensed
version of these rapid—and chaotic—events.

> After this, al-Malik al-Nasir Daʾud, the ruler of Kerak, marched
> there from Kerak and took it in the latter part of the year 644
> (1246–7). It was then recovered by al-Malik al-Salih [Ayyub, of
> Egypt] in the year 645 (1247–8). It remained in his hands and in
> those of his son al-Malik al-Muʾazzam Turanshah after him. Next
> ... the ruler of Aleppo, took control of Damascus, Jordan and
> Palestine, and he held Jerusalem until he made peace with ... the
> ruler of Egypt, for whom he evacuated the city in the year 651

(1253–4). . . . [Then] in the year 652 (16 September–14 October 1254), when al-Malik al-Salih's Bahri [M]amlukes left Egypt to go to al-Malik al-Nasir (Yusuf), the ruler of Damascus, to seek for his help, the latter sent an army to Jerusalem which recovered it.[32]

Thus, as a consequence of Ayyubid rivalries and civil wars, the city of Jerusalem had become a pawn in the larger game of intra-Moslem politics, bouncing like a ball among the various polities of the day. It changed hands fully ten times in the sixteen years from 1239 to 1254 CE.

THE MONGOLS ARRIVE

Jerusalem next passed into the hands of the Mongols, when, in their westward incursions from the steppes of central Asia, they reached the area of Syria and Palestine in 1260 CE. In March and April of 1260 CE, the Mongol leader, Kitbuqa, sent a small reconnaissance force far ahead of his main army. While the rest of the Mongol troops remained north of Damascus, this force, looting and pillaging as it advanced, reached as far south as Gaza. The raiders struck at Jerusalem and the cities of Hebron, Ascalon, and Nablus. Abu Shama, a writer and legal scholar in Damascus at the time of the Mongol invasion, says: "As is customary with them [the Mongols], they killed the men and captured the children and women. They brought back a large amount of prisoners and loot, that included cows, sheep and plunder, and they arrived in Damascus with this."[33]

Ibn al-Furat reports: "when the [Mongols] conquered the lands, they entered Jerusalem and killed some people there. They continued to hold the city until their defeat at ᶜAyn Jalut [in the Jezreel Valley]."[34] His testimony was based on an account originally written by Ibn Shaddad al-Halabi, who is known for his biography of the Mamluke sultan Baibars and who wrote: "When the Mongols gained control over the country, they entered [Jerusalem] and killed people. It remained in their hands until [Qutuz] defeated them at ᶜAyn Jalut." Similarly, Ibn Wasil said: "As for the Mongols who went to Nablus and did what they did, they reached as afar as Gaza. They entered Jerusalem and enslaved and looted."[35]

The Mamluke rulers of Egypt and the Levant reacted quickly, defeating the Mongols at the battle of ᶜAyn Jalut in the Jezreel Valley, near the ancient mound of Megiddo, on September 3, 1260 CE. Even so, seven years after the Mongol raid into southern Palestine, Jerusalem and the surrounding country still remained a wasteland. A Jewish rabbi named Nachmanides (Rambam to his followers) arrived from Spain and described the devastation he found in the land: "And what can I say about the country? Much of it is deserted; the desolation is overwhelming. . . . Jerusalem is more devastated than all else."[36]

Although the Mongols were never again a serious threat to Palestine or Egypt, they did stage one more raid that reached Jerusalem. This occurred nearly forty years later, in 1300 CE, just after the last of the Crusaders had finally been evicted from the Holy Land in 1291 CE.[37] Kutubi, a writer nearly contemporaneous with the events he describes, says that a Mongol officer named Bulay (or Mulay) came raiding with ten thousand horsemen.

> They looted property and [took] booty and prisoners, in such amounts that only God could count it. With his army he fell upon the region of Gaza, the Jordan River Valley and Jerusalem (bayt al-maqdis). . . . Bulay came [to Damascus], and with him his army, from the Jordan River valley, Gaza, Ramla, and Jerusalem (al-quds). With him was an extremely large number of prisoners.[38]

Baybars al-Mansuri, a Mamluke emir who had been dispatched with two hundred horsemen to guard against just such a Mongol raid, corroborated Kutubi's account. He says that there were not ten thousand but twenty thousand Mongols involved and that they "fell upon the Jordan River Valley and Baysan." His report continues: "They wreaked havoc and raided that country. They looted what they found of livestock, supplies and equipment and they killed whoever fell into their hands. Their raids reached Jerusalem and Hebron, and they got as far as Gaza . . ." Another chronicler—Ibn Abiᵓl-Fadaᵓil, an Egyptian Christian author—later noted that when the Mongols reached Jerusalem in 1300 CE, they "killed both Moslems and Christians, drank wine on [the] Haram el-Sharif and took young women and children [as captives]. They did despicable deeds, destroyed, killed, looted and captured children and women."[39]

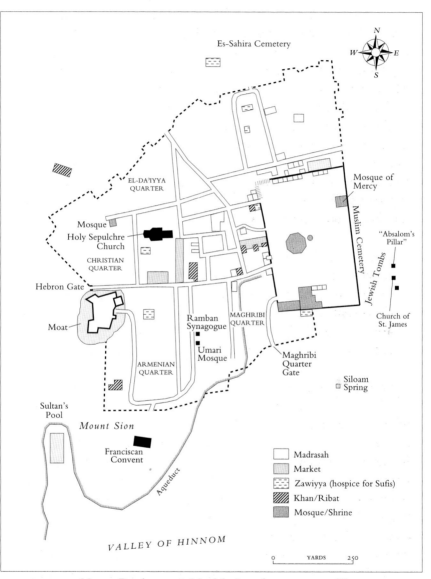

Map 19. Development in Mamluke Jerusalem, 1250–1517 CE

Es-Sahira Cemetery

N
W — E
S

EL-DAʾIYYA
QUARTER

Mosque of
Mercy

Mosque
Holy Sepulchre
Church
CHRISTIAN
QUARTER

Muslim Cemetery

"Absalom's
Pillar"

Jewish Tombs

Hebron Gate

Moat

Ramban
Synagogue

MAGHRIBI
QUARTER

Church of
St. James

Umari
Mosque

ARMENIAN
QUARTER

Maghribi
Quarter
Gate

Siloam
Spring

Sultan's
Pool

Mount Sion

Franciscan
Convent

Aqueduct

Madrasah
Market
Zawiyya (hospice for Sufis)
Khan/Ribat
Mosque/Shrine

VALLEY OF HINNOM

0   YARDS   250

Following the Mongol raid of 1300 CE, the Mamlukes ruled Jerusalem until the coming of the Ottomans under Sultan Selim I in December 1516 CE. During the Mamluke years, Jerusalem was left unfortified, with the exception of the citadel, which was rebuilt in 1310 CE. The city's population was smaller than at most times in its earlier history. Nevertheless, it continued to function as an important religious center, and there were several additional constructions on and around the Haram al-Sherif.[40]

During these centuries, Jerusalem was also a center for scholars and for exiled members of the Egyptian (Mamluke) military aristocracy. Over the years, according to Mamluke official records, "hundreds if not thousands of discharged officers" settled in Jerusalem. Among them were ex-prisoners whose sentences had been commuted. Why the city became a favored place of exile during the Mamluke period is not clear, but certainly the incoming emigrants enhanced and increased the small local population.[41]

The last of the Crusaders had been expelled from Acre in 1291 CE, and the centuries of Mamluke rule are usually described as relatively peaceful for Jerusalem.[42] There were, however, a number of Bedouin raids. In 1348 CE the city was attacked and the inhabitants were driven out.[43] In 1461 CE sixty people were killed by Bedouins just outside the city.[44] In 1480 CE Bedouins from the tribe of Banu Zayd attacked the city in broad daylight because they were angry that the governor of Jerusalem had executed some of their relatives. The governor managed to escape, but the markets and mosques of the city were looted, and a number of prisoners were set free. Warfare between the nomadic Bedouins and city inhabitants was not limited to Jerusalem during this period; Hebron, Ramla, and other cities in Palestine were also attacked.[45]

THE OTTOMANS ARRIVE

After nearly three centuries of Mamluke rule, Sultan Selim I and his Ottoman army captured Jerusalem in December 1516 CE. The Ottomans were a dynasty of Turkish Moslems named for their founder

Osman (or Othman). He had established a small kingdom in Asia Minor, in what is now modern Turkey, during the mid-thirteenth century CE. While the Mamlukes were expanding from Egypt into Palestine, the Ottomans had been seizing territories in Europe and Asia. They captured Constantinople in 1453 CE and thenceforth called this city Istanbul (roughly translated as "in the city")—although the official name was not changed until 1930, nearly five hundred years later. By the time Selim I came to the throne in Istanbul in 1512 CE, the Ottomans were already a major power in the area. The young sultan quickly expanded his empire in new directions, primarily to the east and south. In so doing, he came into conflict with the Safavid dynasty in the area of modern Iran and the Mamlukes in Egypt and Syria. The sultan and his forces triumphed. With the ensuing shift in the balance of power, the Ottoman Empire rapidly spread until it covered much of the Middle East.[46]

The major battle between the Ottomans and the Mamlukes was fought in August 1516, far to the north of Jerusalem, near the city of Aleppo in Syria. The Ottoman victory opened up all of Palestine to the sultan's victorious army, so that he was able to march all the way to Cairo, facing only minor resistance. The Ottomans were able to take Jerusalem without a fight. The sultan entered the city in December 1516 CE.[47] The Ottoman traveler Evliya Chelebi (or Tshelebi) noted:

> all the ʿulema [religious scholars] and pious men went out to meet Selim Shah in A.H. 922 [1516 CE]. They handed him the keys to the Mosque el-Aqsa and the Dome of the Rock of Allah. Selim prostrated himself and exclaimed: "Thanks be to Allah! I am now the possessor of the (Sanctuary of the) first qibla." He then made presents to all the notable people, exempted them from onerous taxes and confirmed them [in their posts].[48]

EARLY OTTOMAN JERUSALEM

With Selim I's conquest, Jerusalem became an Ottoman city, and it remained so for the next four hundred years, until World War I. For most of the period, Jerusalem was an undistinguished provincial city within one of the *sanjaqs* (districts) that made up the larger province of

Damascus. Even its holy aura diminished to some extent during the years of Ottoman rule.[49]

Between the years 1537 and 1541 CE, Sultan Suleiman the Magnificent, son of Selim I, made an attempt to rebuild Jerusalem, so that it might recapture some of the glory it had enjoyed in the days of Saladin. He rebuilt the walls of the city, which had lain mostly in ruins for nearly three hundred years. Suleiman's constructions were primarily functional, insofar as they protected the inhabitants from Bedouin raiders and brought water to its populace, although his wife also authorized the opening of a charitable foundation complex and public soup kitchen within the city.[50] The walls and gates constructed during this period still define much of the Old City of Jerusalem today. The contemporary sixteenth-century CE Jewish chronicler Joseph Ha-Cohen wrote:

> God aroused the spirit of Suleiman, king of Rumelia and Persia, and he set out to build the walls of Jerusalem, the holy city in the land of Judah. And he sent officials who built its walls and set up its gates as in former times and its towers as in bygone days. And his fame spread throughout the land for he wrought a great deed. And they also extended the tunnel into the town lest the people thirst for water.[51]

Suleiman also refurbished the Haram al-Sherif, paying particular attention to the Dome of the Rock. He ordered new blue, green, brown, and black tiles from Iznik in Turkey to decorate its outer facade. As a result of Suleiman's investment in the city, its population began to grow once again. The new settlers were mostly Moslems and Christians, but they also included Jews who had been expelled from Spain in 1492 and who now found a new home in Jerusalem.[52]

It was still necessary to protect the city against Bedouin raiders and other hostile interlopers during these years, as well as to guard against potential threats from the West. Although no attacks from the West materialized during this period, there are reports of periodic attempts by Bedouins to scale the city walls, in some cases by using ropes under cover of darkness. A governor of Jerusalem, Abu Sayfayn, was attacked and killed by Bedouins in 1590 CE.[53] Another governor, Mohammed

Pasha, was overthrown in 1625 CE by a mercenary force led by "the most wicked and evil Mohammed ibn Faroukh, blind in one eye," as one contemporary Jewish eyewitness reported. The same eyewitness continued:

> [ibn Faroukh] entered Jerusalem with three hundred mercenary soldiers who proceeded to depose Mohammed Pasha. Immediately thereafter he set himself against us [the inhabitants of Jerusalem], and mercilessly tortured us and the Arab and Christian residents as well. Placing guards at the exits from the city, he ordered many [of us] to be brought bound and tortured before him so he could extort and confiscate their money. . . . For two years we were persecuted, harassed, and molested so that many fled the city . . .

Ottoman troops under the command of Hassan Pasha liberated the city in 1627/28 CE, but as the same contemporary observer said, "one cannot recount the property losses and personal sufferings endured during those abominable days."[54]

THE *NAQIB AL-ASHRAF* REBELLION

During the years of Ottoman rule, the local governors (who held the title *sanjaq-bey*) were sometimes more concerned with enriching themselves at the expense of Jerusalem's inhabitants than in just government. They imposed onerous taxes and were not above taking bribes. One such governor, Jurji Mohammed Pasha (or Georgi Mehmet Pasha), went so far in these practices that in 1703 CE the inhabitants rose up in what was perhaps the most interesting of the small rebellions that took place in Jerusalem during the Ottoman period. The *naqib al-ashraf* revolt, as it is called, was led by Mustafa al-Husseini, who was the *naqib* (head) of the Jerusalem *al-ashraf*—a prestigious and powerful group of families who were said to be sharifs, or direct descendants of the Prophet Mohammed. It was the first truly popular uprising to be staged against Ottoman rule in Palestine and reflected the lawless and chaotic state into which the area had descended after two centuries of continuous Ottoman presence.[55]

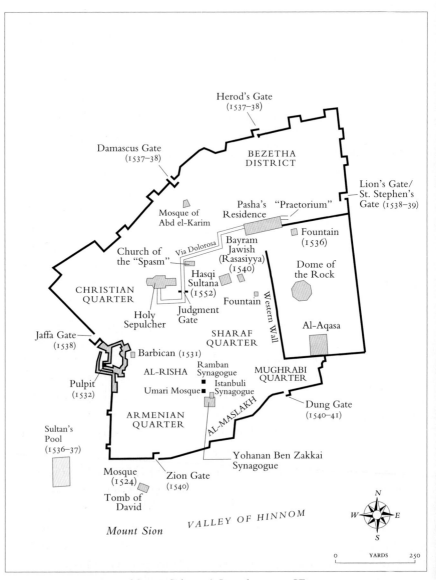

Map 20. Suleiman's Jerusalem, 1540 CE

Accounts of the rebellion come from several contemporary or nearly contemporary sources.[56] According to these accounts, the inhabitants of Jerusalem rebelled after two years of oppression by the governor. The religious judge (*qadi*) of Jerusalem may have aided the rebels. He was the brother-in-law of the Grand Mufti of Istanbul and was thus extremely well connected, although the Franciscan monks described him as a man "of little wisdom."[57]

In any event, on a Friday in May of 1703 CE, after prayers and a fiery sermon at the al-Aqsa Mosque by the qadi, who railed against the oppressions of the governor, armed rebels marched on the citadel. The governor, who was responsible for maintaining order in much of Palestine, was away on a military campaign subduing a rebellion in the region of Nablus. The qadi, whom the governor regarded as a pompous bore and a personal enemy, may well have taken advantage of the governor's absence to stage the coup. It is also possible that the rebels were pawns in a power struggle between the governor and the qadi, both of whom wished to extort money from the local populace.[58] Be that as it may, the rebels soon were in control of the entire city and immediately released from captivity all those who had been imprisoned by the governor.

In the face of the rebellion, the governor hastily fled the area. Mustafa al-Husseini, the naqib, took over as temporary leader and as "head of the city" of Jerusalem, apparently with the support of the qadi. The inhabitants of Jerusalem then proceeded to govern the city by and for themselves, and they apparently fought off several attempts by the exiled governor to regain the city.[59]

More than two years elapsed before the Ottoman administrators were able to turn their attention to the revolt in Jerusalem. They were occupied with another rebellion—the so-called *Edirne vakasi* (Edirne incident)—which occurred in the very heart of Istanbul itself and which resulted in the overthrow and replacing of the reigning sultan, Mustafa II, by his younger brother, Ahmed III. Many scholars agree that these major and minor revolts were the direct result of a change in the nature of Ottoman rule, which had deteriorated from a strong and centralized state in the sixteenth century CE to a weakened and ineffective administration characterized by greedy governors, rapacious tax collectors, and quarreling local leaders in the eighteenth century.[60]

Meanwhile, Mohammed Pasha, the former governor of Jerusalem, had apparently not been disgraced by his ignominious flight. Instead, he received a promotion to *wali* (provincial governor) of Damascus and *amir al-hajj* (leader of the caravan to Mecca), a position of high esteem.[61] Eventually, he appointed a man named Asnam Pasha to occupy his former position as local governor (*sanjaq-bey*) in Jerusalem. After an exchange of messages with the inhabitants of Jerusalem, Asnam Pasha was dispatched to retake the city. Accompanied by some two thousand Janissaries—elite Ottoman troops—he marched to the gates of the city in late October of 1704 CE.

The city's inhabitants, who had been busy strengthening the fortifications, now locked and barred the gates, refusing entry to the new governor. Lacking sufficient forces to take the city, Asnam Pasha and the Janissaries waited outside the walls for several weeks, correctly assuming that the inhabitants were ill prepared to survive a prolonged siege. Ultimately, a compromise was reached in which the inhabitants paid their outstanding taxes, the new governor appointed a deputy to represent him in the city, and the Ottoman troops remained outside the walls.[62]

However, events soon became more complicated. The sultan, in far-off Istanbul, appointed a new and different governor for Jerusalem. The new governor was an older man and was, perhaps surprisingly, welcomed by the rebels within the city, who saw him as no great threat. In the meantime, Mohammed Pasha, still the provincial governor of Damascus, decided to end the rebellion once and for all. He gathered together a larger army, appointed yet another governor for Jerusalem— a man named Mustafa Pasha—and sent an ultimatum to the rebels in Jerusalem, demanding that they surrender. He then marched on the city with twenty-two companies of Janissaries, probably totaling between twenty-two hundred and twenty-five hundred armed men, in late November of 1705 CE.[63]

As Mohammed Pasha and his armies were approaching Jerusalem, turmoil reigned inside the city. The naqib was engaged in a quarrel with the qadi. It has been suggested that the Ottomans secretly financed the opponents of the naqib in order to create internal dissension that would facilitate the retaking of the city.[64] Certainly, the defenders inside Jerusalem, instead of uniting to fight the common enemy, split into two armed camps and began fighting each other. Defender fought defender in bloody clashes that lasted for several days.[65]

When the Ottoman forces under Mohammed Pasha arrived outside the walls of Jerusalem, the naqib and other leaders of the revolt realized that their time was up. They fled under cover of darkness, leaving the city to those who welcomed the return of Ottoman rule. And so, on November 27, 1705 CE, Mohammad Pasha, Mustafa Pasha, and their Ottoman troops entered Jerusalem. Some accounts say that the city gates were wide open and that the Ottoman forces entered without a struggle. Other accounts say that the remaining rebels put up a stiff resistance before they were eventually defeated. In any event, the new Ottoman governor of Jerusalem quickly assumed his duties, and thereafter troops were stationed in the city on a regular basis to forestall further trouble. Mustafa al-Husseini, the naqib al-ashraf, was eventually arrested and sent to Istanbul and was executed in 1707 CE. He was twenty-five years old at the time.[66]

In the aftermath of the rebellion, the Ottoman authorities imposed even greater taxes and duties upon the population of Jerusalem. If the years of the rebellion had been difficult for the inhabitants of Jerusalem, the years immediately following its suppression were disastrous. Rabbi Gedaliah of Siemiatycze described the situation with the following words:

When the powerful Pasha entered the town at the head of a strong army, he plundered and destroyed, leaving no one untouched. As to the Jews, if he knew that one was a rich man, he caught him and forced him to ransom himself for a huge sum. His excuse to the Sultan was ready: they were rebels. And a new army came from the Sultan to live there and see to it that there would be no more rebellion. At this time many wealthy Sephardim fled Jerusalem and settled in other places.[67]

PALM SUNDAY, 1757 CE

Approximately half a century later, religious strife engulfed Jerusalem when the Greek Orthodox inhabitants rose up against the Catholic population on Palm Sunday in 1757 CE. The rioting reflected larger religious conflicts in Europe and the Ottoman Empire at the time. Since approximately 1740 CE, the French had been charged with protecting the rights of Catholics living within the territories of the Ottoman Empire. The Franciscans and other Catholic groups had been granted control of important religious shrines in and around Jerusalem, including the Church of the Holy Sepulcher, the Tomb of the Virgin, and half of Golgatha.[68]

For years, the Greek Orthodox community in Jerusalem had smarted under perceived injustices, and eventually their anger boiled over. Enraged Greek Orthodox rioters attacked the Basilica of the Resurrection, destroyed its lamps and vessels, and chased the Franciscan monks into the Church of St. Savior, which they promptly besieged. The Greek Orthodox patriarch Parthenios quickly traveled to Istanbul, to petition Sultan Uthman III. Although the Christian holy places in Jerusalem had been under control of the Catholics for nearly seventy years, since 1690 CE, the sultan ordered that the Greek Orthodox community should once again assume responsibility for their administration. His ruling still forms part of the basis for the situation in Jerusalem today, whereby individual denominations either control or share control of Christian holy sites around the city.[69]

NAPOLEON AND JERUSALEM

By the eighteenth century, the defenses of Jerusalem were in a dismal state. It was already known in the 1740s that none of the twenty-seven bronze cannon that defended the citadel of Jerusalem actually worked. Forty years later the Ottoman authorities were still ignoring requests for new cannon and ammunition.[70] By this point, the centuries-old constructions of Suleiman the Magnificent, including the walls around the Old City, had fallen into a sad state of disrepair. One European traveler described the city as it appeared in 1784 CE as follows:

> To see its destroyed walls, its debris-filled moat, its city circuit choked with ruins, you would scarcely recognize this famous metropolis which once fought against the most powerful empires in the world; which for a moment held even Rome at bay; and

which, by a bizarre twist of fate, gains honor and respect in its disgrace. In short, you would scarcely recognize Jerusalem.[71]

However, when Napoleon and the French army invaded Egypt in July 1798, the Ottoman officials in Damascus finally heeded the frantic requests for arms and ammunition and made an effort at refortifying the city. In Jerusalem itself, Moslems attacked—and took hostage—the Franciscan monks at the Church of St. Savior, releasing them only at the sultan's insistence.[72] The following year, Napoleon sent a portion of his force—some thirteen thousand French troops—north into the Holy Land, and he won decisive battles at el-Arish, Gaza, and Jaffa. It was the first successful invasion by Europeans since the time of the Crusaders.[73]

Napoleon issued a call for the Jews of Asia and Africa to join him in reestablishing ancient Jerusalem. The inhabitants of Jerusalem prepared to resist Napoleon and his forces, but the expected attack never materialized. Although some French troops did come within three miles of the city on March 2, 1799, Napoleon concentrated on capturing Jaffa and then (unsuccessfully) laid siege to Acre—which was both economically and militarily more important than Jerusalem at the time.[74] When asked by his traveling secretary why he did not wish to conquer a city as famous as Jerusalem, Napoleon reportedly replied: "Jerusalem is not in my line of operation. I do not wish to be annoyed by mountain people in difficult roads."[75] He thus joined with Alexander the Great as one of the few major conquerors or invaders of Syria-Palestine who did not enter Jerusalem.

Despite Napoleon's lack of enthusiasm for Jerusalem, the French incursion into the Holy Land marked the beginning of the reemergence of Western interest in the region. By the 1830s, international travelers, artists, archaeologists, and biblical scholars began to make the long trek to the area.[76]

THE NINETEENTH CENTURY

Several additional conflicts disturbed the city of Jerusalem in the time between Napoleon's withdrawal from the Holy Land in 1799 and the arrival of Western travelers a few decades later. In 1806 the Ottoman governor of Jaffa and Gaza, Mohammed Pasha Abu Maraq, illegally extended his rule to encompass Jerusalem. Rebels in the city took advantage of the situation and rose up against the local governor. Neither the smaller rebellion in Jerusalem nor the larger one of Abu Maraq lasted very long. By 1807 the general unrest had been quelled by the governor of Sidon, who also restored the exiled governor to his place in Jerusalem.[77]

In 1808 CE the Church of the Holy Sepulcher was destroyed by fire. The fire began in the western part of the church, which was under control of the Armenians, and quickly spread, gutting the building and collapsing the pillars supporting the dome. Recriminations began immediately, with the Armenians and the Greek Orthodox priests accusing each other of responsibility for the blaze. Eleven years elapsed before permission was granted to rebuild the church.[78]

No sooner had construction begun in 1819 CE than the local Moslems protested and attempted to prevent the rebuilding. Rioting began and quickly spread throughout the city. The rioters attacked the Greek Orthodox patriarchate and the men working on the Church of the Holy Sepulcher and then occupied the citadel. They besieged the house of the governor of Jerusalem and eventually forced him to flee from the city. In the end, the provincial governor (*wali*) of Damascus sent in troops to put down the rebellion. The Ottoman troops, led by an officer named Abu Dhari'a, besieged the citadel and forced the rebels to surrender. Abu Dhari'a personally decapitated forty-six of the ringleaders and sent their heads to Damascus, thus effectively ending the revolt.[79]

The Greek War of Independence from the Turks began two years later, in 1821. Its repercussions were felt throughout the Ottoman Empire. Jerusalem was not spared. The Ottoman administrators—suspicious of the religious minorities within their borders—forced the Christian inhabitants of Jerusalem to relinquish their weapons, to wear black, and to work on the city's fortifications. Soon thereafter, Jerusalem's Moslem population attacked the Greek Orthodox patriarchate once again. Peace was eventually restored when the Ottoman authorities stepped in, but violence threatened to flare again in 1823, when rumors reached the city of an impending attack by the Greek navy on the city of Beirut. When the attack did not materialize, calm temporarily returned to Jerusalem.[80]

Meanwhile, in 1822, a new provincial governor (wali) was appointed in Damascus. He had the same name as an earlier governor of Jerusalem—Mustafa Pasha. He soon authorized his agents to use force if necessary in collecting taxes, which he increased tenfold. Three years later, this resulted in a repetition of the antitax rebellion of 1703. According to the account of a Greek monk named Neophytos, the peasants living around Jerusalem rebelled first, but they were quickly suppressed by the wali and five thousand men. However, as soon as the wali's army returned to Damascus, the peasants rebelled again. This time, they were aided by the inhabitants, including the upper-class citizens, of Jerusalem proper. On June 5, 1825 CE, they attacked and captured the citadel, seized the stockpiled weapons, and expelled the garrison of soldiers. They also expelled all non-Arabs, including Albanians and Turks, from the city. They appointed two local army officers as their leaders, Yusuf Agha al-Ja°uni and Ahmad Agha al-Asali.[81]

The sultan in Istanbul, Mahmud II, heard news of the rebellion in 1826 CE and ordered it put down. He dispatched Abdullah Pasha, governor of Sidon, with two thousand men—and seven cannon, which were used to bombard Jerusalem from the Mount of Olives. Fierce fighting continued for a week or more, and both private houses and public buildings were hit indiscriminately by cannon fire. Eventually an agreement between the opposing forces was reached, but not until food had become scarce and loss of life inside the city had grown at an alarming rate. The rebels laid down their weapons, while the Ottomans, for their part, agreed to lower taxes, pardon those involved in the revolt, and order the army to refrain from interfering in the internal affairs of the city.[82]

But the Ottoman Empire was slowly disintegrating, and soon similar rebellions broke out in nearby Hebron and Nablus. Then, in November 1831 CE, an Egyptian army invaded the Levant. Mohammed Ali Pasha of Egypt, an Albanian Turk who had once fought with the Ottomans against Napoleon, decided that the time was ripe to wrest control of Palestine and Syria from the Ottomans. A large Egyptian army—estimates of its size range from forty thousand to ninety thousand men—under the command of his son, Ibrahim Pasha, made the long march from Egypt to Syria. En route, a small force of Egyptian soldiers entered and occupied Jerusalem on December 7. Despite the Ottoman sultan's exhortations to the Jerusalemites to rise up and resist the invaders, there was apparently little fuss or fighting in Jerusalem during the Egyptian takeover. The city of Acre, on the coast to the north, was destroyed during the same Egyptian invasion.[83]

It has been said that this invasion in the year 1831 CE marks a turning point in the history of modern Jerusalem. Under Egyptian rule, which lasted until 1840 CE, Christians and Jews in Jerusalem and elsewhere in the region enjoyed, for the first time, the same rights and privileges as their Moslem neighbors. During this period, the city was modernized in a number of other ways, and a new secularized judicial system was introduced.[84]

However, those ten years were not entirely peaceful. Beginning in May of 1834 CE, a major rebellion against the Egyptian authorities took place all across Palestine, including in Jerusalem. The so-called Peasants' Revolt was set into motion in part as a reaction to an Egyptian plan to conscript Palestinians into the Egyptian army, a move that was seen by the local chiefs and leading families as a way to strip them of any remaining power. The rebellion was also underwritten, to a certain extent, by the Ottoman authorities in Istanbul, who issued decrees encouraging the local inhabitants to overthrow the foreign invaders and expel them from the land.[85]

The rebels entered Jerusalem on May 31, reportedly through the Dung Gate (or, according to some, through the water tunnels, like in the story of Joab in David's capture of Jerusalem several millennia earlier). Trapping the Egyptian troops in the citadel, they took control of the city and held it for five short—but bloody—days. Shops were looted, houses destroyed, inhabitants raped and killed. Other uprisings engulfed the Galilee, the coastal region by Gaza, and the districts of Nablus and Hebron. Had these been coordinated, the rebels might have succeeded in driving the Egyptians out of Palestine. As it was, they failed to unite their efforts and were picked off one by one, as Mohammed Ali and the Egyptian army slowly brought each town, village, city, and area—Jerusalem, Safed, Haifa, Tiberias, Hebron, Nablus—back under their control over a period of months. Ibrahim

Pasha himself appeared at the head of the Egyptian army to reduce Jerusalem. By early June the rebellion had been extinguished in the city, although it continued elsewhere in Palestine until finally crushed in August of 1834. Many of the rebel leaders were pursued and executed, while others were sent into exile. Although there were minor problems elsewhere in Palestine from time to time, it has reasonably been said that the uprising of 1834 CE was the last major popular rebellion of the Ottoman period in Palestine.[86]

Not until 1840 CE did the Ottoman rulers, with the help of Britain, France, and Russia, succeed in driving Mohammed Ali and the Egyptian army out of Palestine and Syria. The remaining decades of Ottoman rule, during the Tanzimat, a "reorganization" period of the empire from 1840 CE onward, were fairly peaceful in Jerusalem.[87] Indeed, during those years, life in Jerusalem stagnated to a certain extent. For example, the American author Samuel Clemens—better known to the reading public as Mark Twain—visited Jerusalem in 1867 and reacted just as had the European traveler Comte de Volney eighty years earlier.

> A fast walker could go outside the walls of Jerusalem and walk entirely around the city in an hour. I do not know how else to make one understand how small it is. . . . The streets are roughly and badly paved with stone, and are tolerably crooked—enough so to make each street appear to close together constantly and come to an end about a hundred yards ahead of a pilgrim as long as he chooses to walk in it. . . . The population of Jerusalem is composed of Moslems, Jews, Greeks, Latins, Armenians, Syrians, Copts, Abyssinians, Greek Catholics, and a handful of Protestants. One hundred of the latter sect are all that dwell now in this birthplace of Christianity. The nice shades of nationality comprised in the above list, and the languages spoken by them, are altogether too numerous to mention. It seems to me that all the races and colors and tongues of the earth must be represented among the fourteen thousand souls that dwell in Jerusalem. Rags, wretchedness, poverty and dirt, those signs and symbols that indicate the presence of Moslem rule more surely than the crescent-flag itself, abound. Lepers, cripples, the blind, and the idiotic,

assail you on every hand, and they know but one word of but one language apparently—the eternal "bucksheesh." To see the numbers of maimed, malformed and diseased humanity that throng the holy places and obstruct the gates, one might suppose that the ancient days had come again, and that the angel of the Lord was expected to descend at any moment to stir the waters of Bethesda. Jerusalem is mournful, and dreary, and lifeless. I would not desire to live here.[88]

During the second half of the nineteenth century and the early years of the twentieth century CE, both Zionist and Arab unification movements began, leading to reverberations and ramifications that would define the rest of the twentieth century in Palestine (and elsewhere) in terms of politics, religion, and growing nationalism.[89] Moreover, World War I and the end of the Ottoman Empire in 1917 were looming on the horizon. Jerusalem would have a seminal role to play in some or all of those upcoming events.

TATARS, CRUSADERS, ZIONISTS, AND EXTREMISTS

In a radio broadcast of August 30, 1971, Egyptian president Anwar el-Sadat drew a comparison between the "Zionist invasion" and the Crusades. He prefaced this remark by saying:

This is the lesson we learned from History. . . . As long as we Arabs do not unite, foreign invaders will come and take over our area and humiliate us. But the moment our will is united and our might is one, we shall be able to wipe out any invasion. . . . That had happened before, during the Tatar [Khwarizmian] invasion and during the Crusades. . . . The [Crusader] colonies lasted 80 years, but Saladin united Egypt and Syria and the whole Arab Will, and enabled us to . . . rid ourselves of the Crusaders.[90]

Just six years later, Sadat made his historic visit to Jerusalem. In his address to the Knesset, after calling Jerusalem the "city of peace," he made a momentous declaration, reversing the consistent theme of years of earlier speeches.

> Above all, this city should not be severed from those who have made it their abode for centuries. Instead of reviving the precedent of the Crusades, we should revive the spirit of [U]mar Ibn al-Khattab and Saladin, namely the spirit of tolerance and respect for right. The holy shrines of Islam and Christianity are not only places of worship but a living testimony of our interrupted presence here. Politically, spiritually and intellectually, here let us make no mistake about the importance and reverence we Christians and Moslems attach to Jerusalem.[91]

As I have already noted, Sadat was shot to death four years later by an Egyptian Islamic extremist, a member of the Jamaʾat al-Jihad (Organization for Jihad). Many fundamentalists in the Arab world were outraged by Sadat's 1977 visit to Jerusalem and by his signing of the Camp David Peace Accords the following year. They compared his actions to al-Malik al-Kamil's "traitorous" act of returning Jerusalem to Frederick II and the Crusaders in 1229 CE.[92]

Nearly two decades after Sadat's assassination, Ayman al-Zawahiri, one of the founders of Jamaʾat al-Jihad, merged his organization with that of Osama bin Laden, to form the terrorist group al-Qaeda. In 1998, bin Laden and Zawahiri, acting on behalf of their new World Islamic Front for Jihad against Jews and Crusaders, jointly issued a religious ruling (fatwa) that called for death to Americans and their Zionist allies. Apparently bin Laden and Zawahiri had literally interpreted Sadat's original message of the 1970s linking the "Zionist invasion" and the Crusades and had decided to imitate Saladin in order to "unite Egypt and Syria and the whole Arab Will" and rid themselves of the modern "Crusaders." The original message lived on, although the revised version and the messenger did not.

TABLE 4. Chronology from 1077 CE to 1840 CE

Date	Conqueror	Event
1077 CE	Islam	The Turcomans wrest control of Jerusalem from the Fatamid caliphs ruling from Egypt.
1095–99 CE	Christian Crusaders	Pope Urban II calls for a Crusade (the First Crusade) to retake Jerusalem and the Holy Land from the "infidel." Jerusalem comes under Christian control.
1187 CE	Islam	Saladin and the forces of Islam take Jerusalem and vast territories from the Crusaders. His successors, the Ayyubid dynasty, govern much of the Middle East.
1229 CE	Christian Crusaders	Al-Malik al-Kamil hands over Jerusalem, without a battle, to Frederick II, leader of the Sixth Crusade.
1239 CE	Islam	Al-Nasir Da'ud of Kerak in Syria, an Ayyubid, conquers the city in a twenty-one-day siege.
1241–43 CE	Christian Crusaders	Theobald of Navarre regains Jerusalem through rivalries among Ayyubid rulers of the Middle East.
1244 CE	Islam	Khwarizmian warriors (Tartars) capture Jerusalem and then conquer much of the Levant with the help of the sultan of Egypt.
1246–47 CE	Islam	The Egyptian sultan conquers the city from a renegade band of Khwarizmians.
1246–47 CE	Islam	Al-Nasir Da'ud of Kerak conquers Jerusalem.
1247–48 CE	Islam	The Egyptian sultan recaptures the city.
1250 CE	Islam	The Mamlukes seize control of Egypt and its possessions.
1253–54 CE	Islam	The Ayyubid ruler of Aleppo and Damascus and the Mamluke sultan of Egypt alternately capture and control Jerusalem.
1260 CE	—	The Mongols raid Jerusalem and other cities of Palestine.
1260 CE	Islam	The Mamlukes defeat the Mongols at a great battle near Megiddo and reestablish their control of Jerusalem.
1300 CE	—	The Mongols again briefly raid Jerusalem.
1300–1517 CE	Islam	The Mamlukes rule Jerusalem during a relatively peaceful period interrupted only by Bedouin raids.
1516 CE	Islam	The Ottomans defeat the Mamlukes at Aleppo and take control of Jerusalem and the Levant.
1537–41 CE	Islam	Sultan Suleiman the Magnificent rebuilds the walls of Jerusalem. Jerusalem is part of the Ottoman Empire until 1914.
1703–5 CE	Islam	A rebellion called the *naqib al-ashraf* revolt temporarily overthrows the local Ottoman governor.
1799 CE	Western Christians	The French under Napoleon enter the Holy Land, but Jerusalem is spared.
18th and 19th centuries CE	Islam	Between 1831 and 1840, Egyptians, rather than Ottomans, ruled Jerusalem. A number of relatively minor internal and external conflicts rock Jerusalem during these centuries.

8

PEACE TO THEIR ASHES, HONOR TO THEIR MEMORY

AN APOCRYPHAL STORY told about General Edmund Henry Hyn-man Allenby's entrance into Jerusalem on December 11, 1917, after the British conquest of the city, is that he announced grandly, "Now the Crusades have ended." Forty-one years later, in a speech on March 20, 1958, Egyptian president Gamal Abdel Nasser repeated the story, saying, "It was no accident at all that General Allenby, commander of the British forces, said on arriving in Jerusalem: 'Today the wars of the Crusaders are completed.'"[1]

Although some scholars continue to attribute the original statement to Allenby,[2] the general himself always firmly denied that he had been on a Crusade. In fact, both he and General Liman von Sanders—his German counterpart during the 1918 battles in Palestine—took pains to point out that, technically, Allenby's campaign could not have been a Crusade, since there were Moslems fighting on behalf of the Allies and there were Christians fighting on the side of the Ottomans.[3] In April 1933, Allenby delivered a speech at the Jerusalem YMCA in which he reiterated:

Our campaign has been called "The Last Crusade." It was not a crusade. There is still a current idea that our object was to deliver Jerusalem from the Moslem. Not so. Many of my soldiers were Moslems. The importance of Jerusalem lay in its strategical position. There was no religious impulse in this campaign. The sole object of every man in my army was to win the war.[4]

Nevertheless, the image of a successful Western crusade in the Holy Land captured the public imagination. Allenby's soldiers are still sometimes called "Crusaders" by both Western and Eastern politicians, military leaders, and authors,[5] and the concept continues to be part of the propaganda surrounding the modern city of Jerusalem. The story of Allenby's conquest of Palestine and entrance into Jerusalem begins with British prime minister David Lloyd George's request for a Christmas present and draws to an end with two British army cooks' search for fresh eggs and clean water on a cold December morning.

THE BATTLE FOR JERUSALEM

In June 1917 Prime Minister David Lloyd George asked General Allenby to deliver Jerusalem "as a Christmas present for the British nation." At the time, World War I had been ongoing in the Middle East for more than two years—ever since the Turks tried to capture the Suez Canal in January 1915. By mid-November 1917 all was ready, and the general's campaign to capture the city got underway. It was part of a larger advance that had started with successful attacks on Beersheba on October 27 and on Gaza three days later.[6]

Allenby, who had previously served with the Allied forces in France, was brought in to replace General Sir Archibald Murray as commander of the Egyptian Expeditionary Force (EEF)—as the Allied forces in the Middle East were called. Allenby had a distinguished ancestry that included Oliver Cromwell. Nicknamed "the Bull," Allenby was a large man with a voice to match. After the successful conclusion of the Middle Eastern campaign, his name was further embellished with a title and peerage; he became "Lord Allenby of Megiddo [the site of his most famous victory] and Felixstowe [the ancestral family home]."[7]

Allenby was generally well read and was especially well versed in both military history and the Bible. Stories abound in the reminiscences of his soldiers about his fondness for telling biblical stories and recounting military history, all associated with whatever terrain in Palestine they were passing through at the time. Upon occasion, his knowledge of military history was employed in his own military tactics. When he fought the battle of Megiddo in September 1918, he deliberately employed a strategy used by the Egyptian pharaoh Thutmose III at the same site thirty-four hundred years earlier.[8]

Allenby assumed command of the EEF at midnight on June 28, 1917. His appointment has been described as the war's turning point for the Allies in the Middle East. General Archibald Murray had proven to be a rather lackluster leader, and the Allied advance had bogged down under his command. At the time of Allenby's arrival, the soldiers of the EEF were reeling and demoralized after two failed attempts to capture Gaza. Allenby promptly moved the general headquarters from its base in Cairo up to the front lines, so that he could be with his men. An improvement in morale was immediate, and the successful attacks on Gaza and Beersheba followed at the end of October and in the first week of November. By mid-November, Allenby and his men—eighty thousand frontline troops—were ready to head for Jerusalem.[9]

As the esteemed scholar Sir Martin Gilbert notes, it was at this moment—on November 9, 1917, as Allenby and his men were preparing for their march on Jerusalem—that "the British Government made public a letter from the Foreign Secretary A. J. Balfour, sent to Lord Rothschild a week earlier, in which Balfour promised to use Britain's influence to establish a 'National Home in Palestine' for the Jews."[10] This short letter, almost a note really, quickly became known as the Balfour Declaration. Meant as a "declaration of sympathy with Jewish Zionist aspirations," it read in part, "His Majesty's Government view with favour the establishment in Palestine of a national home for the Jewish people, and will use their best endeavours to facilitate the achievement of this object . . ."[11] Together with other documents issued by British officials, the Balfour Declaration would exert a profound influence on British policy in Palestine during the next several decades. Undoubtedly, the expected quick capture of Jerusalem by Allenby had much to do with the timing of this letter and its release to the public.

The Allied advance on Jerusalem began near Ramla, to the west of Jerusalem, on November 17, 1917. Allenby and his men—including the Seventy-fifth and Fifty-second Divisions, the Yeomanry Mounted Division, and a brigade of the Australian Mounted Division—soon moved off the direct Jaffa-Jerusalem road and marched northeast over the hills. Their intention was to swing north of Jerusalem and isolate it by cutting the Turkish supply line that ran north-south down the Nablus-Jerusalem road. In so doing, Allenby hoped to limit the amount of fighting that would take place within the city itself, since he wished to avoid damaging the holy sites of Jerusalem. He was also well aware that it was nearly impossible to take Jerusalem from the west—as numerous armies before had found out to their dismay—and that he would be much more likely to capture the city if he attacked from the north.[12]

By November 21, after fierce fighting against Turkish Seventh Army artillery positions located high above them, the infantry captured the "key to Jerusalem"—the three-thousand-foot-high peak of Nebi Samwil, reputedly the burial place of the prophet Samuel and the spot from which Richard the Lionheart refused to look at Jerusalem during the Third Crusade. Allenby and his men were poised to take the Nablus-Jerusalem road and, after that, the city of Jerusalem itself.[13]

The Turkish defenders of Jerusalem were certain that they and the city were about to be overrun. On November 23, according to Colonel Richard Meinertzhagen, Allenby's field intelligence officer, a final message was sent in cipher from the Turkish wireless station in Jerusalem. It was intercepted and decoded by the British.

> To Damascus. Important and secret.
> Oh Friends. Let us repudiate all our debts. The enemy is in front of us only half an hour from here. Guns are firing and roaring all round us; our ears can hear nothing else. For three and four days fighting has been going on day and night without cessation. This is our last resistance. There is no lack of British aeroplanes over the city. Adieu from Jerusalem.[14]

Despite the gloomy tone of this dispatch, the Turkish forces suddenly counterattacked, and the British advance stalled. The so-called First Battle for Jerusalem came to a sudden end on November 24. Allenby wrote in his official dispatch, "it was evident that a period of preparation and organization would be necessary before an attack could be delivered in sufficient strength." It would be another ten days before the "Second Battle for Jerusalem" began and just over two weeks before the city was taken.[15]

Allenby reported that all preparations were complete by December 4, despite the fact that the Allies had had to fight running battles and fend off numerous Turkish counterattacks in the intervening days. The arrival of fresh reinforcements was especially important; the Fifty-second and Seventy-fifth Divisions of the Twenty-first Corps were relieved by members of the Tenth, Sixtieth, and Seventy-fourth Divisions of the Twentieth Corps, while some of the Yeomanry Mounted Division were replaced by the Seventh Mounted Brigade. In addition, the Fifty-third Division from the Twentieth Corps was reinforced in its position to the south of Jerusalem and Bethlehem, on the Hebron road north of Beersheba.

In contrast, the Turkish troops defending Jerusalem were unrelieved by fresh forces. There are indications that the German high command in Berlin had "already accepted the abandonment of Jerusalem as inevitable," perhaps as early as November 28.[16] The German commander in the conflict, General von Falkenhayn, had already left Jerusalem by November 17, apparently with no intention of returning. He directed the remainder of the German counterattacks from new headquarters in Nablus.[17]

The final Allied attack on Jerusalem began in driving rain at dawn on December 8 and lasted a little more than twenty-four hours. In his official dispatch on December 16 to the secretary of state for war, Allenby wrote matter-of-factly:

The troops moved into positions of assembly by night, and, assaulting at dawn on the 8th, soon carried their first objectives. They then pressed steadily forward. The mere physical difficulty of climbing the steep and rocky hillsides and crossing the deep valleys would have sufficed to render progress slow, and the opposition encountered was considerable. Artillery support was soon difficult, owing to the length of the advance and the difficulty of moving guns forward. But by about noon London troops had already advanced over two miles, and were swinging north-east to gain the Nablus-Jerusalem road; while the Yeomanry had captured the Beit Iksa spur, and were preparing for a further advance. . . . During the day about 300 prisoners were taken and many Turks killed. Our own casualties were light. Next morning [the ninth] the advance was resumed. The Turks had withdrawn during the night, and the London troops and Yeomanry, driving back rearguards, occupied a line across the Nablus-Jerusalem road four miles north of Jerusalem, while Welsh troops occupied a position east of Jerusalem across the Jericho road. These operations isolated Jerusalem, and at about noon the enemy sent out a parlementaire and surrendered the city.[18]

Lieutenant Colonel (later Field Marshal Viscount) Archibald P. Wavell, author of a volume on the Palestine campaign and a biography of Allenby, reports that by the morning of December 9 the noose tightened around Jerusalem, as the Fifty-third, Sixtieth, and Seventy-fourth Divisions all fought their way into positions surrounding the city. A running battle took place during the afternoon of the ninth (and perhaps again on the morning of the tenth, according to some accounts) on the Mount of Olives, where a few stalwart Turkish troops fought a savage rearguard action against members of the Sixtieth Division. The "official history" of the campaign reports that seventy Turkish soldiers were killed here and another ten taken prisoner, while the British suffered forty-three casualties in this one location.[19]

During the advance upon Jerusalem, the British had put eighteen thousand infantry, eight thousand cavalry, and 172 guns into the field, while the Turks had fifteen thousand infantry, eight hundred cavalry, and 120 guns in their defense of the city.[20] Later, in his official dispatch, Allenby reported that a total of twelve thousand Turkish troops had been taken prisoner between October 31 and December 9. Other official reports give totals of approximately thirty-six hundred Turkish dead and almost twenty-five thousand wounded or missing in action during the battles for Jerusalem between early November and the end of December 1917. The British lost approximately twenty-five hundred dead and 16,400 wounded or missing in action between early November and mid-December 1917. So much for a bloodless conquest of Jerusalem, as some have claimed this was. However, not a single building in Jerusalem had been damaged, for the greater part of the fighting had taken place outside the city walls. Neither attacker nor defender wished to be accused of having damaged anything within the holy city.[21]

THE KEYS TO THE CITY

The mayor, the mufti, the chief of police, and the inhabitants of Jerusalem were uncertain to whom they should surrender the city when it was captured by the British forces. According to official and semiofficial accounts,[22] Ali Faud Pasha, commander of the Turkish troops defending Jerusalem, and Ahmed Cemal Pasha, the Turkish governor of Syria, ordered the evacuation of Jerusalem after nightfall on December 8, after a day of fierce fighting. It is not clear why the order to evacuate was given at that moment, but by midnight the governor of the city, Izzet Bey, had personally smashed the telegraph machine with a hammer, and by dawn Jerusalem was almost empty of Turkish troops. Many were in full flight toward Nablus or Jericho.[23]

The mayor of Jerusalem, Selim al-Husseini, accompanied by various officials, ventured out from the city to surrender and formally hand over the keys to Jerusalem to the conquerors. They first encountered Privates H. E. Church and R. W. J. Andrews—mess cooks attached to the 2/20th Battalion, London Regiment, Sixtieth Division. The two cooks were out searching for clean water and eggs with which to make breakfast for their company. Bewildered by the mayor's attempt to present them with the keys to the city, the cooks refused to accept them and made their way back to their unit.[24]

Frustrated, the mayor and his party continued on. At approximately 8:00 A.M., they encountered Sergeants Frederick Hurcomb and James Sedgewick of the 2/19th Battalion, London Regiment, Sixtieth Division, but the sergeants also refused to accept the keys, deeming themselves insufficiently worthy of the honor.[25]

Next, the mayor's party met Majors W. Beck and F. R. Barry, officers with the Sixtieth Divisional Artillery who were conducting a reconnaissance mission in and around the village of Lifta, northwest of Jerusalem. They also considered themselves unworthy of accepting such a historic surrender, but they promised to return to their unit and to "telephone back news of the surrender."[26]

The mayor and his group had somewhat better luck in their fourth attempt to surrender. Thus far, in each encounter on their journey, they had met ever higher-ranking British soldiers, and they now ran into Lieutenant Colonel H. Bailey, commander of the 303rd Brigade R.F.A., in the suburbs of Jerusalem, on the road leading to Lifta. The Lieutenant Colonel was in the process of moving his artillery pieces closer to Jerusalem when he and Captain R. Armitage, one of his three battery commanders, saw the mayor's group and their white flag of truce from a distance. The Lieutenant Colonel sent Armitage back for reinforcements, while he met the Jerusalem party, accompanied only by his orderly. After questioning the mayor and learning that Jerusalem now lay undefended, Bailey had a telegram sent to Major General John S. M. Shea, who was in charge of the Sixtieth Division. The telegram read simply:

> Priority 60th Division. Jerusalem has surrendered. Colonel Bailey, R.F.A., is now with the Mayor awaiting any General Officer to take over the City. . . . 8.55 a.m.[27]

In the meantime, Lieutenant Colonel Bailey and the mayor's party had been joined by Brigadier General C. F. Watson, who commanded the 180th Brigade. Watson had already seen the telegram sent to Major General Shea. He and Bailey, accompanied by ten armed British soldiers, then rode to the Jaffa Gate with the mayor and entered Jerusalem through the hole that had been created in the city wall for Kaiser Wilhelm's visit back in 1898. Brigadier General Watson was thus the first high-ranking British officer to enter the city on December 9, 1917. By this time it was about 9:30 in the morning. The official report says that he, too, refused to accept the keys to the city, but other reports claim that he was keen to be given the keys and only reluctantly gave them back to the mayor when informed that Major General John Shea was on his way to accept the surrender.[28]

After receiving the telegram confirming the surrender, Major General Shea had taken the time to consult with his own superior, Lieutenant General Sir Philip Chetwode, who commanded the three infantry divisions that made up the Twentieth Corps. Following Sir Chetwode's orders, Shea reached Jerusalem by motorcar at 11:00 A.M. and formally accepted the surrender from the mayor, in the name of General Allenby.[29]

That year, December 9, the day of the surrender of Jerusalem, was coincidentally the first day of Hanukkah—the festival that celebrates the Maccabees' rededication of the cleansed Temple in Jerusalem following the recapture of the city from the Hellenistic Seleucid rulers in 164 BCE. The official British report by Captain Cyril Falls noted this coincidence, which Major Harry Pirie-Gordon had already mentioned in his semiofficial account of events.

> On this same day 2,082 years before, another race of conquerors, equally detested, were looking their last on the city which they could not hold, and . . . it was fitting that the flight of the Turks should have coincided with the national [Jewish] festival of the Hanukah, which commemorates the recapture of the Temple from the heathen Seleucids by Judas Maccabaeus . . .[30]

ALLENBY ARRIVES IN JERUSALEM

Later that same day—December 9—Allenby sent the news of the capture of Jerusalem to the War Cabinet in London. In reply, he received a telegram asking him to keep the news secret until it was officially announced. Prime Minister Lloyd George was ill at the time, and Andrew Bonar Law, chancellor of the exchequer, made the formal announcement in the House of Commons on December 10. Lloyd George and Allenby had succeeded in presenting Britain and the world with the desired "Christmas present." The propaganda value of this "gift" was immense, and great care had to be taken in its packaging and presentation to the world.[31]

When General Allenby finally arrived for the formal acceptance of Jerusalem's surrender, an honor guard of representatives from all of the various Allied troops in Palestine greeted him as he was driven up the

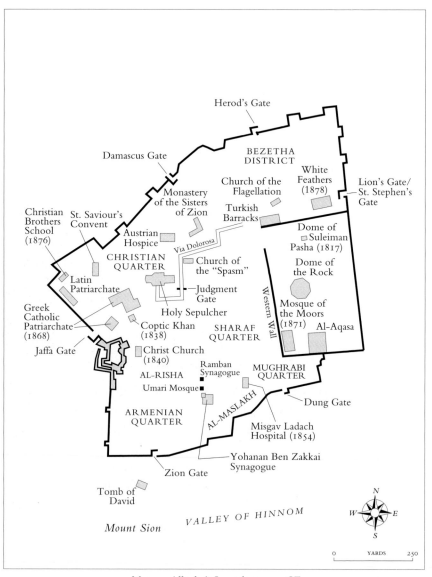

Herod's Gate

BEZETHA
DISTRICT

Damascus Gate

White
Feathers
(1878)

Church of the
Flagellation

Lion's Gate/
St. Stephen's
Gate

Monastery
of the Sisters
of Zion

Turkish
Barracks

Christian
Brothers
School
(1876)

St. Saviour's
Convent

Dome of
Suleiman
Pasha (1817)

Austrian
Hospice

Via Dolorosa

CHRISTIAN
QUARTER

Dome of
the Rock

Church of
the "Spasm"

Latin
Patriarchate

Judgment
Gate

Western Wall

Mosque of
the Moors
(1871)

Greek
Catholic
Patriarchate
(1868)

Holy Sepulcher

Coptic Khan
(1838)

SHARAF
QUARTER

Al-Aqasa

Jaffa Gate

Christ Church
(1840)

Ramban
Synagogue

MUGHRABI
QUARTER

AL-RISHA

Umari Mosque

AL-MASLAKH

Dung Gate

ARMENIAN
QUARTER

Misgav Ladach
Hospital (1854)

Yohanan Ben Zakkai
Synagogue

Zion Gate

Tomb of
David

VALLEY OF HINNOM

N

Mount Sion

W   E

S

0   YARDS   250

Map 21. Allenby's Jerusalem, 1917 CE

Fig. 10. Jerusalem, from the road leading to Bethany. (Painting by David Roberts, Esq., R.A.)

Jaffa Road past members of the 180th Brigade. Cyril Falls says that English, Scottish, Irish, Welsh, Australian, New Zealand, French, and Italian troops were positioned outside and inside the Jaffa Gate awaiting Allenby's arrival. Accompanied by dignitaries of various nationalities, Allenby walked through the Jaffa Gate at noon on December 11, 1917, in an elaborate entrance that had been stage-managed in far-off London.

The decision to enter Jerusalem on foot was deliberate. The Jaffa Gate, after years of disuse, had been reopened for the occasion. The gap in the wall next to the Jaffa Gate, which had been created for Kaiser Wilhelm's motorcade in 1898, was deliberately ignored. As many later writers observed, this was done for its propaganda value, to illustrate the contrast between Teutonic arrogance and British humility and respect.

In the crowd of officers accompanying General Allenby was Major (later Colonel) T. E. Lawrence, now better known as Lawrence of Arabia. He was wearing clothes borrowed for the occasion, which he later described as "the supreme moment of the war." The entire crowd marched to the steps of the citadel within the Old City, where an official proclamation was read in seven different languages and then posted on the walls of Jerusalem.[32]

In the meantime, the War Cabinet in London sent a second telegram to General Allenby, which read:

> War Cabinet wishes to congratulate you on the capture of Jerusalem, which is an event of historic and world-wide significance and has given the greatest pleasure to the British and other Allied peoples. Your victorious campaign for the conquest of Palestine in the face of very great transport and other difficulties constitutes a notable military performance, and the War Cabinet views your continued progress and success with the greatest interest and confidence.[33]

There are reports that the inhabitants of Jerusalem welcomed Allenby with open arms. Perhaps they saw in him the fulfillment of a two-hundred-year-old Arab prophecy that predicted, "when the Nile flows into Palestine, then shall the prophet from the west drive the

Turk from Jerusalem." In a sense, the first part of the prophecy had already been fulfilled by the recently completed British-built pipeline bringing water from the Nile across the Sinai and north to Gaza and beyond. Allenby fulfilled the second part of the prophecy when he conquered the Turks and entered the city. In Arabic "the prophet" is translated as *al nebi*, the name by which Allenby was already known in Palestine. It had also been said that "the conqueror who entered by the Golden Gate . . . would hold Jerusalem forever." However, entering the Old City of Jerusalem via the so-called Golden Gate would have entailed marching through a Moslem graveyard, so Allenby chose to enter Jerusalem through the Jaffa Gate. He entered the city humbly and on foot, in a manner similar to that of Jesus and of Caliph Umar centuries earlier. This image was not lost upon either the local population or the greater world beyond. As Raymond Savage wrote in 1926, "After General Allenby had entered Jerusalem modestly on foot, many of the Arab rulers recalled their cherished prophecy—'He who shall save Jerusalem and exalt her among the nations will enter the city on foot, and his name will be "God, the Prophet"—Allah Nebi!'"[34]

THE PROCLAMATION

On the evening of the day that he entered Jerusalem, Allenby wrote home to his wife. His letter briefly describes the momentous events of the previous few days and contradicts those who say that the Allied capture of Jerusalem in 1917 was bloodless.

> Jerusalem surrendered to me on the 9th. I informed the War Office, but was not allowed to publish the news before the P.M. [Prime Minister David Lloyd George] had announced it in the House. That was done yesterday. Today I entered Jerusalem, on foot; with the French and Italian Commanders—Lt.-Colonel Piepape and Major Agostino—of the detachments in my Army; and the Attache and a few Staff officers. We entered at the Jaffa Gate; and, from the steps of the Citadel—hard by—issued a proclamation in many languages to the assembled multitude. Great enthusiasm—real or feigned—was shown. Then I received the notables and the heads of all the Churches—of which there

are many, including Abyssinian. After this we reformed our procession and returned to our horses—which we had left outside the walls. . . . The Turks are driven 3 or 4 miles down the Jericho road, to the East, and some 6 or 8 miles to the North. . . . Chetwode's Corps, and the Divisions of Generals Shea and Mott, in that Corps, were the lucky ones who had the honour of capturing the Holy City. . . . It was a great feat; and our losses were light. The rocky and mountainous country they fought over is indescribable. Guns could give little support; and the Turks were driven out by rifle and machine-gun fire, followed by the bayonet. A great number of Turks were killed, and about 400 or 500 taken prisoner.[35]

Captain Cyrus Falls notes that the proclamation issued by Allenby had been crafted in London and sent by telegraph to Allenby three weeks before he captured Jerusalem. On December 11, it was read out loud in a number of languages, including English, French, Arabic, Hebrew, Greek, Russian, and Italian.

To the inhabitants of Jerusalem the Blessed and the people dwelling in its vicinity.

The defeat inflicted upon the Turks by the troops under my command has resulted in the occupation of your city by my forces. I therefore here and now proclaim it to be under martial law, under which form of administration it will remain so long as military considerations make it necessary.

However, lest any of you should be alarmed by reason of your experience at the hands of the enemy who has retired, I hereby inform you that it is my desire that every person should pursue his lawful business without fear of interruption. Furthermore, since your city is regarded with affection by adherents of three of the great religions of mankind, and its soil has been consecrated by the prayers and pilgrimages of multitudes of devout people of these three religions for many centuries, therefore do I make known to you that every sacred building, monument, Holy spot, shrine, traditional site, endowment, pious bequest, or customary place of prayer, of whatsoever form of the three religions, will be maintained and protected according to the existing customs and beliefs of those to whose faiths they are sacred.[36]

In an interesting footnote to history, the mayor of Jerusalem, Selim al-Husseini, sickened and died of pneumonia within two weeks of Allenby's triumphal entrance into Jerusalem. Near death, he attributed his impending demise to a cold caught while "standing out in the open and surrendering the city so often!"[37]

THE BRITISH DEFEND JERUSALEM AGAINST A COUNTERATTACK

The Turkish army and its German commanders made one last attempt to recapture Jerusalem from the British, on December 27. But Allenby was expecting the attack: an intercepted Turkish wireless message had given the plan away some days before.[38] Two days prior to the attack, the British celebrated Christmas. As the eminent historian Sir Martin Gilbert has noted, it was the first time since the Crusades—that is, in nearly seven hundred years—that Christmas was celebrated in a Jerusalem under Christian rule.[39]

The Turkish counterattack, which came from the north and east, lasted four days, until December 30, 1917. It was a vicious and bloody battle, fought just to the north of the city proper. It coincided with a planned British advance into that same area. Allenby's official dispatch—dated September 18, 1918, and republished in the *London Gazette*—was typically understated. It read in part:

during the week before Christmas [1917] . . . various movements and concentrations of troops on the part of the enemy indicated that he intended to attack, with the object of recovering Jerusalem.

This proved to be the case. On the night of Dec. 26–27, the enemy attacked with great determination astride the Jerusalem-Nablus road. A counter-attack against the right of his attack was carried out immediately by two divisions. As the result of three days' fighting, not only did the enemy's attempt to recapture Jerusalem fail, but by the end of the third day he found himself seven miles further from Jerusalem than when his attack started.[40]

The British plan to prevent the Turks from retaking Jerusalem was fairly simple. The British greatly outnumbered the Turkish forces. It has been estimated that General Falkenhayn had at most twenty thousand Turkish troops from the Seventh Army, whereas Allenby had approximately thirty-three thousand Allied troops to counter their attack. Allenby therefore positioned the Fifty-third and Sixtieth Divisions of the British Twentieth Corps to the north of Jerusalem, to stand firm between the Turkish forces and the city. At the same time, the Tenth and Seventy-fourth Divisions advanced into enemy territory. By the end of the fighting, not only had the Turks failed to reach the walls of the city, but the British troops had advanced between four thousand yards and two and a half miles further north along a front of some six miles.[41]

Allenby wrote:

The Turkish attempt to recapture Jerusalem had thus ended in crushing defeat. . . . Seven hundred and fifty prisoners, twenty-four machine guns, and three automatic rifles were captured during these operations, and over 1,000 Turkish dead were buried by us. Our own casualties were considerably less than this number.

However, official records indicate that Allenby was minimizing the British casualties, although he was more accurate about the Turkish casualties. The British forces suffered nineteen hundred killed, wounded, or missing in action during the last week of December, of which nearly fourteen hundred were attributable to the defense of Jerusalem. The Turkish forces suffered nearly sixteen hundred casualties in their failed attempt to recapture Jerusalem.[42]

Nine months later, Allenby annihilated the Turkish Seventh and Eighth Armies in a lightning-quick campaign featuring the famous battle of Megiddo (Armageddon), fought in late September 1918.[43] With that victorious mopping-up action, World War I effectively came to a close in the Middle East.

However, the battle of Megiddo did not bring an end to British casualties in Palestine. Those continued to mount during the period of the British mandate from 1920 to 1948, when the British forces underwent a transformation from liberators to peacekeepers of a volatile region. The British soon learned that victory in Jerusalem frequently marks the beginning, not the end, of troubles in the Holy Land. In this they resembled both the Crusaders who preceded them by a thousand years and the Israelis who would succeed them thirty years later.

THE RIOTS OF 1920, 1921, AND 1929

Trouble erupted in Jerusalem early in 1920 when the British announced their intention to implement the Balfour Declaration. In February and March, as many as fifteen hundred Arabs marched in protest through the streets of Jerusalem. Although some Jewish shopkeepers and bystanders were injured in the March protests, it was not until April 4, 1920, that the first deaths from violence in the city over this conflict occurred.[44]

April 4 was Easter Sunday. The Christian holy day coincided with the Moslem celebration of Nebi Musa, an annual festival involving a march from Jerusalem to the presumed burial place of Moses a few miles outside the city. As Professor Karen Armstrong has put it, the processions represented a "symbolic way of taking possession of the Holy City" and so were deliberately held at the same time as the Christian Easter activities. Begun centuries earlier by the Mamlukes as a reaction against the Crusaders, the event had taken on new meaning with the arrival of Allenby and the gradual identification of the British as new "Crusaders." The Arabs of the city were in a state of agitation, especially now that the Balfour Declaration had finally been made public in an Arabic translation nearly two years after its original statement in 1917.[45]

In any event, a riot ensued during the Nebi Musa processions of 1920. The Jewish Quarter was looted, nine people were killed, and another 244 were injured. Nearly all of the victims were Jewish. A few days later, shots were fired at the mufti's house, probably by Zionists bent on revenge.[46]

The Arab rioters of April 4 were reportedly inflamed by angry speeches given by public figures. One of these speakers was Haj Amin al-Husseini, a man with interesting family associations. He was the son of the mufti of Jerusalem and the cousin of the mayor of Jerusalem. He was also the future uncle of Yasser Arafat and the great-uncle of Faisal Husseini, the late Palestinian Authority minister for Jerusalem affairs. Haj Amin al-Husseini was afterward convicted and sentenced in absentia to ten years in prison for his role in the 1920 riot. However, within one year, Sir Herbert Samuel, the first British high commissioner in Palestine, had pardoned him and appointed him as the Grand Mufti of Jerusalem. Later, while exiled from Jerusalem during World War II, al-Husseini allied himself with Hitler, meeting with the führer in November 1941 and broadcasting anti-Jewish and anti-British propaganda in Arabic from Berlin. He has frequently been accused of being responsible—more than any other single person—for the agitations in Jerusalem and throughout Palestine during the 1920s and 1930s and especially of engineering the riots of 1929 and 1936.[47]

About the time that Haj Amin al-Husseini was arrested, twenty Jews were also arrested for their role in the 1920 riot. Among them was Vladimir Jabotinsky, the controversial figure who had co-founded the "Jewish Legion" of the British Army and who founded "Revisionist Zionism" (so called to differentiate his rather bellicose politics from the more moderate Zionist policies of David Ben-Gurion and Chaim Weizman, as well as Herzl and Nordau before them). Jabotinsky had secretly trained six hundred Jews as a "self-defence group" (the Haganah) and thus had violated the British regulation against bearing arms. He received a long prison sentence, which was soon commuted because of protests back in Britain.[48]

Rioting began again in 1921, on the fourth anniversary of the Balfour Declaration. On November 2, Sir Herbert Samuel sent a telegraph to Winston Churchill, who was at that time the British secretary of state for colonial affairs.

A disturbance took place in Jerusalem this morning when a small crowd of Arab roughs appeared in the Jaffa Road. They were dispersed by the police but soon after gathered for an attack on the Jewish Quarter. This was averted by the police. Some shots were exchanged between this crowd and the crowd in the Jewish Quarter. . . . Four Jews and one Arab were killed.[49]

Protests and violence continued and spread throughout Palestine. The Arab population held general strikes in 1925, 1926, 1931, and 1933. An anti-Jewish riot started in August 1929 within the Old City of Jerusalem and quickly spread to other cities, including Hebron and Safed.[50] These so-called Wailing Wall Riots of 1929 had their origin in a decade-long feud over the Jewish practice of bringing benches, chairs, and other objects to the Wailing (or Western) Wall—located on the western side of the Haram al-Sherif and thought to be the only remaining part of the original Temple Mount built by King Solomon. Such objects were specifically forbidden under Ottoman laws that regulated what could and could not be used at this Jewish sacred site. When a screen—to separate the men from the women while praying at the wall—was brought to the site on Yom Kippur in September 1928, it touched off a controversy that eventually resulted in riots a year later.[51]

In mid-August 1929, on Tisha-b'Ab (the anniversary of the destruction of the Temple), the Haganah, the fledgling underground Jewish paramilitary force, organized a large demonstration in Tel Aviv. Soon afterward, six thousand Jewish demonstrators, including numerous members of *Betar* (the militant Zionist youth group founded by Jabotinsky in 1923) made their way to Jerusalem and marched around the walls of the Old City. The next day, they marched through the Arab and Moslem quarters en route to the Wailing Wall, where they raised the Zionist flag and sang the Hebrew anthem "Hatikvah." In retaliation, two thousand Arabs marched to the wall and tore up a Torah scroll.[52]

Then, approximately a week later, the real trouble began when a young Jewish boy was killed while attempting to retrieve a soccer ball from a neighboring Arab yard. Crowds of angry Jews demonstrated at his funeral and throughout Jerusalem. In the course of these demonstrations, an Arab boy was fatally stabbed. In response, on Friday afternoon, August 23, an Arab mob poured out of the al-Aqsa Mosque after midday prayers. Armed with sticks, clubs, knives, and a few guns, they attacked any Jews they encountered, including ultra-Orthodox Jews living in the Mea Shearim quarter just to the north of the Old City. The Jews fought back. Violence flared throughout the country, but mainly in Jerusalem, Hebron, and Safed. By the time the week of hostilities ended, 116 Arabs and 133 Jews were dead, and another 232 Arabs and 339 Jews were wounded. The mufti denied any responsibility for the "Wailing Wall Riots" of 1929, but he later hailed as heroes the Arabs who were arrested for their part in the disturbances.[53]

THE ARAB REVOLT OF 1936
AND ITS AFTERMATH

In May 1936, the newly formed Arab Higher Committee—the representative body for the Arabs of British Palestine, headed by Grand Mufti Haj Amin al-Husseini—called a general strike for all of Palestine. It lasted six months and marked the beginning of the Arab revolt that would consume much of the next three years and would claim hundreds of Jewish, Arab, and British lives. During the later spring and summer of 1936, many Jews were killed, including several students and professors at the Hebrew University of Jerusalem.[54]

A group headed by Lord Peel came from England to examine the disturbances and suggest a means of ending them. The Peel Commission concluded, in its report of July 1937, that the outbreak of the revolt was caused by both the Arabs' desire for independence and their fear of the prospect of a Jewish national home in the region. The commission's recommendation that the country be partitioned into separate Jewish and Arab states created an uproar in the Arab community and contributed to the escalation of the revolt. Although the mufti fled from Palestine into exile, many scholars feel that he continued to direct the revolt from afar, until it ended in 1939.[55]

In the months and years after the report of the Peel Commission, violence continued in Jerusalem. Members of the Jewish group Irgun Zvai Leumi (the "National Military Organization") embarked on a terror campaign in the city with a wave of bombings aimed at civilians. The group—composed of Revisionist Zionist followers of Jabotinsky who had split off from the Haganah—quickly became known to the larger world simply as the Irgun rather than by their Hebrew acronym Etzel. Menachem Begin, later the prime minister of Israel and cosigner of the Camp David Peace Accords and the Egyptian-Israeli Peace Treaty, was the most famous of the Irgun commanders. He was not involved in the violence of 1936–39, however, since he did not arrive in Palestine until the 1940s.[56]

On September 5, 1937, Irgunists threw a bomb at a bus in Jerusalem, killing one Arab and injuring another. Over the next six weeks, they bombed additional buses and killed four more Arabs. After an eight-month hiatus, the Irgunists struck four more times in a two-week period in July 1938. They threw bombs at vegetable markets and a bus station in Jerusalem, killing thirty Arabs and wounding many more. In response, Arabs seized much of the Old City of Jerusalem, only to have it retaken by British forces on October 19, 1938.

Relative peace prevailed for four months, but violence erupted again on February 26, 1939, when Irgunists planted a bomb in a Jerusalem vegetable market, killing four Arabs. Then, on May 18, the British government issued the "White Paper" (promptly nicknamed "the Black Paper") of 1939. This proclamation limited Jewish immigration into Palestine to seventy-five thousand over the next five years and made further immigration after that date effectively subject to Arab approval. In response, Palestinian Jews rioted and destroyed public and private property in Jerusalem and set fire to the Department of Migration, which held the immigration and citizenship records. The day's violence culminated in a baton charge by British police that resulted in more than one hundred Jews injured and a British policeman shot dead in retaliation. Marches and protests continued for the next few days. On May 26, an Arab attacker shot dead a recent Jewish émigré from Germany. On May 29, Jewish terrorists planted two bombs in the Rex Cinema, injuring two Britons and thirteen Arabs. They also shot at Arab buses. By this time, the Irgun had added British targets to their list of Arab targets, thus beginning a process that eventually, in the 1940s, transformed their campaign of terror against Arab civilians into a campaign aimed at driving out the occupying British military force.

In June 1939, matters came to a boil. A bomb planted by the Irgunists in the Jerusalem bus station on June 2 killed five Arabs and wounded nineteen more. Other bombs planted that day and night took out more than half of the Jerusalem telephone system. A bomb planted on June 3 killed nine Arabs and injured forty others. On June 7, an Arab vegetable seller was shot and killed in the Jewish market in Mea Shearim within Jerusalem. On the night of June 8 (while a young John F. Kennedy was staying in the city), Jewish extremists set off at least fourteen bombs throughout Jerusalem, cutting off most of the electricity. Over the next few days, bombs went off in the General Post Office and in the Palestine Broadcasting Building, causing numerous deaths and injuries.[57]

In all, Irgunist bomb attacks killed more than 40 Arabs and wounded at least another 130 Arabs in Jerusalem during the period from 1937 to 1939. There were, in addition, British casualties, but during these years, the targets of the Irgun were primarily Arab civilians. The parallel between the Jewish terror bombings in Jerusalem during 1937–39, on the one hand, and the Arab terror bombings in Jerusalem during 1987–93 and 2000–2004, on the other, is both remarkable and unmistakable. In a very real sense, after a lapse of half a century, the Palestinians of the recent intifada uprisings have turned the early tactics of the Irgunists against the Jews themselves.[58]

Then as now, the violence was by no means confined to Jerusalem. In 1937–39, attacks by and against both Jews and Arabs took place in many areas of Palestine, including Jerusalem, Haifa, Tel Aviv, and other cities. The final death toll from these years has been estimated at 150 British soldiers, five hundred Jews, and more than three thousand Arabs. The Arab casualties include an estimated one thousand "collaborators" killed by fellow Arabs—a situation powerfully reminiscent of recent events in Israel, the West Bank, and Gaza.[59]

EVENTS IMMEDIATELY
FOLLOWING WORLD WAR II

The Arab revolt that began in 1936 had come to an end by the time World War II started on September 1, 1939. The Irgun also agreed to suspend its attacks for the duration of the war. However, in 1944 the violence resumed. By this time, Menachem Begin, a new immigrant to Palestine, had emerged as the leader of the Irgun.[60] On February 1, 1944, they issued a proclamation that read in part:

> We are now entering the final stage of this World War. . . . Our people's destiny shall be determined at this historic juncture. The British regime has violated the armistice agreement which was declared at the outset of the war. . . . Let us fearlessly draw the proper conclusions. There can no longer be an armistice between the Jewish Nation and its youth and a British administration in

the Land of Israel. . . . Our nation is at war with this regime and it is a fight to the finish.[61]

It was no coincidence that violent opposition to the British increased as the likelihood of a German invasion decreased. Palestine was thought to be in imminent danger after the fall of Greece and Crete to the Nazis in 1941. The American Office of Strategic Services even sent the well-known archaeologist and rabbi Nelson Glueck to survey possible escape routes for the British army in Palestine and Transjordan.[62] Only with the defeat of Rommel and his army at the battle of El-Alamein in October 1942 did the threat of a Nazi invasion of the region diminish. By then, despite the rhetoric of the exiled Haj Amin al-Husseini, former Grand Mufti of Jerusalem, and the pledges made by high-ranking Germans—such as Foreign Minister Joachim von Ribbentrop—that the "Jewish National Home" would be "obliterated," it was safe to assume that Palestine would escape the war without suffering invasion.[63]

However, by the summer of 1944 the British found themselves fighting a bitter war within Jerusalem and other cities in Palestine against two principal opponents: the resurgent Irgun, now under the leadership of Menachem Begin, and an offshoot of the Irgun known by the acronym *Lehi*, standing for *Lohamei Herut Yisrael* (fighters for the freedom of Israel). The latter was better known to the British as the Stern Gang, after their first leader, Avraham Stern. It was primarily composed of ultraradical individuals who had split from the Irgun over the decision to suspend attacks during World War II. Although Avraham Stern was killed in February 1942, Lehi remained active until 1949. Yitzhak Shamir was one of the three men who jointly took over the leadership of Lehi after Stern's death. Shamir, like Menachem Begin, would later become prime minister of Israel.

Both the Irgun and Lehi were angered by British policies prohibiting Jewish immigration and were obsessed by a desire to establish a Jewish state in the region without delay. They were committed to driving the British out of Palestine and did not hesitate to use force to further their aims. From 1944 onward they largely abandoned the assassination of Arab civilians in favor of attacking British military targets. In the eyes of some, the Jewish terrorists of the 1930s had become the freedom fighters of the 1940s. Of course, the British recipients of their violence continued to regard them as terrorists, and even the Haganah—by now the official Jewish underground paramilitary force—considered the members of the Irgun and Lehi to be "dissidents."[64]

Both groups successfully carried out numerous "missions" between 1944 and 1948: the British in Palestine were faced with violence from the Irgun and Lehi on a nearly monthly basis. The Irgun attacked immigration offices in Jerusalem, Tel Aviv, and Haifa simultaneously on February 12, 1944. Two weeks later, they attacked the income tax offices in the same three cities. On March 23 an attack on the British intelligence (CID) offices in Jerusalem caused the collapse of the building and the deaths of a British officer and an Irgun fighter. And on July 14 the Irgun bombed the Land Registry Office in Jerusalem, killing two Arab guards.[65]

The most infamous acts of terror involved high-level assassinations and the destruction of prominent landmarks. Members of the Lehi organization assassinated Lord Moyne, the British minister for Middle East affairs, in Cairo on November 6, 1944, and Count Folke Bernadotte, the Swedish United Nations mediator, in Jerusalem on September 17, 1948. In between these acts, the Irgun blew up a wing of the King David Hotel in Jerusalem on July 22, 1946.[66]

Lord Moyne's death outraged the British authorities, and they cracked down on the Jewish terrorists. The two assassins were quickly caught and hanged. The British declared an open *saison* (hunting season) on the Irgun. They were aided by the Haganah and the Jewish Agency for Palestine. The latter group was originally set up in 1929 to encourage immigration, land development, and education, among other services; and by this time, the agency, led by David Ben-Gurion, was essentially the Jewish government in Palestine. The open *saison* lasted six months, until March 1945, and resulted in the killing or capturing of most of the Irgun's top members. The Stern Gang was left alone for the most part, either because the Haganah feared violent retaliation from Lehi members or because of a secret agreement between Lehi and the Haganah.[67]

Then, late in 1945, the situation changed. The Haganah, the Irgun, and Lehi joined together to form Tenuat Hameri (the United Resistance Movement), as a reaction to the British government's decision to allow only fifteen hundred Jewish immigrants per month into Palestine. During the month of October 1945, the Haganah set off five hundred bombs throughout Palestine, in an attempt to disrupt the railway system. As darkness fell on December 27, the Irgun and Lehi together attacked the Jerusalem headquarters of British intelligence (CID), located on Jaffa Road, and also simultaneously attacked targets in Jaffa and Tel Aviv.[68]

Not all of the joint efforts were as successful. On Saturday evening, January 19, 1946, the Irgun and Lehi together attempted to rescue prisoners from the central police headquarters in Jerusalem and to attack the Palestine Broadcasting Service. They ended up suffering casualties and retreated without achieving either goal.[69]

THE BOMBING OF THE KING DAVID HOTEL

Irgun members dressed as Arabs drove a stolen truck containing seven milk churns packed with explosives to the service entrance of the King David Hotel at 11:45 A.M. on July 22, 1946. The entrance also served the kitchens of the Regence Café, located in the hotel. Directly above the café, the southwestern wing of the hotel housed the offices of the British administration, on five separate floors.[70]

The Irgunists rounded up the kitchen staff, held them at gunpoint, and carried the milk churns into the basement of the hotel. Their plan nearly foundered when an alert British officer spied the intruders, but they shot him as he attempted to draw his gun. By the time the Jerusalem police were alerted by an alarm bell at approximately 12:15 P.M., the seven milk churns, with timing devices and detonators attached, were in place around the central pillars in the basement. Israel Levi, the Irgunist in charge, also rigged a booby trap so that the churns could not easily be disarmed. On the churns, he placed signs— in three languages—reading, "Mines—Do Not Touch."[71]

The Irgun raiding party then fled the hotel. Some accounts say they drove away in the stolen truck; others say that most made for a black taxi waiting on a street about two hundred yards northeast of the hotel, while some ran away on foot. At least two of the attackers were hit by British gunfire during the getaway; one later died of his wounds.

A few minutes afterward, a small bomb exploded outside a car dealership just south of the King David Hotel. A second small bomb planted in a street to the north of the hotel failed to explode. Menachem Begin later said that the smaller bombs were intended to frighten people and to encourage them to leave the general area. Some doubt the truth of this statement. In any event, the initial small explosion had the opposite effect. The blast damaged a passing bus and blew out windows in nearby buildings. Wounded passengers from the bus were carried into the hotel, while many of those already inside the hotel gathered in the southwestern corner to see what was going on, without realizing that they were standing on top of a powder keg with a smoldering fuse.

The smaller bomb blast was the signal for an Irgun member, Adina Hay-Nissan, to make three telephone calls, warning of the bombs in the basement and of the impending destruction of the King David Hotel. She later said that she placed the telephone calls—to the hotel, to the French consulate, and to the *Palestine Post*—nearly thirty minutes before the milk churns were set to explode. The Irgun claimed afterward that the highest-ranking British official in the hotel—John Shaw, the chief secretary of the British occupation administration— had ignored their telephoned warning. However, British officials insisted that there had been no advance warning and that the calls were received only after the milk churns exploded at 12:37 P.M., demolishing all six floors of the southwestern wing of the King David Hotel.[72]

After the Irgun blew up the hotel, the temporary alliance between the Haganah, the Irgun, and Lehi disintegrated. The Haganah publicly disavowed the now infamous attack, which had killed ninety-one people, including twenty-eight Britons, seventeen Jews, and forty-one Arabs. To his dying day, Menachem Begin maintained that the Irgun had not intended to cause casualties. Others contend that the evidence indicates otherwise.[73]

The repercussions from the destruction of the King David Hotel were significant. Sympathy for the Jewish cause, already waning, was sharply reduced in Britain and elsewhere. The Irgun became pariahs in the eyes of the world. The Jewish Agency condemned the attack. Its head, David Ben-Gurion, reportedly told a French newspaper reporter that the Irgun was "the enemy of the Jewish people." As the alliance of the Haganah, the Irgun, and Lehi dissolved, the Irgun was forced to issue a statement taking sole responsibility for the heinous act.[74]

After the King David Hotel incident, the violence continued. On October 30, 1946, the Irgun went after the railway station in Jerusalem. Although they were detected, came under fire, and were subsequently arrested, the Irgunists managed to leave two suitcases filled with explosives inside the waiting room of the station. One of the suitcases exploded, destroying the building and killing a policeman who was attempting to pick it up.[75] Then, in quick succession, the Irgun blew up the income tax offices in Jerusalem on November 20 and attacked a police station in the city on November 30.[76]

Three months later, on March 1, 1947, the Irgun attacked Goldschmidt House—the British officers' club located on King George Street in Jerusalem. It was supposedly impregnable, as it was located in the middle of one of the four "security zones" constructed by the British in Jerusalem. These security zones were nicknamed "Bevingrads" by the local Jerusalemites, after Ernest Bevin, who was at the time (1945–51) the British secretary of state for foreign affairs. The entire area was surrounded by a fence with barbed wire, and identity cards were needed to gain entrance. The attack took place on the Sabbath, a day when the British would not have expected observant Jews to conduct a military operation. The Irgun claimed that they scheduled it for that day because the streets would be empty and there would be fewer civilian casualties. The attack began under cover of heavy machine-gun fire. A truck filled with armed Irgun members disguised in British uniforms crashed through the barbed wire fence and came to a halt at the entrance to the Officers' Club. Three of the men ran inside the building. Each carried a backpack containing thirty kilograms of explosives. Dov Salomon, the leader, placed all three backpacks next to the building's supporting pillars and lit the fuse. At 3:00 P.M., Goldschmidt House blew up, killing seventeen British officers and injuring twenty-seven others. That evening, the British imposed martial law in Jerusalem and Tel Aviv. At dawn the next day, more than twenty thousand British troops began a crackdown throughout Palestine, rounding up all suspected Irgunists and other Jewish terrorists. But the British operations, code-named "Hippo" in Jerusalem and "Elephant" in Tel Aviv, were failures, and their widely cast nets caught no one of importance in any of the Jewish resistance groups.[77]

The Irgun continued their attacks, and on March 12 they blew up a building in the Schneller British army base in Jerusalem, killing one British soldier and wounding eight more. The incident made headlines around the world and served to further undermine British authority in the region. Martial law was revoked five days later, on March 17.[78]

A special session of the United Nations to debate the situation in Palestine, originally scheduled for September 1947, was hastily rescheduled for April 28. But the violence continued. On August 2, the Irgun attacked the Royal Air Force Club in Jerusalem. On August 5, a bomb planted in the Jerusalem Labor Department exploded while three British constables were attempting to defuse it; it killed all three instantly.[79]

On August 31, 1947, the United Nations Special Committee on Palestine (UNSCOP) published its report recommending a partitioning of Palestine into two sovereign states—one Jewish, one Arab. Jerusalem would belong to neither; it would become a neutral, demilitarized city governed by an appointee of the United Nations (UN). But the report's recommendations had little effect on the violence in Palestine, which continued throughout the early fall and into November. On the night of November 13, just weeks before the UN vote on the plan to partition, six grenades were thrown at the Ritz Café on King George Avenue, killing one British soldier and injuring twenty-seven other people, while two British policemen were shot nearby.[80]

THE PARTITION

On November 29, 1947, the UN voted to pass the resolution, by the required two-thirds majority (thirty-three for, thirteen against, with ten abstentions). The Jews in Palestine welcomed the news with rejoicing, but the Arabs responded with gunfire. On November 30, Arab gunmen shot at an ambulance on its way to Hadassah Hospital and used hand grenades and machine-gun fire to kill five Jewish passengers on two buses bound for Jerusalem. There was violence elsewhere in the Arab world as well. Three hundred Jewish homes were burned in Aleppo, Syria, as half of the city's four thousand Jews fled in terror. Seventy-six Jews were killed in Aden, Yemen.[81]

The Arab Higher Committee refused to consider the idea of a Jewish state anywhere in Palestine and declared November 29 to be a "day of mourning." They issued a call for a three-day general strike—including a boycott against all Jewish goods—to begin on December 2. On that day, three Jews were killed in the Old City, and two hundred Arabs, mostly teenagers, marched through Jerusalem chanting "Death to the Jews." They looted Jewish shops in the Commercial Center by the Jaffa Gate while British troops looked on. In retaliation, Jews attacked Arab shops and a garage elsewhere in the city. The next day, there were additional shootings and killings in Jerusalem.[82]

Soon the violence intensified, and this time the British were no longer the primary target. Now Arabs killed Jews and Jews killed Arabs. Stabbing, shooting, bombing, lynching, and beating of civilians and combatants on both sides were daily occurrences in Jerusalem and throughout Palestine. On December 5 the Jewish Agency called up all men and women between the ages of seventeen and twenty-five for military duty. On December 11 the Jewish Quarter of the Old City was attacked by an Arab mob. After a six-hour gun battle, three Arabs were killed and the attackers were driven off. On December 13 Irgunists hurled two bombs into a crowd by the Damascus Gate bus station and opened fire; five Arabs were killed and forty-seven injured. In a period of only two weeks, seventy-four Jews, seventy-one Arabs, and nine British were killed in and around Jerusalem.[83] The deaths continued to mount in the city during the rest of December and into the New Year.[84] It was not an auspicious beginning to the idea of the Partition. It was, however, an intimation of what was to come.

POLITICS AND PROPAGANDA

While Allenby may not have made the famous remark that the Crusades had finally come to an end, many others saw—and still see—his campaign and capture of Jerusalem in exactly that light. A poem published in the *New York Times* on December 19, 1917, captured the enthusiasm of some at the moment, who had no way of knowing what lay in store for the British during their occupation of Palestine.

Jerusalem, Jerusalem
Lift up thy gates once more!

The soldiers of the Tenth Crusade
Are at thy temple door!
Oh, raise thine ancient battle hymn
Where Godfrey died of yore!

Jerusalem, Jerusalem
The Coeur de Lion's glance,
Saladin's troth, the lilies on
The breast of knightly France.
The faith of Simon and of John,
Are thine inheritance!

Jerusalem, Jerusalem
From Heaven's heights divine
They bend—thy warriors of old —
Their gaze on Palestine
Where, 'neath their crests, is "Allenby"
Engraven on thy shrine!

Jerusalem, Jerusalem
Oh, set thy gates ajar;
The Infidel and his ally—
The Beast—shall pass afar.
And, on thy soldiers of the cross
Shall rise the Christmas Star.[85]

As Professor Jonathan Newell has pointed out, many autobiographies by British soldiers in the immediate aftermath of the Palestine campaigns contain either the word *Crusade* or the word *Crusaders* in their title, demonstrating that this notion had become embedded in the popular imagination. Interestingly, most of these soldier-authors did not hark back to the successful First Crusade but, rather, chose Richard the Lionheart and the Third Crusade as their model. Perhaps they saw themselves as completing that failed mission.[86]

In an article entitled "The Legacy of the Crusades: An Islamic Perspective," Dr. Hadia Dajani-Shakeel, formerly professor of Middle Eastern studies at the University of Toronto, demonstrates the power still present today in the apocryphal Allenby story.

One popular story, which every child growing up in mandate Palestine may have heard, describes the entry of the British General Allenby into Jerusalem. The story goes that upon entering the Holy City, the General prayed first in the Church of Resurrection, then headed to the Muslim sacred shrines: The Aqsa Mosque and the Dome of the Rock. There, he paused for a minute, then invoking the memory of Richard the Lionheart, he proclaimed, in the presence of the Muslim officials: Now the Crusades have ended.[87]

Even if Allenby did not utter this statement, Moslem paranoia about a Crusader mentality from the West was perhaps not totally unfounded, particularly given Lloyd George's original request for Jerusalem as a "Christmas present" and the subsequent joyful celebration of Christmas in Jerusalem under Christian control for the first time in nearly seven hundred years.

In her magisterial volume on the Crusades as seen from an Islamic perspective, Dr. Carole Hillenbrand, professor of Islamic history at the University of Edinburgh, sums up the situation in a nutshell.

It is not significant in the war of propaganda that Allenby did not actually make his famous "remark." Nevertheless, Allenby's alleged remark was propagated by Sayyid Qutb [the Egyptian fundamentalist writer and "Moslem Brothers" spokesman executed for treason in 1966] and other Muslim writers and it epitomises the way in which the modern Islamic world views the spectre of the Crusades.[88]

It is in this light that one may better understand why many in both the West and the East shuddered when President George W. Bush uttered his infamous "crusade" remarks in the heated aftermath of the World Trade Center and Pentagon terrorist attacks masterminded by Osama bin Laden and al-Qaeda.

Winston Churchill, with his knowledge of history, tried to put Allenby's campaign into accurate political, military, and, above all, religious perspective. When Churchill visited Jerusalem in 1921, in his official capacity as secretary of state for colonial affairs, he attended the dedication service for the British Military Cemetery on Mount Scopus on March 27. Churchill paid homage to the British soldiers buried there who had died in Palestine during World War I, including those who had fallen during the battle for Jerusalem in December 1917. "These veteran soldiers lie where rests the dust of the Khalifs, Crusaders, and Maccabees," said Churchill. He continued: "Their monuments will be maintained not only for centuries, but as long as the British State endures. Peace to their ashes, honour to their memory and may we not fail to complete the work they began."[89]

Churchill thus managed, in a single sentence, to invoke not only the Christian Crusades but also earlier Islamic and Jewish military efforts to capture Jerusalem, thereby demonstrating the importance of the city to all three religions. However, the "British State," as Churchill put it, endured only three decades longer in Palestine. It ended its control with the clarion trumpets of the 1948 war sounding in the immediate distance.

9

JERUSALEM OF GOLD

AS THEY PREPARED for war in the spring of 1948, both Arabs and Jews invoked images of previous battles for Jerusalem. On May 15, the first day of existence of the fledgling Jewish state, Menachem Begin, commander of the Irgun, addressed the nation in a radio broadcast. He, like the Zionists Jabotinsky and Herzl before him, saw a parallel between the efforts of his own day and those of the Maccabees in 167 BCE.

> The Hebrew revolt of 1944–48 has been blessed with success— the first Hebrew revolt since the Hasmonean insurrection that has ended in victory. . . . The State of Israel has arisen in bloody battle. . . . The foundation has been laid—but only the foundation—for true independence. One phase of the battle for freedom, for the return of the whole People of Israel to its homeland, for the restoration of the whole Land of Israel to its God-covenanted owners, has ended. But only one phase.[1]

One year earlier, Abd al-Rahman Azzam, secretary-general of the Arab League (whose members at that time were Egypt, Syria, Lebanon, Transjordan, Iraq, Saudi Arabia, and Yemen), sought to invoke a different and harsher precedent from the past. Anticipating the forthcoming war, he declared: "This will be a war of extermination. It will be a momentous massacre to be spoken of like the Mongolian massacre and the Crusades."[2]

JANUARY–APRIL 1948

The violence that had raged during the final months of 1947 continued into the New Year. Jews and Arabs attacked and counterattacked one another throughout the cities of Palestine, in Jerusalem, Tel Aviv, Jaffa, and Haifa.[3]

On January 7, 1948, two days after a bomb planted by the Haganah killed twenty-six people at the Semiramis Hotel, Irgunists drove a stolen police van containing a fifty-gallon oil drum filled with explosives and scrap metal to the Jaffa Gate in Jerusalem. They lit the fuse, pushed the drum out of the van, and sped off. The drum exploded, killing or wounding more than sixty Arabs waiting at a bus stop. But the Irgunists did not get far. Their van crashed into a nearby traffic island, and British security forces shot all but one Irgunist as they ran from the scene. A second bomb, with its fuse primed and ready to be lit, was still inside the van.[4]

Retaliation was not long in coming. An Arab explosives expert named Fauzi el-Kutub filled a British police pickup truck with TNT. On February 1, two British deserters—police captain Eddie Brown and army corporal Peter Madison—parked the pickup in front of the *Palestine Post* building and walked away. The truck blew up, killing or injuring twenty people, demolishing the front of the building, and damaging all the surrounding structures.[5]

Three weeks later, the three men collaborated again. This time, the two British deserters and some Arabs dressed in British army uniforms drove an armored car and three British army trucks loaded with explosives to Ben Yehuda Street, one of the busiest streets in Jerusalem. They parked the trucks and drove away in the armored car. When the trucks exploded, fifty-two people were killed, and more than one hundred were wounded. The street and its buildings were left in shambles. Soon after, the Irgun and Lehi, bent on revenge, killed ten British soldiers and wounded twenty more.[6]

On March 11, in an audacious attack, el-Kutub and his driver took a Ford belonging to the United States Consulate General (a car flying an American flag from its fender) into the driveway of the Jewish Agency in Jerusalem. They parked the car, which was packed with TNT, directly in front of the doorway of Haganah headquarters and walked away. An alert guard came to investigate and moved the car but did not get very far. The car exploded, killing him and thirteen civilians within the Jewish Agency.[7]

As the British mandate in Palestine drew to a close, the first four thousand British troops left for home in early March of 1948. Before the end of the month, two Jewish convoys attempting to bring food and aid from Tel Aviv to Jerusalem were ambushed, and many of the participants were killed. Soon the Jews in Jerusalem were under attack once again, this time both from within and from outside the city boundaries. Arab irregulars slowly tightened a noose around the Jewish parts of the city, where food and water soon grew scarce. As starvation loomed for the one hundred thousand resident Jews, only armed convoys dared to make the trip from Tel Aviv. Few of them successfully ran the blockade, and none made it through completely unscathed. The state of the Jews within Jerusalem continued to become more desperate as convoy after convoy failed to reach the city. Only when the Haganah launched Operation Nachshon and reopened the Jerusalem corridor from Tel Aviv to Jerusalem in mid-April did the Jewish inhabitants of Jerusalem obtain some brief relief. But that supply line soon closed down again.[8]

On April 9, the Irgun and Lehi, in a joint operation, attacked the village of Deir Yassin, to the west of Jerusalem. The details of the events of that day are contested, but the end result is not questioned. Many of the villagers were killed—perhaps as many as 250 men, women, and children, according to reports at the time, but probably closer to 100 in actuality. The Irgun and Lehi claimed that all had been killed during the fighting, whereas the few survivors insisted that there had been a massacre, with mutilation of the victims as well as raping and looting.

Whatever were the true events of that day, the attack on Deir Yassin subsequently featured in the propaganda of both sides. "Deir Yassin" became—and still remains—a rallying cry for the displaced Arabs of Palestine; the attack is remembered like the massacre by Lebanese militiamen of hundreds of Palestinian civilians in the Sabra and Shatila refugee camps outside Beirut in 1982. Although the Jewish Agency and various other Jewish organizations expressed dismay and officially repudiated the events at Deir Yassin, the quasi-military Jewish organizations such as Irgun and Lehi were thenceforth able to play upon the fears of the Arabs by using the threat of a repetition elsewhere in Palestine to help them win battles—or even to win without having to fight. The situation was not unlike that of three thousand years earlier when the Neo-Assyrian king Sennacherib ordered scenes from the capture and destruction of Judaean Lachish in 701 BCE inscribed upon the walls of his palace at Nineveh. Those scenes were intended, in part, to dissuade other potential rebels from rising up.[9]

Arab vengeance for Deir Yassin came quickly to Jerusalem. On April 10, Jewish areas came under mortar fire. On April 13, a kindergarten in the Jewish Quarter was hit, and more than twenty children were injured. Then, at 9:30 A.M. on April 14, 1948, a ten-vehicle medical convoy bound for Hadassah Hospital—located on Mount Scopus, in the Arab section of Jerusalem—was attacked. The vehicles included two ambulances, several armored buses, and three trucks loaded with hospital supplies. All were clearly marked as belonging to the Magen David Adom—the Jewish version of the Red Cross. In the vehicles were mostly civilians—doctors, nurses, and patients, as well as some Hebrew University personnel. Although there had been isolated incidents previously, the medical people did not really expect trouble, since the hospital had received an assurance from the British high commissioner that any medical traffic going to Mount Scopus would be protected by British soldiers and police.[10]

Nevertheless, a mine in the roadway exploded, disabling three of the first four vehicles, including an ambulance and two buses. Six vehicles turned and fled, but rifle fire, grenades, and Molotov cocktails rained down upon the hapless occupants of the first four. It was a one-sided battle. Only the escorts in the lead vehicle had weapons; the doctors, nurses, and patients were all unarmed. The British did little to help. By the time the Highland Light Infantry came to the assistance of the beleaguered convoy, some six hours had passed, and seventy-seven people were dead, including the director of the hospital, the head of the Cancer Research Department, and some of the foremost medical practi-

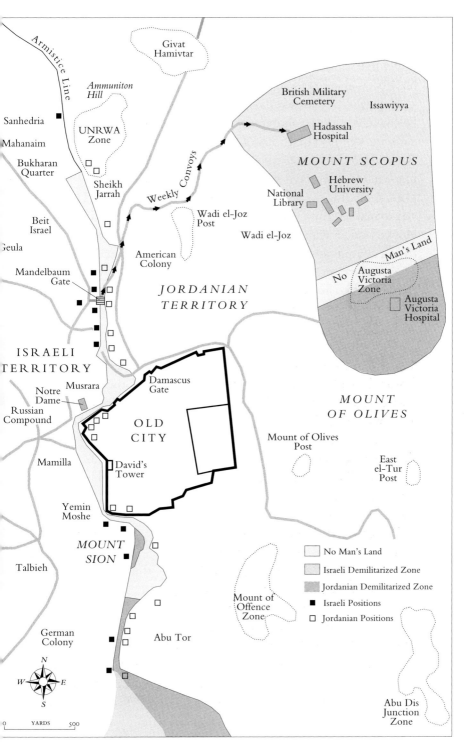

Map 22. The city boundary of Jerusalem, 1948–67 CE

tioners in the land. Some had died inside the burning buses. Afterward, the Arab Higher Committee issued a statement praising the attack and noted that if the British had not interfered, the Arab attackers would have been able to kill all of the Jews, not just seventy-seven.[11]

However, by the next day, the situation improved somewhat for the beleaguered Jewish inhabitants of Jerusalem. A convoy of 131 vehicles carrying five hundred tons of food finally reached the city from Tel Aviv. Two days later, 250 trucks—out of 280 that began the journey—made it through with an additional one thousand tons of supplies, including flour, sugar, milk, fruit, and vegetables. The last convoy to make it through to Jerusalem before the road from Tel Aviv was blocked once again did so on April 20. In this convoy, 294 of 300 trucks completed the journey, but the Jewish commander was killed, as were thirty of the Arab attackers. Damaged and destroyed vehicles that failed to reach the city can still be seen today, enshrined as memorials by the side of the modern highway leading from Tel Aviv to Jerusalem.[12]

The fighting in and around Jerusalem did not occur in a vacuum, and serious battles raged throughout all of Palestine at this time. The British did little to stem the violence; most of their attention was focused on an orderly withdrawal of their own troops from the area. The death toll continued to mount at an alarming rate. According to the *Palestine Post* of May 3, more than 3,500 Arabs, 1,100 Jews, and 150 Britons were killed in the five-month period between December 1947 and the end of April 1948.[13] All this slaughter occurred before war was officially declared.

THE DECLARATION OF INDEPENDENCE

After thirty years of British rule in Palestine, the British mandate was scheduled to end at midnight on May 14, 1948. Earlier that day, the British officially lowered the Union Jack and left Jerusalem. However, hours before the official end of the British occupation, the Haganah seized forward positions inside Jerusalem as fighting erupted throughout the entire country. Because the fourteenth was a Friday and the Jewish Sabbath would commence at sunset, David Ben-Gurion, the head of the provisional government of Israel, read aloud the Declaration of Independence in a live radio broadcast from Tel Aviv at 4:00 P.M. He declared that the state of Israel would come into existence at the stroke of midnight, as the British mandate expired.[14]

Eleven minutes after midnight in Palestine, President Harry S. Truman officially confirmed the recognition of the new state of Israel by the United States of America. It was an unexpected move, and his motivation is still debated today. Pundits quip that there were more Jewish votes than Arab votes in the United States at the time, but of course the situation was much more complicated. Whatever his reasons, Truman's declaration made the United States the first country in the world to recognize the new state of Israel. Some of his cabinet members thereafter referred to Truman as Israel's "midwife," others called him Israel's "godfather."[15]

Israel's Declaration of Independence read in part:

> The State of Israel ... will be based on the principles of liberty, justice and peace as conceived by the Prophets of Israel; will uphold the full social and political equality of all its citizens, without distinction of religion, race, or sex; will guarantee freedom of religion, conscience, education and culture; will safeguard the Holy Places of all religions. ... In the midst of wanton aggression, we yet call upon the Arab inhabitants of the State of Israel to preserve the ways of peace and play their part in the development of the State, on the basis of full and equal citizenship and due representation in all its bodies and institutions—provisional and permanent. We extend our hand in peace and neighborliness to all the neighboring states and their peoples, and invite them to cooperate with the independent Jewish nation for the common good of all.[16]

The plea for cooperation between Jews and Arabs went unheeded. Within hours, Israel was surrounded by the hostile armies of all the members of the Arab League except Yemen. Transjordan, Iraq, Syria, Lebanon, Egypt, and Saudi Arabia joined forces to crush the new nation at its birth on May 15, 1948.[17]

For the first effort against the state of Israel, Transjordan sent its Arab Legion, the best trained of the Arab armies attacking Israel. The legion was led by major general John Bagot Glubb—known as "Glubb Pasha"—with nearly forty other British officers serving as senior commanders. Glubb's commission in the British army had terminated with the end of the mandate, and he was at this time essentially a mercenary in the pay of King Abdullah of Transjordan. Many of the other officers, however, had been seconded from the British army. Glubb, apparently well versed in geography and history, planned to attack Jerusalem from the north. On the night of May 14, the legion moved across the Allenby Bridge into Palestine, to the accompaniment of King Abdullah's cries of "Forward!"—their ears ringing with the sound of his revolver firing into the heavens.[18]

Events rapidly unfolded. By the morning of May 15, fighting was fierce inside the city. An army of Arab irregulars—the so-called Arab Liberation Army, commanded by the explosives expert Fauzi el-Kaukji—overran some suburbs of Jerusalem, while Jewish forces captured the Mea Shearim police station (in the area that is now the center of the Orthodox Jewish population) and the predominantly Arab neighborhoods of Sheikh Jarrah (along the route to Mount Scopus), as well as the German Colony, the Greek Colony, Bakaa, and Talbiyeh. That night, Jewish forces captured the Allenby Barracks (in southern Jerusalem), which was defended by three hundred Iraqi troops. With the capture of the barracks came desperately needed arms and ammunition, including an antitank gun. By the night of the sixteenth, the Haganah had overrun the Jerusalem railway station and the last remaining Arab suburbs in the New City. The next day, a military convoy carrying army supplies from Tel Aviv reached the Jewish forces inside the city.[19]

By this time, the Jewish defenders of the Old City were growing desperate. Although the UN Security Council had earlier declared that the Old City was to be an open, demilitarized zone, it had been under almost constant siege since February, when the Arabs blocked up the Zion Gate and cut off access to the New City. The siege was to continue until the surrender by the Israeli defenders on May 28—the longest siege of the Old City since the time of the Crusaders nearly a thousand years earlier.[20]

Jewish troops outside the walls of the Old City, responding to frantic messages from the defenders inside, attempted to break through the Jaffa Gate. Their attack was planned for the night of May 17 but did not begin until dawn on the eighteenth, by which time the Arab forces inside the gate were well prepared. Jewish explosives experts were killed before they could blow open the gate, and the attacking soldiers were cut down by merciless fire from within the walls. The Jewish forces retreated with heavy losses.[21]

Later that same day, the First Infantry Company of the Arab Legion entered the Old City through St. Stephen's Gate (also known as the Lion's Gate, after the two ornamental stone lions placed on either side by Sultan Suleiman I as part of his rebuilding plan in the early seventeenth century). Men from the legion promptly joined the Arab irregulars fighting for control of the Jewish Quarter. This created panic among the defenders and caused the Jewish soldiers outside the Old City to redouble their efforts to relieve those inside.[22]

An attack through the Zion Gate by the newly formed Harel Brigade of the Palmach—the Palmach were the assault companies of the Haganah—was finally successful in the early hours of May 19. Yitzhak Rabin was in overall command, Colonel Uzi Narkiss was in charge of the battalion, and Major David Elazar was in command of the unit that was chosen for the attack. All three men went on to hold prominent positions in the state of Israel, Rabin becoming prime minister in the 1970s. Following the order to attack, sixty Palmach men first captured Mount Zion to the south and then blew a breach in the Zion Gate to enter the Old City. They soon linked up with the defenders in the Jewish Quarter. They brought food, ammunition, blood plasma, and chlorine for purifying the water of the city's cisterns. They also brought eighty men from the Etzioni Brigade of the Haganah as reinforcements. These joined the 120 Haganah and approximately one hundred Irgun soldiers who had been in place in the Old City since the siege began. There were now about fifteen hundred civilians and three hundred soldiers left to defend the Jewish Quarter of Jerusalem—the same quarter that had housed some twenty-eight thousand Jews fifty years earlier.[23]

Meanwhile, at dawn on the same day (May 19), the Arab Legion recaptured the area of Sheikh Jarrah and then took both the area of French Hill and the British Police Training School (from which they could shell Hadassah Hospital and Mount Scopus). At the same time, a column of Arab Legion troops spearheaded by a squadron of armored cars advanced into the Old City through the Damascus Gate. This force then joined the attack on the Jewish Quarter.[24]

Badly outnumbered, the Palmach withdrew at six in the evening. Their orders had been to link up with and resupply the defenders of the Jewish Quarter but not to help defend the area. The decision to withdraw was controversial and ultimately costly, for no link with the defenders in the Old City was ever reestablished. After the Palmach withdrawal, the Jewish Quarter came under daily heavy artillery fire. In addition, the Arab combatants blew up the water pipeline running between Jerusalem and the coast, creating a severe water shortage in the city.[25]

As these events were unfolding within the Old City, the Arab Legion was shelling the northern suburbs of the city from the area of Sheikh Jarrah, while the Egyptians shelled the southern suburbs from a monastery on the outskirts of Bethlehem. The shelling was indiscriminate, and civilian shops and houses were hit as well as military and administrative targets. Many civilians were killed or wounded. The fighting was also fierce on the outskirts and in the areas immediately surrounding Jerusalem (Kibbutz Ramat Rahel, the Arab village of Shuafat, and the heights of Nebi Samwil) and throughout the rest of Palestine/Israel.[26]

On May 22, Thomas C. Wasson, the American consul in Jerusalem, was shot dead by an Arab sniper. At the time of the attack, Wasson was walking to the American Consulate from the French Consulate, where he had been attending a meeting of the three-person UN Truce Commission. The commission had just sent the UN Security Council a cable that read in part:

> For past 5 days . . . Jerusalem, including old city, subjected indiscriminate attacks and nightly shelling by mortars of Arab legion. Among attacked are hospitals, religious and social institutions

including Hadassah Medical Center on Mount Scopus and mainly non-combatant citizens. Does world intend remaining silent? Will United Nations who expressed fears for peace Holy City permit this to continue? In name Jewish Jerusalem we demand immediate action to patrol Holy City.

Later that same day, the UN Security Council called for a cease-fire throughout Palestine. The Jews promptly agreed, on the condition that the Arabs did as well. But the Arabs asked for a delay while they arranged for a "consultation." Meanwhile, the fighting continued to rage in Jerusalem.[27]

By May 23, Glubb Pasha and the Arab Legion attempted to capture the Notre Dame Monastery, located just outside the New Gate in Jerusalem. The Haganah had taken the monastery on May 14 and had resisted all attempts by the Arabs to recapture it. As the renewed attack began with a push by the Third Regiment of the Arab Legion, Haganah defenders inside the monastery threw Molotov cocktails. They set on fire an armored car and a second vehicle in the street immediately outside, creating a barricade that prevented the approach of additional armored vehicles. The defenders then poured such a murderous barrage of gunfire into the two hundred attacking infantrymen that Glubb Pasha was forced to call off the assault. Nearly half of the Arab Legion forces involved in the attack were either killed or wounded during the intense battle. Glubb later said that it was the worst defeat his men suffered in the war.[28]

On May 26, a Jewish pilot flying in a small plane buzzed the Jewish quarter four times, dropping guns and ammunition. Nothing reached the Jewish defenders, the entire load falling into the hands of the Arab forces. The Jews in the Old City radioed the news to those outside the walls. They had only 170 machine-gun bullets left and asked for the plane to make another run with more weapons. It was not possible.[29]

By the next day, May 27, fully one-third of the Jewish Quarter was in Arab hands, and Arab forces set on fire the main synagogue, the Hurva. There was neither plasma nor anesthetic left in the hospital. Only thirty-six Jewish soldiers were still uninjured and able to fight, and they had only three hundred rounds of ammunition left among them. In the previous week, sixty-two Jews had been killed and more than two hundred wounded during the fighting in the Old City.[30]

Finally, on the morning of May 28, the end came. At 9:15 A.M. two rabbis carrying white flags of surrender set out from the Jewish Quarter toward the Zion Gate. At 4:30 P.M., after seven hours of tense negotiations, Major Abdullah al-Tel, commander of the Arab Legion in the Old City, agreed to accept the surrender of the Quarter. Troops from the Arab Legion quickly occupied the area. Some 340 Jewish soldiers and able-bodied men between the ages of fifteen and sixty, nearly all of them wounded, were taken to Amman as prisoners of war. The remaining civilians and the very seriously wounded—nearly thirteen hundred refugees—were allowed to flee to the western part of the city during a two-hour cease-fire. As they left, they could see smoke and flames begin to rise as the Arab forces systematically set fire to the Jewish Quarter. The departing Jews would not be able to return to their homes and synagogues or to the sacred Wailing Wall until Israeli forces retook the Old City nineteen years later, in 1967.[31]

The next morning, May 29, in the aftermath of the Arab Legion's greatest victory of the 1948 war, the British government ordered all British officers with the legion to remove themselves from command and refrain from further fighting. The operational commanders, the brigade commanders, three of the four officers commanding the infantry units, and the trained artillery officers in the Arab legion were all British. That British officers had been involved in the attack upon the Jewish Quarter had not gone unnoticed by the rest of the world, and the British government was becoming increasingly worried about a potential political backlash.[32]

The loss of the many officers who had been seconded from the British army significantly impaired the fighting capability of the Arab Legion and undoubtedly influenced the outcome of the war, as Glubb Pasha later lamented. However, a number of the British officers and Glubb Pasha himself removed themselves for only forty-eight hours and soon resumed their previous positions of command within the legion. The temporary absence of all the officers, though, allowed the British government to issue a statement denying that any British officers were currently engaged in hostilities against the Jews and to sponsor a second resolution in the UN Security Council, calling for a cease-fire to be followed by four weeks of truce throughout all of Palestine.[33]

The cease-fire and this first truce were not implemented until June 11. In the meantime, the Arab siege of the New City in western Jerusalem intensified, with unrelenting artillery barrages and incessant machine-gun and rifle fire. Civilians could not walk the streets, and it was dangerous to appear even momentarily in a doorway or window. Ricocheting bullets and shrapnel from exploding mortar and artillery rounds were a constant danger. Famine was so intense that the inhabitants and refugees were reduced to eating dandelions, weeds, and other wild plants from their backyards. Water was so scarce that severe rationing was imposed and little or no sanitation was possible. Perhaps some of the more educated among the inhabitants recalled Josephus's description of the siege of Jerusalem by Titus in 70 CE. Lack of sanitation and a diet of wild plants were common elements in the two sieges separated in time by nearly two thousand years.[34]

To relieve the Jews besieged in the New City, a three-mile-long pass known as the Burma Road was eventually carved by hand out of sheer rock and steep hillsides. It bypassed a section of the Tel Aviv-Jerusalem road dominated by the Arab village of Latrun. The village had been the site of frequent ambushes that had effectively closed the road. The bypass was completed on June 9, and supply convoys once again began to reach Jerusalem. Every twenty-four hours, they brought one hundred tons of supplies. A new pipeline running the length of the Tel Aviv-Jerusalem road was also constructed, providing the city with water once again.[35]

On June 11, 1948, the first cease-fire and truce went into effect. During the previous weeks of fighting, from May 14 until June 11, more than ten thousand artillery and mortar shells landed in Old or New Jerusalem, destroying more than two thousand Jewish homes and killing or wounding twelve hundred civilians. Whether, in their turn, Jewish forces fired on the Haram al-Sherif and hit the Dome of the Rock and the al-Aqsa Mosque with gunfire and mortar shells, killing or wounding Moslem worshipers, is uncertain, but a few historians claim that is what happened. After the surrender, Jewish synagogues and other holy places in the Old City were destroyed or used as garbage dumps, latrines, henhouses, and stables.[36]

The first truce of the 1948 war lasted twenty-eight days, from June 11 until July 9. During that period, the United Nations organized official convoys that brought a limited quantity of supplies to Jerusalem—all subject to Arab Legion inspection. The Burma Road, however, was improved and maintained surreptitiously—allowing food and water, as well as military equipment and reinforcements, to enter Jerusalem without inspection. The Arab armies also were able to regroup, rest, and rearm.[37]

There was little fighting in Jerusalem during the first truce, but during this four-week period, the fledgling state of Israel faced its greatest internal rebellion. On May 28 David Ben-Gurion—as head of the provisional government—had signed an order creating a national army, to be known as the Israel Defense Forces (IDF). The order specifically prohibited the existence of any other armed forces—for example, the Irgun or Lehi. On June 20 this was put to the test, when a ship named the *Altalena* arrived off the coast of Israel. On board were nine hundred recruits, as well as arms and ammunition, destined for the Irgun. The IDF and the Irgun fought a pitched battle when the ship ran aground in Tel Aviv; fifteen men were killed, and the ship was eventually sunk. This was the nearest that the Jews had come to a civil war in two millennia, but infighting between Jewish factions before they united against a common enemy was nothing new, as we have seen previously—during the First Jewish Revolt against the Romans, for example. In the end, the IDF won. On June 28 Menachem Begin and other members of the Irgun took an oath of allegiance, and the Irgun officially ceased to exist as an independent organization.[38] Lehi, however, continued its activities during the rest of 1948 and into 1949. They would commit one more major act of aggression that shocked the world.

Meanwhile, the UN mediator, Count Folke Bernadotte of Sweden, proposed a new partition of territory. He suggested giving Galilee to the Israelis and the Negev to the Arabs, that Transjordan govern a portion of Palestine, and that Jerusalem come under the authority and control of the United Nations. This time, all of the involved parties rejected the proposal.[39]

TEN DAYS OF FIGHTING

On July 9 the first truce expired when the Arabs refused to extend it for an additional ten days. Fighting erupted across Palestine once again, from Galilee to the Negev. The renewed conflict lasted only ten days, until Count Bernadotte negotiated another cease-fire and truce. But those few days before the second cease-fire took effect on July 18 saw some of the fiercest fighting of the war, especially along the southern front, near Beersheba and Gaza.[40]

There was also renewed fighting in and around Jerusalem. On July 10 air-raid sirens were heard in Jerusalem for the first time, as an Egyptian Spitfire dropped bombs on the New City. The Arab Legion attacked the New City twice but was beaten back. The Israelis in turn fought to expand the "Jerusalem corridor" leading between Jerusalem and Tel Aviv and also made a number of armed forays in and around the Old City. On the last night before the new cease-fire took effect, the Israelis attacked the Old City in two places. An Irgun unit managed to penetrate through the New Gate but was soon forced to withdraw. A Haganah unit tried to attack through the Zion Gate but was unsuccessful. As a consequence of these failed Israeli attacks, the city continued to be divided into Arab and Jewish sectors, and it remained so for the next nineteen years.[41]

THE SECOND TRUCE AND CEASE-FIRE

During the second truce, Count Bernadotte—the UN mediator—actively continued to push for the partition of Palestine. Although he had revised his original proposal, the plan was still unacceptable to both the Jews and the Arabs. Lehi decided to take matters into their own hands. On September 17, 1948, they assassinated Count Bernadotte in Jerusalem, shooting him and a French aide with pistols at point-blank range. Yitzhak Shamir, one of the Lehi leaders at the time, later admitted the group's involvement. The name of the assassin who fired the fatal shots, Yehoshua Cohen, was quickly circulated, but neither he nor the others involved were ever caught. Bernadotte's murder shocked the world. His partition proposal effectively died with him, although it took longer to expire.[42]

The second truce was frequently disrupted by fighting. Between August and October, Arab forces shelled Mount Zion, attacked Mandelbaum House, bombarded the southern suburbs of Jerusalem, and killed a number of civilians and combatants by sniper fire. On October 31, UN observers noted that there had been "108 instances of Arab firing at Jewish positions in the city during the last week," despite the truce that was ostensibly in effect. The casualties on both sides continued to mount, although the first Arab-Israeli war was to all intents and purposes already over.[43]

A formal cease-fire was declared in Jerusalem on November 28, 1948, and negotiations for a lasting set of agreements between the warring countries began in earnest. In the end, the armistice borders were set where fighting had ended on July 18, and agreements were signed between Israel and Egypt, Lebanon, Transjordan, and Syria between February and July 1949. Israel now possessed more territory than it was originally granted under the UN partition plan, but the fledgling state had suffered a heavy blow—more than six thousand of its citizens, nearly 1 percent of the entire population, had been killed in the fighting. Estimates of casualties from all of the Arab nations that had sent troops range from five thousand to fifteen thousand killed.

With the formal cessation of hostilities, the Israelis controlled the New City in western Jerusalem, from which a reported thirty thousand Arabs had fled or been expelled. Transjordan controlled the Old City (from which two thousand Jews had been expelled), as well as eastern Jerusalem and lands to the east of the city. One year later, King Abdullah formally annexed the area of Palestine that he controlled and named it the West Bank of his Hashemite kingdom of Jordan. The Israelis in turn declared western Jerusalem to be the capital of Israel and then moved their parliament, the Knesset, there in February 1949.[44]

Jerusalem was formally divided into two parts under the armistice agreement signed between Israel and Jordan on April 3, 1949. The so-called Green Line dividing the city ran north-south along the November 1948 cease-fire line. Several demilitarized zones were established, as were several areas designated as "No Man's Land." Neither side was completely happy with the agreement, and accusations and complaints frequently flew back and forth between the two in the ensuing years.

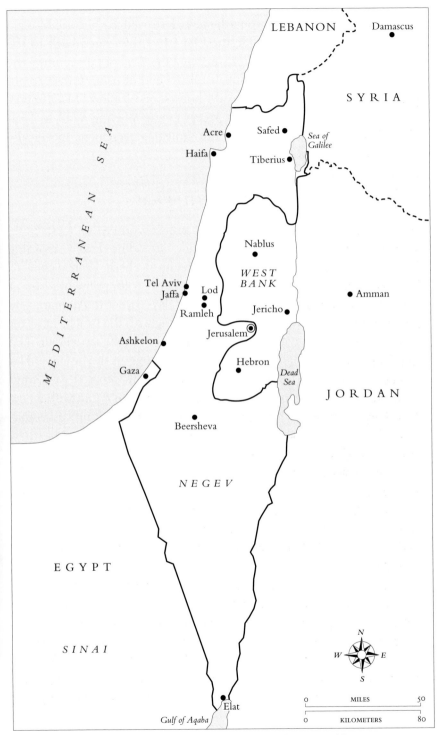

Map 23. The frontiers of the state of Israel, 1949–67 CE

The Arabs were outraged when the Jews destroyed the historic Moslem cemetery in Mamilla (outside the Old City) that dated back to the Arab conquest. The Jews bitterly accused the Arabs of desecrating the Jewish cemetery on the Mount of Olives and of using Jewish tomb-stones as paving material for roads, houses, and latrines. Most impor-tant, Jordan denied the Israelis access to the Wailing Wall in Jeru-salem, although Article VIII of the armistice agreement specifically guaranteed such right of access.[45]

BETWEEN THE WARS

On July 20, 1951, two years after the annexation of the West Bank, King Abdullah was assassinated while attending Friday morning prayers at the al-Aqsa Mosque on the Haram al-Sherif. He had come to Jerusalem to deliver the eulogy for Riad Bey a-Solh, prime minister of Lebanon, who had been assassinated four days earlier in Amman. The two men were rumored to have been meeting with the Israelis in secret negotiations aimed at a separate and permanent peace settlement. The assassin who shot the king was reportedly acting on the orders of Haj Amin al-Husseini—the exiled and by this time deposed ex–Grand Mufti of Jerusalem. King Abdullah had replaced Haj Amin with a new mufti of Jerusalem in December 1948. By ordering the king's assassina-tion, Haj Amin showed that he was still a force to be reckoned with in the Arab world.[46]

Violence flared in East Jerusalem following Abdullah's assassination. The Arab Legion arrested hundreds of Arab demonstrators, shot thirty more, and hanged four men accused of plotting the assassination. Arab-against-Arab violence erupted again five years later, when there were protests in East Jerusalem following the Jordanian elections in October 1956. In dispersing the protestors opposed to the new king, Hussein, the Jordanian army opened fire and killed several Arab men, women, and children. Similar protests in late April 1963 resulted in a similar tragedy, with more demonstrators killed and wounded. In addi-tion to internecine Arab conflicts, there were also additional conflicts between Arabs and Jews in Jerusalem during the years 1952, 1953, 1954, 1956, and 1965.[47]

THE SIX-DAY WAR

Early on the morning of June 5, 1967, the day that began the Six-Day War, General Mordecai "Motti" Hod, the commander of the Israeli air force, sent his men into the air with the following words ringing in their ears:

> The spirit of Israel's heroes accompany us to battle. . . . From Joshua Bin-Nun, King David, the Maccabees, and the fighters of 1948 and 1956, we shall draw the strength and courage to strike the Egyptians who threaten our safety, our independence, and our future. Fly, soar at the enemy, destroy him and scatter him throughout the desert so that Israel may live, secure in its land, for generations.[48]

The war began at approximately 7:45 A.M., when Israeli aircraft attacked ten Egyptian airbases simultaneously, destroying more than three hundred aircraft still on the ground. As General Hod later told Yitzhak Rabin, the Egyptian air force ceased to exist in the span of 180 minutes. The attack was a preemptive strike that caught Egypt totally by surprise, despite the fact that King Hussein of Jordan later said that he warned Egyptian president Gamal Abdel Nasser three separate times in the days before the attack (on May 30, June 3, and June 4), eventually predicting that it would take place on June 5 or 6.[49]

The surprise attack by the Israelis was undertaken with firm knowledge that Egypt was marshaling forces for its own attack against Israel. In the days before the Six-Day War, Egyptian president Nasser had declared:

> During the Crusaders' occupation, the Arabs waited seventy years before a suitable opportunity arose and they drove away the Crusaders. Some people commented that . . . we should shelve the Palestinian question for seventy years, but I say that as a people with an ancient civilization, as an Arab people, we are determined that the Palestine question will not be liquidated or forgotten. The whole question, then, is the proper time to achieve our aims. We are preparing ourselves constantly.[50]

Alongside a multitude of complex issues, Nasser sought revenge for Egypt's 1956 defeat in the Sinai at the hands of Israel. Now, in the spring of 1967, Egypt and Israel had been poised on the brink of war for several weeks. From May 16, the world had waited expectantly for hostilities to begin. Egypt had been readying its military forces after receiving information (erroneous, as it turned out) from Russia that Israel was planning an attack. Syria had already declared that it would be Egypt's ally in whatever action was forthcoming.

In an effort to prevent potential action on a third front, Israel asked Jordan to remain neutral. It sent the request via the United Nations, as well as via British and American contacts. General Odd Bull, the UN commander in Jerusalem, did not deliver the message (which he described as a "threat") until 11:00 A.M. on the morning of June 5. It ended: "Israel will not, repeat not, attack Jordan if Jordan maintains the quiet. But if Jordan opens hostilities, Israel will respond with all of its might." However, Egypt had already invoked its mutual-defense treaty with Jordan two hours earlier. Later that afternoon, Nasser personally telephoned King Hussein.[51]

Before Bull was able to deliver the message to Hussein, sporadic machine-gun fire had been exchanged, and Jordanian mortar shells had hit West Jerusalem—just after 10:00 A.M. on the morning of June 5. Slightly over an hour later, shells from Arab Legion howitzers rained down upon Jewish Jerusalem, from Ramat Rahel at the south to Mount Scopus in the north. The shelling continued for the next ten hours, killing twenty civilians and injuring over one thousand.[52]

The Jordanians had made their allegiance clear. Their attacks began by aiming at Jewish Jerusalem and its immediate vicinity. But their decision to go to war with Israel was to some extent based upon faulty information from Egypt. That morning, the Egyptians had not admitted to the loss of their entire air force; they had claimed instead that they had destroyed 75 percent of the Israeli airplanes and were already fighting deep inside Israeli territory. The Syrians and Iraqis were similarly misled by Egyptian misinformation when they also declared war on Israel.[53]

Soon after the Jordanians began bombarding West Jerusalem, sixteen of their Hawker Hunter fighter aircraft attacked Netanya and two other Israeli towns. At approximately the same time, Syrian and Iraqi

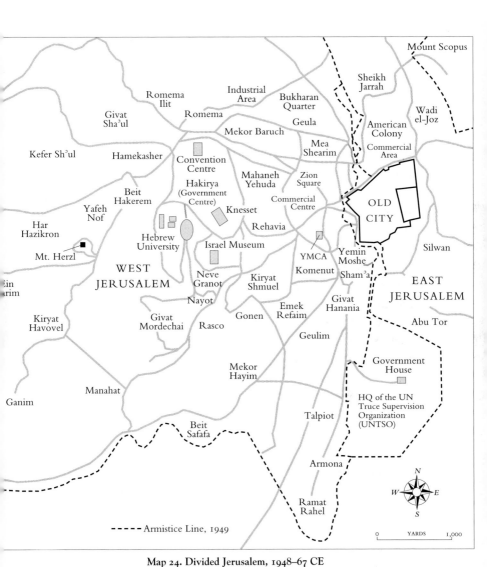

Map 24. Divided Jerusalem, 1948–67 CE

airplanes bombed towns, oil refineries, and airfields elsewhere in Israel. In retaliation, Israeli planes bombed the Amman and Mafraq airfields in Jordan just before 12:30 P.M. and again at 1:10 P.M., destroying the entire Jordanian air force, thus ensuring that Jordanian planes would play no further part in the war. Similar attacks with identical results were made against the Syrian and Iraqi air forces. Israel now had complete control of the skies and would retain control for the rest of the war. Its dominance in the air proved to be a decisive factor in the battle for Jerusalem.[54]

By 1:00 P.M., four hundred Jordanian troops, under the command of Major Badi Awad, crossed the demarcation line, entered the neutral zone, and surrounded the United Nations headquarters in the former British Government House on the so-called Hill of Evil Counsel. They opened fire on the Israeli soldiers in the nearby Allenby Barracks, and the Israelis temporarily withdrew from the area.[55] Then Jordanian troops, advancing westward, crossed the Green Line into Israeli territory. They attacked the first set of buildings that they reached—the Jewish Experimental Farm in an area called Talpiot—but were driven back by three workers and the farm director's wife, armed with ancient Czechoslovakian guns. (An alternative version of the story has it that the attackers were held at bay by a single elderly policeman aided by the farm director's wife.) Before the Jordanians could mount a second assault, two Israeli army companies with Sherman tanks reached the farm, relieving the amateur defenders.[56]

By now it was mid-afternoon of June 5, and the Jordanians withdrew to the United Nations headquarters, where they soon came under attack from the pursuing Israeli forces. The ensuing battle, although it lasted only eleven minutes, was fierce. There were numerous casualties, and several of the Israelis' Sherman tanks were knocked out before the Jordanians evacuated the UN building and retreated.[57]

With the United Nations headquarters now in their hands, Israeli forces captured several additional Jordanian positions located further to the southeast—Antenna Hill and two bunkers nicknamed for their shapes, the "Sausage" and the "Bell." The fighting lasted nearly four hours. Nearly one hundred Jordanians were killed or wounded, while the two Israeli infantry companies had only ten men left standing by the end of the battle.[58]

With the capture of these additional positions by early evening on June 5, the Israelis gained control of the part of southern Jerusalem that lay to the east of the Green Line—an area that had been under the control of Jordan since 1948. The unintended conquest (as historian Michael Oren has called it) of Jordanian Jerusalem, including the Old City, had begun. It would take less than forty-eight more hours to complete, with enduring consequences for the entire region.[59]

At about 9:00 p.m. that evening, Israeli aircraft bombed and strafed a battalion of Patton army tanks from the Jordanian Sixtieth Armored Brigade (coming up from Jericho) and a Jordanian infantry unit, as they both headed for Jerusalem. Neither force reached the city. Several hours later, in the intense darkness just before dawn on June 6, Israeli forces, following in the footsteps of Allenby and Richard the Lionheart, reached Nebi Samwil, just to the west of the city. In a tank battle lasting fifteen minutes, the Israelis captured the heights, and from there they were able to control the northern approaches to Jerusalem.[60]

The Israelis began a three-pronged attack—coordinated by Colonel Mordechai "Motta" Gur, commander of the Fifty-fifth Paratroop Brigade—on the Jordanian positions at the northern and eastern edges of Jerusalem. The paratroopers had been training to fight in the Sinai but were reassigned at the last minute and sent on buses to Jerusalem instead. The fighting was especially intense on Ammunition Hill—so named because Allenby and his men had stored their munitions there during World War I. There the Jordanians had their main outpost, protected by trenches, minefields, coils of barbed wire, and other obstacles. The Israelis captured the hill after a three-hour battle in which seventy-one Jordanian soldiers and thirty-five Israelis died.[61]

Nearby, in the district of Sheikh Jarrah, was the well-protected British Police Training School. It was also attacked and captured at great cost during those early morning hours—at least forty Israeli soldiers and one hundred Arab legionnaires were killed in the fighting. The famous American Colony Hotel was then overrun, as was the Ambassador Hotel. Further to the north, Israeli forces also gained control of Jordanian positions on French Hill, but they came under "friendly fire" from their own air force and tanks and were forced to retire temporarily. By this time, Mount Scopus, northeast of the Old City, was entirely in Israeli hands, and Hadassah Hospital and the old

Hebrew University campus were no longer isolated outposts, as they had been for the previous nineteen years.[62]

At 4:30 A.M. on this second day of the war, while the battles raged for Ammunition Hill and the police school, Israeli intelligence intercepted a radio-telephone call made on an open line. It was Egyptian president Nasser calling King Hussein of Jordan. Nasser had learned the true extent of his losses only late the previous afternoon. His officers had been afraid to tell him the truth about the Israeli early-morning air attack until nearly eight hours after it occurred. Now he was calling the Jordanian king with an ingenious explanation to give to the world. According to Israeli intelligence reports, Nasser suggested that they announce that the United States was fighting on Israel's side, which would explain the "unexpected" success of the Jews. "Will we say that the United States and Britain [are attacking] or just the United States?" he asked. The "United States and England," replied Hussein. And so, three hours later, Radio Cairo and other Arab news sources in Amman, Damascus, and elsewhere began reporting that American and British fighter-bombers were providing air support for Israeli ground forces; that American pilots were flying Israeli planes; and that American warships were blocking the entrance to the Suez Canal. Riots and violent demonstrations against the United States and Britain quickly broke out across the Arab world. Egypt, Syria, Algeria, Yemen, Iraq, Mauritania, and Sudan immediately cut diplomatic relations with the United States. Jordan, however, did not sever its ties with the United States, and a week after the war, King Hussein issued an apology for having been party to the "Big Lie."[63]

By 7:30 A.M. on the second day of the war, Colonel Gur was setting up his forward headquarters in the Palestine Archaeological Museum, after taking out Jordanian positions in East Jerusalem and helping to establish control of the Mount Scopus region. The museum, better known as the Rockefeller Museum, is located just outside the northeast corner of the Old City, between Herod's Gate on the north wall and St. Stephen's Gate on the east wall. Three archaeologists from the Hebrew University of Jerusalem accompanied Gur to the museum. In his memoirs, Uzi Narkiss gives their names as Avraham Biran, Joseph Aviram, and Nahman Avigad, all well-known and well-respected scholars. They were sent at the request of Yigael Yadin—the world-famous Israeli general and archaeologist—to ensure the safety of the ancient artifacts in the Rockefeller Museum, which included some of the Dead Sea Scrolls.[64]

By noon on this second day of fighting, the Israelis had captured most of East Jerusalem, except for the Old City. Uzi Narkiss, Moshe Dayan, and Ezer Weizman had lunch on top of Mount Scopus, with a view of the city stretching out below them. At the time, Narkiss, by now promoted to general, was the commanding officer of Israeli Central Command; General Dayan was the minister of defense; and General Weizman was chief of the General Staff Operations Branch (he later became the seventh president of Israel). In addition to his military skills, Dayan was also an avid amateur archaeologist and historian who had once compared himself to King David's right-hand man Joab and his brothers, the sons of Zeruiah. Narkiss asked permission to attack the Old City, reminding Dayan that the Romans under Titus had taken Jerusalem from the north nearly two thousand years earlier. Dayan refused this request but granted permission to encircle and besiege the Old City, in the hope that the occupants would simply surrender.[65]

By now, the Jordanian troops were in trouble. Although the Syrians and the Saudis had promised reinforcements, their troops stopped at the Jordanian border and refused to cross. Only the Iraqi Eighth Brigade tried to cross into Israel, but they were promptly annihilated by Israeli aircraft while traversing the Jordan River via the Damia Bridge about thirty miles north of Jericho. About the time that the three Israeli generals were having lunch on Mount Scopus, Hussein was cabling Nasser, "To this situation, if it continues, there can be only one outcome: you and the Arab nation will lose this bastion, together with all its forces, after glorious combat that will be inscribed by history in blood."[66]

By that evening, many of the Jordanian troops had already evacuated the region and were withdrawing toward Jericho. The Old City was one of the last areas in Jerusalem still defended by Jordanian soldiers—about six hundred men, commanded by Brigadier Ata Ali Hazzaa. The brigadier set up his headquarters in the Armenian quarter and stationed fifty soldiers at each of the seven gates leading into the Old

City. They went into action when an Israeli battalion sent to capture the Augusta Victoria ridge on the Mount of Olives, just south of Mount Scopus, took a wrong turn in the dark and ended up outside St. Stephen's Gate. The Jordanians released a murderous fire from the ramparts above, and the Israeli troops withdrew after suffering heavy casualties.[67]

At 11:30 P.M. King Hussein ordered all Jordanian troops to retreat back across the Jordan River. Accordingly, soon after midnight, Brigadier Ata Ali Hazzaa declared that all Jordanian soldiers in the Old City who wished to do so could withdraw. Two hours later, with the possibility of a new UN-brokered cease-fire in the offing, King Hussein rescinded his first set of orders, ordering the Jordanian troops to remain and "to kill the enemy wherever you find them with your arms, hands, nails, and teeth."[68]

In the Old City, Brigadier Ata Ali Hazzaa received the new instructions in the early morning hours of June 7, the third day of the war. But it was too late. Three-quarters of the men under his command—450 of the 600—had already left. Most fled via the Dung Gate, which the Israelis had deliberately left unguarded. As the sun rose that morning, only 150 Jordanian soldiers still defended the Old City and the Augusta Victoria ridge. The cease-fire never materialized.[69]

At 5:00 A.M. the Israeli Cabinet, unaware that the Old City was virtually defenseless, met in Tel Aviv to debate the merits of attacking this most sacred part of Jerusalem. Moshe Dayan, a voice of caution for much of the war, argued against an attack, warning that there could be fierce hand-to-hand fighting. Others voiced apprehension that an Islamic holy war would break out once Israel captured the Temple Mount/Haram al-Sherif. In the end, the cabinet decided that Jerusalem must be reunited and gave General Narkiss the instructions that he had been awaiting.[70] The time had come to issue the order to attack the Old City.

> Today Jerusalem is to be liberated. In the south and in the north the city of our ancestors is in our hands. Our army is still poised. Men of this Regional Command, be resolute. Do not waver.
> (signed) Major-General Uzi Narkiss
> G.O.C. Central Command[71]

At 6:00 A.M. the Israelis began shelling the Moslem quarter of the Old City. At 8:30 A.M. Israeli artillery and airplanes attacked Jordanian positions in and around the Augusta Victoria Hotel on the ascent to the Mount of Olives, above and to the east of the Old City. Infantry followed and quickly overran the hotel and then the whole of the Mount of Olives. Ten Israelis died in the attack. The Jordanians suffered many more dead and wounded. Some were trapped in their own trenches and killed by napalm dropped from Israeli jets.[72] Meanwhile, the Israelis had learned that the Old City was now only lightly defended and that they were free to attack. The plan called for the first troops to advance through St. Stephen's Gate, at the northeastern edge of the Old City.[73]

Colonel Gur first requested an artillery strike on the Jordanian defensive positions located on top of the northern and eastern walls of the Old City, above and to either side of St. Stephen's Gate. Just after 9:30 A.M., the city walls shook with the fury of the tank and artillery fire. A bus blocking the gate was blasted aside, and the gate door was blown open. Fifteen minutes after the barrage began, Gur drove a half-track in between the two ornamental stone lions flanking the gate. The lions were the only obvious guardians of this entrance to the Old City, except for a single Jordanian soldier in a nearby minaret. Advancing Israeli troops quickly silenced his Bren gun.[74]

During the barrage, a single mortar round missed its target and fell into the courtyard of the Crusader Church of St. Anne. The Israelis later claimed that no other sacred building was struck during their assault. The reason Moshe Dayan had refused to provide additional artillery or air support was to lessen the chance of damaging sacred places in the Old City, especially in the vicinity of the Haram al-Sherif, where the Arabs had stored ammunition, explosives, and other military equipment in several places.[75]

From St. Stephen's Gate, Colonel Gur and his men headed up the Via Dolorosa, while other Israeli troops spread out across the Old City—to the Damascus, Jaffa, Zion, and Dung Gates; to the Moslem, Christian, Jewish, and Armenian quarters. Gur's half-track reached the Temple Mount/Haram al-Sherif minutes later. There he found no Jordanian soldiers, only the *qadi* (religious judge) of Jerusalem and the Jordanian governor of the Jerusalem district. These two men approached Gur bearing a message saying that there would be no further opposition.[76]

However, a sniper's bullet killed an Israeli soldier moments later, as Gur and his men hurried down from the mount to the Wailing Wall on its western side. The Israeli soldiers quickly dispatched the sniper, as well as several other Jordanian soldiers at the base of the stairs leading down to the wall. The story goes that as soon as the Israelis reached the Wailing Wall, they began to pray, many bursting into tears, overwhelmed by the moment. It was the first time in nineteen years that Jews had been able to pray at one of their most sacred sites. Gur sent Narkiss a simple message—"The Temple Mount is in our hands"—as Rabbi Shlomo Goren, the senior Israeli military chaplain, blew the shofar (the ram's-horn trumpet) at the wall and offered up prayers that were broadcast over Israeli radio. In the background, Israeli soldiers could be heard singing the words to "Yerushala[c]im Shel Zahav" (Jerusalem of gold). The song, with its haunting refrain "Jerusalem of gold, of copper, and of light," had taken the nation by storm after its premiere at the Independence Day celebrations on May 15, just three weeks before the Six-Day War broke out.[77]

By early afternoon on June 7, 1967, the entire Old City was in Israeli hands—868 years to the day since the Crusaders first appeared in front of the walls of Jerusalem in 1099 CE.[78] Dayan, Narkiss, and Rabin made their way via the Temple Mount/Haram al-Sherif to the Wailing Wall, where Dayan slipped a prayer into a crack between the stones. It read, "May peace descend on the whole house of Israel."[79]

With the capture of the Old City, the "unintentional" battle for Jerusalem was over. As historian Michael Oren has stated, the Six-Day War was supposed to be very limited in scope, directed only against the Egyptian air force and the first line of Egyptian defense in the Sinai. Instead, the war had quickly escalated, in large part because of Jordan's mutual-defense treaty with Egypt. The capture of East Jerusalem and the Old City was thus, Oren argues, an unforeseen by-product of the war: "Israelis, when they think of the Six-Day War and of Jerusalem, think of it as the high point of the war, but in fact it was unintentional."[80]

The Six-Day War lasted another three days after the capture of Jerusalem, during which time there was only mopping-up action in the holy city. But the Israeli conquest of Jordanian Jerusalem came with a high price for both sides. In approximately fifty-one hours of fighting within the city limits, 180 Israeli and 350 Jordanian soldiers were killed in action; 14 Israeli and 149 Jordanian civilians also died.[81] Throughout all of Palestine/Israel, some 700 Jordanian troops were killed and another 6,550 were listed as wounded, missing, or captured in the course of the six days of the war. The entire Jordanian air force and half their armor were destroyed. Jordan also lost control of East Jerusalem and of the holy places on the Haram al-Sherif. King Hussein's great-grandfather had lost Mecca and Medina to the Saudis. Now, as a result of his gamble with Nasser, King Hussein had lost the last of the three most sacred Moslem holy places.[82]

THE IMMEDIATE AFTERMATH

At the Wailing Wall on the afternoon of June 7, Defense Minister Moshe Dayan declared:

> We have united Jerusalem, the divided capital of Israel. We have returned to our holiest of holy places, never to part from it again. To our Arab neighbors we extend, also at this hour—and with added emphasis at this hour—our hand in peace. And to our Christian and Muslim fellow citizens, we solemnly promise full religious freedom and rights. We did not come to Jerusalem for the sake of other peoples' holy places, and not to interfere with the adherents of other faiths, but in order to safeguard its entirety, and to live there together with others, in unity.[83]

Although the Israelis promptly bulldozed at least twenty-five Arab houses built against the Wailing Wall (they did so in order to create a plaza for two hundred Jewish worshipers to celebrate Shavuot, the Festival of Weeks), they returned the Haram al-Sherif to the Moslems ten days after its capture. The Moslem trust called the Waqf has been in charge of the Haram al-Sherif and its religious structures ever since. The following Friday, four thousand Moslems—joined by Dayan—prayed on the Haram al-Sherif during the day, then thousands of Jews prayed that evening and the next day at the Wailing Wall, immediately below.[84]

On June 28, 1967, the Knesset formally unified Jerusalem, adding the Old City and East Jerusalem to the state of Israel. The concrete dividers and partitions erected to separate the two sides of the city in the years since 1948 were torn down in a matter of days. Jews visited East Jerusalem, shopping in the souk of the Old City. Arabs crossed into West Jerusalem and freely walked the streets. Jerusalem became a single metropolis once again, for the first time in nearly two decades.[85]

Many believe that the decisions made during and in the immediate aftermath of the 1967 Six-Day War continue to influence events in Jerusalem and Israel to this day. Dayan was extremely cautious in many of his decisions concerning Jerusalem. Some critics believe that the Israelis conquered the Old City not as a result of his decisions but despite them. Moreover, Dayan persuaded the other ministers to hand over the Temple Mount/Haram al-Sherif to the Islamic Waqf within days of the Israeli victory. Some have speculated that had the Temple Mount remained in Israeli hands, many of the problems in Jerusalem would not exist today.[86]

THE RIGHT OF RETURN

In November 1953, President Harry S. Truman (who had just completed his two terms as president of the United States) was visiting the Jewish Theological Seminary in New York when his old friend and business partner Eddie Jacobson pointed to him and said: "This is the man who helped create the State of Israel." Truman retorted instantly, "What do you mean, 'helped create'? I am Cyrus, I am Cyrus." Truman's reference to the Persian king who had allowed the Jews to return to Judah from their exile in Babylon in the year 539 BCE was not lost on his small audience—it was clear that he saw himself as far more than a "midwife" or "godfather" to Israel.[87]

The Israeli leaders, victorious in 1948 and again in 1967, drew many comparisons between their troops and Jewish soldiers of antiquity.[88] For their part, the Palestinians often refer to the loss of their homeland and of West Jerusalem to the Jews in 1948 as the *Nakbeh*—the "catastrophe." The subsequent loss of East Jerusalem and the Old City to the Israelis in 1967 added to this calamity. The Palestinians' ongoing exile from the lands in which they once lived is perceived by many as the equivalent of the Babylonian Exile of the Jews.

While there are some superficial similarities between these two events separated by more than twenty-five hundred years, there are also significant differences. In 586 BCE, for those Judaeans who were sent into exile, the deportation to Babylon was forcibly imposed, not voluntary. In contrast, supporters of Israel's position frequently point out—perhaps disingenuously—that many of the original Arab refugees from modern Palestine, estimated at 500,000–750,000, left their homes voluntarily in 1947 and 1948 (hoping to return quickly after an Arab victory) and that few were forcibly exiled by the Israeli conquerors. However, many—and perhaps most—Palestinians challenge this view. People sympathetic to their cause insist that the refugees did not leave voluntarily but were forced out by the Israeli military and civilians. Whatever the truth of the situation, numerous Arab countries retaliated by expelling a large number of Jews (estimates range from four hundred thousand to eight hundred thousand) during the years immediately following 1948.[89]

After the Six-Day War in 1967, 175,000–300,000 Palestinians fled from the West Bank to Jordan. Some of these were longtime inhabitants of the area, while others were refugees from 1948 who had resettled in the West Bank and now were forced to relocate a second time. Once again, in retaliation, thousands of Jews were expelled from numerous Arab countries after 1967. There were also riots, pogroms, arrests, and confiscations of Jewish property in Egypt, Yemen, Lebanon, Tunisia, Morocco, Libya, Syria, and Iraq.[90]

The so-called right of return for the Palestinians has been a major point of contention between Arabs and Israelis for several decades.[91] However, the concept of a right of return for those conquered in battle and subsequently exiled does not have much support by way of historical precedent in the Middle East. To cite a few examples relevant to the ancient Israelites and Judaeans, the right of return was not applied to the ten tribes of Israel deported by the Neo-Assyrians in 720 BCE or to the Judaeans whom the Romans forced into exile around the world in 70 CE and 135 CE. It took two thousand years for the Jews to return to Israel after their defeats by the Romans. Hopefully it will take considerably less time for the Palestinians to be able to reclaim at least some of the land that they lost in 1948 and 1967.

There may be other lessons to be learned from the history of the region known at various times as Israel, Judaea, Palestine, and, again, Israel—lessons relevant to the ongoing exile of the Palestinians. After the northern kingdom of Israel was destroyed by the Neo-Assyrians in 720 BCE, the conquerors orchestrated the involuntary deportations of most of the ten northern tribes. But there was apparently also a large voluntary emigration, with a flood of Israelites pouring into the southern kingdom of Judah.[92] After the Neo-Assyrian conquest, the northern kingdom of Israel disappeared, along with its ten tribes, but the neighboring kingdom of Judah, with its newly mixed population of Judaeans and Israelites, soon grew strong and prospered.

The dispersed Palestinians number more than four million at last estimate. Certainly it is hard not to sympathize with the plight of any exiled people and in particular with that of refugees, of whom there were an estimated 135,000,000 throughout the world during the twentieth century alone.[93] The lament of the Jews exiled in 586 BCE, inscribed in Psalm 137, might equally be the cry of the modern Palestinian exiles.

By the waters of Babylon, there we sat down and wept, when we remembered Zion. . . . If I forget you, O Jerusalem, let my right hand wither! Let my tongue cleave to the roof of my mouth, if I do not remember you, if I do not set Jerusalem above my highest joy! (Psalm 137:1–6)

10

SPEAK TENDERLY TO JERUSALEM

AT THE OPENING of the sixteenth Maccabiah Games in Jerusalem's Teddy Stadium on July 16, 2001, Prime Minister Ariel Sharon—whom some have dubbed "the modern Judah Maccabee"—declared:

> Approximately 2,100 years ago, the Maccabees lit the torch in Modiᶜin and carried it to the gates of Jerusalem, in the Jewish people's struggle for freedom in its homeland. The same fire of freedom and faith, which was not extinguished during 2,000 years, is, today, passed on to you. . . . You represent the spirit of the Maccabees who fought for Jerusalem and for Jewish rights and independence 2,167 years ago.[1]

Earlier that morning, at 1:30 A.M., in an open field located about a kilometer from the stadium, two Palestinians accidentally blew themselves up when the bomb they were preparing detonated prematurely. The resulting explosion could be heard throughout much of the city. Authorities speculated that the two men, one of whom belonged to the terrorist group Fatah and the other to the Popular Front for the Liberation of Palestine, were planning to set off the bomb during the opening ceremonies of the Maccabiah Games.[2] And so, although the names of the combatants have changed, the fight for control of Jerusalem continues, more than two millennia after the Maccabees disappeared from the face of the earth.

AFTER 1967

On June 11, 1967, immediately after the Six-Day War ended, Moshe Dayan addressed a group of Israeli soldiers, saying:

> The War, the Six Day War, has ended. In those six days we liberated the Temple Mount. . . . We have vanquished the enemy. . . . The battle has died down, but the campaign is far from over. Those who rose up against us have been defeated but they have not made peace with us. Return your swords to their scabbards, but guard and take care of them. For the day of beating them into plowshares is not yet at hand.[3]

Dayan was correct; the battles for Jerusalem and Israel would continue. Numerous incidents of terrorism followed the war. In October 1968, two Moslem girls placed a bomb in the Zion Cinema in Jerusalem. Fortunately, they were observed and the bomb was removed just in time, exploding minutes afterward.[4] One month later, Arab terrorists killed twelve people and injured many more with a powerful car bomb planted in the Mahane Yehuda open-air market on Jaffa Road in Jerusalem.[5]

In 1969, bombs exploded in a Jerusalem supermarket and in the cafeteria of the National Library of the Hebrew University.[6] The already tense situation was further inflamed in August of that year, when a deranged twenty-eight-year-old fundamentalist Christian tourist from Australia named Denis Michael Rohan set fire to the al-Aqsa Mosque on the Haram al-Sherif. The fire destroyed the wooden *minbar* (prayer rostrum or pulpit) that Saladin had installed eight hundred years earlier, and it damaged the ceiling and dome of the mosque. Some Moslem authorities accused the Israelis of underwriting Rohan's attack, and rumors spread that the Israeli firemen had poured gasoline, rather than water, on the blaze. It turned out that Rohan was a psychopath who had acted alone in an attempt to "hasten Christ's Second Coming." The ceiling and dome were quickly rebuilt, but the minbar still had not been replaced more than thirty years later.[7]

In the early years of the 1970s, car bombings, grenade attacks, and letter bombs in Jerusalem were a prelude to the Yom Kippur War. On October 6, 1973, Egypt and Syria simultaneously attacked Israel. Ancient Greece and Rome had often initiated their battles against the rebellious Judaeans on the Jewish Sabbath, when religious Jews were enjoined to worship and forbidden to fight. The Arabs borrowed this technique in 1973 and attacked on Yom Kippur, the Day of Atonement—the most solemn and sacred of the Jewish holidays. The fighting took place far from Jerusalem, but the repercussions were felt in the city long afterward. In the aftermath of this war, Israelis questioned their state of readiness to protect their borders, and some of their heroes from the 1948 and 1967 wars fell into disgrace. Although Egypt and Syria lost the war, the Arab nations demonstrated that they could muster a fighting force to be reckoned with. In this conflict, they saw themselves as having gained an important "moral victory" that eased the humiliation of earlier defeats.[8]

Following the October 1973 war, terrorism continued to haunt the city of Jerusalem. Grenade and bomb attacks occurred with increasing frequency from the end of 1973 through 1976. One of the worst acts took place on July 4, 1975, when a refrigerator left in Zion Square exploded, killing fourteen people and wounding seventy more. The Palestine Liberation Organization (PLO), then—as now—headed by Yasser Arafat, claimed responsibility for the blast.[9]

Egyptian president Anwar Sadat's historic visit to Jerusalem in 1977 did little to stop the violence, and terrorist activities continued apace. A bomb planted by the PLO in a box of fruit exploded in the Mahane Yehuda open-air market in late June 1978, killing two people and injuring nearly fifty more. Throughout the 1980s, terrorist activity continued, with bombings, grenade attacks, and airplane hijackings in Israel and beyond its borders.[10]

Following Denis Rohan's attack on the al-Aqsa mosque in 1968, the Temple Mount/Haram al-Sherif became the focal point for attacks by Jewish extremist religious groups. The extremists' primary aims included the destruction of the Moslem mosques and other buildings on the Haram al-Sherif and the construction in their place of the Third Temple (following the First Temple of Solomon and the Second Temple of Herod). In 1980, Rabbi Meir Kahane, the founder of the Jewish Defense League, was arrested and imprisoned for allegedly plotting to destroy the Dome of the Rock with a long-range missile. In April 1982, an American Jew named Alan Goodman—a volunteer in the Israeli army—opened fire with a machine gun at the Dome of the Rock, killing two Moslem guards, wounding eleven other people, and pockmarking the walls with over a hundred bullet holes. In 1984, a plot to blow up the Dome of the Rock, four years in the planning, was uncovered. The conspirators—eighteen Orthodox Jews—had already planted explosives on the Haram al-Sherif when they were caught. Given the state of the cold war at the time, some have speculated that if the plan had succeeded, it could have ignited World War III.[11]

Elsewhere in Jerusalem, the violence continued with a bus bomb in December 1983 and grenade attacks in February 1984 and October 1986, which killed or maimed numerous Israelis. In November 1986, serious riots and counterdemonstrations took place.[12] Then, in December 1987, the First Intifada erupted.

THE FIRST INTIFADA

It is too early to place the First and Second Intifadas into any reasonable historical perspective.[13] Moreover, they have already involved so many individual incidents that any complete account would have to include a laundry list of explosions and mangled bodies from the last decade of the twentieth century and the first years of the twenty-first century. Nevertheless, even at this early stage, it is possible to take cognizance of some of the most dramatic and traumatic episodes and to make a few observations.

Since 1987, Jerusalem, mirroring events across the length and breadth of Israel, has been the scene of constant agitation and unrest. *Intifada* means "shaking off"—a reference to the "shaking off" of Israeli oppression by Palestinians. The First Intifada began as a spontaneous uprising in December 1987 and quickly evolved into an organized rebellion. Some have suggested that this evolution was encouraged by the Palestinian leadership, which saw an organized uprising as a means by which to achieve their goal of throwing off the shackles of Israeli occupation and dominance in the region. The economic strikes and stone throwing that marked its early days gradually gave way to shootings, knifings, grenade attacks, and bombings, as the Palestinians intensified their struggle to gain independence from the Israeli occupation. On November 15, 1988, the Palestine National Council of the PLO issued a Declaration of Independence, in which they proclaimed the establishment of the state of Palestine, with its capital in Jerusalem.

> The Palestine National Council, in the name of God, and in the name of the Palestinian Arab people; hereby proclaims the establishment of the State of Palestine on our Palestinian territory with its capital Holy Jerusalem (Al-Quds Ash-Sharif).[14]

The number of violent incidents in the early years of the Palestinian uprising and especially after the Palestinian Declaration of Independence was released is astounding. In just the first six months of 1989 alone, the police reported 562 buses and cars stoned, ninety-seven cases of arson, and seventy gasoline bombs in Jerusalem. Many more episodes went unreported, but a bomb that devastated the Mahane Yehuda open-air market on Jaffa Road on May 28, 1990, drew international attention. Riots in East Jerusalem and in the area of the Temple Mount/Haram al-Sherif were a monthly and sometimes weekly occurrence. The most serious disturbance took place on October 8, 1990, when a Jewish fringe group known as the Temple Mount Faithful visited the Temple Mount with the announced intention of laying a symbolic cornerstone for the Third Temple. During the riots touched off by their visit, Israeli police shot and killed twenty-one Arabs on the Haram al-Sherif.[15]

The motive of the Palestinian leadership in encouraging the First Intifada is perhaps best illustrated by a speech given by Yasser Arafat on December 31, 1992, in which he said:

> Our people, O brothers and friends, are the active volcano in the Middle East which will only calm itself when one of the youths of the revolution and the Intifada hoists the flag of your state over Jerusalem, and our homeland Palestine. . . . The vanguard of your

revolution, the Fatah movement, has proven that there is no going back on the jihad for Palestine, on the homeland, or on martyrdom . . .[16]

BETWEEN THE INTIFADAS

During the inter-intifada years—from 1993 to 2000—violence in Jerusalem and elsewhere in Israel continued, although at a somewhat reduced level. Several important events took place during these years. In September 1993, Israeli and Palestinian representatives signed a Declaration of Principles, later called the Oslo Agreement. Many looked upon this agreement as an important first step toward peace in the region. In joint letters exchanged between Yasser Arafat and Yitzhak Rabin on September 9, 1993, the PLO recognized the right of the state of Israel to exist in peace and security, while the Israelis recognized the PLO as the representative of the Palestinian people. The principal signatories received the Nobel Peace Prize for their efforts, and as a result of the Oslo Agreement, a fledgling Palestinian state was established in the West Bank and Gaza Strip. It was governed by the Palestinian Authority, with Yasser Arafat elected as its first president. Adding to the expectation of regional peace engendered by the Oslo Agreement, Israel and Jordan signed a formal peace treaty in late October 1994, concluding nearly fifty years of hostilities between the two countries.[17]

But Palestinian militants had other ideas about the cessation of hostilities. They never relinquished their goal of an independent Palestinian state, with the concomitant destruction of the state of Israel. Instead of laying down their weapons, they continued their undeclared war. Just as the Irgun and Lehi had resorted to bombings and assassinations in the 1930s and 1940s in order to drive the British troops from Palestine, so Hamas, the Palestinian Islamic Jihad, the Fatah Tanzim, and other Palestinian militant groups increasingly turned to bombings and other violence during the inter-intifada years of the 1990s in the hope of driving the Israeli occupiers from the land they perceived as theirs.

Fatah, an Arabic word meaning "conquest by means of jihad," is a reverse acronym of the Arabic *Harakat at-Tahrir al-Wataniyyeh al-Falas-*

tiniyyeh (Movement for the National Liberation of Palestine), which was founded by Yasser Arafat in the 1960s. Fatah eventually became the most prominent faction within the PLO. Members of Fatah are involved in the current political leadership of the Palestinian Authority and are frequently credited with coordinating the activities of the Second Intifada. The Fatah Tanzim is the armed wing of Fatah, consisting of hard-line militia groups over which Arafat claims to have little control. Hamas, whose name comes from an Arabic word meaning "zeal" and is also an acronym for the *Harakat al-Muqawamah al-Islamiyya* (Islamic Resistance Movement), and the Palestinian Islamic Jihad, which incorporates the concept of "holy war" into its name, are two of the more active populist militant organizations that have come to the forefront during the period of the Palestinian uprising. These last two groups have been officially declared terrorist organizations by the United States, as have the Palestine Liberation Front, the Popular Front for the Liberation of Palestine, and the al-Aqsa Martyrs Brigade.[18]

During these years, the Palestinian militants introduced a new weapon, the suicide bomber, into their struggle for nationhood and the expulsion of the Israeli occupiers. Moreover, they added a new, lethal twist in the cycle of violence when they declared all Israelis to be soldiers and thereby justified attacks aimed specifically at civilians. Hamas claimed responsibility when a suicide bomber blew himself up on the No. 18 bus near the Central Bus Station in Jerusalem on February 25, 1996, killing seventeen Israeli civilians and nine soldiers. One month later, sixteen Israeli civilians and three soldiers were killed when another suicide bomber blew himself up on the same route, as the bus was negotiating traffic on Jaffa Road in Jerusalem.[19]

It did not help matters when, on September 26, 1996, Israeli prime minister Benjamin Netanyahu opened up to visitors and tourists a four-hundred-foot-long tunnel dug by archaeologists alongside the western edge of the Temple Mount/Haram al-Sherif and exiting onto the Via Dolorosa. The Palestinians immediately accused the Israelis of having dug the tunnel in an attempt to undermine the Temple Mount and cause the collapse of the mosques upon it. Although the charge was baseless, fifty-four Palestinians and fourteen Israelis were killed in the riots that followed. Further suicide bombings in Jerusalem continued through the end of the twentieth century and into the twenty-first century.[20]

THE SECOND INTIFADA

The Second Intifada, sometimes referred to as the "al-Aqsa Intifada," began immediately after Ariel Sharon, then the Israeli opposition leader, visited the Temple Mount/Haram al-Sherif on September 28, 2000. It would appear that this new intifada was sparked by outrage at Sharon's insensitive expedition and his accompanying entourage, which reportedly included two thousand Israeli soldiers.[21] Yasser Arafat declared as much in a speech at the Arab summit on October 21, 2000.

> The direct reason for holding this extraordinary summit is the wave of savage violence that our Palestinian people have been subjected to. This wave started when [Israeli opposition leader Ariel] Sharon desecrated the al-Aqsa Mosque and its compound [by visiting it on September 28, 2000]. With this premeditated step, that was conducted in concert with the Israeli government, Sharon set off a spark that spread from Jerusalem to every Arab, Muslim, and Christian city and village. . . . This visit was not simply a passing act like those committed by the settlers against our holy shrines; instead, it created a new dimension in the Arab-Israeli struggle. I remind you that when he was defense minister, and a minister in past governments before that, as well as an army commander, he was barred from visiting such holy shrines. Therefore, what took place was planned in collusion with the Israeli Government.[22]

However, the Mitchell Report, authored by Senator George Mitchell and published on April 30, 2001, concluded: "The Sharon visit did not cause the 'Al-Aqsa Intifada.' But it was poorly timed and the provocative effect should have been foreseen; indeed it was foreseen by those who urged that the visit be prohibited." Some Palestinian activists and officials later said that the uprising was not spontaneous and that Yasser Arafat and the Palestinian Authority had been planning the new campaign against Israel for some time—probably since July 2000, after the failure of the Camp David summit. The claim was that the Palestinians simply seized on Sharon's visit as a pretext to begin the violence. Other reports minimized Arafat's rule, saying that while he had not triggered the renewed violence, he "was not displeased at the outbreak of the Intifada."[23]

Although there were riots and a car bomb explosion following Sharon's September 2000 excursion, sustained violence did not erupt in Jerusalem until after Sharon was elected prime minister in February 2001.[24] Upon his elevation to office, car and suicide bombings in the holy city began again and reached a higher level than ever before. The violence was aggravated by a new Israeli policy of assassinating high-ranking members of Palestinian militant organizations and by the Palestinian policy of retaliating with suicide or car bombings after each assassination.

The first bomb exploded in an ultra-Orthodox neighborhood just two days after Sharon became prime minister. It caused only minor injuries and damage but marked the beginning of an extended period of attacks on civilians in Jerusalem. Leaders of Fatah had earlier warned, "the Intifada would escalate if Sharon wins the election." Hamas also threatened to "carry out suicide attacks and to escalate the Intifada," while the Islamic Jihad vowed "to attack targets in Israel in the days to come."[25]

Car bombs exploded (or were defused) and suicide bombers blew themselves up on buses and in cafés during seventeen out of the next eighteen months from February 2001 through July 2002. A period of relative calm followed, but it was shattered by another bombing in November 2002 and then a series of suicide bombings in May, June, August, and September 2003. More than one of the bombers is thought to have come through "Jerusalem's porous northern rim."[26]

The attention of the world was caught by many of the suicide bombings and the consequent horrific loss of life—in the Sbarro pizzeria in August 2001, on the Ben Yehuda pedestrian mall in December 2001, in the ultra-Orthodox neighborhood of Beit Yisrael and in the Moment Café in March 2002, and in the cafeteria of Hebrew University in July 2002, to name but five. The advent of female suicide bombers, who first appeared in Jerusalem with an attack on Jaffa Road in January 2002, was one more step in the undeclared war between the Palestinians and the Israelis. This new approach to warfare is a "first" for Jerusalem, a city that thought it had already witnessed every possible form of barbarism in its millennia-long history.[27]

THE PAST, HAPPENING OVER
AND OVER AGAIN

In the continuing cycles of "Jerusalem violence" that have lasted nearly four thousand years, one constant stands out clearly: the vast majority of the serious conflicts in or about the holy city were inspired by a desire to control its holiest site—the Temple Mount/Haram al-Sherif and the rock that stands upon it. Throughout Jerusalem's history, the names, nationalities, and religious inclinations of the combatants have changed, but this driving force has remained.

All three great monotheistic religions—Judaism, Christianity, and Islam—view Jerusalem as their holy city. Each claims membership in the Abrahamic covenant and each cites scriptural authority to justify their sacred designation for the city. If history is an indication, any conquest of the city by one of these groups at the expense of the others is doomed to be temporary because the others will not rest—indeed, some would argue that their respective faiths do not permit them to rest—until they can make Jerusalem a center for uninhibited worship. Arafat said as much to President Clinton at Camp David in July 2000, "As I've told you, Jerusalem will be liberated, if not now then later: in five, ten, or a hundred years." Arafat's supporters feel the same way; upon his return to Gaza after the failed Accords, one banner waved by a Palestinian marcher read: "Jerusalem is before our eyes; tomorrow it will be in our hands."[28]

Both Palestinians and Israelis have some sort of legitimate claim to the same small pieces of real estate—first the Temple Mount/Haram al-Sherif surmounted by its sacred rock, then Jerusalem, and finally all of Israel/Palestine. Both have claimed Jerusalem as the capital city of their nation—the Israelis in 1948 and the Palestinians in 1988. No negotiator, on either side, can offer to give up their claim to the city without appearing as a traitor to their people. At Camp David, Arafat told Clinton: "I can't betray my people. Do you want to come to my funeral? I'd rather die than agree to Israeli sovereignty over the Haram al-Sherif. . . . I won't go down in Arab history as a traitor." A month later Ehud Barak said essentially the same thing: "No Israeli prime minister will ever confer exclusive sovereignty over the Temple Mount [on the Palestinians]. It's been the cradle and the heart of the identity of the Jewish people for 3,000 years."[29]

Like the Israelis and Palestinians of the current struggle, many—and perhaps most—of those who fought for Jerusalem down through the ages thought that they alone had a God-given right to the Temple Mount/Haram al-Sherif and the surrounding city. But to say that one or another people have a historical or religious right of ownership of the Temple Mount and of Jerusalem is to deny the equally valid claims of other peoples and other religions. A brief glance at table 1 (in the introduction to this book) will confirm that the conquerors of one era have been, in the past, and very likely will be, in the future, the hapless victims of the next generation of conquerors. Even those who controlled Jerusalem for a few hundred or even a thousand years should acknowledge that other peoples may also have prior claims and that ownership at one point in time is not a valid argument for an inalienable right to ownership in either the present or the future. As Saeb Erekat (one of the chief Palestinian negotiators in 1993 and 2000) has said, "There's no such thing as a sovereignty over history. History is in our books, in our memories."[30]

Nevertheless, it is likely that the history of Jerusalem will continue to be used and misused by political and military leaders in the propaganda of present and future conflicts. Meron Benvenisti, the former deputy mayor of Jerusalem, describes this as "the habit of . . . always returning to the quarry of history to dig up arguments to aid them [the Israelis and Palestinians] in their present-day quarrels."[31]

Six months after Ariel Sharon opened the sixteenth Maccabiah Games in the midst of the Second Intifada by invoking the memory of the Maccabees, Yasser Arafat sanctioned continued violence in the holy city. In a speech on January 26, 2002, Arafat called for "jihad [holy war] and martyrdom." Including himself as an active participant in the ongoing struggle for control of Jerusalem, Arafat beseeched Allah: "Please God, give me the honor of being one of the martyrs for holy Jerusalem."[32] Twenty months later, when threatened with expulsion by Israel in the immediate aftermath of the Café Hillel suicide bombing in early September 2003, Arafat declared to a crowd of cheering supporters, "[our] people will not capitulate and will not kneel down until one of our boys or one of our girls raises the Palestinian flag on the domes and churches of Jerusalem." The crowd responded instantly, "To Jerusalem we are marching, martyrs in the millions!"[33]

And so Jerusalem continues as a city besieged. Once again peoples of differing beliefs and national aspirations are contending for the same small piece of ground. Someday it may be possible to proclaim these words from the Book of Isaiah: "Speak tenderly to Jerusalem, and cry to her that her warfare is ended . . ." (Isaiah 40:2). For now, however, in Jerusalem, perhaps more than anywhere else in the world, "There is no present or future—only the past, happening over and over again. . . ."[34]

NOTES

INTRODUCTION

1. As quoted in Mairson 1996, 23. See also Klein 2001, 57, who says "of all these holy sites in East Jerusalem, al-Haram al-Sharif—The Temple Mount—is the one with the greatest potential for an explosion."

2. Corwin 2000, 6. The derivation of the name *Jerusalem* is debated. One possibility is that it comes from the Hebrew words *ir* (city) and *shalom* (peace), which would give the meaning "city of peace." *Harper's Bible Dictionary* (1985, 465) notes: "Jerusalem was understood in rabbinic and Christian writings to mean 'Seeing of Peace.' . . . The interpretation 'City of Peace' became popular after the biblical period." It more likely comes from the Hebrew words *yara* (founded) and *Salem* (the name of the local god), which would give a meaning of "founded by the god Salem" or "the foundation of the god, Salem." See also Kollek and Pearlman 1968, 17; Smith 1972, 250–71; Idinopulos 1991, 6; Armstrong 1996, 7; Armstrong 1998, 5.

3. The numbers given here add up to more than 118, because some of the individual 118 conflicts recorded in table 1 are both an attack and a capture or recapture, a siege and a destruction, a revolt and a period of terrorist attacks, and so on. See table 1 for the specific instances of the 118 separate conflicts, with the date, opponents, and action/result listed for each. Previous studies that variously state that Jerusalem has suffered more than twenty sieges, changed hands more than twenty-five times, been conquered forty times, and was destroyed thirty-seven times in the past four thousand years turn out to be both underestimates and overestimates: cf. Schmelz 1975, 123; Narkiss 1983, 258; Elon 1989, 149; Benvenisti 1996, 242; Cattan 2000a, 12; Wasserstein 2001, x; Enderlin 2003, 177.

4. Finkelstein and Silberman 2001, 132–33. The following description of the topography of Jerusalem is indebted to a number of secondary sources, including Kollek and Pearlman 1968, 37–38; Smith 1972; Schmitt 1980, 101–2; *Harper's Bible Dictionary* 1985, 463–64; Peters 1985, 8; Mazar 1992, 26; Wightman 1993, 13; Benvenisti 1996, 144; Herzog and Gichon 1997, 99–100; Mazar 1997, 52; Schniedewind 1998, 12. See now also Cahill 2003, 13–17.

5. The Kidron Valley is also known as the Jehoshaphat, Siloam, or Silwan Valley. The Central Valley was later called the Tyropoeon Valley. The Hinnom Valley is also known as the Gehenna Valley.

6. The Hinnom Valley, which runs north-south along the western edge of the western hill before turning and running east-west along the southern end of the city, took over the role of protecting Jerusalem's western flank, as well as its southern border, when the city expanded to the west.

7. The full quote is: ". . . the spot was not such as to excite jealousy, nor for which there could be any fierce contention; for it is rocky, and, although well supplied with water, it is surrounded by a barren and waterless territory" (translation following Jones 1930).

8. Gorenberg 2000, 11.

9. Corwin 2000, 6.

10. Fink (1969, 375) describes the Latin kingdom of Jerusalem as "an island in the sea of Islam." For Abdi-Heba's exclamation in Amarna Letter EA 288, see full translation in Moran 1992, 331.

CHAPTER 1

1. Chronicles 11:4–8. Unless otherwise noted, all quotations from the Hebrew Bible, the New Testament, and the Apocrypha follow the New Revised Standard Version (NRSV).

2. An article containing Arafat's Land Day speech on March 30, 2000, from which the quotation of Arafat is taken, appeared in the issue of *Al-Quds* of the same day. I am indebted to Yigal Carmon and the Middle East Media Research Institute (MEMRI) for the original Arabic article and an English translation. Husseini's statement was made during an interview with Jeffrey Goldberg published in the *New York Times Magazine* on October 3, 1999 (Goldberg 1999, 77). See also Stuart Schoffman's article in the July 16, 2001, issue of the *Jerusalem Report* (Schoffman 2001, 47).

3. In the *Wall Street Journal* of September 30, 1996, Amy Dockser Marcus reported, "the Palestinian Authority has begun promoting the notion that the Palestinians are the modern-day successors to the Canaanites, who lived there long before Abraham ever showed up." She quoted Marwan Abu Khalaf, then director of the Institute of Islamic Archaeology in Jerusalem, as saying, "Both the Israelis and Palestinians are determined to prove that their ancestors lived here first" (Marcus 1996, A1). See also Ya'ari 1996, 32; Marcus 2000, 90–91; Klein 2001, 105–6. The assertions by Yasser Arafat and Faisal Husseini that modern Palestinians are descended from the ancient Jebusites may be taking advantage of a statement made in 1996 by Keith Whitelam, then a professor of religious studies at the University of Stirling in Scotland. In his book *The Invention of Ancient Israel*, Whitelam claims that there has been a "silencing of Palestinian history" and that "the struggle for the Palestinian past is only just beginning." He deliberately refers to the ancient people of this region with the term *Palestinians*, rather than using the more usual (and less politicized) scholarly term *Canaanites*, although history tells us that the terms *Palestine* and *Palestinian* were not invented until the Roman period, nearly a millennium after David's conquest of Jerusalem. See Whitelam 1996, 46, 77, 148–49, 236. Objections to Whitelam's use of the term *Palestinians* in place of *Canaanites* have come even from scholars usually considered to be in Whitelam's corner. For instance, Professor Thomas Thompson (1997, 179) wrote: "Of course, Whitelam's references to the population of ancient Palestine as 'Palestinians' is hardly to be accepted as a reference to any historically existent ethnicity. It is at best a term

of convenience referring to the peoples of this region." See also Lemche 1997, 131–32; Shanks 1997a, 50–52; Dever 2001, 34–37.

4. See Asali 1994, 37–39; Armstrong 1996, 420; Gilbert 1996, 358; Khalidi 1997, 214 nn. 12–13; Armstrong 1998, 18; Khalidi 2000, xi–xii. See also Bahat 1992; Mazar 1992; Reich 1992; Tsafrir 1992; Shanks 1995a, xiv, 1, 11–12; Shanks 1995b, 24–28; Benvenisti 1996, 1–10, 49; Silberman 1997; Mazar 2000, 64.

5. See Naʾaman 1994d; Schoville 1994, 158–59; Drews 1998.

6. On the Sea Peoples and the destructions—including those by earthquake—at the end of the Late Bronze Age, see Sandars 1985; Drews 1993; Drews 2000; Nur and Cline 2000; Oren 2000; Nur and Cline 2001; Stiebing 2001; Cline and O'Connor 2003.

7. Translation following Sandars 1985, 143.

8. See Astour 1965; Schoville 1994; Tubb 1998.

9. First there is the biblical text: "Thus says the Lord GOD to Jerusalem: Your origin and your birth are of the land of the Canaanites; your father was an Amorite, and your mother a Hittite" (Ezekiel 16:3; see also Ezekiel 16:45). Then there is the biblical reference to the Jebusite named "Uriah the Hittite," who was unfortunate enough to be married to Bathsheba when she caught King David's fancy (2 Samuel 11:1–27). Finally, the Bible tells us about Araunah, the Jebusite who sold his land on top of Mount Moriah to David (2 Samuel 24:16–25). He seems to have had a Hurrian title also found in Hittite (ewrine, "lord") linked to his name. Elsewhere in the Bible (1 Chronicles 21; 2 Chronicles 3:1), the name of this Jebusite is given as "Ornan" rather than "Araunah," and the original Hebrew text of 2 Samuel 24:16 says "the Araunah" rather than simply "Araunah." Scholars have therefore speculated that Ornan may have been a Jebusite ruler—perhaps the last in Jerusalem, given David's conquest—who bore the Hurrian/Hittite title of "the Araunah" (lord). On the possible connections between the Jebusites and the Hittites, which is not compelling but still tantalizing, see Yadin 1963, 267–70; Harper's Bible Dictionary 1985, 449; The New Encyclopedia of Archaeological Excavations in the Holy Land 1993, 699; Shanks 1995a, 32; Armstrong 1996, 14, 37, 39–40; Bahat 1996a, 23. For a well-written and easily accessible history of the Hittites, see Bryce 1998, with full previous references.

10. The appointment calendar includes a summary of history entitled The Land, Its People and History, within which this statement is made; see Bar-Illan 1992, A8. It is of interest to note that Aamiry (1978, 54), who appears to be far from the "objective historian" that he calls himself (51), also states that the Jebusites built Jerusalem in 4000 BC; one wonders if Aamiry's book was the source of Husseini's misinformation.

11. Sethe 1926; Posener 1940; Kollek and Pearlman 1968, 17; Schmitt 1980, 104–5; Harper's Bible Dictionary 1985, 465; Mazar 1992, 26; Wightman 1993, 13–14; Auld and Steiner 1996, 27–28; Armstrong 1996, 6–7; Armstrong 1998, 15; Bahat 1996a, 20, 22; Franken 2000, 17–18, 20; Talhami 2000, 116; Cahill 2003, 21 n. 38. See Naʾaman 1992a, 278–79, for words of caution about identifying this city as Jerusalem. Six hundred years later, Adonizedek, the king of Jerusalem at the time of Joshua in the twelfth century BCE, also had a good Canaanite name and is also specifically called an Amorite in the biblical text; so are the soldiers in his army (Joshua 10:1–5). Another ruler of Jerusalem—Abdi-Heba, of the fourteenth century BCE—had a good Canaanite name as well. It consisted of a Semitic noun meaning "servant of" attached to the name of a Hurrian goddess (Heba). (Note, however, that Aamiry [1978, 21] refers to Abdi-Heba as the "Arab governor of Jerusalem during the fourteenth century BC.") If the city of Salem is equated with Jerusalem, we have the name of one additional ruler of Jerusalem as well—Melchizedek, the high priest and "king of Salem" who met and blessed Abraham in perhaps the eighteenth century BCE (Genesis 14:18–20; Hebrews 7:1–4). (Whether the biblical city of Salem is also a reference to

Jerusalem is debated, but it is an equation that most scholars accept. See discussions in, for example, *Harper's Bible Dictionary* 1985, 465, 625; Franken 2000, 18–19.) Melchizedek, too, had a good Canaanite name—which may well be Amorite, if its similarity to Adonizedek's name is any indication. We do not know whether there is any subset of Canaanite or Amorite names that are distinctly Jebusite, since this is not territory into which any scholar has yet been willing or able to venture, but certainly none of the rulers of Jerusalem whose names we know have specifically identifiable Jebusite names. I thank Professor Baruch Halpern of Pennsylvania State University and Professor P. Kyle McCarter of Johns Hopkins University for their assistance in these philological and linguistic matters. See also Moran 1975, 146–66; Peters 1985, 8; Mazar 1992, 28; Franken 2000, 23–24, 38.

12. On the foundation and possible date that Jerusalem came under Jebusite control, see discussions in *Harper's Bible Dictionary* 1985, 449, 465; Peters 1985, 8; Bar-Illan 1992, A8; *The New Encyclopedia of Archaeological Excavations in the Holy Land* 1993, 699; Asali 1994, 38; Naʾaman 1994a, 263, 280; Armstrong 1996, 14, 40; Bahat 1996a, 23; Franken 2000, 23–24, 38. If Adonizedek and his army from Jerusalem who fought against Joshua in the twelfth century BCE were indeed Amorites, as the biblical text specifically says (Joshua 10:1–28), the Jebusites may not have taken control of Jerusalem until after the death of Adonizedek and his men. This would mean that they had only been in the city for about a century when David attacked.

13. On the vexed question of the origins of the Israelites, see, most recently, the discussions in Denver 2003; Finkelstein and Silberman 2001, 97–118, 329–39. Important earlier bibliography includes Alt 1925; Albright 1939; Mendenhall 1962; Alt 1966; Mendenhall 1973; Gottwald 1979; Noth 1981; Halpern 1983; Finkelstein 1988; Silberman 1990.

14. Translations of the Amarna Letters presented here follow Moran 1992, 326–27, 330–32.

15. On the Jerusalem Amarna Letters, see especially Moran 1975, 1992. The six Amarna Letters written by Abdi-Heba are numbered EA 285–90; the other two relevant letters that mention Abdi-Heba are EA 280 and 366. See Moran 1975, 146–66; Schmitt 1980, 105–7; Moran 1992, 321–34, 364; Mazar 1992, 28; Naʾaman 1992a, 276–78, 383–88; Wightman 1993, 20–21; Naʾaman 1996a, 19–20, 24, 25 n. 2; Bahat 1996a, 22–23; Armstrong 1996, 13–14; Naʾaman 1998, 42–44; Franken 2000, 19–21. For words of caution, see Franken and Steiner 1992, 110–11; Auld and Steiner 1996, 29.

16. Joshua 10:1–28, 12:7–12. See Kollek and Pearlman 1968, 17; Schmitt 1980, 102–3; *Harper's Bible Dictionary* 1985, 13, 465; Naʾaman 1992a, 287; Shanks 1995a, 4–5; Bahat 1996a, 23; Franken 2000, 21; Kirsch 2000, 151. See especially Naʾaman 1994a, 252–56, 280–81, with full references to earlier publications.

17. Cf. Joshua 12:20–21 and Judges 1:27–28. See, for example, Shanks 1995a, 5; Cline 2000, 45; Kirsch 2000, 151. Separate passages in the Bible have it that Joshua subsequently reallocated the territory of the Jebusites, in one instance to the tribe of Judah and in another to the tribe of Benjamin (Joshua 15:1, 8; 18:11, 16). A frequent interpretation of these two apparently conflicting biblical passages is that the tribes of Judah and Benjamin received lands that were separate but contiguous (but see Naʾaman 1991, 10–12). Jerusalem lay on the border between the tribe of Judah and the tribe of Benjamin, and this may have been a significant factor—there were other factors, as will appear later in this narrative—in David's eventual choice of Jerusalem as a neutral site for the capital of his combined kingdom. In any event, the Book of Judges states that some unspecified time after Joshua's encounter with the king of Jerusalem at Gibeon, the tribe of Judah conquered Jerusalem: "And the men of Judah fought against Jerusalem, and took it, and smote it with the edge of the sword, and set the city on fire" (Judges 1:8). Even this, however, is apparently contradicted in the

Book of Joshua: "But the Jebusites, the inhabitants of Jerusalem, the people of Judah could not drive out; so the Jebusites dwell with the people of Judah at Jerusalem to this day" (Joshua 15:63). The Book of Judges then makes a similar statement about the tribe of Benjamin: "But the people of Benjamin did not drive out the Jebusites who dwelt in Jerusalem; so the Jebusites have dwelt with the people of Benjamin in Jerusalem to this day" (Judges 1:21). Biblical scholars frequently explain away the first statement—that in Judges 1:8—and suggest that the Jebusites were not driven from Jerusalem by either Joshua or the tribes of Judah and Benjamin (see Kollek and Pearlman 1968, 22; Schmitt 1980, 103–4; Miller and Hayes 1986, 170; Na'aman 1991, 10–12; Na'aman 1994a, 260–63, 280; Shanks 1995a, 5, 9; Bahat 1996a, 23; Franken 2000, 24; Kirsch 2000, 334 n. 3). This may imply a Jebusite-held Jerusalem hemmed in by the tribe of Judah on one side and the tribe of Benjamin on the other—or even a shared city. It is, however, entirely possible that the tribe of Judah did indeed capture the city but was unable to rid itself entirely of the Jebusites and that both the tribe of Judah and, later, the tribe of Benjamin were forced to share the city with its established inhabitants. That is not as surprising as it perhaps appears. Cohabitating with a vanquished enemy was certainly not unusual. The later Greeks frequently did so in their colonization of the eastern and western Mediterranean during the Archaic period of the eighth through sixth centuries BCE, and the Roman general Pompey left the majority of the Jewish inhabitants unharmed when he conquered Jerusalem in 63 BCE.

18. See also Joshua 15:8, 18:28; Judges 19:10. The biblical text seems to indicate that the city was known as Jebus at the time of David's conquest, but this may have simply been a later mechanism introduced in specific biblical books in order to differentiate between Israelite Jerusalem and pre-Israelite Jerusalem. A second possibility is that the city's name was indeed temporarily changed during the centuries of Jebusite rule—we know from the Egyptian Execration Texts and the Amarna Letters that the city was known as Jerusalem in the ninteenth, eighteenth, and fourteenth centuries BCE, and we also know that it was called Jerusalem three hundred years later, from the time of David's conquest in the late eleventh century BCE onward. A third possibility is that the names *Jebus* and *Jerusalem* were in use simultaneously during this period, just as the names *Jerusalem* and *Al-Quds* are currently used to refer to the city by Israelis and Arabs, respectively. A fourth possibility is that the clarifying statements equating Jebus and Jerusalem in the biblical text, such as "Jebus (that is, Jerusalem)" in Joshua 18:28, may have been added by later editors who were inaccurate, for the topographical descriptions of Jebus and its surrounding territory found in the Bible do not match the actual topography of Jerusalem and its surrounding territory. (If Jebus and Jerusalem are not identical, then the most likely candidate for the ancient city of Jebus is the site of Sha'fa, located just to the north of Jerusalem, as J. Maxwell Miller has suggested. This would not negate the tradition that Jerusalem was inhabited by the Jebusites during the time of the Israelite invasion, for it still would have lain within Jebusite territory.) For the various discussions concerning the names *Jebus* and *Jerusalem*, see Miller 1974, 115–27; Miller 1975, 154; *Harper's Bible Dictionary* 1985, 449–50; Miller and Hayes 1986, 170; *Anchor Bible Dictionary* 1992, 652–53, 751; Auld and Steiner 1996, 1, 14; Franken 2000, 20.

19. Halpern 2001, 479. See also the following works, which contain full references to earlier publications: Kirsch 2000; McKenzie 2000; Marcus 2000, 105–28; Finkelstein and Silberman 2001, 128–30.

20. The discovery of the Tel Dan inscription has generated numerous publications, most of which cannot be noted here because of space considerations. For the original publication and subsequent translations of the Tel Dan inscription, see Biran and Naveh 1993; Biran and Naveh 1995; Schniedewind 1996, 77–78; Na'aman 1997a, 126. Scholars have

recently suggested that there may be mentions of David or the "House of David" in additional inscriptions as well; see Lemaire 1994; Shanks 1999a.

21. 2 Samuel 5:6–9; 1 Chronicles 11:4–8.

22. See previous discussions in Yadin 1963, 267–70; Kollek and Pearlman 1968, 27–28; Shanks 1975, 31–37; *Harper's Bible Dictionary* 1985, 465; Miller and Hayes 1986, 171; Wightman 1993, 25–27; Shanks 1995a, 12–23; Bahat 1996a, 24; Herzog and Gichon 1997, 99–102; Franken 2000, 24, 38–39; Kirsch 2000, 151–55; McKenzie 2000, 133–34.

23. See discussions in, for example, Davies 1992; Thompson 1992; Whitelam 1996; Shanks 1997a; Lemche 1998; Steiner 1998; Thompson 1999; Marcus 2000; Dever 2001; Finkelstein 2001; Finkelstein and Silberman 2001; Schoffman 2001; Finkelstein 2003; Silberman 2003.

24. For concise compilations of previous suggestions, see Holm-Nielson 1993; Kleven 1994a, 1994b.

25. See Shiloh 1981; Gill 1996; Herzog and Gichon 1997, 101–2; Reich and Shukron 1999; Shanks 1999b; Shanks 1999c; Shanks 1999d; Geva 2000, "Twenty-five Years," 5; Marcus 2000, 86–89; Reich and Shukron 2000; Cahill 2003, 24–25; Killebrew 2003, 334–35.

26. On the size of the Jebusite city and the various second and early first millennia BCE fortification systems, see Kenyon 1967, 12–22; Shanks 1975, 23–26; Shiloh 1984, 16, 26–27; Mazar 1992, 29; *The New Encyclopedia of Archaeological Excavations in the Holy Land* 1993, 701–2; Steiner 1993; Wightman 1993, 14–23; Shanks 1995a, 1–3, 25–29; Auld and Steiner 1996, 24–27, 32; Mazar 1997, 52–54; *The Oxford Encyclopedia of Archaeology in the Near East* 1997, 225–26; Cahill 1998; Steiner 1998, 31; Reich and Shukron 1999; Franken 2000, 24, 38–39; Geva 2000, "Twenty-five Years," 4–5; Cahill and Tarler 2000, 31, 34–35; Mazar 2000, 64–65; Reich and Shukron 2000; Finkelstein 2001; Steiner 2001, 10–53; Cahill 2003, 21–54; Finkelstein 2003; Killebrew 2003; Steiner 2003; Ussishkin 2003.

27. See also 1 Kings 9:24: "But Pharaoh's daughter went up from the city of David to her own house which Solomon had built for her; then he built the Millo"; 1 Kings 9:15: "And this is the account of the forced labor which King Solomon levied to build the house of the LORD and his own house and the Millo and the wall of Jerusalem and Hazor and Megiddo and Gezer"; 1 Kings 11:27: "Solomon built the Millo, and closed up the breach of the city of David his father"; 1 Chronicles 11:8: "And he built the city round about from the Millo in complete circuit; and Joab repaired the rest of the city"; 2 Chronicles 32:5: "He set to work resolutely and built up all the wall that was broken down, and raised towers upon it, and outside it he built another wall; and he strengthened the Millo in the city of David." See also perhaps 2 Kings 12:20.

28. On the identification of the Millo, see, among other works, Kollek and Pearlman 1968, 40; Peters 1985, 8; Miller and Hayes 1986, 171; Auld and Steiner 1996, 13; Mazar 1997, 54; Steiner 1998, 31.

29. See Alfödy 1995; Feldman 2001.

30. All translations of Josephus used here and elsewhere in this volume follow Whiston 1999.

31. Yadin 1963, 267–70. Yadin notes the similarity to an oath sworn by Hittite soldiers who called upon the gods to strike them blind and lame if they should fail in their assigned duties. See also Olyan 1998 and further discussion in many of the references cited in the preceding notes.

32. For the most recent accounts, see especially Dever 2001; Finkelstein and Silberman 2001. Both contain full references to earlier discussions. The writing is unlikely to date, as some "biblical minimalists" have argued, to the Persian and/or Hellenistic periods.

33. See the most recent discussions in Kirsch 2000, 154–55; Finkelstein 2001, 107; Halpern 2001, 319–20.

34. Naᵓaman 1996a, 23. See also Naᵓaman 1997b, 1998.

35. There is, as yet, no archaeological evidence that either the middle or northern sections of the eastern ridge were inhabited at the time of David's assault. Some scholars—for example, Knauf (2000a) and Pace (1978)—have suggested that the Late Bronze Age and Iron Age settlements may have been on the highest point of the eastern ridge (i.e., on the summit of Mount Moriah, where the Temple Mount would later be located) or even on the western ridge, but those suggestions have not been met with much enthusiasm. See now the discussions in Finkelstein 2001, 106–7 and n. 7; Halpern 2001, 320 and n. 9.

36. Armstrong 1988, 9. The Old Testament states that David's son Solomon enslaved the remaining Jebusites (1 Kings 9:20–21; 2 Chronicles 8:7–8). On Masada, see, most recently, Netzer 1991; Shanks 1997b; Ben-Yehuda, Zias, and Meshel 1998. See also discussion below.

37. Ezra 9:1–2; Ezekiel 16:2–3; Zekhariah 9:7.

38. 2 Samuel 24:16–25; 1 Chronicles 21:15–28.

39. 2 Samuel 6, 24; 1 Chronicles 15–16, 21.

40. 2 Chronicles 3.

41. See Ben-Dov 1982, 33; *Harper's Bible Dictionary* 1985, 465–66; Peters 1985, 12–13; Armstrong 1996, 44; Franken 2000, 11.

42. Contra Wasserstein 2001, 318.

43. Naᵓaman 1997b; Cahill 1998; Naᵓaman 1998; Steiner 1998; Finkelstein 2001; Finkelstein and Silberman 2001; Cahill 2003, 73–80; Finkelstein 2003; Killebrew 2003, 338–45; Steiner 2003.

44. Mark Twain (1898) once wrote:

The Egyptian, the Babylonian, and the Persian rose, filled the planet with sound and splendor, then faded to dream-stuff and passed away; the Greek and the Roman followed, and made a vast noise, and they are gone; other peoples have sprung up and held their torch high for a time, but it burned out, and they sit in twilight now, or have vanished. . . . All things are mortal but the Jew; all other forces pass, but he remains.

45. Recent genetic testing has tended to support this belief; see, for instance, Skorecki et al. 1997; Thomas et al. 1998; Hammer et al. 2000; Oppenheim et al. 2000; Nebel et al. 2001. See also Peters 1984, 81–82, on a claimed Jewish presence in the Holy Land throughout the millennia.

46. See, for example, Hammer et al. 2000; Behar et al. 2003. On the conversion of the royal house of the Khazars to Judaism, see, with further bibliography, Dunlop 1967; Koestler 1976; Halpern 1977, 308–9, 315–16; Roth 1977, 228, 230–31; Rosenthal and Mozeson 1990, 153.

47. Asali 1994, 39, following similar statements originally published in Aamiry 1978 (e.g.,: "Jerusalem was founded by Arabs; throughout its existence they never abandoned it, and they always remained the basic population" [51]). Note that Aamiry's scholarly sources (cited on pp. 50–51) are Sir James Frazer, whose specialty was mythology and comparative religion (cf. *The Golden Bough* [1922]); Frances E. Newton, whose book entitled *Fifty Years in Palestine* (1948) has been described as an "inadequate histor[y]" having a "pro-Palestinian Arab viewpoint" (Stein 1991a); and a Mrs. E. A. Finn, "wife of the British Consul," who wrote a book entitled *Palestine Peasantry* (1923) after having "lived in Jerusalem for a period of almost twenty years." For the quotations from the appointment calendar distributed by

Faisal al-Husseini's Palestine Association for Studies of International Affairs in Jerusalem, see Bar-Illan 1992, A8.

48. Cattan (2000a, 21) states emphatically, "The Philistines and the Canaanites are the ancestors of the Palestinians of today." See also Aamiry 1978, 1, 49–51; Hadawi 1983, 43–59; Cattan 2000b, 3.

49. Khalidi 1997, 149, 253 n. 13. See also Khalidi 2000, xv–xvi, in which Khalidi sets out this thesis that was "pressed strongly by Arab scholars and writers after the beginning of the conflict with Zionism in the late nineteenth and early twentieth centuries" and notes, "Although there is some evidence for this proposition as regards Jerusalem specifically, elements of it remain to be proved, and others are unprovable or demonstrably false." See also the discussion of Peters 1984, 137–57, and the reply of Said 1988, 23–31. In the fall of 2003, Khalidi moved to Columbia University in New York to become the first Edward Said Professor of Middle East Studies and director of the Middle East Institute at the university.

50. Davies 1992, 62–63. See also Thompson 1999, 80–81.

51. See, however, the various studies (already cited) published in Skorecki et al. 1997; Thomas et al. 1998; Hammer et al. 2000; Oppenheim et al. 2000; Nebel et al. 2001. Such genetic studies may eventually allow us to begin discussing such questions and ancestral claims on a scientific basis.

CHAPTER 2

1. Quotations follow Gutgold 2001, 9; Winkler 2001; Fam 2001a. See also Fam 2001b; Rees 2001; MacKenzie 2003, and additional Associated Press articles published in the *Jerusalem Post* on March 11 and 12, 2001.

2. Matar 1990, 235 (originally published in 1979). See also Karsh and Rautsi 1991, 122–23, 152–53.

3. Lewis 1989, A4; Burns 1990, A13; Keys 1990, 9; Lamb 1990, A14–15; Laqueur 1990, A27; Miller and Mylroie 1990, 57–58; Baram 1991, 49–51; Bulloch and Morris 1991, 42–45; Dyer and Hunt 1991, 40–41; Henderson 1991, 3; Maranz 1991, 38; Parson 1991, 35–36; Simons 1996, 86; Jehl 1997, A4; Roberts 1997, 222–23. See also Hallote and Joffe 2002, 104.

4. See, for example, Finkelstein and Silberman 2001, 123–45, with further bibliography. See Dever 2001 for references to and critiques of publications by the so-called biblical minimalists who take issue with the biblical account of events during these years. See also Dever 1997; Edelman 1997; Knauf 1997; Millard 1997; Niemann 1997; Handy 1997a; Naʾaman 1997c; other contributions in the 1997 volume on Solomon edited by Lowell K. Handy; Silberman 2003; Ussishkin 2003. See now Cahill 2003, 73–80, with full references and bibliography, for a rebuttal to the various proposals that challenge the historical existence of David and Solomon by using (or misusing) archaeological data from Jerusalem; see also the discussion in Killebrew 2003, 338–43.

5. The bibliography on Shishak and Shoshenq is large and growing exponentially, thanks to debates reignited by Rohl (1997), among others. Occam's razor still seems the best solution, however, and I continue to believe that Shishak and Shoshenq are one and the same.

6. Mazar 1957; Redford 1973; Mazar 1986; Naʾaman 1992b, 79, 83–84; Naʾaman 1996, 22; Shanks 1999a, Cline 2000, 75–82; Halpern 2001, 71–72; Finkelstein and Silberman 2001, 161, 231–32; Finkelstein 2002, 109–35.

7. Note, though, that Josephus says four hundred thousand "footmen" (*Antiquities of the Jews* 8.10.250).

8. Redford 1973; Naʾaman 1992b, 79, 83–86; Naʾaman 1996, 22.

9. Friedman 1997, 44; Miller and Hayes 1986, 231, 237–38, 245–46.

10. See the Monolith Inscription from Nimrud: Miller and Hayes 1986, 258–59, 269–70; Finkelstein and Silberman 2001, 178.

11. 1 Kings 15:16–20; see also 2 Chronicles 16:1–4. See, most recently, Auld and Steiner 1996, 16; Finkelstein and Silberman 2001, 232.

12. 2 Kings 10:32–33; 12:17–18; 13:3, 7, 22.

13. 2 Kings 12:17–18; 2 Chronicles 24:23–25. On Hazael and the kingdom of Israel, see Schniedewind 1996, 83–85; Naʾaman 1997a, 125–27; Finkelstein 1998, 208; Finkelstein 1999, 61, 63; Cline 2000, 82–88; Finkelstein and Silberman 2001, 111, 197.

14. 2 Kings 14:13–14. See also 2 Chronicles 25:23–24; Josephus *Antiquities of the Jews* 9.9.199–204. See, recently, Miller and Hayes 1986, 298–302; Finkelstein and Silberman 2001, 233.

15. 2 Kings 16:5–9; see also Isaiah 7:1–9. See, most recently, Naʾaman 1995a, 1995b; Finkelstein and Silberman 2001, 233–34; previously, among many others, Tadmor and Cogan 1979, 505.

16. Translation following Pritchard 1969, 282. See also 2 Chronicles 28:20–21.

17. 2 Kings 17:4. See Miller and Hayes 1986, 332–37; Finkelstein and Silberman 2001, 199.

18. Sargon II's possible march on Jerusalem hinges almost entirely upon a single line in the Book of Isaiah (10:32), which says, "This very day he [Sargon II] will halt at Nob, he will shake his fist at the mount of the daughter of Zion, the hill of Jerusalem." See discussions in Evans 1980, 159–61; Becking 1992, 54–55; Sweeney 1994; Naʾaman 1994c; Younger 1996; Younger 1998: 216–18.

19. See also 2 Kings 17:6. Cf. Miller and Hayes 1986, 332–37; Finkelstein and Silberman 2001, 199; Stern 2001, 11, 43–45, 49–50.

20. See discussion in Finkelstein and Silberman 2001, 169.

21. Genesis 49:8.

22. Broshi 1974, 25. See relevant discussions regarding the date of the expansion onto the western hill of Jerusalem in Bahat 1993, 581–84; Cahill 2003, 70–71; Geva 2003; Killebrew 2003, 336–37; Reich and Shukron 2003.

23. Naʾaman 1974, 1979, 1994b, 1995c; Finkelstein and Silberman 2001, 251–55. See now discussions in Roberts 2003; Younger 2003; Hoffmeier 2003a, 2003b.

24. From the "Rassam Prism" inscription; translation following Cogan 2001, 43 (following Cogan and Tadmor 1988, 337–39). For the translation of the nearly identical "Oriental Institute Prism" inscription, see Luckenbill 1924, 32–33; Pritchard 1969, 287–88; Broshi 1974, 25; Naʾaman 1979, 62; Stohlmann 1983, 150–51; Finkelstein and Silberman 2001, 260. See also Sennacherib's "Bull Inscription" and the "Nebi Yunus Slab"; translations of both can be found in Pritchard 1969, 288. See also Naʾaman 1974 and 1979 for discussion of a fragment from yet another inscription possibly relating to Sennacherib's Judaean campaign.

25. Ussishkin 1982; Bleibtreu 1990; Bleibtreu 1991; Russell 1991; Naʾaman 1995c, 191–93; Russell 1998; Schoffman 2001, 45.

26. 2 Chronicles 32:27–29.

27. 2 Chronicles 32:2–8; Avigad 1980; Rosovsky 1992, 26–27; Shea 1999, 44; Finkelstein and Silberman 2001, 255–56.

28. Translation following Finkelstein and Silberman 2001, 256. The inscription has recently been the source of much discussion but has now been conclusively dated to around 700 BCE. See, for example, Hendel 1996, 233–37; Rogerson and Davies 1996, 138–49; Shea 1999, 44; Vaughn 1999a, 43–64, especially 58–59; Vaughn 1999b, 17–18; Gugliotta 2003, A03.

29. Finkelstein and Silberman 2001, 257.

30. On his "Rassam Prism" and on the nearly identical "Oriental Institute Prism," Sennacherib says:

> He, Hezekiah, was overwhelmed by the awesome splendor of my lordship, and he sent me after my departure to Nineveh, my royal city, his elite troops and his best soldiers, which he had brought into Jerusalem as reinforcements, with 30 talents of gold, 800 talents of silver, choice antimony, . . . countless trappings and implements of war, together with his daughters, his palace women, his male and female singers. He (also) dispatched his personal messenger to deliver the tribute and to do obeisance. (Translation following Cogan 2001, 43, following Cogan and Tadmor 1988, 337–39)

31. 2 Kings 18:17–35; see also 2 Chronicles 32:9–19.

32. Some scholars suggest that the biblical description is of not one but two separate attacks on Jerusalem—one in 701 BCE that resulted in Sennacherib collecting a large bribe or tribute and a second one in 688 BCE in which Sennacherib's army withdrew because of an outbreak of disease. This idea has recently received much attention in the scholarly literature but has not succeeded in swaying the traditional historians of this period, who still prefer to see a single attack by Sennacherib, in 701 BCE. See discussions in Horn 1966; Naʾaman 1974, 1979, 1995c; Evans 1980; Shea 1985, 1997, 1999; Yurco 1991; Cogan 2001. See also Vaughn 1999b, 7–11.

33. Stohlmann 1983; Halpern 1991; Naʾaman 1993, 114–15; Finkelstein and Silberman 2001, 263–64; Stern 2001, 11.

34. Miller and Hayes 1986, 397–402; Naʾaman 1991, with previous bibliography; Finkelstein and Silberman 2001, 264–81; Sweeney 2001; Tatum 2003.

35. Naʾaman 1991, 51–55; Cline 2000, 89–100; Finkelstein and Silberman 2001, 281–83.

36. Wiseman 1956; Wiseman 1985, 5, 14–15, 22–23; Sack 1991, 13–14, 58–59; Naʾaman 1992c.

37. 2 Kings 24:1. See now the detailed discussion in Lipschits 2002.

38. Wiseman 1985, 22–23, 29–30; Miller and Hayes 1986, 406–8; Cogan and Tadmor 1988, 308, 340; Malamat 1990, 75; Sack 1991, 58–59; Naʾaman 1992c, 41–44; Stager 1996, 58, 77; Malamat 1999, 37, 39–41; Lipschits 1999a, 156–58; Lipschits 1999b, 467–69; Marcus 2000, 154–55; Stern 2001, 304. See also Malamat 1950, 1956, 1968, 1975, 1979, and 1998.

39. Wiseman 1956, 34–35; Sack 1991, 63; Lipschits 2002. On the debate over Jehoiakim's manner of death, see, for example, Bright 1972, 326–27; Green 1982, 103–9; Miller and Hayes 1986, 408; Lipschits 1999b, 470. The Book of Daniel simply adds to the confusion, saying:

> In the third year of the reign of Jehoiakim king of Judah, Nebuchadnezzar king of Babylon came to Jerusalem and besieged it. And the Lord gave Jehoiakim king of Judah into his hand, with some of the vessels of the house of God; and he brought them to the land of Shinar, to the house of his god, and placed the vessels in the treasury of his god. (Daniel 1:1–2)

This is the wrong year for this event—the third year of Jehoiakim's reign was 605 BCE, a time when Nebuchadnezzar was busy fighting at the battle of Carchemish and was not yet king of the Neo-Babylonians—and this error does not inspire confidence in the accuracy of the rest of the statement.

40. Jeremiah (52:28) says that Nebuchadnezzar deported 3,023 Jews from Jerusalem in his seventh year. Although this is usually taken as a variant on the number of deportees from the subsequent siege of 597 BCE, it may actually be an additional corroboration for Josephus's account of an earlier attack and deportation of three thousand "principal persons" in 598 BCE. For a brief relevant discussion, see Malamat 1968, 154.

41. Translation following Grayson 1975, 102. See also Wiseman 1956, 73; Pritchard 1969, 563–64; Cogan and Tadmor 1988, 340; Finkelstein and Silberman 2001, 293.

42. The month of Kislev that year lasted from December 18, 598 BCE, to January 15, 597 BCE; Jerusalem fell to the Neo-Babylonian forces in mid-March 597 BCE.

43. Wiseman 1956, 32–33; Malamat 1968, 144–45; Wiseman 1985, 32; Malamat 1990, 72; Sack 1991, 63; Malamat 1999, 40; Lipschits 1999b, 469–70; Finkelstein and Silberman 2001, 293; Lipschits 2002. Miller and Hayes (1986, 408) point out that the uncertainty over whether the second day of Adar corresponds to the fifteenth or the sixteenth of March is "due to the fact that the Babylonians reckoned the day from dusk to dusk."

44. Some scholars combine all of the numbers given in this biblical account, for a total of eighteen thousand deportees to Babylon in this year; most others see the totals as simply two variations on the same figure—eight thousand versus ten thousand. For example, Sack (1991, 126 n. 24) gives the number eighteen thousand; Malamat (1990, 72; 1999, 40) gives the number ten thousand.

45. On Josiah's death, see, most recently, the discussion in Cline 2000, 90–100.

46. 2 Kings 24:18–20; 2 Chronicles 36:11–13; Jeremiah 52:1–3.

47. Wiseman 1985, 36; Cogan and Tadmor 1988, 322–23; Malamat 1990, 73–74; Malamat 1999, 40–41; Marcus 2000, 171–72.

48. 2 Kings 25:1–21; Jeremiah 39:1–10, 52:1–30. Some scholars, most notably Avraham Malamat, believe that the siege may have actually begun on January 15, 588 BCE (i.e., a year earlier), and that it lasted for nearly thirty months, rather than eighteen months. The difference in opinion is the result of two possible calendrical systems: see Malamat 1968, 151–53; Wiseman 1985, 36–37; Dyer and Hunt 1991, 94–95; Malamat 1990, 74. Here, the traditional view that the siege began on January 15, 587 BCE, and that it lasted for eighteen months will be followed.

49. Jeremiah 34:7. See Finkelstein and Silberman 2001, 293–95.

50. 2 Kings 25:3–4; Jeremiah 39:2, 52:6–7; Josephus *Antiquities of the Jews* 10.7.116, 10.8.135.

51. Malamat 1968, 151–53; Wiseman 1985, 36–37; Dyer and Hunt 1991, 95; Lipschits 1999b, 477. Apart from a statement by Ezekiel that Zedekiah sought military aid from Egypt (e.g., Ezekiel 17:15), other biblical references are hard to find—and the only possible extrabiblical evidence that this "Egyptian interlude" ever took place may come from an obscure reference found at the city of Lachish to the south of Jerusalem: "The commander of the host, Koniahu Son of Elnathan, hath come down in order to go to Egypt" (Lachish Letter III; see Malamat 1968, 151). Malamat has suggested that the Egyptian expedition to relieve Jerusalem was sent about halfway through the siege. Judging from the fact that the siege was immediately renewed, it is clear that the Egyptian force was defeated or withdrew, if the episode ever even occurred.

52. See Bleibtreu 1990, 1991; Stager 1996.

53. Malamat 1968, 153; Malamat 1990, 74; Lipschits 1999b, 476–77; Marcus 2000, 154.

54. Jeremiah 38:7, 39:3. See Malamat 1968, 154–55; Wiseman 1985, 36–37.

55. 2 Kings 25:4–7; Jeremiah 39:4–7, 52:7–11. See also Josephus *Antiquities of the Jews* 10.8.135–41.

56. This toilet seat was found still in situ in a small cubicle attached to the "House of Ahiel" in Area G of Professor Nahman Avigad's excavations in the Jewish Quarter. See Cahill et al. 1991; Marcus 2000, 157.

57. Cahill et al. 1991, 68.

58. Reinhard and Warnock 1996, 21–22.

59. Cahill et al. 1991, 68–69; Marcus 2000, 157.

60. Lipschits 1999b, 477. See also, previously, Malamat 1990, 74.

61. Cf. 2 Kings 25:8–10 and Jeremiah 39:8 with Jeremiah 52:12–14, which variously give the date as either the seventh or tenth day of the month of Ab, rather than the ninth day. See discussions in Malamat 1968, 154–55; Malamat 1990, 74–75; Lipschits 1999b, 477. See also Hallo 1982, 49.

62. Wiseman 1985, 37; Rosovsky 1992, 27–28; Lipschits 1999a, 158; Lipschits 1999b, 473–74, 477; Marcus 2000, 156–57, 169; Finkelstein and Silberman 2001, 295; Stern 2001, 309–10, 323–24.

63. Lipschits 1999b, 473, 480.

64. Friedman 1997; Finkelstein and Silberman 2001, 296–305.

65. The invasion of 582 BCE was probably in retaliation for the massacre of the Neo-Babylonian garrison at Mizpah—the capital of Babylonian Judah, established to the north of Jerusalem—and for the murder of Gedaliah, the puppet king who had been set upon the throne of Judah by Nebuchadnezzar following the destructions of 586 BCE. Jerusalem may or may not have been involved. See Wiseman 1985, 37–39; Zorn 1997; Finkelstein and Silberman 2001, 305–6.

66. See Porten 1968; Finkelstein and Silberman 2001, 305–6.

67. Jeremiah 52:28–30; 2 Kings 24:14. See Miller and Hayes 1986, 419–20; Cogan and Tadmor 1988, 324; Finkelstein and Silberman 2001, 306.

68. Finkelstein and Silberman 2001, 305–6; see also Grabbe 1992, 116–17; Barstad 1996. See now the various contributions in Lipschits and Blenkinsopp 2003, especially Lipschits 2003, 323–76.

69. Lipschits 2003, 364.

70. See now Barstad 2003.

71. Quotation from Winkler 2001. See also Fam 2001b; Lewis 2003, 48–49; Cline 2003a; Cline 2003b.

CHAPTER 3

1. Translation of Herzl following Lewisohn 1955, 303. Translation of Jabotinsky following Stanislawski 2001, 196.

2. See, for instance, the discussions in Bar-Kochva 1985; Nodet 1986.

3. For this traditional view, see Miller and Hayes 1986, 440–48; Finkelstein and Silberman 2001, 297–300, 308; Stern 2001, 357, 431, 531, 545, 548, 580. For the argument that *Ioudaios* (*Yehudi*) was used to indicate "Jew" beginning only in the second century BCE—and always meant "Judaean" before that date—see Cohen 1999, 69–106; Dessel 2002: 59. Cf. the brief discussion in Grabbe 2003, 70–71.

4. See Ezra 4:3 and discussions in Kollek and Pearlman 1968, 73–74; Grabbe 1992, 126–28; Armstrong 1996, 91–95; Stern 2001, 353. Oded Lipschits (1999b, 478–80) has pointed out that we are presented with two points of view in the biblical texts with regard to the people who remained behind in Judah during the Babylonian Exile: (1) the point of view of the exiles in Babylon (2 Kings 25:12, 21; Jeremiah 39:10; Jeremiah 52:16, 27); and (2) the point of view of those who remained in the land (2 Kings 25:22; Jeremiah 40:7, 10–11). See now also Barstad 2003, Fried 2003, and other discussions in the 2003 volume edited by Lipschits and Blenkinsopp.

5. See especially Armstrong 1996, 93–95, with references. Their squabbles may have extended to the reconstruction of other parts of the city, for when Nehemiah arrived in Jerusalem, he found the walls of the city in ruins. It is a matter of scholarly debate whether the walls had been destroyed as the result of a disturbance in the 480s BCE or whether they were still lying where they had fallen during the destruction by Nebuchadnezzar more than a century earlier.

6. Kollek and Pearlman 1968, 74–75; Williamson 1984, 81–88; Grabbe 1992, 132; Shanks 1995a, 120–23; Armstrong 1996, 96–99. See Josephus *Antiquities of the Jews* 11.5.159–83; see also the Book of Nehemiah in the Hebrew Bible and 2 Maccabees 1:20–36 in the Apocrypha.

7. See Genesis through Deuteronomy.

8. On Jerusalem during the Persian period, see now Lipschits 2003, 329–31, with further references and bibliography.

9. Momigliano 1979, 442–48; Cohen 1982–83, 41–68; Peters 1985, 42; Klein 1986, 78; Grabbe 1992, 181–83, 206–8; Armstrong 1996, 103.

10. Bar-Kochva 1989, 477–81; Grabbe 1992, 211–12; Armstrong 1996, 104.

11. Bar-Kochva 1989, 474–81, 484–85.

12. Peters 1985, 45; Armstrong 1996, 107–9; Sacchi 2000, 218. See also the brief discussion in Polybius 16.39.4.

13. Harrington 1988, 38–39; Armstrong 1996, 109–11.

14. See further discussion in chapter 4.

15. 1 Maccabees was written by an anonymous author sometime before 125 BCE and may have been an official Hasmonean version written from the Maccabean point of view, while the preface to 2 Maccabees says that it is an abridgment of a much longer work written by one Jason of Cyrene. See discussion, with further references, in Grabbe 1992, 223–25. It is generally conceded that Josephus used much of the account found in 1 Maccabees, supplemented by additional information probably derived from a history written by Nicolaus of Damascus—secretary to Herod the Great—most of which is now lost. See discussion, with further references, in Grabbe 1992, 227–29.

16. 2 Maccabees 4:7–17. Cf. Peters 1985, 51–52; Harrington 1988, 15; Gruen 1993, 240–43; Armstrong 1996, 112.

17. 2 Maccabees 4:32–50. Cf. Brauer 1970, 5; Peters 1985, 49, 51–52; Harrington 1988, 15, 42–43; Gruen 1993, 243–44; Armstrong 1996, 112–13; Hayes and Mandell 1998, 57.

18. See varying discussions and conflicting interpretations of these and the following events in Brauer 1970, 6–7; Peters 1985, 52; Harrington 1988, 43–45; Grabbe 1992, 274–77, 282–85; Gruen 1993, 244–47; Armstrong 1996, 113; Hayes and Mandell 1998, 57–59; Sacchi 2000, 225–26. Some scholars argue that the rumors of Antiochus III's death and Jason's subsequent rebellion should be linked to the events of 168/167 BCE rather than to those of 170/169 BCE, but there is no consensus on the matter.

19. 2 Maccabees 5:9.

20. See 1 Maccabees 1:29–37; 2 Maccabees 5:23–26; Josephus *Antiquities of the Jews* 12.5.248–56. See also discussions in Brauer 1970, 7; Peters 1985, 52–53; Harrington 1988, 45; Grabbe 1992, 282–85; Shanks 1995a, 125–26; Armstrong 1996, 113; Hayes and Mandell 1998, 59; Sacchi 2000, 225–26. Josephus describes in detail the plundering of the Temple treasures at this time, but this should probably be associated with Antiochus's earlier attack on the city in 170/169 BCE, as per the account in 1 Maccabees.

21. Tsafrir 1975, 501–21; Avigad 1980, 64–65; Peters 1985, 55; Harrington 1988, 60–61; Bar-Kochva 1989, 438, 442–65; Grabbe 1992, 245–46; Reich 1992, 48; Shanks 1995a, 125–26; Armstrong 1996, 113.

22. Kollek and Pearlman 1968, 85; Brauer 1970, 7; Peters 1985, 53–55; Klein 1986, 84; Cohen 1987, 14–15; Harrington 1988, 45–46, 62–63; Grabbe 1991, 59–74; Grabbe 1992, 282–85; Gruen 1993, 247–50; Shanks 1995a, 125–26; Armstrong 1996, 113–14; Hayes and Mandell 1998, 65; Sacchi 2000, 225–26, 235. See also Daniel 9:27, 11:31, and 12:11, for "the abomination that desolates."

23. 1 Maccabees 2:1–30, 42–48; Josephus *Antiquities of the Jews* 12.6.265–78.

24. Kollek and Pearlman 1968, 85–86; Klein 1986, 84; Cohen 1987, 30; Harrington 1988, 62–64; Grabbe 1992, 285–93; Armstrong 1996, 116–17; Duncan and Opatowski 1998, 31–32; Hayes and Mandell 1998, 61, 69–70.

25. 1 Maccabees 3:10–4:35; 2 Maccabees 8:1–9:29; Josephus *Antiquities of the Jews* 12.6.285–12.7.315. Cf. Kollek and Pearlman 1968, 86–87; Peters 1985, 55–56; Harrington 1988, 67–68; Bar-Kochva 1989, xiii; Grabbe 1992, 285–87; Duncan and Opatowski 1998, 32.

26. 1 Maccabees 4:41–51.

27. Kollek and Pearlman 1968, 87–88; Brauer 1970, 8–9; Klein 1986, 84–85; Harrington 1988, 69–70; Grabbe 1992, 287–88; Armstrong 1996, 117; Hayes and Mandell 1998, 73–74; Sacchi 2000, 242.

28. 1 Maccabees 6:60–62. See discussion in Kollek and Pearlman 1968, 88; Brauer 1970, 9; Klein 1986, 86; Harrington 1988, 71–72; Bar-Kochva 1989, 81, 299–301, 543–45; Grabbe 1992, 288–89; Hayes and Mandell 1998, 74–75. See also Josephus *Antiquities of the Jews* 12.9.362–66, 375–82.

29. See 1 Maccabees 5:1–9:22; 2 Maccabees 10:10–15:39; Josephus *Antiquities of the Jews* 12.9.354–12.11.426. See also Harrington 1988, 72, 75–76; Bar-Kochva 1989, xiii; Grabbe 1992, 289–93; Duncan and Opatowski 1998, 32.

30. On Simon's destruction of the Akra, see Armstrong 1996, 117.

31. 1 Maccabees 10:7–11; Josephus *Antiquities of the Jews* 13.2.35–42.

32. 1 Maccabees 11:19–38; Josephus *Antiquities of the Jews* 13.4.120–30.

33. 1 Maccabees 12:35–37; Josephus *Antiquities of the Jews* 13.5.145–48, 181–86.

34. Kollek and Pearlman 1968, 89; Grabbe 1992, 293–97.

35. 1 Maccabees 13:10; Josephus *Antiquities of the Jews* 13.6.201–3.

36. Josephus *Antiquities of the Jews* 13.6.213–14. Grabbe (1992, 297–99) states that Josephus's account is contradicted by 1 Maccabees 14:37, but the relevant lines here in 1 Maccabees do not seem to be describing the Akra.

37. Peters 1985, 57–58; Harrington 1988, 81–82; Grabbe 1992, 297–99; Duncan and Opatowski 1998, 34–35; Sacchi 2000, 250.

38. Kollek and Pearlman 1968, 89; Bar-Kochva 1989, 162; Grabbe 1992, 299; Duncan and Opatowski 1998, 34–35; Hayes and Mandell 1998, 93–95.

39. Cohen 1987: 30–31; Grabbe 1992, 285–86; Sacchi 2000, 239.

40. It remains a matter of scholarly debate whether the Romans intervened and forced

the end of the siege. See the discussion, with earlier references, in Rajak 1981, 65–81. See also Grabbe 1992, 299; Sacchi 2000, 253.

41. Josephus *Antiquities of the Jews* 13.8.245–53. See Peters 1985, 58–59; Hayes and Mandell 1998, 93–94; Sacchi 2000, 253. Excavated remains of Hellenistic arrowheads, ballista stones, and tumbled masonry may be remnants of the siege by Antiochus VII and the subsequent removal of the city wall: see Wightman 1993, 116–17, with previous bibliography; now also see Sivan and Solar 2000, 173–74.

42. Kollek and Pearlman 1968, 89; Peters 1985, 58–59; Reich 1992, 46–48; Shanks 1995a, 129–30; Armstrong 1996, 118.

43. The tower was built adjoining a much older Israelite tower, which had helped in the defense against Nebuchadnezzar and the Neo-Babylonians nearly five hundred years earlier. The stretch of wall that Avigad uncovered is probably part of what Josephus refers to as the "First Wall." This was a defensive wall that ran around the entire city, as opposed to the so-called Second and Third Walls built as protection against Roman attacks from the north in 70 CE. Another massive tower was built on the eastern hill to protect the original City of David—when this was reexcavated by Kathleen Kenyon in the 1960s, she dated its construction securely to the Hasmonean period as well. See Avigad 1980, 65–74; Peters 1985, 59; Bar-Kochva 1989, 162; Shanks 1995a, 129–30.

44. Kollek and Pearlman 1968, 89–91; Brauer 1970, 12–13; Peters 1985, 61; Klein 1986, 88; Grabbe 1992, 302–4; Armstrong 1996, 121; Sacchi 2000, 261.

45. Kollek and Pearlman 1968, 89–91; Brauer 1970, 12–13; Peters 1985, 61; Grabbe 1992, 302–4; Armstrong 1996, 121; Sacchi 2000, 262.

46. Josephus *Antiquities of the Jews* 14.2.19–28. See Kollek and Pearlman 1968, 91; Brauer 1970, 14; Peters 1985, 61; Klein 1986, 88–89; Grabbe 1992, 306–7; Armstrong 1996, 122–24.

47. Josephus *Antiquities of the Jews* 14.2.29–14.3.53.

48. On Pompey and Jerusalem, see Kollek and Pearlman 1968, 92–93; Brauer 1970, 1–2, 14–18; Peters 1985, 61–66; Grabbe 1992, 306–7; Armstrong 1996, 125; Duncan and Opatowski 1998, 38–39; Hayes and Mandell 1998, 102–11; Sacchi 2000, 269–70.

49. See also discussion in Kollek and Pearlman 1968, 95; Brauer 1970, 18; Peters 1985, 65–66; Armstrong 1996, 125–26; Sacchi 2000, 273–75.

50. See Nordau and Nordau 1943; Shavit 1988, 21, 214; Shapira 1992, 14.

51. See the extended discussion in Grabbe 1992, 247–74, with summaries and interpretations of material published by earlier scholars. See also the discussion in Harrington 1988, 88–96.

52. This was not the only instance when rival Jewish factions sought foreign assistance to resolve their differences or overcome their opponents, sometimes to their eventual regret. A number of additional occurrences can be noted in the conflicts already detailed, as well as in some of those that were to follow, during the overall period from 175 BCE to 66 CE.

CHAPTER 4

1. Avigad 1980, 120–39; 1983, 66–72. See also Rosovsky 1992, 28–29; Shanks 1995a, 165–69, 175–77.

2. Technically speaking, the (or a) Jewish Diaspora actually began with Nebuchadnezzar's destruction of the First Temple in 586 BCE, since there were communities of Jews scattered around the Middle East, Egypt, and elsewhere from then on. One could also make

the argument that the (or a) Diaspora began even earlier, with the Neo-Assyrian destruction of Israel in 720 BCE, when the ten lost tribes were carried off to oblivion and many of the other inhabitants fled to Judah and Jerusalem. However, most scholars consider the Roman destruction of the Second Temple in 70 CE and of Jerusalem itself in 70 and 135 CE as beginning the final Jewish Diaspora, for reasons just outlined.

3. Translation following Shapira 1992, 32–33.

4. See Morris 1999, 52–53.

5. Translation following Zohn 1973, 45. See also Zerubavel 1995, 23, 36.

6. Translation following Stanislawski 2001, 91–92. See also Shapira 1992, 14; Marks 1994, 2; Zerubavel 1995, 42–43, 52–53; Stanislawski 2001, 97. Betar, the site of Bar Kokhba's last stand against the Romans, was symbolically and evocatively chosen as the name for the militant Zionist youth group subsequently founded in 1923 by Nordau's student and disciple Vladimir Jabotinsky.

7. Josephus *Antiquities of the Jews* 14.8.127–12.323; *Jewish War* 1.10.195–1.12.247. See Kollek and Pearlman 1968, 95–96; Brauer 1970, 30–31; Armstrong 1996, 126; Duncan and Opatowski 1998, 41.

8. Josephus *Antiquities of the Jews* 14.13.330–31.

9. Kollek and Pearlman 1968, 95–96; Brauer 1970, 30–31; Grabbe 1992, 347; Armstrong 1996, 126; Hayes and Mandell 1998, 124.

10. Brauer 1970, 30–31.

11. Josephus *Antiquities of the Jews* 14.13.342–69; *Jewish War* 1.13.253–73. See Kollek and Pearlman 1968, 95–96; Brauer 1970, 30–33; Grabbe 1992, 347–48; Hayes and Mandell 1998, 124.

12. Josephus *Antiquities of the Jews* 14.14.381–14.15.400; *Jewish War* 1.14.280–1.15.294. See Kollek and Pearlman 1968, 96; Brauer 1970, 34; Armstrong 1996, 126; Duncan and Opatowski 1998, 41.

13. Brauer 1970, 39; Grabbe 1992, 327, 350.

14. See detailed discussion in Grabbe 1992, 326–27, 350–51, regarding the month and year of Herod's capture of Jerusalem. See Dio Cassius *Historia Romana* 49.22.4–5 for the event taking place on the Sabbath.

15. Kollek and Pearlman 1968, 96; Brauer 1970, 40; Grabbe 1992, 327–28, 350; Armstrong 1996, 126.

16. Dio Cassius *Historia Romana* 49.22.6. See also Josephus *Antiquities of the Jews* 14.16.470–91, 15.1.5–10; Josephus *Jewish War* 1.18.354–57; Kollek and Pearlman 1968, 96–97; Brauer 1970, 40–41; Grabbe 1992, 350–51.

17. The exact location of these walls is a matter of debate. For a description of the three walls and the additional fortifications that protected the city, see Josephus *Jewish War* 5.4.136–55. See also Kollek and Pearlman 1968, 98; Broshi 1978, 13–14; Wightman 1993, 111–12; Armstrong 1996, 128–30.

18. Broshi 1978, 13; Reich 1992, 49.

19. Ritmeyer and Ritmeyer 1989, 26; Armstrong 1996, 131–32; Jacobson 2002, 23–24.

20. Kollek and Pearlman 1968, 100–105; Brauer 1970, 85; Peters 1985, 79; Klein 1986, 94–95; Ritmeyer and Ritmeyer 1989, 23–26; Reich 1992, 49; Shanks 1995a, 137–38, 156–57; Armstrong 1996, 130–32; Jacobson 1999, 54.

21. Cf. John 2:20 with Josephus *Antiquities of the Jews* 20.9.219–23.

22. Kollek and Pearlman 1968, 99; Brauer 1970, 83–85; Peters 1985, 76–77, 79; Klein 1986, 94; Grabbe 1992, 357; Shanks 1995a, 137–38, 156–57; Armstrong 1996, 130–32; Jacobson 2002, 19, 22. For arguments about where the Temple was located on the Mount

and for other related details, see, for example, with further bibliography, Bahat 1995; Ritmeyer and Kaufman 2000.

23. The tower is either the one called Hippicus or the one called Phasael and today known erroneously as the "Tower of David."

24. Kollek and Pearlman 1968, 98–99; Peters 1985, 74–77; Ritmeyer and Ritmeyer 1989, 24; Grabbe 1992, 356–57; Wightman 1993, 123–26; Shanks 1995a, 137–38; Armstrong 1996, 128.

25. Brauer 1970, 120; Kokkinos 2002. See also "What Killed Herod?" *Biblical Archaeology Review* 28, no. 2 (March–April 2002), 16, and the responses, some with diagnoses, in the letters to the editor, *Biblical Archaeology Review* 28, no. 4 (July–August 2002).

26. Josephus *Antiquities of the Jews* 17.6.149–81; *Jewish War* 1.33.647–55. See Brauer 1970, 121–22; Armstrong 1996, 139.

27. Josephus *Antiquities of the Jews* 17.9.206–23; *Jewish War* 2.1.1–13. See Brauer 1970, 127–29; Armstrong 1996, 139–40.

28. Josephus *Antiquities of the Jews* 17.10.250–64; *Jewish War* 2.3.39–50.

29. Josephus *Antiquities of the Jews* 17.10.265–70, 286–98; *Jewish War* 2.3.51–2.5.79. See Brauer 1970, 129–35; Rhoads 1976, 26; Grabbe 1992, 366–68; Armstrong 1996, 139–40; Goldsworthy 1996, 89.

30. See, for example, Grabbe 1992, 368.

31. Translation following Rolfe 1930, 157.

32. The soldiers were garrisoned within the Antonia fortress, which lay immediately to the north of the Temple and was connected to the Temple's outermost courts.

33. Josephus *Antiquities of the Jews* 18.3.55–59; *Jewish War* 2.9.167–71. See Brauer 1970, 140–45; Rhoads 1976, 61; Grabbe 1992, 424; Armstrong 1996, 140–42.

34. See also Josephus *Jewish War* 2.9.172–77; Brauer 1970, 146; Rhoads 1976, 61; Grabbe 1992, 424.

35. Klein 1986, 103; Armstrong 1996, 142–43.

36. Luke also wrote:

As Jesus approached Jerusalem and saw the city, he wept over it and said: "If you, even you, had only known on this day what would bring you peace—but now it is hidden from your eyes. The days will come upon you when your enemies will build an embankment against you and encircle you and hem you in on every side. They will dash you to the ground, you and your children within your walls. They will not leave one stone on another, because you did not recognize the time of God's coming to you." (Luke 19:41–44)

We should keep in mind, however, that scholars are divided as to whether the Gospels were written before (50s–60s CE) or after (80s–90s CE) the Roman destruction of Jerusalem. This in turn will have an impact upon whether Jesus did in fact actually predict the siege and fall of Jerusalem forty years before it took place.

37. Josephus *Jewish War* 2.10.184–203; Josephus *Antiquities of the Jews* 18.8.257–309; Philo *Embassy to Gaius* 184–338; Tacitus *Histories* 5.93. See Smallwood 1957, 3–5, 11–12; Rhoads 1976, 62–63; Bilde 1978, 67–69, 75; Schwartz 1990, 78, 80–81; Grabbe 1992, 401–5. It is conceivable that this incident is referred to in the Gospels, with the words "But when you see the desolating sacrilege set up where it ought not to be (let the reader understand), then let those who are in Judaea flee to the mountains" (Mark 13:14; see also Matthew 24:15), although this could also be a reference to the desecration by Hadrian in 132 CE.

38. Rhoads 1976, 62–63; Bilde 1978, 67–69, 75; Armstrong 1996, 149–50. For a description of the three walls and the additional fortifications that protected the city, see earlier discussion. Kathleen Kenyon and other archaeologists believed that this "Third Wall" lies underneath the north wall of the present-day Old City of Jerusalem, where an Ottoman Turkish wall now stands. However, in the 1920s, E. L. Sukenik and L. A. Mayer excavated the remains of another wall with towers on its north face between six hundred and fifteen hundred feet to the north of the present north wall of the Old City. They argued that this was Agrippa's "Third Wall." Many—but by no means all—modern scholars agree with them. See, most recently, Magness 2000. See also Kenyon 1967, 155; Kollek and Pearlman 1968, 106–8; Rhoads 1976, 62–63; Broshi 1978, 13–14; Peters 1985, 70–71; Price 1992, 290–92; Wightman 1993, 161; Shanks 1995a, 172–75.

39. See brief discussions in Brauer 1970, 185; Rhoads 1976, 70; Armstrong 1996, 150. We must take with a grain of salt these estimates of the numbers who died, since they would represent perhaps one-quarter of the entire population of the city at that time.

40. Armstrong 1996, 148–49.

41. But see Harkabi 1983, 6–8; Grabbe 1992, 412–13; Aberbach and Aberbach 2000, 29–30, 32; Horsley 2002, 102–6. The war itself and its possible causes are highly contentious areas of scholarship. Certainly, over the course of the war from 66–70 CE, a full spectrum is covered. One could describe it beginning as a typical rebellion sparked by Florus's looting of the Temple treasury; then morphing into a full-blown revolt with nationalistic and social agendas, only to degenerate into a civil war fought between rival Jewish factions; and finally coming to a united, but ignominious, end at the hands of Titus and his Roman legions. The literature on the First Jewish Revolt is immense. The following sources are some of the more recent publications, which will include earlier bibliography: Goodman 2002; various contributions in Furneaux 1972; Bilde 1979; Gabba 1981; Gichon 1981; Tsafrir 1982; Goodman 1983; Goodman 1985; Price 1992; Berlin and Overman 2002.

42. Josephus *Antiquities of the Jews* 20.11.252–58. See, for example, Brauer 1970, 196; Goodman 1985.

43. Maier 1999, 10–11. For discussions concerning the accuracy and credibility of Josephus's reporting, see Broshi 1983; Cohen 1983; Rajak 1983; Goodman 2002.

44. Josephus *Jewish War* 2.14.293–96. See Kollek and Pearlman 1968, 125; Brauer 1970, 194–95, 197; Rhoads 1976, 98; Harkabi 1983, 7; Grabbe 1992, 446–47; Sheldon 1994, 6; Armstrong 1996, 150; Hayes and Mandell 1998, 182.

45. Brauer 1970, 197; Grabbe 1992, 446–47; Hayes and Mandell 1998, 182.

46. Brauer 1970, 198–99.

47. Josephus *Jewish War* 2.15.325–2.16.335. See Kollek and Pearlman 1968, 126; Brauer 1970, 199; Grabbe 1992, 447–48; Hayes and Mandell 1998, 182.

48. Brauer 1970, 200; Rhoads 1976, 98–99; Grabbe 1992, 448; Sheldon 1994, 6–7.

49. Grabbe 1992, 448–49.

50. Brauer 1970, 200; Rhoads 1976, 100–101.

51. It is thought that they remained there until Passover of 74 CE, several years after the Romans had destroyed Jerusalem. The story of the Roman siege of Masada and of the eventual defeat of the Jews there was recorded by Josephus (*Jewish War* 7.8.252–7.9.406) and figures prominently in the modern history of the fledgling state of Israel, particularly after Yigael Yadin's excavations at the site in the 1960s. Recently, however, Josephus's account has been called into question, and the story of the last stand at Masada is currently being reexamined. See most recently Cohen 1983; Netzer 1991; Ben-Yehuda 1995; Shanks 1997b; Ben-Yehuda, Zias, and Meshel 1998, and Ben-Yehuda 2002. On the Sicarii and the

Zealots, see also Zeitlin 1962; Smith 1971; Horsley 1986; Hengel 1989; Grabbe 1992, 458; Price 1992, 17–21; Sheldon 1994, 2–5.

52. Josephus *Jewish War* 2.18.457–98. See Brauer 1970, 201–2; Grabbe 1992, 448–49.

53. For full discussion, see Gichon 1981. See also Brauer 1970, 202; Grabbe 1992, 449; Sheldon 1994, 7–13; Goldsworthy 1996, 84–85; Hayes and Mandell 1998, 186–87.

54. Gichon 1981, 51–55; Grabbe 1992, 448–49; Sheldon 1994, 8–10; Goldsworthy 1996, 86; Hayes and Mandell 1998, 187.

55. Josephus *Jewish War* 2.19.527–32.

56. Brauer 1970, 203; Rhoads 1976, 101; Gichon 1981, 55–56; Grabbe 1992, 449–50; Sheldon 1994, 10; Goldsworthy 1996, 86–88; Hayes and Mandell 1998, 187.

57. Joshua 10:10–11; 1 Maccabees 3:13–24.

58. Brauer 1970, 203; Bar-Kochva 1976, 57–59; Rhoads 1976, 101; Gichon 1981, 18–21; Sheldon 1994, 10–13; Goldsworthy 1996, 86; Hayes and Mandell 1998, 187.

59. Translation following Rolfe 1930, 289. See also Tacitus *Histories* 5.10; Harkabi 1983, 7; Keppie 1984, 214–15; Price 1992, 11.

60. Keppie 1984, 67. The most famous example of a Roman army losing its standards occurred when an army led by Crassus of the First Triumvirate was annihilated by the Parthians in 53 BCE (Plutarch *Life of Crassus*). The emperor Augustus sent Tiberius against the Parthians in 20 BCE. He regained the standards. Augustus recorded these triumphs in his famous *Res Gestae* inscription, erected just before he died in 14 CE. Tiberius also recovered a standard lost by Decidius Saxa in Syria in 40 BCE and two lost by Mark Antony in Armenia in 36 BCE. All had ended up in the hands of the Parthians; see Colledge 1967, 38–45. The other famous set of lost standards were those belonging to Varus, which were captured by Germanic tribes in the Teutoburg Forest in September of 9 CE, when they massacred his three legions of Roman soldiers. Later campaigns led by Germanicus were launched in 15 and 16 CE, in part to recover the standards lost by Varus. See Keppie 1984, 168–69; Dornberg 1992, with earlier references; Goldsworthy 1996, 18–19; Sheldon 2001. On the logistics of the Roman army during these years, see now Roth 1999.

61. The reconstituted Twelfth Legion was among the troops under Titus's command during the final conquest of Jerusalem in 70 CE. It was once again marching behind a standard in 136 CE, according to a list recorded at that time by Flavius Arrianus, governor of Cappadocia. But it is not specified whether this was their eagle standard or another standard. See Arrian *Ektaxis kata Alanoon*; Keppie 1984.

62. Josephus *Jewish War* 3.1.1–7, 3.4.59–69. See Brauer 1970, 217–18; Grabbe 1992, 454; Sheldon 1994, 12–13.

63. Josephus *Jewish War* 3.7.132–3.8.408. See Brauer 1970, 227; Armstrong 1996, 151–52; Maier 1999, 8; Aviam 2002. On Josephus's life and history, see numerous books and articles by Louis H. Feldman, including Feldman 1965, 1984, 1998.

64. Josephus *Jewish War* 3.9.409–4.2.120, 4.8.440–4.9.490.

65. Brauer 1970, 227–28; Peters 1985, 111; Grabbe 1992, 456–57; Sheldon 1994, 13–15; Syon 2002.

66. See also discussions in Brauer 1970, 239–41; Rhoads 1976, 107; Grabbe 1992, 457–59; Price 1992, 89–94; Hayes and Mandell 1998, 195–96.

67. See Kollek and Pearlman 1968, 128; Brauer 1970, 228, 236–41; Rhoads 1976, 104–7; Grabbe 1992, 457–59; Price 1992, 102–3; Sheldon 1994, 14–15; Armstrong 1996, 150–52; Hayes and Mandell 1998, 195–96.

68. Translation following Moore 1931, 175–77. See Brauer 1970, 244–45; Stern 1974, 63; Harkabi 1983, 9; Sheldon 1994, 16; Hayes and Mandell 1998, 196.

69. Rosenthal and Mozeson 1990, 103; Price 1992, 127–28; Sheldon 1994, 16; Hayes and Mandell 1998, 196.

70. Kollek and Pearlman 1968, 128; Brauer 1970, 245–46; Grabbe 1992, 459; Hayes and Mandell 1998, 197.

71. Translation following Moore 1931, 197. Grabbe 1992, 459; Price 1992, 104–7, 115; Sheldon 1994, 15–16; Hayes and Mandell 1998, 195–96.

72. Translation following Moore 1931, 199. See also Moore 1969, 220–21; Brauer 1970, 262; Stern 1974, 63; Harkabi 1983, 9; Sheldon 1994, 16.

73. Avigad 1970, 7. See now Abu El-Haj 2001, 143–46, 208–13, for an interesting discussion questioning the standard reconstruction of the events leading to the "Burnt House" and the young woman within it; see also, previously, Abu El-Haj 1998, 169–71, 182 n. 12.

74. Josephus *Jewish War* 5.6.266–74, 5.7.296–302.

75. Josephus *Jewish War* 5.7.293–316. See Kollek and Pearlman 1968, 129–30; Brauer 1970, 246–48; Peters 1985, 111–12; Price 1992, 132–33; Sheldon 1994, 16; Armstrong 1996, 151–52; Hayes and Mandell 1998, 197.

76. Kollek and Pearlman 1968, 130; Brauer 1970, 248; Price 1992, 134–35; Sheldon 1994, 16–18; Armstrong 1996, 151–52; Hayes and Mandell 1998, 197.

77. See Josephus *Jewish War* 5.10.437–38, 5.11.446–51. Kollek and Pearlman 1968, 130; Brauer 1970, 249–50; Hayes and Mandell 1998, 199.

78. Josephus *Jewish War* 5.11.466–72. See Kollek and Pearlman 1968, 128, 130; Brauer 1970, 249–50; Peters 1985, 111–12; Rosenthal and Mozeson 1990, 104; Price 1992, 142–43; Sheldon 1994, 18; Hayes and Mandell 1998, 199.

79. Kollek and Pearlman 1968, 132; Rosenthal and Mozeson 1990, 104; Price 1992, 143–44; Sheldon 1994, 18; Hayes and Mandell 1998, 199.

80. For more on John of Gischala, see, for example, Rappaport 1983; see also Price 1992.

81. Josephus *Jewish War* 6.1.1–92. See Kollek and Pearlman 1968, 132; Brauer 1970, 253–54; Peters 1985, 113–15; Sheldon 1994, 18–19; Hayes and Mandell 1998, 199–200.

82. Brauer 1970, 255; Peters 1985, 113–15; Hayes and Mandell 1998, 200.

83. See Brauer 1970, 256; Price 1992, 153–56.

84. Kollek and Pearlman 1968, 132; Brauer 1970, 257; Peters 1985, 113–15; Price 1992, 162–65; Sheldon 1994, 19; Hayes and Mandell 1998, 200.

85. Translation of Josephus here follows Peters 1985, 116–17, which renders the translation more effectively than does the translation in Whiston 1999.

86. Josephus *Jewish War* 6.4.220–70. See Kollek and Pearlman 1968, 132; Brauer 1970, 258–59; Peters 1985, 116–17; Rosenthal and Mozeson 1990, 105; Price 1992, 167–71; Sheldon 1994, 19; Hayes and Mandell 1998, 202.

87. Kollek and Pearlman 1968, 135; Brauer 1970, 258–59; Alon 1977; Peters 1985, 116–17; Shanks 1995a, 175. Josephus actually records the day as "the tenth day of the month Lous [Ab]"–rather than the ninth, as is traditionally thought (*Jewish War* 6.4.250).

88. Ritmeyer and Ritmeyer 1989, 40.

89. Translations following Peters 1985, 116–17. Again, the translations of Josephus in this paragraph follow Peters 1985, which renders the translation more effectively than does the translation in Whiston 1999.

90. Josephus *Jewish War* 6.6.316. See Peters 1985, 116–17.

91. Brauer 1970, 260–61; Price 1992, 171–74; Rosovsky 1992, 28–29; Sheldon 1994, 19; Shanks 1995a, 175–77.

92. Kollek and Pearlman 1968, 135; Shanks 1995a, 175; Hayes and Mandell 1998, 202–3.

93. Kollek and Pearlman 1968, 135; Brauer 1970, 264–65; Klein 1986, 115; Sheldon 1994, 20; Hayes and Mandell 1998, 204.

94. The translation of the Arch of Titus inscription follows Overman 2002, 217, following Lewis and Reinhold 1990, 15. See also Kenyon 1967, 165–66; Kollek and Pearlman 1968, 135.

95. See Klein 1986, 115; Armstrong 1996, 153–54; Hayes and Mandell 1998, 204.

96. Professor Geza Alföldy of Heidelberg University in Germany believes the inscription originally read, "The Emperor Caesar Vespasian Augustus ordered the new amphitheater to be made from the booty." Sometime after Vespasian's death in 79 CE, Titus made a small alteration by adding a *T*—standing for "Titus"—before the word *Caesar*. See Alföldy 1995; Feldman 2001. For reactions from other scholars, see also Hartman 2001; Ostling 2001.

97. We know that Solomon's Temple was plundered at least eight times between about 960 BCE and 586 BCE. In chronological order, it was (1) either looted by Shishak or used by Rehoboam to bribe Shishak in 925 BCE, (2) used by Asa of Judah to bribe Ben-Hadad of Aram-Damascus in 875 BCE, (3) looted by Hazael of Aram-Damascus or used by Jehoash of Judah to bribe Hazael in 800 BCE, (4) looted by Jehoash of Israel in 785 BCE, (5) used by Ahaz of Judah to bribe Tiglath-Pileser III of Assyria in 734 BCE, (6) looted by Sennacherib of Assyria or used by Hezekiah of Judah to bribe Sennacherib in 701 BCE, (7) looted by Nebuchadnezzar of Babylonia in 597 BCE, and (8) looted again by Nebuchadnezzar in 586 BCE. From about 515 BCE until 70 CE, the Second Temple was plundered many times. We know it was (1) robbed by Menelaus in 172 BC; (2) plundered by Antiochus IV in 169 BCE; (3) looted by Pompey in 63 BCE; (4) looted by Crassus in 54 BCE; (5) looted by Sabinus in 4 CE; (6) used by Pontius Pilate about 27 CE; (7) looted by Florus in 66 CE; (8) plundered, with its treasures melted down, by John of Gischala in 70 CE; and (9) looted by Titus late in 70 CE.

98. Peters 1985, 116–17; Hayes and Mandell 1998, 203.

99. Grabbe (1992, 459–60) says:

The noncombatants within the city suffered from famine and from the militants. Exactly how the many atrocities against innocent victims, often leaders and nobles, that are reported by Josephus are to be evaluated is problematic. If Josephus is to be believed, they must all have perished several times over: on several occasions his narrative describes things so that no one among the citizenry could have been left alive, yet the next episode reports more victims.

For further discussions, see Brauer 1970, 261–62; Ben-Dov 1982, 186–87; Rosenthal and Mozeson 1990, 105; Hayes and Mandell 1998, 203; Feldman 2001, 31.

100. Ben-Dov 1982, 185; see also Geva 1997, 35–37.

101. Kenyon 1967, 165–66; Kollek and Pearlman 1968, 135; Brauer 1970, 263; Rhoads 1976, 174; Avigad 1980, 205; Ben-Dov 1982, 185–87; Geva 1984, 239–54; Peters 1985, 120–21; Armstrong 1996, 151–54; Geva 1997, 35–41; Hayes and Mandell 1998, 203; Broshi and Gibson 2000, 153; Geva 2000, "Twenty-five Years," 18–19; . Evidence for the ensuing presence of the Tenth Legion in Jerusalem has been found by archaeologists in the form of roof tiles, bricks, and pipe sections, many bearing the legion's stamp: L(*egio*) X F(*retensis*) or LEG-X-FRE. For recent discussions of this evidence and the location of the Roman camp within Jerusalem, see Ben-Dov 1982; Geva 1984; Geva 1997; Broshi and Gibson 2000; Geva 2000; Magness 2002.

102. Kollek and Pearlman 1968, 137–38; Brauer 1970, 265; Yadin 1971, 17; Rhoads 1976, 174; Netzer 1991, 20–32; Grabbe 1992, 460; Magness 1992c, 58–67.

103. There are also accounts found in the Talmud, Mishnah, and Midrash, but these are probably considerably later. See Yadin 1971, 18–27, 255–59; Schäfer 1981, 74–94; Oppenheimer 1982, 59; Grabbe 1992, 570–71, 585, 601; Marks 1994, 4–5, 209–12.

104. There is much debate as to which came first, the announcement or the rebellion (or even the exclusion and expulsion of the Jews from Jerusalem), but it seems most plausible that the announcement came first. For discussions, see Mantel 1967–68; Kollek and Pearlman 1968, 138–41; Brauer 1970, 272; Yadin 1971, 19–21; Isaac and Roll 1979, 65; Ben-Dov 1982, 189–90; Oppenheimer 1982, 62; Peters 1985, 126; Golan 1986, 226, 237–39; Klein 1986, 116–17; Grabbe 1992, 571–77, 600, 602; Tsafrir 1992, 68; Armstrong 1996, 161–63; Eshel 1997, 46; Geva 1997, 41; Holum 1997, 50–51; Hayes and Mandell 1998, 211. This was the second revolt in two decades. A previous Jewish revolt known as the "War of Quietus"—after the Roman commander who finally suppressed it—lasted from 115–17 CE in Egypt, Cyprus, and Cyrene. That rebellion did not involve Jerusalem.

105. The literature on the Second Jewish Revolt is immense. See, for example, Bietenhard 1948, 81–108; Smallwood 1959, 334, 336–37, 340; Kollek and Pearlman 1968, 138–41; Brauer 1970, 272–73; Yadin 1971, 18–21; Applebaum 1976; Smallwood 1976, 428–66; Gichon 1979; Isaac and Roll 1979, 65; Bowersock 1980; Schäfer 1980; Schäfer 1981; Oppenheimer 1982, 63–68; Applebaum 1983–84; Harkabi 1983, 28–29, 47, 57–58; Isaac 1983–84; Applebaum 1984; Isaac and Oppenheimer 1985; Gichon 1986; Klein 1986, 117–18; Schäfer 1990; Grabbe 1992, 559–60, 570–77, 601–3; Marks 1994, 6–8, 14; Shanks 1995a, 215; Duncan and Opatowski 1998, 43–46; Hayes and Mandell 1998, 211, 214; Eck 1999, 76–89.

106. Translations follow Cary 1925. Note that Dio Cassius's figures have been criticized and called into question by some historians. For discussions see, for example, Brauer 1970, 273–74; Yadin 1971, 19–21; Applebaum 1974; Oppenheimer 1982, 73–74; Harkabi 1983, 35; Klein 1986, 118–19; Rosenthal and Mozeson 1990, 132–33; Grabbe 1992, 605; Marks 1994, 8–9; Armstrong 1996, 163; Duncan and Opatowski 1998, 46.

107. For various opinions and arguments, see Kollek and Pearlman 1968, 138–41; Oppenheimer 1982, 68–69; Harkabi 1983, 35; Isaac and Oppenheimer 1985, 54–55; Peters 1985, 127–28; Klein 1986, 118; Grabbe 1992, 578, 604–5; Marks 1994, 8; Armstrong 1996, 163; Geva 1997, 41–42; Eshel 2002.

108. Harris 1926, 199–206; Kollek and Pearlman 1968, 138–41; Brauer 1970, 273–74; Avigad 1980, 205–7; Bowersock 1980, 137–38; Isaac 1980–81, 31–54; Ben-Dov 1982, 190–91, 210; Oppenheimer 1982, 75; Bowersock 1985, 53; Peters 1985, 129–30; Klein 1986, 119–20; Magen 1988, 48–56; Ritmeyer and Ritmeyer 1989, 24; Rosenthal and Mozeson 1990, 132; Grabbe 1992, 556–57; Mango 1992, 2; Rosovsky 1992, 35–36; Tsafrir 1992, 68; Shanks 1995a, 215–17; Armstrong 1996, 164–66; Eliav 1997, 125–44; Geva 1997, 42–45; Hayes and Mandell 1998, 215; Geva 2000, "Twenty-five Years," 19; Aberbach and Aberbach 2000, 87.

109. Translation following Zerubavel 1995, 52–53 and n. 28, quoting Ben-Gurion's speech in a ceremony of pledging allegiance on June 27, 1948, as reprinted in *Medinat Yisrael ha-Mehudeshet* (Tel Aviv: Am Oved, 1969), 1:207–8.

110. The original Hebrew version appeared in 1980; the English translation consulted here appeared as Harkabi 1983. See discussion and reactions, with further bibliography, in, for example, Marks 1994, 9; Frankel 1984; Zerubavel 1995, 179, 182.

111. Harkabi 1983, xii–xiii, 105; Marks 1994, 4–5, 9; Zerubavel 1995, 179.

112. Friedman 1982, E22. See Zerubavel 1995, 182.

113. Silberman 2002, 237.

114. Harkabi 1983, 50.

CHAPTER 5

1. Ross's statements about Arafat's remark were made in interviews conducted by *FOX News Sunday* on April 21, 2002, in the United States (transcripts available) and by Channel 1 in Israel. See Sennott 2000; Steinberg 2001, 8A; Lazaroff 2002a: 1. A1. Barak's comments (reflecting a discussion with President Clinton) were made in interviews with the Israeli revisionist historian Benny Morris of Ben Gurion University in Beer-Sheva and were published in the *New York Review of Books* on June 13, 2002; see Morris 2002a, 42–45. Arafat's comment to Chirac follows quotation in Enderlin 2003, 281.

2. Quotations follow Lefkovits 2001a, 3A; Lefkovits and Keinon 2001a, 2. See also Sennott 2001, A1.

3. Winer 2002, 4. Additional comments made by Yasser Arafat in 2002 and by Saeb Erekat, one of the chief Palestinian negotiators of the 1993 Oslo Agreement and the 2000 Camp David Accords, have been published by Enderlin (2003, 205): "Arafat, while accepting the principle of Israeli sovereignty over the Wailing Wall, declares that 'the Jews have no claim to the whole area of the Haram al-Sharif. They [the Israelis] excavated everywhere, and they didn't find a single stone from the Temple, just some stones from the Temple of Herod.' And Saeb Erekat adds: 'The fact is that, today, no such thing as a Temple Mount exists. What's there is a mosque. We're dealing with realities.'" See also Hendel 2003, 8.

4. See Wasserstein 2001, 322; see also chapter 9 in the present book.

5. In stating that the Temple was in Nablus rather than Jerusalem, Arafat (followed by Sabri) is clearly invoking the alternate, Samaritan version of the Hebrew Bible, which sees Mount Gerizim as God's chosen holy place and the proper site for the Temple. Mount Gerizim is near ancient Shechem, now modern Nablus, in the West Bank. However, the standard Masoretic version of the Hebrew Bible very clearly places God's chosen holy place and the proper site for the Temple at Jerusalem. See Purvis 1968 for further discussion on the Samaritan Pentateuch and this major ancient controversy that raged between the Samaritans and the Judaeans. Regardless, the Temples of Solomon and Herod built in Jerusalem were completely different entities from the temple built by the Samaritans on Mount Gerizim near Nablus.

6. This is discussed in chapter 4; see the references cited there.

7. Avi-Yonah 1976, 191–204; Avigad 1980, 208; Peters 1985, 146–47; Klein 1986, 121–22; Mango 1992, 3; Shanks 1995a, 225, 230; Gil 1996a, 2.

8. Translation following Peters 1993, 51–52.

9. Kollek and Pearlman 1968, 138–41; Yadin 1971, 22; Avigad 1980, 208; Ben-Dov 1982, 210; Klein 1986, 120; Armstrong 1996, 164–66; Gil 1996a, 2; Geva 1997, 72; Hayes and Mandell 1998, 215; Aberbach and Aberbach 2000, 87.

10. Klein 1986, 120–21.

11. Translation following Mango and Scott 1997, 37; see also 41–43.

12. Avi-Yonah 1976, 165; Avigad 1980, 208–9; Ben-Dov 1982, 210; Peters 1985, 137–40, 161–66; Klein 1986, 120–23; Mango 1992, 3; Shanks 1995a, 225, 230–31; Gil 1996a, 2.

13. Chitty 1966, 155; Avi-Yonah 1976, 258–65; Ben-Dov 1982, 261; Peters 1985, 170–72; Rosenthal and Mozeson 1990, 149; Armstrong 1996, 213–14.

14. Antiochus Strategius *The Capture of Jerusalem by the Persians in the Year 614*; translation following Conybeare 1910, 506–7; cf. Peters 1985, 170–72. An alternate version favored by some scholars is that the city initially surrendered without a fight but then rebelled against the Persians, who were forced to besiege the city in order to retake it. See various discussions in Runciman 1951, 10; Chitty 1966, 155–56; Klein 1986, 124; Rosen-

thal and Mozeson 1990, 149; Gil 1992, 6; Mango 1992, 3–4; Armstrong 1996, 213–14; Reich 1996, 32–33.

15. See various discussions in Hamilton 1940, 7–8; Avi-Yonah 1976, 265; Prawer 1985, 13–14; Wightman 1989, 13, 26–27; Magness 1991, 208–17; Magness 1992a, 67–74; Magness 1992b, 96; Magness 1993, 40, 42; Russell 2001, 48–49.

16. Translation following Conybeare 1910, 506–7; cf. Peters 1985, 170–72. The Byzantine chronicler Theophanes the Confessor says briefly, "In this year the Persians took [the region of] the Jordan, Palestine, and the Holy City by force of arms and killed many people therein" (translation following Mango and Scott 1997, 431; cf. Turtledove 1982, 11). See also Macler 1904, 68–69, for a translation of the account of the Armenian historian Sebeos, which differs somewhat from the preceding accounts, perhaps because Sebeos was not an eyewitness. For discussions, see Runciman 1951, 10; Chitty 1966, 155–58; Avi-Yonah 1976, 263–65; Avigad 1980, 208; Ben-Dov 1982, 241, 261–62; Klein 1986, 124; Rosenthal and Mozeson 1990, 149–51; Gil 1992, 6; Mango 1992, 3–4; Gil 1996a, 1; Armstrong 1996, 213–14; Reich 1996, 32–33; al-Khateeb 1998, 33; Russell 2001, 49.

17. Translation following Conybeare 1910, 507; cf. Peters 1985, 170–72. For full discussions, see Runciman 1951, 10; Chitty 1966, 155–58; Avi-Yonah 1976, 265–66; Avigad 1980, 208; Ben-Dov 1982, 241, 261–62; Klein 1986, 124; Rosenthal and Mozeson 1990, 149–51; Gil 1992, 6; Mango 1992, 3–4; Armstrong 1996, 213–14; Gil 1996a, 1; al-Khateeb 1998, 33.

18. Translation following Conybeare 1910, 507. See also Macler 1904, 68–69; Chitty 1966, 157–58; Avi-Yonah 1976, 266; Mango 1992, 3–4; Armstrong 1996, 214; Reich 1996, 32–33.

19. Reich 1994, 117–18; Reich 1996, 26–33, 60; Russell 2001, 50–51. See also Milik 1960–61, 127–89, for an analysis of the thirty-five sites mentioned by Strategius.

20. Rosenthal and Mozeson 1990, 149; Armstrong 1996, 213–14; Reich 1996, 32–33, 60.

21. The quotation in this paragraph is from Ben-Dov 1982, 261. Cf. Avi-Yonah 1976, 260–63; Avigad 1980, 208; Ben-Dov 1982, 241, 261–62; Klein 1986, 124; Rosenthal and Mozeson 1990, 149–50; Gil 1992, 5–6; Mango 1992, 3–4; Reich 1996, 33; Gil 1996a, 1; al-Khateeb 1998, 33; Horowitz 1998, 1–39.

22. Macler 1904, 68–69; Runciman 1951, 10; Chitty 1966, 157–58; Avi-Yonah 1976, 266; Klein 1986, 124; Rosenthal and Mozeson 1990, 150–51; Shanks 1995a, 233; Reich 1996, 32.

23. Cf. Avi-Yonah 1976, 268; Peters 1985, 173; Mango 1992, 3–4; Armstrong 1996, 214–15; Reich 1996, 33.

24. Cf. Avi-Yonah 1976, 270–71; Ben-Dov 1982, 262–63; Turtledove 1982, 29–30; Peters 1985, 173; Klein 1986, 125; Rosenthal and Mozeson 1990, 152–53; Gil 1992, 7–8; Mango 1992, 3–4; Shanks 1995a, 233; Armstrong 1996, 214–15; Gil 1996a, 2–3; Mango and Scott 1997, 448–57.

25. Translation following Mango and Scott 1997, 458–59; cf. Turtledove 1982, 30. Mango and Scott (1997, 459 nn. 2–3) note that Theophanes must be mistaken about Zacharias being reinstated as patriarch, for Zacharias had died while exiled in Persia; they suggest—based on existing variations of Theophanes' manuscript—that it was probably Modestus who was appointed patriarch by Heraclius. They also give a date of March 21, 630 CE, for Heraclius's triumphant entry into Jerusalem, and they note the many alternate dates that have been suggested, ranging from 628 to 631 CE. See discussions in Avi-Yonah 1976, 268, 271; Ben-Dov 1982, 262–63; Turtledove 1982, 29–30; Peters 1985, 173; Klein 1986,

125; Rosenthal and Mozeson 1990, 152–53; Gil 1992, 7–8; Mango 1992, 3–4; Shanks 1995a, 233; Armstrong 1996, 214–15; Reich 1996, 33, 60; Gil 1996a, 2–3.

26. Klein 1986, 131; Armstrong 1988, 28–29; Lewis 1995, 51–52. On Mohammed and the origins of Islam, see also Peters 1973; Armstrong 1992; Peters 1994; Armstrong 2000.

27. Klein 1986, 131–32; Armstrong 1988, 28–32; Armstrong 1992, 45–47, 82–85; Gil 1992, 11; Peters 1994, 141–43, 191–98; Lewis 1995, 52–53; Duncan and Opatowski 1998, 46, 48; Armstrong 2000, 3–5; Lewis 2003, 33–34.

28. Armstrong 1988, 30, 37–38; Armstrong 1992, 240–44; Gil 1992, 11; Peters 1994, 235–39; Lewis 1995, 52–53; Duncan and Opatowski 1998, 48; Armstrong 2000, 5, 13–15.

29. Lewis 1995, 53–54; Lewis 2003, 5. Cf. Armstrong 1988, 30–31; Armstrong 2000, 8, 10.

30. Armstrong 1988, 40; Armstrong 1992, 255–60; Lewis 1995, 54–55; Lewis 2003, xviii, 7.

31. Armstrong 1988, 40–41. See also Lewis 2003, 29–39.

32. For an account of the Moslem conquest of Syria and adjacent areas, see Donner 1981. Cf. Armstrong 1996, 226; Duncan and Opatowski 1998, 48; Armstrong 2000, 25–29. On Sophronius's complaint in 634 CE, see Peters 1985, 175, 177; Idinopulos 1991, 210; Gil 1992, 51.

33. Lewis 1995, 62.

34. Avi-Yonah 1976, 272; Donner 1981, 112–13, 128–29, 139, 142, 148–49, 151–53; Ben-Dov 1982, 263; Peters 1985, 175; Idinopulos 1991, 154–55, 210–11; Gil 1992, 51; Grabar 1996, 46; Gil 1996a, 5; Duncan and Opatowski 1998, 48–49.

35. Gil 1996a, 6–7. See also Tibawi 1969, 7–8; Donner 1981, 151; Gil 1992, 51–52; Shanks 1995a, 233; Armstrong 1996, 227–28; Grabar 1996, 6. Note that Tabari, who is described by Gil (1996a, 6) as "the greatest of Arab chroniclers" and who also lived during the ninth century CE, gives two dates for the capture of Jerusalem, 636 CE and 637 CE; Gil argues that the date of 638 CE given by Baladhuri "is to be preferred." Peters (1993, 43–44) argues for the date of 635 CE—as have Busse (1986) and Linder (1996, 121)—although Peters (1985, 176–77) previously agreed with the date of 638 CE. Other dates that have been suggested include 637 CE; cf. Duri 2000, 106.

36. Translation following Peters 1985, 190; cf. also Turtledove 1982, 39; Mango and Scott 1997, 471. For modern scholarly discussions of the length of the siege, cf. Donner 1981, 151; Gil 1992, 51–52; Peters 1993, 43–44, 46; Gil 1996a, 6. A few scholars have suggested that the siege lasted only four months, but they do not present their evidence: cf. Klein 1986, 133; al-Khateeb 1998, 129.

37. Translation following Peters 1985, 176–77. See also Tibawi 1969, 7–8; Peters 1993, 43–44; Armstrong 1996, 240–41.

38. The sources include the ninth-century Byzantine chronicler Theophanes and the ninth-century Arab historian Waqidi, among others; see translation and discussion in Peters 1993, 44, 46. See also Runciman 1951, 3; Tibawi 1969, 7–8; Ben-Dov 1982, 263; Turtledove 1982, 39; Armstrong 1988, 46; Idinopulos 1991, 154–55; Gil 1992, 52; Shanks 1995a, 233–34; Armstrong 1996, 228; Grabar 1996, 46; Gil 1996a, 7; Mango and Scott 1997, 471–72; Gorenberg 2000, 71. For a translation of Tabari's account, see Friedmann 1992, 185–94.

39. Aamiry 1978, 47. Benvenisti (1996, 15) similarly claims, "The Arab conquest was accomplished without bloodshed." See also the description and discussion in Armstrong 1996, 228.

40. Gil 1996a, 6; see also Gil 1992, 52.

41. Klein 1986, 126; Grabar 1996, 6.

42. However, he soon changed his mind; the second *qibla* proposed by Mohammed—probably in 624 CE, after his move to Medina—decreed that the faithful should instead face Mecca while praying. Cf. Spuler 1960, 10; Glubb 1970, 136, 170, 287; Donner 1981, 97; Klein 1986, 130; Idinopulos 1991, 215; Friedmann 1992, xviii; Gil 1992, 65–66, 90–91; Peters 1993, 48–49; Armstrong 1996, 224; Grabar 1996, 46–47; Gil 1996a, 3; Gil 1996b, 163, 196–97; Duri 2000, 105–6; Pipes 2001, 50–51; Wasserstein 2001, 10.

43. Cf. Kollek and Pearlman 1968, 155; Tibawi 1969, 8; Lazarus-Yafeh 1974, 213–14; Stendel 1974, 148–49; Peters 1985, 185–91, 195–201; Klein 1986, 135; Idinopulos 1991, 154–55, 214; Friedmann 1992, 195–96; Gil 1992, 52, 65–67; Peters 1993, 44–46; Armstrong 1996, 229–31; Grabar 1996, 47; Gil 1996a, 11–13; al-Khateeb 1998, 129–31; Duri 2000, 108; Gorenberg 2000, 71. It is possible that Umar's temporary mosque was located where the al-Aqsa Mosque stands today, rather than where the Dome of the Rock is presently, but the original placement is debated.

44. Hasson 1996, 353; cf. Talhami 2000, 114–15.

45. See sura 17 of the Koran, called "The Nocturnal Journey." For discussions of the various traditions associated with this night journey and of the relevance of the al-Aqsa Mosque on the Haram al-Sherif, cf. Tibawi 1969, 6–7; Glubb 1970, 136; Stendel 1974, 148–49; Donner 1981, 97; Peters 1985, 182–85; Klein 1986, 127–29; Armstrong 1992, 138–42; Friedmann 1992, 194–95; Peters 1993, 57–58, 64–66; Peters 1994, 144–47; Armstrong 1996, 224, 246; Gil 1996a, 3–4; Hasson 1996, 353, 355–59; al-Khateeb 1998, 107–19; Duri 2000, 105; Gorenberg 2000, 70–71; Talhami 2000, 114; Pipes 2001, 51–53; Wasserstein 2001, 10.

46. The translation and discussion of inscriptions follow Lewis 1995, 69–70; Lewis 2003, 43–44. On al-Malik's construction of the Dome of the Rock, cf. Kollek and Pearlman 1968, 156; Ben-Dov 1982, 278–81; Hawting 1986, 59–61; Klein 1986, 136–37; Rosen-Ayalon 1989, 5–6, 12–14; Idinopulos 1991, 224–27; Elad 1992; Gil 1992, 91–92; Peters 1993, 60–64; Wightman 1993, 227–28; Shanks 1995a, 234–38; Armstrong 1996, 236–42; Grabar 1996, 7, 52–53, 110–13; Bahat 1996a, 86; Gil 1996a, 11–13; Duri 2000, 110; Gorenberg 2000, 71–72; Talhami 2000, 117–18; Wasserstein 2001, 10–11. On al-Walid's construction of the original al-Aqsa Mosque, cf. Kollek and Pearlman 1968, 161; Ben-Dov 1982, 278–79; Klein 1986, 136; Rosen-Ayalon 1989, 4–6; Idinopulos 1991, 233–34; Gil 1992, 95; Peters 1993, 60–61; Wightman 1993, 227–28; Shanks 1995a, 234; Armstrong 1996, 242–43; Bahat 1996a, 82–83; Duri 2000, 111. On the reconstruction and restoration work done on the walls of the Temple Mount and other buildings constructed on the Haram al-Sherif, cf. Bahat 1996a, 73–74, 81–84, 86–87.

47. Cf. Tibawi 1969, 9; Stendel 1974, 148–49; Klein 1986, 136; Rosen-Ayalon 1989, 2; Gil 1992, 114; Raby and Johns 1992; Peters 1993, 47–48; Lewis 1995, 70; Armstrong 1996, 224; Grabar 1996, 112; Gil 1996a, 9–10; Khalidi 1997, 14; al-Khateeb 1998, 26; Hillenbrand 1999, 301; Pipes 2001, 51–53. Tibawi (1969, 9) writes: ". . . Jerusalem's place as the third Holy City in Islam was finally established. Its Roman name was dropped and it became al-Bait al-Muqaddas (the Holy House), in apposition to al-Bait al-Haram (the Sacred House), the appellation of Mecca. A variant of the name was Bait al-Maqdis or simply al-Quds (the Holy City). Later still it became al-Quds ash-Sharif (the Holy and Noble City)." Grabar (1996, 112) says further: "There is, however, one concrete instance in which a Jewish transferal may indeed be proposed for this period; even though it does not immediately affect the Rock, its overall impact was considerable—that is, the use of the words *Bayt al-Maqdis,* "The Holy House," to refer to the Haram area, while *Iliya* (from the Latin name of the city, *Aelia Capitolina*) remained the name of the city. At some

point *Bayt al-Maqdis* became the name of the city and *al-Haram al-Sharif* the name of the sanctuary, but the change was not completed until much later, and for several centuries there was considerable confusion about the matter." Gil (1992, 114) adds: "The term *bayt al-maqdis* became open to various other meanings. Sometimes it meant the Temple Mount and sometimes (in most cases) the city of Jerusalem, but at times also the whole of Palestine."

48. Porath 1975, 355; Klein 1986, 136; Gil 1992, 113; Armstrong 1996, 234; Gil 1996a, 9–10; Talhami 2000, 118–19.

49. Ben-Dov 1982, 300. 324–25; Klein 1986, 143–46; Idinopulos 1991, 246–47; Gil 1992, 87, 295–96, 325–27, 373–74, 409–15; Armstrong 1996, 244, 254, 256–57, 268–70; Bahat 1996b, 70–74; Gil 1996a, 15, 17, 19–21, 23–30, 34–35; Duncan and Opatowski 1998, 54; Duri 2000, 113, 120.

50. Lewis 1995, 62.

51. Lewis 1995, 62–74; Armstrong 2000, 31–37, 41–43.

52. Translation following Turtledove 1982, 112; cf. also translation in Mango and Scott 1997, 584. See also Gil 1992, 87; Armstrong 1996, 244.

53. Lewis 1995, 75–77; Armstrong 2000, 52–53.

54. Klein 1986, 141–42; Gil 1992, 286–88; Gil 1996a, 14; Armstrong 2000, 53–55.

55. Gil 1996a, 15.

56. Gil 1992, 295–96; Armstrong 1996, 254; Gil 1996a, 15; Duri 2000, 113.

57. Armstrong 1996, 256.

58. Klein 1986, 143; Gil 1992, 325–26; Armstrong 1996, 256–57; Gil 1996a, 19.

59. Lewis 1995, 83; Cline 2000, 124.

60. Klein 1986, 143; Gil 1992, 335–54; Armstrong 1996, 257; Gil 1996a, 19–21; Armstrong 2000, 81.

61. Klein 1986, 144–45; Gil 1992, 373–74; Gil 1996a, 24–25.

62. Gil 1992, 386–97; Gil 1996a, 26–27.

63. Lewis 1995, 87–90; Armstrong 2000, 81.

64. For a partial biography of Ibn al-Athir, see Gabrieli 1969, xxvii–xxviii.

65. Translation following Richards 2002, 172.

66. Peters 1985, 250; Klein 1986, 146; Gil 1992, 409–13; Armstrong 1996, 268; Gil 1996a, 34; Duncan and Opatowski 1998, 54; Richards 2002, 172, 190.

67. Runciman 1951, 75–76; Klein 1986, 146; Gil 1992, 412–13; Armstrong 1996, 268–70; Gil 1996a, 34; Duncan and Opatowski 1998, 54; Hiyari 2000, 135–36.

68. Translation following Richards 2002, 192.

69. The earlier destruction of the Church of the Holy Sepulcher in 1009 CE by the Egyptian Fatimid caliph al-Hakim is also thought to have been a contributing factor.

70. Translation following Peters 1971, 272–73; Gabrieli 1969, 10–12. See also the earlier and briefer account in the *Damascus Chronicle* (its title is literally the *Continuation of the Chronicle of Damascus*) of Ibn al-Qalanisi, translated in Gibb 1932, 45.

71. Klein 1986, 149; Hamblin 1991, 35–36; Lev 1991, 51; Gil 1992, 413–14; Jones and Ereira 1995, 68; Armstrong 1996, 270; Gil 1996a, 35; Hillenbrand 1999, 44–47; Duri 2000, 120; Hiyari 2000, 136–37; Boas 2001, 8–9.

72. Armstrong 1996, 270.

73. See the discussion at the beginning of this chapter, with references.

74. Quotations follow Lefkovits and Keinon 2001a, 2; Lefkovits 2001a, 3A. Translation of the 1930 Supreme Moslem Council booklet follows Lefkovits 2001a, 3A.

75. "PA Mufti Denies *Post* Report" 2001, 3.

76. Sennott 2001, A1.

77. Cf. Gil 1992, 114; Gil 1996a, 9–10. See also earlier discussion.

78. Morris 2002a.

79. Ben-Dov 1982, 241.

CHAPTER 6

1. This is the version of Urban's speech that was recorded by Robert of Rheims, a monk who may have been present at Clermont. The translation follows Peters 1971, 26–29. See also Runciman 1951, 106–9; Jones and Ereira 1995, 21.

2. Jones and Ereira 1995, 22, 24; Runciman 1951, 106–9.

3. Hillenbrand 1999, 599, 605–6. For example, the Palestinian historian A. L. Tibawi (1969, 44) writes: "By occupying Palestine the modern crusaders have earned the enmity of all Arabs; by seizing Jerusalem that of all Muslims. Are the modern crusaders bent on forcing history to repeat itself?" See also Tibawi 1969, 43; Sivan 1995, 26–28; Marcus 1996, A1; Halevi 2000, M5; Lewis 2003, 47.

4. Translations following Israeli 1978, 71, 102–3, 198. See also additional references by Sadat to Zionists and Crusaders in Israeli 1978, 57, 71, 73, 92, 200, 211, 368, 415–16; Israeli 1979, 806.

5. Fink 1969, 375.

6. Text as reported on http://www.chretiens-et-juifs.org/BIN_LADEN/Laden_war _amer.htm.

7. Quotation follows Harris 2001, A1. See also Ford 2001, 12; Kennedy 2001, 7.

8. Peters 1971, 25–26, 171.

9. On Fulcher, see McGinty 1941, 3–4. On Peter Tudebode, see Peters 1971, 171, 245–49; Hill and Hill 1974, 112–20. On Raymond of Aguilers, see Krey 1958, 250–62; Hill and Hill 1968, 116–28; Peters 1971, 156, 249–60. On the anonymous author of the *Gesta*, see Krey 1958, 249–50, 256–57; Hill 1962, 87–97; Peters 1971, 25–26, 255–56. On William of Tyre, see Babcock and Krey 1943: 348–78. On the Islamic accounts, see Gabrieli 1969, xxvii–xxviii; Peters 1971, 272–73; Hillenbrand 1999, 63–66.

10. On the Fatimid defenders and their leader, see the account of Ibn al-Athir (translated in Gabrieli 1969, 10–12; Peters 1971, 272–73). See also Ehrenkreutz 1984, 66–72; Jones and Ereira 1995, 68–70. On the Crusaders' journey and the leaders of the Crusaders, see, most recently, Armstrong 1988, 176–77; Jones and Ereira 1995, 22–24; Armstrong 1996, 272–73; Boas 1999, 2–4.

11. Translation following Krey 1958, 249–50. See Runciman 1951, 280; Hill 1962, 87; Armstrong 1988, 177; Armstrong 1996, 273–74; Boas 2001, 9–10.

12. Translation following Krey 1958, 249–50. See Hill 1962, 88.

13. The story is told in the account of Raymond of Aguilers; see translation in Krey 1958, 250–256. See further discussion in Runciman 1951, 281; Prawer 1985, 7–9; France 1994, 333; Jones and Ereira 1995, 70; Duncan and Opatowski 1998, 70; Boas 2001, 10.

14. Translation following Krey 1958, 249–50. See Hill 1962, 88.

15. See Runciman 1951, 279–82; France 1994, 335–36; Jones and Ereira 1995, 70–71; Duncan and Opatowski 1998, 69–70; Boas 1999, 13; Boas 2001, 12.

16. Translation following Babcock and Krey 1943: 351–52.

17. Translation following Babcock and Krey 1943, 354.

18. Translation following Peters 1971, 245–49. See Hill and Hill 1974, 117.

19. Translation following Peters 1971, 256–60. See Krey 1958, 257–62; Hill and Hill

1968, 125. See also Peters 1971, 156, for a brief discussion of Raymond and the date of his manuscript.

20. Translation following Babcock and Krey 1943, 348–49. For additional discussions of the number of Crusaders probably present in the army that besieged Jerusalem, see France 1994, 2–3, 330–31; Jones and Ereira 1995, 70; Boas 1999, 13–14; Boas 2001, 9–10, 13.

21. Translation following Peters 1971, 255–56. See Krey 1958, 256–57; Hill 1962, 90. See also Runciman 1951, 284; France 1994, 347; Jones and Ereira 1995, 71; Boas 2001, 12.

22. Translation following Hill and Hill 1968, 124–25. See Krey 1958, 257–62; Peters 1971, 256–60. See also the accounts of the anonymous Crusader, Peter Tudebode, William of Tyre, and Ibn al-Athir (Babcock and Krey 1943, 360–61; Gabrieli 1969, 10–12; Peters 1971, 272–73; Hill and Hill 1974, 117). Several of these accounts refer to the eastern side of the siege or the eastern side of the city but are referring to the northern side of the city, which was indeed the eastern area of the siege from the Crusader point of view.

23. Translation following Hill and Hill 1968, 124–25. See Krey 1958, 257–62; Peters 1971, 256–60.

24. Translation following Peters 1971, 255–56. See Krey 1958, 256–57; Hill 1962, 90–91. See also Runciman 1951, 284–86; Prawer 1985, 9; France 1994, 349–50.

25. Translation following Peters 1971, 256–60. See Krey 1958, 257–62; Hill and Hill 1968, 125–27. See also the detailed account of William of Tyre, translated in Babcock and Krey 1943, 361–71. See further discussion by Kollek and Pearlman 1968, 175–76; Prawer 1985, 10; Boas 1999, 13–14; Hiyari 2000, 138–40.

26. Prawer 1985, 2–3, 5.

27. Translation following Peters 1971, 256–60. See Krey 1958, 257–62; Hill and Hill 1968, 125–27.

28. Translation following Gabrieli 1969, 10–12. See Peters 1971, 272–73. See also discussion in Ben-Dov 1982, 343; Prawer 1985, 10–11; Armstrong 1988, 178–79; Idinopulos 1991, 167; France 1994, 349–55; Jones and Ereira 1995, 71.

29. Translation following Peters 1971, 255–56. See Krey 1958, 256–57; Hill 1962, 91.

30. Translation following Babcock and Krey 1943, 371. On the al-Aqsa Mosque as the "Temple of Solomon" and other relevant details, see also Ben-Dov 1982, 343; Jones and Ereira 1995, 11–12; Shanks 1995, 238–39.

31. Translation following Peters 1971, 256–60. See Krey 1958, 257–62; Hill and Hill 1968, 127–28; Armstrong 1996, 274.

32. Translation following Peters 1971, 255–56. See Krey 1958, 256–57; Hill 1962, 91. See also Runciman 1951, 285–87.

33. Translation following McGinty 1941, 68–69.

34. Translation following Peters 1971, 26–29. See Runciman 1951, 287; Kollek and Pearlman 1968, 176; Hirst 1974, 6; Klein 1986, 150; Idinopulos 1991, 167; Jones and Ereira 1995, 74; Armstrong 1996, 274; Duncan and Opatowski 1998, 71–72; Hillenbrand 1999, 64.

35. See Babcock and Krey 1943, 378; Runciman 1951, 285–86; Kollek and Pearlman 1968, 176; Jones and Ereira 1995, 74.

36. Translation following Peters 1971, 255–56. See Krey 1958, 256–57; Hill 1962, 92.

37. Translations following McGinty 1941, 70 and Hill and Hill 1974, 119, respectively. See also Peters 1971, 245–49.

38. Translation of Ibn al-Athir follows Gabrieli 1969, 10–12. See Peters 1971, 272–73; also Jones and Ereira 1995, 11–12, 74; Hillenbrand 1999, 65–66. The translation of Fulcher of Chartres follows McGinty 1941, 69.

39. Translation following McGinty 1941, 69. See also Jones and Ereira 1995, 74.

40. Translation following Babcock and Krey 1943, 372.

41. For the accounts of Peter Tudebode and Fulcher of Chartres, see McGinty 1941, 78; Peters 1971, 245–49; Hill and Hill 1974, 120. See also Jones and Ereira 1995, 75; Armstrong 1996, 275; Boas 2001, 12–13.

42. Translation following Hillenbrand 1999, 64–66.

43. Boas 2001, 13 and n. 32. See also Benvenisti 1972, 35; Prawer 1980, 88; Armstrong 1996, 274; Hiyari 2000, 137. Note that Albert of Aix says that only three hundred were killed in the Temple of Solomon; see McGinty 1941, 66–69 n. 4. For William of Tyre's numbers, see Babcock and Krey 1943, 372.

44. Ford 2001, 12; Kennedy 2001, 7.

45. Runciman 1951, 288; Jones and Ereira 1995, 75.

46. On the Crusader architecture of Jerusalem, see especially—and most recently—Bahat 1992; Boas 1999; Hiyari 2000; Meinhardt 2000; Woodfin 2000; Boas 2001. On the churches in particular, see also Ben-Dov 1982, 343; Shanks 1995, 239;

47. Klein 1986, 151–52; Armstrong 1996, 281–83; Duncan and Opatowski 1998, 61; Boas 1999, 21, 24; Hillenbrand 1999, 288. For more on the various Crusader orders, particularly the Templars, see Partner 1982; Burman 1986; Nicholson 1993; Read 1999.

48. Kollek and Pearlman 1968, 161; Ben-Dov 1982, 346; Klein 1986, 153; Jones and Ereira 1995, 78; Armstrong 1996, 275, 277, 281–82; Boas 1999, 21, 24; Hillenbrand 1999, 288; Hiyari 2000, 141; Meinhardt 2000; Woodfin 2000.

49. Kollek and Pearlman 1968, 156; Klein 1986, 151–53; Jones and Ereira 1995, 78; Armstrong 1996, 276–77, 280–81; Boas 1999, 24; Hillenbrand 1999, 288–90; Hiyari 2000, 141; Meinhardt 2000; Woodfin 2000.

50. Ehrenkreutz 1972, 11, 27–29; Lyons and Jackson 1982, 6–7; Lewis 1995, 90–91; Hillenbrand 1999, 23–24; Reston 2001, 4–5.

51. Ehrenkreutz 1972, 23–24, 31–193; Lyons and Jackson 1982, 8–200; Jones and Ereira 1995, 135–36; Lewis 1995, 90–91; Boas 1999, 4–5; Hillenbrand 1999, 23–24, 171; Reston 2001, 4–7.

52. Ehrenkreutz 1972, 161–64; Dajani-Shakeel 1988, 102–3; Dajani-Shakeel 1991, 45, 52–57; Hillenbrand 1999, 71–72. On the original seventh- and eighth-century CE principles of jihad, see Armstrong 1988, 40–41; Lewis 2003, 29–39. On jihad in Islam, see also Mir 1991.

53. Translation following Hillenbrand 1999, 71–74. See also Porath 1975, 353–54; Boas 1999, 4–5.

54. Translation following Dajani-Shakeel 1988, 103.

55. Translation following Dajani-Shakeel 1991, 52–53.

56. Translation following Dajani-Shakeel 1991, 58. See Dajani-Shakeel 1991, 58–62; Hillenbrand 1999, 23–24, 172.

57. Translations of these authors are now available in English. For Ibn al-Athir, see Gabrieli 1969, xxvii–xxviiii, 139–46; for Imad al-Din, see Gabrieli 1969, xxix–xxx, 153–60; for Ibn Shaddad, see Richards 2001, 1–4, 77–78; for al-Maqrizi, see Broadhurst 1980, xix, 36–37, 84–85. See also Hillenbrand, 171, 180–82.

58. Ben-Dov 1982, 344; Armstrong 1988, 253–54; Dajani-Shakeel 1988, 84; Jones and Ereira 1995, 159–60; Boas 1999, 4–5; Hillenbrand 1999, 23–24; Hiyari 2000, 165; Lewis 2003, 47–49. The literature specifically on the battle of Hattin is immense and is not cited here, since it is a separate topic.

59. Al-Athir in Gabrieli 1969, 139. See Dajani-Shakeel 1988, 90.

60. Translation following Dajani-Shakeel 1988, 62. See also al-Athir in Gabrieli 1969,

139; Jones and Ereira 1995, 161; Armstrong 1996, 292–93; Duncan and Opatowski 1998, 73–75; Hillenbrand 1999, 23–24; Hiyari 2000, 167–68; Boas 2001, 15; Ibn Shaddad in Richards 2001, 77.

61. Dajani-Shakeel 1988, 87. On Ernoul, see Morgan 1973.

62. Jones and Ereira 1995, 75; Armstrong 1996, 276.

63. Lane-Poole 1906, 224–28; Gabrieli 1969, 142–43; Dajani-Shakeel 1988, 88–89; Jones and Ereira 1995, 161; Armstrong 1996, 292–93; Boas 2001, 15–16.

64. See translations in Gabrieli 1969, 142–43, 154; Richards 2001, 77. See also discussions in Lane-Poole 1906, 224–28; Lyons and Jackson 1982, 273; Dajani-Shakeel 1988, 86–87; Hiyari 2000, 169, 175–76 n. 115; Boas 2001, 15–16.

65. Translation following Richards 2001, 77.

66. However, al-Athir gives a slightly different account, reporting that Saladin rode around the city for the first five days before deciding how best to attack and then moved his forces directly against the north side. For discussion of the various accounts, see Lane-Poole 1906, 224–28; Gabrieli 1969, 153–54; Lyons and Jackson 1982, 273; Prawer 1985, 13; Dajani-Shakeel 1988, 90–91; Boas 2001, 16.

67. Translation following Gabrieli 1969, 154. See also discussions in Lane-Poole 1906, 224–28; Dajani-Shakeel 1988, 90–92.

68. Lane-Poole 1906, 226–28; Dajani-Shakeel 1988, 90–91; Duncan and Opatowski 1998, 73–75; Edbury 1998, 55–56.

69. Translation following Gabrieli 1969, 140–41.

70. Translation following Gabrieli 1969, 140–41. See also discussions in Lyons and Jackson 1982, 273; Prawer 1985, 13; Dajani-Shakeel 1988, 93–94; Edbury 1998, 56–57; Boas 2001, 16.

71. Translation following Richards 2001, 77–78.

72. Prawer 1985, 13–14, with references in footnotes to work by previous scholars. See also Lane-Poole 1906, 224–28; Lyons and Jackson 1982, 273; Dajani-Shakeel 1988, 94–95; Armstrong 1996, 293; Edbury 1998, 56–57; Boas 2001, 16.

73. Translation following Nicholson 1997, 38.

74. Prawer 1985, 13–14. See also Avi-Yonah 1976, 265; Dajani-Shakeel 1988, 95; Armstrong 1996, 293.

75. Lane-Poole 1906, 228–29; Lyons and Jackson 1982, 274; Dajani-Shakeel 1988, 96; Edbury 1998, 58.

76. Translation following Gabrieli 1969, 141–42. See discussions, based also on Ernoul, the anonymous thirteenth-century author(s) of the *Libellus*, and others, in Lane-Poole 1906, 228–29; Lyons and Jackson 1982, 274; Armstrong 1988, 257–58; Dajani-Shakeel 1988, 96–97; Edbury 1998, 58–59; Boas 2001, 16.

77. Translation following Richards 2001, 77–78.

78. Lane-Poole 1906, 229–30; Newby 1983, 121; Dajani-Shakeel 1988, 97; Jones and Ereira 1995, 162; Armstrong 1996, 293–94. Hillenbrand (1999, 189) suggests that it was deliberate timing on Saladin's part to take possession of the city on the specific anniversary of Mohammed's nocturnal journey.

79. Translation following Gabrieli 1969, 142.

80. Translation following Gabrieli 1969, 142–44. See also al-Maqrizi in Broadhurst 1980, 84–85; Ibn Shaddad in Richards 2001, 77–78; and discussions in Lane-Poole 1906, 229–31; Ben-Dov 1982, 344; Lyons and Jackson 1982, 274–76; Armstrong 1988, 258–59; Dajani-Shakeel 1988, 97–99; Jones and Ereira 1995, 162; Armstrong 1996, 293–94; Edbury 1998, 59–61; Boas 2001, 16.

81. Lane-Poole 1906, 230–31; Gabrieli 1969, 158; Lyons and Jackson 1982, 277;

Dajani-Shakeel 1988, 99; Jones and Ereira 1995, 162. See Edbury 1998, 63, for the figure of eleven thousand.

82. Lane-Poole 1906, 233; Gibb 1973, 54–55; Hirst 1974, 4–5; Klein 1986, 158; Armstrong 1988, 258; Dajani-Shakeel 1988, 99–101; Edbury 1998, 64–65.

83. Translation following Gabrieli 1969, 144. See also Lane-Poole 1906, 235; al-Maqrizi in Broadhurst 1980, 84–85; Ben-Dov 1982, 345; Armstrong 1988, 259–60; Edbury 1998, 66–67; Boas 2001, 16–19; Ibn Shaddad in Richards 2001, 77–78.

84. See Lyons and Jackson 1982, 276; Dajani-Shakeel 1988, 101–2; Boas 2001, 16–19.

85. Al-Athir in Gabrieli 1969, 144–45; al-Maqrizi in Broadhurst 1980, 84–85. See also Lane-Poole 1906, 235; Kollek and Pearlman 1968, 161–62; Ehrenkreutz 1972, 205–6; Ben-Dov 1982, 345; Newby 1983, 122; Klein 1986, 158–59; Armstrong 1988, 258–59; Dajani-Shakeel 1988, 104–6; Hillenbrand 1999, 156–57, 300–301, 606–7; Meinhardt 2000; Woodfin 2000; Boas 2001, 16–18. See also the discussion in chapter 10 in the present book.

86. Quotation from Shadid 2003, A12. See also Hillenbrand 1999, 600; Lewis 2003, 29–30.

87. See the discussion in Mullin 2003, B2.

88. Shadid 2003, A12.

89. Text as reported on http://www.fas.org/irp/world/para/docs/980223-fatwa.htm (last accessed March 14, 2004). See now also the discussion in Lewis 2003, xxiv–xxvii, 157–59.

90. Text of fax as reported in the London *Times*, September 25, 2001.

91. Text of statements reported on http://www.washingtonpost.com/wp-srv/nation /specials/attacked/binladentape_122701.html and in Pincus 2001b, A1, respectively. See also Pincus 2001a, A16.

92. Translation following the Associated Press, as published in the *Washington Post*, February 11, 2003, A14. For other references to "Crusaders" by Osama bin Laden during 2001–3, see the text of a statement as reported by the Associated Press, October 9, 2001; Althaus 2001, A19; Harding 2001, 4; Woodward and Balz 2002, A16; Reuters 2002, A14; Lewis 2003, 157–59. Kurtz (2002, A13) quotes bin Laden in an October 2001 interview with the al-Jazeera network as saying: "We kill the kings of the infidels, kings of the crusaders and civilian infidels in exchange for those of our children they kill. This is permissible in Islamic law and logically."

93. Hillenbrand 1999, 593–99; Dajani-Shakeel 2000, 12–13; Halevi 2000, M5. On Saddam Hussein and Saladin, see Lamb 1990, A15; Williams 1990, A7; Dyer and Hunt 1991, 133–34; Henderson 1991, 52; Rezun 1992, 5; Bengio 1998, 82; Lewis 2003, 48–49.

94. Dajani-Shakeel 2000, 12–13.

95. Dajani-Shakeel 2000, 13.

96. Marcus 1996, A1.

97. Halevi 2000, M5.

98. Morris 2002a.

99. Bengio 1998, 82–83.

100. Chandrasekaran 2003, A1.

101. Marcus 1996, A1.

102. Translation following Dajani-Shakeel 1991, 62. See also Hillenbrand 1999, 600–612, "Modern Manifestations of the Islamic 'Counter-Crusade,'" particularly concerning the city of Jerusalem.

103. Translation following the Associated Press, as published in the *Washington Post*, February 11, 2003, A14.

104. See Hillenbrand 1999, 600–601; Mullin 2003, B2; . See also now Cook 1996, 2002a, 2002b.

CHAPTER 7

1. Text following that published in el-Sadat 1977, 338; Laqueur and Rubin 1985, 598; Quandt 1986, 351–52.

2. Dajani-Shakeel 2000, 13. For the text of the Camp David Peace Accords, see Laqueur and Rubin 1985, 609–15; Quandt 1986, 376–83. For the text of the Egyptian-Israeli Peace Treaty, see Laqueur and Rubin 1985, 615–16; Quandt 1986, 397–401. On discussions of Sadat and Jerusalem at Camp David, see Kamel 1986; Quandt 1986, 222, 243, 251–52, 255, 262, 283, 356–60. On reactions in the Arab world, see Jiryis 1978, 26–61; Laqueur and Rubin 1985, 602–4, 616–21.

3. Runciman 1954, 3–54; Oldenbourg 1966, 445–65; Johnson 1969, 87–114; Painter 1969, 45–73; Ehrenkreutz 1972, 212–16; Lyons and Jackson 1982, 295–333; Duncan and Opatowski 1998, 75–77; Richards 2001, 72–75, 91–165.

4. Runciman 1954, 55–75; Painter 1969, 73–85; Ehrenkreutz 1972, 216–23; Lyons and Jackson 1982, 334–61; Duncan and Opatowski 1998, 77–79.

5. Jones and Ereira 1995, 193; Dajani-Shakeel 1988, 107; Duncan and Opatowski 1998, 75–79; Hillenbrand 1999, 192; Boas 2001, 18–19. See also Reston 2001.

6. Hillenbrand 1999, 201.

7. See Humphreys 1977, 163–64; Ben-Dov 1982, 345; Wightman 1993, 277–78; Jones and Ereira 1995, 219–20; Shanks 1995, 240; Armstrong 1996, 301; Hillenbrand 1999, 215; Broshi and Gibson 2000, 154–55; Hiyari 2000, 168–69, 171; Little 2000, 182–83; Boas 2001, 19. On the fortress at Mount Tabor, see Cline 2000, 136–40.

8. Translation of Abu Shama follows Hillenbrand 1999, 216. Translation of Ibn Wasil follows Broshi and Gibson 2000, 154–55. See also Wightman 1993, 277–78; Armstrong 1996, 301; Hiyari 2000, 168–69, 171; Little 2000, 182–83.

9. See Peters 1985, 364; Klein 1986, 161; Wightman 1993, 283; Armstrong 1996, 302; Duncan and Opatowski 1998, 60; Boas 2001, 19.

10. Translation following Gabrieli 1969, 269–70.

11. Humphreys 1977, 202–3; Ben-Dov 1982, 345; Klein 1986, 161; Wightman 1993, 283; Jones and Ereira 1995, 223; Armstrong 1996, 302; Duncan and Opatowski 1998, 60; Hillenbrand 1999, 216–17; Broshi and Gibson 2000, 155; Hiyari 2000, 171; Lewis 2003, 50.

12. Humphreys 1977, 202–3; Idinopulos 1991, 255–56; Wightman 1993, 283; Armstrong 1996, 302–3; Hillenbrand 1999, 216–17, 221.

13. Translation following Gabrieli 1969, 269–73.

14. Translation following Broadhurst 1980, 206–7.

15. Translation following Gabrieli 1969, 271. See also Hillenbrand 1999, 216–17; Boas 2001, 19.

16. Armstrong 1996, 303–4; Little 2000, 185; Boas 2001, 20.

17. Hillenbrand 1999, 216–17, 221.

18. Klein 1986, 161; Idinopulos 1991, 255; Jones and Ereira 1995, 223, 225; Armstrong 1996, 303; Boas 2001, 20.

19. Translation following Lyons and Lyons 1971, 62.

20. Translation following Broadhurst 1980, 251. For various discussions of the dates of this attack, see Lyons and Lyons 1971, 203; Humphreys 1977, 261; Wightman 1993,

285–86; Duncan and Opatowski 1998, 61; Hillenbrand 1999, 222; Hiyari 2000, 171; Little 2000, 185; Boas 2001, 20.

21. Ibn al-Furat, translation following Lyons and Lyons 1971, 62.

22. Translation following Little 2000, 185. See Humphreys 1977, 264–67, 274; Wightman 1993, 286; Jones and Ereira 1995, 227; Armstrong 1996, 303–4; Duncan and Opatowski 1998, 61; Hillenbrand 1999, 203; Hiyari 2000, 171; Boas 2001, 20.

23. Translation following Lyons and Lyons 1971, 62.

24. Lewis 1995, 96; Armstrong 1996, 304.

25. Ben-Dov 1982, 357; Peters 1985, 368; Idinopulos 1991, 256; Wightman 1993, 286; Armstrong 1996, 303–4; Duncan and Opatowski 1998, 61; Hillenbrand 1999, 222; Hiyari 2000, 171; Boas 2001, 20; Lewis 2003, 50.

26. Translation following Lyons and Lyons 1971, 2–3.

27. Translations following Lyons and Lyons 1971, 2–3. See also discussions in Humphreys 1977, 275; Wightman 1993, 286; Hillenbrand 1999, 222.

28. Ibn al-Furat, translation following Lyons and Lyons 1971, 2–3. See also discussions in Jones and Ereira 1995, 227–28; Hillenbrand 1999, 222; Little 2000, 185; Boas 2001, 20.

29. Translations following Lyons and Lyons 1971, 63.

30. Lewis 1995, 87, 100; Hillenbrand 1999, 225–26; Cline 2000, 144; Little 2000, 186.

31. See Hillenbrand 1999, 225–26; Little 2000, 186.

32. Translation following Lyons and Lyons 1971, 63.

33. Translation following Amitai 1987, 237; see also Amitai-Preiss 1995, 31–32.

34. Translation following Lyons and Lyons 1971, 63. See also Ben-Dov 1982, 357; Little 2000, 186.

35. Translations following Amitai 1987, 238.

36. Translation quoted in Ben-Dov 1982, 357; see also translation in Holtz 1971, 126–27; Amitai 1987, 238, with references. On the battle of Ayn Jalut, see Cline 2000, 142–51, with further bibliographical references.

37. On this Mongol raid, see Amitai 1987, especially 247–48.

38. Translation following Amitai 1987, 244.

39. Translations following Amitai 1987, 244–45.

40. Kenyon 1967, 197; Ben-Dov 1982, 357–58; Little 1984, 73, 77; Wightman 1993, 287–88; Shanks 1995, 241; Little 2000, 186.

41. Quotation follows Shoshan 1984, 100–101. See also Ayalon 1972, 33–35; Shoshan 1984, 94.

42. Wightman 1993, 297; Little 2000, 186.

43. Armstrong 1995, 313. As Armstrong notes, there was also a tremendous outbreak of the Black Death in Jerusalem from 1351 to 1353 CE.

44. Armstrong 1995, 314; Little 2000, 196.

45. Lapidus 1967, 87; Sharon 1975, 15.

46. Klein 1986, 167; Levy 1992, 152–53; Armstrong 1995, 321–22; Ze'evi 1996, 1–2; Quataert 2000, 13–36; Imber 2002, 48.

47. Asali (2000a, 200) says that the Ottoman army took Jerusalem on December 28, 1516 (4 Dhu'l-Hijja 922 AH), and that the sultan himself officially entered the city and received the keys on December 30. He stayed two days, before resuming the journey to Egypt on January 1, 1517 CE (8 Dhu'l-Hijja 922 AH). Bahat (1996, 64) agrees that the sultan entered on December 30. Other scholars—Duncan and Opatowski (1998, 86) and Armstrong (1995, 321–22)—say that the sultan entered the city on December 1. See also Cohen 1989, 1; Shanks 1995, 241; Ze'evi 1996, 1–2; Little 2000, 196; Imber 2002, 47. Note that

Chelebi (cf. Stephan 1980, 59 n. 4) says that a *firman* (decree or mandate) granted by Sultan Selim in 1517 gives the date as March 20, 1517 (25 Safar AH 923).

48. Translation following Stephan 1980, 59. Cf. also Peters 1985, 479; Armstrong 1995, 321–22; St. Laurent 2000, 415; Asali 2000a, 200.

49. Heyd 1960, i, 39–43; Porath 1975, 356; Ben-Dov 1982, 358; Idinopulos 1991, 264–65; Doumani 1995, 34–35; Rafeq 2000, 26.

50. Myres 2000; Rafeq 2000, 25; Singer 2002.

51. Translation following Peters 1985, 479–80. See also Levy 1992, 20–21; Peters 1993, 204; Wightman 1993, 297.

52. On Suleiman and his rebuilding projects in Jerusalem, including addressing the chronic problem of water, see Lamb 1951, 256–57; Kenyon 1967, 197–98; Ben-Dov 1982, 358–59, 362–67; Peters 1985, 479–80; Bahat 1986, 64; Klein 1986, 168–70; Idinopulos 1991, 265–67; Levy 1992, 20–21; Peters 1993, 204; Wightman 1993, 297; Armstrong 1995, 323–25; Shanks 1995, 241; illenbrand 2000, 9–10; Rafeq 2000, 25; St. Laurent 2000, 417–18; Asali 2000a, 200–201.

53. Cohen 1989, 120–21.

54. Translations following Holtz 1971, 137. See also Peters 1985, 487–88.

55. On the revolt, see Rozen 1982, 75–90; Rozen 1984, 249–70; Manna 1989, 49–74; Barnai 1992, 20; Manna 1994, 51–66; Armstrong 1995, 342; Ze'evi 1996, 5, 60–63, 191; Manna 2000, 196–204; Rafeq 2000, 28; Asali 2000a, 215; Wasserstein 2001, 23. For a discussion of rebellious resistance to taxes in Jerusalem and elsewhere during the Ottoman period, see Singer 1994, especially 116–18. A century earlier, in 1603–11, Fakhr al-Din established a Druze polity centered on Mount Lebanon, which eventually included Safed, Ajlun, and Nablus. Although it never included Jerusalem and is not considered a popular revolt, the polity was an earlier challenge to Ottoman authority in Palestine. See Salibi 1988, 123–24, 142; Rafeq 2000, 27. I thank Professor Uzi Baram for information and references.

56. These include the diary of the Armenian patriarch Minas; a chronicle and other documents written by Franciscan monks of the monastery of San Salvador; a report by Rabbi Gedaliah of Siemiatycze (Poland); and French diplomatic correspondence, primarily memoranda written by J. B. Estelle, the French consul based in Saida (now in modern Lebanon). See Rozen 1984, 251, with full bibliographic references.

57. Quoted in Rozen 1984, 252–53.

58. Rozen 1984, 252–55.

59. Rozen 1984, 255; Manna 1994, 54–55; Armstrong 1995, 342; Ze'evi 1996, 60; Manna 2000, 199–200; Asali 2000a, 215.

60. Rozen 1984, 250–51; Manna 1994, 52–53; Ze'evi 1996, 60, 63. On the *Edirne vakasi*, see Abou-El-Haj 1984.

61. Rozen 1984, 255; Manna 1994, 55–56; Armstrong 1995, 342; Ze'evi 1996, 60; Asali 2000a, 215. Note that Manna (1994, 53–56) suggests that Mohammed Pasha was the *wali* (provincial governor) of the entire area all along, rather than beginning as simply the *sanjaq-bey* of Jerusalem and then being promoted sometime after 1703 CE.

62. Rozen 1984, 256–57; Manna 1994, 55–56; Armstrong 1995, 342; Ze'evi 1996, 60; Asali 2000a, 215.

63. Rozen 1984, 257–58; Manna 1994, 56; Armstrong 1995, 342; Ze'evi 1996: 60; Asali 2000a, 215. I am indebted to Dr. Rhoads Murphey of the University of Birmingham in England for his thoughts on the number of men in a company of Janissaries at that point in time.

64. Manna 1994, 55–56.

65. Rozen 1984, 257–58; Manna 1994, 56; Armstrong 1995, 342; Ze'evi 1996, 60–61; Asali 2000a, 215.

66. Rozen 1984, 257–58; Manna 1994, 56–57; Armstrong 1995, 342; Ze'evi 1996, 60–61; Manna 2000, 200; Rafeq 2000, 28; Asali 2000a, 215. Note that some scholars place the capture of the city on October 28, 1705 CE, instead of November 27.

67. Translation following Rozen 1984, 265; see also Rozen 1984, 269–70.

68. Wardi 1975, 390–91; Peters 1985, 540; Armstrong 1995, 344; Asali 2000a, 216; Wasserstein 2001, 24.

69. Wardi 1975, 390–91; Peters 1985, 540; Armstrong 1995, 344; Wasserstein 2001, 24–25.

70. Cohen 1973, 271–72, 278.

71. Constantine François Chasseboeuf (later known as the comte de Volney), translation following Peters 1985, 535; Peters 1993, 203. See now also discussion in Knauf 2000b.

72. Armstrong 1995, 346; Schur 1999, 33–34; Asali 2000a, 222.

73. Klein 1986, 174; Armstrong 1995, 346; Schur 1999, 172; Asali 2000a, 222. See Schur 1999 for a comprehensive account of Napoleon in the Holy Land.

74. Klein 1986, 174; Armstrong 1995, 346; Schur 1999, 15, 33–34, 117–20; Manna 2000, 204–6.

75. For the quotation from Napoleon, see Schur 1999, 54, with references. See now also Wasserstein 2001, 25. Reason: Alexander the Great and Jerusalem, see discussion in chapter 3.

76. Idinopulos 1998, xi–xii, 31–32, 36–39; Schur 1999, 172–76; Silberman 2001, 492. On David Roberts's travels in the Holy Land, see Ballantine 1866; Guiterman 1978; Sim 1984. On William Bartlett's travels in the Holy Land, see Carne 1836; Bartlett 1844. Bartlett made three visits to the Holy Land, beginning in 1834, but it was David Roberts's visit in early 1839 and his subsequent publication of a magnificent series of lithographs that brought the Holy Land directly to the attention of an appreciative audience in England and Europe. (Several of Roberts's lithographs grace the pages of this present volume, and a copy of his famous painting of Titus's destruction of Jerusalem in 70 CE is featured on the cover.) Much has been written about Edward Robinson's journeys to the Holy Land and his archaeological explorations in the region: see, for instance, Silberman 1982; Ben-Arieh 1983; Gilbert 1985.

77. Rafeq 2000, 29.

78. Abir 1975, 297; Armstrong 1995, 347–48; Asali 2000a, 223; Wasserstein 2001, 26.

79. Abir 1975, 297; Armstrong 1995, 347–48; Asali 2000a, 223.

80. Abir 1975, 297–98; Armstrong 1995, 349; Asali 2000a, 223; Wasserstein 2001, 26.

81. Abir 1975, 298; el-Aref 1975, 336; Manna 1994, 58–59; Armstrong 1995, 349; Rafeq 2000, 29–30; Asali 2000a, 224.

82. Abir 1975, 298; el-Aref 1975, 336; Gerber 1985, 7; Manna 1994, 58–60; Armstrong 1995, 349; Rafeq 2000, 30; Asali 2000a, 224; Wasserstein 2001, 26.

83. Abir 1975, 300–309; Ma'oz 1975a, 146; Ben-Arieh 1984, 107; Gerber 1985, 8; Klein 1986, 174; Manna 1994, 60; Armstrong 1995, 349–50; Idinopulos 1998, 43; Karsh and Karsh 1999, 32; Manna 2000, 206–7; Rafeq 2000, 30–31; Schölch 2000, 229; Asali 2000a, 224; Wasserstein 2001, 26.

84. See references in previous note.

85. Abir 1975, 304–10; Ma'oz 1975a, 147; Ben-Arieh 1984, 109; Klein 1986, 174–75; Levy 1992, 162; Kimmerling and Migdal 1993, 6–9; Manna 1994, 60–61; Armstrong 1995, 350; Manna 2000, 208–9; Rafeq 2000, 31; Wasserstein 2001, 26.

86. Manna 1994, 61. See also Stendel 1974, 152; Abir 1975, 310; Ben-Arieh 1984, 109–10; Kimmerling and Migdal 1993, 8–11; Manna 1994, 60–61; Armstrong 1995, 350; Idinopulos 1998, 46–47; Manna 2000, 208–9; Rafeq 2000, 31; Wasserstein 2001, 26–27.

87. Stendel 1974, 152; Ben-Arieh 1984, 111–12; Klein 1986, 175; Abu-Manneh 1990; Manna 1994, 61; Idinopulos 1998, 53, 86; Rafeq 2000, 31–32; Wasserstein 2001, 27.

88. Twain 1895, 558–60; see also Idinopulos 1998, 117–21.

89. Idinopulos 1998, 129–30, 133–34; Silberman 2001.

90. Translation following Israeli 1978, 102–3. See also Israeli 1978, 211, 415–16, for Sadat's references in two additional speeches to Tatars (Khwarizmians), in addition to his more usual references to Crusaders.

91. Text following that published in el-Sadat 1977, 338–39. See Laqueur and Rubin 1985, 598; Quandt 1986, 352.

92. Quandt 1986, 2.

CHAPTER 8

1. Quotations following Dajani-Shakeel 2000, 11–12 and Laffin 1975, 167, respectively. See also Newell 1991a, 225; Newell 1991b, 364–65; Hillenbrand 1999, 604.

2. See, for example, Newell 1991b, 364–65. See also discussion in Hillenbrand 1999, 604; Dajani-Shakeel 2000, 11–12.

3. As pointed out by Newell 1991a, 193–94. See Sanders 1927, 35; Wavell 1941, 230 n. 3; Bullock 1988, 95.

4. Quotation following Newell 1991a, 193.

5. See Whitehair 1918, 331; Meinertzhagen 1960, 224; Armstrong 1996, 370; Hillenbrand 1999, 604.

6. Quotation following Wavell 1946, 155. See Pirie-Gordon 1919, 1–2, text facing plates 3–5; Liddell Hart 1930, 398–99; Lloyd George 1937, 202–3; Wavell 1940, 167; Gardner 1966, 127; James 1993, 129–38; Armstrong 1996, 370; Gilbert 1996, 45–46; Bullock 1998, 89; Wasserstein 2001, 80; Bruce 2002, 2; Mordike 2002, 1, 6–8.

7. Savage 1926, 17; Wavell 1941, 26; Mordike 2002, 2. See also Hughes 1996, 1999, on Allenby in Palestine.

8. Wavell 1929, 3; Wavell 1941, 194–95; Wavell 1944, 10; Gardner 1966, 127; Newell 1991a, 194–95; James 1993, 144; Cline 2000, 6–28.

9. Pirie-Gordon 1919, text facing plates 6–16; Liddell Hart 1930, 398–99; Lloyd George 1937, 202–3; Wavell 1940, 167; Wavell 1946, 155; Gardner 1966, 127; James 1993, 129–38; Armstrong 1996, 370; Gilbert 1996, 45–46; McCarthy 1997, 362–63; Bullock 1998, 89; McCarthy 2001, 104; Wasserstein 2001, 80; Bruce 2002, 2; Mordike 2002, 1–3, 6–8.

10. Gilbert 1996, 46–47. See also discussion in Idinopulos 1998, 144–50.

11. For the text of the Balfour Declaration, see Aronstein 1936, 21; Clarke 1981, 16; Laqueur and Rubin 2001, 16.

12. Pirie-Gordon 1919, 8, text facing plates 17–19; Savage 1926, 249–50; Falls 1930, 188–236; Wavell 1940, 156–62; Wavell 1941, 223–26; Wavell 1946, 188–90; Gardner 1966, 155–56; Bullock 1988, 90–91; James 1993, 138–39; Gilbert 1996, 47; Duncan and Opatowski 1998, 109; Sheffy 1998, 242; Bruce 2002, 155–56.

13. Pirie-Gordon 1919, 8, text facing plates 19–20; Gilbert 1923, 126–28; Savage 1926, 249–50; Falls 1930, 188–236; Wavell 1940, 156–62; Wavell 1941, 223–26; Wavell 1946, 188–90; Gardner 1966, 155–56; Bullock 1988, 90–91; James 1993, 138–39; Gilbert

1996, 47–48; Duncan and Opatowski 1998, 109; Bruce 2002, 157. Later, the Seventy-fifth Division adopted the symbol of a key as the heraldic emblem for their divisional badge, in commemoration of their capture of Nebi Samwil, the "key to Jerusalem"; cf. Bullock 1988, 90.

14. Meinertzhagen 1960, 225. See Sheffy 1998, 242. Note that Gardner (1966, 158) is incorrect in placing the sending of this message just before the actual fall of Jerusalem on December 9; see also Savage 1926, 254–56. On Meinertzhagen and his famous intelligence activities during the war, see Meinertzhagen 1960; Lord 1970; Lawrence 1991, 384.

15. Pirie-Gordon 1919, 8, text facing plates 20–21; Savage 1926, 250–51; Wavell 1941, 226; Wavell 1946, 190; Bullock 1988, 91–92; Gilbert 1996, 48; Bruce 2002, 157–58.

16. This is according to Lawrence James, who published a biography of Allenby entitled *Imperial Warrior* (1993).

17. Pirie-Gordon 1919, 9, 67, text facing plates 22–25; Gilbert 1923, 128; Falls 1930, 237–41, Wavell 1940, 162–65; Wavell 1941, 228; Wavell 1946, 190–92; Bullock 1988, 91–92; James 1993, 139–40; Gilbert 1996, 47–48; Duncan and Opatowski 1998, 110; Sheffy 1998, 242; Bruce 2002, 159.

18. Text from Pirie-Gordon 1919, 9.

19. Wavell 1940, 164–68; Wavell 1941, 228–29; Wavell 1946, 192–93. For other descriptions of the events of December 8–9, see Whitehair 1918, 331; Pirie-Gordon 1919, 67–68, text facing plates 25–27; Gilbert 1923, 136, 142–46; Savage 1926, 251–53; Falls 1930, 241–51, 256–59; Gardner 1966, 158, 160–61; James 1993, 140; Gilbert 1996, 49–51, 54; Bullock 1998, 92–93; Duncan and Opatowski 1998, 110; Bruce 2002, 159–63; Mordike 2002, 7–8.

20. Wavell 1940, 165–67; Gardner 1966, 158, 160–61.

21. Pirie-Gordon 1919, 10; Falls 1930, 262. Gilbert (1977, 66) gives still higher figures: "During the battle for Jerusalem more than 3,600 British and 19,000 Turkish soldiers had been killed in action."

22. The accounts were published by Major (later Lieutenant Colonel) Harry Pirie-Gordon in 1919 and Captain Cyril Falls in 1930.

23. Pirie-Gordon 1919, text facing plates 3 and 26; Falls 1930, 252. See also Savage 1926, 254; Bullock 1988, 91, 93–94; James 1993, 140; Gilbert 1996, 47–49.

24. Falls 1930, 252. See also the stories, with slightly conflicting details, told by Whitehair 1918, 331; Pirie-Gordon 1919, text facing plate 27; Gilbert 1923, 154–66; Savage 1926, 254–56; Thomas 1938, 122–24; Wavell 1941, 229–31; Wavell 1946, 193–94; Gardner 1966, 159; Bullock 1988, 94; James 1993, 140–41; Armstrong 1996, 370; Gilbert 1996, 52–54; Duncan and Opatowski 1998, 110–11; Segev 2000, 50–51; Wasserstein 2001, 78–79; Bruce 2002, 162–63.

25. Falls 1930, 252. See also Savage 1926, 254–56. A famous photograph was taken of this second encounter; it can be found in many of the books that discuss Allenby's capture of Jerusalem.

26. Falls 1930, 252. See also Savage 1926, 254–56.

27. Falls 1930, 252–53. See also Savage 1926, 254–56.

28. Falls 1930, 253–54. See also Savage 1926, 254–56.

29. Falls 1930, 254. See also Savage 1926, 254–56; Mordike 2002, 3.

30. Pirie-Gordon 1919, text facing plate 26. See also Savage 1926, 254–56; Falls 1930, 254; Gilbert 1977, 67; Newell 1991a, 193; Gilbert 1996, 50–51.

31. Falls 1930, 264; Wavell 1941, 230–31; Wavell 1946, 194; Gardner 1966, 160–61; Newell 1991a, 189–90; Newell 1991b, 372; James 1993, 142–44; Gilbert 1996, 55; Idinopulos 1998, 144.

32. Quotation following Lawrence 1935, 453. On Allenby's entrance into Jerusalem, see Whitehair 1918, 331; Pirie-Gordon 1919, text facing plate 28; Savage 1926, 256–57; Falls 1930, 259–61; Lawrence 1935, 453; Wavell 1941, 230; Wavell 1946, 193–94; Gardner 1966, 159; Clarke 1981, 15–17; Narkiss 1983, 257–58; Bullock 1988, 94–95; Newell 1991a, 189–90; James 1993, 140–41; Gilbert 1996, 54–55; Idinopulos 1998, 143–44; Gorenberg 2000, 84–85; Wasserstein 2001, 79–80; Bruce 2002, 163–64; Mordike 2002, 8. On the visit of Kaiser Wilhelm, see Silberman 2001, 494–95.

33. Text following Gardner 1966, 160–61.

34. Savage 1926, 258. On Allenby and the prophecy, see Pirie-Gordon 1919, text facing plate 28; Gilbert 1923, 177–78; Savage 1926, 256–58; Meinertzhagen 1960, 225; Gardner 1966, 161; Clarke 1981, 17; Newell 1991a, 189–90, 192; Gilbert 1996, 56.

35. Text following Wavell 1941, 231–32. See Gardner 1966, 161; Bruce 2002, 164.

36. Falls 1930, 260–61. See also Pirie-Gordon 1919, text facing plate 28; Savage 1926, 257–58; Gardner 1966, 161–62; Bullock 1988, 95; Idinopulos 1998, 143–44; Wasserstein 2001, 80.

37. Quotation following Thomas 1938, 124. See Gilbert 1923, 169–70; Wasserstein 2001, 79.

38. Falls 1930, 278; Wavell 1940, 171; Wavell 1941, 232; Wavell 1946, 194–95; Bruce 2002, 168–69.

39. Gilbert 1996, 61.

40. Pirie-Gordon 1919, 12–13. See also Falls 1930, 279–81.

41. Pirie-Gordon 1919, 68, text facing plates 30–31; Savage 1926, 258–61; Falls 1930, 265, 278–91; Wavell 1940, 170–72; Wavell 1941, 232; Wavell 1946, 194–95; Gilbert 1996, 56; Bullock 1998, 97; Sheffy 1998, 242–43; Bruce 2002, 168–69.

42. Pirie-Gordon 1919, 13; Falls 1930, 290; Bullock 1998, 97.

43. Pirie-Gordon 1919, 29–31, text facing plates 41–45. See now the discussion, with full bibliography, in Cline 2000, 6–28.

44. Mattar 1988, 16–17; Gilbert 1996, 82.

45. Armstrong 1996, 374–375. See Mattar 1988, 16–17; Idinopulos 1998, 149–50, 165–66; Wasserstein 2001, 101–4.

46. Tibawi 1969, 33; Laffin 1975, 165; Sachar 1979, 123; Mattar 1988, 16–17; Idinopulos 1991, 292; Armstrong 1996, 374–75; Gilbert 1996, 82–84; Idinopulos 1998, 165–67; Segev 2000, 127–29, 132–39; Wasserstein 2001, 104.

47. Churchill and Churchill 1967, 10–11; Prittie 1974, 54–55; Laffin 1975, 165; Armstrong 1988, 100; Mattar 1988, 16–17, 102–3; Armstrong 1996, 383–84; Gilbert 1996, 83–84, 149, 151–52; Idinopulos 1998, 166–67; Segev 2000, 127–29, 132–39; Pipes 2001, 57–58; Wasserstein 2001, 104–8, 116. See, however, Mattar 1988, for a defense against some of these accusations. Regarding the life and times of Haj Amin al-Husseini, see also Schechtman 1965; Jbara 1985. On the mufti's meeting with Hitler, see, in addition to many of the sources already cited, Laqueur and Rubin 2001, 51–55.

48. Quotation following Gilbert 1996, 83. See Bell 1977, 18; Mattar 1988, 17; Gilbert 1996, 83–84; Idinopulos 1998, 166–67; Segev 2000, 137–43.

49. Gilbert 1975, 637.

50. Prittie 1974, 54–55; Laffin 1975, 165; Gilbert 1996, 83; Gorenberg 2000, 82–83; Wasserstein 2001, 324–27.

51. Tibawi 1969, 35; Hirst 1974, 8–9; Prittie 1974, 54–55; Lundsten 1978, 3–27; Sachar 1979, 173; Mattar 1988, 33–35; Idinopulos 1991, 292–93; Gerner 1994, 25; Armstrong 1996, 380–81; Gilbert 1996, 119–20; Idinopulos 1998, 192, 194–96; Hudson 2000, 254–55; Pappé 2003, 6–16.

52. Lorch 1968, 27–28; Tibawi 1969, 36; Hirst 1974, 9; Lundsten 1978, 23; Sachar

1979, 173; Mattar 1988, 45–46; Armstrong 1996, 381–82; Gilbert 1996, 120; Idinopulos 1998, 192; Segev 2000, 309–10; Pappé 2003, 15.

53. Tibawi 1969, 36–37; Sachar 1979, 173–74; Mattar 1988, 33, 46–48, 118–19; Gerner 1994, 25–26; Armstrong 1996, 381–82; Gilbert 1996, 120–26; Idinopulos 1998, 192, 194, 196–97; Segev 2000, 310, 314–27; Wasserstein 2001, 324–27. Twenty-nine Jews and thirty-eight Arabs were killed in Jerusalem alone during the violence that accompanied the "Wailing Wall Riots."

54. Marlowe 1946, 144–45, 150–51; Bauer 1966, 49, 53, 55–56; Laffin 1975, 165–66; Bethell 1979, 26–28; Sachar 1979, 199–201; Mattar 1988, 68–69, 73–74; Idinopulos 1991, 293; Khalidi 1991, 189; Gerner 1994, 26–27, 36; Armstrong 1996 383–84; Gilbert 1996, 134, 136, 140–42; Hudson 2000, 256.

55. Marlowe 1946, 173; Bethell 1979, 30; Sachar 1979, 201–8; Mattar 1988, 99; Khalidi 1991, 189–90; Armstrong 1996, 384–85; Gilbert 1996, 142–43, 147–48; Idinopulos 1998, 206–10; Laqueur and Rubin 2001, 41–43; Wasserstein 2001, 110.

56. Bell 1977; Bethell 1979, 41; Silver 1984; Zadka 1995; Segev 2000, 384.

57. On all of the incidents of violence mentioned and on the White Paper of 1939, see Marlowe 1946, 200–205; Pritie 1974, 55–56; Bethell 1979, 35–49; Sachar 1979, 210–13, 222–26; Khalidi 1991, 192–95; Armstrong 1996, 385; Gilbert 1996, 150–51, 154–60; Idinopulos 1998, 210–12; Hudson 2000, 256; Wasserstein 2001, 115–16. Note that Walid Khalidi's 1991 chronology (pp. 192–95) itemizes the Palestinian victims in Jerusalem but makes no mention of the Jewish dead and injured during that same period.

58. The Irgunists were similarly imitating and turning upon the Palestinians terror tactics begun by the Arabs during the first year (1936) of the Arab revolt and perhaps even earlier (i.e., during the 1920s). In addition, Zadka (1995, xii) says: "the PLO has often said that it tried to emulate it [the Irgun] in its own struggle against Israel. Some of the Irgun's operations were taught in its [the PLO's] military courses and every book on the subject was widely read by Palestinian leaders." For additional discussion of both similarities and differences between the First Intifada and the 1936–39 Arab revolt, see Stein 1991a.

59. Marlowe 1946, 200–205; Khalidi 1991, 192–95; Gerner 1994, 36; Armstrong 1996, 383–84; Gilbert 1996, 151. On potential similarities between Palestinian and Irgunist terrorism, see the brief discussion in Carr 2002 (210–15) and a spirited response in Klinghoffer 2002.

60. The descriptions and discussions here of the events in Jerusalem from 1944 onward are based on material presented in numerous secondary sources—especially Lorch 1968, Bell 1977, Zadka 1995, and Gilbert 1996—as well as various personal narratives and reminiscences, such as Levin 1950.

61. Text following Zadka 1995, 186–88; see also 28–30.

62. On Glueck's work for the OSS, see Fierman 1985, 1986; Horstman 1999; Time, December 13, 1963, 50–60 (Glueck is the only biblical archaeologist ever to be portrayed on the cover of Time). On the perceived danger to Palestine and Jerusalem in 1941, see Gilbert 1996, 162.

63. Quotation following Gilbert 1996, 165. See Zadka 1995, 32.

64. Bell 1977, 268–69. See Katz 1968, 55; Lorch 1968, 27–28, 35–36; Silver 1984; Armstrong 1988, 105–6; Heller 1995; Zadka 1995, 21–24, 32–36; Gilbert 1996, 172; Gorenberg 2000, 91–92.

65. Bell 1977, 86–87, 113–20; Zadka 1995, 38–41, 191.

66. Katz 1968, 93–95; Bell 1977, 95–98; Sachar 1979, 388; Armstrong 1988, 106; Gilbert 1996, 235–36.

67. Bell 1977, 95–100, 128, 133–36; Zadka 1995, 44, 52–63, 156.

68. Bell 1977, 151; Zadka 1995, 45–46, 56–57, 60–63, 74, 191; Duncan and Opatowski 1998, 118.

69. Bell 1977, 154; Zadka 1995, 73–74, 192.

70. This account of the bombing of the King David Hotel is derived from the various descriptions and information found in Katz 1968, Bell 1977, Bethell 1979, Clarke 1981, Zadka 1995, and Gilbert 1996. See those sources, with specific page numbers as listed below, for additional references and bibliography.

71. Bell 1977, 169–70; Bethell 1979, 258–60; Zadka 1995, 86–87; Gilbert 1996, 172.

72. On the above, see Bell 1977, 170–72; Bethell 1979, 260–63; Zadka 1995, 86–88; Gilbert 1996, 172.

73. See discussions in Katz 1968, 93–95; Bell 1977, 168–73; Bethell 1979, 258–67; Clarke 1981; Zadka 1995, 63, 86–89, 192; Gilbert 1996, 172–73.

74. Quotation follows Gilbert 1996, 173. See Bell 1977, 173; Bethell 1979, 263–64, 266–67. On the increase of anti-Semitism as a result of attacks on the British in Palestine, see Zadka 1995, 170–72.

75. Bell 1977, 182; Zadka 1995, 192.

76. Zadka 1995, 192.

77. Katz 1968, 125; Bell 1977, 190; Sachar 1979, 277; Zadka 1995, 72, 149, 159–60, 192.

78. Katz 1968, 126–27; Bell 1977, 190–91; Zadka 1995, 72, 160–68, 192.

79. Bell 1977, 239; Zadka 1995, 192; Wasserstein 2001, 125–26.

80. Bell 1977, 245–46; Gilbert 1996, 173–75; Wasserstein 2001, 126–28.

81. Lorch 1968, xxix–xxx, 46; Bell 1977, 249–50; Sachar 1979, 291–92, 298; Gilbert 1996, 176–77; Duncan and Opatowski 1998, 126; Klein 2001, 43; Wasserstein 2001, 128–31.

82. Lorch 1968, 19–20, 46–48; Palumbo 1987, 34; Gilbert 1996, 176–80.

83. Bell 1977, 254–55; Palumbo 1987, 35; Gilbert 1996, 180–82.

84. Bell 1977, 256; Gilbert 1996, 183–85.

85. Maysi 1917, 9. The poem was signed "Kadra Maysi," which was Katherine Drayton Mayrant Simons's pen name.

86. Newell 1991a, 191. See, for examples, Sommers 1919; Whitehair 1919; Maxwell 1920; Gilbert 1923. See also Bruce 2002; Bruce uses the title *The Last Crusade* for his study of the Palestine campaign of World War I.

87. Dajani-Shakeel 2000, 11–12.

88. Hillenbrand 1999, 604.

89. Churchill's words were reported in a brief note in the London *Times* on March 28, 1921. I would like to thank Allen Packwood (director) and Rachel Lloyd (archives assistant) of the Churchill Archives Centre for their assistance in tracking down Churchill's words. Gilbert (1975, 559; 1996, 88) gives a slightly different version of Churchill's brief speech, based on the report that appeared in the *Egyptian Gazette* on March 29, 1921. On Churchill's visit to the cemetery, see also Hurwitz 1995, 8.

CHAPTER 9

1. Begin 1977, 373; see also Marks 1994, 2.

2. Quotation following Laquer and Rubin 1985, 152; see also Laffin 1975, 166; Sachar 1979, 333–34. The secretary-general was not always quite as confident, however, for according to Efraim Karsh (2001, 27), he also told a group of Zionists in September of 1947:

"We succeeded in expelling the Crusaders, but lost Spain and Persia, and may lose Palestine. But it is too late for a peaceable solution."

3. As noted previously, the events in Jerusalem from 1948 onward are extremely well known and have been written about extensively by many previous scholars and eyewitnesses. The descriptions and discussions presented here depend heavily upon a number of detailed secondary sources—especially Lorch 1968, Bell 1977, and Gilbert 1996—as well as various personal narratives and reminiscences, including Levin 1950.

4. Bell 1977, 266–67; Wasserstein 2001, 134.

5. Lorch 1968, 55–56; Syrkin 1974, 63; Bell 1977, 267–68; Gilbert 1996, 190; Wasserstein 2001, 134. Gilbert identifies one of the British deserters as Peter Marsden, rather than Peter Madison.

6. Lorch 1968, 55–56; Syrkin 1974, 63; Bell 1977, 268; Gilbert 1996, 195; Wasserstein 2001, 134.

7. Lorch 1968, 55–56; Syrkin 1974, 63; Bell 1977, 268; Gilbert 1996, 196–97; Wasserstein 2001, 134.

8. Levin 1950, back cover; Lorch 1968, 67–70, 92–96; Padon 1974, 85; Syrkin 1974, 61, 63–66, 67, 82; Bell 1977, 268–71, 273–74, 279–82; Sachar 1979, 324; Herzog 1984, 29–31; Gilbert 1996, 196, 198–99; Duncan and Opatowski 1998, 127; Wasserstein 2001, 142–43.

9. On the above, see Lorch 1968, 96; Bell 1977, 294–96; Sachar 1979, 333–34; Herzog 1984, 31; Flapan 1987b, 10–11; Palumbo 1987, xviii, 102, 104, 206; Armstrong 1988, 106–7; Armstrong 1996, 386–87, 389–90; Gilbert 1996, 199–200, 203; Duncan and Opatowski 1998, 128; Karsh 2000b, 31; Wasserstein 2001, 144.

10. Lorch 1968, 123–24; Herzog 1984, 38–40; Palumbo 1987, 102; Gilbert 1996, 202–3; Duncan and Opatowski 1998, 131–32; Wasserstein 2001, 144.

11. Lorch 1968, 123–24; Syrkin 1974, 63; Herzog 1984, 38–40; Gilbert 1996, 203–5; Wasserstein 2001, 144.

12. Lorch 1968, 125–26; Syrkin 1974, 67; Bell 1977, 296–97; Sachar 1979, 306–7; Herzog 1984, 29–31; Gilbert 1996, 206–7; Duncan and Opatowski 1998, 128–29; Wasserstein 2001, 143.

13. Gilbert 1996, 208. As Sir Gilbert notes, this was more than thirty deaths per day.

14. Sachar 1979, 311; Wasserstein 2001, 149–51.

15. Schoenbaum 1993, 34; Benson 1997, 168. See discussions in Katz 1968, 229; Elath 1981, 105–10; Cohen 1990, 207–22; Schoenbaum 1993, 34–62; Benson 1997, 166–68; Merkley 1998, 189–90; Bass 2003, 30–33. For further analysis on Truman and Israel, see also Snetsinger 1974; Ganin 1979; and the additional contributions in Weinstein and Ma'oz 1981.

16. Text from Laqueur and Rubin 2001, 81–83.

17. Lorch 1968, 150–51; Herzog 1984, 23–24; Gilbert 1996, 212.

18. Glubb 1957, 82–85, 99–101; Lorch 1968, 203–5; Kirkbride 1976, 28, 35–36; Sachar 1979, 315, 321; Herzog 1984, 23; Gilbert 1996, 213–14; Wasserstein 2001, 154; Morris 2002b, 121–23, 149–52. On Glubb himself, see with full notes and references Lunt 1984; Royle 1992; Morris 2002b. On the role of Glubb and the other British officers in the battle for Jerusalem, see Lunt 1984, 134–45; Royle 1992, 353–67; Wasserstein 2001, 154–57; Morris 2002b, 149–70.

19. Lorch 1968, 206–20; Herzog 1984, 23, 44; Gilbert 1996, 214–15.

20. Levin 1950, back cover; Lorch 1968, 209–12; Syrkin 1974, 61, 71–75; Herzog 1984, 61; Idinopulos 1991, 298–99; Duncan and Opatowski 1998, 133. Some writers give the dates of the siege as April 22 (the date that they give for the last supply convoy reach-

ing Jerusalem) until June 11 (the date of the first truce), but this is a reference to the siege of the entire city of Jerusalem (including the New City), rather than simply the Jewish Quarter within the Old City. On the siege, see also Kurzman 1970, 343–402.

21. Lorch 1968, 213–14; Syrkin 1974, 75; Herzog 1984, 61; Gilbert 1996, 215–16; Duncan and Opatowski 1998, 133.

22. Glubb 1957, 111–13; Kirkbride 1976, 31–32; Sachar 1979, 324; Herzog 1984, 44–45; Gilbert 1996, 217–18; Morris 2002b, 160–61, 163.

23. Lorch 1968, 215–16; Syrkin 1974, 73, 76; Sachar 1979, 324–25; Herzog 1984, 38, 61–62, 171; Gilbert 1996, 217; Duncan and Opatowski 1998, 133.

24. Glubb 1957, 114–15; Syrkin 1974, 77; Sachar 1979, 324; Herzog 1984, 44–45; Gilbert 1996, 217–18; Morris 2002b, 163.

25. Syrkin 1974, 77; Sachar 1979, 324; Herzog 1984, 44–45; Gilbert 1996, 217–18.

26. Syrkin 1974, 70; Sachar 1979, 324; Herzog 1984, 44–45, 60–61; Gilbert 1996, 218–19; Morris 2002b, 163.

27. Syrkin 1974, 70–71; Gilbert 1996, 220; Wasserstein 2001, 145.

28. Glubb 1957, 124–27; Lorch 1968, 207–8; Sachar 1979, 324; Herzog 1984, 59–60; Gilbert 1996, 220–21; Duncan and Opatowski 1998, 133; Morris 2002b, 165–67.

29. Syrkin 1974, 77–78; Gilbert 1996, 222–23.

30. Syrkin 1974, 78; Herzog 1984, 62; Gilbert 1996, 223–24.

31. Glubb 1957, 129–30; Lorch 1968, 216–17; Syrkin 1974, 78–79; Kirkbride 1976, 32–33; Sachar 1979, 324–25; Herzog 1984, 62; Idinopulos 1991, 299; Gilbert 1996, 223–25; Duncan and Opatowski 1998, 133.

32. Herzog 1984, 23; Lunt 1984, 145; Royle 1992, 365–67; Gilbert 1996, 226; Wasserstein 2001, 156; Morris 2002b, 121–23, 171–72.

33. Herzog 1984, 23; Lunt 1984, 145; Royle 1992, 365–67; Gilbert 1996, 226; Wasserstein 2001, 156; Morris 2002b, 122–23, 172.

34. See discussion in chapter 4. See also Syrkin 1974, 63, 70, 79–82; Herzog 1984, 44–45, 62.

35. Syrkin 1974, 82–83; Sachar 1979, 325–27; Herzog 1984, 45; Gilbert 1996, 227–28; Duncan and Opatowski 1998, 129–30.

36. Tibawi 1969, 40–41; Syrkin 1974, 79; Sachar 1979, 325; Idinopulos 1991, 299; Gilbert 1996, 229; Hudson 2000, 259; Wasserstein 2001, 152.

37. Herzog 1984, 74–75.

38. Lorch 1968, 278–79, 301–3; Bell 1977, 317–27; Herzog 1984, 75. See now Sprinzak 1999.

39. Herzog 1984, 76; Gilbert 1996, 230; Wasserstein 2001, 159–60.

40. Herzog 1984, 76–87; Gilbert 1996, 231; Wasserstein 2001, 160–61.

41. Lorch 1968, 331–33, 348–50; Padon 1974, 86; Herzog 1984, 79–84; Gilbert 1996, 231–33; Duncan and Opatowski 1998, 133–35.

42. Lorch 1968, 398; Bell 1977, 336–40; Sachar 1979, 338; Herzog 1984, 87–88; Marton 1994; Gilbert 1996, 234–36, 239; Sprinzak 1999, 40–48; Wasserstein 2001, 162.

43. Quotation following Gilbert 1996, 238. See Lorch 1968, 457–62; Gilbert 1996, 234–38.

44. Lorch 1968, 535–46; Padon 1974, 86–87; Mattar 1983, 57–59; Herzog 1984, 105–6; Idinopulos 1991, 300–301; Armstrong 1996, 387, 389–90; Gilbert 1996, 238–40, 244–45; Wasserstein 2001, 162–67.

45. Hirst 1974, 13–15; Idinopulos 1991, 299; Armstrong 1996, 387–89; Benvenisti 1996, 240–42; Gilbert 1996, 241; Hudson 2000, 260; Wasserstein 2001, 167; Oren 2002, 307.

46. Padon 1974, 97; Herzog 1984, 111; Elon 1989, 100; Armstrong 1996, 387; Gilbert 1996, 239, 248; Wasserstein 2001, 182–83.

47. Gilbert 1996, 248, 261–62, 266; Wasserstein 2001, 183, 191.

48. As quoted in Oren 2002, 170. The following section on the Six-Day War is especially indebted to the excellent book published by Michael B. Oren in 2002, as well as to Sachar 1979, Herzog 1984, and Gilbert 1996. Other sources include personal narratives, such as Schleifer 1972, Narkiss 1983, and Rabinovich 1987. See also Neff 1984 and papers and discussions in Parker 1996. Where numbers, quantities, and times differ between the various secondary sources, Oren 2002 has been followed unless otherwise noted.

49. On this opening salvo of the war, see Churchill and Churchill 1967, 78; Hussein 1969, 55–56; Dayan 1976, 350–52; Sachar 1979, 639–40; Herzog 1984, 149–53; Mutawi 1987, 108–9, 122–23; Slater 1991, 265–66; Armstrong 1996, 396–98; Duncan and Opatowski 1998, 163; Oren 2002, 170–76.

50. Speech to Arab Trade Unionists, May 26, 1967; translation following Laqueur and Rubin 1985, 175–79, especially 178.

51. Text following Oren 2002, 184. See Hussein 1969, 60–61, 64, 71; Tibawi 1969, 41; Hirst 1974, 3; Bull 1976, 113; Dayan 1976, 366; Narkiss 1983, 105; Herzog 1984, 149–51, 169–70; Mutawi 1987, 74, 93–95; Armstrong 1996, 396–97; Gilbert 1996, 272–73; Duncan and Opatowski 1998, 163; Klein 2001, 53; Wasserstein 2001, 205; Laqueur 2002, 13B.

52. Schleifer 1972, 161–62, 167; Hirst 1974, 3–4; Bull 1976, 113; Dayan 1976, 355–56; Sachar 1979, 643–44; Narkiss 1983, 103–4; Herzog 1984, 171; Slater 1991, 268; Gilbert 1996, 274, 277; Duncan and Opatowski 1998, 163; Wasserstein 2001, 205–6; Oren 2002, 183, 187.

53. Hussein 1969, 60–61; Schleifer 1972, 160; Bull 1976, 113; Sachar 1979, 643; Herzog 1984, 153, 169–70, 172–73; Mutawi 1987, 123, 149–51; Oren 2002, 184–85.

54. Hussein 1969, 61–75; Schleifer 1972, 167; Dayan 1976, 352–53, 356, 366; Sachar 1979, 644; Herzog 1984, 153, 172–73; Mutawi 1987, 127–28; Wasserstein 2001, 206; Oren 2002, 186–88.

55. Schleifer 1972, 170; Bull 1976, 114–15; Dayan 1976, 366; Sachar 1979, 644; Narkiss 1983, 97–98, 113, 115; Herzog 1984, 171; Mutawi 1987, 132; Gilbert 1996, 274–75; Duncan and Opatowski 1998, 163; Oren 2002, 189.

56. Sachar 1979, 643–44; Gilbert 1996, 275, 277; Oren 2002, 189, 191.

57. Schleifer 1972, 171–72; Bull 1976, 115; Dayan 1976, 366; Sachar 1979, 650; Narkiss 1983, 115–19, 123–27; Herzog 1984, 171; Mutawi 1987, 132; Gilbert 1996, 275; Duncan and Opatowski 1998, 164; Wasserstein 2001, 206; Oren 2002, 191. The numbers given as killed and wounded differ in each of the secondary accounts.

58. Narkiss 1983, 127–35; Gilbert 1996, 275; Duncan and Opatowski 1998, 164; Oren 2002, 191–92. The numbers given as killed and wounded differ in each of the secondary accounts.

59. Oren 2002, 311–12. See also Laqueur 2002, 13B; Meyer 2002, 4.

60. Schleifer 1972, 176; Herzog 1984, 174–76; Mutawi 1987, 133–34; Gilbert 1996, 276–77; Oren 2002, 206–7, 219.

61. Schleifer 1972, 178–79; Dayan 1976, 367–68; Sachar 1979, 650–52; Narkiss 1983, 111–12, 170–79; Herzog 1984, 173, 176; Mutawi 1987, 133; Gilbert 1996, 277; Duncan and Opatowski 1998, 164–65; Wasserstein 2001, 207; Oren 2002, 192, 206, 219–22, 224. The numbers given as killed and wounded differ in each of the secondary accounts.

62. Schleifer 1972, 180–81; Dayan 1976, 367–68; Sachar 1979, 650–52; Narkiss 1983, 181–84, 213–16; Herzog 1984, 176; Gilbert 1996, 278; Duncan and Opatowski 1998, 165; Oren 2002, 220–22, 224.

63. Text following Oren 2002, 226. See Hussein 1969, 81–86; Sachar 1979, 645; Mutawi 1987, 151–52, 159; Oren 2002, 178, 209, 211, 216–18, 225–26. Oren reports that Cairo's radio broadcast "Voice of the Arabs" already had been broadcasting announcements of America's involvement since 6:00 P.M. the previous afternoon, two hours after Nasser first learned the extent of the disaster that had befallen his air force. In a later cable sent by Nasser to Hussein on Wednesday, June 7, Nasser attempted to justify his earlier assertion: "The High Command of our Armed Forces deduced that beyond a shadow of a doubt, the United States and Great Britain were aiding Israel. The basis for this deduction was the intensity of the enemy's air offensive. We could not believe these vast resources belonged to Israel alone" (Hussein 1969, 94).

64. Schleifer 1972, 203; Sachar 1979, 650–52; Narkiss 1983, 188, 201, 208–9; Silberman 1995, 151–54; Armstrong 1996, 402; Gilbert 1996, 282–83; Duncan and Opatowski 1998, 165; Silberman 2001, 498; Oren 2002, 192, 223–24.

65. Lau-Lavie 1968, 9; Narkiss 1983, 217–19; Herzog 1984, 150, 153; Slater 1991, 269; Gilbert 1996, 278; Gorenberg 2000, 98–99; Oren 2002, 231–32.

66. Translation following Oren 2002, 226. See also Hussein 1969, 87–88; Mutawi 1987, 128–29, 138–39, 155; Oren 2002, 226.

67. Schleifer 1972, 184, 188–89; Narkiss 1983, 238–43; Herzog 1984, 174; Gilbert 1996, 280–81; Duncan and Opatowski 1998, 165; Oren 2002, 228.

68. Translation and details following Oren 2002, 238–40. See also Schleifer 1972, 189–90; Gilbert 1996, 282; Meyer 2002, 4.

69. Schleifer 1972, 189–90; Mutawi 1987, 134; Gilbert 1996, 282; Oren 2002, 238–41. See also Meyer 2002, 4.

70. Narkiss 1983, 243–48; Gilbert 1996, 282; Oren 2002, 242–43.

71. Text following Narkiss 1983, 233.

72. Schleifer 1972, 191–92; Teveth 1973, 336; Sachar 1979, 654; Narkiss 1983, 248–49; Herzog 1984, 181; Gilbert 1996, 283; Duncan and Opatowski 1998, 166; Oren 2002, 243.

73. Dayan 1976, 368; Gilbert 1996, 283; Oren 2002, 243.

74. Schleifer 1972, 193–94; Sachar 1979, 654; Narkiss 1983, 250–52; Herzog 1984, 180–82; Gilbert 1996, 283–84; Wasserstein 2001, 207; Oren 2002, 244–45.

75. Schleifer 1972, 200 n. 9; Narkiss 1983, 247, 251; Herzog 1984, 181; Gilbert 1996, 284; Oren 2002, 242–43, 245; Oren, personal communication, September 1, 2003. Hudson (2000, 268) claims, "In the course of the fighting the Israelis had fired shells into the Haram al-Sharif." Similarly, Schleifer (1972, 195; see also 198) states, "The door of al-Aqsa [Mosque] had been blasted open by a bazooka shell that also damaged the upper façade." Neither Schleifer nor Hudson provides any documentation or further references to back up their statements. In contrast, General Uzi Narkiss notes in his memoirs: "Hastily, I visited the [al-Aqsa] Mosque and was delighted to find no damage, except to a glass door from the brief battle in the courtyard. There had apparently been resistance from inside. As the cleaning up continued, I told Motta [Gur] once again to make sure that no holy places or shrines were touched" (Narkiss 1983, 254). Michael Oren's detailed 2002 volume contains no mention of damage to either the Haram al-Sherif or the al-Aqsa Mosque, and he states (personal communication, September 1, 2003) that he knows "of no evidence to support the claims . . . regarding damage caused by Israel to the Haram in 1967." In his book, Oren instead emphasizes—as do most, if not all, serious historical accounts—the care that the Israelis took not to damage any of the holy sites in Jerusalem, whether Moslem, Christian, or Jewish, for fear of igniting "yet another international crisis" (Oren 2002, 245).

76. Schleifer 1972, 194; Sachar 1979, 654; Herzog 1984, 180–82; Gilbert 1996,

284–85; Duncan and Opatowski 1998, 166; Gorenberg 2000, 99; Wasserstein 2001, 207; Oren 2002, 245.

77. Schleifer 1972, 194; Sachar 1979, 654–55; Narkiss 1983, 252–56; Elon 1989, 88; Armstrong 1996, 398–400; Benvenisti 1996, 102; Gilbert 1996, 284–87; Gorenberg 2000, 99–100; Oren 2002, 245–46. See also Wasserstein 2001, 328–29. On "Jerusalem of Gold," see Gottlieb 1967, 112–15; Sachar 1979, 654–55; Armstrong 1996, 397; Gilbert 1996, 271; Gorenberg 2000, 96–97, 102. As Naomi Shemer, its author, listened to the radio on June 7 and heard the soldiers singing her song, she reportedly added a new stanza then and there, celebrating the capture of the Old City and the renewed Jewish link between antiquity and the present.

78. Schleifer (1972, 7) notes the coincidence of the day but erroneously says that 859 years separated the two anniversaries. Those in the media who compare modern Israelis to the Crusaders have not yet picked up on this minor coincidence.

79. Translation following Dayan 1985, 184. See also Narkiss 1983, 260–62; Slater 1991, 271; Oren 2002, 246. The various secondary accounts each give slightly different variations of the exact words in Dayan's prayer. I follow here the quotation given in the memoir written by his daughter. In entering the Old City, Dayan, Narkiss, and Rabin walked three abreast through St. Stephen's Gate. It was a masterful "photo opportunity" orchestrated by Dayan, who made certain that the photographers went through the gate before them. Including Narkiss and Rabin in the picture was an afterthought for Dayan, but it ensured that the photograph was published on the front page of every major newspaper in the world the next morning. Markedly (and some said deliberately on the part of Dayan), Prime Minister Levi Eshkol was not present for the picture, having been told that the area was still too dangerous and that his safety could not be ensured. See Dayan 1976, 368; Narkiss 1983, 260; Slater 1991, 270–71, 279; Gorenberg 2000, 101–2; Wasserstein 2001, 207; Meyer 2002, 4; Oren 2002, 246.

80. Quote from interview in Meyer 2002, 4. On the mutual-defense treaty between Jordan and Egypt, see Mutawi 1987, 108–11.

81. Mutawi 1987, 135; Gilbert 1996, 285–86. Sachar (1979, 654) states that there were 1,756 Israeli casualties overall during the 1967 battle for Jerusalem, taking into account all of the battles fought in the surrounding mountains and adjacent territory. See Oren 2002, 305, for the total number of Israeli, Egyptian, Syrian, and Jordanian casualties during the six days of the war.

82. Sachar 1979, 654; Herzog 1984, 182–83; Oren 2002, 241–42, 247, 305–6.

83. Hirst 1974, 4; Narkiss 1983, 262; Slater 1991, 271; Gilbert 1996, 287; Wasserstein 2001, 205; Oren 2002, 246. Again, the various secondary accounts give slightly different versions of the exact words that Dayan spoke. I follow here the version quoted by Gilbert.

84. Schleifer 1972, 204–5; Hirst 1974, 9–10; Mattar 1983, 59; Slater 1991, 292; Armstrong 1996, 402–3; Benvenisti 1996, 73; Gilbert 1996, 289–96; Gorenberg 2000, 102–3; Hudson 2000, 268; Silberman 2001, 498; Wasserstein 2001, 225, 329–30 (giving the number of houses demolished in the Maghrebi area as 135, rather than simply 25); Oren 2002, 307.

85. See Schleifer 1972, 215; Sachar 1979, 673–74; Mattar 1983, 59; Narkiss 1983, 277; Slater 1991, 279, 291; Armstrong 1996, 403–4; Hudson 2000, 268–69; Wasserstein 2001, 208. The unification was against the wishes of the United Nations, which passed a resolution in July 1967 asking Israel to rescind its action. When this resolution was ignored, the United Nations then passed Resolution 242 (in November 1967), which declared that Israel must withdraw from the territories it had captured during the Six-Day War. The latter resolution is still a point of contention today.

86. Dayan's image is beginning to come under closer scrutiny. For his alleged involvement in illegal archaeological excavation and antiquities-collecting activities, see Kletter 2001. For his autobiography and for biographies of (and commentaries upon) Dayan in English, see Lau-Lavie 1968; Teveth 1973; Dayan 1976; Dayan 1985; Slater 1991; Elon 1997, 51–62. For discussions of Dayan and his Jerusalem-based decisions during the Six-Day War, see Churchill and Churchill 1967, 60–61; Teveth 1973, 335; Sachar 1979, 644, 652, 654; Slater 1991, 269; Gilbert 1996, 282, 295–96; Oren 2002, 190, 192, 207–8, 231–32, 242–43, 307.

87. Davis 1972, 43; Davis 1981, 82–83. See also Ganin 1981, 111; Schoenbaum 1993, 34–35; Benson 1997, 168, 189–90; Merkley 1998, 190–92; Bass 2003, 15. Moshe Davis, who is the sole source for this anecdote, says that he was present during the exchange and that it took place during a private conversation with Professor Alexander Marx and seminary president (and professor) Louis Finkelstein. Contra Bass, neither Davis nor Schoenbaum (whom Bass cites) say that the exchange occurred during an introduction to a speech Truman was about to make. The comparison to Cyrus was apparently first brought to Truman's attention by the chief rabbi of Israel, Isaac Halevi Herzog, when he visited Truman at the White House in the spring of 1949. Eliahu Elath, Israel's first ambassador to the United States, relates this story and notes its lasting impact upon Truman; see Elath 1977, 48–49.

88. See the translations and summaries of statements by David Ben-Gurion, Chaim Weizman, and Moshe Dayan in Zerubavel 1995, 52–53; in Sachar 1979, 674; and in historical document no. 3 at http://www.mfa.gov.il/mfa/go.asp?MFAH019co (last accessed March 14, 2004).

89. The number of publications on this topic is immense and still growing. For estimates of the numbers involved and for examples of forays into this debate, see Sachar 1979, 332–36; Glazer 1980, 96–118; Herzog 1984, 105–6; Morris 1987; Palumbo 1987, xiv–xix, 203–10; Flapan 1987a, 81–118; Flapan 1987b, 3–26; Armstrong 1988, 76, 107, 121; Tessler 1989, 90–91; Morris 1990; Pappé 1992, 87–101; Kimmerling and Migdal 1993, 146–47, 152–53; Krystall 1998, 5–22; Morris 1999; Yahya 1999, 6–7, 27–33; Cattan 2000b; Karsh 2000a; Karsh 2000b, 30–31, 34; Karsh 2001, 26–31; Khalidi 2001, 12–36; Merkley 2001, 10–12; Morris 2001, 37–59; Reinhart 2002, 7–9, 52–53; the various contributions in Karmi and Cotran 1999, especially Pappé 1999. On the Jewish refugees from Arab countries after 1948, see most recently Davis and Radler 2003, 4; Edwards 2003, A7; Freedman 2003, B11; Radler 2003a, 4; Radler 2003b, 7.

90. For the 1967 figures, see (in addition to discussions in the references already cited) Mutawi 1987, 171; Masalha 1999; Oren 2002, 306–7.

91. As examples of the various positions within the debate, see, for instance, Said and Hitchens 1988; Abu-Sitta 1999; Al-Qasem 1999; Khalidi 1999; Quigley 1999; Karsh 2000b; Karsh 2001.

92. Broshi 1974, 21, 23–26; Marcus 2000, 135; Finkelstein 2001, 105; Finkelstein and Silberman 2001, 243, 245–46.

93. Pipes 2003, 7. The Palestinians thus make up only 3 percent of all the twentieth-century refugees, but as Pipes points out, they are just about the only group that has not effectively been resettled and assimilated somewhere else. Pipes and other scholars blame this on the other Arab nations rather than on Israel. In comparison, Israel offered sanctuary to all of the Jews who were expelled from Arab countries after the wars of 1948 and 1967, so that there is no parallel outstanding Jewish refugee problem and, until recently, almost never any discussion of a "right to return" for those expelled Jews, recently estimated at nearly nine hundred thousand (see now the newspaper reports by Davis and Radler 2003, 4; Edwards 2003, A7; Freedman 2003, B11; Radler 2003a, 4; Radler 2003b, 7).

CHAPTER 10

1. Translation following that at http://www.israel-mfa.gov.il/mfa/go.asp?MFAH0k7f0 (last accessed March 14, 2004). On Sharon being called a modern Judah Maccabee, see Bar-Kochva 1985, 22.

2. Lefkovits 2001b, 1.

3. Text following Slater 1991, 278.

4. Armstrong 1996, 410–12; Gilbert 1996, 302–3.

5. Armstrong 1996, 410–12; Gilbert 1996, 302–3.

6. Armstrong 1996, 410–12.

7. Quotation following Armstrong 1996, 413. See Ben-Dov 1982, 345; Klein 1986, 159; Elon 1989, 97–100; Idinopulos 1991, 321–22; Armstrong 1996, 412–13; Gilbert 1996, 308–9; Gorenberg 2000, 107–10; Klein 2001, 61; Wasserstein 2001, 331–32. In October 2002 it was announced that the country of Jordan finally planned to fulfill the late King Hussein's pledge to replace the *minbar*—at an estimated cost of two million dinars (approximately $2,800,000); cf. Associated Press 2002.

8. Gilbert 1996, 317–18. Numerous volumes have been published on the 1973 Yom Kippur War, but they are not the focus of the discussions here.

9. Gilbert 1996, 319; Wasserstein 2001, 228.

10. Gilbert 1996, 324, 330–31.

11. Elon 1989, 100–105; Idinopulos 1991, 322–23; Armstrong 1996, 414–16; Gilbert 1996, 330; Sprinzak 1999, 146–68; Gorenberg 2000, 14–17, 128, 131–37; Klein 2001, 61; Wasserstein 2001, 334–38.

12. Gilbert 1996, 330–31; Wasserstein 2001, 253.

13. Despite the lack of historical distance, or perhaps because of it, there are numerous books and edited volumes already published on the First Intifada; see, for example, Lockman and Beinin 1989; Peretz 1990; Schiff and Ya'ari 1990; Freedman 1991; O'Ballance 1998. See also Wasserstein 2001, 255–65; Enderlin 2003.

14. Translation following Laqueur and Rubin 2001, 356. See Armstrong 1996, 416–17; Gilbert 1996, 334–36; Duncan and Opatowski 1998, 152; Hudson 2000, 273–75; Klein 2001, 106; Wasserstein 2001, 255–56, 260.

15. Makovsky 1989, 2; Shapiro and Kampeas 1990, 1; Kampeas 1990a, 1; Klein 2001, 62; Wasserstein 2001, 337–38. For a sample of murders, riots, and clashes that took place in Jerusalem during 1989 and 1990, see Horovitz 1989, 1; Izenberg 1989, 8; Rees 1989, 12; Dudkevitch 1990, 4; Guthartz 1990, 9; Kampeas and Hutman 1990, 1; Kampeas and Dudkevitch 1990, 2; Rees 1990, 1; Kampeas 1990b, 18; Kampeas 1990c, 8; Gilbert 1996, 335–39, 342; O'Ballance 1998, 51–94.

16. Translation following Laqueur and Rubin 2001, 407–8.

17. See Armstrong 1996, 417; Gilbert 1996, 349–55; O'Ballance 1998, 155–59, 171–88, 197–206; Klein 2001, 137–57; Wasserstein 2001, 263–64. For compilations of violence in Jerusalem during these years, see http://www.israel-mfa.gov.il/mfa/go .asp? MFAH0i5d0 and http://www.israel-mfa.gov.il/mfa/go.asp?MFAH occ40 (last accessed March 14, 2004). For the text of the Oslo Agreement (known more formally as the Declaration of Principles on Interim Self-Government Arrangements) and for the letters exchanged between Rabin and Arafat, see Laqueur and Rubin 2001, 413–28. See also the subsequent Cairo Agreement made between Israel and the PLO on March 4, 1994 (Laqueur and Rubin 2001, 442–59). For the text of the peace treaty between Israel and Jordan, see Laqueur and Rubin 2001, 477–86.

18. See http://www.iris.org.il/whofatah.htm, http://www.us-israel.org/jsource/Terror-

ism/Fatah.html, http://www.idf.il/6880031/english/b1.html, http://www.ict.org.il/inter_ter
/orgdet.cfm?orgid=82, http://slate.msn.com/id/1006301/, http://usinfo.state.gov/topical/pol
/terror/texts/03043004.htm; http://www.fas.org/irp/world/para/fr100203.html; and http:
//www.hamasonline.com (last accessed March 14, 2004). See also Laqueur and Rubin 2001,
130–31, "Fatah: The Seven Points."

19. Hutman and Keinon 1996, 1; Immanuel 1996, 3; Keinon 1996, 5; Enderlin 2003,
31–32.

20. Immanuel and O'Sullivan 1996, 1; Dudkevitch 1997, 1; Rodan et al. 1997, 1; Tepperman 1997, 5; Keinon 1998, 3; Klein 1998, 3; O'Ballance 1998, 203–4, 226–27; Wohlgelernter and Klein 1998, 1; Feldman 2000, 14–15; Gorenberg 2000, 182–85; Levin 2000;
Romey 2000, 20; Klein 2001, 274–77; Wasserstein 2001, 296, 341–42; Cabbage 2002, A1;
Enderlin 2003, 53–58, 72.

21. Greenberg 2000, 11; Lahoud 2000, 1; Lefkovits 2000a, 3; Lefkovits 2000b, 4;
Wasserstein 2001, 317.

22. Text from Laqueur and Rubin 2001, 556.

23. Quotations follow Mitchell 2001, 7 and Enderlin 2003, 325, respectively. See also
Silberman 2001, 487–88, 501–2; Abu Toameh 2002, 3B, Reinhart 2002, 88, 93–95; Enderlin 2003, 293–94, 324–25.

24. Lazaroff 2000, 3; Sontag 2000, 1; Lefkovits 2000c, 4.

25. Quotations follow Lahoud 2001a, 2 and Lahoud 2001b, 2. See also Dudkevitch
2001, 2; Lahoud 2001c, 2A; Lefkovits and Keinon 2001b, 1A.

26. See compilations on http://www.israel-mfa.gov.il/mfa/go.asp?MFAH0i5do and
http://www.israel-mfa.gov.il/mfa/go.asp?MFAH0cc40 (last accessed March 14, 2004). On
the porousness of Jerusalem's northern border, see citation in Dudkevitch et al. 2002, 1.

27. Lefkovits 2001c, 1; Lefkovits 2001d, 4; Lefkovits 2001e, 2; Lefkovits 2001f, 2;
Lefkovits 2001g, 1A; Lefkovits 2001h, 1; Lefkovits 2001i, 1; Lefkovits 2001j, 3; Lefkovits
2001k, 2; Lefkovits 2001l, 1; Lefkovits 2001m, 3; Lefkovits and Dudkevitch 2001, 3;
Lefkovits and O'Sullivan 2001, 1; Lazaroff 2002, 1; Lefkovits 2002a, 1; Lefkovits 2002b, 3A;
Lefkovits 2002c, 3; Lefkovits 2002d, 1A; Lefkovits 2002e, 3; Lefkovits 2002f, 1; Lefkovits
2002g, 1; Lefkovits 2002h, 1; Lefkovits 2002i, 1A; Lefkovits and Rudge 2002, 1; Lefkovits
et al. 2002, 1; Rudge and Lefkovits 2001, 1; Anderson and Moore 2003, 1; Lefkovits 2003a,
1; Lefkovits 2003b, 1; Lefkovits 2003c, 3; Moore 2003, 1; Moore and Anderson 2003, 1;
Schechter 2003, 1; Siegel and Lazaroff 2003, 1.

28. Quotations follow Enderlin 2003, 253, 265. See also Klein 2001, 57

29. Quotations from Arafat and Barak follow Enderlin 2003, 253, 274.

30. Quotation following Enderlin 2003, 205.

31. Benvenisti 1996, 17. He says further, "The myths of the ancient forefathers are the
essence of local politics, and on the shoulders of the living the heritage of past generations
weighs as heavily as their tombstones" (234).

32. Quoted in Hockstader 2002, A17.

33. Quoted in Anderson 2003, A19.

34. O'Neill 1952, 128.

BIBLIOGRAPHY

Aamiry, M. A. 1978. *Jerusalem: Arab Origin and Heritage*. New York: Longman.

Aberbach, Moshe, and David Aberbach. 2000. *The Roman-Jewish Wars and Hebrew Cultural Nationalism*. New York: St. Martin's Press.

Abir, Mordechai. 1975. Local Leadership and Early Reforms in Palestine, 1800–1834. In *Studies on Palestine during the Ottoman Period*, ed. Moshe Ma²oz, 284–310. Jerusalem: Magnes Press.

Abou-El-Haj, Rifa²at Ali. 1984. *The 1703 Rebellion and the Structure of Ottoman Politics*. Leiden: Nederlands Historisch-Archaeologisch Instituut te Istanbul.

Abu El-Haj, Nadia. 1998. Translating Truths: Nationalism, the Practice of Archaeology, and the Remaking of Past and Present in Contemporary Jerusalem. *AE* 25:166–88.

———. 2001. *Facts on the Ground: Archaeological Practice and Territorial Self-Fashioning in Israeli Society*. Chicago: University of Chicago Press.

Abu Manneh, Butrus. 1990. Jerusalem in the Tanzimat Period: The New Ottoman Administration and the Notables. *WI* 30:1–44.

Abu-Sitta, Salman. 1999. The Feasibility of the Right of Return. In *The Palestinian Exodus: 1948–1998*, ed. Ghada Karmi and Eugene Cotran, 171–96. Reading, UK: Ithaca Press.

Abu Toameh, Khaled. 2002. How the War Began. *Jerusalem Post*, September 20, 3B.

Albright, William F. 1939. The Israelite Conquest of Canaan in the Light of Archaeology. *BASOR* 74:11–23.

Alföldy, Géza. 1995. Eine Bauinschrift aus dem Colosseum. *ZPE* 109:195–226.

al-Khateeb, Mohammed Abdul Hameed. 1998. *Al-Quds: The Place of Jerusalem in Classical Judaic and Islamic Traditions*. London: Ta-Ha Publishers.

Alon, Gedalia. 1977. The Burning of the Temple. In *Jews, Judaism, and the Classical World: Studies in Jewish History in the Times of the Second Temple and Talmud*, trans. Israel Abrahams, 252–68. Jerusalem: Magnes Press.

Al-Qasem, Anis. 1999. The Right of Return in International Law. In *The Palestinian Exodus: 1948–1998*, ed. Ghada Karmi and Eugene Cotran, 123–49. Reading, UK: Ithaca Press.

Alt, Albrecht. 1925. *Die Landnahme der Israeliten in Palaestina*. Leipzig: Reformationsprogramm der Universitaet.

———. 1966. The Settlement of the Israelites in Palestine. In *Essays on Old Testament History and Religion*, 133–69. Garden City, NY: Doubleday.

Althaus, Dudley. 2001. America Responds; Bin Laden Allegedly Criticizes Pakistan; Statement Condemns Aid to "Christian Crusade." *Houston Chronicle*, November 2, A19.

Amitai, Reuven. 1987. Mongol Raids into Palestine (A.D. 1260 and 1300). *JRAS*, 236–55.

Amitai-Preiss, Reuven. 1995. *Mongols and Mamluks: The Mamluk-Ikhanid War, 1260–1281*. Cambridge: Cambridge University Press.

Anchor Bible Dictionary. 1992. Edited by David Noel Freedman. New York: Doubleday.

Anderson, John Ward. 2003. Israel Threatens Removal of Arafat: Cabinet Approves Action, but without Specifics; Some Say Move Could Backfire. *Washington Post*, September 12, A19.

Anderson, John Ward, and Molly Moore. 2003. Suicide Bombers Kill at Least Thirteen. *Washington Post*, September 10, 1.

Applebaum, Shimon. 1976. *Prolegomena to the Study of the Second Jewish Revolt (A.D. 132–135)*. Oxford: British Archaeological Reports.

———. 1983–84. Points of View on the Second Revolt. *SCI* 7:77–87.

———. 1984. The Second Jewish Revolt (A.D. 131–35). *PEQ* 116:35–37.

Armstrong, Karen. 1988. *Holy War: The Crusades and Their Impact on Today's World*. New York: Doubleday.

———. 1992. *Muhammad: A Biography of the Prophet*. San Francisco: HarperSanFrancisco.

———. 1996. *Jerusalem: One City, Three Faiths*. New York: Alfred A. Knopf.

———. 1998. The Holiness of Jerusalem: Asset or Burden? *JPS* 27, no. 3:5–19.

———. 2000. *Islam: A Short History*. New York: Modern Library.

Aronstein, Philipp. 1936. *Speeches of British Statesmen on Judaism and Zionism*. Berlin: Im Schochken Verlag.

Asali, Kamil J. 1994. Jerusalem in History: Notes on the Origins of the City and Its Tradition of Tolerance. *ASQ* 16, no. 4:37–45.

———. 2000a. Jerusalem under the Ottomans, 1516–1831 AD. In *Jerusalem in History*, ed. Kamil J. Asali, 200–227. New York: Olive Branch Press.

———, ed. 2000b. *Jerusalem in History*. New York: Olive Branch Press.

Associated Press. 2002. Jordan to Renovate Pulpit at Jerusalem's Al-Aqsa Mosque. Associated Press Worldstream, International News, October 3.

Astour, Michael C. 1965. The Origin of the Terms "Canaan," "Phoenician," and "Purple." *JNES* 24, 346–50.

Auld, Graeme, and Margreet Steiner. 1996. *Jerusalem*. Vol. 1, *From the Bronze Age to the Maccabees*. Cambridge: Lutterworth Press.

Auld, Sylvia, and Robert Hillenbrand, eds. 2000. *Ottoman Jerusalem: The Living City, 1517–1917*. London: Altajair World of Islam Trust.

Aviam, Mordechai. 2002. Yodefat/Jotapata: The Archaeology of the First Battle. In *The First Jewish Revolt: Archaeology, History, and Ideology*, ed. Andrea M. Berlin and J. Andrew Overman, 121–33. London: Routledge.

Avigad, Nahman. 1970. Excavations in the Jewish Quarter of the Old City of Jerusalem, 1969/70 (Preliminary Report). *IEJ* 20:1–8.

———. 1980. *Discovering Jerusalem*. New York: Thomas Nelson Publishers.

———. 1983. Jerusalem in Flames: The Burnt House Captures a Moment in Time. *BAR* 9, no. 6:66–72.

Avi-Yonah, Michael. 1976. *The Jews of Palestine: A Political History from the Bar Kokhba War to the Arab Conquest*. New York: Schocken Books.

Ayalon, David. 1972. Discharges from Service, Banishments, and Imprisonments in Mamluk Society. *IOS* 2:25–50.

Babcock, Emily A., and A. C. Krey. 1943. *A History of Deeds Done beyond the Sea by William, Archbishop of Tyre*. Vols. 1 and 2. New York: Columbia University Press.

Bahat, Dan. 1986. *Carta's Historical Atlas of Jerusalem*. Jerusalem: Carta.

———. 1992. The Crusaders. In *Jerusalem: Five Thousand Years of History*, special issue, *LDA*, March, 88–99.

———. 1993. Was Jerusalem Really That Large? In *Biblical Archaeology Today, 1990: Proceedings of the Second International Congress on Biblical Archaeology, Jerusalem, June–July 1990*, ed. Avraham Biran and Joseph Aviram, 581–84. Jerusalem: Israel Exploration Society.

———. 1995. Jerusalem Down Under: Tunneling along Herod's Temple Mount Wall. *BAR* 21, no. 6:30–47.

———. 1996a. *The Illustrated Atlas of Jerusalem*. Jerusalem: Carta.

———. 1996b. The Physical Infrastructure. In *The History of Jerusalem: The Early Muslim Period, 638–1099*, ed. Joshua Prawer and Haggai Ben-Shammai, 38–100. Jerusalem: Yad Izhak Ben-Zvi.

Ballantine, James. 1866. *The Life of David Roberts, R.A.* Edinburgh: Adam and Charles Black, North Bridge.

Baram, Amatzia. 1991. *Culture, History, and Ideology in the Formation of Bathist Iraq, 1968–1989*. New York: St. Martin's Press.

Bar-Illan, David. 1992. The History of Palestine according to the Gospel of Faisal Husseini. *Jerusalem Post*, November 27, A8.

Bar-Kochva, Bezalel. 1976. Seron and Cestius Gallus at Beith Horon. *PEQ* 108:13–21.

———. 1985. The Perception of the Battles of Judas Maccabaeus and Their Impact on Modern Israel. In *Antike in der Moderne*, ed. Wolfgang Schuller, 15–23. Konstanz: Universitätsverlag Konstanz.

———. 1989. *Judas Maccabaeus: The Jewish Struggle against the Seleucids*. Cambridge: Cambridge University Press.

Barnai, Jacob. 1992. *The Jews in Palestine in the Eighteenth Century*. Trans. Naomi Goldblum. Tuscaloosa: University of Alabama Press.

Barstad, Hans M. 1996. *The Myth of the Empty Land*. Oslo: Scandinavian University Press.

———. 2003. After the "Myth of the Empty Land": Major Challenges in the Study of Neo-Babylonian Judah. In *Judah and the Judeans in the Neo-Babylonian Period*, ed. Oded Lipschits and Joseph Blenkinsopp, 3–20. Winona Lake, IN: Eisenbrauns.

Bartlett, William H. 1844. *Walks about the City and Environs of Jerusalem*. London: Hall, Virtue.

Bass, Warren. 2003. *Support Any Friend: Kennedy's Middle East and the Making of the U.S.-Israel Alliance*. Oxford: Oxford University Press.

Bauer, Yehuda. 1966. The Arab Revolt of 1936. *New Outlook: Middle East Monthly* 9, no. 6:49–57; no. 7:21–28.

Becking, Bob. 1992. *The Fall of Samaria: An Historical and Archaeological Study*. Leiden: E. J. Brill.

Begin, Menachem. 1977. *The Revolt*. New York: Nash Publishing.

Behar, Doron M., et al. 2003. Multiple Origins of Ashkenazi Levites: Y Chromosome Evidence for Both Near Eastern and European Ancestries. *AJHG* 73, no. 4:768–79.

Bell, J. Bowyer. 1977. *Terror Out of Zion: Irgun Zvai Leumi, Lehi, and the Palestine Underground, 1929–1949*. New York: St. Martin's Press.

Ben-Arieh, Yehoshua. 1983. *The Rediscovery of the Holy Land in the Nineteenth Century*. Jerusalem: Israel Exploration Society.

———. 1984. *Jerusalem in the Nineteenth Century*. New York: St. Martin's Press.

Ben-Dov, Meir. 1982. *In the Shadow of the Temple: The Discovery of Ancient Jerusalem*. Trans. Ina Friedman. New York: Harper and Row.

Bengio, Ofra. 1998. *Saddam's Word: Political Discourse in Iraq*. New York: Oxford University Press.

Benson, Michael T. 1997. *Harry S. Truman and the Founding of Israel*. Westport, CT: Praeger.

Benvenisti, Meron. 1972. *The Crusaders in the Holy Land*. New York: Macmillan and Company.

———. 1996. *City of Stone: The Hidden History of Jerusalem*. Berkeley: University of California Press.

Ben-Yehuda, Nachman. 1995. *The Masada Myth: Collective Memory and Mythmaking in Israel*. Madison: University of Wisconsin Press.

———. 2002. *Sacrificing Truth: Archaeology and the Myth of Masada*. Amherst, NY: Humanity Books.

Ben-Yehuda, Nachman, Joseph Zias, and Ze'ev Meshel. 1998. Questioning Masada. *BAR* 24, no. 6:30–53, 64–66, 68.

Berlin, Andrea M., and J. Andrew Overman, eds. 2002. *The First Jewish Revolt: Archaeology, History, and Ideology*. London: Routledge.

Bethell, Nicholas. 1979. *The Palestine Triangle: The Struggle between the British, the Jews, and the Arabs, 1935–48*. New York: G. P. Putnam's Sons.

Bietenhard, Hans. 1948. Die Freiheltskriege der Juden unter den Kaisern Trajan und Hadrian und der messianische Tempelbau. *Judaica* 4:81–108.

Bilde, Per. 1978. The Roman Emperor Gaius (Caligula)'s Attempt to Erect His Statue in the Temple of Jerusalem. *ST* 32:67–93.

———. 1979. The Causes of the Jewish War according to Josephus. *JJS* 10:179–202.

Biran, Avraham, and Joseph Naveh. 1993. An Aramaic Stele Fragment from Tel Dan. *IEJ* 43:81–98.

———. 1995. The Tel Dan Inscription: A New Fragment. *IEJ* 45:1–18.

Bleibtreu, Erika. 1990. Five Ways to Conquer a City. *BAR* 16, no. 3:37–44.

———. 1991. Grisly Assyrian Record of Torture and Death. *BAR* 17, no. 1:52–61, 75.

Boas, Adrian J. 1999. *Crusader Archaeology: The Material Culture of the Latin East*. London: Routledge.

———. 2001. *Jerusalem in the Time of the Crusades: Society, Landscape, and Art in the Holy City under Frankish Rule*. London: Routledge.

Bowersock, Glen W. 1980. A Roman Perspective on the Bar Kokhba Revolt. In *Approaches to Ancient Judaism*, vol. 2, ed. William S. Green, 131–41. Chico, CA: Scholars Press.

———. 1985. Palestine: Ancient History and Modern Politics. *JPS* 14/4:49–57.

Brauer, George C., Jr. 1970. *Judaea Weeping: The Jewish Struggle against Rome from Pompey to Masada, 63 B.C. to A.D. 73*. New York: Thomas Y. Crowell Company.

Bright, John. 1972. *A History of Israel*. 2d ed. Philadelphia: Westminster.

Broadhurst, R. J. C. 1980. *A History of the Ayyubid Sultans of Egypt: Translated from the Arabic of al-Maqrizi*. Boston: G. K. Hall and Company.

Broshi, Magen. 1974. The Expansion of Jerusalem in the Reigns of Hezekiah and Manasseh. *IEJ* 24:21–26.

————. 1978. Estimating the Population of Ancient Jerusalem. *BAR* 4, no. 2:10–15.

————. 1983. The Credibility of Josephus. In *Essays in Honour of Yigael Yadin*, ed. Geza Vermes and Jacob Neusner, 379–84. Totowa, NJ: Published for the Oxford Centre for Postgraduate Studies by Allanheld, Osmun, and Company.

Broshi, Magen, and Shimon Gibson. 2000. Excavations along the Western and Southern Walls of the Old City of Jerusalem. In *Ancient Jerusalem Revealed*, ed. Hillel Geva, rev. ed., 147–55. Jerusalem: Israel Exploration Society.

Bruce, Anthony P. C. 2002. *The Last Crusade: The Palestine Campaign in the First World War*. London: John Murray.

Bryce, Trevor R. 1998. *The Kingdom of the Hittites*. Oxford: Oxford University Press.

Bull, Odd. 1976. *War and Peace in the Middle East: The Experiences and Views of a U.N. Observer*. London: Leo Cooper.

Bulloch, John, and Harvey Morris. 1991. *Saddam's War: The Origins of the Kuwait Conflict and the International Response*. London: Faber and Faber.

Bullock, David L. 1988. *Allenby's War: The Palestine-Arabian Campaigns, 1916–1918*. London: Blandford Press.

Burman, Edward. 1986. *The Templars: Knights of God*. Rochester, VT: Destiny Books.

Burns, John F. 1990. New Babylon Is Stalled by a Modern Upheaval. *New York Times*, October 11, A13.

Busse, Heribert. 1986. Omar's Image as the Conqueror of Jerusalem. *JSAI* 8:149–68.

Cabbage, Michael. 2002. Politics Dog Archaeologists in Holy Land. *Orlando Sentinel*, August 4, A1.

Cahill, Jane M. 1998. David's Jerusalem: Fiction or Reality? Part 2, It Is There: The Archaeological Evidence Proves It. *BAR* 24, no. 2:34–41, 63.

————. 2003. Jerusalem at the Time of the United Monarchy: The Archaeological Evidence. In *Jerusalem in Bible and Archaeology: The First Temple Period*, ed. Andrew G. Vaughn and Ann E. Killebrew, 13–80. Atlanta: Society of Biblical Literature.

Cahill, Jane M., Karl Reinhard, David Tarler, and Peter Warnock. 1991. It Had to Happen: Scientists Examine Remains of Ancient Bathroom. *BAR* 17, no. 3:64–69.

Cahill, Jane M., and David Tarler. 2000. Excavations Directed by Yigal Shiloh at the City of David, 1978–1985. In *Ancient Jerusalem Revealed*, ed. Hillel Geva, rev. ed., 31–45. Jerusalem: Israel Exploration Society.

Carne, John. 1836. *Syria, the Holy Land, Asia Minor, &c. illustrated; in a series of views drawn from nature by W. H. Bartlett, William Purser, &c.; with descriptions of the plates*. London: Fisher, Son, and Company.

Carr, Caleb. 2002. *The Lessons of Terror: A History of Warfare against Civilians; Why It Has Always Failed and Why It Will Fail Again*. New York: Random House.

Cary, Earnest. 1925. *Dio's Roman History, vol. 8: Books 61–70*. London: William Heineman.

Cattan, Henry. 2000a. *Jerusalem*. London: Saqi Books.

————. 2000b. *The Palestine Question*. London: Saqi Books.

Chandrasekaran, Rajiv. 2003. Baghdad Looks Back for Its Future. *Washington Post*, March 10, A1.

Chitty, Derwas J. 1966. *The Desert a City: An Introduction to the Study of Egyptian and Palestinian Monasticism under the Christian Empire*. Oxford: Basil Blackwell.

Churchill, Randolph S., and Winston S. Churchill. 1967. *The Six Day War*. Boston: Houghton Mifflin Company.

Clarke, Thurston. 1981. *By Blood and Fire: The Attack on the King David Hotel*. New York: G. P. Putnam's Sons.

Cline, Eric H. 2000. *The Battles of Armageddon: Megiddo and the Jezreel Valley from the Bronze Age to the Nuclear Age*. Ann Arbor: University of Michigan Press.

———. 2003a. Does Saddam Think He's a Modern-Day Saladin? *History News Network*, March 10. http://hnn.us/articles/1305.html.

———. 2003b. Saddam Hussein and History 101. *ByGeorge* 15, no. 11 (March 4): 2.

Cline, Eric H., and David O'Connor. 2003. The Mystery of the "Sea Peoples." In *Mysterious Lands*, ed. David O'Connor and Stephen Quirke, 107–38. London: UCL Press.

Cogan, Mordechai. 2001. Sennacherib's Siege of Jerusalem. *BAR* 27, no. 1:40–45, 69.

Cogan, Mordechai, and Hayim Tadmor. 1988. *II Kings: A New Translation with Introduction and Commentary*. Anchor Bible Series 11. Garden City, NY: Doubleday.

Cohen, Amnon. 1973. *Palestine in the Eighteenth Century: Patterns of Government and Administration*. Jerusalem: Magnes Press.

———. 1989. *Economic Life in Ottoman Jerusalem*. Cambridge: Cambridge University Press.

Cohen, Amnon, and Gabriel Baer, eds. 1984. *Egypt and Palestine: A Millennium of Association (868–1948)*. New York: St. Martin's Press.

Cohen, Michael. 1990. *Truman and Israel*. Berkeley: University of California Press.

Cohen, Shaye J. D. 1982–83. Alexander the Great and Jaddus the High Priest according to Josephus. *AJS Review* 7–8:41–68.

———. 1983. Masada: Literary Tradition, Archaeological Remains, and the Credibility of Josephus. In *Essays in Honour of Yigael Yadin*, ed. Geza Vermes and Jacob Neusner, 385–405. Totowa, NJ: Published for the Oxford Centre for Postgraduate Studies by Allanheld, Osmun, and Company.

———. 1987. *From the Maccabees to the Mishnah*. Philadelphia: Westminster.

———. 1999. *The Beginnings of Jewishness: Boundaries, Varieties, Uncertainties*. Berkeley: University of California Press.

Colledge, Malcolm A. R. 1967. *The Parthians*. New York: Frederick A. Praeger.

Conybeare, Frederick C. 1910. Antiochus Strategos' Account of the Sack of Jerusalem in A.D. 614. *EHR* 25:502–16.

Cook, David B. 1996. Muslim Apocalyptic and Jihad. *JSAI* 20:66–104.

———. 2002a. America, the Second ᶜAd: The Perception of the United States in Modern Muslim Apocalyptic Literature. *Yale Center for International and Area Studies Publications* 5:150–93.

———. 2002b. Suicide Attacks or Martyrdom Operations in Contemporary Jihad Literature. *Nova Religio* 6, no. 1:7–44.

Corwin, Norman. 2000. O Jerusalem, Jerusalem. *Los Angeles Times*, October 15, 2000, *Sunday Book Review*, 6.

Dajani-Shakeel, Hadia. 1988. Some Medieval Accounts of Salah al-Din's Recovery of Jerusalem (Al-Quds). In *Studia Palaestina: Studies in Honour of Constantine K. Zurayk*, ed. Hisham Nashshabah, 83–113. Beirut: Institute for Palestine Studies.

———. 1991. A Reassessment of Some Medieval and Modern Perceptions of the Counter-Crusade. In *The Jihad and Its Times: Dedicated to Andrew Stefan Ehrenkreutz*, ed. Hadia Dajani-Shakeel and Ronald A. Messier, 41–70. Ann Arbor: University of Michigan Press.

———. 2000. The Legacy of the Crusades: An Islamic Perspective. In *Approaching Jerusalem: The Legacy of the Crusades in the Twenty-first Century*, ed. Penny J. Cole and Hadia Dajani-Shakeel, 10–23. Regina, Canada: Campion College.

Dajani-Shakeel, Hadia, and Ronald A. Messier, eds. 1991. *The Jihad and Its Times: Dedicated to Andrew Stefan Ehrenkreutz*. Ann Arbor: University of Michigan Press.

Davies, Philip R. 1992. *In Search of "Ancient Israel."* JSOT Supplement Series 148. Sheffield: Sheffield Academic Press.

Davis, Douglas, and Melissa Radler. 2003. UK to address issue of Jewish refugees from Arab lands. *Jerusalem Post*, July 2, 4.

Davis, Moshe. 1972. America and the Holy Land; A Colloquium. *American Jewish Historical Quarterly* 62:5–62.

———. 1981. Reflections on Harry S. Truman. In *Truman and the American Commitment to Israel: A Thirtieth Anniversary Conference,* ed. Allen Weinstein and Moshe Ma'oz, 82–85. Jerusalem: Magnes Press.

Dayan, Moshe. 1976. *Moshe Dayan: Story of My Life.* New York: Morrow.

Dayan, Yael. 1985. *My Father, His Daughter.* New York: Farrar, Straus, and Giroux.

Dessel, J. P. 2002. Review of *Archaeology of the Land of the Bible,* vol. 2, by Ephraim Stern. *BAR* 28, no. 6:58–59.

Dever, William G. 1997. Archaeology and the "Age of Solomon": A Case Study in Archaeology and Historiography. In *The Age of Solomon: Scholarship at the Turn of the Millennium,* ed. Lowell K. Handy, 217–51. Leiden: E. J. Brill.

———. 2001. *What Did the Biblical Writers Know and When Did They Know It? What Archaeology Can Tell Us about the Reality of Ancient Israel.* Grand Rapids, MI: William B. Eerdmans Publishing.

———. 2003. *Who Were the Early Israelites and Where Did They Come From?* Grand Rapids, MI: William B. Eerdmans Publishing.

Donner, Fred M. 1981. *The Early Islamic Conquests.* Princeton: Princeton University Press.

Dornberg, John. 1992. Battle of the Teutoberg Forest. *Archaeology* 45, no. 5:26–33.

Drews, Robert. 1993. *The End of the Bronze Age.* Princeton: Princeton University Press.

———. 1998. Canaanites and Philistines. JSOT 81:39–61.

———. 2000. Medinet Habu: Oxcarts, Ships, and Migration Theories. *JNES* 59:161–90.

Dudkevitch, Margot. 1990. Riots Plague City in Slaying Aftermath. *Jerusalem Post*, May 25, 4.

———. 1997. Thirteen Killed in Jerusalem Blast; Hamas Claims Market Attack. *Jerusalem Post*, July 31, 1.

———. 2001. Violence in Territories Surges amid Calls to Intensify Intifada. *Jerusalem Post*, February 7, 2.

Dudkevitch, Margot, Etgar Lefkovits, and David Rudge. 2002. Jerusalem, Haifa on Red Alert; Bomber Reportedly in Capital. *Jerusalem Post*, June 18, 1.

Dunlop, D. M. 1967. *The History of the Jewish Khazars.* New York: Schocken Books.

Duri, Abdul Aziz. 2000. Jerusalem in the Early Islamic Period, 7th–11th Centuries AD. In *Jerusalem in History,* ed. Kamil J. Asali, 105–29. New York: Olive Branch Press.

Dyer, Charles H., and Angela E. Hunt. 1991. *The Rise of Babylon: Sign of the End Times.* Wheaton: Tyndale House Publishers.

Eck, Werner. 1999. The Bar Kokhba Revolt: The Roman Point of View. *JRS* 89:76–89.

Edbury, Peter W. 1998. *The Conquest of Jerusalem and the Third Crusade: Sources in Translation.* Aldershot: Ashgate.

———, ed. 1985. *Crusade and Settlement: Papers Read at the First Conference of the Society for the Study of the Crusades and the Latin East and Presented to R. C. Smail.* Cardiff: University College Cardiff Press.

Edelman, Diana V. 1997. Foreword to *The Age of Solomon: Scholarship at the Turn of the Millennium,* ed. Lowell K. Handy. Leiden: E. J. Brill.

Edwards, Steven. 2003. Don't Forget Jewish Refugees, Study Urges. Papers show Arab states orchestrated persecution: experts. *Ottawa Citizen*, June 24, A7.

Ehrenkreutz, Andrew S. 1972. *Saladin*. Albany: State University of New York Press.

———. 1984. The Fatimids in Palestine: The Unwitting Promoters of the Crusades. In *Egypt and Palestine: A Millennium of Association (868–1948)*, ed. Amnon Cohen and Gabriel Baer, 66–72. New York: St. Martin's Press.

Elad, Amikam. 1992. Why Did Abd al-Malik Build the Dome of the Rock? A Re-examination of the Muslim Sources. In *Bayt al-Maqdis: ʿAbd al-Malik's Jerusalem*, ed. Julian Raby and Jeremy Johns, 33–58. Oxford: Oxford University Press.

el-Aref, Aref. 1975. The Closing Phase of Ottoman Rule in Jerusalem. In *Studies on Palestine during the Ottoman Period*, ed. Moshe Maʾoz, 334–40. Jerusalem: Magnes Press.

Elath, Eliahu. 1977. Harry S. Truman: The Man and Statesman. First Annual Harry S. Truman Lecture, Hebrew University of Jerusalem, May 18.

———. 1981. The Fourteenth of May 1948 in Washington, D.C. In *Truman and the American Commitment to Israel: A Thirtieth Anniversary Conference*, ed. Allen Weinstein and Moshe Maʾoz, 105–10. Jerusalem: Magnes Press.

Eliav, Yaron. 1997. Hadrian's Actions in the Jerusalem Temple Mount according to Cassius-Dio and Xiphilini Manus. *JSQ* 4, no. 2:125–44.

Elon, Amos. 1989. *Jerusalem: City of Mirrors*. Boston: Little, Brown, and Company.

———. 1997. *A Blood-Dimmed Tide: Dispatches from the Middle East*. New York: Columbia University Press.

el-Sadat, Anwar. 1977. *In Search of Identity: An Autobiography*. New York: Harper and Row.

Enderlin, Charles. 2003. *Shattered Dreams: The Failure of the Peace Process in the Middle East, 1995–2002*. Trans. Susan Fairfield. New York: Other Press.

Eshel, Hanan. 1997. Jerusalem No More. *BAR* 23, no. 6:46–48, 73.

———. 2002. Documents of the First Jewish Revolt from the Judean Desert. In *The First Jewish Revolt: Archaeology, History, and Ideology*, ed. Andrea M. Berlin and J. Andrew Overman, 157–63. London: Routledge.

Evans, Carl D. 1980. Judah's Foreign Policy from Hezekiah to Josiah. In *Scripture in Context: Essays on the Comparative Method*, ed. Carl D. Evans, William W. Hallo, and John B. White, 157–78. Pittsburgh: Pickwick Press.

Falls, Cyril. 1930. *Military Operations: Egypt and Palestine; From June 1917 to the End of the War*. Part 1. London: His Majesty's Stationery Office.

Fam, Mariam [Miriam]. 2001a. Iraqis Take to Streets Calling for "Liberating Palestine" under Saddam Hussein. Associated Press, August 15.

———. 2001b. Iraqi "Jerusalem Army" Championing Palestinians. *Jerusalem Post* (Internet edition), September 30 (http://www.jpost.com/Editions/2001/09/03/LatestNews.35488.html).

Feldman, Louis H. trans. 1965. *Josephus: The Jewish Antiquities, vol. 9*. Loeb Classical Library. Cambridge: Harvard University Press.

———. 1984. *Josephus and Modern Scholarship, 1937–1980*. Berlin: Walter de Gruyter.

———. 1998. *Josephus' Interpretation of the Bible*. Berkeley: University of California Press.

———. 2001. Financing the Colosseum. *BAR* 27, no. 4:20–31, 60–61.

Feldman, Steven. 2000. Furor over Temple Mount Construction. *BAR* 26, no. 2:14–15.

Fierman, Floyd S. 1985. Nelson Glueck and the OSS during World War II. *Journal of Reform Judaism* 32, no. 3:1–20.

———. 1986. Rabbi Nelson Glueck: An Archaeologist's Secret Life in the Service of the OSS. *BAR* 12, no. 5:18–22.

Fink, Harold S. 1969. The Foundation of the Latin States, 1099–1118. In *A History of the*

Crusades, vol. 1, The First Hundred Years, ed. Kenneth Setton and Marshall W. Baldwin, 368–409. Madison: University of Wisconsin Press.

Finkelstein, Israel. 1988. The Archaeology of the Israelite Settlement. Jerusalem: Israel Exploration Society.

———. 1998. Notes on the Stratigraphy and Chronology of Iron Age Taʾanach. TA 25:208–18.

———. 1999. Hazor and the North in the Iron Age: A Low Chronology Perspective. BASOR 314:55–70.

———. 2001. The Rise of Jerusalem and Judah: The Missing Link. Levant 33:105–15.

———. 2002. The Campaign of Shoshenq I to Palestine: A Guide to the Tenth Century BCE Polity. ZDPV 118:109–35.

———. 2003. The Rise of Jerusalem and Judah: The Missing Link. In Jerusalem in Bible and Archaeology: The First Temple Period, ed. Andrew G. Vaughn and Ann E. Killebrew, 81–101. Atlanta: Society of Biblical Literature.

Finkelstein, Israel, and Nadav Naʾaman, eds. 1994. From Nomadism to Monarchy: Archaeological and Historical Aspects of Early Israel. Jerusalem: Israel Exploration Society.

Finkelstein, Israel, and Neil A. Silberman. 2001. The Bible Unearthed: Archaeology's New Vision of Ancient Israel and the Origin of Its Sacred Texts. New York: Free Press.

Finkelstein, Louis, ed. 1997. The Jews: Their History. New York: Schocken Books.

Flapan, Simha. 1987a. The Birth of Israel: Myths and Realities. New York: Pantheon Books.

———. 1987b. The Palestinian Exodus of 1948. JPS 16/4: 3–26.

Ford, Peter. 2001. Europe Cringes at Bush "Crusade" against Terrorists. Christian Science Monitor, September 19, 12.

France, John. 1994. Victory in the East: A Military History of the First Crusade. Cambridge: Cambridge University Press.

Frankel, Jonathan. 1984. Bar Kokhba and All That. Dissent 31:192–202.

Franken, Hendricus J. 2000. Jerusalem in the Bronze Age, 3000–1000 BC. In Jerusalem in History, ed. Kamil J. Asali, 11–41. New York: Olive Branch Press.

Franken, Hendricus J., and Margreet L. Steiner. 1992. Urusalim and Jebus. ZAW 104:110–11.

Freedman, Robert O., ed. 1991. The Intifada: Its Impact on Israel, the Arab World, and the Superpowers. Miami: Florida International University Press.

Freedman, Samuel G. 2003. Are Jews Who Fled Arab Lands Refugees, Too? New York Times, October 11, B11.

Fried, Lizbeth S. 2003. The Land Lay Desolate: Conquest and Restoration in the Ancient Near East. In Judah and the Judeans in the Neo-Babylonian Period, ed. Oded Lipschits and Joseph Blenkinsopp, 21–54. Winona Lake, IN: Eisenbrauns.

Friedman, Jane. 1982. For Israelis, Bar Kochba Isn't Ancient History. New York Times, January 31, E22.

Friedman, Richard E. 1997. Who Wrote the Bible? San Francisco: HarperCollins.

Friedmann, Yohanan. 1992. The History of al-Tabari v. XII: The Battle of al-Qadisiyyah and the Conquest of Syria and Palestine. Albany: State University of New York Press.

Fritz, Volkmar, and Philip R. Davies, eds. 1996. The Origins of the Ancient Israelite States. JSOT Supplement Series 228. Sheffield: Sheffield Academic Press.

Furneaux, Rupert. 1972. The Roman Siege of Jerusalem. New York: David McKay Company.

Gabba, Emilio. 1981. La rivolta giudaica del 66 c.e. In Atti del congresso internazionale di studi vespasianei: Rieti, settembre 1979, 153–73. Rieti: Centro di Studi Varroniani Editore.

Gabrieli, Francesco. 1969. Arab Historians of the Crusades. Trans. E. J. Costello. Berkeley: University of California Press.

Ganin, Zvi. 1979. *Truman, American Jewry, and the Creation of Israel, 1945–1948*. New York: Holmes & Meier Publishers.

———. 1981. Truman, American Jewry, and the Creation of Israel. In *Truman and the American Commitment to Israel: A Thirtieth Anniversary Conference*, ed. Allen Weinstein and Moshe Ma'oz, 111–21. Jerusalem: Magnes Press.

Gardner, Brian. 1966. *Allenby of Arabia: Lawrence's General*. New York: Coward-McCann.

Gerber, Haim. 1985. *Ottoman Rule in Jerusalem: 1890–1914*. Berlin: Klaus Schwarz Verlag.

Gerner, Deborah J. 1994. *One Land, Two Peoples: The Conflict over Palestine*. Boulder, CO: Westview Press.

Geva, Hillel. 1984. The Camp of the Tenth Legion in Jerusalem: An Archaeological Reconsideration. *IEJ* 34:239–54.

———. 1997. Searching for Roman Jerusalem. *BAR* 23, no. 6:34–45, 72–73.

———. 2000. Twenty-five Years of Excavations in Jerusalem, 1968–1993: Achievements and Evaluation. In *Ancient Jerusalem Revealed*, ed. Hillel Geva, rev. ed., 1–30. Jerusalem: Israel Exploration Society.

———. 2003. Western Jerusalem at the End of the First Temple Period in Light of the Excavations in the Jewish Quarter. In *Jerusalem in Bible and Archaeology: The First Temple Period*, ed. Andrew G. Vaughn and Ann E. Killebrew, 183–208. Atlanta: Society of Biblical Literature.

———, ed. 1994. *Ancient Jerusalem Revealed*. Jerusalem: Israel Exploration Society.

———. 2000. *Ancient Jerusalem Revealed*. Rev. ed. Jerusalem: Israel Exploration Society.

Gibb, Sir Hamilton A. R. 1932. *The Damascus Chronicle of the Crusades: Extracted and Translated from the Chronicle of Ibn al-Qalanisi*. London: Luzac and Company.

———. 1973. *The Life of Saladin: From the Works of 'Imad ad-Din and Baha' ad-Din*. Oxford: Clarendon Press.

Gichon, Mordechai. 1979. The Bar Kokhba War: A Colonial Uprising against Imperial Rome. *Revue Internationale d'Histoire Militaire* 42:82–97.

———. 1981. Cestius Gallus's Campaign in Judaea. *PEQ* 113:39–62.

———. 1986. New Insight into the Bar Kokhba War and a Reappraisal of Dio Cassius 69.12–13. *JQR* 77:15–43.

Gil, Moshe. 1992. *A History of Palestine, 634–1099*. Cambridge: Cambridge University Press.

———. 1996a. The Political History of Jerusalem during the Early Muslim Period. In *The History of Jerusalem: The Early Muslim Period, 638–1099*, ed. Joshua Prawer and Haggai Ben-Shammai, 1–37. Jerusalem: Yad Izhak Ben-Zvi.

———. 1996b. The Jewish Community. In *The History of Jerusalem: The Early Muslim Period 638–1099*, ed. Joshua Prawer and Haggai Ben-Shammai, 163–200. Jerusalem: Yad Izhak Ben-Zvi.

Gilbert, Martin. 1975. *Winston S. Churchill*. Vol. 4, *1916–1922*. *The Stricken World*. Boston: Houghton Mifflin Company.

———. 1977. *Jerusalem History Atlas*. New York: Macmillan Publishing.

———. 1996. *Jerusalem in the Twentieth Century*. New York: John Wiley and Sons.

Gilbert, Vivian. 1923. *The Romance of the Last Crusade, with Allenby to Jerusalem*. New York: William B. Feakins.

Gill, Dan. 1996. The Geology of the City of David and Its Ancient Subterranean Waterworks. In *Excavations at the City of David*, vol. 4, *1978–1985: Various Reports*, ed. Donald T. Ariel and Alon De Groot, Qedem 35, 1–28. Jerusalem: Institute of Archaeology, Hebrew University of Jerusalem.

Glazer, Steven. 1980. The Palestinian Exodus in 1948. *JPS* 9/4:96–118.

Glubb, John B. 1957. *A Soldier with the Arabs*. New York: Harper & Brothers Publishers.

———. 1970. *The Life and Times of Muhammad*. New York: Stein and Day.

Golan, David. 1986. Hadrian's Decision to Supplant "Jerusalem" by "Aelia Capitolina." *Historia* 35:226–39.

Goldberg, Jeffrey. 1999. Israel's Y2K Problem. *New York Times Magazine*, October 3, 38–43, 52, 65, 76–77.

Goldsworthy, Adrian K. 1996. *The Roman Army at War: 100 BC–AD 200*. Oxford: Clarendon Press.

Goodman, Martin. 1983. The First Jewish Revolt: Social Conflict and the Problem of Debt. In *Essays in Honour of Yigael Yadin*, ed. Geza Vermes and Jacob Neusner, 417–27. Totowa, NJ: Published for the Oxford Centre for Postgraduate Studies by Allanheld, Osmun, and Company.

———. 1985. On the Abuse of the Roman Procurator Florus Described in *BJ* II. *JJS* 36:195–99.

———. 2002. Current Scholarship on the First Revolt. In *The First Jewish Revolt: Archaeology, History, and Ideology*, ed. Andrea M. Berlin and J. Andrew Overman, 15–24. London: Routledge.

Gorenberg, Gershom. 2000. *The End of Days: Fundamentalism and the Struggle for the Temple Mount*. New York: Free Press.

Gottlieb, Linda. 1967. The Song That Took a City. *Reader's Digest*, December, 112–15.

Gottwald, Norman K. 1979. *The Tribes of Yahweh: A Sociology of the Religion of Liberated Israel, 1250–1050 BCE*. New York: Orbis Books.

Grabar, Oleg. 1996. *The Shape of the Holy: Early Islamic Jerusalem*. Princeton: Princeton University Press.

Grabbe, Lester L. 1991. Maccabean Chronology: 167–164 or 168–165 B.C.E.? *JBL* 110:59–74.

———. 1992. *Judaism from Cyrus to Hadrian*. Minneapolis: Augsburg Fortress Press.

———. 2003. Review of *The Beginnings of Jewishness*, by Shaye J. D. Cohen. *JNES* 62:70–71.

———, ed. 1997. *Can a "History of Israel" Be Written?* JSOT Supplement Series 245. Sheffield: Sheffield Academic Press.

———. 1998. *Leading Captivity Captive: "The Exile" as History and Ideology*. JSOT Supplement Series 278. Sheffield: Sheffield Academic Press.

Grayson, A. Kirk. 1975. *Assyrian and Babylonian Chronicles*. Locust Valley, NY: J. J. Augustin.

Green, Alberto R. 1982. The Fate of King Jehoiakim. *AUSS* 20:103–9.

Greenberg, Joel. 2000. Sharon Touches a Nerve, and Jerusalem Explodes. *New York Times*, September 29, 11.

Gruen, Erich S. 1993. Hellenism and Persecution: Antiochus IV and the Jews. In *Hellenistic History and Culture*, ed. Peter Green, 238–74. Berkeley: University of California Press.

Gugliotta, Guy. 2003. Scientists Confirm Ancient Date of Jerusalem Conduit: Siloam Tunnel May Have Been Planned to Offset Siege. *Washington Post*, September 11, A03.

Guiterman, Helen. 1978. *David Roberts R.A.: 1796–1864*. London: Dramrite Printers.

Gutgold, Shira. 2001. Mideast Notes: Saddam Hussein Forms a "Jerusalem Liberation Army." *Jerusalem Post*, February 13, 9.

Guthartz, Ron. 1990. City Takes Steps to Put End to Riots. *Jerusalem Post*, August 17, 9.

Hadawi, Sami. 1983. Who Are the Palestinians? *Journal of Historical Review* 4, no. 1:43–59.

Halevi, Yossi Klein. 2000. Commentary: Palestinians See Israelis as the Crusaders. *Los Angeles Times*, November 19, M5.

Hallo, William W. 1982. Nebukadnezar Comes to Jerusalem. In *Through the Sound of Many Voices: Writings Contributed on the Occasion of the Seventieth Birthday of W. Gunther Plaut*, ed. Jonathan V. Plaut, 40–57. Toronto: Lester and Orpen Dennys.

Hallote, Rachel S., and Alexander H. Joffe. 2002. The Politics of Israeli Archaeology: Between 'Nationalism' and 'Science' in the Age of the Second Republic. *Israel Studies* 7/3:84–116.

Halpern, Baruch. 1983. *The Emergence of Israel in Canaan*. Chico, CA: Scholars Press.

———. 1991. Jerusalem and the Lineages in the Seventh Century BCE: Kinship and the Rise of Individual Moral Liability. In *Law and Ideology in Monarchic Israel*, ed. Baruch Halpern and D. W. Hobson, 11–107. Sheffield: Sheffield Academic Press.

———. 2001. *David's Secret Demons: Messiah, Murderer, Traitor, King; The Bible in Its World*. Grand Rapids, MI: William B. Eerdmans Publishing.

Halpern, Israel. 1977. The Jews in Eastern Europe: From Ancient Times until the Partitions of Poland, 1772–1795. In *The Jews: Their History*, ed. Louis Finkelstein, 305–42. New York: Schocken Books.

Hamblin, William. 1991. To Wage Jihad or Not: Fatimid Egypt during the Early Crusades. In *The Jihad and Its Times: Dedicated to Andrew Stefan Ehrenkreutz*, ed. Hadia Dajani-Shakeel and Ronald A. Messier, 31–39. Ann Arbor: University of Michigan Press.

Hamilton, Robert W. 1940. Excavations against the North Wall of Jerusalem, 1937–38. *QDAP* 10:1–57.

Hammer, Michael F., et al. 2000. Jewish and Middle Eastern Non-Jewish Populations Share a Common Pool of Y-Chromosome Biallelic Haplotypes. *PNAS* 97, no. 12:6769–74.

Handy, Lowell K. 1997a. On the Dating and Dates of Solomon's Reign. In *The Age of Solomon: Scholarship at the Turn of the Millennium*, ed. Lowell K. Handy, 96–105. Leiden: E. J. Brill.

———, ed. 1997b. *The Age of Solomon: Scholarship at the Turn of the Millennium*. Leiden: E. J. Brill.

Harding, Luke. 2001. Attack on Afghanistan; Propaganda—Bin Laden Letter Urges Muslims to Fight "Crusaders" of West; Pakistanis Get Call to Arms on al-Jazeera. *Guardian* (London), November 2, 4.

Harel, Menashe. 1974. The Jewish Presence in Jerusalem throughout the Ages. In *Jerusalem*, ed. John M. Oesterreicher and Anne Sinai, 137–47. New York: John Day Company.

Harkabi, Yehoshafat. 1983. *The Bar Kokhba Syndrome: Risk and Realism in International Politics*. Trans. Max D. Ticktin. Chappaqua, NY: Rossel Books.

Harper's Bible Dictionary. 1985. Ed. Paul J. Achtemeier. San Francisco: Harper and Row.

Harrington, Daniel J. 1988. *The Maccabean Revolt: Anatomy of a Biblical Revolution*. Wilmington, DE: Michael Glazier.

Harris, John F. 2001. Bush Gets More International Support for U.S. "Crusade" against Terrorism; Officials Warn New Attacks Are Possible. *Washington Post*, September 17, A1.

Harris, Rendel. 1926. Hadrian's Decree of Expulsion of the Jews from Jerusalem. *HTR* 19:199–206.

Hartman, Carl. 2001. Scholar Says Roman Colosseum Was Built with Loot That Soldiers Took from Temple in Jerusalem. Associated Press, August 31.

Hasson, Izhak. 1996. The Muslim View of Jerusalem: The Qur²an and Hadith. In *The History of Jerusalem: The Early Muslim Period, 638–1099*, ed. Joshua Prawer and Haggai Ben-Shammai, 349–85. Jerusalem: Yad Izhak Ben-Zvi.

Hawting, G. R. 1986. *The First Dynasty of Islam: The Umayyad Caliphate, AD 661–750*. London: Croom Helm.

Hayes, John H., and Sara R. Mandell. 1998. *The Jewish People in Classical Antiquity: From Alexander to Bar Kochba*. Louisville, KY: Westminster John Knox.

Heller, Joseph. 1995. *The Stern Gang: Ideology, Politics, and Terror, 1940–1949*. London: Frank Cass.

Hendel, Ronald S. 1996. The Date of the Siloam Inscription: A Rejoinder to Rogerson and Davies. *BA* 59:233–37.

———. 2003. Was There a Temple in Jerusalem? *BR* 19, no. 5:8, 42.

Henderson, Simon. 1991. *Instant Empire: Saddam Hussein's Ambition for Iraq*. San Francisco: Mercury House.

Hengel, Martin. 1989. *The Zealots: Investigations into the Jewish Freedom Movement in the Period from Herod I until 70 A.D.* Trans. David Smith. Edinburgh: T. and T. Clark.

Herzog, Chaim. 1984. *The Arab-Israeli Wars: War and Peace in the Middle East from the War of Independence through Lebanon*. Rev. ed. New York: Vintage Books.

Herzog, Chaim, and Mordechai Gichon. 1997. *Battles of the Bible*. London: Greenhill Books.

Heyd, Uriel. 1960. *Ottoman Documents on Palestine, 1552–1615: A Study of the Firman according to the Mühimme Defteri*. Oxford: Clarendon Press.

Hill, Rosalind, M. T. trans. 1962. *Gesta francorum et aliorum Hierosolymytanorum* (The deeds of the Franks and the other pilgrims to Jerusalem). London: Thomas Nelson and Sons.

Hill, John H., and Laurita L. Hill. 1962. *Raymond IV: Count of Toulouse*. Syracuse: Syracuse University Press.

———. 1968. *Raimond d'Aguilers: Historia Francorum Qui Ceperunt Iherusalem*. Philadelphia: American Philosophical Society.

———. 1974. *Peter Tudebode: Historia de Hierosolymitano Itinere*. Philadelphia: American Philosophical Society.

Hillenbrand, Carole. 1999. *The Crusades: Islamic Perspectives*. Chicago: Fitzroy Dearborn Publishers.

Hillenbrand, Robert. 2000. Introduction: Structure, Style, and Context in the Monuments of Ottoman Jerusalem. In *Ottoman Jerusalem: The Living City, 1517–1917*, ed. Sylvia Auld and Robert Hillenbrand, 1–23. London: Altajair World of Islam Trust.

Hirst, David. 1974. Rush to Annexation: Israel in Jerusalem. *JPS* 3/4:3–31.

Hiyari, Mustafa A. 2000. Crusader Jerusalem. In *Jerusalem in History*, ed. Kamil J. Asali, 130–76. New York: Olive Branch Press.

Hockstader, Lee. 2002. Blast Hits Central Jerusalem. *Washington Post*, January 28, A1, A17.

Hoffmeier, James K. 2003a. Egypt's Role in the Events of 701 B.C. in Jerusalem. In *Jerusalem in Bible and Archaeology: The First Temple Period*, ed. Andrew G. Vaughn and Ann E. Killebrew, 219–34. Atlanta: Society of Biblical Literature.

———. 2003b. Egypt's Role in the Events of 701 B.C.: A Rejoinder to J. J. M. Roberts. In *Jerusalem in Bible and Archaeology: The First Temple Period*, ed. Andrew G. Vaughn and Ann E. Killebrew, 285–89. Atlanta: Society of Biblical Literature.

Holm-Nielsen, Svend. 1993. Did Joab Climb "Warren's Shaft"? In *History and Traditions of Early Israel*, ed. Andre Lemaire and Benedikt Otzen, 38–49. Leiden: E. J. Brill.

Holum, Kenneth. 1997. Hadrian's Imperial Tour. *BAR* 23, no. 6:5–51, 76.

Horn, Siegfried H. 1966. Did Sennacherib Campaign Once or Twice against Hezekiah? *AUSS* 4:1–28.

Horovitz, David. 1989. Five Policemen, Pupils Hurt In Violent Disturbances in East Jerusalem. *Jerusalem Post*, October 17, 1.

Horowitz, Elliott. 1998. "The Vengeance of the Jews Was Stronger than Their Avarice":

Modern Historians and the Persian Conquest of Jerusalem in 614. *Jewish Social Studies* 4, no. 2:1–39.

Horsley, Richard A. 1986. The Zealots, Their Origin, Relationships, and Importance in the Jewish Revolt. *NT* 28, no. 2:159–92.

———. 2002. Power Vacuum and Power Struggle in 66–7 C.E. In *The First Jewish Revolt: Archaeology, History, and Ideology*, ed. Andrea M. Berlin and J. Andrew Overman, 87–109. London: Routledge.

Horstman, Barry M. 1999. Dr. Nelson Glueck: Rabbi dug up truth. *The Cincinnati Post*, 26 May 1999.

Hudson, Michael C. 2000. The Transformation of Jerusalem, 1917–2000 AD. In *Jerusalem in History*, ed. Kamil J. Asali, 249–85. New York: Olive Branch Press.

Hughes, Matthew D. 1996. General Allenby and the Palestine Campaign, 1917–18. *JSS* 19, no. 4:59–88.

———. 1999. *Allenby and British Strategy in the Middle East, 1917–1919*. London: Frank Cass.

Humphreys, R. Stephen. 1977. *From Saladin to the Mongols: The Ayyubids of Damascus, 1193–1260*. Albany: State University of New York Press.

Hurwitz, David L. 1995. Churchill and Palestine. *Judaism* 44, no. 1:3–32.

Hussein ibn Talal. 1969. *My "War" with Israel*. As told to Vick Vance and Pierre Lauer. New York: Morrow.

Hutman, Bill, and Herb Keinon. 1996. Hamas Suicide Bomb Kills Eighteen in Jerusalem: Peres—We Are at War with Hamas. *Jerusalem Post*, March 4, 1.

Idinopulos, Thomas A. 1991. *Jerusalem Blessed, Jerusalem Cursed*. Chicago: Ivan R. Dee.

———. 1998. *Weathered by Miracles: A History of Palestine from Bonaparte and Muhammad Ali to Ben-Gurion and the Mufti*. Chicago: Ivan R. Dee.

Imber, Colin. 1990. *The Ottoman Empire, 1300–1481*. Istanbul: Isis Press.

———. 2002. *The Ottoman Empire, 1300–1650*. New York: Palgrave Macmillan.

Immanuel, Jon. 1996. Hamas Claims Sunday's Attacks. *Jerusalem Post*, March 1, 3.

Immanuel, Jon, and Arieh O'Sullivan. 1996. Four Killed in Clashes between IDF, PA Police. *Jerusalem Post*, September 26, 1.

Isaac, Benjamin. 1980–81. Roman Colonies in Judaea: The Foundation of Aelia Capitolina. *Talanta* 12–13:31–54.

———. 1983–84. Cassius Dio on the Revolt of Bar Kokhba. *SCI* 7:68–76.

Isaac, Benjamin, and Aharon Oppenheimer. 1985. The Revolt of Bar Kokhba: Ideology and Modern Scholarship. *JJS* 36:3–35.

Isaac, Benjamin, and Israel Roll. 1979. Judaea in the Early Years of Hadrian's Reign. *Latomus* 38:54–66.

Israeli, Raphael. 1978. *The Public Diary of President Sadat*. Part 1, *The Road to War (October 1970–October 1973)*. Leiden: E. J. Brill.

———. 1979. *The Public Diary of President Sadat*. Part 2, *The Road of Diplomacy (November 1973–May 1975)*. Leiden: E. J. Brill.

Izenberg, Dan. 1989. Security Crackdown Planned after Temple Mount Riot. *Jerusalem Post*, April 9, 8.

Jackson, John. 1969. *Tacitus: The Annals, Books I–III*. Cambridge, MA: Harvard University Press.

Jacobson, David. 1999. Sacred Geometry: Unlocking the Secret of the Temple Mount. Part 2. *BAR* 25, no. 5:54–63, 74.

———. 2002. Herod's Roman Temple. *BAR* 28, no. 2:19–27, 60–61.

James, Lawrence. 1993. *Imperial Warrior: The Life and Times of Field-Marshal Viscount Allenby, 1861–1936*. London: Weidenfeld and Nicolson.

Jbara, Taysir. 1985. *Palestinian Leader Hajj Amin Al-Husayni: Mufti of Jerusalem*. Princeton: Kingston Press.

Jehl, Douglas. 1997. Babylon Journal: Look Who's Stealing Nebuchadnezzar's Thunder. *New York Times*, June 2, A4.

Jiryis, Sabri. 1978. The Arab World at the Crossroads: An Analysis of the Arab Opposition to the Sadat Initiative. *JPS* 7/2:26–61.

Johnson, Edgar N. 1969. The Crusades of Frederick Barbarossa and Henry VI. In *A History of the Crusades*, vol. 2, *The Later Crusades, 1189–1311*, ed. Kenneth Setton, Robert L. Wolff, and Harry W. Hazard, 87–122. Madison: University of Wisconsin Press.

Jones, Horace L. 1930. *The Geography of Strabo*. London: William Heinemann.

Jones, Terry, and Alan Ereira. 1995. *Crusades*. New York: Facts on File.

Kamel, Mohamed I. 1986. *The Camp David Accords: A Testimony*. London: KPI Limited.

Kampeas, Ron. 1990a. Twenty-one Arabs Die as the Police Quell Temple Mount Riot. 125 Arabs Injured; Nineteen Israelis Hurt as Moslems Pelt Succot Worshippers at Western Wall. *Jerusalem Post*, October 9, 1.

———. 1990b. Riots—and Festivities—in the Jerusalem Area. *Jerusalem Post*, November 16, 18.

———. 1990c. Violent Clashes in East Jerusalem. *Jerusalem Post*, November 18, 8.

Kampeas, Ron, and Margot Dudkevitch. 1990. Capital Suffers Extraordinary Week of Violence. *Jerusalem Post*, March 16, 2.

Kampeas, Ron, and Bill Hutman. 1990. Curfews Set on Three Jerusalem Neighbourhoods after More Riots. *Jerusalem Post*, June 24, 1.

Karmi, Ghada, and Eugene Cotran, eds. 1999. *The Palestinian Exodus: 1948–1998*. Reading, UK: Ithaca Press.

Karsh, Efraim. 2000a. *Fabricating Israeli History: The "New Historians."* 2d ed. London: Frank Cass.

———. 2000b. Were the Palestinians Expelled? *Commentary* 110, no. 1:29–34.

———. 2001. The Palestinians and the "Right of Return." *Commentary* 111, no. 5:25–31.

Karsh, Efraim, and Inari Karsh. 1999. *Empires of the Sand: The Struggle for Mastery in the Middle East, 1789–1923*. Cambridge: Harvard University Press.

Karsh, Efraim, and Inari Rautsi. 1991. *Saddam Hussein: A Political Biography*. New York: Free Press.

Katz, Samuel. 1968. *Days of Fire*. New York: Doubleday.

Keinon, Herb. 1996. Gruesome Feeling Left at Site after Smoke Clears. *Jerusalem Post*, February 26, 5.

———. 1998. A History of Terror. *Jerusalem Post*, November 8, 3.

Kennedy, Helen. 2001. W Apologizes to Arab World for His "Crusade" Battle Cry. *Daily News*, September 19, 7.

Kenyon, Kathleen M. 1967. *Jerusalem: Excavating Three Thousand Years of History*. New York: McGraw-Hill Book Company.

Keppie, Lawrence J. F. 1984. *The Making of the Roman Army: From Republic to Empire*. London: B. T. Batsford.

Keys, David. 1990. Crisis in the Gulf: Saddam Harks Back to a Glorious Past. *Independent* (London), August 11, 9.

Khalidi, Rashid. 1997. *Palestinian Identity: The Construction of Modern National Consciousness*. New York: Columbia University Press.

———. 1999. Truth, Justice, and Reconciliation: Elements of a Solution to the Palestinian

Refugee Issue. In *The Palestinian Exodus: 1948–1998*, ed. Ghada Karmi and Eugene Cotran, 221–41. Reading, UK: Ithaca Press.

———. 2000. Introduction to *Jerusalem in History*, ed. Kamil J. Asali. New York: Olive Branch Press.

———. 2001. The Palestinians and 1948: The Underlying Causes of Failure. In *The War for Palestine: Rewriting the History of 1948*, ed. Eugene L. Rogan and Avi Shlaim, 12–36. Cambridge: Cambridge University Press.

Khalidi, Walid. 1991. *Before Their Diaspora: A Photographic History of the Palestinians, 1876–1948*. Washington, DC: Institute for Palestine Studies.

Kimmerling, Baruch, and Joel S. Migdal. 1993. *Palestinians: The Making of a People*. New York: Free Press.

Killebrew, Ann E. 2003. Biblical Jerusalem: An Archaeological Assessment. In *Jerusalem in Bible and Archaeology: The First Temple Period*, ed. Andrew G. Vaughn and Ann E. Killebrew, 329–45. Atlanta: Society of Biblical Literature.

Kirkbride, Alec. 1976. *From the Wings: Amman Memoirs 1947–1951*. London: Frank Cass.

Kirsch, Jonathan. 2000. *King David: The Real Life of the Man Who Ruled Israel*. New York: Ballantine Books.

Klein, Amy. 1998. Carnage and Half-Priced Fruit. *Jerusalem Post*, November 8, 3.

Klein, Herbert A. 1986. *Temple beyond Time: Mount Moriah; From Solomon's Temple to Christian and Islamic Shrines*. Malibu: Joseph Simon Pangloss Press.

Klein, Menachem. 2001. *Jerusalem: The Contested City*. Trans. Haim Watzman. New York: New York University Press.

Kletter, Raz. 2003. A Very General Archaeologist: Moshe Dayan and Israeli Archaeology. *JHS* 4, article 5:1–42. Available online at http://www.purl.org/jhs.

Kleven, Terence. 1994a. Up the Waterspout: How David's General Joab Got Inside Jerusalem. *BAR* 20, no. 4:34–35.

———. 1994b. The Use of *snr* in 2 Sam. 5:8: Hebrew Usage and Comparative Philology. *VT* 44:195–204.

Klinghoffer, Judith A. 2002. Jewish Terrorism. *History News Network*, July 8. http://hnn.us/articles/832.html.

Knauf, Ernst Axel. 1997. Le Roi est Mort, Vive Le Roi! A Biblical Argument for the Historicity of Solomon. In *The Age of Solomon: Scholarship at the Turn of the Millennium*, ed. Lowell K. Handy, 81–95. Leiden: E. J. Brill.

———. 2000a. Jerusalem in the Late Bronze and Early Iron Ages: A Proposal. *TA* 27:75–90.

———. 2000b. Ottoman Jerusalem in Western Eyes. In *Ottoman Jerusalem: The Living City, 1517–1917*, ed. Sylvia Auld and Robert Hillenbrand, 73–76. London: Altajair World of Islam Trust.

Koestler, Arthur. 1976. *The Thirteenth Tribe: The Khazar Empire and Its Heritage*. New York: Random House.

Kokkinos, Nikos. 2002. Herod's Horrid Death. *BAR* 28, no. 2:28–35, 62.

Kollek, Teddy, and Moshe Pearlman. 1968. *Jerusalem: Sacred City of Mankind: A History of Forty Centuries*. London: Weidenfeld and Nicolson.

Krey, August C. 1958. *The First Crusade: The Accounts of Eye-Witnesses and Participants*. Gloucester, MA: Peter Smith.

Krystall, Nathan. 1998. The De-Arabization of West Jerusalem 1947–50. *JPS* 27/2:5–22.

Kurtz, Howard. 2002. U.S. Doomed, Bin Laden Says on Tape. *Washington Post*, February 1, A13.

Kurzman, Dan. 1970. *Genesis 1948: The First Arab-Israeli War.* New York: World Publishing.

Laffin, John. 1975. *The Arab Mind Considered: A Need for Understanding.* New York: Taplinger Publishing.

Lahoud, Lamia. 2000. Rajoub Warns of Riots if Sharon Visits Temple Mount Today. *Jerusalem Post,* September 28, 1.

———. 2001a. PA Preparing for Sharon Victory. *Jerusalem Post,* February 5, 2.

———. 2001b. Fatah: Sharon Will Face Violence. *Jerusalem Post,* February 6, 2.

———. 2001c. US Condemns Capital Car Bombing; Bush Urges Arafat to Stop Violence. *Jerusalem Post,* February 9, 2A.

Lamb, David. 1990. Saddam Hussein Held Hostage by His Obsession with the Arab Myth. *Los Angeles Times,* October 12, A14–15.

Lamb, Harold. 1951. *Suleiman the Magnificent: Sultan of the East.* Garden City, NY: Doubleday.

Lane-Poole, Stanley. 1906. *Saladin and the Fall of the Kingdom of Jerusalem.* New York: G. P. Putnam's Sons.

Lapidus, Ira M. 1967. *Muslim Cities in the Later Middle Ages.* Cambridge: Harvard University Press.

Laqueur, Walter. 1990. Like Hitler, but Different. *Washington Post,* August 31, A27.

———. 2002. Unintended War, Unintended Consequences. *Jerusalem Post,* May 31, 13B.

Laqueur, Walter, and Barry Rubin, eds. 1985. *The Israel-Arab Reader: A Documentary History of the Middle East Conflict.* 4th ed. New York: Facts on File.

———. 2001. *The Israel-Arab Reader: A Documentary History of the Middle East Conflict.* 6th ed. New York: Penguin Books.

Lau-Lavie, Naphtali. 1968. *Moshe Dayan: A Biography.* London: Vallentine, Mitchell.

Lawrence, Thomas E. 1935. *The Seven Pillars of Wisdom.* New York: Doubleday, Doran, and Company.

Lazaroff, Tovah. 2000. The Aftershock of a Bomb: Mahaneh Yehuda Shopkeepers Say They're Not Afraid. *Jerusalem Post,* November 10, 3.

———. 2002a. Ross: Arafat Said Temple Was in Nablus. *Jerusalem Post,* May 15, 1.

———. 2002b. Eight Killed, 86 Wounded in Hebrew U. Attack: Hamas Claims Responsibility; Says It "Avenged Shehadeh." *Jerusalem Post,* August 1, 1.

Lazarus-Yafeh, Hava. 1974. The Sanctity of Jerusalem in Islam. In *Jerusalem,* ed. John M. Oesterreicher and Anne Sinai, 211–25. New York: John Day Company.

Lefkovits, Etgar. 2000a. Sharon's Planned Visit to Temple Mount Angers Palestinians. *Jerusalem Post,* September 27, 3.

———. 2000b. Thirty-four Hurt in Riot after Sharon's Visit to Mount. *Jerusalem Post,* September 29, 4.

———. 2000c. Islamic Jihad Says It Was Responsible for Car Bomb. *Jerusalem Post,* November 3, 4.

———. 2001a. 1930 Moslem Council Guide: Jewish Temple Mount Connection "beyond dispute." *Jerusalem Post,* January 26, 3A.

———. 2001b. Sixteenth Maccabiah Games Open; Two Terrorists Die Nearby while Preparing Bomb. *Jerusalem Post,* July 17, 1.

———. 2001c. Two Bombs Rock Jerusalem. *Jerusalem Post,* March 28, 1.

———. 2001d. Bomb Disaster Averted by Jerusalem Pub Owner. *Jerusalem Post,* May 20, 4.

———. 2001e. Weekend Bombs Rock Central Jerusalem. *Jerusalem Post,* May 29, 2.

———. 2001f. Watermelon Bomb Discovered by Bus Driver. *Jerusalem Post,* July 29, 2.

———. 2001g. Fifteen Killed in Jerusalem Suicide Bombing; Cabinet Deliberates Retaliation for Attack. *Jerusalem Post,* August 10, 1A.

———. 2001h. Jerusalem Car Bomb Fails to Trigger Larger Bomb. *Jerusalem Post,* August 22, 1.

———. 2001i. Four Bombings in Seven Hours Shake Jerusalem. *Jerusalem Post,* September 4, 1.

———. 2001j. Car Bomb Explodes in Southern Jerusalem. *Jerusalem Post,* October 3, 3.

———. 2001k. No Injuries in King David Explosion. *Jerusalem Post,* November 19, 2.

———. 2001l. Terrorists Strike in Jerusalem Center: Eleven Dead, 160 Wounded in Kikar Zion Suicide Attacks. *Jerusalem Post,* December 2, 1.

———. 2001m. Suicide Bomber Wounds Two in Capital. *Jerusalem Post,* December 6, 3.

———. 2002a. Bomber Kills Eleven in Jerusalem; Two Babies among Dead, Fifty-seven Wounded in Beit Yisrael Attack. *Jerusalem Post,* March 3, 1.

———. 2002b. Waiter Foils Jerusalem Café Bombing. *Jerusalem Post,* March 8, 3A.

———. 2002c. Suicide Bomber Attacks Bus in Jerusalem. *Jerusalem Post,* March 18, 3.

———. 2002d. Suicide Bomber Kills Three in Jerusalem. *Jerusalem Post,* March 22, 1A.

———. 2002e. Female Suicide Bomber Kills Two at Capital Supermarket. *Jerusalem Post,* March 31, 3.

———. 2002f. Six Killed, Eighty-four Wounded in Jerusalem Bombing. *Jerusalem Post,* April 14, 1.

———. 2002g. Nineteen Killed in Jerusalem Bus Bombing. *Jerusalem Post,* June 19, 1.

———. 2002h. Six Killed in North Jerusalem Attack. *Jerusalem Post,* June 20, 1.

———. 2002i. Eleven Die in Jerusalem Bus Bombing: Grandmother, Grandson, Mother, Son among Dead. *Jerusalem Post,* November 22, 1A.

———. 2003a. Seven Killed in Jerusalem Bus Bombing; Bomber Was Dressed as a Religious Jew. *Jerusalem Post,* May 19, 1.

———. 2003b. At Least Eighteen Killed in Jerusalem Bus Bombing: Many Children among Victims; Both Jihad, Hamas Claim Responsibility. *Jerusalem Post,* August 20, 1.

———. 2003c. Jerusalem Remains on "Red Alert." *Jerusalem Post,* September 11, 3.

Lefkovits, Etgar, and Margot Dudkevitch. 2001. Jerusalem Bomb Injures Two Workers. *Jerusalem Post,* November 15, 3.

Lefkovits, Etgar, and Herb Keinon. 2001a. Concern at New Digging on Temple Mount. *Jerusalem Post,* January 22, 2.

———. 2001b. Unknown Groups Claim Jerusalem Car Bombing. *Jerusalem Post,* February 9, 1A.

Lefkovits, Etgar, Herb Keinon, and Margot Dudkevitch. 2002. Female Suicide Bomber Kills One in Capital; Over 150 Treated in Second Jaffa Road Attack in Five Days. *Jerusalem Post,* January 28, 1.

Lefkovits, Etgar, and Arieh O'Sullivan. 2001. IDF Reinforces Jerusalem after Suicide Bombing. *Jerusalem Post,* September 5, 1.

Lefkovits, Etgar, and David Rudge. 2002. Eleven Killed in Jerusalem Suicide Attack. *Jerusalem Post,* March 10, 1.

Lemaire, Andre. 1994. "House of David" Restored in Moabite Inscription. *BAR* 20, no. 3:30–37.

Lemche, Niels Peter. 1997. Clio Is Also among the Muses! Keith W. Whitelam and the History of Palestine: A Review and a Commentary. In *Can a "History of Israel" Be Written?* ed. Lester L. Grabbe, 123–55. Sheffield: Sheffield Academic Press.

———. 1998. *The Israelites in History and Tradition.* Louisville, KY: Westminster John Knox.

Lev, Yaacov. 1991. *State and Society in Fatimid Egypt*. Leiden: E. J. Brill.

Levin, Andrea. 2000. Media Mute on the Temple Mount Desecrations. *On Camera*, July 14. http://world.std.com/~camera/docs/oncamera/octemple.html.

Levin, Harry. 1950. *Jerusalem Embattled: A Diary of the City under Siege*. London: Cassell.

Levy, Avigdor. 1992. *The Sephardim in the Ottoman Empire*. Princeton, NJ: Darwin Press.

Lewis, Bernard. 1995. *The Middle East: A Brief History of the Last Two Thousand Years*. New York: Scribner.

————. 2002. *What Went Wrong? Western Impact and Middle Eastern Response*. Oxford: Oxford University Press.

————. 2003. *The Crisis of Islam: Holy War and Unholy Terror*. New York: Modern Library.

Lewis, Naphtali, and Meyer Reinhold. 1990. *Roman Civilization*. Vol. 2. 3d ed. New York: Columbia University Press.

Lewis, Paul. 1989. Ancient King's Instructions to Iraq: Fix My Palace. *New York Times*, April 19, A4.

Lewisohn, Ludwig. 1955. *Theodor Herzl: A Portrait for This Age*. New York: World Publishing.

Liddell Hart, Basil H. 1930. *History of the First World War*. London: Cassell and Company.

Linder, Amnon. 1996. Christian Communities in Jerusalem. In *The History of Jerusalem: The Early Muslim Period, 638–1099*, ed. Joshua Prawer and Haggai Ben-Shammai, 121–62. Jerusalem: Yad Izhak Ben-Zvi.

Little, Donald P. 1984. Relations between Jerusalem and Egypt during the Mamluk Period according to Literary and Documentary Sources. In *Egypt and Palestine: A Millennium of Association (868–1948)*, ed. Amnon Cohen and Gabriel Baer, 73–93. New York: St. Martin's Press.

————. 2000. Jerusalem under the Ayyubids and Mamluks, 1197–1516 AD. In *Jerusalem in History*, ed. Kamil J. Asali, 177–99. New York: Olive Branch Press.

Lipschits, Oded. 1999a. The History of the Benjamin Region under Babylonian Rule. *TA* 26:155–90.

————. 1999b. Nebuchadrezzar's Policy in "Hattu-Land" and the Fate of the Kingdom of Judah. *UF* 30: 467–87.

————. 2000. Judah, Jerusalem, and the Temple (586–539 B.C.). *Actes du Ve Colloque international. La Transeuphratene a l'epoque perse: religions, croyances, rites et images*, 120–34. Paris: Institut Catholique.

————. 2002. "Jehoiakim slept with his father . . ." (II Kings 24:6)—Did He? *JHS* 4, article 1:1–27. Available online at http://www.purl.org/jhs.

————. 2003. Demographic Changes in Judah between the Seventh and the Fifth Centuries B.C.E. In *Judah and the Judeans in the Neo-Babylonian Period*, ed. Oded Lipschits and Joseph Blenkinsopp, 323–76. Winona Lake, IN: Eisenbrauns.

Lipschits, Oded, and Joseph Blenkinsopp, eds. 2003. *Judah and the Judeans in the Neo-Babylonian Period*. Winona Lake, IN: Eisenbrauns.

Lloyd George, David. 1937. *War Memoirs of David Lloyd George: 1918*. Boston: Little, Brown, and Company.

Lockman, Zachary, and Joel Beinin, eds. 1989. *Intifada: The Palestinian Uprising against Israeli Occupation*. Boston: South End Press.

Lorch, Netanel. 1968. *Israel's War of Independence: 1947–1949*. 2d ed. Hartford, CT: Hartmore House.

Lord, John. 1970. *Duty, Honour, Empire: The Life and Times of Colonel Richard Meinertzhagen*. London: Hutchinson.

Lundsten, Mary Ellen. 1978. Wall Politics: Zionist and Palestinian Struggles in Jerusalem, 1928. *JPS* 8/1:3–27.

Lunt, James. 1984. *Glubb Pasha: A Biography*. London: Harvill Press.

Lyons, Malcolm C., and D. E. P. Jackson. 1982. *Saladin: The Politics of the Holy War*. Cambridge: Cambridge University Press.

Lyons, Ursula, and Malcolm C. Lyons. 1971. *Ayyubids, Mamlukes, and Crusaders: Selections from the Tarikh al-Duwal waʾl-Muluk of Ibn al-Furat*. Vol. 2, *The Translation*. Cambridge: W. Heffer and Sons.

MacKenzie, Hilary. 2003. "We Are Ready to Die": On the Twelfth Anniversary of the Persian Gulf War, One Hundred Units of the Al-Quds Army Parade through the Northern City of Mosul. *Montreal Gazette*, February 6, A18.

Macler, Frédéric. 1904. *Histoire d'Héraclius par L'évèque Sebèos*. Paris: Imprimerie Nationale.

Magen, Menahem. 1988. Recovering Roman Jerusalem: The Entryway Beneath Damascus Gate. *BAR* 15, no. 3:48–56.

Magness, Jodi. 1991. The Walls of Jerusalem in the Early Islamic Period. *BA* 54:208–17.

———. 1992a. A Reexamination of the Archaeological Evidence for the Sassanian Destruction of the Tyropoeon Valley. *BASOR* 287:67–74.

———. 1992b. Review of *The Damascus Gate, Jerusalem*, by Gregory J. Wightman. *BASOR* 287:96.

———. 1992c. Masada: Arms and the Man. *BAR* 18, no. 4:58–67.

———. 1993. *Jerusalem Ceramic Chronology*. Sheffield: Sheffield University Press.

———. 2000. The North Wall of Aelia Capitolina. In *The Archaeology of Jordan and Beyond: Essays in Honor of James A. Sauer*, ed. Lawrence E. Stager, Joseph A. Greene, and Michael D. Coogan, 328–39. Winona Lake, IN: Eisenbrauns.

———. 2002. In the Footsteps of the Tenth Roman Legion in Judea. In *The First Jewish Revolt: Archaeology, History, and Ideology*, ed. Andrea M. Berlin and J. Andrew Overman, 189–212. London: Routledge.

Maier, Paul L. 1999. Introduction to *The New Complete Works of Josephus*, trans. William Whiston. Grand Rapids, MI: Kregel Publications.

Mairson, Alan. 1996. The Three Faces of Jerusalem. *National Geographic*, 189, no. 4 (April): 2–31.

Makovsky, David. 1989. Intifada Violence Down in Capital. *Jerusalem Post*, July 5, 2.

Malamat, Avraham. 1950. The Last Wars of the Kingdom of Judah. *JNES* 9:218–27.

———. 1956. A New Record of Nebuchadrezzar's Palestinian Campaigns. *IEJ* 6:246–55.

———. 1968. The Last Kings of Judah and the Fall of Jerusalem: An Historical-Chronological Study. *IEJ* 18:137–55.

———. 1975. The Twilight of Judah in the Egyptian-Babylonian Maelstrom. *VT* Suppl. no. 28, 123–45.

———. 1979. The Last Years of the Kingdom of Judah. In *The Age of the Monarchies: Political History*, vol. 4, part 1. ed. Abraham Malamat and Israel Ephʾal, 205–21. Jerusalem: Massada Press.

———. 1990. The Kingdom of Judah between Egypt and Babylon. *ST* 44:65–77.

———. 1998. Let My People Go and Go and Go and Go. *BAR* 24, no. 1:62–66, 85.

———. 1999. Caught between the Great Powers. *BAR* 25, no. 4:34–41, 64

Mango, Cyril. 1992. The Temple Mount, AD 614–638. In *Bayt al-Maqdis: ʿAbd al-Malik's Jerusalem*, ed. Julian Raby and Jeremy Johns, 1–16. Oxford: Oxford University Press.

Mango, Cyril, and Roger Scott. 1997. *The Chronicle of Theophanes Confessor*. Oxford: Clarendon Press.

Manna, Adel. 1989. The Rebellion of Naqib al-Ashraf in Jerusalem, 1703–1705 [in Hebrew]. *Cathedra* 42:49–74.

———. 1994. Eighteenth and Nineteenth-Century Rebellions in Palestine. *JPS* 24, no. 1:51–66.

———. 2000. Jerusalem sous les Ottomans. In *Jerusalem: Le sacré et le politique*, ed. Farouk Mardam-Bey and Elias Sanbar, 196–204. Arles: Sindbad.

Mantel, Hugo. 1967–68. The Causes of the Bar Kokhba Revolt. *JQR* 58:224–42, 274–96.

Ma^ɔoz, Moshe 1975a. Changes in the Position of the Jewish Communities of Palestine and Syria in the Mid-Nineteenth Century. In *Studies on Palestine during the Ottoman Period*, ed. Moshe Ma^ɔoz, 142–63. Jerusalem: Magnes Press.

———, ed. 1975b. *Studies on Palestine during the Ottoman Period*. Jerusalem: Magnes Press.

Maranz, Felice. 1991. Alas, Babylon. *Jerusalem Post*, March 7, 38.

Marcus, Amy Dockser. 1996. Time Sharing: In Mideast Politics, Controlling the Past Is a Key to the Present—Clash over Tunnel Illustrates Volatility of Intertwining the Daily and the Divine—Ancient Stories Are Rewritten. *Wall Street Journal*, September 30, A1.

———. 2000. *The View from Nebo: How Archaeology Is Rewriting the Bible and Reshaping the Middle East*. Boston: Little, Brown, and Company.

Marks, Richard G. 1994. *The Image of Bar Kokhba in Traditional Jewish Literature: False Messiah and National Hero*. University Park: Pennsylvania State University Press.

Marlowe, John. 1946. *Rebellion in Palestine*. London: Cresset Press.

Marton, Kati. 1994. *A Death in Jerusalem*. New York: Pantheon Books.

Masalha, Nur. 1999. The 1967 Palestinian Exodus. In *The Palestinian Exodus: 1948–1998*, ed. Ghada Karmi and Eugene Cotran, 63–109. Reading, UK: Ithaca Press.

Matar, Fuad. 1990 (originally published 1979). *Saddam Hussein: A Biographical and Ideological Account of His Leadership Style and Crisis Management*. London: Highlight Publications.

Mattar, Ibrahim. 1983. From Palestinian to Israeli: Jerusalem 1948–1982. *JPS* 12/4:57–63.

Mattar, Philip. 1988. *The Mufti of Jerusalem: Al-Hajj Amin al-Husayni and the Palestinian National Movement*. New York: Columbia University Press.

Maxwell, Donald. 1920. *The Last Crusade*. London: John Lane Company.

Maysi, Kadra [Katherine Drayton Mayrant Simons]. 1917. A Christmas Hymn. *New York Times*, December 19, A9.

Mazar, Amihai. 1992. The Beginnings. In Jerusalem: Five Thousand Years of History, special issue, *LDA*, March, 24–31.

Mazar, Benjamin. 1957. The Campaign of Pharaoh Shishak to Palestine. *VT* 4:57–66.

———. 1986. Pharaoh Shishak's Campaign to the Land of Israel. In *The Early Biblical Period: Historical Studies*, ed. Shmuel Ahituv and Baruch A. Levine, 139–50. Jerusalem: Israel Exploration Society.

Mazar, Eilat. 1997. Excavate King David's Palace! *BAR* 23, no. 1:50–57, 74.

———. 2000. The Royal Quarter of Biblical Jerusalem: The Ophel. In *Ancient Jerusalem Revealed*, ed. Hillel Geva, rev. ed., 64–72. Jerusalem: Israel Exploration Society.

McCarter, P. Kyle, Jr. 1984. *II Samuel: A New Translation with Introduction, Notes, and Commentary*. Anchor Bible Series 9. Garden City, NY: Doubleday.

McCarthy, Justin. 1997. *The Ottoman Turks: An Introductory History to 1923*. London: Longman.

———. 2001. *The Ottoman Peoples and the End of Empire*. New York: Oxford University Press.

McGinty, Martha E. 1941. *Fulcher of Chartres: Chronicle of the First Crusade*. Philadelphia: University of Pennsylvania Press.

McKenzie, Steven L. 2000. *King David: A Biography*. New York: Oxford University Press.

Meinertzhagen, Richard. 1960. *Army Diary, 1899–1926*. London: Oliver and Boyd.

Meinhardt, Jack. 2000. When Crusader Kings Ruled Jerusalem. *AO* 3, no. 5:20–26.

Mendenhall, George E. 1962. The Hebrew Conquest of Palestine. *BA* 25:66–87.

———. 1973. *The Tenth Generation: The Origins of the Biblical Tradition*. Baltimore: Johns Hopkins University Press.

Merkley, Paul C. 1998. *The Politics of Christian Zionism: 1891–1948*. London: Frank Cass.

———. 2001. *Christian Attitudes towards the State of Israel*. Montreal: McGill-Queen's University Press.

Meyer, Michal. 2002. A City Won by Accident. *Jerusalem Post*, May 31, 4.

Milik, Josef T. 1960–61. La topographie de Jérusalem vers la fin de l'époque Byzantine. *Mélanges de l'Université Saint Joseph, Beyrouth* 37:127–89.

Millard, Alan. 1997. King Solomon in His Ancient Context. In *The Age of Solomon: Scholarship at the Turn of the Millennium*, ed. Lowell K. Handy, 30–53. Leiden: E. J. Brill.

Miller, J. Maxwell. 1974. Jebus and Jerusalem: A Case of Mistaken Identity. *ZDPV* 90:115–27.

———. 1975. Geba/Gibeah of Benjamin. *VT* 25:145–66.

Miller, J. Maxwell, and John Hayes. 1986. *A History of Ancient Israel and Judah*. Philadelphia: Westminster.

Miller, Judith, and Laurie Mylroie. 1990. *Saddam Hussein and the Crisis in the Gulf*. New York: Random House.

Mir, Mustansir. 1991. Jihad in Islam. In *The Jihad and Its Times: Dedicated to Andrew Stefan Ehrenkreutz*, ed. Hadia Dajani-Shakeel and Ronald A. Messier, 113–26. Ann Arbor: University of Michigan Press.

Mitchell, George J., et al. 2001. *Sharm El-Sheikh Fact-Finding Committee Final Report*. April 30. http://usinfo.state.gov/regional/nea/mitchell.htm.

Momigliano, Arnaldo. 1979. Flavius Josephus and Alexander's Visit to Jerusalem. *Athenaeum* 57:442–48.

Moore, Clifford H. 1931. *Tacitus: The Histories, Books IV–V*. Cambridge: Harvard University Press.

Moore, Molly. 2003. Instead of a Wedding, a Double Funeral in Jerusalem. *Washington Post*, September 11, 1.

Moore, Molly, and John Ward Anderson. 2003. Blast Devastates U.N. Baghdad Offices; Suicide Bomber Strikes Jerusalem Bus. *Washington Post*, August 20, 1.

Moran, William L. 1975. The Syrian Scribe of the Jerusalem Amarna Letters. In *Unity and Diversity: Essays in the History, Literature, and Religion of the Ancient Near East*, ed. Hans Goedicke and J. J. M. Roberts, 146–66. Baltimore: John Hopkins Press.

———. 1992. *The Amarna Letters*. Baltimore: Johns Hopkins University Press.

Mordike, John. 2002. *General Sir Edmund Allenby's Joint Operations in Palestine, 1917–18*. Paper no. 6. Fairbairn, Australia: Aerospace Centre.

Morgan, Margaret R. 1973. *The Chronicle of Ernoul and the Continuations of William of Tyre*. Oxford: Oxford University Press.

Morris, Benny. 1987. *The Birth of the Palestinian Refugee Problem, 1947–1949*. Cambridge: Cambridge University Press.

———. 1990. *1948 and After: Israel and the Palestinians*. Oxford: Clarendon Press.

———. 1999. *Righteous Victims: A History of the Zionist-Arab Conflict, 1881–1999*. New York: Alfred A. Knopf.

———. 2001. Revisiting the Palestinian Exodus of 1948. In *The War for Palestine: Rewriting the History of 1948*, ed. Eugene L. Rogan and Avi Shlaim, 37–59. Cambridge: Cambridge University Press.

———. 2002a. Camp David and After: An Exchange. 1, An Interview with Ehud Barak. *New York Review of Books*, June 13, 42–45.

———. 2002b. *The Road to Jerusalem: Glubb Pasha, Palestine, and the Jews*. London: I. B. Tauris Publishers.

Mullin, Dennis. 2003. Call It by Any Other Name, It Still Adds up to a Crusade. *Washington Post*, January 5, B2.

Murphey, Rhoads. 1999. *Ottoman Warfare, 1500–1700*. New Brunswick, NJ: Rutgers University Press.

Mutawi, Samir A. 1987. *Jordan in the 1967 War*. Cambridge: Cambridge University Press.

Myres, David. 2000. Al-ʿImara Al-ʾAmira: The Charitable Foundation of Khassaki Sultan (959/1552). In *Ottoman Jerusalem: The Living City, 1517–1917*, ed. Sylvia Auld and Robert Hillenbrand, 539–81. London: Altajair World of Islam Trust.

Naʾaman, Nadav. 1974. Sennacherib's "Letter to God" on His Campaign to Judah. *BASOR* 214:25–39.

———. 1979. Sennacherib's Campaign to Judah and the Date of the LMLK Stamps. *VT* 29:61–86.

———. 1991. The Kingdom of Judah under Josiah. *TA* 18:3–71.

———. 1992a. Canaanite Jerusalem and Its Central Hill Country Neighbours in the Second Millennium B.C.E. *UF* 24:275–91.

———. 1992b. Israel, Edom, and Egypt in the Tenth Century B.C.E. *TA* 19:71–93.

———. 1992c. Nebuchadrezzar's Campaign in Year 603 BCE. *BN* 62:41–44.

———. 1993. Population Changes in Palestine Following Assyrian Deportations. *TA* 20:104–24.

———. 1994a. The "Conquest of Canaan" in the Book of Joshua and in History. In *From Nomadism to Monarchy: Archaeological and Historical Aspects of Early Israel*, ed. Israel Finkelstein and Nadav Naʾaman, 218–81. Jerusalem: Israel Exploration Society.

———. 1994b. Hezekiah and the Kings of Assyria. *TA* 21:235–54.

———. 1994c. The Historical Portion of Sargon II's Nimrud Inscription. *State Archives of Assyria Bulletin* 8:17–20.

———. 1994d. The Canaanites and Their Land: A Rejoinder. *UF* 26:397–418.

———. 1995a. Rezin of Damascus and the Land of Gilead. *ZDPV* 111:105–17.

———. 1995b. Tiglath-Pileser III's Campaigns against Tyre and Israel (734–732 B.C.E.). *TA* 22:268–78.

———. 1995c. The Debated Historicity of Hezekiah's Reform in the Light of Historical and Archaeological Research. *ZAW* 107:105–17.

———. 1996. The Contribution of the Amarna Letters to the Debate on Jerusalem's Political Position in the Tenth Century B.C.E. *BASOR* 304:17–27.

———. 1997a. Historical and Literary Notes on the Excavations of Tel Jezreel. *TA* 24, 1:122–28.

———. 1997b. Cow Town or Royal Capital? Evidence for Iron Age Jerusalem. *BAR* 23, no. 4:43–47, 67.

———. 1997c. Sources and Composition in the History of Solomon. In *The Age of Solomon: Scholarship at the Turn of the Millennium*, ed. Lowell K. Handy, 57–80. Leiden: E. J. Brill.

———. 1998. David's Jerusalem: Fiction or Reality? Part 3, It Is There: Ancient Texts Prove It. *BAR* 24, no. 2:42–44.

Narkiss, Uzi. 1983. *The Liberation of Jerusalem: The Battle of 1967.* London: Vallentine, Mitchell.

Nebel, Almut, et al. 2001. The Y Chromosome Pool of Jews as Part of the Genetic Landscape of the Middle East. *AJHG* 69, no. 5:1095–1112.

Neff, Donald. 1984. *Warriors for Jerusalem: The Six Days That Changed the Middle East.* New York: Linden Press/Simon and Schuster.

Nelson, Richard. 1983. *Realpolitik* in Judah (687–609 B.C.E.). In *Scripture in Context*, vol. 2, *More Essays on the Comparative Method*, ed. William W. Hallo, James C. Moyer, and Leo G. Perdue, 177–89. Winona Lake, IN: Eisenbrauns.

Netzer, Ehud. 1991. The Last Days and Hours at Masada. *BAR* 17, no. 6:20–32.

Newby, Percy H. 1983. *Saladin in His Time.* London: Faber and Faber.

Newell, Jonathan Q. C. 1991a. Allenby and the Palestine Campaign. In *The First World War and British Military History*, ed. Brian Bond, 189–226. Oxford: Clarendon Press.

———. 1991b. Learning the Hard Way: Allenby in Egypt and Palestine, 1917–19. *JSS* 14, no. 3:363–87.

The New Encyclopedia of Archaeological Excavations in the Holy Land. 1993. Ed. Ephraim Stern, Ayelet Lewinson-Gilboa, and Joseph Aviram. New York: Simon and Schuster.

Nicholson, Helen J. 1993. *Templars, Hospitallers, and Teutonic Knights: Images of the Military Orders, 1128–1291.* Leicester: Leicester University Press.

———. 1997. *Chronicle of the Third Crusade: A Translation of the Itinerarium peregrinorum et gesta Regis Ricardi.* Aldershot: Ashgate.

Niemann, H. Michael. 1997. The Socio-Political Shadow Cast by the Biblical Solomon. In *The Age of Solomon: Scholarship at the Turn of the Millennium*, ed. Lowell K. Handy, 252–99. Leiden: E. J. Brill.

Nodet, E. 1986. La Dédicace, les Maccabées et le Messie. *RB* 93:321–75.

Nordau, Anna, and Maxa Nordau. 1943. *Max Nordau: A Biography.* New York: Nordau Committee.

Nordau, Max. 1941. *Max Nordau to His People: A Summons and a Challenge.* New York: Scopus Publishing.

Noth, Martin. 1981. *The Deuteronomistic History.* Sheffield: Sheffield Academic Press.

Nur, Amos, and Eric H. Cline. 2000. Poseidon's Horses: Plate Tectonics and Earthquake Storms in the Late Bronze Age Aegean and Eastern Mediterranean. *JAS* 27:43–63.

———. 2001. What Triggered the Collapse? Earthquake Storms. *AO* 4, no. 5:31–36, 62–63.

O'Ballance, Edgar. 1998. *The Palestinian Intifada.* New York: St. Martin's Press.

Oesterreicher, John M., and Anne Sinai, eds. 1974. *Jerusalem.* New York: John Day Company.

Oldenbourg, Zoé. 1966. *The Crusades.* Trans. Anne Carter. New York: Pantheon Books.

Olyan, Saul. 1998. "Anyone blind or lame shall not enter the house": On the Interpretation of Second Samuel 5:8b. *CBQ* 60:218–27.

O'Neill, Eugene. 1952. *A Moon for the Misbegotten.* New York: Random House.

Oppenheim, Ariella, et al. 2000 High-Resolution Y Chromosome Haplotypes of Israeli and Palestinian Arabs Reveal Geographic Substructure and Substantial Overlap with Haplotypes of Jews. *Human Genetics* 107, no. 6:630–41.

Oppenheimer, Aharon. 1982. The Bar Kokhba Revolt. *Immanuel* 14:58–76.

Oren, Eliezer D., ed. 2000. *The Sea Peoples and Their World: A Reassessment.* University Museum Monograph 108. Philadelphia: University Museum, University of Pennsylvania.

Oren, Michael B. 2002. *Six Days of War: June 1967 and the Making of the Modern Middle East.* Oxford: Oxford University Press.

Ostling, Richard N. 2001. Was Rome's Colosseum Paid for by Plundering Jerusalem Temple? Associated Press, July 23.

Overman, J. Andrew. 2002. The First Revolt and Flavian Politics. In *The First Jewish Revolt: Archaeology, History, and Ideology,* ed. Andrea M. Berlin and J. Andrew Overman, 213–20. London: Routledge.

The Oxford Encyclopedia of Archaeology in the Near East. 1997. Ed. Eric M. Meyers. New York: Oxford University Press.

PA Mufti Denies *Post* Report. 2001. *Jerusalem Post,* January 28, 3.

Pace, Guiseppe. 1978. Jebus sul monte e Shalem sul colle. *BeO* 20:213–24.

Padon, Gabriel. 1974. The Divided City: 1948–1967. In *Jerusalem,* ed. John M. Oesterreicher and Anne Sinai, 85–107. New York: John Day Company.

Painter, Sidney. 1969. The Third Crusade: Richard the Lionhearted and Philip Augustus. In *A History of the Crusades,* vol. 2, *The Later Crusades, 1189–1311,* ed. Kenneth Setton, Robert L. Wolff, and Harry W. Hazard, 45–85. Madison: University of Wisconsin Press.

Palumbo, Michael. 1987. *The Palestinian Catastrophe: The 1948 Expulsion of a People from Their Homeland.* London: Faber and Faber.

Pappé, Ilan. 1992. *The Making of the Arab-Israeli Conflict 1947–1951.* London: I. B. Tauris.

———. 1999. Were They Expelled?: The History, Historiography, and Relevance of the Palestinian Refugee Problem. In *The Palestinian Exodus: 1948–1998,* ed. Ghada Karmi and Eugene Cotran, 37–61. Reading, UK: Ithaca Press.

———. 2003. Haj Amin and the Buraq Revolt. *Jerusalem Quarterly File* 18:6–16.

Parker, Richard B., ed. 1996. *The Six-Day War: A Retrospective.* Gainesville: University Press of Florida.

Parson, Erwin R. 1991. The Psychology of the Persian Gulf War. Part 1, Gulf-Nam and Saddam Hussein's Nebuchadnezzar Imperial Complex: A Political Psychological Analysis. *Journal of Contemporary Psychotherapy* 21, no. 1:25–52.

Partner, Peter. 1982. *The Murdered Magicians: The Templars and Their Myth.* Oxford: Oxford University Press.

Peretz, Don. 1990. *Intifada: The Palestinian Uprising.* Boulder, CO: Westview Press.

Peters, Edward. 1971. *The First Crusade: The Chronicle of Fulcher of Chartres and Other Source Materials.* Philadelphia: University of Pennsylvania Press.

Peters, Francis E. 1973. *Allah's Commonwealth: A History of Islam in the Near East, 600–1100 A.D.* New York: Simon and Schuster.

———. 1985. *Jerusalem: The Holy City in the Eyes of Chroniclers, Visitors, Pilgrims, and Prophets from the Days of Abraham to the Beginnings of Modern Times.* Princeton: Princeton University Press.

———. 1993. *The Distant Shrine: The Islamic Centuries in Jerusalem.* New York: AMS Press.

———. 1994. *Muhammad and the Origins of Islam.* New York: State University of New York Press.

Peters, Joan. 1984. *From Time Immemorial: The Origins of the Arab-Jewish Conflict over Palestine.* New York: Harper and Row.

Pincus, Walter. 2001a. New Videotape Features Pale Bin Laden: Al Qaeda Leader's Message Was Made in Early December, U.S. Officials Say. *Washington Post,* December 27, A16.

———. 2001b. Bin Laden Fatalistic, Gaunt in New Tape. *Washington Post,* December 28, A1.

Pipes, Daniel. 2001. The Muslim Claim to Jerusalem. *Middle East Quarterly,* fall, 49–66.

———. 2003. The Refugee Curse. *Jerusalem Post,* August 20, 7.

Pirie-Gordon, Charles Harry C. 1919. *A Brief Record of the Advance of the Egyptian Expeditionary Force under the Command of General Sir Edmund H. H. Allenby, G.C.B., G.C.M.G., July 1917 to October 1918*. 2d ed. London: Her Majesty's Stationery Office.

Porath, Yehoshua. 1975. The Political Awakening of the Palestinian Arabs and Their Leadership Towards the End of the Ottoman Period. In *Studies on Palestine during the Ottoman Period*, ed. Moshe Ma'oz, 351–81. Jerusalem: Magnes Press.

Porten, Bezalel. 1968. *Archives from Elephantine: The Life of an Ancient Jewish Military Colony*. Berkeley: University of California Press.

Posener, Georges. 1940. *Princes et pays d'Asie et de Nubie: Textes hiératiques sur des figurines d'envoûtement du Moyen Empire*. Brussels: Fondation Égyptologique Reine Elizabeth.

Prawer, Joshua. 1980. *Crusader Institutions*. Oxford: Oxford University Press.

———. 1985. The Jerusalem the Crusaders Captured: A Contribution to the Medieval Topography of the City. In *Crusade and Settlement: Papers Read at the First Conference of the Society for the Study of the Crusades and the Latin East and Presented to R. C. Smail*, ed. Peter W. Edbury, 1–16. Cardiff: University College Cardiff Press.

Prawer, Joshua, and Haggai Ben-Shammai, eds. 1996. *The History of Jerusalem: The Early Muslim Period, 638–1099*. Jerusalem: Yad Izhak Ben-Zvi.

Price, Jonathan J. 1992. *Jerusalem under Siege: The Collapse of the Jewish State, 66–70 C.E.* Leiden: E. J. Brill.

Prittie, Terence. 1974. Jerusalem under the Mandate. In *Jerusalem*, ed. John M. Oesterreicher and Anne Sinai, 53–60. New York: John Day Company.

Purvis, James D. 1968. *The Samaritan Pentateuch and the Origin of the Samaritan Sect*. Cambridge: Harvard University Press.

Quandt, William B. 1986. *Camp David: Peacemaking and Politics*. Washington, DC: Brookings Institution.

Quataert, Donald. 2000. *The Ottoman Empire, 1700–1922*. Cambridge: Cambridge University Press.

Quigley, John. 1999. The Right of Displaced Palestinians to Return to Home Areas in Israel. In *The Palestinian Exodus: 1948–1998*, ed. Ghada Karmi and Eugene Cotran, 151–69. Reading, UK: Ithaca Press.

Rabinovich, Abraham. 1987. *The Battle of Jerusalem: June 5–7, 1967*. Philadelphia: Jewish Publication Society.

Raby, Julian, and Jeremy Johns. 1992. *Bayt al-Maqdis: ʿAbd al-Malik's Jerusalem*. Oxford: Oxford University Press.

Radler, Melissa. 2003a. Report presses for reparations for Jewish refugees from Arab lands. *Jerusalem Post*, June 25, 4.

———. 2003b. WJC asks UN to address Jewish refugee issue. *Jerusalem Post*, August 13, 7.

Rafeq, Abdul-Karim. 2000. The Political History of Ottoman Jerusalem. In *Ottoman Jerusalem: The Living City, 1517–1917*, ed. Sylvia Auld and Robert Hillenbrand, 25–36. London: Altajair World of Islam Trust.

Rajak, Tessa. 1981. Roman Intervention in a Seleucid Siege of Jerusalem? *GRBS* 22:65–81.

———. 1983. *Josephus: The Historian and His Society*. London: Duckworth.

Rappaport, Uriel. 1983. John of Gischala: From Galilee to Jerusalem. In *Essays in Honour of Yigael Yadin*, ed. Geza Vermes and Jacob Neusner, 479–93. Totowa, NJ: Published for the Oxford Centre for Postgraduate Studies by Allanheld, Osmun, and Company.

Read, Piers P. 1999. *The Templars*. New York: St. Martin's Press.

Redford, Donald B. 1973. Studies in Relations between Palestine and Egypt during the First Millennium B.C. Part 2, The Twenty-Second Dynasty. *JAOS* 93:3–17.

Rees, Matt. 2001. Saddam's Move. *Time*, August 27, 31.

Rees, Robert. 1989. Twenty-one Arrested as Funeral for E. Jᵓlem Youth Turns into a Riot. *Jerusalem Post*, December 12, 12.

———. 1990. Violent Rioting in East Jerusalem: Two Killed. *Jerusalem Post*, March 11, 1.

Reich, Roni [Ronny]. 1992. Back From Babylon: The Second Temple. In Jerusalem: Five Thousand Years of History, special issue, *LDA*, March, 46–55.

———. 1994. The Ancient Burial Ground in the Mamilla Neighborhood, Jerusalem. In *Ancient Jerusalem Revealed*, ed. H. Geva, 111–18. Jerusalem: Israel Exploration Society.

———. 1996. God Knows Their Names. *BAR* 22, no. 2:26–33, 60.

Reich, Roni [Ronny], and Shukron, Eli. 1999. Light at the End of the Tunnel: Warren's Shaft Theory of David's Conquest Shattered. *BAR* 25, no. 1:22–33, 72.

———. 2000. The System of Rock-Cut Tunnels near Gihon in Jerusalem Reconsidered. *RB* 107:5–17.

———. 2003. The Urban Development of Jerusalem in the Late Eighth Century B.C.E. In *Jerusalem in Bible and Archaeology: The First Temple Period*, ed. Andrew G. Vaughn and Ann E. Killebrew, 209–18. Atlanta: Society of Biblical Literature.

Reinhard, Karl J., and Peter Warnock. 1996. Archaeoparasitology and the Analysis of the Latrine Pit Soils from the City of David. In *Illness and Healing in Ancient Times*, ed. Ofra Rimon, 20–23. Haifa: University of Haifa.

Reinhart, Tanya. 2002. *Israel/Palestine: How to End the War of 1948*. New York: Seven Stories Press.

Reuters. 2002. Excerpts of Purported Statement by Bin Laden. *Washington Post*, October 15, A14.

Rezun, Miron. 1992. *Saddam Hussein's Gulf Wars: Ambivalent Stakes in the Middle East*. London: Praeger.

Rhoads, David M. 1976. *Israel in Revolution, 6–74 C.E.: A Political History Based on the Writings of Josephus*. Philadelphia: Fortress Press.

Richards, Donald S., trans. 2001. *The Rare and Excellent History of Saladin, by Bahaᵓ al-Din Ibn Shaddad*. Aldershot: Ashgate.

———. 2002 *The Annals of the Saljuq Turks: Selections from al-Kamil fiᵓl-Taᵓrikh of ʿIzz al-Din Ibn al-Athir*. London: RoutledgeCurzon.

Ritmeyer, Kathleen, and Leen Ritmeyer. 1989. Reconstructing Herod's Temple Mount in Jerusalem. *BAR* 15, no. 6:23–42.

Ritmeyer, Leen, and Asher Kaufman. 2000. Where Was the Temple? The Debate Goes On. *BAR* 26, no. 2:52–61, 69.

Roberts, J. J. M. 2003. Egypt, Assyria, Isaiah, and the Ashdod Affair: An Alternative Proposal. In *Jerusalem in Bible and Archaeology: The First Temple Period*, ed. Andrew G. Vaughn and Ann E. Killebrew, 265–83. Atlanta: Society of Biblical Literature.

Roberts, Paul William. 1997. *The Demonic Comedy: Some Detours in the Baghdad of Saddam Hussein*. New York: Farrar, Straus, and Giroux.

Rodan, Steve, Elli Wohlgelernter, and Margot Dudkevitch. 1997. Four Die in Triple Suicide-Bombing; PM After Jᵓlem Attack—We Can't Continue This Way. *Jerusalem Post*, September 5, 1.

Rogerson, John, and Philip R. Davies. 1996. Was the Siloam Tunnel Built by Hezekiah? *BA* 59:138–49.

Rohl, David M. 1997. *Pharaohs and Kings: A Biblical Quest*. New York: Crown Publishers.

Rolfe, J. C. 1930. *Suetonius*, vol. 2. New York: William Heineman.

Romey, Kristin M. 2000. Jerusalem's Temple Mount Flap. *Archaeology* 53, no. 2:20.

Rosen-Ayalon, Myriam. 1989. *The Early Islamic Monuments of al-Haram al-Sharif: An Icono-*

graphic Study. Qedem 28. Jerusalem: Institute of Archaeology, Hebrew University of Jerusalem.

Rosenthal, Monroe, and Isaac Mozeson. 1990. *Wars of the Jews: A Military History from Biblical to Modern Times*. New York: Hippocrene Books.

Rosovsky, Nitza. 1992. A Thousand Years of History in Jerusalem's Jewish Quarter. *BAR* 18, no. 3:22–40, 78.

Roth, Cecil. 1977. The European Age in Jewish History (to 1648). In *The Jews: Their History*, ed. Louis Finkelstein, 225–58. New York: Schocken Books.

Roth, Jonathan. 1999. *The Logistics of the Roman Army at War* (264 B.C.–A.D. 235). Leiden: E. J. Brill.

Royle, Trevor. 1992. *Glubb Pasha*. London: Little, Brown, and Company.

Rozen, Minna [Rosen, Minna]. 1982. The Mutiny of Nakib el Ashraf in Jerusalem (1702–1706) and Its Impact on the *Dhimmis* [in Hebrew]. *Cathedra* 22:75–90.

———. 1984. The Naqib al-Ashraf Rebellion in Jerusalem and Its Repercussions on the City's *Dhimmis*. *Asian and African Studies* 19:249–70.

Rudge, David, and Etgar Lefkovits. 2001. Car Bomb Explodes in Capital. *Jerusalem Post*, July 30, 1.

Runciman, Steven. 1951. *A History of the Crusades*. Vol. 1, *The First Crusade and the Foundation of the Kingdom of Jerusalem*. Cambridge: Cambridge University Press.

———. 1954. *A History of the Crusades*. Vol. 3, *The Kingdom of Acre and the Later Crusades*. Cambridge: Cambridge University Press.

Russell, James. 2001. The Persian Invasions of Syria/Palestine and Asia Minor in the Reign of Heraclius: Archaeological, Numismatic, and Epigraphic Evidence. In *The Dark Centuries of Byzantium (7th–9th c.)*, ed. E. Kountoura-Galake, 41–71. Athens: National Hellenic Research Foundation, Institute for Byzantine Research.

Russell, John M. 1991. *Sennacherib's Palace without Rival at Nineveh*. Chicago: University of Chicago Press.

———. 1998. *The Final Sack of Nineveh: The Discovery, Documentation, and Destruction of King Sennacherib's Throne Room at Nineveh, Iraq*. New Haven: Yale University Press.

Sacchi, Paolo. 2000. *The History of the Second Temple Period*. JSOT Supplement Series 285. Sheffield: Sheffield Academic Press.

Sachar, Howard M. 1979. *A History of Israel: From the Rise of Zionism to Our Time*. New York: Alfred A. Knopf.

Sack, Ronald H. 1991. *Images of Nebuchadnezzar: The Emergence of a Legend*. London: Associated University Presses.

Said, Edward W. 1988. Conspiracy of Praise. In *Blaming the Victims: Spurious Scholarship and the Palestinian Question*, ed. Edward W. Said and Christopher Hitchens, 23–31. London: Verso.

Said, Edward W., and Christopher Hitchens, eds. 1988. *Blaming the Victims: Spurious Scholarship and the Palestinian Question*. London: Verso.

Salibi, Kamal S. 1988. *A House of Many Mansions: The History of Lebanon Reconsidered*. Berkeley: University of California Press.

Sandars, Nancy K. 1985. *The Sea Peoples*. Rev. ed. London: Thames and Hudson.

Sanders, Liman von. 1927. *Five Years in Turkey*. Annapolis, MD: U.S. Naval Institute.

Savage, Raymond. 1926. *Allenby of Armageddon*. Indianapolis: Bobbs-Merrill Company.

Schäfer, Peter. 1980. Rabbi Aqiva and Bar Kokhba. In *Approaches to Ancient Judaism*, vol. 2, ed. William S. Green, 113–30. Chico, CA: Scholars Press.

———. 1981. The Causes of the Bar Kokhba Revolt. In *Studies in Aggadah, Targum, and*

Jewish Liturgy in Memory of Joseph Heinemann, ed. Jakob Petuchowski and Ezra Fleischer, 74–94. Jerusalem: Magnes Press.

———. 1990. Hadrian's Policy in Judaea and the Bar Kokhba Revolt: A Reassessment. In *A Tribute to Geza Vermes: Essays on Jewish and Christian Literature and History*, ed. Philip R. Davies and Richard T. White, 281–303. Sheffield: Sheffield Academic Press.

Schechter, Erik 2003. Suicide Bomber Kills Sixteen in Jerusalem; Hamas Terrorist Disguised as Haredi. *Jerusalem Post*, June 12, 1.

Schechtman, Joseph. 1965. *The Mufti and the Fuehrer: The Rise and Fall of Haj Amin el-Huseini*. New York: Thomas Yoseloff.

Schiff, Ze'ev, and Ehud Ya'ari. 1990. *Intifada: The Palestinian Uprising; Israel's Third Front*. Ed. and trans. Ina Friedman. New York: Simon and Schuster.

Schleifer, Abdullah. 1972. *The Fall of Jerusalem*. New York: Monthly Review Press.

Schmelz, Uziel O. 1975. Some Demographic Peculiarities of the Jews of Jerusalem in the Nineteenth Century. In *Studies on Palestine during the Ottoman Period*, ed. Moshe Ma'oz, 119–141. Jerusalem: Magnes Press.

Schmitt, John J. 1980. Pre-Israelite Jerusalem. In *Scripture in Context: Essays on the Comparative Method*, ed. Carl D. Evans, William W. Hallo, and John B. White, 101–21. Pittsburgh: Pickwick Press.

Schniedewind, William M. 1996. Tel Dan Stela: New Light on Aramaic and Jehu's Revolt. *BASOR* 302:75–90.

———. 1998. David's Jerusalem: The Lessons of Historical Geography. *BAR* 24, no. 6:12.

Schoenbaum, David. 1993. *The United States and the State of Israel*. New York: Oxford University Press.

Schoffman, Stuart. 2001. Looking beneath the Surface. *Jerusalem Report*, July 16, 45–47.

Schölch, Alexander. 2000. Jerusalem in the Nineteenth Century (1831–1917 AD). In *Jerusalem in History*, ed. Kamil J. Asali, 228–48. New York: Olive Branch Press.

Schoville, Keith N. 1994. Canaanites and Amorites. In *Peoples of the Old Testament World*, ed. Alfred J. Hoerth, Gerlad L. Mattingly, and Edwin M. Yamauchi, 157–82. Grand Rapids, MI: Baker Books.

Schwartz, Daniel R. 1990. *Agrippa I: The Last King of Judaea*. Tübingen: J. C. B. Mohr (Paul Siebeck).

Segev, Tom. 2000. *One Palestine, Complete*. New York: Metropolitan Books.

Sennott, Charles M. 2000. Sacred Site Holds Key to Mideast Peace: At Temple Mount, Faith and Nationalism Collide. *Boston Globe*, October 22, A1.

———. 2001. History, Animosity Vie at the Temple Mount. *Boston Globe*, March 15, 2001, A1.

Sethe, Kurt. 1926. *Die Ächtung feindlicher Fürsten, Völker und Dinge auf altägyptischen Tongefässcherben des mittlern Reiches*. Berlin: Preussische Akademie der Wissenschaften.

Shadid, Anthony. 2003. Scholars Urge Jihad in Event of Iraq War. *Washington Post*, March 11, A12.

Shanks, Hershel. 1975. *The City of David: A Guide to Biblical Jerusalem*. Washington, DC: Biblical Archaeology Society.

———. 1995a. *Jerusalem: An Archaeological Biography*. New York: Random House.

———. 1995b. Jerusalem 3,000: A Yearlong Celebration. *BAR* 21, no. 6:24–28.

———. 1997a. The Biblical Minimalists: Expunging Ancient Israel's Past. *BR* 13, no. 3, 32–39, 50–52.

———. 1997b. Masada. *BAR* 23, no. 1:58–63.

———. 1999a. Has David Been Found in Egypt? *BAR* 25, no. 1:34–35.

———. 1999b. First Person: New Life for an Old Theory. *BAR* 25, no. 1:6, 70–72.

———. 1999c. I Climbed Warren's Shaft (but Joab Never Did). *BAR* 25, no. 6:30–35.

———. 1999d. Everything You Ever Knew about Jerusalem Is Wrong (Well, Almost). *BAR* 25, no. 6:20–29.

Shapira, Anita. 1992. *Land and Power: The Zionist Resort to Force, 1881–1948*. Trans. William Templer. New York: Oxford University Press.

Shapiro, Haim, and Ron Kampeas. 1990. Riot Erupts in Old City. *Jerusalem Post*, April 13, 1.

Sharon, Moshe. 1975. The Political Role of the Bedouins in Palestine in the Sixteenth and Seventeenth Centuries. In *Studies on Palestine during the Ottoman Period*, ed. Moshe Ma°oz, 11–30. Jerusalem: Magnes Press.

Shavit, Yaacov. 1988. *Jabotinsky and the Revisionist Movement: 1925–1948*. London: Frank Cass.

Shea, William H. 1985. Sennacherib's Second Palestinian Campaign. *JBL* 104:401–18.

———. 1997. The New Tirhakah Text and Sennacherib's Second Palestinian Campaign. *AUSS* 35:181–87.

———. 1999. Jerusalem under Siege: Did Sennacherib Attack Twice? *BAR* 25, no. 6:36–44, 64.

Sheffy, Yigal. 1998. *British Military Intelligence in the Palestine Campaign, 1914–1918*. London: Frank Cass.

Sheldon, Rose Mary. 1994. Taking on Goliath: The Jews against Rome, AD 66–73. *Small Wars and Insurgencies* 5, no. 1:1–28.

———. 2001. Slaughter in the Forest: German Insurgency and Roman Intelligence Mistakes. *Small Wars and Insurgencies* 12, no. 3:1–38.

Shiloh, Yigal. 1981. Jerusalem's Water Supply during Siege: The Rediscovery of Warren's Shaft. *BAR* 7, no. 4:24–39.

———. 1984. *Excavations at the City of David*. Vol. 1, *1978–1982: Interim Report of the First Five Seasons*. Qedem 19. Jerusalem: Institute of Archaeology, Hebrew University of Jerusalem.

Shoshan, Boaz. 1984. On the Relations between Egypt and Palestine: 1382–1517 A.D. In *Egypt and Palestine: A Millennium of Association (868–1948)*, ed. Amnon Cohen and Gabriel Baer, 94–101. New York: St. Martin's Press.

Siegel, Judy, and Tovah Lazaroff. 2003. Father, Daughter Buried the Day of Her Wedding. *Jerusalem Post*, September 11, 1.

Silberman, Neil A. 1982. *Digging for God and Country: Exploration, Archeology, and the Secret Struggle for the Holy Land, 1799–1917*. New York: Alfred A. Knopf.

———. 1992. Who Were the Israelites? *Archaeology* 45, no. 2:22–30.

———. 1995. *The Hidden Scrolls*. New York: Grosset Books.

———. 1997. Structuring the Past: Israelis, Palestinians, and the Symbolic Authority of Archaeological Monuments. In *The Archaeology of Israel: Constructing the Past, Interpreting the Present*, ed. Neil A. Silberman and David B. Small, 62–81. Sheffield: Sheffield Academic Press.

———. 2001. If I Forget Thee, O Jerusalem: Archaeology, Religious Commemoration, and Nationalism in a Disputed City, 1801–2001. *Nations and Nationalism* 7, no. 4:487–504.

———. 2002. The First Revolt and Its Afterlife. In *The First Jewish Revolt: Archaeology, History, and Ideology*, ed. Andrea M. Berlin and J. Andrew Overman, 237–52. London: Routledge.

———. 2003. Archaeology, Ideology, and the Search for David and Solomon. In *Jerusalem in Bible and Archaeology: The First Temple Period*, ed. Andrew G. Vaughn and Ann E. Killebrew, 395–405. Atlanta: Society of Biblical Literature.

Silberman, Neil A., and David B. Small, eds. 1997. *The Archaeology of Israel: Constructing the Past, Interpreting the Present. JSOT* Supplement Series 237. Sheffield: Sheffield Academic Press.

Silver, Eric. 1984. *Begin: The Haunted Prophet.* New York: Random House.

Sim, Katharine. 1984. *David Roberts R.A., 1796–1864: A Biography.* London: Quartet Books.

Simons, Geoff. 1996. *Iraq: From Sumer to Saddam.* New York: St. Martin's Press.

Singer, Amy. 1994. *Palestinian Peasants and Ottoman Officials: Rural Administration around Sixteenth-Century Jerusalem.* Cambridge: Cambridge University Press.

———. 2002. *Constructing Ottoman Beneficence: An Imperial Soup Kitchen in Jerusalem.* Albany: State University of New York Press.

Sivan, Emmanuel. 1995. *Mythes Politiques Arabes.* Translated from the Hebrew by Nicolas Weill. Paris: Librairie Arthème Fayard.

Sivan, Renée, and Giora Solar. 2000. Excavations in the Jerusalem Citadel, 1980–1988. In *Ancient Jerusalem Revealed,* ed. Hillel Geva, rev. ed., 168–76. Jerusalem: Israel Exploration Society.

Skorecki, Karl, et al. 1997. Y Chromosomes of Jewish Priests. *Nature* 385:32.

Slater, Robert. 1991. *Warrior Statesman: The Life of Moshe Dayan.* New York: St. Martin's Press.

Slaughter, Gertrude E. T. 1955. *Saladin (1138–1193): A Biography.* New York: Exposition Press.

Smallwood, E. Mary. 1957. The Chronology of Gaius' Attempt to Desecrate the Temple. *Latomus* 16:3–17.

———. 1959. The Legislation of Hadrian and Antoninus Pius against Circumcision. *Latomus* 18:334–47.

———. 1976. *The Jews under Roman Rule.* Leiden: E. J. Brill.

Smith, George A. 1972. *Jerusalem: The Topography, Economics, and History from the Earliest Times to A.D. 70.* New York: Ktav Publishing House.

Smith, Morton. 1971. Zealots and Sicarii: Their Origins and Relations. *HTR* 64:1–19.

Snetsinger, John. 1974. *Truman, the Jewish Vote, and the Creation of Israel.* Stanford: Hoover Institution Press.

Sommers, Cecil. 1919. *Temporary Crusaders.* London: John Lane Company.

Sontag, Deborah. 2000. Battle at Jerusalem Holy Site Leaves Four Dead and Two Hundred Hurt. *New York Times,* September 30, 1.

Sprinzak, Ehud. 1999. *Brother against Brother: Violence and Extremism in Israeli Politics from Altalena to the Rabin Assassination.* New York: Free Press.

Spuler, Bertold. 1969. *The Age of the Caliphs.* Trans. F. R. C. Bagley. Princeton, NJ: Markus Wiener Publishers.

Stager, Lawrence E. 1996. The Fury of Babylon: Ashkelon and the Archaeology of Destruction. *BAR* 22, no. 1:56–69, 76–77.

Stanislawski, Michael. 2001. *Zionism and the Fin de Siècle: Cosmopolitanism and Nationalism from Nordau to Jabotinsky.* Berkeley: University of California Press.

Stein, Kenneth W. 1991a. A Historiographic Review of Literature on the Origins of the Arab-Israeli Conflict. *AHR* 96, no. 5:1450–65.

———. 1991b. The Intifada and the 1936–1939 Uprising: A Comparison of the Palestinian Arab Communities. In *The Intifada: Its Impact on Israel, the Arab World, and the Superpowers,* ed. Robert O. Freedman, 3–36. Miami: Florida International University Press.

Steinberg, Gerald M. 2001. Arafat's Rewriting of History. *Jerusalem Post,* July 27, 8A.

Steiner, Margreet. 1993. The Jebusite Ramp of Jerusalem: The Evidence from the Macalister, Kenyon, and Shiloh Excavations. In *Biblical Archaeology Today, 1990: Proceedings of the Second International Congress on Biblical Archaeology, Jerusalem, June–July 1990*, ed. Avraham Biran and Joseph Aviram, 585–88. Jerusalem: Israel Exploration Society.

———. 1998. David's Jerusalem: Fiction or Reality? Part 1, It's Not There: Archaeology Proves a Negative. *BAR* 24, no. 2:26–33, 62–63.

———. 2001. *Excavations by Kathleen M. Kenyon in Jerusalem, 1961–1967*. Vol. 3, *The Settlement in the Bronze and Iron Ages*. Copenhagen International Series 9. London: Sheffield Academic Press.

———. 2003. The Evidence from Kenyon's Excavations in Jerusalem: A Response Essay. In *Jerusalem in Bible and Archaeology: The First Temple Period*, ed. Andrew G. Vaughn and Ann E. Killebrew, 347–63. Atlanta: Society of Biblical Literature.

Stendel, Ori. 1974. The Arabs in Jerusalem. In *Jerusalem*, ed. John M. Oesterreicher and Anne Sinai, 148–63. New York: John Day Company.

Stephan, St. H., trans. 1980. *Evliya Tshelebi's Travels in Palestine (1648–1650)*. Jerusalem: Ariel Publishing House.

Stern, Ephraim. 2001. *Archaeology of the Land of the Bible*. Vol. 2, *The Assyrian, Babylonian, and Persian Periods (732–332 B.C.E.)*. New York: Doubleday.

Stern, Menahem, ed. 1974. *Greek and Latin Authors on Jews and Judaism*. Vol. 2, *From Tacitus to Simplicius*. Jerusalem: Israel Academy of Sciences and Humanities.

Stiebing, William H., Jr. 2001. When Civilization Collapsed: Death of the Bronze Age. *AO* 4, no. 5:16–26, 62.

St. Laurent, Beatrice. 2000. The Dome of the Rock Restorations and Significance, 1540–1918. In *Ottoman Jerusalem: The Living City, 1517–1917*, ed. Sylvia Auld and Robert Hillenbrand, 415–24. London: Altajair World of Islam Trust.

Stohlmann, Stephen. 1983. The Judaean Exile after 701 B.C.E. In *Scripture in Context*, vol. 2, *More Essays on the Comparative Method*, ed. William W. Hallo, James C. Moyer, and Leo G. Perdue, 145–75. Winona Lake, IN: Eisenbrauns.

Stone, Michael E. 1982. Reactions to Destructions of the Second Temple. *JJS* 13:195–204.

Sweeney, Marvin A. 1994. Sargon's Threat against Jerusalem in Isaiah 10:27–32. *Biblica* 75:457–70.

———. 2001. *King Josiah of Judah: The Lost Messiah of Israel*. Oxford: Oxford University Press.

Syon, Danny. 2002. Gamla: City of Refuge. In *The First Jewish Revolt: Archaeology, History, and Ideology*, ed. Andrea M. Berlin and J. Andrew Overman, 134–53. London: Routledge.

Syrkin, Marie. 1974. The Siege of Jerusalem. In *Jerusalem*, ed. John M. Oesterreicher and Anne Sinai, 61–84. New York: John Day Company.

Tadmor, Hayim, and Michael Cogan. 1979. Ahaz and Tiglath-Pileser in the Books of Kings: Historiographic Considerations. *Biblica* 60:491–508.

Talhami, Ghada Hashem. 2000. The Modern History of Islamic Jerusalem: Academic Myths and Propaganda. *Middle East Policy* 7, no. 2:113–29.

Tatum, Lynn. 2003. Jerusalem in Conflict: The Evidence for the Seventh-Century B.C.E. Religious Struggle over Jerusalem. In *Jerusalem in Bible and Archaeology: The First Temple Period*, ed. Andrew G. Vaughn and Ann E. Killebrew, 291–306. Atlanta: Society of Biblical Literature.

Tepperman, Jonathan. 1997. Previous Bombings in Mahaneh Yehuda. *Jerusalem Post*, July 31, 5.

Tessler, Mark. 1989. Arabs in Israel. In *Israel, Egypt, and the Palestinians: From Camp David to Intifada*, ed. Ann M. Leach and Mark Tessler, 89–124. Bloomington, IN: Indiana University Press.

Teveth, Shabtai. 1973. *Moshe Dayan: The Soldier, the Man, the Legend*. Trans. Leah and David Zinder. Boston: Houghton Mifflin Company.

Thomas, Lowell, with Kenneth B. Collings. 1938. *With Allenby in the Holy Land*. London: Cassell and Company.

Thomas, Mark G., et al. 1998. Origins of Old Testament Priests. *Nature* 394:138–40.

Thompson, Thomas L. 1992. *Early History of the Israelite People from the Written and Archaeological Sources*. Leiden: E. J. Brill.

———. 1997. Defining History and Ethnicity in the South Levant. In *Can a "History of Israel" Be Written?* ed. Lester L. Grabbe, 166–87. Sheffield: Sheffield Academic Press.

———. 1999. *The Mythic Past: Biblical Archaeology and the Myth of Israel*. New York: Basic Books.

Tibawi, Abdul L. 1969. *Jerusalem: Its Place in Islam and Arab History*. Beirut: Institute for Palestine Studies.

Tsafrir, Yoram. 1975. The Location of the Seleucid Akra. *RB* 82:501–21.

———. 1982. The Desert Fortresses in Judaea in the Second Temple Period. In *The Jerusalem Cathedra: Studies in the History, Archaeology, Geography and Ethnography of the Land of Israel*, vol. 2, ed. Lee I. Levine, 120–145. Jerusalem: Yad Izhak Ben-Zvi Institute.

———. 1992. Roman and Byzantine Jerusalem. In Jerusalem: Five Thousand Years of History, special issue, *LDA*, March, 66–77.

Tubb, Jonathan N. 1998. *The Canaanites*. Norman, OK: University of Oklahoma Press.

Turtledove, Harry. 1982. *The Chronicle of Theophanes*. Philadelphia: University of Pennsylvania Press.

Twain, Mark. 1895. *The Innocents Abroad*. Hartford: American Publishing.

———. 1898. Concerning the Jews. *Harper's Magazine*, March.

Ussishkin, David. 1982. *The Conquest of Lachish by Sennacherib*. Tel Aviv: Sonia and Marco Nadler Institute of Archaeology of Tel Aviv University.

———. 2003. Solomon's Jerusalem: The Text and the Facts on the Ground. In *Jerusalem in Bible and Archaeology: The First Temple Period*, ed. Andrew G. Vaughn and Ann E. Killebrew, 103–15. Atlanta: Society of Biblical Literature.

Vaughn, Andrew G. 1999a. Palaeographic Dating of Judaean Seals and Its Significance for Biblical Research. *BASOR* 313:43–64.

———. 1999b. *Theology, History, and Archaeology in the Chronicler's Account of Hezekiah*. Atlanta: Society of Biblical Literature.

Vaughn, Andrew G., and Ann E. Killebrew, eds. 2003. *Jerusalem in Bible and Archaeology: The First Temple Period*. Atlanta: Society of Biblical Literature.

Wardi, Chaim. 1975. The Question of the Holy Places in Ottoman Times. In *Studies on Palestine during the Ottoman Period*, ed. Moshe Ma'oz, 385–93. Jerusalem: Magnes Press.

Wasserstein, Bernard. 2001. *Divided Jerusalem: The Struggle for the Holy City*. New Haven: Yale University Press.

Wavell, Archibald P. 1929. *The Palestine Campaigns*. 2d ed. London: Constable and Company.

———. 1940. *The Palestine Campaigns*. 3d ed. London: Constable and Company.

———. 1941. *Allenby: A Study in Greatness*. New York: Oxford University Press.

———. 1944. *Allenby in Egypt (Being Volume II of Allenby: A Study in Greatness)*. New York: Oxford University Press.

———. 1946. *Allenby: Soldier and Statesman*. London: George G. Harrap and Company.

Weinstein, Allen, and Moshe Maʾoz, ed. 1981. *Truman and the American Commitment to Israel: A Thirtieth Anniversary Conference.* Jerusalem: Magnes Press.

Whiston, William. 1999. *The New Complete Works of Josephus.* Rev. ed. Grand Rapids, MI: Kregel Publications.

Whitehair, Charles W. 1918. An Old Jewel in the Proper Setting: An Eyewitness's Account of the Reconquest of the Holy Land by Twentieth Century Crusaders. *National Geographic* 34, no. 4:325–44.

Whitelam, Keith W. 1996. *The Invention of Ancient Israel: The Silencing of Palestinian History.* London: Routledge.

Wightman, Gregory J. 1989. *The Damascus Gate, Jerusalem: Excavations by C.-M. Bennett and J. B. Hennessy at the Damascus Gate, Jerusalem, 1964–66.* British Archaeological Reports International Series 519. Oxford: British Archaeological Reports.

———. 1993. *The Walls of Jerusalem: From the Canaanites to the Mamluks.* Mediterranean Archaeology Supplement 4. Sydney: Meditarch.

Williams, Daniel. 1990. The New King of Babylon? *Los Angeles Times,* September 6, A7.

Williamson, Hugh G. M. 1984. Nehemiah's Walls Revisited. *PEQ* 116:81–88.

Winer, Stuart. 2002. Mount Destruction. *Jerusalem Post,* February 1, 4.

Winkler, Claudia. 2001. The Iraq Report. *Weekly Standard,* October 17.

Winter, Michael. 1984. Military Connections between Egypt and Syria (including Palestine) in the Early Ottoman Period. In *Egypt and Palestine: A Millennium of Association (868–1948),* ed. Amnon Cohen and Gabriel Baer, 139–49. New York: St. Martin's Press.

Wiseman, Donald J. 1956. *Chronicles of Chaldean Kings (626–556 B.C.) in the British Museum.* London.

———. 1985. *Nebuchadrezzar and Babylon: The Schweich Lectures of the British Academy, 1983.* Oxford: Oxford University Press.

Wohlgelernter, Elli, and Amy Klein. 1998. Islamic Jihad Claims Jerusalem Bombing. *Jerusalem Post,* November 8, 1.

Woodfin, Warren T. 2000. The Holiest Ground in the World: How the Crusaders Transformed Jerusalem's Temple Mount. *AO* 3, no. 5:27–37.

Woodward, Bob, and Dan Balz. 2002. Combating Terrorism: "It Starts Today." *Washington Post,* February 1, A1, A16.

Yaʾari, Ehud. 1996. The New Canaanites. *Jerusalem Report,* September 19, 32.

Yadin, Yigael. 1963. *The Art of Warfare in Biblical Lands.* Jerusalem: International Publishing.

———. 1971. *Bar-Kokhba: The Rediscovery of the Legendary Hero of the Second Jewish Revolt against Rome.* New York: Random House.

Yahya, Adel H. 1999. *The Palestinian Refugees: 1949–1998.* Al-Bireh, Palestine: Abu Ghush Press.

Younger, Lawson K., Jr. 1996. Sargon's Campaign against Jerusalem: A Further Note. *Biblica* 77:108–10.

———. 1998. The Deportations of the Israelites. *JBL* 117:201–27.

———. 2003. Assyrian Involvement in the Southern Levant at the End of the Eighth Century B.C.E. In *Jerusalem in Bible and Archaeology: The First Temple Period,* ed. Andrew G. Vaughn and Ann E. Killebrew, 235–63. Atlanta: Society of Biblical Literature.

Yurco, Frank J. 1991. The Shabaka-Shebitku Co-regency and the Supposed Second Campaign of Sennacherib against Judah: A Critical Assessment. *JBL* 110:35–45.

Zadka, Saul. 1995. *Blood in Zion: How the Jewish Guerrillas Drove the British out of Palestine.* London: Brassey's.

Zeitlin, Solomon. 1962. Zealots and Sicarii. *JBL* 82:395–98.

Zerubavel, Yael. 1995. *Recovered Roots: Collective Memory and the Making of Israeli National Tradition*. Chicago: University of Chicago Press.

Zohn, Harry, trans. 1973. *Zionist Writings: Essays and Addresses; Theodor Herzl*. Vol. 1, January, 1896–June, 1898. New York: Herzl Press.

Zorn, Jeffrey. 1997. Mizpah: Newly Discovered Stratum Reveals Judah's Other Capital. *BAR* 23, no. 5:29–38, 66.

INDEX

Note: Page numbers in italics indicate maps, illustrations, and tables.

1 Chronicles, 19, 21, 28
1 Kings, 39
1 Maccabees, 76, 78, 80–82, 85–86
2 Chronicles, 39, 41, 44, 53, 56, 60, 62–63
2 Kings, 39, 42, 45–46, 48–52, 54–55, 59, 62–65
2 Maccabees, 75–76, 78–80, 82
2 Samuel, 21–22, 26

Aaron, 154
Ab, 61, 138. *See also* Ninth of Ab; Tisha-bᵓAb
al-Abbas, 157
Abbasid(s), 9, 156–57, 186
Abd al-Malik, 151, 154
Abd al-Rahman Azzam, 267
Abdi-Heba, 6, 8, 18
Abdullah (king of Transjordan), 274, 282, 284
Abdullah al-Tel, 278
Abdullah Pasha, 229
Abraham, 5, 30, 154
Abu Bakr, 148–49, 200
Abu Dhariᵓa, 228
Abu Harb Tamim, 9, 157
Abu Moslem, 156

Abu Sayfayn, 220
Abu Shama, 204, 215
Abu Ubaydah ibn Jarrah, 149–50
Acre, 114, 116, 202–4, 207, 213, 218, 227, 230. *See also* Akko
Adam, 154
Adar, 54
al-Adil, 204
Adonizedek, 19
Aegean region, 13, 15
Aelia, 149, 155
Aelia Capitolina, 131, 133–34, 137, 139
Aelia Hadrianus, 131
al-Afdal, 160–61
Agrippa, 111, 119
Ahab, 42
Ahaz, 8, 44
Ahmed III, 223
Akhenaten, 18
Akhetaten, 18
Akiba ben Yosef, Rabbi, 131, 134
Akkad, 54
Akko, 114. *See also* Acre
Akra, 8, 79, 81–82, 85–87
el-Alamein, 257
Al-Azhar University, 196

Aleppo, 195, 213–14, 219, *234*, 262
Aleppoans, *10*
Alexander Jannaeus, 8, 89–90, 99
Alexander the Great, 68–70, 73–74, 76, *94*, 227
Alexandria, 114, 116, 119, 166
Algeria, 290
Ali Faud Pasha, 241
Allah, 32, 167, 200, 219, 309
Allah Nebi, 247
Allenby, Edmund H. H., *10*, 150, 235–40, *243–44*, 246–51, 263–65, 274, 288–89
Allenby Barracks, 274, 288
Allenby Bridge, 274
Alptakin, 9, 158
Al-Qaeda, 233, 265
Al-Quds, 155
Al-Quds Ash-Sharif, 303
Altalena, 280
Amarna Letters, 18
Amaziah, 8, 44
Ambassador Hotel, 289
Amenhotep III, 18
American Colony Hotel, 289
Amorite(s), 15–17, 19, 32, 34, 115
Amr ibn al-As, 149
Anatolia, 3, 15–16, 212
Andrews, R. W. J., 241
Ankara, 15
Antenna Hill, 288
Antigonus, 9, 99–102
Antioch, 102, 114, 116, 145, 161
Antiochus Strategius, 142
Antiochus III (the Great), 8, *74–75*, 94
Antiochus IV (Epiphanes), 8, 69, 77–80, 82
Antiochus V, 8
Antiochus VI, 86
Antiochus VII, 8, 29, 87–89
Antipater, 8, 90, 99
Antiquities of the Jews (Josephus), 27, 53, 56, *58–59, 73–76, 80, 88, 90, 92, 100–101, 106, 110–12*
Antonia (fortress), 102, *104*, 114, 124–25
Anwar al-Sadat. *See* al-Sadat, Anwar
Apocrypha, 75–76
Apollonius, 79
al-Aqsa Intifada, 306. *See also* Second Intifada
al-Aqsa Martyrs Brigade, 305
al-Aqsa Mosque, 105, 137, 154, 156, 178–79, 181–83, 186, 195–96, 211, 223, 253, 279,

284, 301, 306. *See also* Masjid al-Aqsa; Palatium Salomonis; Templum Salomonis
aquila, 116. *See also* Eagle standard
Arab(s), 6, 9–*10*, 12–13, 29, 33, 35–37, 119, 149, 154, 166–68, 196–99, 201–2, 221, 229, 232, 233, 246–47, 251–60, 262–63, 267–70, 272–82, 284–86, 289–91, 293, 295–97, 300–301, 303, 306, 309
Arab Higher Committee, 254, 262, 272
Arabia, 33, 50, 147, 167
Arabian Peninsula, 148
Arabic, 3, 13, 30, 143, 155, 162, 247–48, 251–52, 304–5
Arab League, 267, 273
Arab Legion, 29, 275–78, 280–81, 284, 286
Arafat, Yasser, 6, 12, 136–37, 162, 197–98, 252, 301, 303–10
Aramaic, 28, 117
Aram-Damascus, 42, 44, 67
Araunah, 30
Archangel Gabriel, 146–47, 154
Archelaus, 9, 106, 108
Aretas III, 8, 90
el-Arish, 227
Aristobulus II, 8, 90–93, 95, 99–100
Armageddon, 37, 204, 250
Armenia, 91
Armitage, R., 242
Armstrong, Karen, 148, 251
Arsuf, 187, 203
Artaxerxes I, 70
Artuq, 161
Asa, 8, 42
Asali, Kamil, 33
Ascalon, 179, 187–88, 215. *See also* Ashkelon
Ashkelon, 44, 52, 114. *See also* Ascalon
Ashkenazi, 33
Asia, 75, 148, 155, 212, 215, 219, 227
Asia Minor, 159, 168
Asnam Pasha, 224
Assad, Hafez, 197–98
Associated Press, 36
Assyria, 18. *See also* Neo-Assyria
Assyrian(s), 15. *See also* Neo-Assyrian(s)
Ata Ali Hazzaa. *See* Hazzaa, Ata Ali
Atsiz ibn Uwaq, 159–60
Augusta Victoria Hotel, 293
Augusta Victoria ridge, 292
Augustus, 106, 108, 109
Avigad, Nahman, 48, 96, 121, 290
Aviram, Joseph, 290

Awad, Badi, 288
Ayyub, al-Malik al-Salih. *See* al-Malik al-Salih Ayyub
Ayyubids, 204–5, 209, 211
Azariah, 44
Azekah, 58
Azzam, Abd al-Rahman. *See* Abd al-Rahman Azzam

Baalbek, 183, 212
Baasha, 8, 42
Babylon, 5, 37, 45, 52–56, 58–60, 62–65, 69, 73, 102, 296–98
Babylonia, 18, 58, 64, 69. *See also* Neo-Babylonia
Babylonian(s), 15. *See also* Neo-Babylonian(s)
Babylonian Chronicles, 52, 54–55, 57
Babylonian Exile, 30, 64–67, 94, 297
Babylonian Talmud, 73
Baghdad, 37, 157, 197–99
Bailey, H., 242
Baladhuri, 149
Balfour, A. J., 237
Balfour Declaration, 237, 251–52
Balian (of Ibelin), 188, 192–94
Banu Zayd, 218
Barak, Ehud, 136, 198, 309
Bar Giora, Simon, 9, 117–18, 121, 128
Bar Kathros, 96, 127
Bar Kokhba, Shimon, 6, 94, 98, 132, 134–35
Bar Kokhba Rebellion, 97, 131, 135
Bar Kokhba Syndrome (Harkabi), 135
Bar Kosiba, Shim'on. *See* Bar Kokhba, Shimon
Barry, F. R., 241
Bar Simon, Eleazar, 9, 117, 121
Barzapharnes, 100
Basilica of the Resurrection, 226
Battering rams, 48, 62, 91, 123–24, 126, 142, 172
Battle of Hattin, 188
Battle of Manzikert, 159
Bayt al-Maqdis, 155, 162
Beck, W., 241
Bedouin(s), 10, 157–59, 218, 220, 234
Beersheba, 236–37, 239, 281
Begin, Menachem, 254, 256–57, 260, 267, 280
Beit ha-Miqdash, 155
Bengio, Ofra, 198
Ben-Gurion, David, 252, 258, 260, 272, 280

Ben-hadad, 42
Benjamin (tribe of), 8, 20
Benvenisti, Meron, 1, 309
Bernadotte, Count Folke, 258, 280–81
Betar, 253
Bethany, 245
Bethesda, 104, 232
Beth Horon, 115
Bethlehem, 149, 181, 239, 276
Bevin, Ernest, 261
Bible, 11, 13, 16, 19, 21–22, 26, 28–30, 32, 38–39, 42, 45–46, 49, 53–54, 57, 60, 199, 237. *See also names of individual books*
bin Laden, Osama, 6, 167, 195–97, 199–200, 233, 265
al-Bira, 206
Biran, Avraham, 290
Bir Salim, 12
Boas, Adrian, 181
Britain, 197, 231, 237, 243, 252, 260, 290
British, 5, 10, 13, 25, 29, 46, 150, 213, 235–43, 246–47, 249–52, 254–66, 268–70, 272–74, 278, 286, 290, 304
British Government House, 288
British Museum, 46
British Police Training School, 276, 289
Brown, Eddie, 268
Bukhara, 159
Bulay, 216
Bull, Odd, 286
al-Buraq, 154, 193
Burma Road, 279–80
Burnt House, 121
Bush, George W., 167, 181, 197, 265
Byblos, 187
Byzantine(s), 9, 137–40, 142–43, 144–46, 149, 155–59, 163
Byzantium, 139

Caesarea, 109, 112–14, 117, 155, 187
Café Hillel, 310
Cahan, Yaakov, 97
Cairo, 18, 158, 184, 196, 219, 237, 258, 290
Caligula, 9, 109–11
Caliph Umar. *See* Umar ibn al-Khattab (caliph)
Camp David, 136, 307–8
Camp David Peace Accords, 201, 233, 254
Canaan, 1, 13–19, 33, 51, 69
Canaanite(s), 2, 6–8, 12–13, 15–19, 25–26, 32–35, 39, 150

Carchemish, 51–52, 67
Cardo Maximus, 132
Carter, Jimmy, 201
Catholics, 10, 225–26
Central Valley, 2–3
Cestius Gallus, 9, 29, 113–15, 119
Chaldeans, 54, 58, 60, 62
Charlemagne, 157
Chechnya, 200
Chelebi (Tshelebi), Evliya, 219
Chetwode, Philip, 243
Chirac, Jacques, 136
Chislev, 81
Christ, 98, 138, 171, 175, 300. See also Jesus
Christian(s), 9, 30, 32, 37, 111, 137–39, 142,
    144–47, 149–50, 154, 157–59, 164–67,
    172–73, 182–83, 186, 194–95, 198, 203,
    206–7, 213, 216, 220–21, 226, 228, 230,
    233–35, 249, 251, 265–66, 293, 295, 300,
    306
Christianity, 64, 138, 155–56, 181, 231, 233,
    308
Chronicler, 39, 41, 44
Chronicles, Book of. See 1 Chronicles;
    2 Chronicles
Church, H. E., 241
Churchill, Sir Winston, 252, 265–66
Church of St. Anne, 182, 293
Church of St. Savior, 226–27
Church of St. Sion, 139
Church of St. Stephen, 171
Church of the Holy Sepulcher, 139, 146, 154,
    157–59, 195, 226, 228
Church of the Purification, 141
Church of the Resurrection, 158, 194
Cilicia, 91
Circumcision, 80, 131, 165, 179
Citadel (Jerusalem), 247
City of David, 2, 22, 70. See also Stronghold
    of Zion
City of peace, 1, 201, 232
Claudius, 109
Clemens, Samuel, 231
Clermont, 164
Clinton, Bill, 136, 308
Colosseum, 26, 129
Constantine, 138–39, 150
Constantinople, 138–39, 144, 164, 204, 219
Crassus, 9, 91, 93
Cromwell, Oliver, 236
Crusade(s), 159–60, 166–67, 185, 197, 202–3,

    205, 232–35, 249, 263–66, 268. See also
    individual Crusades, e.g., First Crusade;
    Fifth Crusade
Crusader(s), 5–6, 9–10, 29, 35, 105, 142, 151,
    156, 160–61, 164, 166–69, 171–98, 201–8,
    211–14, 216, 218, 227, 232–36, 251,
    264–66, 275, 285, 293–94
Cumanus, 9, 111
Cyprus, 15
Cyrus (the Great), 65, 69–70, 94, 145, 248,
    296

Daimbert, 183
Dajani-Shakeel, Hadia, 264
Damascenes, 10
Damascus, 150, 156–58, 183–84, 211–16, 220,
    224, 227–29, 234, 238, 290
Damascus Gate, 142, 170, 263, 276, 293
Dark Ages, 15
Daʾud, al-Nasir. See al-Nasir Daʾud
ad-Daula, Iftikhar. See Iftikhar ad-Daula
David, King, 3, 5–8, 11–13, 17–22, 24–33,
    37–38, 50, 63, 67, 68–69, 87–88, 95, 104,
    150, 160, 177, 204, 230, 285, 291
David's Tower, 204, 211. See also Tower of
    David
Davies, Philip, 34
Dayan, Moshe, 137, 198, 291–93, 294–96,
    300
Dead Sea Scrolls, 291
Declaration of Independence (Israel), 272–73
Declaration of Independence (Palestine),
    303
Declaration of Principles, 304
Decumanus, 132
Deir Yassin, 269–70
Demetrius I, 8, 86
Deuteronomistic History, 64
Diaspora, 32, 97–98, 134
al-Din, Nur. See Nur al-Din
ad-Din, Salah. See Saladin
Dio Cassius, 131–32
Diodochoi, 73, 94
Dome of the Rock, 5, 30, 137, 151, 153–54,
    160, 179, 182–83, 194–95, 206, 219–20,
    265, 302. See also Templum Domini
Domitian, 119
Dung Gate, 230, 292–93

Eagle standard, 116, 119
East Jerusalem, 284, 290–91, 294–96, 303

Edirne vakasi, 223
Edom, 57, 88
EEF. *See* Egyptian Expeditionary Force
Egypt, 3, 13, 15, 18, 25, 34, 38–39, 44, 46,
    50–52, 58, 64–67, 69–70, 73–75, 77–79,
    91, 94, 114, 116, 130, 155, 158, 160, 166,
    168, 183–87, 197, 199–201, 205, 207–8,
    211–16, 219, 227, 229–30, 232–34, 267,
    273, 282, 285–86, 290, 294, 297, 301
Egyptian(s), 6, 8, *10*, 13, 15–18, 39, 41,
    50–52, 56, 58–59, 67, 75, 87, 130, 158–59,
    161, 166, 179, 186, 201–2, 207–8, 211–14,
    216, 218, 229–35, 254, 265, 276, 281,
    285–86, 290, 294, 301
Egyptian Expeditionary Force (EEF), 236–37
Egyptian-Israeli Peace Treaty, 201
Ekkehard of Aura, 176
Elasa, 82
Elazar, David, 275
Eleazar bar Simon. *See* Bar Simon, Eleazar
Elephantine (island), 64
Elijah, 154
End Times, 37
Erekat, Saeb, 309
Ernoul, 186–89, 191–92
Etzel, 254
Eudocia, 139
Euphrates, 15, 51, 212
Eusebius, 131
Eutychius, 137–38
Execration Texts, 16, 25
Exodus, 32, 35
Ezekiel, 5, 53–54, 59–60, 64

Falkenhayn, General von, 239, 250
Falls, Cyril, 243, 246
Famine, 59, 86, 118, 123–25, 128, 132
Fatah, 299, 304–5, 307
Fatah Tanzim, 304–5
Fatima, 155, 158
Fatimid(s), 9, 158–61, 164, 166, 168, 184
Feast of Tabernacles, 89, 114
Federation of Arab Republics, 166
Festival of Lights, 69
Fifteenth Legion, 116, 119, 124
Fifth Crusade, 204
Fifth Legion, 116, 119, 124
Filastin, 13
Finkelstein, Israel, 48
First Crusade, 9, 168, 178, 234, *264*
First Intifada, *10*, 302

First Jewish Revolt, 96, 98, 102, 106, 111–12,
    135, 280
First Qibla, 151
First Temple, 30, 38, *43*, *94*, 129, 301. *See
    also* Temple of Solomon
First Triumvirate, 91, 99
Flavian dynasty, 119
Florus, 9, 112–13
Fourth Crusade, 204
France, 164, 197, 202, 214, 231, 236,
    264
Franks, 161, 168, 181, 190, 193, 202–4,
    206–8, 211–12
Frederick Barbarossa, 202
Frederick II (Hohenstaufen), 9, 205–6,
    233–34
Fulcher of Chartres, 168, 179–81
Further Mosque, 151, 154, 193

Gabinius, 8, 93
Gabriel (archangel), 146–47, 154
Gadara, 117
Galba, 119
Galilee, 86, 100, 114, 116–17, 230, 280–81
Gamala, 117
Gate of Benjamin (Jerusalem), 60
Gaugamela, 73
Gaul, 108
Gaza, 73, 188, 213, 215–16, 227–28, 230,
    236–37, 247, 256, 281, 304, 308
Gaza Strip, 6, 34
Gedaliah of Siemiatycze, 225
Gehenna (valley). *See* Valley of Gehenna
Genghis Khan, 212
Genoa, 172
Gesta, 168, 171, 174
Gezer, 38
al-Ghazzali, 185, 196
Gibeon, 19
Gihon Spring, 2, 22, 25–26, 48
Gilbert, Martin, 237, 249
Glubb, John Bagot (Glubb Pasha), 274,
    277–78
Glueck, Nelson, 257
Godfrey of Bouillon, 168, 171, 174–75, 182,
    191, 264
Golan Heights, 117
Golden Gate, 247
Golgatha, 226
Goliath, 20
Goodman, Alan, 302

Goren, Shlomo, 294
Gorenberg, Gershom, 3
Gospels, 110, 138. *See also* Luke; Mark; Matthew
Grand Mufti (of Istanbul), 223
Grand Mufti (of Jerusalem), 136, 162, 252, 254, 257, 284
Greece, 70, 78, 257, 301
Greek(s), 26, 32, 69, 73, 80, 93–94, 97, 136, 139, 144, 148, 165, 173, 229, 231, 248, 274
Greek Orthodox, 10, 225–26, 228
Greek War of Independence, 228
Green Line (Jerusalem), 282, 288–89
Gregory VII, 160, 164
Gur, Colonel Mordechai "Motta," 289–90, 293–94
Guy de Lusignan, 186–87, 202

Habiru, 7
Ha-biryonim (Cahan), 97
Hadassah Hospital, 262, 270, 276, 289
Hadassah Medical Center, 277
Hadrian, 9, 131–32, 134, 137–38, 145
Haganah, 252–54, 258–60, 268–69, 272, 274–75, 277, 281
Haifa, 187, 202, 230, 256, 258, 268
Haj Amin al-Husseini. *See* al-Husseini, Haj Amin
al-Hakim, 158
Halpern, Baruch, 19
Hamas, 304–5, 307
Hanukkah, 69, 82, 85, 93, 243
Hanukkiah, 69
ha-Qodesh, 155
Haram al-Sherif, 3, 30, 105, 136–37, 151, 154, 162, 182–83, 206, 213, 216, 218, 220, 253, 279, 284, 292–96, 300–303, 305–6, 309. *See also* Temple Mount
Harkabi, Yehoshafat, 135
Harun al-Rashid. *See* al-Rashid, Harun
HaShomer, 98
Hasmon, 95
Hasmonean(s), 8, 80, 84, 87–88, 94–95, 99, 101–2, 124, 267
Hasmonean kingdom, 83, 85, 87, 89, 94
Hassan ibn Mufarrij, 159
Hassan Pasha, 221
Hatikvah, 253
Hatti, 46
Hattin, 187–88
Hattusas, 15

Hazael, 8, 20, 42, 67
Hazael of Aram, 8
Hazor, 38
Hazzaa, Ata Ali, 291–92
Hebrew Bible, 17, 42, 44–46, 51–52, 55, 58, 64, 75
Hebrew University, 89, 254, 270, 290, 300, 307
Hebrews, 11, 20, 30, 32–33, 147, 154
Hebron, 20, 187, 207, 211, 215–16, 218, 229–30, 239, 253
Helena, 139
Heliodoros, 8, 75
Heliopolis, 156
Hellenistic age, 73
Heraclius, 9, 142, 145–46
Herod (the Great), 3, 9, 29–30, 70, 88, 99, 100–102, 105–6, 108, 111, 130, 137, 142, 178, 182, 290, 302
Herod Agrippa, 111
Herodian Jerusalem, 103
Herod's Temple. *See* Temple of Herod
Herzl, Theodor, 6, 68, 94, 98, 252, 267
Hezekiah, 8, 46, 48–50, 67
Hijra, 147
Hillenbrand, Carole, 265
Hill of Evil Counsel, 288
Hinnom Valley, 2
Hippicus, 102, 104, 130
Hitler, Adolf, 252
Hittites, 15, 16, 18
Hod, General Mordecai "Motti," 285
Holy City, 146, 149, 201–2, 248, 251, 265, 277
Holy House, 136, 149–50
Holy Land, 168, 183–84, 198, 202, 205, 216, 227, 234, 251
Holy war, 5, 148, 164, 167, 184, 292, 305, 309
Homs, 211–13
Horns of Hattin, 186
Hoshea, 44, 46
Hospitallers, 182, 194, 208
House of David, 63
Hugh de Payens, 182
Hurcomb, Frederick, 241
Hussein (king of Jordan), 285–86, 290, 292, 295
Hussein, Saddam, 6, 36–37, 65, 66, 184, 197–99, 284, 286, 290–91
Husseini, Adnan, 137
Husseini, Faisal, 12, 16, 33, 252

al-Husseini, Haj Amin, 252, 254, 257, 284
al-Husseini, Mustafa, 221, 223, 225
al-Husseini, Selim, 241, 249
Hyrcanus II, 8, 90–93, 95, 99–100

Ibn Abi'l-Fada'il, 216
Ibn al-As, Amr. *See* Amr ibn al-As
Ibn al-Athir, 159–61, 168, 177, 179, 186–90,
    192–95
Ibn al-Furat, 208, 211–15
Ibn al-Jawzi, 168
Ibn al-Khattab, Umar (caliph). *See* Umar ibn
    al-Khattab (caliph)
Ibn al-Qalanisi, 168
Ibn Jarrah, Abu Ubaydah. *See* Abu Ubaydah
    ibn Jarrah
Ibn Mufarrij, Hassan. *See* Hassan ibn Mufarrij
Ibn Muyassar, 168
Ibn Shaddad, 186, 188–89, 191–92, 199, 215
Ibn Uwaq, Atsiz. *See* Atsiz ibn Uwaq
Ibn Wasil, 204–6
Ibrahim Pasha, 230
Idumea, 88, 90, 99, 108, 117
Idumean(s), 9, 90, 101
Iftikhar ad-Daula, 161
Ikhshidids, 9
Ilghazi, 161
Iliya, 155
Imad al-Din al-Isfahani, 186, 189, 194, 203
India, 200
Intifada(s), 302–4, 306–7. *See also* al-Aqsa
    Intifada; First Intifada; Second Intifada
Iran, 142, 219
Iraq, 6, 13, 36–37, 142, 146, 183, 197, 267,
    273, 290, 297
Iraqi(s), 36, 37, 149, 274, 286, 288, 291
Irgun, 10, 254–62, 267–70, 275, 280–81, 304
Irgunists, 254–56, 259, 261, 263, 268
Isaac, 5, 30
Isabel of Brienne, 205
Isaiah, Book of, 48, 64, 310
al-Isfahani, Imad al-Din. *See* Imad al-Din
    al-Isfahani
Ishbaal, 20
Ishbosheth, 20
Islam, 30, 35, 37, 137, 139, 142, 146–48, 151,
    154–57, 159, 162, 166–67, 184, 194,
    196–97, 212–13, 233–34, 308
Islamic Waqf, 137, 295–96
Israel, 1–2, 6–8, 13, 17, 19–21, 32–34, 38–42,
    44–45, 50, 55, 57–58, 67, 69, 74, 79, 81,

85–86, 93, 96–97, 100, 116, 134–36, 148,
    162, 166, 197–98, 201, 256–57, 259, 267,
    273–76, 280, 282–83, 285–86, 288,
    290–92, 294–98, 300–302, 304, 307–8,
    310
Israel Defense Forces (IDF), 280
Israeli(s), 6, 10, 12, 29, 33–35, 135, 166, 168,
    196, 198, 205, 251, 280–82, 284–85,
    288–89, 291–97, 300–302, 304–5, 308–9
Israelite(s), 3, 5–8, 11–13, 15, 17, 19, 26–28,
    30, 33–35, 42, 45, 297–98
Istanbul, 48, 219, 223–26, 229–30
Iznik, 220
Izzet Bey, 241

Jabotinsky, Vladimir, 6, 68, 94, 252–54, 267
Jacob, 38, 45
Jaffa, 172, 187, 227–28, 238, 259, 268. *See also*
    Joppa; Treaty of Jaffa
Jaffa Gate, 106, 144, 179, 242, 246–47, 263,
    268, 275, 293
Jaffa Road, 246, 252, 259, 300, 303, 305,
    307
Janissaries, 224
Japha, 117
Jason, 8, 76–79
al-Ja'uni, Yusuf Agha. *See* Yusuf Agha
    al-Ja'uni
Jebus, 16, 19, 21
Jebusite(s), 3, 5–8, 11–13, 15–17, 19, 21–22,
    25–30, 32–35, 37, 150
Jehoahaz (Jehoash), 8, 42, 44
Jehoiachin, 53–56
Jehoiakim, 52–54, 56, 67
Jehoshaphat, Valley of, 175. *See also* Kidron
    Valley
Jeremiah, 57–59, 62–65
Jericho, 60, 87, 117, 240–41, 248, 289, 291
Jerusalem, 1–3, 5–8, 10–13, 16–34, 36–39,
    41–50, 53–66, 69–75, 77–82, 84–91,
    93–96, 98–103, 106, 108–14, 116–23, 125,
    127–32, 134, 136–40, 142–46, 148–52,
    154–64, 166–75, 177, 179–84, 186–91,
    193–95, 197–99, 201–9, 211–59, 261–72,
    274–77, 279–82, 284, 286–96, 298–310
Jerusalem Army, 36, 65
Jerusalem of Gold, 294
Jerusalem Post, 162
Jerusalem 3000, 12
Jesus, 30, 108, 110, 130, 138, 147, 154, 175,
    247. *See also* Christ

Jew(s), 10, 12–13, 20, 29, 32–33, 35, 37–38,
  46, 56, 64–67, 68–70, 74–82, 85–86,
  88–89, 92–94, 97–98, 100–102, 105,
  108–9, 111–16, 119, 122–24, 127–29,
  134–39, 145–46, 161–63, 167, 179, 196,
  201, 220, 225, 227, 230–31, 233, 237,
  252–56, 260–63, 267–69, 272–73, 275,
  277–82, 284, 290, 294–98, 301–2
Jewish Agency, 260, 263, 269–70
Jewish Diaspora. See Diaspora
Jewish Experimental Farm, 288
Jewish Legion, 252
Jewish Quarter, 61, 251–52, 263, 270, 275–78
Jewish State (Herzl), 68
Jewish War (Josephus), 101, 106, 112–15,
  117–31
Jezebel, 42
Jezreel Valley, 19–20, 51, 204, 215–16
Jihad, 185–86, 196, 233, 305, 307
Joab, 11, 21–22, 25–27, 230, 291
Joash, 8, 42, 44
John Hyrcanus, 8, 87–90, 94, 124
John of Gischala, 9, 117, 121, 124, 128
John Tzimisces, 158
John VII, 158
Jonathan (son of Saul), 20
Joppa, 117, 172. See also Jaffa
Jordan, 13, 33, 57, 100, 149, 200, 214, 282,
  284, 286, 288–90, 294–95, 297, 304
Jordanian(s), 286, 288–89, 292–93
Jordan River, 42, 216, 291–92
Joseph, 154
Joseph ben Mattathias, 117. See also Josephus
Joseph Ha-Cohen, 220
Josephus, 21, 26–29, 53–54, 56–59, 73–76, 78,
  80, 82, 85–90, 92–93, 96, 100–101, 105–6,
  108, 110–15, 117–31, 279. See also Joseph
  ben Mattathias; Yosef bar Mattathyahu
Joshua, 8, 19, 115, 285
Joshua, Book of, 19
Josiah, 28, 50–51, 56, 67
Jotapata, 117
Judaea, 58, 68, 73–74, 78, 86–88, 90, 93–95,
  97–99, 101–2, 106, 108–9, 111, 116–17,
  119, 131–32, 134, 155, 298
Judaea Capta, 129
Judaea Devicta, 129
Judaean(s), 2, 5, 8–9, 44, 46, 52, 59, 63–67,
  70, 82, 85, 87, 91, 94, 100, 116–17,
  128–29, 131–32, 135, 270, 297–98, 301
Judah, 8, 20, 28, 32, 34, 38–39, 40–42,

  44–58, 64–67, 68–69, 80–82, 85, 94, 115,
  148, 220, 296, 298–99
Judaism, 29, 30, 33, 64, 88–90, 138, 155,
  308
Judea. See Judaea
Judges, Book of, 42
Julian the Apostate, 137
Julius Caesar, 91, 99
Jund Filastin, 155
Jupiter, 134, 137
Jurji Mohammed Pasha, 221
Justinian, 139, 141, 145, 150, 163

Kahane, Meir, 302
al-Kamil, al-Malik. See al-Malik al-Kamil
Kamil at-Tawarihh (Ibn al-Athir), 159,
  186
Karnak, 39, 41
Karsh, Efraim, 199
Kashmir, 200
Kawad Sheroe, 146
Kenyon, Kathleen, 25
Kerak, 187, 208, 211–14, 234
Kerakians, 10
Khalidi, Rashid, 33
Khalifs, 266
Khazars, 33
Khosrau II, 145–46, 191
Khwarizmian(s), 10, 211–13, 232–34
Kidron Valley, 2, 22, 26, 175, 312n. 5
King David Hotel, 258–61
King of the Jews, 101. See also Herod (the
  Great)
Kings, Book of. See 1 Kings; 2 Kings
Kislev, 54
Kitbuqa, 215
Knesset, 201, 211, 232, 282, 296
Knights Templar, 182, 194–95, 208
Koran (Qur'an), 147–48, 151, 154,
  193
Kotel, 105. See also Wailing Wall
el-Kutub, Fauzi, 268
Kutubi, 216
Kuwait, 12

Lachish, 46, 49, 58, 270
Lamentations, Book of, 60
Late Bronze Age, 13
Latrines, 61, 195, 279, 284
Latrun, 279
Law, Andrew Bonar, 243

Lawrence, T. E. (Lawrence of Arabia),
246
Lebanon, 13, 16, 57, 100, 168, 202, 267, 273,
282, 284, 297
Legio X Fretensis, 131. *See also* Tenth Legion
Legio XII Fulminata, 114. *See also* Twelfth
Legion
Lehi, 257–60, 268–70, 280–81, 304
Lethold, 175
Levant, 13, 50–52, 54, 56, 59, 73, 74, 139,
146, 157, 211, 216, 229, 234
Libellus, 186
Libya, 297
Libyans, 39
Lifta, 242
Lipschits, Oded, 62, 65
Lloyd George, David, 236, 243, 247, 265
Lohamei Herut Yisrael, 257
Los Angeles Times, 198
Louis IX, 214
Luke, Gospel of, 110, 130
Luxor, 18
Lydda, 187
Lysimachus, 8, 77

Maccabaeus, Judas, 243. *See also* Maccabee,
Judah
Maccabean(s), 6, 82, 85. *See also* Maccabees
Maccabean rebellion/revolt, 68–69, 73,
75–77, 80, 86–87, 93–95, 97
Maccabee, Jonathan, 8, 85–86, 89
Maccabee, Judah, 8, 69, 80–81, 85, 115, 299.
See also Maccabaeus, Judas
Maccabee, Simon, 8, 80, 85–87, 89, 94
Maccabees, 68–69, 73–74, 77, 81–82, 85, 87,
93–95, 97, 243, 266–67, 285, 299–300,
309. *See also* 1 Maccabees; 2 Maccabees;
Maccabean(s)
Maccabiah Games, 299
Macedonia, 70
Madinat Bayt al-Maqdis, 155, 162
Madison, Peter, 268
Mahane Yehuda, 300–301, 303
Mahmud II, 229
Makarios, 138
Malichus, 99
al-Malik, Abd. *See* Abd al-Malik
al-Malik al-Kamil, 201–2, 205–8, 211, 233–34
al-Malik al-Salih Ayyub, 212
Mamilla, 284
Mamluke(s), 5, 10, 35, 214–18, 234, 251

Manasseh, 50, 67
al-Mansuri, Baybars, 216
Manzikert, battle of, 159
al-Maqdis, 155
al-Maqrizi, 186, 207
Marcus, Amy Dockser, 198
Mariamne, 100, 102, 130
Mark, Gospel of, 110, 130
Mark Antony, 101–2
Marwan II, 156
Masada, 29, 100–101, 114, 131
Masjid al-Aqsa, 192, 194, 206. *See also*
al-Aqsa Mosque
Matar, Fuad, 36
Mattaniah, 55
Mattathias, 80–81, 86, 117
Matthew, Gospel of, 110, 130, 138
Mauritania, 290
McCarter, P. Kyle, 22
Mea Shearim, 253, 274
Mecca, 147, 151, 154, 196, 224, 295
Medina, 147, 154, 295
Mediterranean region, 3, 13, 32, 132, 199
Megiddo, 19, 38, 51, 56, 204, 216, 234,
236–37, 250–51
Meinertzhagen, Richard, 238
Menelaus, 8, 76–79
Merneptah, 17
Mesopotamia, 3, 13, 15, 42, 44, 51, 73, 99,
142, 183, 186
Michelangelo, 19
Middle Bronze Age, 25
Middle East, 6, 7, 12, 32–33, 95, 142, 148,
155, 166, 181, 195–200, 204, 214, 219,
234, 236–37, 250, 297, 303
Millo, 21–22, 26
Minoans, 15
Mitchell Report, 306
Moab, 57
Modein (Modiᶜin), 80, 85, 299
Mohammed, 5, 30, 139, 146–48, 151, 154,
156, 193
Mohammed Ali, 10, 229–31
Mohammed ibn Faroukh, 10, 221
Mohammed Pasha, 220–21, 224–25, 228
Mohammed Pasha Abu Maraq, 228
Mongol(s), 10, 35, 212, 215–16, 218,
234
Morocco, 200, 297
Morris, Benny, 162, 198
Moses, 30, 154, 251

Moslem(s), 1, 5, 6, 9–10, 13, 30, 37, 105,
136–37, 146–52, 154–64, 166–68, 172–74,
177–81, 183–88, 190, 192–99, 202–3,
205–8, 211, 213, 215–16, 218, 220,
227–28, 230–31, 233–36, 247, 251, 253,
265, 279, 284, 293, 295, 300–302. See also
Muslim(s)
Mosque of Omar, 151, 153
Mosul, 36, 183
Mount Moriah, 30
Mount of Olives, 121–22, 170–71, 177, 229,
240, 284, 292–93
Mount Scopus, 115, 266, 270, 274, 276–77,
289–92
Mount Tabor, 204
Mount Zion, 82, 139, 171, 275, 282
Moyne, Lord (Baron Edward Walter
Guinness), 258
al-Muʾazzam, 204–5, 214
al-Mubarqa, 157
Mufti (of Jerusalem). See Grand Mufti (of
Jerusalem)
Mulay, 216
Murray, Archibald, 236–37
Muslim(s), 148, 150, 265, 295, 306. See also
Moslem(s)
Mustafa al-Husseini. See al-Husseini, Mustafa
Mustafa Pasha, 224–25, 229
Mustafa II, 223
Mycenaeans, 15

Naʾaman, Nadav, 28, 41
Nabateans, 90
Nablus, 136, 162, 198, 207, 215, 223, 229–30,
238–41, 249
Nachmanides, 216
Nakbeh, 296
Napoleon, 226–27, 229, 234
Naqib Al-ashraf Rebellion, 221
Narkiss, Uzi, 275, 290–92, 294
al-Nasir Daʾud, 208, 211, 214
al-Nasir Yusuf, 214
Nasser, Gamal Abdel, 197, 235, 285–86,
290–91, 295
Navarre, 211, 234
Nea (church), 139, 141, 145, 163
Near East, 4, 15, 34, 37, 51, 77, 91, 93, 94,
199
Nebi Musa, 251
Nebi Samwil, 203, 276, 289
Nebuchadnezzar Imperial Complex, 37

Nebuchadnezzar II, 5–6, 8, 29, 36–37, 50–67,
69–70, 75, 94, 178
Nebuchadrezzar. See Nebuchadnezzar II
Nebuzaradan, 62–65
Necho II, 51–52
Negev, 39, 41, 280–81
Nehemiah, 70, 72
Neo-Assyria, 75. See also Assyria
Neo-Assyrian(s), 8, 13, 34–35, 41–42, 44–46,
49–52, 59, 67, 199, 270, 297–98. See also
Assyrian(s)
Neo-Babylonia, 75. See also Babylonia
Neo-Babylonian(s), 8, 12, 35, 37, 50–52, 54,
56–67, 69–70, 94, 145, 199. See also Baby-
lonian(s)
Neo-Babylonian Empire, 69
Neophytos, 229
Nero, 109, 111–12, 115–18
Netanya, 286
Netanyahu, Benjamin, 305
New Church of St. Mary, 139, 145
New City (Jerusalem), 274, 279, 281–82
Newell, Jonathan, 264
New Testament, 75, 109–10
New York, 135, 197, 263, 296
Nicolaus, 323n. 15
Night Journey (of Mohammed), 30
Ninth of Ab, 62, 127. See also Tisha-bʾAb
Noah, 154
Nobel Peace Prize, 304
Nordau, Max, 6, 94, 98
Normandy, 174
North Africa, 148, 158, 186
Notre Dame Monastery, 277
Nur al-Din, 183–86, 195, 203

Odysseus, 26
Office of Strategic Services (OSS), 257
Old City (Jerusalem), 106, 132, 137, 220, 226,
246–47, 253, 255, 263, 274–79, 281–82,
284, 290–94, 296
Onias III, 76–77
Operation Nachshon, 269
Oren, Michael, 289, 294
Ornan, 30
Oslo Agreement, 304
Osman (Othman), 218–19
Otho, 119
Ottoman(s), 5, 10, 29, 35, 151, 218–33, 235,
253
Ottoman Empire, 151, 219, 226, 229, 232–34

Palace of Solomon, 182. *See also* al-Aqsa
  Mosque
Palaestina Prima, 155
Palaestina Tertia, 155
Palashtu, 13, 34
Palastina, 13, 134
Palatium Salomonis, 182. *See also* al-Aqsa
  Mosque
Palestine, 6, 13, 16, 33–34, 36–37, 39, 65, 93,
  98, 107, 114, 134, 142, 145–46, 149,
  155–59, 162, 168, 182, 186, 197, 203, 208,
  214–16, 218–19, 221, 223, 227, 229–33,
  235–37, 240, 243, 246–47, 251–66,
  268–70, 272–74, 276–77, 279–82, 285,
  290, 295, 297–99, 301, 303–5, 308
Palestine Archaeological Museum, 290
Palestine Liberation Front, 305
Palestine Liberation Organization (PLO), 12,
  301, 303–5
Palestine National Council, 303
Palestinian(s), 5, 6, 10, 12–13, 33–35, 230,
  256, 296–99, 302–3, 305, 307–9
Palestinian Authority, 12, 33, 136, 205, 252,
  304–6
Palestinian Islamic Jihad, 304
Palmach, 275–76
Palm Sunday, 157, 225
Parthians, 9, 88, 93, 99–100
Passover, 106, 111, 121, 129, 134
Paul (apostle), 9, 111
Peel Commission, 254
Pekah, 8, 44
Peleset, 13
Pentagon, attack on (2001), 167, 181, 197,
  265
Pentateuch, 64
Persia, 63, 65, 70, 94, 142, 145–46, 220
Persian(s), 9, 69–71, 73, 94, 137, 139,
  142–46, 156, 163, 165, 191, 296
Petra, 90
Pharisees, 89–90
Phasael, 9, 99–100, 102, 130
Philip Augustus, 202
Philistia, 13, 34
Philistine(s), 13, 16, 20, 33–35, 50
Phocas, 144
Phoenician(s), 16, 42
Pirie-Gordon, Harry, 243
PLO. *See* Palestine Liberation Organization
Pompey, 8, 29, 89, 91–95, 99
Pontius Pilate, 9, 108–9

Pool of Mamilla, 144
Popes, 160, 164, 166, 234
Prawer, Joshua, 192
Prime minister (Israel), 36, 198, 254, 257
Procurator, 108–9, 112
Prophet, 5, 148, 155–58, 167, 193, 221, 247
Psammetichus I, 51
Ptolemaic dynasties, 87
Ptolemais, 114, 116
Ptolemies, 73–74, 77
Ptolemy (son-in-law of Simon Maccabee), 87
Ptolemy I, 8, 73–75, 79, 94
Ptolemy IV (Philopater), 8, 74–75
Ptolemy V (Epiphanes), 75
Ptolemy VI, 78

Qadesh, 15
Qarmatians, 158
Qur'an. *See* Koran
Qutb, Sayyid, 265
Qutuz, 215

Rabin, Yitzhak, 275, 285, 294, 304
Ramadan, 146
Ramat Rahel (kibbutz), 276, 286
Rambam, 216
Ramla, 155, 158–59, 187–88, 216, 218,
  238
al-Rashid, Harun, 157
Raymond of Aguilers, 174, 177–78
Redford, Donald, 41
Rehoboam, 8, 38–39, 41
Reich, Roni (Ronny), 25, 144
Reynald of Chatillon, 186–87
Rezin, 8, 44
Riad Bey a-Solh, 284
Riblah, 60
Richard the Lionheart, 195, 202, 238,
  264–65, 289
Roberts, David, 24, 104, 141, 153, 170, 210,
  245
Robert the Norman, 171
Rockefeller Museum, 290–91
Rohan, Denis, 301
Roman(s), 9, 13, 26, 29, 32, 34–35, 70,
  91–94, 96–102, 106–18, 120–32, 134–39,
  142, 145, 155, 168, 178, 205–6, 280, 291,
  297
Roman Empire, 6, 97, 130
Roman Republic, 93
Roman Senate, 99–101, 116, 128

Rome, 26, 91, 93, 97, 99–101, 106, 108–9,
    111, 116, 118–19, 128–31, 139, 226, 301
Rommel, Erwin, 257
Royal Air Force Club (Jerusalem), 262
Rushalimum, 17
Russia, 33, 231, 286

Sabbath, 73–74, 79, 80, 92, 101, 115, 261,
    272, 301
Sabinus, 9, 108, 331n. 97
Sabri, Ekrima, 136–37, 162
al-Sadat, Anwar, 166, 201–2, 211, 232, 233,
    301
Saddam Hussein. See Hussein, Saddam
Sadducee(s), 89
Saladin, 6, 9, 29, 142, 167–68, 181, 183–204,
    206–7, 220, 232–34, 264, 300
Salah ad-Din. See Saladin
Salomonis, 182
Samaria, 44–45, 50, 64, 86, 88, 108, 155
Samuel, Book of. See 2 Samuel
Samuel, Sir Herbert, 252
Sanders, General Liman von, 235
Saracen(s), 5, 166, 171, 173–78, 180, 195
Sargon II, 44–45, 67
Sasanian, 142, 145, 191
Sasanids, 142
Saudi Arabia, 196, 200, 267, 273
Saul, 20
Savage, Raymond, 247
Sayyid Qutb. See Qutb, Sayyid
Sbarro pizzeria, 307
Scaurus, 91
Scriptores Historiae Augustae, 131
Sea of Galilee, 117, 186
Sea Peoples, 13, 15, 17
Second Intifada, 10, 302, 305–6, 309. See also
    al-Aqsa Intifada
Second Jewish Revolt, 98, 131–32, 135
Second Temple, 26, 30, 32, 64, 69–70, 75, 94,
    102, 116, 129–31, 134. See also Temple of
    Herod
Second Triumvirate, 99
Seleucid(s), 69, 73–77, 79–82, 85–88, 93–95,
    243
Seleucus IV, 8, 75
Selim al-Husseini. See al-Husseini, Selim
Selim I, 10, 218–20
Seljuk(s), 9, 159, 161, 176, 183
Senate. See Roman Senate
Sennacherib, 5, 8, 41, 46, 48–50, 67, 75, 270

Seventh Army, 238, 250
Shahr-Baraz (the Wild Boar), 9, 142
Shalmaneser V, 44, 67
Shamir, Yitzhak, 257, 281
Sharon, Ariel, 36, 111, 299, 306–7, 309
Shavuot, 295
Shea, John S. M., 242–43, 248
Sheikh Jarrah, 274, 276, 289
Shiites, 155
Shiloh, Yigal, 25
Shimron, 19
Shirkuh, 183–84
Shishak, 5, 8, 38–39, 41, 67. See also
    Shoshenq
Shoshenq, 8, 39, 41, 75. See also Shishak
Shuafat, 276
Shukron, Eli, 25
Sicarii, 114
Sidon, 10, 16, 57, 228–29
Siege, 27, 44, 46, 48, 54–55, 58–61, 63, 82,
    85–86, 91–92, 100–101, 110, 117–18,
    122–26, 129, 132, 142, 144, 149–50,
    160–61, 171–72, 174–75, 177, 181, 191,
    202–3, 208, 211, 224, 227, 234, 274–75,
    279
Siege embankments, 125–26
Silberman, Neil Asher, 48, 135
Siloam Inscription, 48
Simon, 264
Simon bar Giora. See Bar Giora, Simon
Sinai, 30, 247, 286, 289, 294
Six-Day War, 137, 285, 294, 296–97,
    300
Sixth Crusade, 9, 205, 207, 234
Sodom, 125
Sohaemus, 119
a-Solh, Riad Bey. See Riad Bey a-Solh
Solomon, 3, 5, 26, 30–32, 38–39, 41, 55, 67,
    68–69, 87, 94–95, 105, 129, 137, 150, 253
Solomon's Stables. See Stables of Solomon
Solomon's Temple. See Temple of Solomon
Sophronius, 148, 150
Sossius, 101–2
Southeastern Turkey, 91
Spain, 148, 157, 216, 220
Spartans, 78
SPQR, 116
Stables of Solomon, 105, 182
St. Anne's Church. See Church of St. Anne
Stepped-Stone Structure, 25
Stern, Avraham, 257

Stern Gang, 258
Strabo, 3, 92
Strategius, 143–44
Stronghold of Zion, 21–22, 25–26, 29–30. See
    also City of David
St. Stephen's Gate, 275, 290, 293
Sudan, 290
Suez Canal, 236, 290
Suez crossing, 202
al-Sulami, 184–85, 196
Suleiman, 220, 222, 226, 234, 275
Sunij, 161
Sunni, 155–56, 196
Suqman ibn Artuq, 161
Syria, 8, 13, 15–16, 34, 39, 41–42, 44, 46, 51,
    54, 58, 60, 73–74, 77, 86, 91, 93–94,
    100–101, 108, 113–14, 116, 119, 129, 134,
    142, 146, 148, 159, 168, 183–87, 197–98,
    204–5, 208, 212–13, 215, 219, 227,
    229–34, 241, 262, 267, 273, 282, 286, 290,
    297, 301
Syria-Mesopotamia, 74, 86
Syrian(s), 76, 101, 108, 115, 179, 184, 199,
    203, 286, 288
Syria Palastina, 34, 93, 94, 134
Syria-Palestine, 41, 46, 54, 148, 204

Taanach, 19
Tabernacle, 30
Tacitus, 119, 121
Talpiot, 288
Tammuz, 58, 61
Tancred, 171, 177, 179
Tapeworms, 61
Tatars, 212, 232
Tebet, 57
al-Tel, Abdullah. See Abdullah al-Tel
Tel Aviv, 28, 62, 117, 197–98, 253, 256,
    258–59, 261, 268–69, 272–74, 279–81, 292
Tel Aviv University, 28, 62, 198
Tel Dan, 20, 28
Templars. See Knights Templar
Temple Mount, 1, 3, 5, 8, 30, 32, 56, 82, 89,
    91–92, 101–2, 105–6, 110, 127, 130, 134,
    136–38, 143, 145, 148, 151, 154, 160,
    162–63, 178–79, 182, 206, 211, 253,
    293–94, 296, 300–301, 303, 305–6, 308–9.
    See also Haram al-Sherif
Temple Mount Faithful, 303
Temple of Herod, 3, 178, 301–2. See also Sec-
    ond Temple

Temple of Marduk, 56
Temple of Solomon, 30, 137, 151, 162, 175,
    177–78, 181–82, 301. See also First Temple;
    Templum Salomonis
Templum Domini, 183. See also Dome of the
    Rock
Templum Salomonis, 182. See also al-Aqsa
    Mosque; Temple of Solomon
Ten Commandments, 30
Tenth Legion, 116, 119, 121–22, 124, 131.
    See also Legio X Fretensis
Tenuat Hameri, 258
Tetrarchs, 99
Teutonic Knights, 182
Theobald, 211, 234
Theodosius II, 139
Theophanes the Confessor, 138, 146, 149,
    156
Thibaut, 211
Third Crusade, 197, 202–3, 238, 264
Third Legion, 119
Third Wall, 111
Thomas "the Undertaker," 144
Thompson, Thomas, 312n. 3
Thutmose III, 237
Tibawi, A. L., 338n. 3
Tiberius, 109
Tiferet Israel Street, 96
Tiglath-Pileser III, 44
Tigris, 15, 51
Tikrit, 183, 198
Tisha-b'Ab, 253. See also Ninth of Ab
Titus, 5, 9, 26, 29, 96, 98, 116, 119–20,
    122–31, 134, 137, 279, 291
Toilet seat, 61
Tomb of the Virgin, 226
Tower of David, 104, 179, 207–8. See also
    David's Tower
Transjordan, 88, 257, 267, 273–74, 280, 282
Treaty of Jaffa, 206
Troy, 26
True Cross, 202–3
Truman, Harry S., 273, 296
Tryphon, 8, 86
Tshelebi, Evliya. See Chelebi (Tshelebi),
    Evliya
Tsinnor, 22, 25, 27
Tudebode, Peter, 168, 173, 179–80
Tunisia, 297
Turanshah, 214
Turcoman(s), 9, 159–61, 164, 166, 234

Turkey, 15–16, 91, 159, 168, 212, 219–20
Twain, Mark, 231
Twelfth Legion, 114–16, 119, 124. *See also* Legio XII Fulminata
Twenty-second Dynasty, 39
Twenty-second Legion, 119
Tyre, 16, 57, 91, 187, 194, 199, 202
Tyropoeon (valley), 102

Ugarit, 15
Umar ibn al-Khattab (caliph), 9, 149–51, 154, 247
Umayyad(s), 9, 151, 154, 156–57
United Monarchy, 20, 32, 38, 67
United Nations, 258, 262, 274, 276–78, 280–82, 286, 288, 292
United Nations Security Council, 274, 276–78
United Nations Truce Commission, 276
University of London, 199
Upper City (Jerusalem), 96
Urban II, 160, 164, 166, 179, 181, 234
Urusalim, 6, 17
Urushamem, 17
Uthman III, 226
Uzbekistan, 159
Uzziah, 44

Valley of Gehenna, 191
Varus, 9, 108. *See also* War of Varus
Vespasian, 5, 26, 116–19, 129, 131
Vienna, 98
Vitellius, 119

Wailing Wall, 105, 154, 253–54, 278, 284, 294–95
Wailing Wall Riots, 253–54
al-Walid, Caliph, 154, 156
Wasson, Thomas C., 276
Waqf. *See* Islamic Waqf
War of Varus, 106, 108
Wars of the Jews (Josephus), 76
Watson, C. F., 242
Weizman, Chaim, 252
Weizman, Ezer, 291
Welt, Die, 136
West Bank, 6, 34, 198, 256, 282, 284, 297, 304
Western Wall. *See* Wailing Wall
West Semitic language, 17

Whipworms, 61
"White Paper," 255
Wilhelm II (kaiser), 242, 246
William of Tyre, 168, 172, 174, 178–81
World Trade Center, attack on (2001), 181, 197
World War I, 213, 219, 232, 236, 250, 266, 289
World War II, 256–57
World War III, 302

Yadin, Yigael, 27, 291
Yahweh, 22
Ya³qubi, 149–50
Yaquti, 161
Yathrib, 147
Year of the Four Emperors, 118
Yehud, 69–71, 73
Yehudi, 322n. 3
Yehudim, 69
Yemen, 33, 158, 186, 200, 262, 267, 273, 290, 297
Yom Kippur, 74, 253, 301
Yom Kippur War, 301
Yoqneam, 19
Yosef bar Mattathyahu, 117. *See also* Josephus
Yusuf, al-Nasir. *See* al-Nasir Yusuf
Yusuf Agha al-Ja³uni, 229
Yusuf Salah ad-Din bin Ayyub. *See* Saladin

Zacharias, 142, 145–46
Zadok, 95
Zangi, 183, 185
al-Zawahiri, Ayman, 233
Zealots, 9
Zedekiah, 55–58, 60, 67, 94
Zerubbabel, 70, 102
Zeruiah, 21, 27, 291
Zion, 96, 298. *See also* Mount Zion; Stronghold of Zion
Zion Cinema, 300
Zion Gate, 274–75, 278, 281, 293
Zionism, 68, 93, 97, 166, 252
Zionist(s), 6, 68, 94–95, 97–98, 166–67, 232, 233, 237, 251–54, 267
Zion Square, 301
Zoroastrians, 144
Zvai Leumi, 254